READING THE
MIDDLE AGES

READING THE
MIDDLE AGES

SOURCES FROM
EUROPE, BYZANTIUM, AND
THE ISLAMIC WORLD

EDITED BY BARBARA H. ROSENWEIN · THIRD EDITION

VOLUME I: FROM *c.*300 TO *c.*1150

UNIVERSITY OF TORONTO PRESS

Toronto Buffalo London

LIBRARY AND ARCHIVES CANADA CATALOGUING IN PUBLICATION

Reading the Middle Ages: sources from Europe, Byzantium, and the Islamic world / edited by Barbara H. Rosenwein. — Third edition.

Also published in one volume.
Includes bibliographical references and index.
Contents: v. 1. From c.300 to c.1150.
Issued in print and electronic formats.
ISBN 978-1-4426-3677-4 (v. 1: softcover).—ISBN 978-1-4426-3678-1 (v. 1: PDF).—
ISBN 978-1-4426-3679-8 (v. 1: HTML)

1. Middle Ages—Sources. I. Title.

D113.R38 2018b   909.07   C2018-901350-8
                                                        C2018-901351-6

We welcome comments and suggestions regarding any aspect of our publications—please feel free to contact us at news@utphighereducation.com or visit our Internet site at www.utorontopress.com.

North America
5201 Dufferin Street
North York, Ontario, Canada, M3H 5T8

2250 Military Road
Tonawanda, New York, USA, 14150

ORDERS PHONE: 1–800–565–9523
ORDERS FAX: 1–800–221–9985
ORDERS E-MAIL: utpbooks@utpress.utoronto.ca

UK, Ireland, and continental Europe
NBN International
Estover Road, Plymouth, PL6 7PY, UK
ORDERS PHONE: 44 (0) 1752 202301
ORDERS FAX: 44 (0) 1752 202333
ORDERS E-MAIL: enquiries@nbninternational.com

Every effort has been made to contact copyright holders; in the event of an error or omission, please notify the publisher.

The University of Toronto Press acknowledges the financial support for its publishing activities of the Government of Canada through the Canada Book Fund.

Printed in the U.S.A.

Funded by the Financé par le
Government gouvernement
of Canada du Canada

 Canadä

For Frank and Amy

IMPORTANT PLACES
MENTIONED
IN THE SOURCES

Yet research continues, and it continues to be fruitful, because historians are not passive instruments, and because they read the same old documents with fresh eyes and with new questions in mind.

Georges Duby, *History Continues*

Contents

II   THE EMERGENCE OF SIBLING CULTURES (*c.*600–*c.*750)

The Resilience of Byzantium

The Formation of the Islamic World

The Impoverished but Inventive West

III   CREATING NEW IDENTITIES (*c.*750–*c.*900)

The Material Basis of Society

IV POLITICAL COMMUNITIES REORDERED (*c.*900–*c.*1050)

Reading through Looking

Following page 268

Preface

The major difference between *Reading the Middle Ages* and other medieval history source books is its systematic incorporation of Islamic and Byzantine materials alongside Western readings. This third edition adds still more readings for those cultures, especially the Islamic world. By organizing the sources topically rather than by region, students and teachers are invited to make comparisons and contrasts within and across cultures. Each source is provided with an introduction followed by one or (usually) two apposite questions. More questions are available on the website for *Reading the Middle Ages* (www.utphistorymatters. com); those pertaining to sources in the second edition were composed by Bruce Venarde, while questions for the new sources have been created by Riccardo Cristiani. Although this book may be used independently or alongside any textbook, it is particularly designed to complement the fifth edition of *A Short History of the Middle Ages*. The chapters have the same titles and chronological scope; the readings here should help expand, deepen, sharpen, and modify the knowledge gained there.

The sources in *Reading the Middle Ages* are varied; there are, for example, records of sales, biographies, hagiographies, poems, and histories.[1] There are two collections of material sources: "Reading through Looking," and an entirely new set of illustrations on "Weapons and Warfare" composed by Riccardo Cristiani. Some teachers may wish to assign all the readings in each chapter; others may wish to concentrate on only a few texts from each chapter. It is also easy to organize readings thematically by region, since the index groups together all the sources pertaining to Italy, Spain, France, and so on.

The introduction to the first text in this book includes a discussion of how to read a primary source. The same project is repeated in chapter 4, this time with a very different sort of document. It should become clear to users of this book that the kinds of questions one brings to all documents are initially the same, but the answers lead down very different paths that suggest their own new questions and approaches. Each reader's curiosity,

---

[1] To make the texts translated from the Greek, Slavic languages, and Arabic more accessible, I have left out diacritical marks and non-Latin letters. Users of this book should, however, keep in mind that Arabic terms such as *sura* and names such as al-Bukhari should more properly be spelled *sūra* and al-Bukhārī, Slavic names such as Boleslaw are more correctly written Bolesław, and Greek terms such as *lorikion* and *komes* are more accurately *lōrikion* and *komēs*.

personality, and interests become part of the process; this, even more than the discovery of hitherto unknown sources, is the foundation of new historical thought.

This is the place for me to acknowledge—with pleasure and enormous gratitude—the many debts that I have incurred in the preparation of this book. All those who contributed translations for this third edition deserve my first thanks: Phil Booth, Riccardo Cristiani, and Joseph O'Callaghan.

Very special thanks go to Dionysios Stathakopoulos and Julia Bray. The former supplied me with numerous—and even annotated—suggestions for readings connected to the Byzantine world, while Julia did the same for medieval Islamic civilizations. It is literally true that the revisions of this book were made possible by these two generous scholars.

Maps were ably made by Erik Goosmann, whose expertise in history as well as cartography was invaluable at every step.

For special help, I thank University of Toronto Press people with whom I worked: Judith Earnshaw, Natalie Fingerhut, Beate Schwirtlich, and Matthew Jubb at Em Dash Design.

Above all, I am grateful to Riccardo Cristiani: for the web questions and the pictorial insert, as mentioned above, but also for his thoughtful and careful reading of the entire manuscript, which led to numerous corrections and clarifications, and his index, which provides the user with numerous reference tools, such as dates for all persons and titles of all readings and their dates. He also helped coordinate all names, places, and facts in this book with those in *A Short History*.

Finally, I thank my husband, Tom, for supporting my work in every way.

Abbreviations and Symbols

AH	Anno Hijra = year 1 of the Islamic calendar, equivalent to 622 CE
b.	before a date = born
b.	before a name = son of (*ibn*, *ben*)
BCE	before common era. Interchangeable with BC. See CE below.
bef.	On timelines = before
bt.	daughter of (*bint*)
cent.	century (used after an ordinal number, e.g. 6th cent. means "sixth century")
c.	circa (used before a date to indicate that it is approximate)
CE	common era. Interchangeable with AD. Both reflect Western dating practices, which begin "our" era with the birth of Christ. In *Reading the Middle Ages*, all dates are CE unless otherwise specified or some confusion might arise.
d.	date of death
d.	dinar = *denarius*, penny
Douay	The standard English version of the Vulgate (Latin) version of the Bible. Ordinarily the books are the same as in the Authorized Version (AV) (see below). The chief differences are that (1) the Douay version accepts some books considered apocryphal in the AV; and (2) the Psalm numbers sometimes differ. The Douay numbers follow the psalm numbering in the Greek Bible, whereas the AV and other Protestant Bibles follow the numbering of the Hebrew text.
e.g.	*exempli gratia* = for example
fl.	*floruit* (used—when birth and death dates are not known—to mean that a person "flourished" or was active at the time of the date)
ibid.	in the same place, referring to the reference in the preceding note
i.e.	that is (from the Latin *id est*)
£	pound (from the first letter of the Latin word *libra*)
MS	manuscript
pl.	plural
r.	ruled
s.	shilling = *solidus*, sous
sing.	singular
...	Ellipses, indicating that words or passages of the original have been left out.

[]   Brackets, indicating words or passages that are not in the original but have been added by the editor to aid in the understanding of a passage.

A date such as Boethius (d. 524/526) means that the exact date of his death is not known or disputed, but it is, at least, within the date range of 524 to 526.

Authorized Version of the Bible

In *Reading the Middle Ages*, references to the Bible are to the Authorized Version (AV). (Psalms are cited in both AV and Douay versions.) The standard abbreviations for the books of the AV are set out below. The Revised Standard Version of the Bible, which is perhaps the best translation in English, derives from the AV, which is based on the King James Version.

Old Testament

Genesis / Gen.
Exodus / Exod.
Leviticus / Lev.
Numbers / Num.
Deuteronomy / Deut.
Joshua / Josh.
Judges / Judges
Ruth / Ruth
1 Samuel / 1 Sam.
2 Samuel / 2 Sam.
1 Kings / 1 Kings
2 Kings / 2 Kings
1 Chronicles / 1 Chron.
2 Chronicles / 2 Chron.
Ezra / Ezra
Nehemiah / Neh.
Esther / Esther
Job / Job
Psalms / Ps.
Proverbs / Prov.
Ecclesiastes / Eccles.
Song of Solomon /
    Song of Sol.
      (This is also often called the
      Song of Songs)

Isaiah / Isa.
Jeremiah / Jer.
Lamentations / Lam.
Ezekiel / Ezek.
Daniel / Dan.
Hosea / Hos.
Joel / Joel
Amos / Amos
Obadiah / Obad.
Jonah / Jon.
Micah / Mic.
Nahum / Nah.
Habakkuk / Hab.
Zephaniah / Zeph.
Haggai / Hag.
Zechariah / Zech.
Malachi / Mal.

New Testament

Matthew / Matt.
Mark / Mark
Luke / Luke
John / John
Acts of the Apostles / Acts
Romans / Rom.
1 Corinthians / 1 Cor.

2 Corinthians / 2 Cor.
Galatians / Gal.
Ephesians / Eph.
Philippians / Phil.
Colossians / Col.
1 Thessalonians / 1 Thess.
2 Thessalonians / 2 Thess.
1 Timothy / 1 Tim.
2 Timothy / 2 Tim.
Titus / Titus
Philemon / Philem.
Hebrews / Heb.
James / James
1 Peter / 1 Pet.
2 Peter / 2 Pet.
1 John / 1 John
2 John / 2 John
3 John / 3 John
Jude / Jude
Revelation / Rev.

Apocrypha

1 Esdras / 1 Esd.
2 Esdras / 2 Esd.
Tobit (Tobias) / Tob.
Judith / Jth.

The Rest of Esther /
    Rest of Esther
The Wisdom of Solomon /
    Wisd. of Sol.
Ecclesiasticus / Ecclus.
Baruch / Bar.

The Song of the Three Holy
    Children / Song of Three
    Children
Susanna / Sus.
Bel and the Dragon / Bel
    and Dragon

Prayer of Manasses / Pr. of
    Man.
1 Maccabees / 1 Macc.
2 Maccabees / 2 Macc.

I

Prelude: The Roman World Transformed (c.300–c.600)

A CHRISTIANIZED EMPIRE

1.1 Toleration or favoritism? *The Edict of Milan* (313). Original in Latin.

No edict (an order issued to governors throughout the empire) was issued at Milan. But Emperors Constantine (r.306–337) and Licinius (r.308–324) met there in 313 and agreed to the provisions of what would be promulgated a few months later—the so-called *Edict of Milan*. It gave notice that Constantine and Licinius agreed to tolerate Christianity along with other religions and that they determined to restore the properties that the Church had lost under Emperor Diocletian (r.284–305). The current owners of the property might be compensated from the emperors' private funds if they applied to their "vicar," an imperial administrator with regional authority.

   The Edict of Milan is the first source in this collection. Let us use it to begin a discussion of how to read primary sources. Each primary source calls for its own methodology and approach; there is no one way to handle all of them. Moreover, as the epigraph of this book points out, readers should bring their own special insights to old sources. Nevertheless, it is usually helpful to begin by asking a standard series of questions.

Who wrote it, and for what audience was it written? Normally this is fairly easy to answer, but often it is not. In this case, it seems that Emperors Constantine and Licinius conceived of the statement, though civil servants in an imperial writing office drafted and published it. The immediate recipients were provincial governors, each referred to as "your Excellency" in this document; they were expected to publish—that is, publicize—the contents to the public.

When was it written? Your editor has given the date 313, which is the year in which the document was issued. At this stage in your historical work, you need not worry about how this date was arrived at. It is more important for you to consider the circumstances and historical events in the context of which this date takes on meaning. In this instance, you should be thinking that the date is pertinent to the history of the Roman Empire; that it comes directly after Constantine won a major battle at the Milvian Bridge in 312; that he attributed his victory to a sign from the Christian God; that immediately thereafter he took over administration of the western portion of the Roman Empire and soon (in 313) allied with Licinius; and that a few months later Licinius became ruler of the eastern half of the Empire. Therefore, you should expect the document to have to do with both imperial authority and religion, which is precisely what you will discover when you read it.

Where was it written? In this case "Milan" is not the right answer. In fact, the *Edict* was issued by Licinius at Nicomedia (today Izmit), in the eastern half of the Empire. But sometimes you will not know so specific an answer, and you must work with what information you have.

Why was it written? Often you will find a provisional answer to this question right in the text of the primary source. Ostensibly the *Edict* was written, as it says, "to give both to Christians and to all others free facility to follow the religion which each may desire." But you should go beyond this obvious answer to ask what other motives might have been at work, what sorts of negotiations may have been involved in its writing, and who benefited.

What is it? In this case, you know that it is *called* an *Edict* but is something a bit different. You might choose to call it an "imperial ordinance," an "official document," or even a "policy statement."

What does it say? This is the most important question of all. To answer it, you need to analyze the document for its various provisions, taking care to understand them fully and seeking further information (if necessary) about its vocabulary.

What are the implications of what it says? This requires you to ask many questions about matters that lie behind the text. Important questions to ask are: *What does the document reveal about such institutions as family, power, social classes and groups, religion, and education and literacy in the world that produced it? What are its underlying assumptions about human nature, agency, and goals; about the nature of the divine? Does the source apply to men and women in the same way?*

How reliable is it? If the document is authentic—if it really is what it purports to be—then at the very least you can know that it was issued by its writer(s). In this case, you can be sure that Constantine and Licinius did indeed want *The Edict of Milan* to be promulgated. You may wish to speculate about how much of it was Constantine's idea and how much Licinius's by considering what else you know about their religious convictions and political motives. The document certainly tells you about the ideals and intentions that they wanted the world to believe they had. But it alone cannot tell you whether the provisions were carried out. To know that, you need other documents and evidence about the nature of Roman imperial power at the time. One document that may help here is the *Creed* declared by the Council of Nicaea (p. 11 below), since Constantine presided over that council.

Are there complicating factors? Medieval texts were all handwritten, and they were "published"—in the sense of being made public and distributed—in relatively small numbers. In many cases we do not have them in their original state. *The Edict of Milan* was issued in multiple handwritten copies in Latin, but none of them has survived. We know its contents because it was incorporated into the writings of two Christian apologists:[1] Lactantius's *On the Deaths of the Persecutors* (written perhaps in 318) and Eusebius's *History of the Church* (the first edition of which was published at some time between 303 and 312). Eusebius's text of the *Edict*, which he translated and presented in Greek, is not entirely the same as the one given by Lactantius. Scholars think that the one in Lactantius is the original, and that is the one printed here. But you should not be content with that. You should instead ask yourself at least two questions about these intermediary sources: *What motives might lead a later source to reproduce a text? What new meanings does the original source take on when it is embedded in a larger document with its own agenda?* You might also consider the fact that the *Edict* was not considered important enough to be drawn upon by the legal experts who compiled *The Theodosian Code* (438; see below, p. 4) or the later *Codex Justinianus* (529).

You should ask these sorts of questions of every source you read. Soon you will see how different the answers are for each document, for every one of them poses special challenges. If you like, look ahead to p. 171 to see this point clearly demonstrated in connection with a very different source, al-Tabari, *The Defeat of the Zanj Revolt*.

[Source: *Church and State Through the Centuries: A Collection of Historic Documents with Commentaries*, trans. and ed. Sidney Z. Ehler and John B. Morrall (Westminster, MD: Newman Press, 1954), pp. 5–6.]

We, Constantine and Licinius the Emperors, having met in concord at Milan and having set in order everything which pertains to the common good and public security, are of the opinion that among the various things which we perceived would profit men, or which should be set in order first, was to be found the cultivation of religion; we should therefore give both to Christians and to all others free facility to follow the religion which each may desire, so that by this means whatever divinity is enthroned in heaven may be gracious and favorable to us and to all who have been placed under our authority. Therefore we are of the opinion that the following decision is in accordance with sound and true reasoning: that no one who has given his mental assent to the Christian persuasion or to any other which he feels to be suitable to him should be compelled to deny his conviction, so that the Supreme Godhead ("Summa Divinitas"), whose worship we freely observe, can assist us in all things with his usual favor and benevolence. Wherefore it is necessary for your Excellency to know that it is our pleasure that all restrictions which were previously put forward in official pronouncements concerning the sect of the Christians should be removed, and that each one of them who freely and sincerely carries out the purpose of observing the Christian religion may endeavor to practice its precepts without any fear or danger. We believed that these points should be fully brought to your attention, so that you might know that we have given free and absolute permission to practice their religion to the Christians. Now that you perceive what we have granted to them, your Excellency must also learn that for the sake of peace in our time a similar public and free right to practice their religion or cult is granted to others, so that every person may have free opportunity to worship according to his own wish. This has been done by us to avoid any appearance of disfavor to any one religion. We have decided furthermore to decree the following in respect of the Christians: if those places at which they were accustomed in former times to hold their meetings (concerning which a definite procedure was laid down for your guidance in previous communications) have been at any previous time acquired from our treasury or from any other person, let the persons

---

[1] An "apologist" is someone who justifies or argues in favor of a doctrine or ideology.

concerned be willing and swift to restore them to the Christians without financial recompense and without trying to ask a price. Let those who have received such property as a gift restore whatever they have acquired to the Christians in similar manner; if those who have bought such property or received it as a gift seek some recompense from our benevolence, let them apply to the vicar, by whom their cases will be referred to our clemency. You are to consider it your duty that all these things shall be handed over to the Christian body immediately and without delay by your intervention. And since the aforesaid Christians are known to have possessed not only those places at which they are accustomed to assemble, but others also pertaining to the law of their body, that is of the churches, not of private individuals, you are to order in accordance with the law which we have described above the return of all those possessions to the aforesaid Christians, that is to their bodies and assemblies without

any further hesitation or argument. Our previous statement is to be borne in mind that those who restore this property without price may, as we have said, expect some compensation from our benevolence.

You ought to bring into play your very effective intervention in all these matters concerning the aforesaid Christian body so that there may be a swift fulfillment of our Edict, in which the interests of public quiet have been consulted by our clemency. Let all this be done, so that as we stated above, the divine favor, of which we have experienced so many instances, may continue with us to bless our successors through all time with public well-being. In order that the character of this our perpetual benevolence can reach the knowledge of all, it will be well for you to circulate everywhere, and to bring to the awareness of all, these points which have been written to you as above, so that the enactment of this our benevolence may not be hidden.

1.2 Law: *The Theodosian Code* (438). Original in Latin.

The Theodosian Code, a massive compilation of imperial edicts and letters issued in 438 under the Roman emperor Theodosius II (r.408–450), was meant to serve as an authoritative standard for determining legal cases throughout the Empire. Covering topics as diverse as legal procedure, marriage, the army, and the Church, the *Code* was immediately adopted by Roman judicial authorities and later was a model for the laws drawn up in Rome's barbarian successor states. The *Code* divided its topics into "Books," which were further subdivided into "Titles." Under each Title were arranged excerpts from pertinent imperial legislation. These were followed, when the compilers thought necessary, by legal interpretations. The passages below concern marriage and divorce.

1. How and why did the *Code* attempt to control social and moral behavior, such as that involved in marriage and divorce?
2. What sort of rights did women have in a Roman divorce?

[Source: *The Theodosian Code and Novels and the Sirmondian Constitutions*, trans. Clyde Pharr (Princeton, NJ: Princeton University Press, 1952), pp. 76–77 (slightly modified).]

Book 3, Title 14: *Marriages with Foreigners*

1. EMPERORS VALENTINIAN AND VALENS AUGUSTUSES TO THEODOSIUS, MASTER OF THE HORSE. [368–373]
No provincial, of whatever rank or class he may be, shall marry a barbarian wife, nor shall a provincial woman

be united with any foreigner. But if there should be any alliances between provincials and foreigners through such marriages and if anything should be disclosed as suspect or criminal among them, it shall be expiated by capital punishment.

Interpretation: No Roman shall presume to have a barbarian wife of any nation whatever, nor shall any

Roman woman be united in marriage with a barbarian. But if they should do this, they shall know that they are subject to capital punishment.

Title 16: Notices of Divorce

1. EMPEROR CONSTANTINE AUGUSTUS TO ABLAVIUS, PRAETORIAN PREFECT. [331]

It is Our[1] pleasure that no woman, on account of her own depraved desires, shall be permitted to send a notice of divorce to her husband on trumped up grounds, as, for instance, that he is a drunkard or a gambler or a philanderer, nor indeed shall a husband be permitted to divorce his wife on every sort of pretext. But when a woman sends a notice of divorce, the following criminal charges only shall be investigated, that is, if she should prove that her husband is a homicide, a sorcerer, or a destroyer of tombs, so that the wife may thus earn commendation and at length recover her entire dowry. For if she should send a notice of divorce to her husband on grounds other than these three criminal charges, she must leave everything, even to her last hairpin, in her husband's home, and as punishment for her supreme self confidence, she shall be deported to an island. In the case of a man also, if he should send a notice of divorce, inquiry shall be made as to the following three criminal charges, namely, if he wishes to divorce her as an adulteress, a sorceress, or a procuress.[2] For if he should cast off a wife who is innocent of these crimes, he must restore her entire dowry, and he shall not marry another woman. But if he should do this, his former wife shall be given the right to enter and seize his home by force and to transfer to herself the entire dowry of his later wife in recompense for the outrage inflicted upon her.

Interpretation: The right to send notice of divorce is extended to a wife or husband for certain approved reasons and causes; for they are forbidden to dissolve a marriage for a trivial charge. If perchance a woman should say that her husband is either a drunkard or given to licentiousness, she shall not send him notice of divorce on that account. But if perchance she should prove that he is either a homicide, a sorcerer, or a violator of tombs, the husband who

is convicted of these crimes appears to be justly divorced, without any fault of the woman; and she may recover her dowry and depart. If the woman should not be able to prove such crimes, she shall be subjected to the following punishment: namely, that she shall forfeit both the dowry which she had given or which had been given on her behalf and the gift[3] which she received, and she shall also be liable to exile by relegation.[4] But if a man should cast off his wife, he also is not permitted to divorce her for a trivial quarrel, as often happens, unless perhaps he should be able to prove that she is guilty of certain crimes, that is, if he is able to prove that she is an adulteress, a sorceress, or a procuress. But if he cannot prove this, he shall restore her dowry to the woman, and he shall not presume to take another wife. But if perchance he should attempt to do so, the woman who was cast off, though innocent, shall have the right to vindicate [claim] for herself her husband's home and all his substance. It is recognized that this is ordained in order that if a woman should be unjustly divorced, she is ordered to acquire the dowry of the second wife also.

2. EMPERORS HONORIUS, THEODOSIUS, AND CONSTANTIUS AUGUSTUSES TO PALLADIUS, PRAETORIAN PREFECT. [421]

If a woman should serve notice of divorce upon her husband and separate from him and if she should prove no grounds for divorce, the gifts shall be annulled which she had received when betrothed. She shall also be deprived of her dowry, and she shall be sentenced to the punishment of deportation. We deny her not only the right to a union with a subsequent husband, but even the right of postliminium.[5] But if a woman who has revolted against her marriage should prove merely flaws of character and ordinary faults, she shall lose her dowry and restore to her husband all gifts, and never at all shall she be associated in marriage with any man. In order that she may not defile her unmarried state with wanton debauchery, We grant to the repudiated husband the right to bring an accusation.[6]

1. It remains to say that if a woman who withdraws[7] should prove serious grounds and a conscience involved

---

[1] This is the "imperial 'we'"—the emperor refers to himself, as representative of the state, in the plural.

[2] I.e., a madam or prostitute.

[3] The betrothal and prenuptial gifts.

[4] There were two forms of punishment by exile: in the harshest, the exile lost all civil rights. In exile by relegation, he or she retained these rights.

[5] The right to return home and resume her former life.

[6] On grounds of immorality.

[7] From her marriage.

in great crimes, she shall obtain possession of her dowry and shall also retain the betrothal bounty, and she shall regain the right to marry after a period of five years from the day of the divorce. For then it will appear that she has done this from loathing of her own husband rather than from a desire for another husband.[1]

2(1). Certainly if the husband should be the first to give notice of divorce and if he should charge his wife with a grave crime, he shall prosecute the accused woman in accordance with the law, and when he has obtained his revenge, he shall both get possession of her dowry and recover his bounty [gifts] to her, and he shall acquire the unrestricted right to marry another woman immediately. 3. If it is a fault of character and not of criminality, the husband shall recover his gifts but relinquish the dowry, and he shall have the right to marry another woman after a period of two years. 4. But if the husband should wish to dissolve the marriage because of a mere disagreement and should charge the repudiated woman with no vices or sins, he shall lose both his gifts and the dowry and be compelled to live in perpetual celibacy; he shall suffer punishment for his insolent divorce in the sadness of solitude; and the woman shall be granted the right to marry after the termination of a year. Moreover, We order to be preserved the guarantees of the ancient law in regard to the retentions from dowries, on account of children.

Interpretation: If a woman should be the first to serve a notice of divorce upon her husband and should not prove the statutory grounds for divorce, she shall forfeit the betrothal bounty, and she shall not recover that which she gave her husband as dowry. In addition, she shall also be sent into exile by relegation, and she shall not have the right to marry or to return to her own.[2] Indeed, if she should prove slight faults in her husband, for which she appears to seek a divorce, she shall forfeit her dowry and shall restore the betrothal gifts, and she shall not have the right to marry another man. If, however, after divorcing her husband, she should become involved in adultery, her husband shall have the right to prosecute her even after the divorce. But if a woman who has separated from her husband should prove that he is guilty of grave and definite crimes, she shall both recover her dowry and vindicate that which her husband bestowed upon her as a betrothal bounty, and she shall have the unrestricted right of marriage after five years.

Indeed, if the husband should be the first to serve notice of divorce, he shall secure his revenge on grounds approved by law, he shall vindicate the dowry of his repudiated wife, shall recover his betrothal gifts, and shall have the right to marry another woman immediately if he wishes. If indeed there were no definite crimes, but, as often happens, the husband is displeased with the frivolity of his wife's character, he shall recover his gifts and shall restore to her immediately anything which he has received from her, and after a period of two years he shall have the right to marry another wife. But if no defect of character should be proved but merely mental discord, the innocent woman who is rejected by her husband shall both vindicate the gifts made to her by the man and shall recover her dowry. But he shall remain alone forever and shall not presume to associate himself in marriage with another woman. The woman, however, is permitted to proceed to another marriage after a year if she should so wish. But for the sake of their common children, if there should be any, the Emperor orders those rules to be observed which have been established in the law concerning retentions according to the number of children, which law Paulus sets forth in his *Book of Responses* under the title, *A Wife's Property*.[3] ...

1.3 Plague: Gregory the Great, *Letter to Bishop Dominic of Carthage* (600). Original in Latin.

The Plague of Justinian lasted from 541 to *c.*750. Named after the emperor under whom it first appeared, the plague spread across the Mediterranean and beyond, from the Middle East to Europe. Pope Gregory the Great (590–604) was well known for spearheading a drive to convert the English to Christianity (see Bede, below, p. 95), for his commentaries on the

----

[1] The husband of another woman?

[2] That is, she shall not have the right of postliminium—to return home and resume her normal life.

[3] The juridical writings of Julius Paulus (*fl. c.*200) were considered authoritative.

Book of Job and other exegetical works, and for his "biography" (in fact the second book of his *Dialogues* on the holy men of Italy) of Saint Benedict of Nursia (for whose *Rule* see below, p. 20). Gregory was also a devoted pastor who wrote a *Pastoral Rule* that served as a handbook for priests throughout the Middle Ages. In his letter to Dominic, who held the important position of bishop of Carthage, Gregory set forth in brief many of the ideas about the purposes of tribulation in this world that earlier had been elaborated in detail by Augustine (see *The City of God*, below p. 16). To counter the plague at Rome, Gregory organized penitential processions there at the beginning of his papacy and probably again *c.*602; these were among the "good deeds and tears of penitence" that he mentioned in his letter to Dominic.

1. Why would Gregory, based in the city of Rome, be concerned about an African bishop?
2. In what ways did Gregory consider the plague to be a "positive" event?

[Source: *Gregorii Magni Registrum epistularum libri VIII-XIV* 10.20, ed. Dag Norberg, Corpus Christianorum, Series Latina 140A (Turnhout: Brepols, 1982), pp. 850–51. Translated by Carole Straw.]

Gregory to Dominic, Bishop of Carthage

We already know how great a plague has invaded Africa;[1] and since not even Italy is free from the attack of this scourge, the groans of our grief are doubled. But amidst these evils and other innumerable calamities, dearest brother,[2] our heart would fail in tribulation without hope unless the Lord's voice had forearmed our frailty. For long ago, the trumpet of the Gospel text resounded for the faithful, foreshadowing the impending end of the world: pestilence, wars and many other things that up to now, as you know, we awaited in fear, and will come. But since we suffer these things that we foreknow, surely we ought not to be afflicted by them as if they were unknown to us. For often even the kind of death is a consolation, considering other ways of dying. How many mutilations and cruelties have we seen for which only death was the remedy, when life was torture? When the choice of a death was offered David, did he not decide that his people should die at the hand of God, rejecting famine and the sword?[3] You realize from this how much grace there is for those who die from a divine blow, when they die in the way that was offered as a gift to the holy prophet. And so, let us give thanks in every adversity to our Creator and, trusting in his mercy, let us endure everything with patience,

for we suffer even less than we deserve. And since we are scourged in this life so that we may by no means be left without the consolation of eternal life, it is necessary that the more we know the nearness of the judgment to come—as these signs declare—the more we should safeguard the accounts we must render to his examination, through the zeal of good deeds and tears of penitence. In this way, by means of the favor of His grace, such great blows do not become for us the beginning of damnation, but the blessing of purification. But since the nature of our weakness is that we cannot help but grieve for those dying, let this teaching of your fraternity be a comfort to those in tribulation. Let it inculcate into them the stability of the promised good things [of Heaven], so that, strengthened by the most certain hope, they learn not to grieve for the loss of passing things, in comparison to the gift to come. Let your word prevent them (as we believe it does) more and more from perpetrating wicked deeds, let it set forth in full the reward of the good and the punishment of evil so that those who love good the less should at least thoroughly fear wrongdoing and restrain themselves from what must be punished. For those who live among the scourges, to commit deeds worthy of scourges is a special form of pride against the punisher, and it is to irritate all the more the anger of the one who lashes.[4] And

---

[1] Gregory is using the "royal we" here; he means himself.

[2] Why would Gregory invoke the metaphor of brotherhood with Dominic even though they were not blood brothers?

[3] In 2 Sam. 24, David orders a census to count the number of fighting men in Israel and Judah. Then he repents. God gives him three ways to die: seven years' famine, three months' flight from the enemy in hot pursuit, or three days of pestilence. Afraid of falling into human hands, David chooses death at God's hand, namely by pestilence. Many die, but he does not.

[4] The "punisher" and "the one who lashes" refer to God.

it is the first kind of madness not to want someone justly to cease his evil deeds, and unjustly to wish that God would check his punishment. But since we need divine assistance in these things, let us, beloved brother, with joined prayers beseech the clemency of almighty God that he may allow us to accomplish things worthily, and may goad the hearts of the people mercifully to do these things, so that as we conform our actions wholesomely in fear of God, we may merit to be rescued from the evils assailing us and to reach to heavenly joys, led by his grace, without which we can do nothing.

HERESY AND ORTHODOXY

1.4 Heretics: *Manichaean Texts* (before 350?). Original in Coptic.

The Manichaeans were founded by Mani (216–277), a Persian prince who early in life joined an ascetic group devoted to spreading the message of Christ. In 240, when he was 24 years old, driven by visions and revelations, he left that group to found a new religion with its own rituals and texts. Spread through active missionizing, especially in India and Egypt, Mani's teachings were enormously popular. At its height, it had followers both in the east and west and engaged (and argued) with Zoroastrianism, Christianity, Taoism, Buddhism, and, later, Islam.

Styling himself the "apostle of Jesus Christ," Mani considered his religion to be the ultimate one, subsuming and fulfilling all the others. In the late Roman Empire, Manichaeism was a lively rival of the Roman brand of Christianity, attracting even the young Augustine (for whom see two readings below, pp. 12 and 16). Although in detail very elaborate and complex, Mani's teachings must here be summed up briefly. The universe had two principles: light (which was good and equivalent to life) and darkness (which was evil and equivalent to death). Originally, these two were separate; then (in our own historical time) they mingled; finally, at the end of time, light (along with goodness and life) will triumph. Human beings represent a mingling: their materiality, carnality and sexuality is death; their soul is divine and is life itself. The task of this period of history is to liberate and save the soul. The Manichaean "elect" delighted in knowing about the many emanations of the divine, in practicing lives of strict asceticism, and in anticipating their triumphant entry into eternal life. Habitual sinners could expect eternal death; ordinary believers could look forward to rebirth in new bodies—with a new chance at election.

The two documents presented here witness to the Manichaean message. The first, Psalm 223, was probably originally composed in Aramaic, perhaps just after Mani's death. It seems to have circulated in a variety of formats alongside other psalms composed by different authors. Although the version here comes from a finely produced Coptic Manichaean Psalm book dating from the late 4th or early 5th century, it is probably safe to assume that the psalm itself comes from before 350.

The second document, "The Chapters of the Teacher"—the *kephalaia*—was probably written around the same time as the psalms, perhaps also in Aramaic. Purporting to report the very words of Mani, it was no doubt very much reworked in the form that we have it. Chapter 79, given here, probably reflects the beliefs and practices of the elect in the 4th century.

1. Imagine and describe the audience that might have read or listened to these texts.
2. How might these texts have appealed to people living in the newly Christianized Roman Empire?

[Source: *Manichaean Texts from the Roman Empire*, ed. Iain Gardner and Samuel N.C. Lieu (Cambridge: Cambridge University Press, 2004), pp. 176–79, 240 (notes added).]

[Psalm] 223

Let us worship the Spirit of the Paraclete.[1]

Let us bless our lord Jesus who has sent to us
  the Spirit of truth. He came and separated us from
    the error
  of the world, he brought us a mirror, we looked,
  we saw the all in it.   5

When the Holy Spirit came he revealed to us
  the way of truth and taught us that there are two
  natures, that of light and that of darkness,
  separate one from the other from the beginning.

The kingdom of light, on the one hand consisted in
    five   10
  greatnesses, and they are the Father and his twelve
  aeons and the aeons of the aeons, the living air,
  the land of light; the Great Spirit breathing in them,
  nourishing them with its light.

However, the kingdom of darkness consists of five
    storehouses,   15
  which are smoke and fire
  and wind and water and darkness; their counsel
  creeping in them, moving them and raising them
  to make war with one another.

Now, as they were making war with one another they
    dared   20
  to make an attempt upon the land of light, thinking
    that they
  would be able to conquer it. Yet they know not that
    which they have
  thought to do they will bring down upon their own
    heads.

And there was a multitude of angels in the land of the
    light,
  having the power to go forth to subdue the enemy 25
  of the Father, whom it pleased that by his word that
  he would send, he should subdue the rebels who
    desired
  to exalt themselves above that which was more
    exalted than they.

Like unto a shepherd that shall see a lion coming to
  destroy his sheep-fold: for he uses guile and takes 30
  a lamb and sets it as a snare that he may catch him
  by it; for by a single lamb he saves his
  sheep-fold. After these things he heals the lamb that
  has been wounded by the lion.

This too is the way of the Father, who sent his   35
  strong son; and he produced from himself his
  virgin equipped with five powers, that
  she might fight against the five abysses of the dark.

When the watcher stood by the border
  of the light, he showed to them his virgin who   40
  is his soul; they bestirred themselves in their abyss,
    desiring
  to exalt themselves over her, they opened their
    mouth desiring
  to swallow her.

He held fast her crown, he spread her over them, like
  nets over fishes, he made her rain down upon them
        45
  like purified clouds of water, she thrust herself
  within them like piercing lightning. She crept in
    their
  inward parts, she bound them all, they not knowing
    it.

---

[1] The Paraclete is mentioned in John 14:16 as the one who will take the place of Jesus. This is Mani.

When the First Man had perfected his war,
 the Father sent his second son. 50
 He came and helped his brother out of the abyss;
 he established this whole universe out of the mixture
   that
 took place of the light and the darkness.

He spread out all the powers of the abyss to ten heavens
   and
 eight earths, he shut them up in this universe 55
 for a season; while he made it a prison for all the
   powers of darkness,
 it is also a place of purification for the soul that was
 swallowed in them.

The sun and moon he founded, he set them on high, to
 purify the soul. Daily they take up the refined part 60
 to the heights, but the dregs however they scrape
 down to the abyss, what is mixed they convey
 above and below.

This entire universe stands firm for a season, there
 being a great building which is being built outside
   this 65
 world. So soon as that Builder shall finish,
 the whole universe will be dissolved and set on fire
 that the fire may smelt it away.

All life, the relic of light wheresoever it be, he will
 gather to himself and of it depict a Statue. 70
 And the counsel of death too, all the darkness,
 he will gather together and paint its very self for a
   [bond (?)]¹
 for the ruler.

In an instant the Living Spirit will come ...
 ... he will succor the light. However, the counsel of
   death 75
 and the darkness he will shut up in the tomb
 that was established for it, that it might be bound in
   it for ever.

There is no other means to bind the enemy save this
   means;
 for he will not be received to the light because he is a
   stranger to it;

nor again can he be left in his land of darkness, that
 he may 80
 not wage a war greater than the first.

A new aeon will be built in the place of this universe
 that shall dissolve, that in it the powers of the light
   may
 reign, because they have performed and fulfilled the
   will
 of the Father entire, they have subdued the hated
   one, they have 85
 ... over him for ever.

This is the knowledge of Mani, let us worship him
 and bless him. Blessed is he every one that believes
   in him,
 for he it is who may live with all the righteous.

Glory and victory to our lord Mani, the Spirit of 90
 truth that comes from the Father, who has unveiled
   for us
 the beginning, the middle and the end.
Victory to the soul of the blessed Maria, Theona, Pshai,
 Jmnoute.²

The Chapters of the Teacher (kephalaia) 79: "Concerning the Fasting of the Saints"

Once more the enlightener speaks to his disciples: "The fasting that the saints fast by is profitable for four great works.

The first work: Shall the holy man punish his body by fasting, he subdues the entire ruling-power that exists in him.

The second: This soul that comes in to him in the administration of his food, day by day; it shall be made holy, cleansed, purified, and washed from the adulteration of the darkness that is mixed in with it.

The third: That person shall make every deed a holy one; the mystery of the children of light in whom there is neither corruption nor ... the food, nor [do they] wound it. Rather, they are holy, there is nothing in them that defiles, as they live in peace.

The fourth: They make a ... the Cross, they restrain their hands from the hand [that harms and] ... not

---

¹ The word "bond" is a conjecture by the editors. The ellipses (...) below mean that one or more words are missing.
² Maria, etc. Perhaps these names refer to Manichaean martyrs.

destroy the living soul.

The fasting is profitable to the saints for these four great works should they persist; that is if they are constant in them daily, and cause the body to make its members to fast with a holy fast.

... [The Catechumens of the] faith. They who have not strength to fast daily should make their fast on the lord's day. They too make a contribution to the works and the fasting of the saints by their faith and their alms."

1.5 Orthodoxy's declaration: *The Nicene Creed* (325). Original in Greek.

A dispute between Bishop Alexander of Alexandria and Arius, an Alexandrian priest, concerning the relationship between the Father and the Son (Jesus Christ) within the Godhead had such far-flung repercussions that Emperor Constantine (r.306–337) called the Council of Nicaea (325), the first "ecumenical" (universal) council, to adjudicate the matter. We do not know precisely what Arius taught, but he clearly subordinated the Son to the Father. The council declared that the Son was of the "same substance" (*homousios*) as the Father and thus not subordinate, a formulation that Arius could not accept. Although Arius was excommunicated, some of his supporters remained in high positions. When Constantius II (r.337–361) came to the imperial throne, he favored the position that the Orthodox called "Arian" and supported Ulfila, whose missionary work among the Goths led to their adoption of "Arianism." Although—or perhaps because—the Goths were allowed into the empire in 376, the Council of Constantinople, held in 381, affirmed the ban on Arianism, in effect branding as heretics the Goths and other barbarian tribes who adopted the Arian position.

1. What are the implications of making the Son of God of one substance with the Father?
2. What are points of comparison (the similarities and the differences) between Orthodox Christian beliefs as set forth in the Nicene Creed and those of the Manichaeans as espoused in Psalm 223?

[Source: John N.D. Kelly, *Early Christian Doctrines*, 2nd ed. (New York: Harper and Row, 1958), p. 232.]

We believe in one God, the Father almighty, maker of all things, visible and invisible;

And in one Lord Jesus Christ, the Son of God, begotten from the Father, only-begotten, that is, from the substance of the Father, God from God, light from light, true God from true God, begotten not made, of one substance [*homousios*] with the Father, through Whom all things came into being, things in heaven and things on earth, Who because of us men and because of our salvation came down and became incarnate, becoming man, suffered and rose again on the third day, ascended to the heavens, and will come to judge the living and the dead;

And in the Holy Spirit. But as for those who say, There was when He was not, and, Before being born He was not, and that He came into existence out of nothing, or who assert that the Son of God is from a different hypostasis or substance, or is created, or is subject to alteration or change—these the Catholic Church anathematizes.[1]

---

[1] I.e., excommunicates.

PATRISTIC THOUGHT

1.6 Conversion: Augustine, *Confessions* (397–401). Original in Latin.

The man who would become bishop of Hippo (today Annaba, in Algeria) in 396 and the preeminent Church Father in the West by the time he died, Augustine (354–430) was the son of a pagan father, Patricius, and a Christian mother, Monica. Educated in rhetoric at schools near his home in Roman North Africa, he seemed headed for a prestigious professional career in law. He threw himself with passion into various modes of life, all (until the last one) recounted with regret in his autobiographical *Confessions*. Involved in a long-term relationship with a woman he never named, he had a son, Adeodatus (meaning: "given by God"). Around the same time, he was attracted to Manichaeism (see above, p. 8) and, after reading Cicero's *Hortensius*, decided to devote himself to philosophy. At that point, he quit studying to become a lawyer and began to teach. All the while his mother prayed that he would convert to the Roman Church, and once Theodosius I became emperor (r.379–395) and made Christianity the official religion, there was yet another good reason to make the conversion. But Augustine did not do so right away. He had first to become disillusioned with the Manichaeans and to hear the sermons of Bishop Ambrose of Milan, which taught him how to understand the Bible spiritually. The excerpt that follows from Book 7, Chapters 5–7 and 12 of his *Confessions* begins around this time, when a Christian named Simplicianus told Augustine about a rhetorician and teacher, Victorinus, who had had the courage to give up his career to follow Christ.

1. What were Augustine's two wills and which one won in the end?
2. Why doesn't Augustine consider his conversion to be his own achievement?

[Source: *The Confessions of St. Augustine*, trans. Rex Warner (New York: Mentor, 1963), pp. 167–74, 181–83 (notes added).]

5. When this man of yours, Simplicianus, told me all this about Victorinus,[1] I was on fire to be like him, and this, of course, was why he had told me the story. He told me this too—that in the time of the Emperor Julian (r.361–363), when a law was passed forbidding Christians to teach literature and rhetoric, Victorinus had obeyed the law, preferring to give up his talking-shop rather than your Word, by which you make even the tongues of infants eloquent. In this I thought that he was not only brave but lucky, because he had got the chance of giving all his time to you. This was just what I longed for myself, but I was held back, and I was held back not by fetters put on me by someone else, but by the iron bondage of my own will. The enemy [i.e., the Devil] held my will and made a chain out of it and bound me with it. From a perverse will came lust, and slavery to lust became a habit, and the habit, being constantly yielded to, became a necessity. These were like links, hanging each to each (which is why I called it a chain), and they held me fast in a hard slavery. And the new will which I was beginning to have

---

[1] "This man of yours": "yours" refers to God, to whom the *Confessions* are addressed. Victorinus had been a celebrated teacher and champion of the pagan gods. Eventually, however, he was willing to jeopardize his fame and publicly declare himself a Christian. This happened in the mid-fourth century, before the 380s, when a series of laws made Christianity the official religion of the Roman Empire.

and which urged me to worship you in freedom and to enjoy you, God, the only certain joy, was not yet strong enough to overpower the old will which by its oldness had grown hard in me. So my two wills, one old, one new, one carnal, one spiritual, were in conflict, and they wasted my soul by their discord.

In this way my personal experience enabled me to understand what I had read—that "the flesh lusteth against the spirit and the spirit against the flesh."[1] I, no doubt, was on both sides, but I was more myself when I was on the side which I approved of for myself than when I was on the side of which I disapproved. For it was no longer really I myself who was on this second side, since there to a great extent I was rather suffering things against my will than doing them voluntarily. Yet it was my own fault that habit fought back so strongly against me; for I had come willingly where I now did not will to be. And who has any right to complain when just punishment overtakes the sinner? Nor did I have any longer the excuse which I used to think I had when I said that the reason why I had not yet forsaken the world and given myself up to your service was because I could not see the truth clearly. Now I could see it perfectly clearly. But I was still tied down to earth and refused to take my place in your army. And I was just as frightened of being freed from all my hampering baggage as I ought to have been frightened of being hampered. The pack of this world was a kind of pleasant weight upon me, as happens in sleep, and the thoughts in which I meditated on you were like the efforts of someone who tries to get up but is so overcome with drowsiness that he sinks back again into sleep. Of course no one wants to sleep forever, and everyone in his senses would agree that it is better to be awake; yet all the same, when we feel a sort of lethargy in our limbs, we often put off the moment of shaking off sleep, and, even though it is time to get up, we gladly take a little longer in bed, conscious though we may be that we should not be doing so. In just the same way I was quite certain that it was better to give myself up to your charity rather than to give in to my own desires; but, though the former course was a conviction to which I gave my assent, the latter was a pleasure to which I gave my consent. For I had no answer to make to you when you called me; "Awake, thou that sleepest, and arise from the dead, and Christ shall give thee light."[2] And, while you showed me wherever I looked that what you said was true, I, convinced by the truth, could still find nothing at all to say except lazy words spoken half asleep: "A minute," "just a minute," "just a little time longer." But there was no limit to the minutes, and the little time longer went a long way. It was in vain that "I delighted in Thy law according to the inner man, when another law in my members rebelled against the law of my mind, and led me captive under the law of sin which was in my members."[3] For the law of sin is the strong force of habit, which drags the mind along and controls it even against its will—though deservedly, since the habit was voluntarily adopted. "Who then should deliver me this wretched from the body of this death, by Thy grace only, through Jesus Christ our Lord?"[4]

6. Now, Lord, my helper and my redeemer, I shall tell and confess to your name how it was that you freed me from the bondage of my desire for sex, in which I was so closely fettered, and from my slavery to the affairs of this world. I was leading my usual life; my anxiety was growing greater and greater, and every day I sighed to you. I went often to your Church, whenever I had time to spare from all that business under the weight of which I was groaning. Alypius[5] was with me. He was free from his official legal work after a third term as assessor and was now waiting to sell his legal advice to anyone who came along, just as I was selling the ability to make speeches—if such an ability can be imparted by teaching. Nebridius, as an act of friendship to us, had consented to teach under Verecundus, a great friend of us all, a citizen and elementary schoolmaster of Milan. He had been very eager to have Nebridius on his staff and indeed had claimed it as something due from our friendship that one of us should come and give him the help and support which he badly needed. Nebridius was not influenced by any desire for profit; he could have done better for himself by teaching literature, if he had wanted. But he was the kindest and best of friends, and, being always ready to help others, would not turn down our request. He conducted himself very carefully in his work, being unwilling to become known in what are regarded by the world as "distinguished circles," and avoiding everything which could disturb his peace of mind; for he wanted to have his

---

[1] Gal. 5:17.

[2] Eph. 5:14.

[3] Rom. 7:22–23.

[4] Rom. 7:24.

[5] Alypius was one of Augustine's friends.

mind free and at leisure for as many hours as possible so as to pursue wisdom, to read about it, or to hear about it.

One day, when Alypius and I were at home (Nebridius, for some reason which I cannot remember, was away) we were visited by a man called Ponticianus who, coming from Africa, was a fellow countryman of ours and who held an important appointment at the emperor's court. He had something or other which he wanted to ask us, and we sat down to talk. In front of us was a table for playing games on, and he happened to notice a book lying on the table. He took it, opened it, and found that it was the apostle Paul. He was quite surprised at this, since he had imagined it would be one of the books over which I wearied myself out in the course of my profession. Next he began to smile and, looking closely at me, told me that he was not only surprised but pleased at his unexpected discovery that I had this book and only this book at my side. For he was a Christian, and baptized. He often knelt before you, our God, in Church, praying long and frequently to you. I told him that I gave the greatest attention to these works of Scripture, and then, on his initiative, a conversation began about the Egyptian monk Antony, whose name was very well known among your servants, although Alypius and I up to this time had never heard of him. When Ponticianus discovered this he talked all the more about him, since he wanted us in our ignorance, at which he was much surprised, to learn more about such a great man. And we were amazed as we heard of these wonderful works of yours which had been witnessed by so many people, had been done in the true faith and the Catholic Church, and all so recently—indeed practically in our own times. All of us were full of wonder, Alypius and I at the importance of what we were hearing, Ponticianus at the fact that we had never heard the story before.

He went on to speak of the communities living in monasteries, of their way of life which was full of the sweet fragrance of you, and of the fruitful deserts in the wilderness, about which we knew nothing. There was actually a monastery in Milan outside the walls of the city. It was full of good brothers and was under the care of Ambrose, but we had not even heard of this. So Ponticianus went on speaking and we sat quiet, listening to him eagerly. In the course of his talk he told us how once, when the emperor was at Trier and busy with holding the chariot races in the Circus, he himself with three friends had gone for a walk in the afternoon through the gardens near the city walls. It happened that they walked in two groups, one of the three going one way with him, and the others going another way by themselves. These other two, as they strolled along, happened to come to a small house which was inhabited by some of your servants, "poor in spirit, of whom is the kingdom of heaven,"[1] and there they found a book in which was written an account of the life of Antony. One of the two friends began to read it. He became full of wonder and excitement, and, as he read, he began to think of how he himself could lead a life like this and, abandoning his profession in this world, give his service to you. For these two men were both officials in the emperor's civil service. Suddenly, then, he was filled with a holy love; he felt a sober shame, and, angry with himself, he looked toward his friend and said: "Tell me now; in all this hard work which we do, what are we aiming at? What is it that we want? Why is it that we are state officials? Can we have any higher hope at court than to become friends of the emperor? And is not that a position difficult to hold and full of danger? Indeed does one not have to go through danger after danger simply to reach a place that is more dangerous still? And how long will it take to get there? But, if I want, I can be the friend of God now, this moment." After saying this, he turned back to the book, troubled and perplexed by the new life to which he was giving birth. So he read on, and his heart, where you saw it, was changed, and, as soon appeared, his mind shook off the burden of the world. While he was reading and the waves in his heart rose and fell, there were times when he cried out against himself, and then he distinguished the better course and chose it for his own. Now he was yours, and he said to his friend: "I have now broken away from all our hopes and ambitions and have decided to serve God, and I am entering on this service now, this moment, in this place. You may not like to imitate me in this, but you must not oppose me."

The other replied that he would stay with him and be his comrade in so great a service and for so great a reward. Both of them were now yours; they were building their own fortress at the right cost—namely, the forsaking of all that they had and the following of you.

At this point Ponticianus and his companion, who had been walking in a different part of the garden, looking for their friends, came and found them in this place. When they found them, they suggested that they should go back, as it was now nearly sunset. The others however told them of the decision which they had reached and what they proposed to do; they described how the whole thing had started and how their resolution was now fixed, and they begged their friends, if they would not now join

---

[1] Matt. 5:3.

them, not to interfere with their purpose. Ponticianus and his friends, while not changing from their former ways, did (as Ponticianus told us) weep for themselves and, devoutly and sincerely congratulating the others, asked them to remember them in their prayers; then, with their own hearts still down on the earth, they went off to the palace. But the other two, with their hearts fixed on heaven, remained there in the cottage. Each of these two was engaged to be married, and when the girls to whom they were engaged heard what had happened, they also dedicated their virginity to you.

7. This was what Ponticianus told us. But you, Lord, while he was speaking, were turning me around so that I could see myself; You took me from behind my own back, which was where I had put myself during the time when I did not want to be observed by myself, and you set me in front of my own face so that I could see how foul a sight I was—crooked, filthy, spotted, and ulcerous. I saw and I was horrified, and I had nowhere to go to escape from myself. If I tried to look away from myself, Ponticianus still went on with his story, and again you were setting me in front of myself, forcing me to look into my own face, so that I might see my sin and hate it. I did know it, but I pretended that I did not. I had been pushing the whole idea away from me and forgetting it.

But now the more ardent was the love I felt for those two men of whom I was hearing and of how healthfully they had been moved to give themselves up entirely to you to be cured, the more bitter was the hatred I felt for myself when I compared myself with them. Many years (at least twelve) of my own life had gone by since the time when I was nineteen and was reading Cicero's *Hortensius* and had been fired with an enthusiasm for wisdom. Yet I was still putting off the moment when, despising this world's happiness, I should give all my time to the search for that of which not only the finding but merely the seeking must be preferred to the discovered treasures and kingdoms of men or to all the pleasures of the body easily and abundantly available. But I, wretched young man that I was—even more wretched at the beginning of my youth—had begged you for chastity and had said: "Make me chaste and continent, but not yet." I was afraid that you might hear me too soon and cure me too soon from the disease of a lust which I preferred to be satisfied rather than extinguished. And I had gone along evil ways, following a sacrilegious superstition—not because I was convinced by it, but simply preferring it to the other

doctrines into which I never inquired in a religious spirit, but merely attacked them in a spirit of spite.

I had thought that the reason why I was putting off from day to day the time when I should despise all worldly hopes and follow you alone was because I could see no certainty toward which I could direct my course. But now the day had come when in my own eyes I was stripped naked and my conscience cried out against me: "Can you not hear me? Was it not this that you used to say, that you would not throw off the burden of vanity for a truth that was uncertain? Well, look. Now the truth is certain, and you are still weighed down by your burden. Yet these others, who have not been so worn out in the search and not been meditating the matter for ten years or more, have had the weight taken from their backs and have been given wings to fly."

So I was being gnawed at inside, and as Ponticianus went on with his story I was lost and overwhelmed in a terrible kind of shame. When the story was over and the business about which he had come had been settled he went away, and I retired into myself. Nor did I leave anything unsaid against myself. With every scourge of condemnation I lashed my soul on to follow me now that I was trying to follow you. And my soul hung back; it refused to follow, and it could give no excuse for its refusal. All the arguments had been used already and had been shown to be false. There remained a mute shrinking; for it feared like death to be restrained from the flux of a habit by which it was melting away into death.

...

12. And now from my hidden depths my searching thought had dragged up and set before the sight of my heart the whole mass of my misery. Then a huge storm rose up within me bringing with it a huge downpour of tears. So that I might pour out all these tears and speak the words that came with them I rose up from Alypius (solitude seemed better for the business of weeping) and went further away so that I might not be embarrassed even by his presence. This was how I felt and he realized it. No doubt I had said something or other, and he could feel the weight of my tears in the sound of my voice. And so I rose to my feet, and he, in a state of utter amazement, remained in the place where we had been sitting. I flung myself down on the ground somehow under a fig tree and gave free rein to my tears; they streamed and flooded from my eyes, an "acceptable sacrifice to Thee."[1]

---

[1] Recalling Phil. 4:18.

And I kept saying to you, not perhaps in these words, but with this sense: "And Thou, O Lord, how long? How long, Lord; wilt Thou be angry forever? Remember not our former iniquities."[1] For I felt that it was these which were holding me fast. And in my misery I would exclaim: "How long, how long this 'tomorrow and tomorrow'? Why not now? Why not finish this very hour with my uncleanness?"

So I spoke, weeping in the bitter contrition of my heart. Suddenly a voice reaches my ears from a nearby house. It is the voice of a boy or a girl (I don't know which) and in a kind of singsong the words are constantly repeated: "Take it and read it. Take it and read it." At once my face changed, and I began to think carefully of whether the singing of words like these came into any kind of game which children play, and I could not remember that I had ever heard anything like it before. I checked the force of my tears and rose to my feet, being quite certain that I must interpret this as a divine command to me to open the book and read the first passage which I should come upon. For I had heard this about Antony: he had happened to come in when the Gospel was being read, and as though the words read were spoken directly to himself, had received the admonition: "Go, sell all that thou hast, and give to the poor, and thou shalt have treasure in heaven, and come and follow me."[2] And by such an oracle he had been immediately converted to you.

So I went eagerly back to the place where Alypius was sitting, since it was there that I had left the book of the Apostle when I rose to my feet. I snatched up the book, opened it, and read in silence the passage upon which my eyes first fell: "Not in rioting and drunkenness, not in chambering and wantonness, not in strife and envying:

but put ye on the Lord Jesus Christ, and make not provision for the flesh in concupiscence."[3] I had no wish to read further; there was no need to. For immediately I had reached the end of this sentence it was as though my heart was filled with a light of confidence and all the shadows of my doubt were swept away.

Before shutting the book I put my finger or some other marker in the place and told Alypius what had happened. By now my face was perfectly calm. And Alypius in his turn told me what had been going on in himself, and which I knew nothing about. He asked to see the passage which I had read. I showed him and he went on further than the part I had read, nor did I know the words which followed. They were these: "Him that is weak in the faith, receive."[4] He applied this to himself and told me so. He was strengthened by the admonition; calmly and unhesitatingly he joined me in a purpose and a resolution so good, and so right for his character, which had always been very much better than mine.

The next thing we do is to go inside and tell my mother. How happy she is! We describe to her how it all took place, and there is no limit to her joy and triumph. Now she was praising you, "Who art able to do above that which we ask or think";[5] for she saw that with regard to me you had given her so much more than she used to ask for when she wept so pitifully before you. For you converted me to you in such a way that I no longer sought a wife nor any other worldly hope. I was now standing on that rule of faith, just as you had shown me to her in a vision so many years before. And so you had changed her mourning into joy, a joy much richer than she had desired and much dearer and purer than that which she looked for by having grandchildren of my flesh.

1.7 Relating this world to the next: Augustine, *The City of God* (413–426). Original in Latin.

As a young man, St. Augustine (354–430) wanted to be an orator and teacher—that is, a rhetorician—but his restless quest for life's meaning led him to make a dramatic conversion, chronicled in his *Confessions* (above, p. 12). Later, as bishop of Hippo in North

---

[1] See Ps. 6:3.

[2] Matt. 19:21.

[3] Rom. 13:13.

[4] Rom. 14:1.

[5] Eph. 3:20.

Africa (r.395–430), he became the most influential churchman of his day and for centuries to come, especially in the Roman Catholic West. Counted among the Church Fathers, Augustine formulated many of the key themes of Western Christianity until at least the twelfth century. Perhaps the most enduring of his works was *The City of God*, which, by postulating two cities—the City of God and the City of Man—permitted Augustine to explore the mingling of the sacred with the secular realms, the uses of adversity in the world, the vision of Heaven as a place of total peace, and the idea that the life of man on earth is a pilgrimage—a holy trek—from home (the here-and-now) to a longed-for place of succor (the City of God). In spite of these universal and timeless themes, the book was written in response to a very specific historical event: the sack of Rome by the Visigoths under their leader Alaric in 410.

1. What does Augustine mean when he says that the City of God exists as "a stranger among the ungodly, living by faith"?
2. What are the evils of human society in Augustine's view, and why does he say that nevertheless the "life of the saints" is "social"?

[Source: Augustine, *Concerning the City of God against the Pagans*, trans. Henry Bettenson (New York: Penguin, 1972), pp. 5–7, 13–17, 858–59, 881, 891–92.]

Book 1

PREFACE. THE PURPOSE AND ARGUMENT OF THIS WORK

Here, my dear Marcellinus,[1] is the fulfilment of my promise, a book in which I have taken upon myself the task of defending the glorious City of God against those who prefer their own gods to the Founder of that City. I treat of it both as it exists in this world of time, a stranger among the ungodly, living by faith,[2] and as it stands in the security of its everlasting seat. This security it now awaits in steadfast patience, until "justice returns to judgment,"[3] but it is to attain it hereafter in virtue of its ascendancy over its enemies, when the final victory is won and peace established. The task is long and arduous; but God is our helper.[4]

I know how great is the effort needed to convince the proud of the power and excellence of humility, an excellence which makes it soar above all the summits of this world, which sway in their temporal instability, overtopping them all with an eminence not arrogated by human pride, but granted by divine grace. For the King and Founder of this City which is our subject has revealed in the Scripture of his people this statement of the divine Law, "God resists the proud, but he gives grace to the humble."[5] This is God's prerogative; but man's arrogant spirit in its swelling pride has claimed it as its own, and delights to hear this verse quoted in its own praise: "To spare the conquered, and beat down the proud."[6]

Therefore I cannot refrain from speaking about the city of this world, a city which aims at dominion, which

---

[1] Marcellinus (d.413) was an intimate disciple of St. Augustine sent by the Emperor Honorius to preside over the council summoned at Carthage to settle the dispute between Catholics and Donatists. Marcellinus was anxious to convert Volusianus (d.437), proconsul of Africa. Volusianus showed interest, but among his objections to Christianity was the charge that it had undermined the Roman Empire. Marcellinus wrote to ask for help from St. Augustine (who had already corresponded with Volusianus), and this led eventually to the writing of *The City of God*.

[2] See Hab. 2:4; Rom. 1:17; Gal. 3:11; Heb. 10:38.

[3] Ps. 94:15; Douay Ps. 93:15.

[4] See Ps. 118:7; Douay Ps. 117:7.

[5] 1 Pet. 5:5.

[6] Virgil, *Aeneid* 6.853.

holds nations in enslavement, but is itself dominated by that very lust of domination. I must consider this city as far as the scheme of this work demands and as occasion serves.

1. THE ENEMIES OF CHRISTIANITY WERE SPARED BY THE BARBARIANS AT THE SACK OF ROME, OUT OF RESPECT FOR CHRIST

From this world's city there arise enemies against whom the City of God has to be defended, though many of these correct their godless errors and become useful citizens of that City. But many are inflamed with hate against it and feel no gratitude for the benefits offered by its Redeemer. The benefits are unmistakable; those enemies would not today be able to utter a word against the City if, when fleeing from the sword of their enemy, they had not found, in the City's holy places, the safety on which they now congratulate themselves.[1] The barbarians spared them for Christ's sake; and now these Romans assail Christ's name. The sacred places of the martyrs and the basilicas of the apostles bear witness to this, for in the sack of Rome they afforded shelter to fugitives, both Christian and pagan. The bloodthirsty enemy raged thus far, but here the frenzy of butchery was checked; to these refuges the merciful among the enemy conveyed those whom they had spared outside, to save them from encountering foes who had no such pity. Even men who elsewhere raged with all the savagery an enemy can show, arrived at places where practices generally allowed by laws of war were forbidden and their monstrous passion for violence was brought to a sudden halt; their lust for taking captives was subdued.

In this way many escaped who now complain of this Christian era, and hold Christ responsible for the disasters which their city endured. But they do not make Christ responsible for the benefits they received out of respect for Christ, to which they owed their lives. They attribute their deliverance to their own destiny; whereas if they had any right judgment they ought rather to attribute the harsh cruelty they suffered at the hands of their enemies to the providence of God. For God's providence constantly uses war to correct and chasten the corrupt morals of mankind, as it also uses such afflictions to train men in a righteous and laudable way of life, removing to a better state those whose life is approved, or else keeping them in this world for further service.

Moreover, they should give credit to this Christian era for the fact that these savage barbarians showed mercy beyond the custom of war—whether they so acted in general in honor of the name of Christ, or in places specially dedicated to Christ's name, buildings of such size and capacity as to give mercy a wider range. For this clemency our detractors ought rather to give thanks to God; they should have recourse to his name in all sincerity so as to escape the penalty of everlasting fire, seeing that so many of them assumed his name dishonestly, to escape the penalty of immediate destruction. Among those whom you see insulting Christ's servants with such wanton insolence there are very many who came unscathed through that terrible time of massacre only by passing themselves off as Christ's servants. And now with ungrateful pride and impious madness they oppose his name in the perversity of their hearts, so that they may incur the punishment of eternal darkness; but then they took refuge in that name, though with deceitful lips, so that they might continue to enjoy this transitory light....

8. BLESSINGS AND DISASTERS OFTEN SHARED BY GOOD AND BAD

No doubt this question will be asked, "Why does the divine mercy extend even to the godless and ungrateful?" The only explanation is that it is the mercy of one "who makes his sun rise on the good and on the bad, and sends rain alike on the righteous and the unrighteous."[2] Some of the wicked are brought to penitence by considering these facts, and amend their impiety, while others, in the words of the Apostle, "despise the riches of God's goodness and forbearance, in the hardness and impenitence of their hearts, and lay up for themselves a store of wrath in the day of God's anger and of the revelation of the just judgment of God, who will repay every man according to his actions."[3] Yet the patience of God still invites the wicked to penitence, just as God's chastisement trains the good in patient endurance. God's mercy embraces the good for their cherishing, just as his severity chastens the wicked for their punishment. God, in his providence, decided to prepare future blessings for the righteous, which the unrighteous will not enjoy, and

---

[1] This refers to Alaric's clemency toward those who took sanctuary in Christian shrines, and especially in the basilicas of St. Peter and St. Paul.

[2] Matt. 5:45.

[3] Rom. 2:4–6; "the Apostle" refers always to St. Paul in the works of the early Fathers of the Church.

sorrows for the ungodly, with which the good will not be tormented. But he has willed that these temporal goods and temporal evils should befall good and bad alike, so that the good things should not be too eagerly coveted, when it is seen that the wicked also enjoy them, and that the evils should not be discreditably shunned, when it is apparent that the good are often afflicted with them.

The most important question is this: What use is made of the things thought to be blessings, and of the things reputed evil? The good man is not exalted by this world's goods; nor is he overwhelmed by this world's ills. The bad man is punished by misfortune of this kind just because he is corrupted by good fortune....

Book 19

5. SOCIAL LIFE; ITS VALUE AND ITS DANGERS
The philosophies hold the view that the life of the wise man should be social; and in this we support them much more heartily. For here we are, with the nineteenth book in hand on the subject of the City of God; and how could that City have made its first start, how could it have advanced along its course, how could it attain its appointed goal, if the life of the saints were not social? And yet, who would be capable of listing the number and the gravity of the ills which abound in human society amid the distresses of our mortal condition? Who would be competent to assess them? Our philosophers should listen to a character in one of their own comedies, voicing a sentiment with which all mankind agrees:

I married a wife; and misery I found!
Children were born; and they increased my cares.[1]

Again, think of the disorders of love, as listed in another quotation from Terence:

Wrongs and suspicions, enmities and war—
Then, peace again.[2]

Have they not everywhere filled up the story of human experience? Are they not of frequent occurrence, even in the honorable love of friends? The story of mankind is full

of them at every point; for in that story we are aware of wrongs, suspicions, enmities and war—undoubted evils, these. And even peace is a doubtful good, since we do not know the hearts of those with whom we wish to maintain peace, and even if we could know them today, we should not know what they might be like tomorrow. In fact, who are, in general, more friendly, or at any rate ought to be, than those within the walls of the same home? And yet, is anyone perfectly serene in that situation, when such grievous ills have so often arisen from the secret treachery of people within those walls? And the bitterness of these ills matches the sweetness of the peace that was reckoned genuine, when it was in fact only a very clever pretense.

This explains why some words of Cicero come so close to our hearts that we cannot but sigh when we read:

No treachery is more insidious than that which is hidden under a pretense of loyalty, or under the name of kinship. For against an open adversary you could be on your guard and thus easily avoid him; but this hidden evil, within the house and family, not only arises before you are aware but even overwhelms you before you can catch sight of it and investigate it.[3]

Hence also that inspired utterance, "A man's enemies are those of his own household,"[4] is heard with deep sorrow of heart. For even if anyone is strong enough to bear these ills with equanimity, or watchful enough to guard with foresight and discretion against the contrivances of pretended friendship, nevertheless he cannot but feel grievous anguish, if he himself is a good man, at the wickedness of the traitors, when by experience he knows their utter viciousness, whether they were always evil and their goodness was a sham, or whether they suffered a change from good-nature to the malice that they now display. If, then, safety is not to be found in the home, the common refuge from the evils that befall mankind, what shall we say of the city? The larger the city, the more is its forum filled with civil lawsuits and criminal trials, even if that city be at peace, free from the alarms or—what is more frequent—the bloodshed, of sedition and civil war. It is true that cities are at times

---

[1] Terence, *Adelphi* 5.4.13–14.
[2] Terence, *Eunuchus* 1.1.14–15.
[3] Cicero, *Actio in Verrem* 2.1.13.
[4] Matt. 10:36.

exempt from those occurrences; they are never free from the danger of them....

20. THE FELLOW-CITIZENS OF THE SAINTS ARE IN THIS LIFE MADE HAPPY BY HOPE

We see, then, that the Supreme Good, of the City of God is everlasting and perfect peace, which is not the peace through which men pass in their mortality, in their journey from birth, to death, but that peace in which they remain in their immortal state, experiencing no adversity at all. In view of this, can anyone deny that this is the supremely blessed life, or that the present life on earth, however full it may be of the greatest possible blessings of soul and body and of external circumstances, is, in comparison, most miserable? For all that, if anyone accepts the present life in such a spirit that he uses it with the end in view of that other life on which he has set his heart with all his ardor and for which he hopes with all his confidence, such a man may without absurdity be called happy even now, though rather by future hope than in present reality. Present reality without that hope is, to be sure, a false happiness, in fact, an utter misery. For the present does not bring into play the true goods of the mind; since no wisdom is true wisdom if it does not direct its attention, in all its prudent decisions, its resolute

actions, its self-control and its just dealings with others, towards that ultimate state in which God will be all in all,[1] in the assurance of eternity and the perfection of peace....

26. ..."Blessed is the people, whose God is the Lord."[2] It follows that a people alienated from that God must be wretched. Yet even such a people loves a peace of its own, which is not to be rejected; but it will not possess it in the end, because it does not make good use of it before the end. Meanwhile, however, it is important for us also that this people should possess this peace in this life, since so long as the two cities are intermingled we also make use of the peace of Babylon—although the People of God is by faith set free from Babylon, so that in the meantime they are only pilgrims in the midst of her. That is why the Apostle instructs the Church to pray for kings of that city and those in high positions, adding these words: "that we may lead a quiet and peaceful life with all devotion and love."[3] And when the prophet Jeremiah predicted to the ancient People of God the coming captivity, and bade them, by God's inspiration, to go obediently to Babylon, serving God even by their patient endurance, he added his own advice that prayers should be offered for Babylon, "because in her peace is your peace"[4]—meaning, of course, the temporal peace of the meantime, which is shared by good and bad alike.

1.8 Monasticism: *The Benedictine Rule* (c.530–c.560). Original in Latin.

St. Benedict (d.c.550–c.560), founder of several monasteries near Rome, wrote the most famous *Rule* for monks. In large measure it is an organized and institutionalized presentation of biblical directives, especially those inspired by the Gospels. The key virtue of the monk in Benedict's *Rule* is obedience. The key duty is the Work of God, the hours of daily chant—known as the offices[5]—centered on the Psalter, all 150 psalms of which the monks were to complete each week. Within a half-century or so, Benedict's *Rule* had been incorporated alongside others in many Western monasteries. In the ninth century, it was adopted as the official norm for the monasteries of the Carolingian Empire. Compare its notions of human virtue and life on earth with those expressed in Augustine's *City of God*, p. 16 above.

---

[1] 1 Cor. 15:28.

[2] Ps. 144:15; Douay Ps. 143:15.

[3] 1 Tim. 2:2.

[4] Jer. 29:7.

[5] These are Vigils (the Night Office), Matins, Prime, Terce, Sext, None, Vespers, and Compline.

1. What role does obedience play in the life of the monk, and why?
2. Imagine that you were the abbot of a Benedictine monastery. What would be your job description?

[Source: *The Rule of St. Benedict*, ed. and trans. Bruce L. Venarde (Cambridge, MA: Harvard University Press, 2011), pp. 3, 7, 11, 13, 15, 17, 19, 21, 23, 29, 31, 33, 35, 37, 45, 47, 57, 59, 61, 79, 85, 87, 89, 97, 123, 125, 139, 141, 143, 161, 163, 177, 179, 187, 189, 191, 193, 229 (notes modified).]

In the name of our Lord Jesus Christ, here begins the prologue of the Rule by the great father Saint Benedict

Listen carefully, my son, to the teachings of a master and incline the ear of your heart. Gladly accept and effectively fulfill the admonition of a loving father so that through the work of obedience you may return to him from whom you had withdrawn through the sloth of disobedience. To you, therefore, my word is now directed—to whoever, renouncing his own will in order to fight for the Lord Christ, the true king, takes up the brilliant and mighty weapons of obedience....

Therefore our hearts and bodies must be prepared to fight for holy obedience to his instructions and what is not possible in us by nature let us ask God to order the aid of his grace to supply us. And if, fleeing the punishments of hell, we desire to attain eternal life, while there is still time and we are in this body and there is time to carry out all these things by the light of this life, we must hurry and do now what would profit us for eternity.

Thus we must found a school for the Lord's service.[1] In its design we hope we will establish nothing harsh, nothing oppressive. But if, according to the dictates of fairness, there emerges something a little severe in the interest of amending sins or preserving love, do not at once be frightened by fear and flee the path of salvation, which can only be narrow at the start. Instead, by progress in monastic life and faith, with hearts expanded in love's indescribable sweetness, we run along the path of God's commands so that, never turning away from his instruction and persevering in his doctrine in the monastery until death, through patience we may share the sufferings of Christ and also deserve to be sharers in his kingdom. Amen.

Here begins the text of the Rule. It is called that because it rules the conduct of those who obey it.

Chapter 1
The Kinds of Monks

It is clear there are four kinds of monks. First are the cenobites, those in a monastery serving under a rule and an abbot. The second kind are anchorites, that is, hermits, those no longer fresh in the fervor of monastic life but long tested in a monastery, who have learned, by now schooled with the help of many, to fight against the Devil. Well trained among a band of brothers for single combat in the desert, by now confident even without another's encouragement, they are ready with God's help, to fight the vices of body and mind with hand and arm alone. The third, a very vile kind, are the sarabaites, tested by no rule nor instructed by experience, like gold in the furnace; but softened like lead, still keeping faith with worldly ways, they are known to lie to God by having tonsures.[2] They go around in pairs or threes or, of course, singly with no shepherd, shut in their own sheepfolds, not the Lord's, and the pleasure of their desires is their law, since they call holy whatever they have thought or chosen and they deem forbidden what they have not wished to do. The fourth kind of monks are those called gyrovagues,[3] who

---

[1] In the Latin of this period, "school" could mean not only a place where instruction was received, but also the group receiving instruction, as well as, more generally, a vocational corporation (such as a guild) of people devoted to a common craft or service. A similar usage can be seen in the English "school of painters" or "school of porpoises."

[2] The tonsure is a haircut, reminiscent of male-pattern baldness, characteristic of monks. Interestingly, Benedict does not mention it elsewhere in the *Rule*.

[3] A combination word from the Greek for "circle" and the Latin for "to wander," reminiscent of the English idiom "to go around in circles."

spend their whole lives lodging in different regions and different monasteries three or four days at a time, always wandering and never stable, serving their own wills and the lure of gluttony worse than sarabaites in every way. It is better to keep silent than to discuss the utterly wretched monastic ways of all these people. Therefore, leaving them aside, with God's help let us proceed to specifications for a very strong kind of monk, the cenobites.

Chapter 2
What Sort of Man the Abbot Should Be

An abbot who is worthy to lead a monastery should always remember what he is called and fulfill the name of "superior" in his deeds. For he is believed to act in the place of Christ in the monastery when he is called by Christ's title, as the apostle says: "You have received the spirit of the adoption of sons, in which we cry out 'Abba, Father.'"[1] Therefore, the abbot must not teach or establish or decree anything that is outside the Lord's commandments, but instead, his decrees and his teaching should sprinkle the yeast of divine justice in the minds of his disciples. The abbot must always be mindful that there will have to be a trial in God's fearsome court concerning two matters: his teaching and his disciples' obedience. And an abbot should know that whatever use the father of the household finds lacking in the sheep will be blamed on the shepherd. It will be equally the case that if all assiduous diligence is applied to a shepherd's unsettled and disobedient flock and every effort to cure its unhealthiness is applied, let their shepherd, acquitted in the Lord's judgment, say to the Lord, with the prophet, "I did not hide your justice in my heart and I spoke your truth and your salvation,[2] yet they scornfully rejected me."[3] And then in the end the punishment for disobedient sheep in his care will be death itself prevailing over them....

Chapter 3
Summoning the Brothers for Counsel

Whenever there is important business to do in the monastery, the abbot should call the whole community together and tell the brothers what it is about. After hearing the brothers' counsel, he should mull things over and do what he judges most beneficial. We said that all should be called to counsel because often the Lord reveals what is best to a junior brother.[4] Thus the brothers should give advice with all humble deference and not presume to defend their views too insistently, and instead let the decision depend on the abbot's judgment so that all may comply with what he has deemed most salutary. But just as it is fitting for disciples to obey their master, so too is it seemly for him to arrange everything justly and prudently.

Everybody therefore, should follow the Rule as a master in all things and nobody should rashly deviate from it. Nobody in the monastery should follow his own heart's will, nor presume to argue with the abbot insolently or outside the monastery.[5] Anyone who so presumes should be subject to the discipline of the Rule.[6] However, the abbot himself should do everything in fear of God and in observance of the Rule, knowing beyond all doubt that he will have to render an account concerning all his decisions to God, the most just judge.

If minor business concerning monastic interests is to be done, let the abbot take only the advice of the senior monks, as it is written: "Do everything with counsel and you will not regret it later."[7]

Chapter 4
The Tools of Good Works

First of all, "to love the Lord God with your whole heart, whole soul, and whole strength," then "your neighbor

---

[1] Rom. 8:15.

[2] Ps. 40:11; Douay Ps. 39:11.

[3] Ezek. 20:27.

[4] Junior could mean "younger" or "lesser in rank."

[5] The meaning here is obscure; as it stands, it means that respectful disagreement with the abbot is permitted only within the cloister but never outside. Some manuscripts read "inside or out," which would restrict much more severely the brothers' opportunities to question the abbot's decision.

[6] This discipline is described in chapters 23–30. It mainly involved "excommunication," that is, an internal shunning and restriction of privileges in the community.

[7] Ecclus. 32:24.

as yourself."[1] Then "not to kill, commit adultery, steal, covet, or give false testimony; honor all men,"[2] and never do to another what you do not want done to yourself.[3] "Renounce yourself to follow Christ. Punish your body,"[4] do not embrace pleasure, love fasting. Give relief to the poor, clothe the naked, visit the sick, bury the dead. Help those in trouble, comfort those in mourning. Make yourself a stranger to the ways of the world, put nothing above the love of Christ.

Do not give in to anger, or waste time holding a grudge. Keep no deceit in your heart, nor give false peace, nor abandon charity. Do not swear oaths, lest by chance you perjure yourself, speak truth with heart and tongue. "Do not return evil for evil."[5] Do no injury, but even bear patiently those done to you. "Love your enemies."[6] Do not curse in return those who curse you, but bless them instead. "Endure persecution for the sake of justice. Do not be proud, nor overly fond of wine,"[7] nor a glutton, a sluggard, "slothful," a grumbler, or a detractor....

Look: these are the tools of the spiritual craft. When we have used them day and night without ceasing and given them back on the Day of Judgment, we will receive in return the reward God himself promised: "What the eye has not seen nor the ear heard, God has prepared for those who love him."[8] The workshops where we should industriously carry all this out are the cloisters of the monastery and stability in the community....

Chapter 7
Humility

Divine Scripture calls out to us, brothers, saying, "Everyone who exalts himself will be humbled, and he who humbles himself will be exalted."[9] When it says these words, it shows us that all exaltation is a kind of pride, which the prophet shows he guards against, saying, "Lord, my heart

is not exalted, nor my eyes lifted up, nor did I move among great affairs or marvels that are beyond me." But what "if I did not understand humbly if I exalted my soul, would you refuse me in my soul like a weaned child on his mother's lap?"[10] So, brothers, if we want to reach the summit of the greatest humility and arrive quickly at that heavenly exaltation toward which we ascend through humility in this present life, as we ascend through our deeds we must raise the ladder that appeared to Jacob in his dream, on which ascending and descending angels were shown to him. We understand without a doubt that this descent and ascent can be nothing other than to descend by exaltation and ascend by humility. That raised ladder is our life in the world, which, in humble hearts, should be hoisted by the Lord to heaven. For we say that the sides of the ladder are our body and soul, in which our divine calling has placed the various rungs of humility and discipline we must climb.

The first step of humility, therefore, is that, placing the fear of God before his eyes at all times, one should altogether shun forgetfulness and always remember everything God commanded so that he always turns over in his mind both how hell burns those who scorn God for their sins and the eternal life prepared for those who fear God. Guarding himself at all times from sins and vices, those of thought, the tongue, the hands, the feet, and of his own will, but also the desires of the flesh, let him consider that he is always observed by God from heaven at all times and that his actions everywhere are seen by the divine gaze and reported by angels at all times....

Chapter 8
Divine Offices at Night

In wintertime, that is, from the first of November until Easter, reason dictates that monks should rise at the eighth hour of the night, so that after resting a little past midnight,

---

[1] Matt. 22:37, 39; Mark 12:30–31; Luke 10:27.

[2] Rom. 13:9; 1 Pet. 2:17.

[3] Tob. 4:16.

[4] Matt. 16:24; Luke 9:23; 1 Cor. 9:27.

[5] 1 Thess. 5:15.

[6] Matt. 5:44; Luke 6:27.

[7] Matt. 5:10; Titus 1:7.

[8] 1 Cor. 2:9.

[9] Luke 18:14.

[10] Ps. 131:1–2, Douay Ps. 130:1–2.

they should rise with digestion complete.[1] The time remaining after Vigils should be for study of the Psalter and readings by brothers who need it. From Easter to the abovementioned first of November, the schedule should be regulated so that, Vigils complete, there is a very brief break during which the brothers may go out for the necessities of nature, then Matins follows immediately, at first light.

Chapter 9
How Many Psalms Should Be Said[2] at the Night Offices

During wintertime as defined above, first this verse is to be said three times: "Lord, you will open my lips, and my mouth will proclaim your praise."[3] To that should be added Psalm 3 and the Gloria.[4] After that, Psalm 94 with an antiphon,[5] or at least chanted. Then an Ambrosian hymn[6] should follow, and then six psalms with antiphons. That done, after the verse is said, the abbot should give a blessing, and with everyone sitting down on benches, three readings should be recited in turn by brothers from the books on the lectern, and three responsories[7] should be chanted in between the readings. Two responsories should be said without the Gloria, but after the third reading, the chanter should say the Gloria. When the chanter begins it, all should rise from their seats at once out of honor and reverence for the Holy Trinity. Books of divine authority should be read at Vigils, from both the Old and New Testaments, and also commentaries on them written by well-known orthodox Catholic Fathers. After these three readings with their responsories, there should follow the remaining six psalms, sung with an Alleluia. After those, there should follow a reading from

the apostle, recited by heart, the verse, and the supplication of the litany that is, the Kyrie Eleison.[8] And Vigils should be concluded in this way....

Chapter 16
How Divine Works Should Be Done During the Day

As the prophet says, "I praised you seven times a day."[9] This sacred number seven will be completed by us if we fulfill the duties of our service at Matins, Prime, Terce, Sext, None, Vespers, and Compline, because he said concerning these daytime hours, "I praised you seven times a day."[10] Concerning nighttime Vigils, the same prophet says, "I rose in the middle of the night to confess your name."[11] Therefore at these times we should praise our creator "for the judgments of his justice,"[12] that is, at Matins, Prime, Terce, Sext, None, Vespers, Compline, and at night we should rise to profess his name....

Chapter 18
The Order in Which Psalms Should Be Said

... We urge this in particular: if this distribution of the psalms happens to displease someone, he should arrange it otherwise if he thinks it better, although in any case he must ensure that the entire Psalter is sung every week, the full complement of 150 psalms, and it is taken up again from the beginning, at Sunday Vigils. For those monks who sing less than the entire Psalter with the customary canticles in the course of a week show themselves lazy in the service of devotion, since what—as we read—our

---

[1] "Midnight" probably means "in the middle of the night," a time that varies according to the season.

[2] Benedict used verbs meaning "say," "sing," and "chant psalms" somewhat haphazardly, but it is likely that the psalms were sung rather than spoken. Certainly that was soon the case in most monasteries.

[3] Ps. 51:17; Douay Ps. 50:17. The "verses" that Benedict refers to are brief excerpts from scripture.

[4] That is, this short hymn of praise or doxology:
   Glory to the Father, the Son, and the Holy Spirit
   As it was in the beginning, is now, and will always be, forever. Amen.

[5] Here, "antiphon" probably means that Psalm 94 was to be sung interspersed with the repetition of a short phrase from scripture.

[6] I.e., a hymn by Saint Ambrose of Milan (d.397).

[7] Short, sung responses from scripture.

[8] Greek for "Lord, have mercy."

[9] Ps. 119:164; Douay Ps. 118:164.

[10] Ps. 119:164; Douay Ps. 118:164.

[11] Ps. 119:62; Douay Ps. 118:62.

[12] Ps. 119:164; Douay Ps. 118:164.

Holy Fathers energetically completed in a single day we, more lukewarm as we are, ought to manage in an entire week....

Chapter 22
How Monks Should Sleep

Each one should sleep in his own bed. They should get bedding suited to their monastic life according to their abbot's determination.[1] If possible, all monks should sleep in one place; if their number does not allow that, they should rest in tens or twenties with senior monks to take care of them. A candle should burn in that room continually until morning. They should sleep clothed, girded with belts or cords, so they do not have their knives at their sides when they sleep, lest by chance they wound another sleeper when dreaming and so that the monks are always ready and, arising immediately at the signal, may hasten to be the first to do the work of God, yet with all seriousness and modesty. Younger brothers should not have beds next to one another, but be interspersed among seniors. Rising for the work of God, they should gently encourage one another, to counter the excuses of the sleepy....

Chapter 33
Whether Monks Should Have Any Private Property

This vice in particular should be torn out at the roots in the monastery: no one should presume to give or receive anything without the abbot's permission, or have any private property, nothing at all, no book or tablets or stylus, but absolutely nothing, since the brothers my not have either their bodies or their wills under their own control. They should look to the father of the monastery for everything they need and not be allowed to have anything that the abbot has not given or permitted. "All things should be common to all," as it is written, "lest somebody say something is his,"[2] or presume it is. If anyone is caught

indulging in this most wicked vice, let him be warned once, then a second time; if he does not amend, let him undergo correction.

Chapter 34
Whether Everyone Should Accept Necessities in Equal Measure

As it is written, "There was allotment to individuals according to their need."[3] By which I do not say that there should be favoritism,[4] God forbid, but consideration of weaknesses, so that he who needs less should thank God and not be upset, but he who needs more should be humbled by his weakness, not puffed up because of the mercy shown him, and in this way all members will be at peace. Most of all, the evil of grumbling should not show itself for any reason or in any word or sign whatsoever; anyone caught at it should be subjected to very severe discipline....

Chapter 39
The Measure of Food

For the daily meal, whether at the sixth or ninth hour, we believe that two cooked dishes for every table will suffice, taking into account individual weaknesses, so that he who cannot eat one may eat the other. Therefore, two cooked dishes should be enough for all the brothers, and if fruit or fresh vegetables are available, they may be added as a third course. A generous pound of bread should suffice for the day, whether there is one meal or both dinner[5] and supper.[6] If the brothers are to have supper, a third of the pound should be set aside by the cellarer for distribution at supper.

If the workload happens to be increased, the abbot will have the choice and the power to increase the portion somewhat, if it is expedient, but above all excess is to be avoided so that indigestion never steals up on a monk, because nothing is so inappropriate to every Christian as excess, our Lord says: "See to it that your hearts are not

---

[1] The meaning here is uncertain: does the abbot hand out bedding appropriate to the level of communal asceticism, or does he treat each individual differently?

[2] Acts 4:32.

[3] Acts 4:35.

[4] See Rom. 2:11.

[5] That is, the midday meal.

[6] The evening meal.

weighed down by overindulgence."[1] Younger boys should not be served the same amount, but less than their elders, frugality being maintained in all things. They should all abstain entirely from the consumption of the meat of quadrupeds, except the gravely ill.

Chapter 40
The Measure of Drink

"Everyone has his own gift from the Lord, one this, another that,"[2] and therefore it is with some uneasiness that we fix the portion of others' sustenance. Nevertheless, contemplating the frailty of the weak, we think that one *hemina*[3] of wine each per day is enough. Those to whom God gives the endurance to abstain should know that they will have their own reward. But if circumstances of the place or work or summer heat demand more, let it be up to the judgment of the superior, who must always take care lest excess or drunkenness creep in. Although we read that wine is not for monks at all, but since in our times monks cannot be persuaded of this, let us at least agree that we should not drink to excess but sparingly "because wine makes even the wise lose their way."[4] If the circumstances of the place are such that not even the aforementioned measure can be obtained, but much less or none at all, those who live there should bless God and not grumble. We caution this, above all: brothers should refrain from grumbling.

Chapter 41
At What Times the Brothers Should Eat

From holy Easter until Pentecost, the brothers should dine at the sixth hour and have supper in the evening.[5] From Pentecost through the summer, if the monks do not have work in the fields and excessive heat does not bother them, they should fast until the ninth hour on Wednesday and Friday. On other days they should dine at the sixth hour, and keep dinner at the sixth hour regularly if they have work in the fields or the summer heat is too great, according to the abbot's decision. The abbot must regulate and arrange everything so that souls are saved and what the brothers do they do without justifiable grumbling.

From the ides of September until the beginning of Lent, they should always eat at the ninth hour. But in Lent until Easter they should eat in the evening; Vespers should be done so that the monks do not need lamplight to eat, but everything should be finished in daylight. Both supper and dinner hours should always be adjusted so that everything may be done in daylight....

Chapter 48
Daily Manual Labor

Idleness is the enemy of the soul. Therefore, the brothers should be occupied at set times in manual labor, and again at other set times in divine reading. Therefore we think that the times for each should be established according to this arrangement, that is: from Easter until the [first] of October, brothers leaving Prime in the morning should work until almost the fourth hour at whatever is necessary; from the fourth hour until almost the sixth they should be free for reading. Rising from the table after Sext, they should rest in their beds in complete silence, and those who want to read to themselves should do so as not to disturb others; and None should be done a little early, at the middle of the eighth hour, and again they should work at whatever is needed until Vespers. They should not be upset if the circumstances of the place or poverty demand they do their own harvesting of produce, because then they are truly monks if they live by the work of their hands, like our Fathers and the apostles. Yet all tasks should be done in moderation out of consideration for the weak.

From the [first] of October until the beginning of Lent, they should be free for reading until the end of the second hour; Terce should be done at the second hour, and then all should work at the tasks assigned to them until None. At the first signal for None, each should set aside his work and be ready when the second signal sounds. After the meal, they should be free for their reading or psalms....

---

[1] Luke 21:34.

[2] 1 Cor. 7:7.

[3] The equivalent modern measure is unknown. Estimates generally range from a pint to a quart.

[4] Ecclus. 19:2.

[5] That is, the traditional Mediterranean pattern in which the largest meal is in the middle of the day.

Chapter 54
If a Monk Should Receive Letters or Anything Else

In no way should it be allowed for a monk to receive letters, gifts, or keepsakes, not from his relatives, any other person, or another monk, nor should he give them, without the abbot's permission. But if something has been sent to him by his relatives, he should not presume to receive it unless the abbot is informed beforehand. But if the abbot orders it to be received, it should be in his power to command to whom it should be given and the brother to whom it happened to have been sent should not be upset, lest "the Devil be given an opportunity."[1] Let anyone who presumes to do otherwise be subject to the discipline of the Rule.

Chapter 55
The Brothers' Clothing and Shoes

Clothing should be given to the brothers according to the nature and the climate of the place where they live, since more is required in colder regions, less in warmer ones. This consideration is the abbot's concern. However, we believe that in milder places, a cowl and a tunic for each monk will suffice—a woolen cowl in winter, a light or worn one in the summer—a scapular for work[2] and footwear: leggings and boots. Monks should not object to the color or coarseness of any of these items, but have what is available in the region where they live and can be purchased cheaply....

Chapter 58
The Discipline of Receiving Brothers

Easy entry to the religious life should not be granted to a newcomer, but as the apostle says, "Test the spirits to see if they are from God."[3] Therefore, if one comes knocking, perseveres, and, after four or five days, seems to suffer patiently ill-treatment directed at him and the difficulty of entry and persists in his request, let entry be granted him and let him stay in the guest quarters for a few days. After that, he should be in the novices' quarters, where they study, eat, and sleep. A senior monk should be assigned to them, someone suited to win souls, in order to watch over them very carefully.

The concern should be whether he truly seeks God, if he is attentive to the work of God, to obedience, and to reprimands. All the difficult and harsh things involved in the approach to God should be made clear to him. If he promises perseverance in his stability, after two months this Rule should be read to him straight through and let this be said to him: "This is the law under which you want to serve. If you can observe it, enter, but if you cannot, you are free to go." If he still stays, he should then be led into the abovementioned novices' quarters and have his patience thoroughly tested again. After six months, the Rule should be read to him so he knows what he is getting into. And if he still stays, after four months the same Rule should be read to him again. And if, after deliberating within himself, he promises to take care in all things and carry out every task given him, then let him be received into the community, knowing that it is stated in the law of the Rule that from that day forward it is not permitted to him to leave the monastery, nor shake his neck from the yoke of the Rule that he was free to reject or accept after such exacting deliberation.

Moreover, the one to be received should give assurances in the oratory, before everyone, concerning his stability, religious life and ways, and obedience. Before God and his saints, let him know that if ever he does otherwise, he will be damned by the one he mocks. He should make a petition concerning this promise of his in the name of the saints whose relics[4] are there and of the abbot who is present....

If he has any property, he should either distribute it to the poor beforehand or, having made a solemn donation, give it to the monastery, keeping none of it whatsoever for himself, since indeed he knows that from that day forward, he will not even have control over his own body. Right there in the oratory, let him be stripped of the clothes in which he is dressed and put on the monastery's clothes. Let the clothing he removed be put in the wardrobe for safekeeping, so that if ever he gives in to the Devil's urging that he should leave the monastery, God forbid, then let him be thrown out, stripped of the monastery's clothes. However,

---

[1] 1 Tim. 5:14.

[2] It is not clear exactly what this garment was. A plausible explanation is that it was an overshirt, smock, or apron-like garment meant to keep other clothes from getting dirty or torn during manual labor.

[3] 1 John 4:1.

[4] Bones or other remnants of a saint.

he should not get back the petition that the abbot took from the altar, which should be kept in the monastery.

Chapter 59
Sons of Nobles and the Poor Who Are Offered

If it happens that a nobleman offers his son to the monastery, if the boy is young, his relatives should make the petition we discussed above, and they should tie together the petition and the boy's hand in an altar cloth, with the oblation,[1] and offer him that way. Concerning his property, they should either promise under oath in this same petition that they will never give him anything themselves, nor through a third party nor by any means, nor offer him the opportunity to own anything. Of course, if they do not want to do that and desire to offer something to the monastery for their own reward, let them make a donation to the monastery of the property they wish to give, keeping usufruct[2] themselves if they so desire. In this way everything is closed off, so that the boy cannot harbor any hope by which, God forbid, he could be deceived and ruined, which we have learned through experience.

Let poorer people do likewise. Those who have no property at all should simply draw up the petition and offer their son before witnesses, with the oblation....

Chapter 73
Not Every Practice of Justice Is Set Out in This Rule

We have sketched this Rule so that those of us practicing it in monasteries may show that we have some honor in our ways and the rudiments of monastic life. But for one who hastens toward perfection in monastic life, there are the teachings of the Holy Fathers, observance of which should direct a man to the peak of perfection. For which page, which word of the divine authority of the Old and New Testament is not the most righteous guide for human life? And which book by the Holy Catholic Fathers does not resound with how we may arrive at our creator by a straight path? As for the *Conferences, Institutes,* and *Lives of the Fathers,* as well as the Rule of our holy father Basil,[3] what else are they but tools of virtue for good and obedient monks? For us, lazy, wicked, and neglectful, they cause a blush of shame.

Therefore, whoever you are, hastening toward your heavenly home, with Christ's help carry out this little Rule sketched as a beginning, and then at last you will reach those greater heights of learning and virtues we mentioned above, with God's protection. Amen.

SAINTLY MODELS

1.9 The virginal life: Jerome, *Letter 24 (To Marcella)* (384). Original in Latin.

St. Jerome (c.347–419/420) was born in the Roman province of Dalmatia, near present-day Ljubljana. As a youth he went to Rome to study rhetoric and philosophy, and there, increasingly ashamed of his reckless student ways, he converted to Christianity. He subsequently lived in Trier, Aquileia, Antioch, and again in Rome; he spent the last decades of his life in

---

[1] Apparently this means at the offering of the bread and wine during the Mass, an oblique indication of the circumstances of profession. Here as elsewhere, Benedict assumes his readers know a great deal already.

[2] Meaning that the gift is in trust; the donors receive any profit or return during their lifetimes, and then the property is transferred to the monastery.

[3] The *Conferences* and *Institutes* refer to the works of John Cassian (d.c.435), who spent the first part of his life as a monk in Bethlehem, Egypt, and Constantinople. Later he founded two monasteries, one for men and the other for women, at Marseille. The *Lives of the Fathers* is probably a reference to Athanasius, *The Life of St. Antony* (see below, p. 30), along with other monastic biographies. The Rule of Basil was a collection of precepts written by Basil (d.379) in Greek for Byzantine monks, but it was available to Western monks through a Latin translation made by Rufinus of Aquileia in 397.

a hermit's cell near Bethlehem. His most famous work is his translation of the entire Bible into Latin: the Old Testament from the original Hebrew and the New Testament from the original Greek. This so-called Vulgate Bible, completed around 405, was the standard in the Christian West for the next millennium. Jerome also wrote biblical commentaries, history, theological tracts, and more than a hundred letters. *Letter 24* dates to his second period in Rome, during which time he was surrounded by a circle of elite women, including Marcella, a well-educated and wealthy widow who had already begun a life of Christian asceticism before Jerome arrived. The letter describes the way of life of the virgin Asella, Marcella's sister (although Jerome never says so explicitly). As a girl, Asella exchanged a gold necklace for a humble dark garment. She lived in a tiny cell and devoted herself to prayer and self-denial amidst the hustle and bustle of Rome, probably on a patch of family property.

1. Jerome offers no specific rationale for why virginity is the ideal state for a Christian woman. What can you gather on this subject from the contents of the letter?
2. What were the joys of the ascetic life?

[Source: *Sancti Eusebii Hieronymi Epistulae pars 1: Epistulae I-LXX*, 2nd ed., ed. Isidorus Hilberg, Corpus Scriptorum Ecclesiasticorum Latinorum 54 (Vienna: Verlag der Österreichischen Akademie der Wissenschaften, 1996), pp. 214–17. Translated and introduced by Bruce L. Venarde.]

To Marcella, concerning the life of Asella.

1. Nobody should find fault that I praise or carp at certain people in my letters, since in exposing the wicked there is a reproach to others and zeal for virtue is spurred by preaching the best deeds of good people. The day before yesterday we had spoken concerning a certain Lea of blessed memory; immediately it pricked my conscience and came to mind that it is not fitting for me, having spoken of the second order of chastity,[1] to keep silent concerning a virgin. Therefore I must briefly sketch the life of our Asella, to whom I ask you not read this letter, since she finds praise of herself burdensome. I ask instead that you deem it worthy to read to young women who, instructing themselves by her example, may think that her way of life is the standard of perfection.

2. I pass over the fact that before she was born, she was blessed in her mother's womb. She was presented to her father, in his sleep, as a virgin in a bowl of gleaming glass more pure than any mirror; still wrapped in infants'

clothing, scarcely ten years old, she was consecrated with the honor of future blessedness.[2] May everything that was before her work be attributed to grace,[3] although God, knowing the future in advance, blessed Jeremiah in the womb and made John [the Baptist] leap in his mother's womb and before the creation of the world set [Saint] Paul apart to preach his son [Christ] [see Jer. 1:5, Luke 1:41, and Eph. 1:5]. I now come to the things that she, by the sweat of her brow, chose, took up, held onto, began, and completed after her twelfth year.

3. Shut up in one narrow cell, she enjoyed the expanse of paradise. Likewise, the soil of the earth was her place of prayer and peace. Fasting was her pleasure and hunger her refreshment. When the human condition, rather than the desire to eat, drew her to food she stirred up hunger more than she suppressed it on a diet of bread, salt, and cold water. And since I nearly forgot what I should have said in the beginning, when she first took up her plan for living, she sold a gold necklace that is commonly called a *murenula* (because, the metal being made supple in little

---

[1] I.e., Lea, however holy, was a chaste widow, not a virgin, and thus she belonged to the "second order" of chastity. She was a wealthy Roman widow who gave up her privileges for a life of asceticism and prayer, directing a community of Christian virgins.

[2] This means that she vowed herself virginity at age ten. The reference to swaddling clothes, the material in which Mary wrapped the infant Jesus, is poetic license that stresses Asella's innocence.

[3] That is, before her "adult" work starting at age twelve, mentioned at the end of the paragraph.

bars, a flexible sort of chain is woven together)[1] without her parents' knowledge. She put on a dark garment that she was unable to obtain from her mother; dressed in a pious portent of her undertaking, she quickly vowed herself to the Lord, so that all her kind would know that they would not be able to force anything out of one who had already condemned the world by means of her clothing.[2]

4. But, as I began to say, she always behaved with such restraint and guarded herself in the retreat of her room to the point that she never set foot in public, nor conversed with men. What is even more astonishing, she loved her virgin sister rather than seeing her.[3] She worked with her hands, knowing what is written: he who does not work does not eat [see 2 Thess. 3:10]. In prayer and psalm-singing she spoke to her bridegroom. She hastened nearly unseen to martyrs' shrines, and although she took joy in her plan, she was all the more greatly pleased that nobody recognized her. Not only fasting all year, eating every two or three days, in Lent she stretched out her sails to the fullest, nearly joining week to week in abstinence with a cheerful face. And because what is perhaps impossible for men to believe is possible with God's help, living this way she reached her fiftieth year, without stomach pain and free from bowel torments. The dry ground on which she lay did not harm her body, nor was her skin, roughened by sackcloth, subject to stench or abrasion. Sound in body and sounder still in mind, she thought her solitude a delight and found a monk's retreat in a busy city.

5. I have learned these few things from you, who know them better. Your eyes have also seen the hardness of camels' knees—the result of frequent prayer—on her holy little body. I offer what I can know. Nothing is more delightful than her seriousness or more serious than her delightfulness; nothing is sadder than her laugh or sweeter than her sadness. The paleness of her face, although it demonstrates continence, does not smack of ostentation. Her speech is silent and her silence speaks; her walk is neither fast nor slow; her bearing likewise. She gives no thought to neatness and her unstylish clothing is style without style. She has earned, by the quality of her life alone, that in a city of ostentation, lewdness, and pleasures, in which it is a misery to be humble, the good acclaim her and the wicked do not dare to disparage her. Let widows and virgins imitate her, married women cherish her, evil women fear her, and priests admire her.

1.10 The eremitical life: Athanasius, *The Life of St. Antony of Egypt* (357). Original in Greek.

Athanasius, bishop of Alexandria (d.373), a ferocious upholder of the Nicene—and therefore anti-Arian—view of the Trinity, saw St. Antony (or Anthony, d.c.356) as the living embodiment of his notion of salvation through Christ. His *Life of St. Antony*, which was translated into Latin in the later fourth century, was the first of what would become an enormously popular genre in the Middle Ages: the saint's biography, or hagiography. The virtues that Athanasius ascribed to Antony—seriousness of vocation even in childhood; resistance to all the temptations of the Devil; application to prayer, vigils, and fasts—were copied in nearly every subsequent saint's Life. This was not mechanical imitation, for Antony's Life was meant to be not just the story of one person but also the model for all Christians. At the same time, Antony's vocation as a solitary—a monk—became the ideal that even many Christians active in the hurly-burly of worldly life admired and strove to imitate.

---

[1] *Murenula* is a diminutive for *murena*, the moray eel. The necklace, made of many tiny pieces of metal joined together, has the supple character of an eel in motion.

[2] It is a commonplace in writing about holy people that families resisted the desires of individuals to "leave the world." Asella's mother did not, it seems, want to offer her virgin daughter something that was, in the Roman world, a mourning costume.

[3] This is almost certainly a reference to Marcella, the addressee of this letter, who would have stayed in the family home before her marriage. Although Asella did sometimes leave her cell, as noted below, apparently her only destinations were Christian shrines.

1. How did Antony's life compare with that of Asella (above, p. 28)?
2. In what ways might *The Life of St. Antony* have influenced Augustine's ideas about the City of God (above, p. 16)?

[Source: Athanasius of Alexandria, *Life of St. Antony of Egypt*, trans. David Brakke, in *Medieval Hagiography: An Anthology*, ed. Thomas Head (New York: Garland, 2000), pp. 7–12, 14 (notes modified).]

LETTER OF ATHANASIUS, ARCHBISHOP OF ALEXANDRIA, TO THE MONKS IN FOREIGN PLACES CONCERNING THE LIFE OF THE BLESSED ANTONY THE GREAT

(Preface.) It is a good competition that you have begun with the monks in Egypt by seeking either to equal or surpass them in your discipline in virtue.[1] For at last there are monasteries among you as well, and the reputation of the [Egyptian] monks is the basis of their organization: therefore, this plan [of yours] deserves praise; may God bring it to completion through your prayers.

Inasmuch as you have asked me about the blessed Antony's way of life and want to learn about how he began the discipline, who he was before this, what the end of his life was like, and if the things that have been said about him are true, so that you might guide yourselves by imitation of him, I have received your charge with great enthusiasm. Indeed, for me as well it is of great profit just to remember Antony, and I know that once you have heard about him, in addition to admiring the man, you too will want to imitate his determination, since monks have in Antony's lifestyle a sufficient pattern for their discipline.

Therefore, do not disbelieve what you have heard from those who have brought reports of him; rather, think that you have heard only a little from them, for even they scarcely can have completely related such great matters. And since I too, urged by you, am telling you what I can by letter, I am sending only a few of the things that I have remembered about him. You for your part should not stop questioning those persons who sail from here, for it is likely that after each person tells what he knows, the account concerning him will still hardly do him justice. Therefore, when I received your letter, I decided to send for certain monks, particularly those who had spent the most time with him, in the hope that I could learn more and send you the fullest possible account. But since the sailing season was coming to an end and the letter carrier was ready to go, I hurried to write to your piety what I know—for I saw him often—and what I was able to learn from the man who followed Antony no short period of time and who poured water on his hand.[2] I have in every place kept my mind on the truth, so that no one, having heard too much, would disbelieve it, or, having learned less than necessary, would look down on the man.

(1.) Antony was an Egyptian by birth, and his parents were well-born and possessed considerable wealth. Since they were Christians, he was raised in a Christian manner. As a child, he lived with his parents and was familiar with nothing other than them and their house. When he grew to become a boy and became older, he did not put up with learning letters because he wanted to be removed even from the companionship of children. It was his complete desire, as it is written, to live in his house as an unformed person.[3] He would go to church with his parents. As a boy, he was not lazy, nor did he become rude as he got older. Rather, he was obedient to his parents, and by paying attention to the readings,[4] he preserved in himself what was beneficial in them. Although as a boy he lived in moderate wealth, he did not trouble his parents for diverse and expensive foods, nor did he seek such pleasures. He was happy merely with whatever he found and asked for nothing more.

---

[1] Athanasius presents his biography in the form of a letter to monks in places outside Egypt, most likely in areas of the western Mediterranean, such as North Africa and southern Europe. Many of the sentences in this opening section appear complicated and obscure to us because we do not know the exact situation in which Athanasius writes and because such a style is typical of prefaces to ancient works, in which the writer hopes to impress his readers with his rhetorical skill.

[2] See 2 Kings 3:11.

[3] See Gen. 25:27.

[4] See 1 Tim. 4:13.

(2.) After the death of his parents, he was left alone with one small sister; he was about eighteen or twenty, and it was his responsibility to care for the house and his sister. Not six months after his parents' death, he was going to church as usual, and he was thinking to himself and considering all this: how the apostles abandoned everything and followed the Savior;[1] how the people in Acts [of the Apostles] sold their possessions and brought the proceeds and laid them at the feet of the apostles for distribution to the needy;[2] and how such a great hope was stored up for these people in heaven.[3] Considering these things, he entered the church, and it happened that just then the Gospel was being read, and he heard the Lord saying to the rich man, "If you wish to be perfect, go, sell all your possessions, and give the proceeds to the poor, and come, follow me, and you will have treasure in heaven."[4] And Antony, as if the remembrance of the saints had been placed in him by God and as if the readings had been made on his account, left the church immediately and gave to the villagers the possessions he had received from his ancestors—three hundred *arourae* of fertile and very beautiful land—so that they would no longer trouble him and his sister.[5] He sold all their other movable possessions, collecting a sizable sum of money, and gave it to the poor, although he kept a little for his sister's sake.

(3.) But when he again entered the church and heard in the Gospel the Lord saying, "Do not worry about tomorrow,"[6] he could not stay: he went out and gave even that [little money remaining] to the common people. When he had delivered his sister to known and faithful virgins in order to be brought up for virginity, he at last devoted himself to the discipline outside the house, attending to himself and guiding himself with patience. For there were not yet so many monasteries in Egypt, and no monk knew the great desert; rather, each of those who wanted to attend to himself practiced the discipline alone, not far from his own village. Now, at this time there was

an old man in the neighboring village who had practiced the solitary life from his youth: when Antony saw him, he imitated him in virtue.[7] At first he too began by remaining in the places around the village; then if he heard of some zealous one somewhere, like the wise bee, he went and sought that person, and he did not return to his own place until he had seen the man and had received from him, so to speak, travel supplies for the road to virtue.

And so, spending time there at first, he strengthened his intention never to return to the things of his parents nor to remember his relatives, but he directed all his desire and all his zeal toward the effort required by the discipline. Therefore, he worked with his hands, since he had heard, "Let not the idle one eat,"[8] and he spent some of the money on bread and some for the needy. He prayed continuously since he knew that it is necessary to pray in secret without ceasing.[9] For indeed he so devoted himself to the reading that nothing of what is written fell from him to the ground,[10] but he retained everything, so that his memory replaced books for him.

(4.) Conducting himself in this way, then, Antony was loved by everyone. He sincerely submitted to the zealous ones whom he visited, and he learned thoroughly the advantage in zeal and discipline that each one possessed in comparison to himself. He contemplated the graciousness of one and the devotion to prayers of another; he observed one's lack of anger and another's love of people; he attended to the one who kept vigils and the other who loved to study; he admired one for his perseverance and another for his fasting and sleeping on the ground; he watched closely the gentle nature of one and the patience of another; but in all he noticed piety toward Christ and love for one another. And when he had been filled in this way, he returned to his own place of discipline, and then he gathered into himself the virtues of each and strove to display them all in himself. Indeed, he was not contentious with those of his own age, except only that

---

[1] See Matt. 4:20; 19:27.

[2] See Acts 4:35–37.

[3] See Col. 1:5.

[4] Matt. 19:21.

[5] Three hundred *arourae* may have been around two hundred acres; thus, Antony is portrayed as very wealthy by the standards of third-century Egypt.

[6] Matt. 6:34.

[7] See Gal. 4:18.

[8] See 2 Thess. 3:10.

[9] See Matt. 6:6; 1 Thess. 5:17.

[10] See 1 Sam. 3:19.

he should not appear to be second to them in the better things. And he did this in such a way that he did not hurt anyone's feelings; rather, they rejoiced in him. And so when the people of the village and the lovers of virtue with whom he associated saw that he was this kind of person, they all called him "Beloved of God"; some welcomed him as a son, others as a brother.

(5.) But the devil, who hates and envies the good, could not bear to see such resolution in a young man, but set out to do against Antony the kinds of things he usually does. First he tried to dissuade him from the discipline by suggesting the memory of possessions, the care of his sister, the intimacy of family, love of money, love of glory, the varied pleasure of food, and the other indulgences of life—and finally the difficulty of virtue and the great effort that it requires. He introduced the weakness of the body and the long duration of time. In short, he raised up a dust cloud of thoughts in Antony's mind, desiring thereby to separate him from his upright intention.

But the enemy saw that he himself was weak in the face of Antony's resolve and saw instead that he was defeated by the other's stubbornness, overthrown by his faith, and falling due to Antony's constant prayers. Then he took confidence in the weapons of the belly's navel[1] and, boasting in these—for they are his primary means of trapping the young—he advanced against the youth, troubling him at night and harassing him by day so that those who watched could sense the struggle that was going on between the two. The one would suggest dirty thoughts, and the other would turn them back with prayers; the one would titillate, and the other, as if seeming to blush, would fortify his body with faith and fasts. And the miserable devil dared at night to dress up like a woman and imitate one in every way merely to deceive Antony. But Antony, by thinking about Christ and the excellence one ought to possess because of him, and by considering the soul's rational faculty, extinguished the ember of the other's deception.

Once again the enemy suggested the ease of pleasure. But Antony, like someone fittingly angry or grieved,

thought about the threat of fire and the torment of the worm, and by setting these thoughts against [those of the enemy], he passed through these things unharmed. All this was a source of shame for the enemy, for he who had considered himself to be like God[2] was now being mocked by a youth, and he who boasted over flesh and blood was being overthrown by a human being who wore flesh. For working with Antony was the Lord, the one who for our sake took flesh and gave to the body the victory over the devil, so that each of those who truly struggle says, "Not I, but the grace of God that is with me."[3]

(6.) At last, when the dragon could not defeat Antony in this way but instead saw himself thrust out of his heart, he gnashed his teeth, as it is written.[4] As if he were beside himself, he finally appeared to Antony in his form just as he is in his mind, as a black boy. And as though he had fallen down, he no longer attacked Antony with thoughts—for the crafty one had been tossed down—but finally he used a human voice and said, "Many people I have deceived, and most I have defeated, but now coming against you and your efforts as I have against others, I have been weakened." Antony asked, "Who are you who say such things to me?" Immediately he answered with a pitiful voice, "It is I who am fornication's lover. It is I who have been entrusted with its ambushes and its titillations against the youth, and I am called the spirit of fornication. How many persons who desired to be prudent I have deceived! How many persons who professed to be so I have persuaded to change by titillating them! It is I on whose account even the prophet blames those who have fallen, saying, 'You have been deceived by the spirit of fornication.'[5] For it was through me that they were tripped up. It is I who so often troubled you and who as often was overthrown by you." But Antony gave thanks to the Lord and took courage in him, and he said to him, "You are very despicable then, for you are black in your mind and as weak as a boy. From now on I will have no anxiety about you, 'for the Lord is my helper, and I will look down on my enemies.'"[6] When he heard this, the

---

[1] See Job 40:16.

[2] See Isa. 14:14; Ezek. 28:2.

[3] 1 Cor. 15:10.

[4] See Ps. 35:16; 37:12; 112:10; Douay Ps. 34:16; 36:12; 111:10.

[5] Hos. 4:12.

[6] Ps. 118:7; Douay Ps. 117:7.

black one immediately fled, cowering before these words and afraid even to approach the man.[1]

(7.) This was Antony's first struggle against the devil, or rather this was the achievement in Antony of the Savior, "who condemned sin in the flesh so that the righteousness of the Law might be fulfilled in us, who walk not according to the flesh, but according to the spirit."[2] But Antony did not, because the demon had fallen, now become negligent and take no thought of himself, nor did the enemy, because he had been defeated, stop lying in ambush. For the enemy went around again like a lion, looking for some opportunity against him.[3] But Antony, since he had learned from the Scriptures that the wiles of the enemy are numerous,[4] practiced the discipline intensely, figuring that, even if the enemy had been unable to deceive his heart through bodily pleasure, he would attempt to trap him by another method. For the demon is a lover of sin....

(8.) Having constrained himself in this way, Antony departed to the tombs, which happened to lie far outside the village. He commanded one of his acquaintances to bring him bread every several days, and he himself entered one of the tombs; when the other had shut the door, he remained inside by himself. Then, when the enemy could not bear this but was afraid that in a short time Antony would fill the desert with the discipline, he came one night with a crowd of demons and so cut Antony with wounds that he lay on the ground speechless from the tortures. For he used to maintain that the pains were so severe that he would say that blows inflicted by human beings could not have inflicted such torture. But by God's Providence—for the Lord does not neglect those who hope in him—his acquaintance came the next day to bring him the bread. When he opened the door and saw Antony lying on the ground as if dead, he lifted him up, carried him to the village church, and laid him on the ground. Many of his relatives and the villagers sat around Antony as if beside a corpse. But around midnight Antony came to himself and got up; when he saw everyone asleep and only his acquaintance keeping watch, he motioned with his head for him to approach and then asked him to pick him up again and carry him to the tombs without waking anybody.

(14.) For nearly twenty years he continued to discipline himself in this way, not going out himself and being seen by others only rarely. After this, when many eagerly desired to imitate his discipline, and others of his acquaintances came and were pulling down and wrenching out the door by force, Antony emerged, as if from some shrine, initiated into the mysteries and filled with God. Now for the first time he appeared outside the fort to those who had come to him. And they, when they saw him, were amazed to see that his body had its same condition: it was neither fat as if from lack of exercise nor withered as if from fasting and fighting demons, but it was such as they had known it before his withdrawal. The disposition of his soul was pure again, for it was neither contracted from distress, nor dissipated from pleasure, nor constrained by levity or dejection. Indeed, when he saw the crowd, he was not disturbed, nor did he rejoice to be greeted by so many people. Rather, he was wholly balanced, as if he were being navigated by the Word and existing in his natural state.

Therefore, through Antony the Lord healed many of the suffering bodies of those present, and others he cleansed of demons. He gave Antony grace in speaking, and thus he comforted many who were grieved and reconciled into friendship others who were quarreling, exhorting everyone to prefer nothing in the world to the love for Christ. While he discussed and recalled the good things to come and the love for humanity that has come to us from God, "who did not withhold his own son, but gave him up for all of us."[5] he persuaded many to choose the solitary life. And so at last there came to be monasteries even in the mountains, and the desert was made a city of monks, who left their homes and enrolled in the heavenly commonwealth.[6]

---

[1] The symbolism of this scene is on two levels. First, the appearance of the devil as a boy reflects the homoerotic interest in male adolescents pervasive in the ancient world and condemned by Christian leaders such as Athanasius. Second, the devil's black skin illustrates the prejudice based on skin color present in late antique Egypt, which was a multiethnic society. Most Alexandrians such as Athanasius were descendants of the Greeks who founded the city in the fourth century BCE and so were of lighter skin color than those of more sub-Saharan African descent.

[2] Rom. 8:3–4.

[3] See 1 Pet. 5:8.

[4] See Eph. 6:11.

[5] Rom. 8:32.

[6] See Phil. 3:20; Heb. 12:23. Compare with Augustine's idea of the City of God, above, p. 16.

1.11 The active life: Sulpicius Severus, *The Life of St. Martin of Tours* (397). Original in Latin.

Sulpicius Severus (*c.*360–*c.*420), a well-to-do and well-educated man of Aquitaine (southern Gaul), became a monk later in life. He met St. Martin (d.397) in 393 or 394 and, impressed by the holy man, wrote his *Life* shortly afterwards. It was a great success: St. Martin soon became the subject of a number of supplementary accounts—letters concerning his death; descriptions of his miracles—and was adopted as the patron saint of the Merovingian kings. Unlike St. Antony, Martin was a bishop, and thus Sulpicius needed to find a way to combine the model of the ascetic monk with that of the active life of a man in the world.

1. If you were a soldier in a fourth- or fifth-century army and you learned about Martin's life, what message would you take away from it?
2. What ideals of behavior did Martin's *Life* offer to bishops?

[Source: *Medieval Saints: A Reader*, ed. Mary-Ann Stouck (Toronto: University of Toronto Press, 1999), pp. 139–42, 144–49 (slightly modified).]

Martin, then, was born at Sabaria in Pannonia [modern Hungary], but was brought up at Ticinum [Pavia], which is situated in Italy. In terms of worldly dignity, his parents were not of the lowest rank, but they were pagans. His father was at first simply a soldier, but afterwards a military tribune. He himself took up a military career while a youth and was enrolled in the imperial guard, first under king Constantine,[1] and then under the Caesar Julian.[2] This, however, was not done of his own free will, for, almost from the earliest years of his holy childhood, this distinguished boy aspired rather to the service of God. For when he was ten years old, against the wish of his parents, he fled to a church and begged to become a catechumen [to begin instruction in Christianity]. Soon afterwards, in a wonderful manner he became completely devoted to the work of God, and when he was twelve years old, he longed for a life in the desert [to become a hermit]; and he would have made the necessary vows if his youthfulness had not been an obstacle. His mind, however, was always intent upon hermitages or the Church, and already meditated in his boyish years on what he later fulfilled as a religious. But since an edict was issued by the rulers of the state that the sons of veterans should be enrolled for military service,

his father (who grudged his pious behavior) delivered him up when he was fifteen years old, and he was arrested and put in chains and was bound by the military oath. He was content with only one servant as his attendant, and then, reversing roles, the master waited on the servant to such a degree that, for the most part, it was he who pulled off his [servant's] boots and he who cleaned them with his own hand; and while they took their meals together, it was he who more often served them. For nearly three years before his baptism, he was a professional soldier, but he kept completely free from those vices in which that class of men become too frequently involved. He showed great kindness towards his fellow-soldiers, and wonderful affection, and his patience and humility surpassed what seemed possible to human nature. There is no need to praise the self-denial which he displayed: it was so great that, even at that date, he was regarded not so much as being a soldier as a monk. By all these qualities he had so endeared himself to the whole body of his comrades that they held him in extraordinary affection. Although not yet regenerated in Christ, by his good works he acted the part of a candidate for baptism.[3] This he did, for instance, by aiding those who were in trouble, by giving help to the wretched, by supporting the needy, by clothing the naked,

---

[1] Constantine I (r.306–337).

[2] Julian was at this time Caesar in Gaul. Later, when emperor (r.361–363), he was known as "the Apostate."

[3] In this era, infant baptism was unusual; most Christians were baptized in adulthood.

while he reserved nothing for himself from his military pay except what was necessary for his daily sustenance. Even then, far from being a senseless hearer of the Gospel, he took no thought for the morrow.[1]

So it happened one day when he had nothing except his weapons and his simple military dress, in the middle of a winter which had been very bitter and more severe than usual, so that the extreme cold had caused the death of many, he chanced to meet at the gate of the city of Amiens a poor naked man. He [the beggar] was entreating the passers-by to have pity on him, but all passed the wretched man without notice, when Martin, that man full of God, recognized that the beggar to whom others showed no pity was reserved for him. But what should he do? He had nothing except the cloak in which he was dressed, for he had already parted with the rest of his garments for similar purposes. Taking, therefore, his sword, which he was wearing, he divided his cloak in half, and gave one part to the beggar, and clothed himself again with what was left. At this, some of the bystanders laughed, because he was now an unsightly object in his mutilated clothing. Many, however, who were of sounder understanding, regretted deeply that they themselves had done nothing similar. They especially felt this because, possessing more than Martin, they could have clothed the poor man without reducing themselves to nakedness.

The following night while he slept Martin had a vision of Christ wearing the part of his cloak with which he had clothed the beggar. He was told to regard the Lord with the greatest care, and to recognize [the Lord's] robe as his own. Before long, he heard Jesus saying in a clear voice to the multitude of angels standing round, "Martin, who is still only a catechumen, clothed me with this robe." Truly the Lord remembered his own words, which he had spoken [while on earth]: "Inasmuch as ye have done these things to one of the least of these, ye have done them unto me,"[2] when he declared that he himself had been clothed in that beggar; and he confirmed the testimony he bore to such a good deed by condescending to show himself in that very garment which the beggar had received.

After this vision the sainted man was not puffed up with vainglory, but he acknowledged the goodness of God in his own action, and as he was now twenty years old he rushed off to receive baptism. However, he did not immediately retire from military service, but gave into the entreaties of his tribune, whom he served as one of

his private staff. For the tribune promised that, after his term of office had expired, he too would retire from the world. Martin was held back by this expectation, and continued to act the part of a soldier (although only in name) for nearly two years after he had received baptism.

In the meantime, the barbarians were invading the two divisions of Gaul, and the Caesar [Julian] brought an army together at the city of Worms, and began to distribute a donative [bonus] to the soldiers. As the custom was, they were called forward, one by one, until it came to Martin's turn. Then, indeed, thinking it a good time to ask for his discharge—for he did not think it would be proper for him to receive a donative if he did not intend to continue as a soldier—he said to Caesar, "Until now I have served you as a soldier: permit me now to be a soldier for God. Let the man who is to fight for you receive your donative; I am a soldier of Christ: it is not lawful for me to fight." Then the tyrant began to rage at what he said, declaring that [Martin] was withdrawing from military service from fear of the battle which was to take place the next day, and not from any religious motive. But Martin, full of courage, and all the more resolute in the face of this attempt at intimidation, said, "If this is attributed to cowardice and not to faith, tomorrow I will confront the battle-line unarmed, and in the name of the Lord Jesus, protected by the sign of the cross and not by shield or helmet, I will advance unarmed into the ranks of the enemy." Then he was ordered to be thrown back into prison, so that he might keep his promise by exposing himself unarmed to the barbarians. But the next day, the enemy sent ambassadors to negotiate peace, surrendering themselves and everything they possessed. From these circumstances, who can doubt that this victory was indeed due to the saintly man? For it was granted him that he should not be sent unarmed into battle. And although the good Lord could have preserved his own soldier even from the swords and spears of the enemy, yet he removed all necessity for fighting so that [Martin's] blessed eyes might not have to witness the death of others. For Christ could not have granted any victory on behalf of his own soldier other than subduing the enemy without bloodshed or the death of anyone.

After leaving military service, [Martin] sought out blessed Hilary [d.c.367], bishop of the city of Poitiers whose proven faith in the things of God was highly regarded, and he stayed with him for some time.... [Later, Martin left Hilary in order to return home to convert his

---

[1] Matt. 6:34.

[2] Matt. 25:40.

parents. Hilary, meanwhile, was exiled and lived for a time in Italy. When he was allowed to return to Poitiers, Martin joined him there.]

After he [Martin] had been most joyfully welcomed by him [Hilary], he established for himself a monastery not far from the town [at Ligugé]. At this time he was joined by a certain catechumen who wished to have instruction in the teachings of the most holy man. Only a few days later, however, the catechumen fell suddenly ill, suffering from a high fever. It so happened that Martin was then away from home. He was absent for three days, and on his return he found the lifeless body; and death had been so sudden, that he had left this world without receiving baptism. The body had been laid out in public, and the grieving brethren were visiting it as their sad duty required, when Martin hurried up, weeping and lamenting. But with his soul completely filled with the Holy Spirit, he ordered the others to leave the cell in which the body was lying; and bolting the door, he stretched himself at full length on the dead limbs of the departed brother. After he had stayed lying there for some time in prayer, and had become aware through the Spirit that the power of God was present, he rose up for a short time, and fixing his gaze on the dead man's face he waited with confidence for the result of his prayer and the mercy of the Lord. And after scarcely two hours had passed he saw the dead man begin to move all his limbs little by little, and his eyes trembling and blinking as he recovered his sight. Then indeed he raised a loud voice to the Lord and gave thanks, filling the cell with cries. Hearing the noise, those who had been standing at the door immediately rushed inside. And truly a marvelous spectacle met them, for they beheld the man alive whom they had left for dead....

At about the same time, Martin was sought after to be bishop of the church at Tours,[1] but when he could not easily be persuaded to leave his monastery, a certain Rusticius, one of the citizens, pretended that his wife was ill, and by throwing himself down at [Martin's] knees, prevailed on him to leave. A crowd of citizens had previously been posted along the road on which he traveled, and in this way he was escorted to the city as if under guard. In an amazing manner, an incredible number of people not only from that town but also from the neighboring cities had assembled to give their votes. They all had only the same wish, the same desire, the same opinion: that Martin was most worthy of being bishop, and that the Church would be happy with such a priest....

And now it is beyond my power to describe completely what Martin was like after he became bishop, and how he distinguished himself. For with the utmost constancy he remained the same as he had been before. There was the same humility in his heart and the same simplicity of clothing. Filled with both authority and courtesy, he kept up the position of a bishop properly, yet in such a way as not to abandon the life and virtues of a monk. For some time he lived in a cell adjacent to the church; but afterwards, when he could not tolerate the disturbance caused by the numbers of visitors, he established a monastery for himself about two miles outside the city.

This spot [Marmoutier] was so hidden and remote that he no longer had to wish for the solitude of a hermit. For on one side it was surrounded by the steep rock of a high mountain, while the rest of the land had been enclosed in a gentle curve of the Loire river; there was only one means of access, and that was very narrow. Here, then, he inhabited a cell built of wood, and a great number of the brothers were housed in the same fashion, but most of them had made themselves shelters by hollowing caves out of the overhanging rock. There were about eighty disciples who were instructed by the example of their holy master. There, no one possessed anything of his own; everything was held in common. No one was allowed either to buy or to sell anything, as is the custom among many monks. No art was practiced there, except that of the scribes, and even this was assigned to the younger brothers while the elder spent their time in prayer. It was rare for any of them to leave his cell, except to gather at the place of prayer. After a period of fasting was over, they all ate their meals together. No one used wine, except when illness compelled them to do so. Most of them wore garments of camel's hair; softer clothing was considered a serious fault there. This must be considered all the more remarkable, because many of them were considered to be of high rank, brought up in a very different fashion, and yet they had forced themselves to accept humility and patience; and we have seen many of these afterwards made bishops. For what city or church would not want a priest from the monastery of Martin?[2] But let me go on to describe the other virtues that Martin displayed as a bishop....

[At this point, Sulpicius describes various miracles wrought by Martin.]

---

[1] In 371.

[2] Compare the standards at Marmoutier with those described in *The Benedictine Rule* (above, p. 20).

On another occasion, in a certain village he demolished a very ancient temple, and set about cutting down a pine-tree that stood close to the temple. The chief priest of that place and a crowd of other pagans began to oppose him. And although these people had, at the Lord's command, been quiet while the temple was being destroyed, they could not endure the cutting-down of the tree. Martin carefully impressed upon them that there was nothing sacred in the trunk of a tree, and urged them instead to honor God whom he himself served; the tree had to be cut down because it was dedicated to a demon.

Then one of them who was bolder than the others said, "If you have any trust in your God, whom you say you worship, we ourselves will cut down this tree, and you stand in its path; for if, as you say, your Lord is with you, you will not be hurt." Then Martin, courageously trusting in the Lord, promised to do so. Upon this, all that crowd of pagans agreed to the condition; for they held the loss of their tree a small matter, so long as they got the enemy of their religion buried under its fall. Since that pine-tree was leaning to one side, so that there could be no question as to which way it would fall when it was cut, Martin was bound to the spot where the tree would certainly fall, as the pagans had stipulated.

Then they began to cut down their own tree, with great delight and rejoicing. A wondering crowd stood some distance away. Little by little the pine-tree began to shake, and, on the point of falling, threatened its own ruin. The monks at a distance grew pale and, terrified by the approaching danger, they lost all hope and faith, expecting only Martin's death. But he, trusting in the Lord, waited courageously, even as the falling pine made a cracking noise, even as it was falling and as it rushed down upon him: simply lifting his hand against it, he held up the sign of salvation. Then, indeed—you would have thought it driven back like a spinning top—it swept round to the opposite side, so that it almost crushed the peasants, who had stood in what seemed to be a safe spot.

Then a shout went up to heaven: the pagans were amazed by the miracle while the monks wept for joy, and the name of Christ was proclaimed by them all together. And as it is well known, on that day salvation came to that region. For there was hardly one of that huge crowd of pagans who did not long for the laying-on of hands [to become a catechumen] and, abandoning their impious errors, they believed in the Lord Jesus. Certainly, before Martin's time, very few, indeed hardly any in those regions had received the name of Christ. Through his virtues and example that name has prevailed to such an extent that now there is no region that is not filled either with crowded churches or monasteries. For wherever he destroyed pagan temples, there immediately he used to build either churches or monasteries.

1.12 The cult of saints: Gregory of Tours, *The Life of Monegundis* (580s). Original in Latin.

Gregory, bishop of Tours (r.573–594), was the most prolific writer of sixth-century Francia and an important witness to the Merovingian period. When he set out to write an account of the saints of his own time, he stressed that all had followed but one "way of life" by giving his book the odd title, *The Life of the Fathers*, with the word "life" in the singular. Moreover, he included one woman, Monegundis, among the "Fathers." What particularly attracted Gregory to this saint was her devotion to St. Martin, the holy patron of Gregory's own see at Tours and the very model of a saint for many bishops (for Martin's *Life* see above, p. 35). Like a mirror reflecting a mirror, Monegundis became the focus of a cult, while she in turn was a pilgrim to Martin's tomb and a devotee of his relics.

1. How do Monegundis's acts and virtues compare with those of St. Antony (above, p. 30) and St. Martin (above, p. 35)?
2. How does Gregory justify including a woman among the Fathers?

[Source: *Gregory of Tours: Life of the Fathers*, trans. Edward James (2d ed., Liverpool: Liverpool University Press, 1991), pp. 118–24 (notes modified).]

About the Blessed Monegundis

The excellent gifts of divine favors that have been offered from heaven to mankind cannot be conceived by the senses nor expressed by words nor represented in writing, since the Savior of the world Himself, from the time of the creation, was seen by the patriarchs, announced by the prophets and in the end deigned to be enclosed in the womb of Mary, ever virgin and ever pure, and the omnipresent and immortal Creator suffered Himself to be clothed in mortal flesh, to go to death for the redemption of men, who were dead through sin, and to rise again victorious. Although we were gravely wounded by the arrows of our sins and covered with wounds received from brigands who had lain in wait, He mingled oil and wine, and led us to the tavern of celestial medicine, that is to say, to the dogma of the Holy Church. He exhorts us to live after the example of the saints and to fortify ourselves by His incessant precepts. He gives us as models not only men, but also the lesser sex, who fight not feebly, but with a virile strength; He brings into His celestial kingdom not only men, who fight as they should, but also women, who exert themselves in the struggle with success. This we can see now in the blessed Monegundis, who left her native land (just like that prudent queen who came to listen to the wisdom of Solomon)[1] and came to the church of Saint Martin to admire the miracles which took place there daily and to drink there as from a priestly well, by which she was able to throw open the door to the grove of Paradise.

1. The most blessed Monegundis was from the city of Chartres. She had been married according to her parents' wishes, and had two daughters, which brought her a profound joy, so that she used to say "God has made me fertile so that two daughters might be born to me." But the bitterness of this world soon dissipated this earthly joy, for both were brought to their death by a light fever. From that time the mother was desolate; mourning and lamenting for the death of her children she did not stop weeping, day and night, and neither her husband nor her friends nor any of her relations could console her. Finally she came to herself, and said, "If I do not receive any consolation for the death of my daughters I fear I may offend my Lord Jesus Christ. Thus forgetting these laments I shall sing with the blessed Job, consoling myself thus: The Lord gave, and the Lord taketh away; blessed be the name of the Lord (Job 1:21)." And saying that she took off her mourning clothes, and had a small room arranged for her, which only had one small window, by which she could see a little daylight. There, despising the vanities of the world and having nothing more to do with her husband, she devoted herself entirely to God, in whom she confided, praying for her sins and for the sins of the people. She had only one girl with her as her servant, to provide her with what was necessary. She took barley flour and ashes mixed with water, kneaded it all with care and made a dough from which she formed loaves with her own hands, and she baked them herself, and thus she comforted herself after long fasts. The rest of the food coming from her house she gave to the poor. It happened one day that the girl who used to serve her (I believe that she was seduced by the wiles of our enemy[2] who always wishes to harm the good) withdrew from her service, saying "I cannot remain with a mistress who practices such abstinence; I prefer to go into the world, where I can eat and drink as much as I like." Five days passed after the departure of this girl, and her devout mistress had not taken her accustomed flour and water; she remained motionless, with Jesus Christ in her heart, in Whom the one who trusts cannot be overthrown, not by any whirlwind or storm. Nor did she think to sustain her life by any mortal food, but only by the word of God, as it is written,[3] recalling the proverb of the wisdom of Solomon, "The Lord will not suffer the soul of the righteous to famish" (Prov. 10:3), and again "The just shall live by faith" (Rom. 1:17). But as the human body cannot survive without using earthly things, she asked by a humble prayer that He who produced manna from heaven for a people when it was hungry,[4] and water from a rock when it was thirsty, might deign to give her the food necessary to sustain her weak body. Immediately, at her prayer, snow fell from the sky and covered the ground. She thanked God, and reached out of her window and collected some snow from the wall, and with this water she made bread as usual, which gave her food for another five days.

She had, next to her cell, a small garden in which she used to walk for exercise. She entered it one day, and walked around looking at the plants. A woman who had put wheat on the roof of her house in order to dry it, because it was a high place, began to watch the saint in an

---

[1] The queen of Sheba; see 1 Kings 10.

[2] The Devil.

[3] Deut. 8:2; Matt. 4:4.

[4] See Exod. 16.

indiscreet way, filled with worldly thoughts. Soon her eyes darkened and she became blind. Recognizing her fault she came to find the saint, and told her what had happened. [Monegundis] hastened to pray, and said, "Woe on me, if for a small offence done against my humble person, someone could have their eyes closed." And when she had finished her prayer she put her hand on this woman. As soon as she had made the sign of the cross the woman recovered her sight. A man from the same region, who had long since lost his hearing, came full of devotion to the cell of the saint, and his relations begged her to deign to put her hands on him. But she said that she was not worthy that Christ should deign to work such things through her; nevertheless, she fell to the ground, as if she wished to kiss the traces of the feet of the Lord, and begged humbly for divine clemency for the man. While she was still lying on the ground the ears of the deaf man opened and he returned home joyfully, delivered from all sadness.

2. Glorified among her relations because of such prodigies, Monegundis, in order to avoid the trap of vainglory, left her husband, her family, her whole house, and went, full of faith, to the basilica of the holy bishop Martin. While on her way she came to a village of the Touraine called Esvres, where relics of the blessed confessor Medard of Soissons were preserved; that very night vigils were being celebrated. The saint [Monegundis] passed the night in attentive prayer, and then returned at the given time with the people to celebrate Mass. While the priests were in the midst of the service a young girl came up, swollen by the poison of a malignant pustule, and threw herself at her feet, saying, "Help me, for cruel death is going to snatch life from me." And she, prostrate in prayer in the usual fashion, prayed to God, the creator of all things, for this girl. Then she got up and made the sign of the cross. As a result, the tumor opened, split into four, and the pus came out: the young girl was saved from importunate death. After that the blessed Monegundis arrived at the basilica of St Martin, and there, on her knees in front of the tomb, she gave thanks to God for being able to see the holy tomb with her own eyes. She settled herself in a small room in which she gave herself every day to prayer, fasts and vigils. And indeed this place was made glorious by her miracles. The daughter of a certain widow came there with her hands all contracted, and she was besought to pray and make the sign of salvation, and then she began to rub the fingers of the girl with her own hands, straightening out the fingers and tendons and finally freeing the palms and leaving

her hands healthy. While these things were happening, her husband, having heard of the reputation of the saint, assembled his friends and neighbors and came after her and brought her back with him and put her in that same cell in which she had lived before. But she did not cease from the work she was used to, and she gave herself over to continual prayer and fasting, so that in the end she might reach the place where she wanted to be. Again she began the path which she desired, begging for the help of St Martin, that he who gave her the desire might give her the means. She came to the basilica and returned to the same cell she had inhabited before; she stayed there without any trouble, without being sought for again by her husband. She gathered together a small number of nuns in that place, and stayed there, persevering in faith and in prayer, eating only bread made of barley and not drinking any wine, except a little on feast-days, and then only diluted with much water. She did not have a soft bed of hay or fresh straw, but only one of interlaced twigs, which are commonly called "mats"; she put this upon a bed-frame or on the ground, and it served her as a bench, a mattress, a pillow, a bed-spread, in a word all that she needed for a bed. She taught those whom she had brought to live with her how to make these mats. And living there, praising God, she gave to many sick people, after she had prayed, healing cures.

4. But already the time was approaching when God would call her to Him, and her strength began to desert her. Seeing this, the nuns who were with her wept bitterly and said "And to whom do you leave us, holy mother? To whom do you entrust your daughters whom you have assembled here to look on God?" She told them, weeping, "If you keep peace and holiness, God will protect you, and you will have the great bishop Saint Martin as shepherd. And I shall not be far from you, for if you invoke me I shall be in your hearts." But the nuns implored her, saying, "Many sick people will come to us, asking to receive your blessing, and what shall we do when they see that you are no more? We shall be confused, and send them away, since we shall no longer contemplate your face. We beg you, then, since you are going from our eyes, that you deign at least to bless some oil and salt that we can give to the sick who ask for a blessing." And she blessed some oil and salt for them, which they preserved with great care. And thus the blessed woman died in peace; she was buried in her cell, and she manifested herself thereafter by many miracles, for many sick people were cured, after her death, by the blessing which we have just mentioned.

BARBARIAN KINGDOMS

1.13 Gothic Italy as Rome's heir: Cassiodorus, *Variae (State Papers)* (*c.*507–536). Original in Latin.

Theodoric and his successor kings of the Ostrogoths saw themselves as continuators of Roman traditions. Depending on classically educated men such as Cassiodorus (d.583) to work for them as writers and publicists, they issued edicts, gave orders, and negotiated with other rulers. The documents here were among the papers that Cassiodorus compiled into his twelve-book *Variae* (or *State Papers*) *c.*537, when the Ostrogothic king Witigis was at war with Emperor Justinian (r.527–565). In 2.27 (i.e., *Variae* book 2, document no. 27), Theodoric demonstrates his adherence to Roman law: even though he considers Jews "destitute of God's grace," he grants them the right, as enshrined in the laws of Theodosius II (see above, p. 4), to maintain their synagogues. In 2.40 he responds to the request of the Frankish king Clovis (r.481/482–511) to send a lyre-player, a symbol of classical refinement and rulership, by writing to Boethius (d.524/526). Trained in the classics like Cassiodorus, Boethius had just written a book on music theory. Writing in Theodoric's name, Cassiodorus borrows some of Boethius's ideas, thereby both flattering Boethius and burnishing the king's reputation for learning. In 3.1, Theodoric presents himself as a peaceful elder statesman mediating between the Frankish king Clovis and the Visigothic leader Alaric (whom Cassiodorus calls "king"). Theodoric's aims were frustrated, however, since Clovis soon attacked the Visigoths and defeated them at the battle of Vouillé (507).

1. Imagine that you were King Theoderic. What would be your "job description"?
2. Why would a barbarian king want to show off his knowledge of music?

[Source: *The* Variae *of Magnus Aurelius Cassiodorus Senator*, trans. S.J.B. Barnish (Liverpool: Liverpool University Press, 1992), pp. 34–35, 38–39, 45–46, 142–43 (notes modified).]

2.27 King Theodoric to All Jews Living at Genoa (507–12)

As it is my desire, when petitioned, to give a lawful consent, so I do not like the laws to be cheated through my favors, especially in that area where I believe reverence for God to be concerned. You, then, who are destitute of His grace, should not seem insolent in your pride.

Therefore, by this authority, I decree that you add only a roof to the ancient walls of your synagogue, granting permission to your requests just so far as the imperial decrees allow.[1] It is unlawful for you to add any ornament, or to stray into an enlargement of the building. And you must realize that you will in no way escape the penalty of the ancient ordinance if you do not refrain from illegalities. Indeed, I give you permission to roof or strengthen the walls themselves only if you are not affected by the thirty year limitation.[2] Why do you wish for what you ought to shun? I grant leave, indeed; but, to my praise, I condemn the prayers of erring men. I cannot command your faith, for no one is forced to believe against his will....

---

[1] This refers to a new law (a "Novel") by Emperor Theodosius II that prohibited Jews from building new synagogues but granted them the right to strengthen those already standing if they threatened to collapse.

[2] This probably means "if no one, for thirty years, has legally challenged the right of your synagogue to exist on that site, and in that form." Theodoric considered property arrangements in place before his conquest of Italy (489–493) to be valid.

2.40 King Theodoric to the Patrician Boethius (506)

Although the king of the Franks, tempted by the fame of my banquets, has earnestly requested a lyre-player from me, I have promised to fulfill his wishes for this reason only, that I know you to be skilled in musical knowledge. To choose a trained man is a task for you, who have succeeded in attaining the heights of that same discipline.

For what is more glorious than music, which modulates the heavenly system with its sonorous sweetness, and binds together with its virtue the concord of nature which is scattered everywhere? For any variation there may be in the whole does not depart from the pattern of harmony. Through [music] we think with efficiency, we speak with elegance, we move with grace. Whenever, by the natural law of its discipline, it reaches our ears, it commands song. The artist changes men's hearts as they listen; and, when this artful pleasure issues from the secret place of nature as the queen of the senses, in all the glory of its tones, our remaining thoughts take to flight, and it expels all else, that it may delight itself simply in being heard. Harmful melancholy he turns to pleasure; he weakens swelling rage; he makes bloodthirsty cruelty kindly, arouses sleepy sloth from its torpor, restores to the sleepless their wholesome rest, recalls lust-corrupted chastity to its moral resolve, and heals boredom of spirit which is always the enemy of good thoughts. Dangerous hatreds he turns to helpful goodwill, and, in a blessed kind of healing, drives out the passions of the heart by means of sweetest pleasures....

Among men all this is achieved by means of five *toni* [scales or modes], each of which is called by the name of the region where it was discovered.[1] Indeed, the divine compassion distributed this favor locally, even while it assuredly made its whole creation something to be praised. The Dorian *tonus* bestows wise self-restraint and establishes chastity; the Phrygian arouses strife, and inflames the will to anger; the Aeolian calms the storms of the soul, and gives sleep to those who are already at peace; the Iastian [Ionian] sharpens the wits of the dull, and, as a worker of good, gratifies the longing for heavenly things among those who are burdened by earthly desire. The Lydian was discovered as a remedy for excessive cares and weariness of the spirit: it restores it by relaxation, and refreshes it by pleasure....

3.1 King Theodoric to Alaric, King of the Visigoths (507)

Although the countless numbers of your clan gives you confidence in your strength, although you recall that the power of Attila yielded to Visigothic might,[2] nevertheless, the hearts of a warlike people grow soft during a long peace. Therefore, beware of suddenly putting on the hazard men who have assuredly had no experience in war for many years. Battle terrifies those who are unused to it, and they will have no confidence in a sudden clash, unless experience gives it in advance. Do not let some blind resentment carry you away. Self-restraint is fore-sighted, and a preserver of tribes; rage, though, often precipitates a crisis; and only when justice can no longer find a place with one's opponent, is it then useful to appeal to arms.

Wait, therefore, until I send my envoys to the Frankish king [Clovis], so that the judgment of friends may terminate your dispute. For I wish nothing to arise between two of my marriage kinsmen that may, perhaps, cause one of them to be the loser.[3] There has been no slaughter of your clansmen to inflame you; no occupied province is deeply incensing you; the quarrel is still trivial, a matter of words. You will very easily settle it if you do not enrage yourself by war. Though you are my relative, let me set against you the notable tribes allied to me, and justice too, which strengthens kings and quickly puts to flight those minds which it finds are so armed against it. And so, giving first the honor of my greeting, I have seen fit to send you X and Y[4] as my envoys. They will convey my instructions, as requisite, and, with your approval, will hasten on to my brother Gundobad and the other kings, lest you should be harassed by the incitements of those who maliciously rejoice in another's war. May Providence prevent that wickedness from overcoming you. I judge your enemy to be our common trouble. For he who strives against you will find in me his due opponent....

---

[1] Tones were a way to categorize melodic practices, and theorists differed on their number.

[2] The Visigoths, fighting as part of the Roman army, won a battle over Attila's Huns in 451.

[3] Theodoric's wife was the sister of Clovis, while Alaric's wife was Theodoric's daughter.

[4] The letters were drafted for specific situations but also for use as models for future correspondence. Here we have the form of the model.

1.14 The conversion of the Franks: Bishop Avitus of Vienne, *Letter to Clovis* (508?). Original in Latin.

This letter was written by the Catholic bishop of Vienne, advisor to the Burgundian kings, to congratulate Clovis, king of the Franks, on his conversion to Catholicism and his baptism. Historians have long been influenced by the *Histories* of Gregory of Tours (for which see an excerpt below, p. 48), which claimed that Clovis had been a pagan until 496, when he had a miraculous conversion to Catholic Christianity and turned all his energies to fighting the Arians. The letter from Avitus suggests a very different scenario. It begins by pointing out that Clovis had been interested in Arianism (one of the "schisms" that Avitus refers to) until he saw the light. It continues with effusive praise of Clovis, words that could probably not have been uttered by a close associate of Burgundian royalty until after that kingdom became allied with the Franks, in 508. Thus Avitus's letter suggests that Clovis's conversion was in 508. By then it is very likely that the Burgundian kings themselves had already given up Arianism for the Catholic faith. Key to Avitus's letter is the idea, which would be influential only later, that the king should send out missionaries to spread Catholicism to "more distant races."

1. For what reasons, according to Avitus, might a king hesitate to change his religion?
2. What benefits does Avitus see in store for Clovis now that he is baptized?

[Source: *Avitus of Vienne: Letters and Selected Prose*, trans. Danuta Shanzer and Ian Wood, Translated Texts for Historians 38 (Liverpool: Liverpool University Press, 2002), pp. 369–73 (notes modified).]

Avitus the bishop to Clovis the king

The chasers after various schisms,[1] by their opinions, different in nature, many in number, but *all* empty of truth, tried to conceal, under the cover of the name "Christian," the lies that have been uncovered by the keen intelligence of Your Subtlety. While we save such things (i.e., the lies) for eternity, while we reserve for future examination[2] the question of who is right on what, even in our present circumstances a ray of truth has shone through. Divine foresight has found a certain judge for our age. In making a choice for yourself, you judge on behalf of everyone. Your faith is our victory.

Many in this very situation, seeking true belief, if they are moved to the suggestion, encouraged by priests or their friends, usually invoke the custom of their race and the rites of ancestral observance as stumbling-blocks.

Thus, to their own detriment, they prefer due reverence to salvation. While they maintain a token respect for their ancestors in continuing to be unbelievers, they demonstrate that they somehow do not know what to choose. Therefore let the dangerous [sense of] shame abandon this excuse after the miracle of your decision! You [alone] among your ancient clan, content with nobility alone,[3] wished whatever could adorn all your lofty ancestry to start from you for the benefit of your race. You have ancestors who did good [deeds], but you wished to be the author of better [ones]. You are the equal of your great-grandfathers in that you reign in the temporal world; for your descendants you have established your rule in heaven.

Therefore let Greece,[4] to be sure, rejoice in having an orthodox ruler, but she is no longer the only one to

---

[1] By schism here, Avitus means heresy.

[2] Presumably the Last Judgment.

[3] Avitus hints at the idea of the divine origin of German kings but suggests that Clovis has rightly given up this idea, and the glory reflected upon his descendants will start from his choice.

[4] I.e., Byzantium, the eastern half of the Roman Empire.

deserve so great a gift. Now her bright glory adorns *your* part of the world also, and in the West, <u>in the person of a new king</u>, the ray of an age-old light shines forth. It is fitting that it began to shine on the birthday of our Redeemer, so that the vivifying water appropriately gave birth to you in your salvation[1] on the very day when the world received the Lord of Heaven born for its redemption. On the day on which the birthday of our Lord is celebrated, let yours be too—the day on which Christ was born to the world, and you to Christ, the day on which you consecrated your soul to God, your life to those present, and your reputation to posterity.

What can be said about the glorious celebration of your regeneration? Even if I was not present at the rites in the flesh, I was not absent from communion in its joys—above all since divine kindness has added this further cause for thankfulness to our part of the world. Before your baptism a message came to me of the most sublime humility,[2] in which you stated that you were a candidate for baptism. Therefore after this waiting-period, Christmas Eve found me finally sure of you. I was turning things over in my mind and wondering how it would be when a large company of bishops united, striving in the sacred service, would lap the royal limbs in the life-giving waters, when he would bow before the servants of the Lord the head that should be so feared by pagans, when locks grown long beneath a helmet[3] would put on the helmet of the sacred chrism, when his spotless limbs, the breastplate removed, would shine as white as his baptismal clothes. Have no fear, O most prosperous of Kings! From now on the very softness of that clothing will cause the hardness of your armor to be all the more effective: whatever good luck has offered you in the past, holiness will now provide.

I would like to add some exhortation to my praise of you, were anything escaping either your knowledge or your watchfulness. Certainly I am not going to preach to you the faith that you saw without a preacher *before* your baptism once you have found it. Or should I preach humility perhaps? You had long ago paid it to me by your service, even though only now do you owe it to me through your profession of faith. Or perhaps I should preach the sense of pity that a people, up till recently captive, once released by you, by its joy conveys to the world and by its tears to God?

There is only one thing that I would like to be increased. Because God has made your race completely his own through you, please offer the seeds of faith from the treasure-house of your heart to more distant races too: since they still live in their natural ignorance, no seeds of heresy have corrupted. Do not be ashamed or find it troublesome even to take the step of sending missions for this purpose to build up the party of the God who has raised up yours so greatly. To the extent that whatever foreign pagan peoples there are, ready to serve you for the first time because of the rule of your religion, while they still seem to have some other distinctive quality, let them be distinguished by their race rather than through their ruler ... [Here the text of the letter breaks off.]

1.15 Gothic Spain converts: *The Third Council of Toledo* (589). Original in Latin.

In 589, sixty-three bishops and other clerics, abbots, and nobles met at Toledo in Spain at the request of King Reccared (r.586–601). They were there to "restore ecclesiastical discipline" by converting the kingdom from the Arian form of Christianity to the Catholic. In 587, Reccared had announced his own conversion, and even before that, in 580, an Arian council at Toledo had accepted part (though not all) of the Catholic Creed on the Trinity, agreeing that the Father and Son were equal and co-eternal, but not the Holy Spirit. The Third Council of Toledo added Catholic teaching on the Holy Spirit and instituted all the

---

[1] The "vivifying water" is that of Clovis's baptism.

[2] The implication seems to have been that Avitus was invited to the ceremony.

[3] Long hair was the identifying mark of the Merovingians.

canons (laws) of the Catholic Church. Since opposition to the conversion of 589 seems to have been very weak, it is likely that most Visigoths were happy to accept Catholicism, which brought them into agreement with the large Hispano-Roman population in Spain.

1. What was the role of the king at the council meeting?
2. How did the conversion to Catholicism affect the daily lives of people at all levels in Spain?

[Source: *Medieval Iberia: Readings from Christian, Muslim, and Jewish Sources*, ed. Olivia Remie Constable with the assistance of Damian Zurro, 2nd ed. (Philadelphia: University of Pennsylvania Press, 2012), pp. 12–20. Translated by David Nirenberg.]

In the name of our Lord Jesus Christ, in the fourth year of the reign of the most glorious, most pious and most faithful to God Lord Reccared, king, on the eighth day of the Ides of May, era 627 [589],[1] this sacred council was celebrated in the royal city of Toledo, by the bishops of all Spain and of the Gauls who are inscribed below.

This most glorious prince having commanded, because of the sincerity of his faith, that all the prelates of his kingdom should convene in one [council] in order that they might exult in the Lord, both for his conversion and for the renewal of the Gothic people, and that they should at the same time give thanks to the divine dignity for such an extraordinary gift, this same most blessed prince addressed the venerable council saying: "I do not believe that you are unaware of the fact, most reverend bishops, that I have summoned you into our serene presence for the restoration of ecclesiastical discipline. And because throughout past times the threatening heresy [of Arianism] did not allow a synod [council] of all the Catholic Church to be convened, God, whom it pleased to eliminate the said heresy through us, admonished us to repair the institutions of the customs of the church...."

Upon [hearing] this, the entire council, giving thanks to God and acclaiming the most religious prince, decreed in that instant a fast of three days. And all the bishops of God having come together again on the eighth day of the Ides of May, after the preliminary oration [prayer], each of the bishops was again seated in his proper place, when behold, among them appeared the most serene prince, having joined himself to the oration of the bishops of God, and filled thereafter with divine inspiration,

he began to address [the bishops] saying: "We do not believe that your holinesses are unaware of how long a time Spain labored under the error of the Arians, and how, not long after our father's death, when it was known that we had associated ourselves with your holy Catholic faith, there [arose] everywhere a great and eternal rejoicing. And therefore, venerable fathers, we decided to unite you [in order] to celebrate this council, so that you yourselves may give eternal thanks to the Lord for the peoples newly come to Christ. The rest of the agenda that we present before your priestliness concerning our faith and hope which we profess, we have written down in this book. Read it, therefore, among yourselves. And [then] approved by the judgment of council and decorated with this testimony of faith, our glory shall shine throughout all times to come."

The... book the king offered was received, therefore, by all the bishops of God, and [it] being read in a clear voice by the clerk, the following was heard: Although the omnipotent God has, for the benefit of the populace, given us charge of the kingdom, and has delivered the governance of not a few peoples into our royal stewardship, nevertheless we remember that we too are of mortal condition, and that we cannot merit the happiness of future blessedness unless we esteem the cult of the true faith, and, at least, please our creator with the creed of which he is worthy. For which reason, the higher we are extolled above our subjects by royal dignity, the more we should provide for those things that pertain to God, both to increase our faith, and to take thought for the people God has entrusted to us....

---

[1] In the Spanish system of dating, used until the fourteenth century, the year 1 began in what is today 38 BCE. The calculation of the day of the month, however, followed the ancient Roman dating system: the eighth day of the Ides of May was the seventh day counting backwards from May 15, so May 8.

Therefore, most holy fathers, these most noble peoples, who have been brought near to the Lord by our diligence, I offer to the eternal God through your hands, as a holy and propitiating sacrifice. Truly it shall be for me an unfading crown and a delight in the reward of the just if these peoples, who because of our dexterity have rushed to the unity of the church, remain rooted and firm within it. And truly, just as it was [entrusted] to our care by the divine will to bring these peoples to the unity of the Church of Christ, it is your duty to instruct them in the dogmas of the Catholics so that, instructed in the full knowledge of the truth, they [shall] know [how] stolidly to reject the errors of the pernicious heresy, and to keep to the path of the true faith through love, embracing the communion of the Catholic Church with an ever more ardent desire....

To these my true confessions I added the sacred decrees of the abovementioned councils, and I signed them, with God [as my] witness, in all innocence of heart....

I, Reccared, king, faithful to this holy and true creed, which is believed by the Catholic Church throughout the world, holding it in my heart, affirming it with my mouth, signed it with my right hand, [under] God's protection.

I, Bado, glorious queen, signed with my hand and with all my heart this creed, which I believed and professed.

Then the entire council broke into acclamations, praising God and applauding the prince....

Here begin the decrees that, in the name of God, were established by the third holy synod in the city of Toledo.

1. THAT THE STATUTES OF THE COUNCILS AND THE DECREES OF THE ROMAN PONTIFFS BE MAINTAINED

After the condemnation of the Arian heresy and the exposition of the holy Catholic faith, the holy council decreed the following: that since in some Spanish churches, whether because of heresy or paganism, canonical discipline was passed over, license for transgression abounded, and the option of discipline was denied, so that any excess of heresy found favor and an abundance of evil made lukewarm the strictness of discipline, [because of these things,] the mercy of Christ having restored peace to the church, [we order that] all that which the authority of the ancient canons[1] prohibited, let it also be restricted by the revived discipline, and let that be performed which [the canons said] ought to be performed....

2. THAT IN ALL THE CHURCHES THE CREED[2] SHOULD BE RECITED ON SUNDAY...

4. THAT IT IS PERMITTED THE BISHOP TO CONVERT A CHURCH IN HIS PARISH INTO A MONASTERY...

5. THAT BISHOPS AND DEACONS SHOULD LIVE CHASTELY WITH THEIR WIVES

It has come to the attention of the holy council that the bishops, presbyters, and deacons who are coming out of heresy [i.e., Arians] copulate with their wives out of carnal desire. So that this shall not be done in the future, we decree what prior canons had already determined: that they are not allowed to live in libidinous union, but rather with the conjugal bond remaining between them they should mutually help each other, without living in the same room. Or if [his] virtue is strong enough, let him make his wife live in some other house, as good witness to [his] chastity, not only before God, but also before men. But if any should choose to live obscenely with his wife after this accord, let him be a lector.[3] [And concerning any of] those who have always been subjected to ecclesiastical canons [i.e., Catholics], if against ancient command they have had consort in their cells with women who could provoke a suspicion of infamy, let them be punished canonically, the women being sold [into slavery] by the bishop, their price being distributed to the poor....

9. THAT THE CHURCHES OF THE ARIANS SHALL BELONG TO THE CATHOLIC BISHOPS IN WHOSE DIOCESES THEY ARE LOCATED...

10. THAT NO ONE COMMIT VIOLENCE AGAINST THE CHASTITY OF A WIDOW, AND THAT NO ONE MARRY A WOMAN AGAINST HER WILL

In the interests of chastity (the increase of which the council should most avidly incite) and with the agree-

---

[1] Canons were the laws determined by Church councils.

[2] See *The Nicene Creed* (above, p. 11), to which was added the "filioque," which said that Holy Spirit proceeded from the Father *and* the Son.

[3] A demotion to minor orders.

ment of our most glorious lord king Reccared, this holy council affirms that widows who wish to maintain their chastity may not be forced with any violence into a second marriage. And if before taking a vow of chastity they wish to be married, let them marry him who of their own free will they wish to have as husband. The same should be maintained concerning virgins, [for] they should not be forced to take a husband against their parents' will or their own. If anyone impedes the desire of a widow or virgin to remain chaste, let him be held a stranger from holy communion and the thresholds of the church.

11. THAT PENITENTS DO PENANCE

[We are] aware of the fact that in some churches of Spain men do penitence for their sins, not in accordance with the canons, but in a disgusting way: as often as they wish to sin, they ask the presbyter to be reconciled. Therefore, in order to eliminate such an execrable presumption, the council decrees that penitence be given in accordance with the form of the ancient canons, that is: that he who repents should first be separated from communion, and he should avail himself often of the laying on of hands, along with the other penitents. Once his time of satisfaction is finished, he should be restored to communion as the bishop sees fit. But those who return to their old vice, whether during the time of penitence or afterwards, shall be condemned in accordance with the severity of the ancient canons....

14. CONCERNING THE JEWS

At the suggestion of the council, our most glorious lord has commanded [that the following] be inserted in the canons: It is not permitted for Jews to have Christian women as wives or concubines, nor to purchase slaves for their personal use. And if children are born of such a union, they should be taken to the baptismal font. They may not be assigned any public business by virtue of which they [might] have power to punish Christians. And if any Christians have been stained by them, [or] by Jewish ritual, or been circumcised, let them return to liberty and the Christian religion without paying the price [of their freedom]....

16. THAT BISHOPS ALONG WITH JUDGES DESTROY THE IDOLS, AND THAT LORDS FORBID THEIR SERVANTS IDOLATRY

Because the sacrilege of idolatry is taking root in nearly all of Spain and Gaul, the holy synod, with the consent of the glorious prince, commands the following: that each bishop in his respective area, along with the judge

of that region, should diligently search out the aforesaid sacrilege, and should nor refrain from exterminating that which they find, and should correct those who participate in such error with any punishment available, save that which endangers life....

17. THAT THE BISHOPS AND THE JUDGES CORRECT WITH BITTER DISCIPLINE THOSE WHO MURDER THEIR OWN CHILDREN

Among the many complaints which have come to the ears of the holy council, there has been denounced to it a crime so great, that the ears of the present bishops cannot bear it, and this is that in some parts of Spain, parents kill their own children, [because they are] eager to fornicate, and know nothing of piety. Those to whom it is troublesome to have many children should first refrain from fornication. [For once] they have contracted marriage under the pretext of procreation, they make themselves guilty of parricide and fornication, who, by murdering their own children, reveal that they were married not for procreation but for libidinous union. Our most glorious lord king Reccared, having taken account of such evil, his glory has deigned to instruct the judges of those regions to inquire diligently concerning such a horrible crime, in conjunction with the bishops, and to forbid it with all severity. Therefore this sacred council sorrowfully urges the bishops of [those] regions that together with the judges they diligently inquire [about this crime], and forbid it with the most severe penalties, excepting death....

23. THAT DANCES BE PROHIBITED ON THE BIRTHDAYS OF THE SAINTS

That unreligious custom which the vulgar people practice on the feast days of the saints must be completely destroyed. That is, that the people who ought to attend to the divine offices instead dedicate themselves to unseemly songs and dances, injuring not only themselves, but also interfering with the offices of the religious. The holy council commends [this] to the care of the bishops and judges: that this custom may be banished from all of Spain.

HERE BEGINS THE EDICT OF THE KING IN CONFIRMATION OF THE COUNCIL

... We decree that all these ecclesiastical rules which we have summarized briefly above [should be] maintained with eternal stability as is amply explained in the canons. If any cleric or layperson does not wish to obey these decrees, [let them be punished as follows]: If they are a bishop, presbyter, deacon, or cleric, let them be subject to excommunication by the entire council. If they are laypeople of substance in their region, let them give [as a fine] half of their possessions to the fisc,[1] and if they are people of inferior status in their region, let them lose [all] their possessions and be sent into exile.

I, Flavius Reccared, have signed as confirmation these decrees that we established with the holy synod.

[There follow the signatures of the bishops, etc.]

1.16 Merovingian Gaul's bishop-historian: Gregory of Tours, *Histories* (576–594). Original in Latin.

Bishop of Tours from 573 until his death in 594, Gregory, who also wrote *Lives* of many saints (e.g., see Monegundis, above, p. 38), began his *Histories* with the Creation itself but soon turned to Gaul and to his own day, which he chronicled in the Augustinian spirit (see *The City of God*, p. 16 above), with both good and bad people and events intermingled. As the successor of St. Martin as bishop of Tours (see *The Life of St. Martin*, above p. 35), Gregory was responsible for the well-being of his flock. But the authority of bishops like Gregory was checked and balanced by that of dukes, counts, and kings. In the excerpt below, Bishop Praetextatus of Rouen was hauled before the Merovingian king Chilperic (r.561–584) on charges of treason. In particular, he was made to answer for his actions regarding Merovech, Chilperic's disinherited son. Merovech had tried to win his father's throne by marrying Brunhild, the widow of Chilperic's rival (and brother) in Francia. Praetextatus was accused of helping further Merovech's plans. The incident illustrates the power of the Frankish king over the episcopacy. But it also shows the immense prestige and authority wielded by bishops.

1. What does Gregory report as his own role during these events?
2. How was Praetextatus punished and what was the justification for this punishment?

[Source: *Gregory of Tours: The Merovingians*, trans. and ed. Alexander Callander Murray (Toronto: University of Toronto Press, 2005), pp. 89–96 (slightly modified).]

Book 5

18. [King] Chilperic [r.561–584] heard that Praetexta-tus, bishop of Rouen, was giving people gifts contrary to the king's interests and had him summoned to his presence. He examined him and discovered that the bishop was in possession of property entrusted to him by Queen Brunhild.[2] This was confiscated, and the king ordered him kept in exile until the bishops could convene a hearing.

The council met, and Bishop Praetextatus was brought before it. The bishops who attended convened in the basilica of the holy apostle Peter in Paris.

"Bishop," said the king to Praetextatus, "why did you think to join in marriage my enemy Merovech,[3] who

---

[1] The fisc was the property or treasury of the state, in this case the king.

[2] Brunhild was the widow of Chilperic's half-brother and rival king, Sigibert (r.561–575). The events of this chapter take place in 577.

[3] Merovech was Chilperic's son by Audovera. When Chilperic married Fredegund, she made sure that Merovech would not gain the throne. Merovech tried to outwit her by marrying Queen Brunhild. He did not succeed.

ought to have acted as a son, with his aunt, that is, his uncle's wife? Or were you unacquainted with what the canons have established for such a case? Also, not only did you demonstrably go too far in this matter, but you even acted in conjunction with Merovech to give gifts to bring about my assassination. You have made a son an enemy of his father, you have led the people astray with money, so that none of them would maintain the loyalty they had for me, and you have tried to hand my kingdom into the hands of another."

When he said this, the crowd of Franks let out a roar and tried to break open the church doors, intending to drag the bishop out and stone him, but the king stopped this happening.

When Bishop Praetextatus denied having done what the king charged, false witnesses came forward who showed various valuable articles.

"These and these you gave us," they said, "on condition we pledge our loyalty to Merovech."

"You're right that you have often received gifts from me," he said in response to these charges, "but it was not for the purpose of driving the king from the kingdom. Since you furnished me with excellent horses and other things, what else could I do but pay you back at the same value?"

The king returned to his quarters, but we remained seated as a group in the sacristy of the basilica of the blessed Peter. As we were talking together, suddenly Aetius, archdeacon of the bishopric of Paris, came in and greeted us.

"Hear me, bishops of God, gathered here together," he said. "In this hour you shall either exalt your name and show that you deserve a glowing reputation, or instead, if you don't have the sense to stand up for yourselves or if you allow your brother to be destroyed, hereafter no one will take you for bishops of God."

When he said this, none of the bishops said anything in reply. For they feared the savage anger of the queen [Fredegund], at whose instigation these proceedings were being conducted.

As they considered these words, with their fingers on their lips, I said, "Please listen to what I have to say, most holy bishops, especially you who seem to be on quite friendly terms with the king; furnish him with advice as befits holy men and priests, so that he is not destroyed

by God's anger, losing his kingdom and reputation in an outburst against a servant of God."

When I said this, all were silent.

Since no one spoke, I added, "My lord bishops, remember the word of the prophet: 'If the watchman sees the iniquity of a person and does not speak, he shall be guilty for a lost soul [cf. Ezek. 33:6].' Therefore do not remain silent, but speak out, and set this king's sins before his own eyes, in case some evil comes upon him, and you are held responsible for his soul. Surely you can't be unaware of what has happened in modern times? How Chlodomer[1] captured Sigismund[2] and threw him in prison, and Avitus, God's priest, said to him: 'Do not lay hands on him and when you go to Burgundy you will win the victory.' But he disregarded what was said to him by the priest and went ahead and killed him with his wife and sons. And Chlodomer went to Burgundy and was overcome by the enemy and killed. What about the emperor Maximus? When he forced the blessed Martin[3] to associate with a certain bishop who was a homicide, and Martin gave in to the impious king in order to help free those condemned to death, Maximus was pursued by the judgment of the eternal King and, driven from the imperial throne, was condemned to the vilest death."

When I said this, no one said anything in reply, but all stared in astonishment.

However, two flatterers among them—it is sad to have to say that of bishops—gave a report to the king, telling him that he had no greater opponent of his interests than me. Promptly a court attendant was sent to bring me before him.

When I arrived, the king was standing beside a bower made of branches; on his right stood Bishop Bertram and on his left Ragnemod. There was a table covered with bread and various dishes in front of them.

On seeing me, the king said, "Bishop, you are supposed to confer justice freely on all. But look now, I don't get justice from you. As I see it, you are giving in to iniquity: your actions are an example of the proverb that the crow does not tear out the eye of another crow."

"If any one of us, king, tries to leave the path of justice," I replied, "he can be corrected by you. But if you abandon it, who shall take you to task? We speak to you, but you pay attention only if you wish. And if you refuse

---

1   King Chlodomer (r.511–524) was a son of King Clovis (r.481–511).

2   Sigismund (r.516–524) was king of the Burgundians.

3   St. Martin (d.397) was bishop of Tours. Maximus was a usurping emperor (r.383–388).

to listen, who will pass sentence on you if it is not He who has proclaimed that He is justice?"

He had been inflamed against me by his flatterers and replied, "I have found justice with everyone, but with you I cannot find it. I know what I shall do to disgrace you before the people and reveal to all that you are unjust. I shall assemble the people of Tours and tell them, 'You may cry out against Gregory that he is an unjust man and renders justice to no one.' And to those who shout this, I will reply, 'I who am king cannot get justice from him. Shall you who are less than I find it?'"

"You do not know whether I am unjust," I said. "He to whom the secrets of the heart are revealed knows my conscience. What people falsely cry out when you revile me means nothing, for everyone knows it is your doing. This is why not I but you will be the one disgraced by the outcries. But why go on with this? You have the law and the canons; search them carefully and then you will know that the judgment of God hangs over you if you do not follow their commands."

Thinking that I did not understand his artfulness, he turned to the broth that was set in front of him, as if this would soothe me.

"I had this broth prepared for you," he said. "There is nothing else in it but fowl and a few chickpeas."

Recognizing his flattery, I replied, "My food is doing the will of God, without at all overlooking whatever he commands, not partaking of the pleasures of these delicacies. As for you who find fault with others in matters of justice, promise first that you will not neglect the law and the canons. Then I shall believe that you follow justice."

Then he stretched out his right hand and swore by almighty God that he would in no way overlook the teaching of the law and the canons. After that I took bread and wine and departed.

That night, when the hymns for the night had been sung, I heard heavy knocking on the door of my lodging. From the servant I sent to answer it, I learned that messengers from Queen Fredegund were there. They were brought in, and I received greetings from the queen. Then her servants asked me not to take a position contrary to her interests and, at the same time, promised two hundred pounds of silver if I attacked Praetextatus, and he was convicted.

"We already have the word of all the bishops," they said. "Don't be the only one in opposition."

"Even if you were to give me a thousand pounds of silver and gold," I said to them, "what else can I do but what the Lord tells me to do? I will promise one thing only, that I will follow what the others agree to in accordance with the canons."

Not understanding what I was saying, they thanked me and went away. In the morning some of the bishops came to me bearing a similar message; to them I gave the same answer.

We met in the morning in Saint Peter's basilica, and the king was present.

"The authority of the canons provides that a bishop detected in theft should be removed from the office of bishop," he said.

We asked who the bishop might be against whom the charge of theft was made.

"You saw the articles of value which he stole from me," the king answered.

Three days before the king had shown us two bundles full of costly articles and treasures of different sorts, valued at more than three thousand solidi,[1] as well as a bag of coined gold, the weight of which suggested about two thousand pieces. The king said this had been stolen from him by the bishop.

The bishop answered, "I believe you remember that I came to you when Queen Brunhild left Rouen and told you that I was holding her property in trust, namely, five parcels, and that her servants came to me quite frequently to retrieve them but I would not release them without your advice. And king, you said to me, 'Rid yourself of this stuff and let the woman have her property back, in case hostility arises between me and my nephew Childebert[2] over these goods.' I went back to the city and gave one roll to the servants, as they could carry no more. They returned a second time and asked for the others. I again sought the advice of your magnificence. And you gave me orders, 'Get rid of this stuff, bishop, get rid of it, so it won't be the cause of a quarrel.' I again gave them two bundles and two more remained in my possession. Why now do you make a false charge and accuse me of theft, when this case should be considered one not of theft but of custody?"

"If this property was considered as being in your possession for safekeeping," responded the king, "why did you open one of these bundles, cut in pieces a belt woven of gold thread, and distribute it to men who were to drive me from the kingdom?"

---

1 A *solidus* was a gold coin.
2 Childebert (r.575–596) had succeeded his father, Sigibert, as king.

"I told you before," answered Praetextatus, "that I had received their gifts, and as I had nothing at hand to give, I therefore presumed to take this and give it in return for their gifts. It seemed to be my property because it belonged to my son Merovech, whom I received from the baptismal font."[1]

King Chilperic saw that he could not convict him with false charges, and being thoroughly confounded and disturbed by his conscience, he left us and summoned certain of his flatterers.

"I confess," he said to them, "I've been beaten by the bishop's replies and I know that what he says is true. What can I do now if the queen's will is to be done with regards to him?"

Then he said, "Go, approach him and say, as if giving your own advice, 'You know that King Chilperic is pious and tender-hearted and readily moved to mercy; humble yourself before him and say that you are guilty of the charges he laid. Then we will all throw ourselves at his feet and prevail on him to pardon you.'"

Bishop Praetextatus was deceived by them and promised he would do as they suggested.

In the morning we met at the usual place. The king approached the bishop.

"If you conferred gifts on these men in return for gifts," he said, "why did you ask them for oaths that they stay loyal to Merovech?"

"I confess," replied the bishop, "I did seek to gain their friendship for him; and I would have summoned to his aid not just a mere mortal but an angel from heaven, had it been right; for he was my spiritual son from the baptismal font, as I have often said."

When the dispute had gone on for a while, Bishop Praetextatus threw himself on the ground.

"I have sinned against heaven and against you, most merciful king," he said. "I am an unspeakable homicide; I wanted to kill you and raise your son to the throne."

When Praetextatus said this, the king fell at the feet of the bishops and said, "Most holy bishops, listen to the guilty confess his accursed crime."

In tears we raised the king from the ground, and he ordered Praetextatus to leave the basilica.

Chilperic himself went to his quarters and sent a book of canons, into which [new pages] had been added containing the so-called apostolic canons. The following was among them: "A bishop found to have committed homicide, adultery, or perjury shall be removed from office."

This was read, and while Praetextatus stood there in shock, Bishop Bertram said, "Pay heed, brother and fellow-bishop, that you do not have the king's favor. For that reason, you cannot benefit from our friendship until you win the king's pardon."

After these events, the king asked that Praetextatus's robe should be torn off him, or that Psalm 108, which contains the curses against [Judas] Iscariot, be read over his head, or at the least that judgment be entered against him, excommunicating him forever. These proposals I opposed on grounds that the king had promised that nothing would be done unauthorized by the canons. Then Praetextatus was taken from our sight and placed under guard. He was beaten severely trying to escape custody one night and was sent into exile on an island in the sea off the coast of the city of Coutances.

After this there was news that Merovech was trying to reach the basilica of Saint Martin [in Tours] for the second time. But Chilperic gave orders to guard the church and close every access. The guards left open one door for a few of the clergy to enter for services but kept all the rest closed. This was a cause of considerable inconvenience to people.

When I was staying in Paris signs appeared in the sky, that is twenty rays in the north part, rising in the east and moving to the west; one of these was more extended and rose above the rest and, when it reached a great height, soon faded away, and in the same way, the rest that followed disappeared. I believe they announced Merovech's death.

As for Merovech, he was lurking in the champaign country near Reims, fearing to entrust himself to the Austrasians openly, and was tricked by the people of Thérouanne, who said they would desert his father Chilperic and submit to him if he would come to them. He took his best fighting men and went quickly to them. They sprung the trap they had prepared: shutting him up in a certain villa, they surrounded him with armed men and sent messengers to his father. On hearing the news, Chilperic got ready to hurry there. But while Merovech was being forced to wait in some lodging-house, he began to fear that he would have to suffer many penalties to satisfy the vengeance of his enemies. He summoned Gailen his confidential servant.

"Up to now," said Merovech, "we have shared the same heart and mind. I ask you not to allow me to fall into the hands of my enemies. Take a sword and run me through."

---

[1] Merovech was thus the godson of Praetextatus.

Without hesitating, Gailen stabbed him with his blade. When the king came, he found his son dead.

20. Then disturbances sprang up against bishops Salonius and Sagittarius.

They had been raised by Saint Nicetius, bishop of Lyons [r.552–573], and appointed to the diaconate. During his episcopate, Salonius was made bishop of the city of Embrun and Sagittarius bishop of the church of Gap. But once they had received episcopal office, their true wilfulness took over; in a mad fury, they appropriated property and committed beatings, homicides, adulteries, and various crimes. At one point, when Victor, bishop of St-Paul-Trois-Châteaux, was celebrating his birthday, they attacked him, sending a force armed with swords and bows against him. The attackers ripped his clothes, struck down servants and took away vessels and all the utensils of the feast, leaving the bishop grossly insulted.

When King Guntram learned of it, he had a synod assemble at Lyons [c.570]. The bishops gathered along with the patriarch, blessed Nicetius, and matters were investigated; they found the accused clearly guilty of the crimes with which they were charged and commanded those who could commit such offenses to be deprived of the office of bishop. But since Salonius and Sagittarius knew the king was still well-disposed to them, they approached him, claiming that they had been unjustly removed from office and imploring him to give them permission to take the matter to the pope of Rome. The king granted their request, gave them letters, and allowed them to leave.

Coming before Pope John [III, 561–574] they explained how they were removed for no good reason. The pope sent letters to the king ordering them restored to their positions. Without delay, the king brought this about, chastising them first with a long lecture. Worse yet, what resulted was not improvement.

They did, however, seek peace with Bishop Victor, surrendering the men who had been involved in the disturbance. But he, mindful of the Lord's command not to return evil for evil against one's enemies, did nothing to these wicked men and let them go free. For this reason, he was later excommunicated because he had made a public charge but privately spared his enemies without the participation of the brothers before whom he had made the charge. Nevertheless, through the good will of the king, he was restored to communion again.

TIMELINE FOR CHAPTER ONE

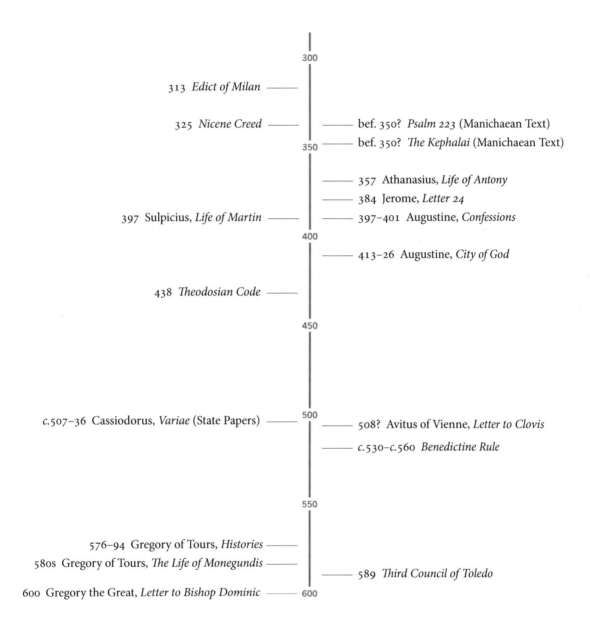

300

313 *Edict of Milan* ──────

325 *Nicene Creed* ────── | ────── bef. 350? *Psalm 223* (Manichaean Text)

350 ────── bef. 350? *The Kephalai* (Manichaean Text)

────── 357 Athanasius, *Life of Antony*

────── 384 Jerome, *Letter 24*

397 Sulpicius, *Life of Martin* ────── ────── 397–401 Augustine, *Confessions*

400

────── 413–26 Augustine, *City of God*

438 *Theodosian Code* ──────

450

c.507–36 Cassiodorus, *Variae* (State Papers) ────── 500 ────── 508? Avitus of Vienne, *Letter to Clovis*

────── c.530–c.560 *Benedictine Rule*

550

576–94 Gregory of Tours, *Histories* ──────

580s Gregory of Tours, *The Life of Monegundis* ──────

────── 589 *Third Council of Toledo*

600 Gregory the Great, *Letter to Bishop Dominic* ────── 600

To test your knowledge and gain deeper understanding of this chapter, please go to **www.utphistorymatters.com** for Study Questions.

The Emergence of Sibling Cultures (c.600–c.750)

THE RESILIENCE OF BYZANTIUM

2.1 The Siege of Constantinople: *The Easter Chronicle* (630). Original in Greek.

Much like Gregory of Tours' *Histories* (see above, p. 48), so too the anonymous *Easter Chronicle* began with the creation of the world, presenting historical events as part of God's plan. Unlike histories, however, which could consider events in a variety of ways, chronicles were written like diary entries, with occurrences discussed by year. The year 626, reproduced here, merited a very long entry. In trying to explain the defeat of an attack on the nearly undefended Constantinople by a coalition of Persians, Slavs, and Avars, the chronicler demonstrated the close intermingling of politics, war, and religion in seventh-century Byzantine thought. Indeed, it seems that the chronicle was compiled shortly after this event to celebrate this and other victories that rolled back the Persian conquests by 628. See Map 2.1 to figure out the movements of each side.

1. What roles does religious belief play in the chronicler's account?
2. Put yourself in the place of the Avar Khagan. What would be your motives in attacking Constantinople?

[Source: *Chronicon Paschale, 284–628 AD*, trans. Michael Whitby and Mary Whitby (Liverpool: Liverpool University Press, 1989), pp. 169–81 (notes and some names and titles modified).]

[626] It is good to describe how now too the sole most merciful and compassionate God, by the welcome intercession of his undefiled Mother, who is in truth our Lady Mother of God and ever-Virgin Mary, with his mighty hand saved this humble city of his from the utterly godless enemies who encircled it in concert, and redeemed the people who were present within it from the imminent sword, captivity, and most bitter servitude; no-one

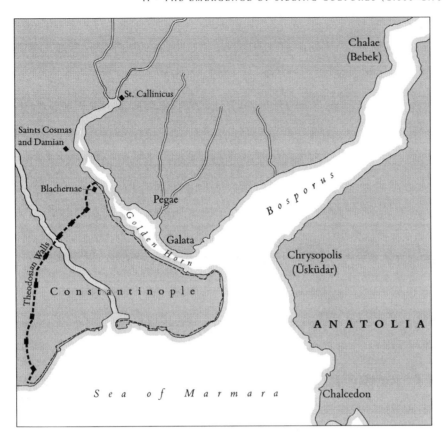

Map 2.1 The Siege of Constantinople

will find a means to describe this in its entirety. For the accursed Shahrbaraz, commander of the Persian army, while he was awaiting (as it seems and was indeed finally revealed by deeds) the arrival of the utterly godless Khagan of the Avars, had for these very many days past been at Chalcedon; he impiously burnt all the suburbs and palaces and houses of prayer, and thereafter remained, awaiting the advent of that man [the Avar Khagan].

And so on the 29th of the month June of the present indiction 14, that is on the day of the Feast of the holy and glorious chief apostles, Peter and Paul, a vanguard of the God-abhorred Khagan arrived, about 30,000. He had spread the rumor by means of reports that he would capture both the Long Wall and the area within it, and as a result, on the same day, which was a Lord's Day, the excellent cavalry who were present outside the city came inside the new Theodosian Wall of this imperial city. The same advance guard remained in the regions of Melantias,[1] while a few of them made sallies at intervals as far as the wall, and prevented anyone from going out or collecting provisions for animals at all.

In the meantime, when as many as ten days in succession had elapsed and none of the enemy appeared near the wall, soldiers went out with camp followers and civilians, with the intention of harvesting a few crops about ten miles distant; it happened that the enemy encountered them, that some fell on either side, and that some of the soldiers' camp followers and of the civilians who had gone out with them were also apprehended. For if it had not happened that the soldiers were diverted to the defence of their camp followers and the civilians, a considerable number of the enemy would have been slaughtered on that day.

Shortly afterwards some of the enemy, as many as 1,000, approached the venerated church of the Holy Maccabees on the far side at Galata; they made themselves

---

[1] The Long Wall was to the west of the Theodosian Walls, too far to the west to be included on Map 2.1. The Theodosian Walls, constructed in the early fifth century, consisted of both inner and outer walls separated by a terrace. Just to the west of the Theodosian Walls was a broad and deep moat. The wall was pierced by nine main gates, many of them mentioned in this text.

visible to the Persians, who had congregated in the regions of Chrysopolis, and they made their presence known to each other by fire signals.

In the meantime the accursed Khagan dismissed Athanasius, the most glorious patrician from the regions of Adrianopolis, after saying to him, "Go and see how the people of the city are willing to conciliate me, and what they are willing to give me to make me retire." And so when the same most glorious Athanasius entered and announced this to Bonus, the most glorious patrician and *magister*,[1] and to the other officials, they reproached him for having thus cringed before the accursed Khagan and for having promised that the people of the city would perform acts of conciliation for him. Then the most glorious Athanasius said that these had been his instructions from the most glorious officials at the time when he was dispatched on embassy; thereafter he had not learnt that the defenses had been strengthened thus and that an army was present here; however, he was ready to tell the Khagan without alteration the message given to him. Then, after the same most glorious Athanasius requested that he first wished to inspect the army that was in the city, a muster was held and about 12,000 or more cavalry resident in the city were present. And then the officials gave him a response that was intended by every means to cause the accursed Khagan [not] to approach the wall, that is the city. Then, after the most glorious Athanasius had reached the vicinity of that man, he was not received, but the cursed Khagan said that he would not give way at all unless he obtained both the city and those who were in it.[2]

On the 29th of the month July the same God-abhorred Khagan reached the wall with the whole of his horde, and showed himself to those in the city.[3] After one day, that is on the 31st of the same month July, he advanced, arrayed for battle, from the gate called Polyandrion as far as the gate of the Pempton and beyond with particular vigor: for there he stationed the bulk of his horde, after stationing Slavs within view along the remaining part of the wall. And he remained from dawn until hour 11 fighting first [along] with unarmored Slav infantry, and in the second rank with infantry in corslets. And towards evening he stationed a few siege engines and mantelets from Brachialion as far as Brachialion.[4]

And again on the following day he stationed a multitude of siege engines close to each other against that part which had been attacked by him, so that those in the city were compelled to station very many siege engines inside the wall. When the infantry battle was joined each day, through the efficacy of God, as a result of their superiority our men kept off the enemy at a distance. But he bound together his stone-throwers and covered them outside with hides; and in the section from the Polyandrion gate as far as the gate of St. Romanus he prepared to station 12 lofty siege towers, which were advanced almost as far as the outworks, and he covered them with hides.[5] And as for the sailors who were present in the city, even they came out to assist the citizens.[6] And one of these sailors constructed a mast and hung a skiff on it, intending by means of it to burn the enemies' siege-towers. Bonus, the all-praiseworthy *magister*, gave commendation to this sailor for having dismayed the enemy not inconsiderably.

But the same most renowned *magister*, after the enemy's approach to the wall, did not cease from urging him to take not only his agreed tribute but also any other condition for the sake of which he had come as far as the

---

[1] Emperor Heraclius, who was in Anatolia fighting the Persians, left Bonus in charge of the administration of Constantinople. The Avar attack was deliberately timed to take advantage of the city's relative defenselessness.

[2] It seems that Athanasius had been sent to the Avar Khagan to dissuade him from approaching Constantinople. In the meantime, unknown to Athanasius, Heraclius had sent extra defenders to the city. Further reinforcements, which arrived at the end of the siege, were brought by Heraclius' brother. However, the city's defenders relied primarily on the strength of the walls of Constantinople, along with their superior naval power. They did not try to engage the main Avar army outside the walls and repeatedly attempted to persuade the Khagan to retire.

[3] The Khagan apparently thought that by showing himself personally, he would intimidate the defenders. But the Patriarch of Constantinople, Sergius, counteracted the effect by parading on the walls himself.

[4] Corselets were body armor. For siege engines, see "Weapons and Warfare in the Middle Ages," in "Reading through Looking," pp. X–XXIV. Mantelets—wooden frames covered with animal hides—were set up to protect the archers. The meaning of "from Brachialion as far as Brachialion" is unclear.

[5] The hides reduced the risk of fire.

[6] These were not the crews of the Byzantine warships (who had to be ready to oppose the canoes of the Slavs) but rather of trading vessels in the Byzantine harbor. Heraclius had sent instructions for everyone to be involved in the defense.

wall. And he did not accept, but said, "Withdraw from the city, leave me your property, and save yourselves and your families." He was anxious to launch to sea the canoes which he had brought with him, and was prevented by the cutters.[1] Finally he prepared for these to be launched at the bridge of St. Callinicus after a third day of the fighting.[2] It was for this reason that he prepared for the canoes to be launched there, because the area was shallow and the cutters were unable to approach there. But the cutters remained within sight of the canoes from St. Nicholas as far as St. Conon on the far side at Pegae, preventing the canoes from going past.[3]

On Saturday in the evening, that is on the second of the month August, the Khagan asked for officials to converse with him. And there went out to him George the most glorious patrician, and Theodore the most glorious *commerciarius* for woad, and Theodosius the most glorious patrician and logothete, and Theodore *syncellus* most dear to God, and Athanasius the most glorious patrician.[4] And when they had set out, the Khagan brought into their sight three Persians dressed in pure silk who had been sent from Shahrbaraz. And he arranged that they should be seated in his presence, while our ambassadors should stand. And he said, "Look, the Persians have sent an embassy to me, and are ready to give me 3,000 men in alliance. Therefore, if each of you in the city is prepared to take no more than a cloak and a shirt, we will make a compact with Shahrbaraz, for he is my friend: cross over to him and he will not harm you; leave me your city and property. For otherwise it is impossible for you to be saved, unless you can become fish and depart by sea, or birds and ascend to the sky. For look—as the Persians themselves say—neither has your emperor invaded Persia nor is your army arrived." But the most glorious George said to him, "These men are imposters and do not speak a word of truth, since our army is arrived here and our most pious lord is in their country, utterly destroying

it." Then one of the Persians was infuriated and in the presence of the Khagan insulted the said most glorious George, and he himself replied to him, "It is not you who insult me, but the Khagan." But the most glorious officials who had come out to him also said this to the Khagan, "Although you have such great hordes, you need Persian help." And he said, "If I wish, they will provide me with men in alliance, for they are my friends." And again our officials said to him, "'We will never relinquish the city, for we came out to you in the expectation of discussing something material. So if you do not wish to discuss with us peace proposals, dismiss us." And he dismissed them.

Straightway, during the night preceding the Lord's Day, through the efficacy of the good and mercy-loving God, the same Persians who had been on the embassy to the Khagan, while they were crossing over to Chrysopolis by way of Chalae, encountered our skiffs, in which there were also some of those from the orphanage.[5] And one of these Persians was found after he had thrown himself into a small skiff known as a *sandalos*, face down and beneath the coverings, and was crossing over to Chrysopolis thus; but the sailor who was in this skiff and was steering it, adroitly signaled to those from the orphanage who pulled back and removed the coverings, and found this Persian unharmed and lying face down; they slew him and removed his head. They overpowered the other two Persians along with the sailor as well, while they were crossing over in another boat, and these they brought at dawn to the wall. Our men chopped off the two hands of one of the surviving Persians, tied round his neck the head of the man slain in the skiff, and sent him to the Khagan.

The other was thrown into a skiff and taken off alive to Chalcedon; when he had been exhibited to the Persians our men beheaded him just as he was in the skiff, and threw his head onto land with a message that read like this: "The Khagan, after making terms with us, sent us the

---

1   A cutter is a type of boat designed for speed.

2   For St. Callinicus see Map 2.1.

3   The Slavs launched their canoes at the head of the Golden Horn, to the northwest of Constantinople. The Byzantine fleet was deployed all across the Golden Horn, from the Blachernai to Galata.

4   Theodore *commerciarius* was a customs officer; Theodosius was the official responsible for military finances; Theodore *syncellus* lived with the patriarch; Athanasius had already (see above) served on an embassy to the Khagan.

5   There were several orphanages in Constantinople; it is not clear which one is referred to here. It seems that in 626 the beneficiaries of the orphanage had been commandeered to assist in the defense of the city by patrolling the Bosporus to intercept communications between Persians and Avars. Chalae, today Bebek, is located along the west coast of the Bosporus, to the north of Constantinople. Chrysopolis, today Üsküdar, is near Chalcedon, which, in 626, was in Persian hands. It seems that the Persians did not cross the Bosporus in force because they had a weak navy; the Byzantines controlled the waters.

ambassadors who were dispatched to him by you; two of them we have beheaded in the city, while look! you have the head of the other."

On the same Lord's Day the accursed Khagan set out for Chalae and put to sea canoes which were intended to set out for the opposite side and bring the Persians to him, in accordance with their promise. When this was known, in the evening about 70 of our skiffs sailed up towards Chalae, even though the wind was against them, so as to prevent the canoes from crossing over. And towards evening the accursed Khagan retired to the vicinity of the wall, and some food and wine were sent to him from the city. Hermitzis, commander of the Avars, came to the gate, saying, "You have committed a grave deed in killing those who ate with the Khagan yesterday, and furthermore in sending him the head and the other with his hands cut off." But they said, "We are not concerned about him." In the night then, as Monday was dawning, their canoes were able to escape our watch and cross to them....[1]

... They sank them and slew all the Slavs found in the canoes.[2] And the Armenians too came out from the wall of Blachernae and threw fire into the portico which is near St. Nicholas.[3] And the Slavs who had escaped by diving from the canoes thought, because of the fire, that those positioned by the sea were Avars, and when they came out there they were slain by the Armenians. A few other Slavs who had escaped by diving, and who came out in the region where the godless Khagan was positioned, were slain at his injunction. And at God's command through the intercession of our Lady the Mother of God, in a single instant, calamity at sea came to him. Our men drove all the canoes onto the land, and after this had happened, the accursed Khagan retired to his rampart, took away from the wall the siege engines which he had

set beside it and the palisade which he had constructed, and began to dismantle the siege towers which he had constructed: by night he burnt his palisade and the siege towers and the mantelets, after removing the hides, and retreated.

Some people said that the Slavs, when they saw what had happened, withdrew and retreated, and for this reason the cursed Khagan was also forced to retreat and follow them.

And this is what the godless Khagan said at the moment of the battle: "I see a woman in stately dress rushing about on the wall all alone."[4] When he was on the point of retreating, he declared, "Do not imagine that I am retreating because of fear, but because I am constrained for provisions and did not attack you at an opportune moment. I am departing to pay attention to supplies, and will return intending to do to you whatever you have accomplished against me."

On the Friday a rearguard of cavalry remained in the vicinity of the wall, setting fire to many suburbs on the same day up till hour 7; and they withdrew. They burnt both the church of Saints Cosmas and Damian at Blachernae and the church of St. Nicholas and all the surrounding areas. However, after approaching the church of our Lady the Mother of God and the Holy Reliquary, the enemy were completely unable to damage any of the things there, since God showed favor, at the intercession of his undefiled Mother. And [the Khagan] requested the most glorious *commerciarius* to converse with him,[5] and Bonus the all-praiseworthy *magister* declared this to him: "Until the present I had the power to talk and make terms with you. But now the brother of our most pious lord has arrived together with the God-protected army. And look! he is crossing over and pursuing you as far as your territory. And there you can talk with one another."[6]

---

[1] The manuscript is missing a page at this point. The Avars were so unskilled in nautical matters that they had to await the arrival of Slav canoes before attempting to slip across the Bosporus by night.

[2] The narrative picks up with a slightly later Slav naval attack along the Golden Horn. Meanwhile, the Khagan was preparing for a concerted land and sea attack.

[3] Emperor Heraclius sent the Armenians to help defend Constantinople. The Avars hoped that the appearance of the Slav flotilla would cause confusion within the city and allow them to overrun the walls. But the Byzantines had advance knowledge of the plan of attack and organized their fleet accordingly. The Slav boats were destroyed; survivors who struggled ashore near Blachernae (where they expected to find Avar besiegers) were killed by both the Byzantines and the enraged Khagan.

[4] The chronicler inserts this to confirm the divine intervention of the Virgin Mary.

[5] This was probably Theodore, who participated in an earlier embassy to the Khagan.

[6] The "brother of our most pious lord" was Theodore, brother of Heraclius.

2.2 Purifying practice: *The Quinisext Council* (691/692). Original in Greek.

As it became clear that Islam and its conquests were going to be a permanent challenge to Byzantium, Emperor Justinian II (r.685–695; 705–711) called a council of bishops to meet in Constantinople to hammer out the rules of Christian discipline. The council divided its canons (102 in all) among the three categories of persons traditional in the east: the secular clergy (e.g., bishops and priests); monks and nuns; and laypeople. Justinian meant for the council to be ecumenical and to include the pope at Rome. But the pope, Sergius I (687–701) did not attend and later refused to sign the document. Sergius objected to two canons, one permitting priests to have wives if their marriage had taken place before their ordination, the other prohibiting certain days of fasting. Later popes, however, approved the council canons, though with reservations.

The canons included here cover some lay practices and new attitudes toward icons.

1. What pastimes did the canons condemn, and why?
2. How separate do the lives of clergy and laypeople seem to have been according to the evidence of the canons?

[Source: R.H. Percival, trans., *The Canons of the Council in Trullo, often called The Quinisext Council* (https://legacy.fordham.edu/halsall/basis/trullo.asp, slightly modified and notes added.]

CANON 50.

No one at all, whether cleric or layman, is from this time forward to play at dice. And if any one hereafter shall be found doing so, if he be a cleric he is to be deposed, if a layman let him be cut off.[1]

CANON 51.

This holy and ecumenical synod altogether forbids those who are called "players [actors]," and their "spectacles," as well as the exhibition of hunts, and the theatrical dances. If anyone despises the present canon, and gives himself to any of the things which are forbidden, if he be a cleric he shall be deposed, but if a layman let him be cut off.

CANON 61.

Those who give themselves up to soothsayers [fortune-tellers] or to those who are called *hecatontarchs* or to any such, in order that they may learn from them what things they wish to have revealed to them, let all such, according to the decrees lately made by the Fathers concerning them, be subjected to the canon of six years.[2] And to this [penalty] they also should be subjected who carry about she-bears or animals of the kind for the diversion and injury of the simple; as well as those who tell fortunes and fates, and genealogy, and a multitude of words of this kind from the nonsense of deceit and imposture. Also those who are called expellers of clouds, enchanters, amulet-givers, and soothsayers.

And those who persist in these things, and do not turn away and flee from pernicious and Greek pursuits of this kind, we declare are to be thrust out of the Church, as also the sacred canons say. "For what fellowship hath light with darkness?" as the Apostle says, "or what agreement is there between the temple of God and idols? or what part hath he that believeth with an infidel? And what concord hath Christ with Belial?" [2 Cor. 6:14–16].

---

[1] Deposition means that the cleric is removed from office. The layman is "cut off" from communion, i.e., from the body of the faithful. No provision is offered for penance and reintegration.

[2] *Hecatontarchs* were old people, mainly women, reputed to have special knowledge. They sold medicines or amulets made of the hair of the female bears or other animals referred to in the next sentence. The "canon of six years" refers to a penance of six years.

CANON 62.

The so-called Calends [first day of the month], and what are called Bota [feasts in honor of Pan] and Brumalia [feasts in honor of Bacchus], and the full assembly which takes place on the first of March, we wish to be abolished from the life of the faithful. And also the public dances of women, which may do much harm and mischief. Moreover, we drive away from the life of Christians the dances given in the names of those falsely called gods by the Greeks whether of men or women, and which are performed after an ancient and un-Christian fashion; decreeing that no man from this time forth shall be dressed as a woman, nor any woman in the garb suitable to men. Nor shall he assume comic, satyric, or tragic masks;[1] nor may men invoke the name of the execrable Bacchus when they squeeze out the wine in the presses; nor when pouring out wine into jars, practicing in ignorance and vanity the things which proceed from the deceit of insanity. Therefore, those who in the future attempt any of these things which are written, having obtained a knowledge of them, if they be clerics we order them to be deposed, and if laymen to be cut off.

CANON 65.

The fires that are lighted on the new moons by some before their shops and houses, upon which (according to a certain ancient custom) they are wont foolishly and crazily to leap, we order henceforth to cease. Therefore, whosoever shall do such a thing, if he be a cleric, let him be deposed; but if he be a layman, let him be cut off.

For it is written in the Fourth Book of the Kings: "And Manasses built an altar to the whole host of heaven, in the two courts of the Lord, and made his sons to pass through the fire, he used lots and augurs and divinations by birds and made ventriloquists and multiplied diviners, that he might do evil before the Lord and provoke him to anger." [2 Kings 21:5–6]

CANON 66.

From the holy day of the Resurrection of Christ our God until the next Lord's day, for a whole week,[2] in the holy churches the faithful ought to be free from labor, rejoicing in Christ with psalms and hymns and spiritual songs; and celebrating the feast, and applying their minds to the reading of the holy Scriptures, and delighting in the Holy Mysteries; for thus shall we be exalted with Christ and together with him be raised up. Therefore, on the aforesaid days there must not be any horse races or any public spectacle.

CANON 71.

Those who are taught the civil laws must not adopt the customs of the Gentiles, nor be induced to go to the theatre, nor to keep what are called Cylestras,[3] nor to wear clothing contrary to the general custom; and this holds good when they begin their training, when they reach its end, and, in short, all the time of its duration. If anyone from this time shall dare to do contrary to this canon he is to be cut off.

CANON 73.

Since the life-giving cross has shown to us Salvation, we should be careful that we render due honor to that by which we were saved from the ancient fall. Wherefore, in mind, in word, in feeling giving veneration (*proskynesis*)[4] to it, we command that the figure of the cross, which some have placed on the floor, be entirely removed therefrom, lest the trophy of the victory won for us be desecrated by the trampling under foot of those who walk over it. Therefore, those who from this present represent on the pavement the sign of the cross, we decree are to be cut off.

CANON 76.

It is not right that those who are responsible for reverence to churches should place within the sacred bounds an eating place, nor offer food there, nor make other sales. For God our Savior teaching us when he was tabernacling [i.e., living] in the flesh commanded not to make his Father's house a house of merchandise. He also poured out the small coins of the money-changers, and drove out all those who made common the temple. If, therefore, anyone shall be taken in the aforesaid fault let him be cut off.

CANON 77.

It is not right that those who are dedicated to religion, whether clerics or ascetics, should wash in the bath with

---

[1] These were the masks worn by actors in tragedy, comedy, and satyr plays in ancient Greece. The Quinisext canons are the last extant references to these ancient practices.

[2] I.e., the whole week after Easter.

[3] Uncertain meaning.

[4] Bowing or prostrating oneself to show honor to something.

women, nor should any Christian man or layman do so. For this is severely condemned by the heathens. But if anyone is caught in this thing, if he is a cleric let him be deposed; if a layman, let him be cut off.

CANON 78.

No one may drive any beast into a church except perchance a traveler, urged there by the greatest necessity, in default of a shed or resting-place, may have turned aside into said church. For unless the beast had been taken inside, it would have perished, and he, by the loss of his beast of burden, and thus without means of continuing his journey, would be in peril of death. And we are taught that the Sabbath was made for man: wherefore also the safety and comfort of man are by all means to be placed first. But should anyone be detected without any necessity such as we have just mentioned, leading his beast into a church, if he be a cleric let him be deposed, and if a layman let him be cut off.

CANON 82.

In some pictures of the venerable icons, a lamb is painted to which the Precursor[1] points his finger, which is received as a type of grace, indicating beforehand through the Law, our true Lamb, Christ our God. Embracing therefore the ancient types and shadows as symbols of the truth, and patterns given to the Church, we prefer "grace and truth," receiving it as the fulfillment of the Law. In order therefore that "that which is perfect" may be delineated to the eyes of all, at least in colored expression, we decree that the figure in human form of the Lamb who taketh away the sin of the world, Christ our God, be henceforth exhibited in images, instead of the ancient lamb, so that all may understand by means of it the depths of the humiliation of the Word of God, and

that we may recall to our memory his conversation in the flesh, his passion and salutary death, and his redemption which was wrought for the whole world.

CANON 91.

Those who give drugs for procuring abortion, and those who receive poisons to kill the fetus, are subjected to the penalty of murder.

CANON 92.

The holy synod decrees that those who in the name of marriage carry off women and those who in any way assist the ravishers, if they be clerics, they shall lose their rank, but if they be laymen they shall be anathematized.

CANON 96.

Those who by baptism have put on Christ have professed that they will copy his manner of life which he led in the flesh. Those therefore who adorn and arrange their hair to the detriment of those who see them, that is by cunningly devised intertwinings [elaborate hairstyles or wigs] and by this means put a bait in the way of unstable souls, we take in hand to cure paternally with a suitable punishment: training them and teaching them to live soberly, in order that having laid aside the deceit and vanity of material things, they may give their minds continually to a life which is blessed and free from mischief, and have their conversation in fear, pure [and holy]; and thus come as near as possible to God through their purity of life; and adorn the inner man rather than the outer, and that with virtues, and good and blameless manners, so that they leave in themselves no remains of the left-handedness of the adversary [the Devil]. But if any shall act contrary to the present canon let him be cut off.

2.3 The iconoclastic argument: *The Synod of 754. Original in Greek.*

Byzantine emperor Leo III (r.717–741) may have launched iconoclasm, but he treated icons as an abuse, not a heresy. His son, Constantine V (r.741–775), took the next step, calling a Church council in 754 to declare the veneration of icons a violation of "the fundamental doctrine of our salvation." The synod, whose proceedings survive only because they were included in the account of the later iconodule (pro-icon) synod of 787, compared

---

[1] John the Baptist. In John 1:29 he sees Jesus and says "Behold the Lamb of God."

"unlawful art" to the great heresies of Nestorius and Arius, who challenged the orthodox view concerning the nature of the persons of the Trinity. No representation of Christ, the iconoclastic bishops argued, could accurately portray the correct union of His two natures, man and God. The synod included no patriarch or papal representative, but it did involve over 300 bishops—a very large number.

1. Why do the bishops of the synod argue that artists who depict Christ "introduce a fourth person into the Trinity"?
2. How might you argue that iconoclasm was more popular in its day than later iconodule propaganda might suggest?

[Source: *A Select Library of Nicene and Post-Nicene Fathers of the Christian Church*, 2nd ser., ed. Philip Schaff and Henry Wace, vol. 14: *The Seven Ecumenical Councils* (Grand Rapids, MI: Wm. B. Eerdmans, 1971), pp. 543–45 (slightly modified and notes added).]

The holy and Ecumenical synod, which by the grace of God and most pious command of the God-beloved and orthodox Emperors, Constantine and Leo[1] now assembled in the imperial residence city, in the temple of the holy and inviolate Mother of God and Virgin Mary, surnamed in Blachernai[2] have decreed as follows.

Satan misguided men, so that they worshiped the creature instead of the Creator. The Mosaic law and the prophets co-operated to undo this ruin; but in order to save mankind thoroughly, God sent his own Son, who turned us away from error and the worshiping of idols and taught us the worshiping of God in spirit and in truth. As messengers of his saving doctrine, he left us his Apostles and disciples, and these adorned the Church, his Bride, with his glorious doctrines. This ornament of the Church the holy Fathers and the six Ecumenical Councils have preserved inviolate. But the before-mentioned demiurgos of wickedness [i.e., Satan] could not endure the sight of this adornment and gradually brought back idolatry under the appearance of Christianity. As then Christ armed his Apostles against the ancient idolatry with the power of the Holy Spirit and sent them out into all the world, so has he awakened against the new idolatry his servants our faithful Emperors and endowed them with the same wisdom of the Holy Spirit. Impelled by the Holy Spirit they could no longer be witnesses of the Church being laid waste by the deception of demons and summoned the sanctified assembly of the God-beloved bishops, that they might institute at a synod a scriptural examination into the deceitful coloring of the pictures which draws down the spirit of man from the lofty adoration of God to the low and material adoration of the creature, and that they, under divine guidance, might express their view on the subject.

Our holy synod therefore assembled, and we, its 338 members, follow the older synodal decrees and accept and proclaim joyfully the dogmas handed down, principally those of the six holy Ecumenical Synods. In the first place the holy and ecumenical great synod assembled at Nicaea, etc.[3]

After we had carefully examined their decrees under the guidance of the Holy Spirit, we found that the unlawful art of painting living creatures blasphemed the fundamental doctrine of our salvation—namely, the Incarnation of Christ—and contradicted the six holy synods. These condemned Nestorius because he divided the one Son and Word of God into two sons, and on the other side, Arius, Dioscorus, Eutyches, and Severus, because they maintained a mingling of the two natures of the one Christ.[4]

---

[1] Constantine V (r.741–775); his son Leo was only four years old when the Synod of 754 met; he eventually ruled as Leo IV (r.775–780).

[2] A church at Constantinople, the shrine of the Virgin at the west end of the Theodosian Walls.

[3] A shorthand way to refer to the other synods.

[4] Nestorius, Arius, Dioscorus, Eutyches, and Severus represent the heresiarchs (the originators of the heresies) of early Christianity. Each had a different view of the nature of the persons of the Trinity.

Wherefore we thought it right to make clear with all accuracy in our present definition the error of such as make and venerate these, for it is the unanimous doctrine of all the holy Fathers and of the six Ecumenical Synods that no one may imagine any kind of separation or mingling in opposition to the unsearchable, unspeakable, and incomprehensible union of the two natures in the one hypostasis or person. What avails, then, the folly of the painter, who from sinful love of gain depicts that which should not be depicted—that is, with his polluted hands he tries to fashion that which should only be believed in the heart and confessed with the mouth? He makes an image and calls it Christ. The name *Christ* signifies *God and man*. Consequently, it is an image of God and man, and consequently he has in his foolish mind, in his representation of the created flesh, depicted the Godhead which cannot be represented and thus mingled what should not be mingled. Thus, he is guilty of a double blasphemy—the one in making an image of the Godhead and the other in mingling the Godhead and manhood. Those fall into the same blasphemy who venerate the image, and the same woe rests upon both, because they err with Arius, Dioscorus, and Eutyches, and with the heresy of the Acephali.[1] When, however, they are blamed for undertaking to depict the divine nature of Christ, which should not be depicted, they take refuge in the excuse: We represent only the flesh of Christ which we have seen and handled. But that is a Nestorian error.[2] For it should be considered that that flesh was also the flesh of God the Word, without any separation, perfectly assumed by the divine nature and made wholly divine. How could it now be separated and represented apart? So is it with the human soul of Christ which mediates between the Godhead of the Son and the dullness of the flesh. As the human flesh is at the same time flesh of God the Word, so is the human soul also soul of God the Word, and both at the same time, the soul being deified as well as the body, and the Godhead remained undivided even in the separation of the soul from the body in his voluntary passion. For where the soul of Christ is, there is also his Godhead; and where the body of Christ is, there too is his Godhead. If then in his passion the divinity remained inseparable from these, how do the fools venture to separate the flesh from the Godhead and represent it by itself as the image

of a mere man? They fall into the abyss of impiety since they separate the flesh from the Godhead, ascribe to it a subsistence of its own, a personality of its own, which they depict, and thus introduce a fourth person into the Trinity. Moreover, they represent as not being made divine that which has been made divine by being assumed by the Godhead. Whoever, then, makes an image of Christ either depicts the Godhead which cannot be depicted and mingles it with the manhood (like the Monophysites),[3] or he represents the body of Christ as not made divine and separate and as a person apart, like the Nestorians.

The only admissible figure of the humanity of Christ, however, is bread and wine in the holy Supper. This and no other form, this and no other type, has he chosen to represent his incarnation. Bread he ordered to be brought, but not a representation of the human form, so that idolatry might not arise. And as the body of Christ is made divine, so also this figure of the body of Christ, the bread, is made divine by the descent of the Holy Spirit; it becomes the divine body of Christ by the mediation of the priest who, separating the oblation [offering] from that which is common, sanctifies it.

The evil custom of assigning names to the images does not come down from Christ and the Apostles and the holy Fathers; nor have these left behind them any prayer by which an image should be hallowed or made anything else than ordinary matter.

If, however, some say we might be right in regard to the images of Christ on account of the mysterious union of the two natures, but it is not right for us to forbid also the images of the altogether spotless and ever-glorious Mother of God, or of the prophets, apostles, and martyrs, who were mere men and did not consist of two natures; we may reply, first of all: If those fall away, there is no longer need of these. But we will also consider what may be said against these in particular. Christianity has rejected the *whole* of heathenism, and so not merely heathen sacrifices, but also the heathen worship of images. The Saints live on eternally with God, although they have died. If anyone thinks to call them back again to life by a dead art, discovered by the heathen, he makes himself guilty of blasphemy. Who dares attempt with heathenish art to paint the Mother of God, who is exalted above all heavens and the Saints? It is not permitted to Christians, who have

---

[1] The Acephali was another name for the followers of Eutyches.

[2] The "error of Nestorius" was to stress the independence of the two natures—divine and human—of Christ.

[3] The Monophysites, like the followers of Eutyches, rejected both the Orthodox assertion of the hypostatic (or "underlying") union of the "two natures" of Christ and the Nestorian assertion of a union that was not hypostatic but rather accidental.

the hope of the resurrection, to imitate the customs of demon-worshipers and to insult the Saints, who shine in so great glory, by common dead matter....

Supported by the Holy Scriptures and the Fathers, we declare unanimously, in the name of the Holy Trinity, that there shall be rejected and removed and cursed out of the Christian Church every likeness which is made out of any material and color whatever by the evil art of painters.

Whoever in future dares to make such a thing, or to venerate it, or set it up in a church, or in a private house, or possesses it in secret, shall, if bishop, presbyter, or deacon, be deposed; if monk or layman, be anathematized[1] and become liable to be tried by the secular laws as an adversary of God and an enemy of the doctrines handed down by the Fathers. At the same time, we ordain that no incumbent of a church shall venture, under pretext of destroying the error in regard to images, to lay his hands on the holy vessels in order to have them altered because they are adorned with figures. The same is provided in regard to the vestments of churches, cloths, and all that is dedicated to divine service. If, however, the incumbent of a church wishes to have such church vessels and vestments altered, he must do this only with the assent of the holy Ecumenical patriarch and at the bidding of our pious Emperors. So also no prince or secular official shall rob the churches, as some have done in former times, under the pretext of destroying images. All this we ordain, believing that we speak as does the Apostle, for we also believe that we have the spirit of Christ; and as our predecessors who believed the same thing spoke what they had synodically defined, so we believe and therefore do we speak and set forth a definition of what has seemed good to us following and in accordance with the definitions of our Fathers.

(1) If anyone shall not confess, according to the tradition of the Apostles and Fathers, in the Father, the Son and the Holy Ghost one godhead, nature and substance, will and operation, virtue and dominion, kingdom and power in three subsistences, that is in their most glorious Persons, let him be anathema.[2]

(2) If anyone does not confess that one of the Trinity was made flesh, let him be anathema.

(3) If anyone does not confess that the holy Virgin is truly the Mother of God, etc.

(4) If anyone does not confess one Christ both God and man, etc.

(5) If anyone does not confess that the flesh of the Lord is life-giving because it is the flesh of the Word of God, etc.

(6) If anyone does not confess two natures in Christ, etc.

(7) If anyone does not confess that Christ is seated with God the Father in body and soul, and so will come to judge, and that he will remain God forever without any grossness, etc.

(8) If anyone ventures to represent the divine image of the Word after the Incarnation with material colors, let him be anathema!

(9) If anyone ventures to represent in human figures by means of material colors by reason of the incarnation, the substance or person of the Word, which cannot be depicted, and does not rather confess that even after the Incarnation he [i.e., the Word] cannot be depicted, let him be anathema!

(10) If anyone ventures to represent the hypostatic union of the two natures in a picture and calls it Christ and thus falsely represents a union of the two natures, etc.

(11) If anyone separates the flesh united with the person of the Word from it and endeavors to represent it separately in a picture, etc.

(12) If anyone separates the one Christ into two persons and endeavors to represent Him who was born of the Virgin separately and thus accepts only a relative union of the natures, etc.

(13) If anyone represents in a picture the flesh deified by its union with the Word, and thus separates it from the Godhead, etc.

(14) If anyone endeavors to represent by material colors God the Word as a mere man, who, although bearing the form of God, yet has assumed the form of a servant in his own person, and thus endeavors to separate him from his inseparable Godhead so that he thereby introduces a quaternity into the Holy Trinity, etc.

(15) If anyone shall not confess the holy ever-virgin Mary, truly and properly the Mother of God, to be higher than every creature whether visible or invisible and does not with sincere faith seek her intercessions as of one having confidence in her access to our God, since she bore him, etc.

(16) If anyone shall endeavor to represent the forms of the Saints in lifeless pictures with material colors which are of no value (for this notion is vain and introduced by

---

[1] I.e., excommunicated from the Church.

[2] I.e., excommunicated from the Church.

the devil) and does not rather represent their virtues as living images in himself, etc.

(17) If anyone denies the profit of the invocation of Saints, etc.

(18) If anyone denies the resurrection of the dead and the judgment and the condign [appropriate] retribution to everyone, endless torment and endless bliss, etc.

(19) If anyone does not accept this our Holy and Ecumenical Seventh Synod, let him be anathema from the Father and the Son and the Holy Ghost and from the seven holy Ecumenical Synods!

[At this point the making or teaching of any other faith is prohibited, and the penalties for disobedience are enumerated.]

The divine Kings Constantine and Leo said: Let the holy and ecumenical synod say, if with the consent of all the most holy bishops the definition just read has been set forth.

The holy synod cried out: Thus we all believe, we all are of the same mind. We have all with one voice and voluntarily subscribed. This is the faith of the Apostles. Many years to the Emperors! They are the light of orthodoxy! Many years to the orthodox Emperors! God preserve your Empire! You have now more firmly proclaimed the inseparability of the two natures of Christ! You have banished all idolatry! You have destroyed the heresies of Germanus [of Constantinople], George and Mansur.[1] Anathema to Germanus, the double-minded, and worshiper of wood! Anathema to George, his associate, to the falsifier of the doctrine of the Fathers! Anathema to Mansur, who has an evil name and Saracen[2] opinions! To the betrayer of Christ and the enemy of the Empire, to the teacher of impiety, the perverter of Scripture, Mansur, anathema! The Trinity has deposed these three!

......

THE FORMATION OF THE ISLAMIC WORLD

2.4 The sacred text: *Qur'an Suras* 1, 53:1–18, 81, 87, 96, 98 (*c*.610–622). Original in Arabic.

Muhammad (*c*.570–632), born in Mecca, orphaned, raised by an uncle, married to Khadija, heard (*c*.610) what he understood to be revelations from God. He recited them (Qur'an means "recitation"), scribes wrote them down, and they became the foundation of a new religion, Islam. New research suggests that somewhat variant editions of Qur'an may have been compiled as early as during Muhammad's lifetime. It begins with a prayer (the *fatihah*, or "Opening"), followed by chapters (suras) that gradually diminish in length. While different from the odes of the pre-Islamic period, the verses of the Qur'an are poetry, and they often take up the traditional themes: remembrance of the beloved (who is now God), a journey (turned into a spiritual quest), and a boast (a celebration of God's generosity and justice). The earliest suras generally are found toward the end of the book. Muhammad's first vision is described in Sura 53, "The Star"; his first auditory revelation was probably "Recite in the name of your lord who created...," which is found in Sura 96, "The Embryo." Other suras come from the period after Muhammad made the *hijra*, or emigration, to Medina (622; the year 1 in the Islamic calendar). Most of those presented here are from Muhammad's earliest Meccan period. Note that there is relatively little punctuation (mirroring the Arabic); this is the translator's way of suggesting the open and multiple meanings of the verses.

---

[1] Germanus I (r.715–730) was the Patriarch of Constantinople. He opposed iconoclasm and was sent into exile. Mansur ("Victorious") was the Arabic surname of John of Damascus, a Syrian monk and saint, who also opposed iconoclasm.

[2] I.e., Arab.

1. What are the characteristics of God as they emerge from these texts?
2. What is the proper attitude and behavior of the believer?

[Source: *Approaching the Qur'an: The Early Revelations*, trans. Michael Sells (Ashland, OR: White Cloud Press, 1999), pp. 42, 44, 48, 50, 72, 96, 104, 106.]

1: The Opening

In the name of God
   the Compassionate the Caring
Praise be to God
   lord sustainer of the worlds
the Compassionate the Caring
master of the day of reckoning
To you we turn to worship   5
   and to you we turn in time of need
Guide us along the road straight
the road of those to whom you are giving
   not those with anger upon them
   not those who have lost the way

53: 1–18 The Star

In the Name of God the Compassionate the Caring
   By the star as it falls
   Your companion[1] has not lost his way nor is he
      deluded
   He does not speak out of desire
   This is a revelation
   taught him by one of great power   5
   and strength that stretched out over
   while on the highest horizon—
   then drew near and came down
   two bows' lengths or nearer
   He revealed to his servant what he revealed   10
   The heart did not lie in what it saw
   Will you then dispute with him his vision?
   He saw it descending another time
   at the lote tree of the furthest limit
   There was the garden of sanctuary   15
   when something came down over the
      lote tree, enfolding

His gaze did not turn aside nor go too far
He had seen the signs of his lord, great signs

81: The Overturning

In the Name of God the Compassionate the Caring
   When the sun is overturned
   When the stars fall away
   When the mountains are moved
   When the ten-month pregnant camels
      are abandoned
   When the beasts of the wild are herded together   5
   When the seas are boiled over
   When the souls are coupled
   When the girl-child buried alive
   is asked what she did to deserve murder
   When the pages are folded out   10
   When the sky is flayed open
   When Jahim[2] is set ablaze
   When the garden is brought near
   Then a soul will know what it has prepared
   I swear by the stars that slide,   15
   stars streaming, stars that sweep along the sky
   By the night as it slips away
   By the morning when the fragrant air breathes
   This is the word of a messenger ennobled,
   empowered, ordained before the lord of the throne,   20
   holding sway there, keeping trust
   Your friend[3] has not gone mad
   He saw him on the horizon clear
   He does not hoard for himself the unseen
   This is not the word of a satan   25
      struck with stones
   Where are you going?
   This is a reminder to all beings
   For those who wish to walk straight

---

[1] "Your companion" is ordinarily interpreted as referring to Muhammad.

[2] A term for the Day of Reckoning.

[3] "Your friend" refers to Muhammad.

Your only will is the will of God   30
    lord of all beings

87: The Most High

In the Name of God the Compassionate the Caring
    Holy be the name of your lord most high
    Who created then gave form
    Who determined then gave guidance
    Who made the meadow pasture grow
    then turned it to a darkened flood-swept remnant   5

We will make you recite. You will not forget
    except what the will of God allows
He knows what is declared
    and what lies hidden
He will ease you to the life of ease
So remind them if reminder will succeed[1]
Those who know awe will be brought to remember 10
He who is hard in wrong will turn away
He will be put to the fire
neither dying in it nor living
He who makes himself pure will flourish
who remembers the name of his lord and   15
    performs the prayer

But no. They prefer the lower life
Better is the life ultimate, the life that endures
As is set down in the scrolls of the ancients
    the scrolls of Ibrahim and Musa[2]

96: The Embryo

In the Name of God the Compassionate the Caring
    Recite in the name of your lord who created—
    From an embryo created the human
    Recite your lord is all-giving
    who taught by the pen
    Taught the human what he did not know before   5

The human being is a tyrant
He thinks his possessions make him secure
To your lord is the return of every thing

Did you see the one who stopped a servant
from performing his prayer?   10
Did you see if he was rightly guided
or commanded mindfulness?
Did you see him call lie and turn away?
Did he not know God could see?

But no. If he does not change   15
    we will seize him by the forelock
the lying, wrongful forelock
Let him call out his gang
We will call out the Zabaniya[3]
Do not follow him
    Touch your head to the earth in prayer
    Come near

98: The Testament[4]

In the Name of God the Compassionate the Caring
    Those who denied the faith—
        from the peoples of the book
        or the idolaters—
        could not stop calling it a lie   5
        until they received the testament

A messenger of God
    reciting pages that are pure
Of scriptures that are sure

Those who were given the book   10
    were not divided one against the other
    until they received the testament

And all they were commanded
    was to worship God sincerely
    affirm oneness, perform the prayer   15

---

[1] Muhammad is to "remind" people about God and justice. There is no notion of "original sin" in Islam, but people "forget" the purpose of human life and the Day of Reckoning.

[2] Ibrahim is Abraham in the Bible; Musa is Moses.

[3] The Zabaniya are probably a species of *jinn*, half-spirit creatures.

[4] This sura is from a later period in Muhammad's career, after he experienced the rejection of not only polytheists but also the "peoples of the book"—Christians and Jews—he had expected to join him.

and give a share of what they have	Those who keep the faith
That is the religion of the sure	and perform the prayer 25
	they are the best of creation
Those who deny the faith—	As recompense for them with their lord—
from the peoples of the book	gardens of Eden
or the idolaters— 20	waters flowing underground
are in Jahannam's fire,[1]	eternal there forever 30
eternal there	God be pleased in them
They are the worst of creation	and they in God

That is for those who hold their lord in awe

....

2.5 Muslim conquests: John of Nikiu, *Chronicle* (*c.*690). Original in Ethiopic.

Probably by "John bishop of Nikiu," who is otherwise known to have been active at the end of the seventh century, this universal chronicle has 123 chapters. Starting with creation, it ends with the Muslim conquest of Egypt, which had previously been under Byzantine rule. John of Nikiu was an adherent of the patriarch of Alexandria, whose brand of Christianity ("Miaphysite" or "Monophysite," later known as Coptic) deviated from the form (called "Chalcedonian") practiced at Constantinople. The *Chronicle* presents numerous problems of interpretation. It survives only in a seventeenth-century Ethiopic translation of an Arabic paraphrase of a Coptic original, and this original in turn depended on various Greek sources, and included various Greek loanwords. The process of transmission has therefore introduced many confusions, omissions, and mistakes. It is evident, for example, that the Arabic translator has misunderstood various words or phrases in Coptic, and that some words (in particular proper nouns) have been transcribed incorrectly or incompletely from Coptic into Arabic and/or Arabic into Ethiopic. Various details, therefore, remain uncertain. But the *Chronicle* is nevertheless our earliest, most reliable, and most important witness to the Muslim conquest of Egypt (640–642).

The identifiable places mentioned in the *Chronicle* are on Map 2.2 below.

1. What evidence can you cite for individuals and groups living in Egypt who supported the Islamic conquest, and what might have been their reasons?
2. What, for John of Nikiu, are the most important causes of the Muslim conquest?

[Source: H. Zotenberg, *Chronique de Jean, évêque de Nikiou, texte éthiopien publié et traduit* (Paris, 1883), 197–214. Introduced and translated by Phil Booth.]

---

[1] The fire of eternal punishment.

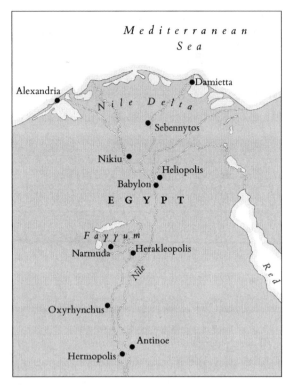

Map 2.2 The Muslim Conquest of Egypt

Chapter 111[1]

Now Theodore was head of the leading generals of Egypt. When the messengers of Theodosius the dux [Byzantine military leader] of Arcadia informed him of the death of John, head of the forces,[2] he thereafter turned back with all the men of Egypt and the troops who were helping him, and he went to Loqyun, which is an island.[3] He feared the rebellion of the people of that region, lest the Muslims come and seize the riverbank at Lukyun, and cause the congregation of God's servants who were loyal

to the Roman [i.e., Byzantine] empire to depart. And his grief was greater than the grief of David over Saul, when he said, "How the mighty have fallen, and the weapon of war perished!"[4] For not only had John head of the forces died, but also John the general from the city of Maros[5] was killed in battle, and the fifty troops who were with him. I will acquaint you in brief with what happened to the leading men of the Fayyum.

For John and the troops who were with him, the forces whom we mentioned before, were appointed by the Romans to watch over the region. They then stationed another guard near the rock of the city of Lahun[6] in order that they stand on permanent guard and report to the leader of the forces the movements of their enemies. After that they prepared a few horses and an assembly of troops and archers and they went for battle with the Muslims, thinking that they might hold them back. But thereafter the Muslims went into the desert and seized many sheep and goats from the mountains, and indeed the men of Egypt were unaware of it. When they arrived at the city of Bahnasa,[7] all the troops who were on the riverbank came with John. And they were not able to come at that time to the region of Fayyum.

Indeed Theodosius the general heard of the arrival of the Ishmaelites [Muslims]. He began to go from place to place in order to see what might happen at the hands of those enemies. But the same Ishmaelites came and killed without pity the leader of the troops and all those who were with him. Immediately they took the region by assault and killed everyone who came out to them, and they did not spare anyone, not the old, not the young, not women. Then they came against the general John. He seized every horse and they hid themselves in the farms and plantations lest their enemies become aware of them. During the night they rose up and came to the great river of Egypt near 'Abuyet,[8] in order that they might be safe. For this was the will of God. But the robber chief who was with Jeremias[9] informed the Muslim troops about

---

[1] The table of contents summarizes this chapter thus: "Concerning the appearance of the Muslims at the edge of the Fayyum and the defeat of the Romans who were living there."

[2] John was perhaps the otherwise attested North African general, John of Barca.

[3] The location is not clear.

[4] 2 Sam. 1:27.

[5] Perhaps a town to the south of Hermopolis.

[6] An ancient irrigation work at the mouth of the Fayyum.

[7] Bahnasa is the Greek Oxyrhynchus.

[8] To the northeast of the Fayyum (and later called "Boyt").

[9] Otherwise unknown.

the Roman men who were hidden, and they seized them and put them to death.

This news came to the ears of the official Theodosius and Anastasius. These two were far from the city of Nikiu at a distance of twelve miles. Immediately they went to the citadel of Babylon [Old Cairo] and remained there, and sent the official Domentianus to the city of 'Abuyet. This man was obese, powerless and ignorant in matters of war. When he arrived he found the troops of Egypt and Theodore fighting the Muslims, and continually coming from the region of Fayyum in order that they might take the region. He took half of the troops and they went to Babylon in order to inform the lords,[1] and the other half of the troops remained with Theodore.

Theodore sought with great diligence for the body of John who had been drowned in the river. With much grief he fetched it with a net, placed it in a coffin and sent it to the lords. The lords for their part sent it to [Byzantine emperor] Heraclius. Those were present in Egypt sought shelter in the citadel of Babylon, and furthermore they were awaiting Theodore the general in order that they might join in the killing of the Ishmaelites before the rise of the water of the river, and the arrival of the time for sowing, when they would not be able to do battle lest their seeds perish and they die through famine with their children and livestock.

Chapter 112[2]

On account of the accusation of the emperor[3] there was much indignation between the leader Theodore and the lords. Theodosius and Anastasius both went out to the city of 'Awn,[4] on horseback with a large number of infantry in order that they might do battle with 'Amr b. al-'As.[5] The Muslims did not know the region of Misr before now.[6] They left alone the fortified cities and came to the place which is called Tendunyas,[7] and went in ships on the [Nile] river. 'Amr with great diligence and with strong mind began to seize the region of Misr. He became distressed of heart concerning his separation from the Muslim troops, and they were separated into two divisions, one division to the east of the river, and one division to the west of the river, and they went to the city which is called 'Aynshems, that is, 'Awn, which is on top of a mountain.

'Amr b. al-'As sent a letter to 'Umar b. al-Khattab[8] in the region of Palestine in which he said, "If you do not send me reinforcement from the Muslims I will not be able to take Egypt." And he sent to him 4,000 Muslim warriors; and the name of their general was Walwarya, and he was of barbarian descent. He divided the warriors who were with him into three divisions: one of the divisions he established at Tendunyas; the second division he established to the north of Babylon of Egypt; and he for his part made preparations with one division at the city of 'Awn. He ordered them thus and said, "Watch out, and if the Roman army come out to kill us, you rise up behind them, and we moreover will be in front of them, and we will bring them between us and kill them." When the Roman troops in ignorance came from the citadel to fight the Muslims, thereafter these Muslims came from behind them as they had planned, and there was a great battle between them. When the Muslim numbers increased against them the Roman troops fled and went in ships. The Muslim soldiers seized the city of Tendunyas. For the forces which were within it were destroyed, and did not survive except a force of 300. These for their part fled and entered into the fortress and shut the gate against them. When they saw the great battle which was happening, they were afraid and fled in ships to Nikiu in much sadness and grief.

Then Domentianus of the city of Fayyum rose up at night without telling the people of Boyt[9] that he was fleeing from the Muslims. They went in a ship to Nikiu.

---

[1] I.e., Theodosius and Anastasius.

[2] The table of contents summarizes thus: "Concerning the first battle of 'Amr with the Romans at the city of 'Awn."

[3] One presumes that the accusation was the failure to mount an effective counter-campaign against the Muslims.

[4] The Greek Heliopolis, or Arabic 'Ain-Shams, near the apex of the Delta.

[5] The famous Arab conqueror of Egypt.

[6] Here "region of Misr" must mean not "region of Egypt" as elsewhere (*misr* being the Arabic for Egypt) but rather, from John's later perspective, the area around the Arab capital at Fustat (also called *misr* in Arabic, perhaps after the word for "garrison town").

[7] Perhaps identical with the Umm Dunayn of the Arabic historiographical tradition. It must have been near Heliopolis.

[8] I.e., the second caliph.

[9] See above, p. 70, n. 8.

When the Muslims learnt that Domentianus had fled they went in joy and seized the region of the Fayyum and of Boyt, and they spilled much blood there.

Chapter 113[1]

Indeed when the Muslims seized the Fayyum with all its environs 'Amr sent to Apa Cyrus of the city of Delas[2] in order that they might bring the ships of Rif[3] in order that they might bring the Ishmaelites who were present on the west of the river across to the east. He gathered all the troops to him in order to wage a great battle. He sent a letter to the official George[4] in order that he might make for him a bridge near the river of the city of Qalyub,[5] in order that he might capture all of the cities of Egypt and also, moreover, the city of 'Atrib and of Kyrdis.[6] And they undertook to help the Muslims. They seized the cities of 'Atrib and Manuf[7] and all of their environs. Moreover he made a great bridge over the river near Babylon[8] lest the ships pass through to Nikiu and Alexandria and Upper Egypt and in order that horses might cross without effort from the west of the river to the east. They subdued the entire region of Misr.

But 'Amr was not satisfied with what he ['Amr] had done, and seized the Roman officials and bound their hands and feet with fetters of iron and wood. He forcibly pillaged much property and he doubled the taxes on the labourers and compelled them to carry their horses' food. He perpetrated many innumerable evils.

Those who were present in the city of Nikiu amongst the lords[9] fled and went to the city of Alexandria, and they left Domentianus with a small force in order that they might protect the city. Furthermore they sent to Dars,[10] head of the generals of the city of Samnud, in order that he might protect the region of the two rivers.[11] Thereafter there was fear in all the cities of Misr. All the men of the region began to flee and enter into the city of Alexandria, and they cast aside all of their properties, treasuries and livestock.

Chapter 114[12]

When those Muslims came with those Egyptians who had renounced the Christian faith and joined the faith of the beast, the Muslims seized all the properties of those Christians who had fled, and they began to call the servants of God the enemies of God. 'Amr for his part left many of his companions at the citadel of Babylon of Egypt and he himself went eastwards to Theodore the general, in the direction of the two rivers. He sent Yaqbari and Satfari[13] in order to capture the city of Samnud and give battle with the Muslims.[14] When they reached the assembly of partisans, all the partisans refused to fight the Muslims. Indeed they joined battle and killed many

---

[1] The table of contents summarizes thus: "How the Jews all gathered in the city of Manuf through fear of Islam and the annoyance of 'Amr and the seizure of their properties, until they left open the gate of Misr and fled to Alexandria; and how oppressors multiplied at the beginning of oppression, and began to help him in the destruction of the men of Egypt."

[2] The Greek Nilopolis in central Egypt. Apa Cyrus is perhaps the same as the Apa Cyrus who was a Roman official at Herakleopolis Magna and who appears in Greek and Arabic documents from the earliest period of occupation.

[3] In the *Chronicle* this designates Upper Egypt.

[4] Otherwise unknown.

[5] To the northwest of Cairo.

[6] 'Atrib is the Greek Athribis; Kyrdis is the Arabic Busir Quredis/Abusir al-Malaq. These towns were situated to the north and south of Cairo.

[7] The Greek Onouphis Ano in the southern Delta.

[8] Not the Babylon of Mesopotamia but rather a town and fortress now part of Cairo.

[9] See above, p. 71, n. 1.

[10] The original name of this person is not clear.

[11] "The region of the two rivers"—used throughout the *Chronicle* to describe the river-locked area around Samnud, the Greek Sebennytos in the central Delta.

[12] The table of contents summarizes thus: "How the men of Samnud so despised 'Amr as not to receive him, and the return of Kaladji to the Romans. And how they seized his mother and wife and concealed them in Alexandria, because he had participated in helping Islam."

[13] The names are corrupted.

[14] Perhaps the text here is corrupted. It is hard to see why 'Amr would want to battle Muslims.

of the Muslims who were with them. The Muslims were not able to perpetrate evil against the cities which were in the two rivers since the water was a wall for them, and the horses were not able to enter it on account of the great waters which were surrounding them.

They [the Muslims] abandoned them [the Romans in the Delta] and went to the region of Rif and came to the city of Budir.[1] They fortified the city and the roads which they had earlier seized. At that time Theodore the general came to Kaladji[2] and petitioned him and said, "Return to us, return to the Romans." Kaladji for his part gave Theodore much money, fearing that they might kill his mother and wife, for they had been hidden in Alexandria. And Theodore the general prevailed over the mind of Kaladji. The latter rose up in the night while the Muslims were asleep, and he went on foot with his companions and reached Theodore the general, and from there he went to the city of Nikiu and joined with Domentianus to do battle with the Muslims. Thereafter Sebendis[3] devised a virtuous plan and fled from the hands of the Muslims during the night. He came to the city of Damietta to John the official, and the latter then sent him to the city of Alexandria with a letter confessing his sin before the lords with many tears in which he said, "This act I have committed because of the slap in the face and the disgrace which I experienced at the hands of John, without shame for my old age. It was for this reason that I joined with Islam. Indeed previously I had led a very quiet life with the Romans."

Chapter 115[4]

Indeed 'Amr leader of the Muslims spent twelve months warring against the Christians who were present in the north of Egypt, but he was not able to take their region. In the fifteenth year of the cycle when it was summer he went to the city of Saka[5] and Nuhu Dumsay,[6] being impatient to kill the Egyptians before the water of the river overflowed.[7] But he was not able to do them any evil. At the city of Damietta, moreover, they did not receive him, and he wanted to burn their plantations with fire. But marching back to his troops who were present at the citadel of Babylon in Egypt, he gave them all the plunder which he had taken from the region of Alexandria. He destroyed the houses of the Alexandrians who had fled, and he took their timbers and iron, and ordered them to construct a road from the citadel of Babylon until they reached that region of the two rivers in order that they might burn the same region with fire. When the people of that region heard this they took their possessions and fled, and left their region a desert. Indeed the Muslims burnt that region. But the people of that region came in the night and extinguished the fire. The Muslims then went to the two cities[8] in order to wage war on them, and they plundered the property of the Egyptians and perpetrated evil against them. The general Theodore and Domentianus were not able to perpetrate evil with the men of the region on account of the Muslims who were between them.

Indeed 'Amr abandoned the coastal region of Egypt and went to Rif in order to wage war on them; and he sent a few Muslims to the city of Antinoe. When the Muslims saw the Romans' weakness and their hatred towards the Emperor Heraclius on account of the persecution which visited upon all of the region of Egypt on account of the orthodox faith, through Cyrus the Chalcedonian patriarch [of Alexandria], they took heart and were strengthened in war. The men of the city took counsel with John their dux in order to wage war upon the Muslims. But he refused and rose up suddenly with his troops and gathered all the tax revenue from the city and went to the city of Alexandria. For he knew that he would not be able to overcome the Muslims, and feared lest the same fate befall him as befell the people of Fayyum. For all the people of the region were subject to the Muslims and paid them taxes. All the Roman troops whom they

---

[1] This designates Busir in Upper Egypt.

[2] Otherwise unidentified. Probably the Coptic name Koloje.

[3] Perhaps an original "Senouthios" or "Senouthes." Otherwise unknown.

[4] The table of contents summarizes thus: "How the Muslims seized Misr in the fourteenth year of the cycle; and in the fifteenth year they seized the fortress of Babylon." The cycle referred to here seems to be Alexandrian lunar cycle. The fifteenth year thus began in April 641.

[5] The Greek Xois in the central Delta.

[6] Perhaps a corrupted combination of the Arabic names for Greek Leontopolis and Damsis, both in the central Delta.

[7] The flood of the Nile began in June.

[8] One suspects a mistake for "rivers."

encountered they killed. The Roman troops were in a citadel. The Muslims besieged them and took their siege engines and destroyed their towers and expelled them from the citadel.[1] They fortified the citadel of Babylon and took the city of Nikiu and were established in it.

Chapter 116[2]

Heraclius was grieved of heart concerning the death of John head of the forces and John the official, whom the Muslims killed, and concerning the defeat of the Romans who were present in the region of Misr. Through the will of God who rules over the souls, officials and armies of kings, Heraclius fell ill with a fever and died in the thirty-first year of his reign, in the month of Yakatit of the Egyptians, and in the months of the Romans February, in the fourteenth year of the lunar cycle, the 357th year of Diocletian.[3]

But people began to say, "Truly, the death of Heraclius has happened because of the striking of gold coins with the image of three emperors, that is, one image of him and two of his sons, one to his right and one to his left, and they did not find a place where they might write the name of the Roman empire." After the death of Heraclius those three images were removed.

When Heraclius the Elder died, Cyrus, the patriarch of Constantinople,[4] disregarded his sister Martina[5] and her children, and he appointed Constantine who was born of the Empress Eudocia[6] and established him as head of the empire after his father. And the two kings were settled with honour and glory. But David and Martin[7] arrested

Cyrus the Roman Chalcedonian patriarch and exiled him to an island in the west of the region of Africa without anyone knowing what had been done.

It happened as Severus the Great, patriarch of Antioch, wrote to the patrician Caesarea, saying, "No son of a Roman emperor will sit upon the throne of his father while the Chalcedonian sect has power in the world."[8]

Constantine the son of Heraclius after he became emperor gathered together a large number of ships and entrusted them to Kiryos and to Salakeryos,[9] and sent them to the patriarch Cyrus in order that they might bring him to him and he might take counsel with him and give tribute to the Muslims—if he were able to fight or not[10]—and he might meet him in the imperial city during the Feast of the Holy Resurrection, and all the people of Constantinople would join with him and perform this act. Thereupon he sent to Anastasius that he should come to him and leave Theodore to protect Alexandria and the cities which were situated on the coastline. He promised Theodore that he would send to him to him in the summer a large force of soldiers so that they might fight the Muslims. But when at the emperor's command they prepared the ships for setting out, the emperor Constantine then fell ill, and contracted a serious illness, and vomited blood from his mouth. When there was no more of that blood he then died. He remained in this illness for one hundred days, that is, his entire reign, he who became emperor after his father Heraclius.[11] People began to mock the emperor Heraclius and his son Constantine.

Men of the Gaianites[12] for their part gathered in their church in the city of Dafasher, near the bridge of the

---

[1] For siege engines, see "Weapons and Warfare in the Middle Ages," in "Reading through Looking," pp. XII–XIV.

[2] The table of contents summarizes thus: "On the death of the emperor Heraclius and the return of Cyrus the patriarch from exile, and his coming to Misr in order to give tribute to the Muslims."

[3] The synchronism is precise for February 641. Scholars disagree as to whether Heraclius died on the 11th January or the 11th February, 641.

[4] The text should here read "Pyrrhus, the patriarch of Constantinople."

[5] Martina was the niece of Heraclius, not his sister, and his second wife.

[6] I.e., Heraclius Constantine/Constantine III, son of Heraclius's first wife, Eudocia.

[7] The young Caesars, sons of Heraclius and Martina.

[8] The passage appears in an extant letter by Severus of Antioch (d.538). A branch of the Miaphysite form of Christianity was sometimes called Severan.

[9] Perhaps a corruption of "Philagrius the Sakellarios," a high-ranking official at Heraclius's court.

[10] The meaning of the text is here obscure.

[11] Since the *Chronicle* places Heraclius's death in February it therefore places Constantine III's death in May or June. Most scholars place the emperor's death in April.

[12] The Gaianites are a sect named after the anti-Chalcedonian counter-patriarch Gaianus, who held the Alexandrian see for a brief period in 565.

apostle St Peter.[1] Cyrus the patriarch had despoiled much of the church's wealth during the time of persecution,[2] without the order of officials. But when the men of the Gaianites wished to raise their hands again Cyrus the patriarch, at that time Eudocianus the brother of the dux Domentianus sent troops against them in order to shoot them with arrows, and prevent them for carrying out their purpose. There were some amongst them whom they beat to death, and others whose hands they cut off, without legal sanction. A herald began to cry out in the city saying, "Let every man amongst you go to his church, and let no one do evil against another illegally."

But God who preserves justice did not forsake the world, and exacted vengeance on the oppressors. He did not pity them, for they had acted treacherously against him, and he delivered them into the hands of the Ishmaelites. Thereupon the Muslims rose up and captured the entire region of Misr. After Heraclius died and at the return of Cyrus, he did not abandon the defeat and persecution of the people of God, but began to heap evil upon evil.

Chapter 117[3]

'Amr the head of the Muslim troops remained outside the citadel of Babylon and besieged the troops who were present inside it. Those same men received word from him that he would not kill them, and they for their part that they would leave for him all the instruments of war, for they were much tormented. Thereupon he ordered them to depart from the citadel. They took a small amount of gold and went. At this the Muslims seized the citadel of Babylon in Egypt on the second day after the Resurrection.[4] God punished them because they did not

honor the life-giving passion of our Lord and Saviour Jesus Christ, who gives life to all those who believe in him. Because of this God delivered them before them.

On the same day of the Feast of the Holy Resurrection, some orthodox prisoners were released. But those enemies of Christ did not leave them without evil, but beat them and cut off their hands. They began to weep, and tears flowed upon their cheeks on that day, and they [the orthodox] reviled them [the heretics].[5] [...][6]

Chapter 118[7]

When the Muslims seized the fortress of Babylon and also Nikiu, there was great sadness amongst the Romans. When 'Amr concluded the business of war he entered into the fortress of Babylon and prepared many ships, great and small, and tied them up at the fortress which he was in.

For his part, Menas, who became head of the Greens, and Cosmas, son of Samuel who was commander of the Blues,[8] besieged the city of Misr and tormented the Romans in the time of the Muslims.

Warriors embarked on ships to the west of the river in pride and pomp and they set out during the night. Indeed 'Amr and an army of Muslims on horseback went by land until they reached the region of Keberyas of 'Abadya.[9] For this reason they waged war against the general Domentianus. When he understood that the Muslim army were approaching his position he climbed into a ship and fled on the ship and abandoned the troops with their ships. He wanted to pass over into a small canal which Heraclius had dug during his reign. But when he discovered that it had been closed off he went and entered the city

---

[1] Dafasher was near Alexandria.

[2] Later Coptic texts also remember the 630s, under the Chalcedonian patriarch Cyrus, as a time of persecution.

[3] The table of contents summarizes thus: "How God delivered the Romans into the hands of the Muslims on account of their division and schism, and the persecution which they visited upon the Christians of Egypt."

[4] I.e., April 10, 641.

[5] In chapter 119 below we discover that the "enemies of Christ" here described were Chalcedonians, and not the Muslims.

[6] I omit an extended quotation, from an unidentified source, comparing its unnamed targets (namely, the Chalcedonians) to pagans, barbarians, and Arians, and bemoaning their persecution.

[7] The table of contents summarizes thus: "How 'Amr subdued 'Abshadi, that is, Nikiu, and the flight of Domentianus the general and the death of his troops in the waters. And the great massacre which occurred in the city of Nikiu, and in all the remaining cities, until 'Amr came to the city of Sawna, which is under the rule of Nikiu and its island, on the 18th of the month of Genbot, in the fifteenth year of the cycle."

[8] These "Greens" and "Blues" refer in the first place to the two "sides" in Byzantine games and entertainments at the hippodrome, but they were also often involved in political conflicts.

[9] Unidentified.

of Alexandria. When the troops saw that their general had fled they abandoned their weapons and entered into the river before their enemies. Then the Muslim troops slew them with the sword in the river, and none survived except one man alone, whose name was Zacharias, who was a champion and a warrior. When the men on the ships saw the flight of the troops they too fled and entered their city. Thereupon the Muslims entered into Nikiu and seized it, and did not encounter any warriors. They began to kill everyone whom they encountered in the street and the churches—men, women and children—and they did not have mercy on anyone.

After they seized the city they went to other places and they pillaged and killed everyone whom they found. They came to the city of Da'[1] and they found 'Esqutaws[2] and those with him, who were in a vineyard, and thereupon the Muslims seized and killed them. They were from the family of Theodore the official.

Let us now be silent, for it is not possible to relate the evils which the Muslims perpetrated when they captured the island of Nikiu on Sunday the 18th of the month of Genbot in the fifteenth year of the cycle,[3] and furthermore the evil which occurred in the city of Caesarea in Palestine.

Theodore the general, commander of the city of Kilunas,[4] left that city and went to Egypt, and left Stephen with the troops who were protecting the city, and they did battle with the Muslims. There was a Jew with the Muslims and he went to the region of Egypt. But with much blood and toil they destroyed the wall of the city and immediately seized it, and killed thousands from the people of the city, and they went and seized much plunder and took the women and children captive, and they divided them between them and left the city desolate. A short time after the Muslims went to the region of Cyprus and killed Stephen and those with him.

Chapter 119[5]

Misr moreover was enslaved to Satan. There was a great quarrel among them with the men of the coast and they

were divided in two. One side allied with Theodore and the other wanted to join with the Muslims. Thereupon one side rose up against the other and plundered their possessions, and burnt their cities with fire. Indeed the Muslims began to fear them.

'Amr then sent many Muslims to Alexandria, and they seized Keryun,[6] which is outside the city. Theodore with his troops who were present in that place fled and entered into the city of Alexandria. The Muslims undertook to wage war on them, and were not able to approach the city's citadel, for they were pelted with stones from atop the citadel, and they were forced outside the city.

The men of Misr began to wage war upon the men of the coast, and there was great strife. But after a short time they made peace. But when their opposition came to an end Satan stirred up another opposition in the city of Alexandria. For Domentianus the official and Menas the general were opposed to each other on account of love of office and other reasons. Theodore the general allied with Menas and opposed Domentianus on account of his flight from Nikiu and abandonment of the troops. Menas was very much angry with Eudocianus the elder brother of Domentianus the official, for the reason that he sinned against the people of the Christians during the Holy Passion, on account of the faith. Domentianus gathered a large number of Blues; and when Menas heard this, he for his part gathered many Greens and the troops who were present in the city. They remained in mutual opposition. Thereupon came Philiades the dux of the region of Arcadia. Domentianus began to oppose the patriarch Cyrus and showed him no honor. For he was his son-in-law, and before had loved him, but thereafter opposed him for no reason. But Menas moreover began to protect Philiades, and he did not despise spiritual love, and he called him to him all the time on account of the honor of the priesthood. For he was the brother of the patriarch George, and was charitable and a lover of God, and had a care for the oppressed.[7] But Philiades did not preserve the love, but began secretly to injure and to preserve evils.

In the time of Theodore the general, a discussion arose concerning the city which is called Mamuna,[8] and

---

[1] Perhaps the Greek Sais in the Delta.

[2] The name of this person is unclear. Greek Isakios?

[3] I.e., the 13th May. This fell on a Sunday in 641, suggesting that the "cycle" is the Alexandrian lunar cycle.

[4] Perhaps a corruption of Greek Askalon, in modern Israel.

[5] The table of contents for chapters 119 and 120 do not correspond to the text.

[6] The Greek Chaireon, southeast of Alexandria.

[7] The patriarch George replaced Cyrus as Chalcedonian patriarch for a brief period in late 640 to September 641.

[8] Unidentified.

concerning the pay of the troops and also the land on which they were established. At that time that wicked man took counsel and said, "Instead of twelve men, one is better. For there will be one man to receive the pay of twelve, and the matter of food and the pay of the troops will have been reduced." For this reason, Menas found cause against Domentianus. All the troops loved him, and believed in him. Menas indeed loved the honor of all men, not because he received a vain glory, but on account of his wisdom and humility.

For the same man was present in the great Church of Caesarion with all the people.[1] All the people of the city gathered against Philiades and wanted to kill him. The same man fled and hid in a church. At that time they went into his house and burnt it with fire, and pillaged all his possessions. But they had pity on the persons whom they found in that church and did not kill them. But when Domentianus discovered this he sent the men of the Blues in order to wage war on them. There was a great battle between them and six men of them died, and many were injured. But with much blood and sweat Theodore established peace between them. He deposed the general Domentianus and established 'Artana as master of the ten grades, who is called Furyans.[2] They returned all the possessions of Philiades which they plundered from his house. For it was said that this battle and quarrel were on account of the faith. [...][3]

Chapter 120

[...] [Theodore] entered the city of Alexandria during the night on the 17th of Maskaram, on the day of the Feast of the Holy Cross.[4] All the people of Alexandria—men and women, old and young—gathered to the patriarch Cyrus, rejoicing and giving praise on account of the return of the patriarch of the city of Alexandria.[5]

But Theodore departed in secret and went to a church of the Theodosians[6] with the patriarch, and closed the doors. He sent for and brought into his presence Menas, and appointed him general, and he chased Domentianus from the city. All of the people began to cry out, "Be gone from the city!" After the arrival of the patriarch Cyrus, George was held in honour by the lord Anastasius. For he had taken office from Heraclius the Younger,[7] and when he had grown older he had received power over all. The patriarch, furthermore, also granted him power.

When the patriarch Cyrus came to the great Church of Caesarion, people strewed all the ground with carpets and sang songs for him, until man trampled on man. Thereafter, with much effort, they brought him to the church. He extolled the pit which contained the holy cross which he had received from the official John before his exile. Moreover he took the glorious cross from a monastery of the Theodosians. But when they began the liturgy on the day of the holy Resurrection, the deacon omitted the psalm sung on the day of the Resurrection, that is: "This is the day which the Lord has made, let us rejoice and be glad at it."[8] In this he wanted to honor the patriarch and to praise him on account of his return, but he introduced another psalm which was not fitting. When the people heard this they said, "This psalm which is not fitting is not a good sign for the patriarch Cyrus, and he will not see again a Feast of the Resurrection in the city of Alexandria." All the congregation of the church and the monks predicted thus in public: "He did what has not been established in the canons." But no-one who heard their words believed them.

Thereafter the patriarch Cyrus rose up and went to Babylon to the Muslims, wanting to make peace and give them tribute in order that they put an end to the war in the region of Egypt. 'Amr welcomed his arrival and said, "You have done well in coming to us." Cyrus answered him and said, "God has given this land to you. Henceforth let there be no enmity between you and the Romans. Before this no quarrel abided with you." They determined the matter of the tribute which he would give. On their side the Ishmaelites would in no way exchange

---

[1] The Caesarion was the main cathedral church of Alexandria.

[2] The name and the role of this person are not clear, although it is possible that Furyans is a corruption of an original *decuriones*, hence "master of the ten grades."

[3] I omit a section of text detailing the restoration of the Chalcedonian patriarch of Alexandria Cyrus, which seems to derive from an independent source, and also a section on Theodore's attempt to reach Libyan Pentapolis.

[4] I.e., the 14th September [641].

[5] Note that John uses here a positive source on Cyrus, and has not altered its tone.

[6] The "Theodosians" designates a Christian sect named after their patriarch Theodosius (536–566).

[7] "Heraclius the Younger" should designate Heraclius's son Heraclonas, who ruled in the central months of 641.

[8] Ps. 118:24.

words but would remain alone for eleven months. The Romans troops who were in Alexandria would take up their weapons and treasures and go by sea. And none of the Roman troops would return again. Those who wanted to go by land would pay tribute each month. The Muslims would seize 150 troops and 50 men of the city as security, and they would make peace. The Romans would put an end to waging war upon the Muslims, and the Muslims to taking churches, and the Muslims would not be involved in any of the affairs of the churches. The Hebrews [i.e., the Jews] they would allow to live in the city of Alexandria.

When the patriarch had finished, he went to the city of Alexandria and told Theodore and the official Constantine in order that they relate this to the emperor Heraclius[1] and confirm it with him. Thereafter all the troops, Alexandrians, and Theodore the official gathered together and paid homage to Cyrus the patriarch. He related to them everything which he had agreed in treaty with the Muslims, and he persuaded them all in this matter. While he was there, thereafter the Muslims came to receive the tribute, of which the men of Alexandria were ignorant. When they saw them, the Alexandrians prepared for war. The troops and the generals took counsel, and said, "We are not able to fight the Muslims, let it be as the patriarch Cyrus says." But the people of the city rose up against the patriarch, and wanted to stone him. But he said to them, "I have done this that I might save you, along with your children." And he besought them with much weeping and sorrow. After that the Alexandrians were ashamed before him, and they gave to much gold to give to the Ishmaelites along with the tribute which they had determined for them. The men of Egypt who fled and entered the city of Alexandria for fear of the Muslims besought the patriarch and said to him, "Get an assurance for us from the Muslims that we might return to our cities, and we will submit to them." And he did for them as they said. The Muslims seized all of the region of Egypt, north and south, and they increased the amount of tax over them threefold.

There was a man whose name was Menas, and who was appointed by the emperor Heraclius over the coastal region. He was proud of heart, ignorant of letters, and he very much hated the Egyptians. After the Muslims had seized the whole region of Egypt they maintained him in his office. They appointed a man called Senuthius[2] over the region of Rif; and they also appointed someone called Philoxenus[3] over the region of Arcadia, that is, the Fayyum. These three loved the pagans [i.e., the Muslims] and hated the Christians, and they forced the Christians to bear fodder for cattle and compelled them to bear milk, honey, fruit, leeks, and many other things. And all this was in addition to grain. They did this through unceasing fear.

They also appointed them to excavate the canal of Hadrian, which had for a long time disappeared, in order that water might flow through it from Babylon in Egypt to the Red Sea. The yoke with which they burdened the Egyptians was greater than that with which Pharaoh had burdened Israel, whom God judged with a righteous judgement and submerged in the Red Sea, he along with all his army, after the great plague with which he plagued them, from man to beast. When God's judgment has come over these Ishmaelites, may he act towards them as he acted towards Pharaoh before. But it is on account of our sins that he has allowed them to act thus towards us. But in the breadth of our lord and saviour Jesus Christ's spirit, he will watch us and protect us. We have faith moreover that he will destroy the enemies of the Cross, as the book which does not lie says.

2.6 Umayyad diplomacy: *The Treaty of Tudmir* (713). Original in Arabic.

Although the Islamic conquests seemed to take place with lightning speed, they were at times piecemeal and even non-violent. Five years after Islamic forces entered Spain in 711, almost the entire peninsula was under the rule of the caliph. Yet documents such as the *Treaty of Tudmir* (713) suggest that in some cases the take-over was peaceful, accomplished

---

[1] I.e., Heraclonas. This indicates that the negotiation took place in or before November 641, the usual date for Heraclonas's fall.

[2] He is probably identical with the *dux* of Antinoe Senuthius who appears in several documents and texts of the period.

[3] This Philoxenus "dux of the province of Arcadia" also appears in a contemporaneous document.

via agreements with local rulers. In this case 'Abd al-'Aziz (d.716), son of Musa (the governor of much of North Africa and a leader in the conquest of Spain), came to an agreement with Theodemir, the local Visigothic commander of the region of Murcia (in the southeast corner of Spain). The Murcians were not to aid any enemies of the Muslims, and they had to pay a modest tax in money and kind. In return, they were offered local autonomy and permission to practice their Christian religion. The Arabic for Theodemir was Tudmir, which for years afterwards was the Arabic name for the region of Murcia.

1. What is the meaning of peace in this document?
2. Who will enforce the peace?

[Source: *Medieval Iberia: Readings from Christian, Muslim, and Jewish Sources*, ed. Olivia Remie Constable (Philadelphia: University of Pennsylvania Press, 1997), pp. 37–38. Translated by Olivia Remie Constable.]

In the name of God, the merciful and the compassionate.

This is a document [granted] by 'Abd al-'Aziz ibn Musa ibn Nusair to Tudmir, son of Ghabdush, establishing a treaty of peace and the promise and protection of God and his Prophet (may God bless him and grant him peace). We ['Abd al-'Aziz] will not set special conditions for him or for any among his men, nor harass him, nor remove him from power. His followers will not be killed or taken prisoner, nor will they be separated from their women and children. They will not be coerced in matters of religion, their churches will not be burned, nor will sacred objects be taken from the realm, [so long as] he [Tudmir] remains sincere and fulfills the [following] conditions that we have set for him. He has reached a settlement concerning seven towns: Orihuela, Valentilla, Alicante, Mula, Bigastro, Ello, and Lorca. He will not give shelter to fugitives, nor to our enemies, nor encourage any protected person to fear us, nor conceal news of our enemies. He and [each of] his men shall [also] pay one dinar every year, together with four measures of wheat, four measures of barley, four liquid measures of concentrated fruit juice, four liquid measures of vinegar, four of honey, and four of olive oil. Slaves must each pay half of this amount.

[Names of four witnesses follow, and the document is dated from the Muslim month of Rajab, in the year 94 of the *hijra* (April 713).]

2.7 Administration: *Letters to 'Abd Allah b. As'ad* (*c*.730–750). Original in Arabic.

Islamic conquerors made use of many of the institutions and professional personnel that they found in the regions they took over. In Egypt, the breadbasket of the Roman world, they found a ready-made tax and requisitioning system that they used for their own benefit. The many administrative documents from this region—papyrus sheets preserved underground in the dry Egyptian climate—allow us to glimpse a well-organized command system designed to carry out orders and respond to problems on the ground. At the top of the hierarchy was the *amir*, the governor of Egypt. Under him were regional officials, pagarchs, and under the pagarchs were various still more local officials and their underlings. All the documents here concern the Fayyum, a region (like so many others in Egypt) made up of small agricultural communities. (See Map 2.2 on p. 70 above.)

The administration of Egypt was no doubt largely carried out through oral directives, but the written word was very important to this society, and many directives were written out by scribes (who sometimes gave their names), in the form of letters. Fayyum's pagarch was Najid b. Mulim, and most of the letters reproduced here were sent by him to 'Abd Allah b. As'ad, an administrative underling who occupied a position somewhere between the pagarch and a village headman. The final letter here, however, is from one al-Salt b. al-Muhajir (otherwise unknown) to 'Abd Allah. Its elaborate opening and blessing are characteristic of private—rather than official—letters.

Many of the letters are fragmentary. Unreadable or lost passages are indicated by ellipses (...). Often you must use your imagination to fill in the blanks, but sometimes, because many phrases are formulaic, the missing words may be supplied from other documents.

1. Why were the opening greetings, however formulaic, important for the functioning of the administration?
2. What sorts of goods and services did the letters talk about?

[Source: Petra M. Sijpesteijn, *Shaping a Muslim State: The World of a Mid-Eighth-Century Egyptian Official* (Oxford: University of Oxford Press, 2013), pp. 285–86, 292–93, 299, 315–16, 344–45, 353, 417. (Editorial interventions silently removed and notes added.)]

Letter 1: Request for Deliveries in Kind

Side A:
In the name of God, the Compassionate, the Merciful.
From Najid b. Muslim to 'Abd Allah b. As'ad.
Peace be upon you and I praise for you God, besides Whom there is no god but He.[1]
Further, and the *amir*, may God preserve him, wrote me urging me with what I owe from what is imposed on the people of the Fayyum in their instalment of this year ... of the ... and the garments[2] and the ... So send it to ... send to me what we are obliged to and what is incumbent upon us of that.... For you know that I assigned to you and the term that I imposed on you. So write to me about the collection of that. And let there not be for anything you owe obstruction and no delay. And may you make your assistance beneficial to us concerning the work that you were put in charge of and may you be reliable. Then do it quickly! And I hope that you will be of the best of my assistants in terms of assisting me, God willing. For you are the most entitled of them to that. And peace be upon you and God's mercy. Humran[3] wrote [it] on Thursday.

Side B:
From Najid b. Muslim [to]   'Abd Allah b. As'ad

Letter 2: Collecting Taxes in Kind

Side A:
In the name of God the Merciful, the Compassionate.
From Najid b. Muslim to 'Abd Allah b. As'ad.
Peace be upon you and I praise for you God besides Whom there is no god but He.
Further, the *amir*, may God make him prosper, wrote to me with what he has calculated for me, of the amount in coin of the people of the province of their taxes in kind. So pay this to him and ... self to me the amount in coin of that ... So hurry to me the amount in money and write me (so) that I pay in coin what you have paid of that and collect their taxes in kind ... of the scribes and we have calculated what the people of every village have to pay of the taxes in kind and its (different) sorts and what has to be paid in coin of it. So inform the people of each village what fell on them in coin and let them give it to the solvent amongst

---

[1] This is a standard greeting and blessing. Compare it to the opening of Letter 2, for example.

[2] Garments: this means that clothes were collected as taxes.

[3] Humran was the scribe for this letter.

them. And write ... and the quota of the tax in kind in its entirety so that your scribe transfers (it) to us, God willing, that which has fallen on the men, of wheat and barley and beans and what was assigned to them of this in coin. And inform your scribe that he is your instrument concerning the execution of this in ..., God willing. And peace be upon you and God's mercy. And 'Abd al-Rahman wrote it.

Side B:

From Najid b. Muslim to	'Abd Allah b. As'ad

Letter 3: Order from the Amir Concerning the Delivery of Grapes

Side A:

In the name of God the Compassionate, the Merciful. From Najid b. Muslim to 'Abd Allah b. As'ad.

Peace be upon you and I praise for you God besides Whom there is no god but He.

Further, the *amir* (may he be made to prosper by God) wrote me concerning the grapes ordering me to send these and to (take care of it?) myself. Thus hand over to him what the people of each village ... deposited with you. And as for whom you appointed over the execution ... that of your scribes over the *amir*'s business which he ordered me (to do), if God wills it. And write me how you acted concerning my letter and concerning the grapes.

Side B:

From Najid h. Muslim	to 'Abd Allah b. As'ad

Letter 4: Instructions to collect sadaqa and zakat

Side A:

In the name of God, the Compassionate the Merciful. From Najid b. Muslim to 'Abd Allah b. As'ad.

Peace be upon you and I praise for you God besides Whom there is no god but He.

Further, God sent His prophet Muhammad, may God praise him, with the guidance and the true religion and everything which God was contended with for his worshippers. Those belonging to the people of the religion of Islam, of the right religion, God has imposed *sadaqa* on their property in order to purify them.... from ... God

through what ... Islam ... and the prayers and the *zakat* payments.... through the *zakat* and on ... and through *zakat* on their possessions ... purification of the people of Islam until you have received from them the ... what God imposed upon them of its *zakat*.[1] Then seal what you have received of it with the seal which has been brought to you. And whoever agrees from amongst the collectors of the tax-levy to hand over the *sadaqa* according to what you wrote, give it to him after you have sealed it from this, *dinars* and carry the free-grazing goats and sheep. And give a document (containing) what you gathered to him from this all together and what was due from everyman of that and what you have received from him with his name and the name of his father and his tribe and the village ... to whom ... lives ... of all that you have received from every village so that it will be all together combining it with the *sadaqa* of another village. And do not delay from the *sadaqa* of the village anything so that it is in one payment. Then hurry instalment upon instalment of the *sadaqas* of the villages according to what you used to calculate and collect before. And peace be upon you and the mercy of God.

Side B:

From Najid b. Muslim to	'Abd Allah b. Asa'd
Concerning the remainders.	

Letter 5: Organization of the Delivery of Oil

Side A:

In the name of God the Merciful the Compassionate. From Najid b. Muslim to 'Abd Allah b. As'ad.

Peace be upon you and I praise for you God besides Whom there is no god but He.

I have sent you Peter, the *symmachos*[2] to collect what the people of your district owe in oil. When this letter of mine comes to you, send with him your *symmachoi* for the collection of that. For I have ordered him, that, in case you delay for him its collection and transport, he should come to me with your scribe and your *symmachoi* so that I may give through them other scribes belonging to your colleagues and their *symmachoi*. So hurry to carry out what I have ordered you of that. And be trustworthy in what you have to do. And let him not use you as a reason for delay in anything of what I assigned to him of the collection of the oil and the coins. And peace be upon you and the mercy of God.

---

[1] The gist of these fragmentary lines is that the *zakat* and *sadaqa* are both godly and purifying.

[2] The *symmachos* (pl. *symmachoi*) was a low-level official who went on site to gather the taxes, in this case oil. He was paid by the Islamic bureaucracy, not by Najid. Byzantine taxes had also been collected by *symmachoi*.

Side B:
From Najid b. Muslim to   'Abd Allah b. As'ad

Letter 6: Assigning Water to Narmuda

Side A:
In the name of God the Compassionate, the Merciful.
From Najid b. Muslim to 'Abd Allah b. As'ad.
Peace be upon you and I praise for you God besides
Whom there is no god but He.
Further, your letter has reached me, mentioning that the
people of Narmuda do not have any water. I have sent
Juzayy and Rashid, the two managers of water, ordering
them to give them water whatever is appropriate and to
water their land. And I have written to Qarina,[1] the one
in charge of Nuwayra, about this. And spare me what is
your affair, and be trustworthy concerning it. Peace be
upon you and the mercy of God.

Side B:
From Najid b. Muslim to   'Abd Allah b. As'ad

Letter 7: Purchase of Various Commodities

Side A:
In the name of God the Merciful, the Compassionate.
From al-Salt b. al-Muhajir to 'Abd Allah b. As'ad.
Peace be upon you and I praise for you God, besides
Whom there is no God but He.

Further, may God be satisfied with us and with you in
all things in His mercy and may He make us and you
of the people of paradise through His strength and His
power. As I am writing to you we are, thanks to God, in
complete wellbeing and health, we ask God for the best for
us and you. Your letter has reached me mentioning your
health and that has pleased me. And I wrote to so-and-so
concerning the ... to you and ... from ... the letter but for a
shortage of messengers. And you wrote me that I buy you
for two *dinars* a Himsi overcoat and I have indeed done
so and I have sent it through Zayd, your servant. And you
wrote me that I send you the ten *dinars* with Zayd; he has
come to me and I counted what I have but no more than
five *dinars* were counted out to him. And I have sent with
him three *dinars* and I paid two *dinars* as the price for the
overcoat.[2] And I will send to you, God willing, the five
remaining ones after gold has given me a profit in Lower
Egypt and I will send them to you with Abu Zayd the ... to
your credit. And I did not hope that my collection ... and
do not order him to do this. And upon my life, if I did not
owe you them (the *dinars*), you would not have written to
me that I lend you money (and) I would have made you
pleased.[3] Do write me about your state, your condition
and any need you may have. For you are amongst the
people I would like to cherish and have a friendly relation
with. And peace be upon you and God's mercy.

Side B:
From al-Salt b. al-Muhajir to   'Abd Allah b. As'ad

2.8 Praising the caliph: Al-Akhtal, *The Tribe Has Departed* (*c.*692). Original in Arabic.

When Caliph 'Abd al-Malik (r.685–705) suppressed a major rebellion, and established his
rule, he needed a way to legitimize his authority and assert its roots in Arabic tradition.

---

[1] Qarina was the headman of a village near Narmuda, which was suffering from a water shortage. Water allocation in the region
was under Najid's supervision, and, as here, he had to make sure that part of the scarce supply available reached every village.
Juzayy and Rashid were water managers; Najid sent them to ensure that the villagers of Narmuda would have enough water for
their personal needs and to irrigate their lands.

[2] The purchase of just one overcoat likely means that 'Abd Allah ordered it for his personal use.

[3] Al-Salt possibly got the overcoat on credit. He certainly owed money to 'Abd Allah, who was obliged in this letter to put pressure
on him to get it back. But al-Salt could render only the overcoat and some of the money; he was hoping to obtain more money
during a trip north to the Nile Delta (Lower Egypt).

This he did largely by patronizing poets, for poetry was both highly valued and adaptive to a variety of purposes. In Syria, where the Umayyads established their capital, most of the population was Christian, but that did not prevent the Christian al-Akhtal (*c.*640–*c.*710) from becoming one of the caliph's most important poetic eulogists. In *The Tribe Has Departed*, al-Akhtal drew on traditional forms: a departure, a journey, and a boast. The parts are labeled here by your editor.

1. What are the virtues and the powers of the "Caliph of God" in this poem?
2. What does the poet say about himself, his feelings, and his role in the events that his poem recounts?

[Source: Suzanne Pinckney Stetkevych, *The Poetics of Islamic Legitimacy: Myth, Gender, and Ceremony in the Classical Arabic Ode* (Bloomington: Indiana University Press, 2002), pp. 89–94, 96–97 (notes added).]

[The Departure]

1. Those that dwelt with you have left in haste,
     departing at evening or at dawn,
   Alarmed and driven out by fate's caprice,
     they head for distant lands.

2. And I, on the day fate took them off,
     was like one drunk
   On wine from Hims or Gadara
     that sends shivers down the spine,

3. Poured generously from a brimming wine-jar
     lined with pitch and dark with age,
   Its clay seal broken
     off its mouth,

4. A wine so strong it strikes
     the vital organs of the reveler,
   His heart, hungover, can barely
     sober up

5. I was like that, or like a man
     whose limbs are racked with pain,
   Or like a man whose heart is struck
     by charms and amulets,

6. Out of longing for them and yearning
     on the day I sent my glance after them
   As they journeyed in small bands
     on Kawkab Hill's two slopes.[1] ...

[The Journey]

17. They alighted in the evening,
      and we turned aside our noble-bred camels:
    For the man in need, the time had come
      to journey

[The Boast]

18. To a man whose gifts do not elude us,
      whom God has made victorious,
    So let him in his victory
      long delight!

19. He who wades into the deep of battle,
      auspicious his augury,
    The Caliph of God
      through whom men pray for rain

20. When his soul whispers its intention to him
      he resolutely sends it forth,
    His courage and his caution
      like two keen blades.

21. In him the common weal resides,
      and after his assurance
    No peril can seduce him
      from his pledge.

22. Not even the Euphrates when its tributaries

---

[1] Kawkab Hill is southwest of Damascus.

pour seething into it
And sweep the giant swallow-wort from its two banks
    into the middle of its rushing stream,

23. And the summer winds churn it
    until its waves
Form agitated puddles
    on the prows of ships,

24. Racing in a vast and mighty torrent
    from the mountains of Byzance[1]
Whose foothills shield them from it
    and divert its course,

25. Is ever more generous than he is
    to the supplicant
Or more dazzling
    to the beholder's eye.

26. They did not desist from their treachery and cunning
    against you
Until, unknowingly, they portioned out
    the maysir players' flesh.[2] ...

29. Like a crouching lion, poised to pounce,
    his chest low to the ground,
For a battle in which there is
    prey for him,

30. [The caliph] advances with an army
    two hundred thousand strong,
The likes of which no man or jinn[3]
    has ever seen.

31. He comes to bridges which he builds
    and then destroys,
He brands his steeds with battle scars,
    above him fly banners and battle dust,

32. Until at al-Taff
    they wreaked carnage,

And at al-Thawiyyah
    where no bowstring twanged.[4]

33. The tribesmen saw clearly
    the error of their ways,
And he straightened out the smirk
    upon their faces....

44. O Banu Umayyah, your munificence
    is like a widespread rain;
It is perfect,
    unsullied by reproach.

45. O Banu Umayyah, it was I
    who defended you
From the men of a tribe
    that sheltered and aided [the Prophet].

46. I silenced the Banu Najjar's endless braying
    against you
With poems that reached the ears
    of every chieftain of Ma'add,

47. Until they submitted,
    smarting from my words—
For words can often pierce
    where sword points fail.

48. O Banu Umayyah, I offer you
    sound counsel:
Don't let Zufar dwell secure
    among you,[5]

49. But take him as an enemy:
    for what you see of him
And what lies hid within
    is all corruption.

50. For in the end you'll meet
    with ancient rancor
That, like mange,[6] lies latent for a while

---

[1] Byzantium.

[2] Maysir means gambling; pre-Islamic maysir players would gamble for the parts of a sacrificed animal. Here the enemies of the caliph are likened to maysir players, but the flesh they gamble for and cut apart is their own.

[3] Jinn are half-spirit creatures.

[4] Al-Taff is where an enemy leader was slain, while al-Thawiyyah was the burial site of another enemy leader.

[5] Zufar was initially an enemy of Caliph al-Malik, but by the time of this poem, he rivaled al-Akhtar and his clan, the Banu Taghlib, for the caliph's favors.

[6] Mange is a skin disease.

only to spread the more.

51. Through us you were victorious,
      O Commander of the Faithful,
    When the news reached you
      within al-Ghutah [of Damascus],

52. They identified for you the head
      of Ibn al-Hubab,
    Its nose bridge now marked
      by the sword.

53. Ears deaf, never will he

hear a voice;
Nor will he talk till stones
  begin to speak.[1]...

78. And remember the Banu Ghudanah
      like herds of young slit-eared goats,
    Runty ones, for whom
      corrals are built,

79. That pee on their forelegs
      when they're hot,
    And shiver with cold
      when wet with rain.[2] ...

THE IMPOVERISHED BUT INVENTIVE WEST

2.9 The private penitential tradition: *Penitential of Finnian* (late 6th cent.). Original in Latin.

The purpose of penance is to achieve reconciliation with God after sinning. In early Christian practice, penance was public, dramatic, and humiliating. But within the Celtic, Anglo-Saxon, and Frankish worlds a different sort of penance became popular: the "tariffed" penance of the penitentials. Drawing on biblical passages, canons (decisions or laws) of early church councils, monastic practices, and perhaps secular laws, these penitentials listed sins and the penances due for them (the tariffs) as a matter of regular religious discipline. The penitential of Finnian, drawn up in the late sixth century in either Ireland or Brittany, is one of the earliest of these books. Although it was probably created in a monastic context, it was directed mainly to clerics and the laity rather than monks. Since clerics were considered "secular" (worldly) because of their pastoral duties, and laypeople were ordinary men and women—not in orders, not of clerical or monastic status, and normally married—the audience at whom this is aimed is itself evidence of the monastic desire to make an impact on the behavior of those "in the world."

1. In what ways is the monastic life itself (as, for example, exemplified by *The Benedictine Rule*) a model for this penitential?
2. What sorts of sins does this penitential focus on?

[Source: *The Irish Penitentials*, ed. Ludwig Bieler (Dublin: Dublin Institute for Advanced Studies, 1963), pp. 75, 77, 79, 81, 87 (notes added).]

---

[1] Al-Akhtar here boasts that his clan defeated and beheaded al-Hubab, the leader of an enemy clan, while the caliph himself relaxed in the park of al-Ghutah.

[2] For a society that values camels above all other animals, it is a great slur to liken the Ghudanah to runty goats.

In the name of the Father and of the Son and of the Holy Ghost.

1. If anyone has sinned by thought in his heart and immediately repents, he shall beat his breast and seek pardon from God and make satisfaction, and [so] be whole.

2. But if he frequently entertains [evil] thoughts and hesitates to act on them, whether he has mastered them or been mastered by them, he shall seek help from God by prayer and fasting day and night until the evil thought departs and he is whole.

3. If, however, he has thought evil and intended to do it and has not been able to do it, since opportunity has failed him, it is the same sin but not the same penance; for example, if he intended fornication or murder, he has, by his intention, already committed the sin in his heart which he did not complete by a deed; but if he quickly does penance, he can be helped. His penance is this: half a year he shall do penance on an allowance of bread and water, and he shall abstain from wine and meat for a whole year.

4. If anyone has sinned in word by inadvertence and immediately repented and has not said any such thing of set purpose, he ought to submit to penance, but he shall keep [only] one special fast; but thereafter let him be on his guard throughout his life, lest he commit further sin.

5. If one of the clerics or ministers of God makes strife, he shall do penance for a period of seven days with bread and water and salt, and seek pardon from God and his neighbor, with full confession and humility; and thus can he be reconciled to God and his neighbor.

6. If anyone has decided on a scandalous deed and plotted in his heart to strike or kill his neighbor, if [the offender] is a cleric, he shall do penance for half a year with an allowance of bread and water and for a whole year abstain from wine and meat, and thus he will be reconciled to the altar; 7. but if he is a layman, he shall do penance for a period of seven days; since he is a man of this world, his guilt is lighter in this world and his reward less in the world to come.

8. But if he is a cleric and strikes his brother or his neighbor and sheds blood, it is the same as if he had killed him, but the penance is not the same: he shall do penance with bread and water and salt and be deprived of his clerical office for an entire year, and he must pray with weeping and tears, that he may obtain mercy of God, since Scripture says: "Whosoever hateth his brother is a murderer";[1] how much more he who strikes him. 9. But if he is a layman, he shall do penance forty days and give some money to him whom he has struck, according as some priest or arbiter determines. A cleric, however, ought not to give money to either man or woman.

10. But if one who is a cleric falls miserably through fornication and loses his crown,[2] if it happens once [only] and it is concealed from men but known before God, he shall do penance for an entire year with an allowance of bread and water and for two years abstain from wine and meat, but he shall not lose his clerical office. For, we say, sins can be absolved in secret by penance and by very diligent devotion of heart and body.

11. If, however, they have long been in the habit of sin and it has not come to the notice of men, he shall do penance for three years with bread and water and lose his clerical office, and for three years more he shall abstain from wine and meat, since it is not a smaller thing to sin before God than before men.

12. But if one of the clerical order falls to the depths of ruin and begets a son and kills him, great is the crime of fornication with homicide, but it can be expiated through penance and God's mercy. He shall do penance three years with an allowance of bread and water, in weeping and tears and prayers by day and night, and he shall implore the mercy of the Lord to perchance have remission of sins;[3] and he shall abstain for three more years from wine and meat, deprived of his clerical office; and for the forty-day periods[4] in the last three years he shall fast with bread and water; and [he shall] be an exile from his own country, until a period of seven years is completed, and so by the judgment of a bishop or a priest he shall be restored to his office.

13. If, however, he has not killed the child, the sin is less, but the penance is the same.

14. But if one of the clerical order is on familiar terms with any woman and he has himself done no evil with her, neither by cohabiting nor by lascivious embraces, this is his penance: For such time as he has her he shall withdraw from the communion of the altar and do penance for forty days and nights with bread and water and tear out of his heart his fellowship with the woman, and so be restored to the altar.

---

[1] 1 John 3:15.

[2] The crown of virginity.

[3] "Remission" of sins means "forgiveness" of sins.

[4] In the penitentials, three forty-day periods of fasting were prescribed in the course of the Church year: before Easter (Lent), before Christmas, and after Pentecost.

15. If, however, he is on familiar terms with many women and has given himself to association with them and to their lascivious embraces, but has, as he says, preserved himself from ruin, he shall do penance for half a year with an allowance of bread and water, and for another half year he shall abstain from wine and meat, but he shall not lose his clerical office; and after an entire year of penance, he shall join himself to the altar.[1]

16. If any cleric lusts after a virgin or any woman in his heart but does not speak with his lips, if he sins thus but once he ought to do penance for seven days with an allowance of bread and water.

17. But if he continually lusts and is unable to indulge his desire, since the woman does not admit him or since he is ashamed to speak, still he has committed adultery with her in his heart—yet it is in his heart, and not in his body; it is the same sin whether in the heart or in the body, yet the penance is not the same. This is his penance: let him do penance for forty days with bread and water.

18. If any cleric or woman who practices magic have led astray anyone by their magic, it is a monstrous sin, but it can be expiated by penance. [Such an offender] shall do penance for six years, three years on an allowance of bread and water, and during the remaining three years he shall abstain from wine and meat.

19. If, however, such a person has not led astray anyone but has given [a potion] for the sake of wanton love to someone, he shall do penance for an entire year on an allowance of bread and water.

20. If a woman by her magic destroys the child she has conceived of somebody, she shall do penance for half a year with an allowance of bread and water, and abstain for two years from wine and meat and fast for the six forty-day periods with bread and water.

21. But if, as we have said, she bears a child and her sin is manifest, [she shall do penance] for six years [with bread and water], as is the judgment in the case of a cleric, and in the seventh year she shall be joined to the altar, and then we say her crown can be restored and she may don a white robe and be pronounced a virgin. So a cleric who has fallen ought likewise to receive the clerical office in the seventh year after the labor of penance, as Scripture says: "Seven times a just man falleth and ariseth,"[2] that is, after seven years of penance he who fell can be called "just" and in the eighth year evil shall not lay hold on him, but for the remainder [of his life] let him preserve himself carefully lest he fall, since, as Solomon says, as a dog returning to his vomit becomes odious, so is he who through his own negligence reverts to his sin."[3] ...

32. We prescribe and urge contributing for the redemption of captives. By the teaching of the Church, money is to be spent fruitfully on the poor and needy.

33. We are also obliged to serve the churches of the saints and, within our means, have pity on all who are in need; pilgrims are to be received into our houses, as the Lord has commanded; the infirm are to be visited; those who are in chains are to be ministered to; and all commandments of Christ are to be performed, "from the least unto the greatest."[4]

34. If any man or woman is nigh unto death, although he [or she] has been a sinner, and asks for the communion of Christ, we say that it is not to be denied to such a person if that person promise God to take the vow, and do well and be received by Him. If he is restored to this world, let him fulfil that which he has vowed to God; but if he does not fulfil the vow which he has vowed to God, [the consequences] will be on his own head, and we will not refuse what we owe to him: we are not to cease to snatch prey from the mouth of the lion or the dragon, that is of the devil, who ceases not to snatch at the prey of our souls, even though we may have to follow up and strive [for his soul] at the very end of a man's life.

35. If one of the laity is converted from his evil-doing unto the Lord, and if he has wrought every evil deed—by committing fornication, that is, and shedding blood—he shall do penance for three years and go unarmed except for a staff in his hand, and shall not live with his wife, but in the first year he shall fast on an allowance of bread and water and salt and not live with his wife; after a penance of three years he shall give money for the redemption of his soul and the fruit of his penance[5] into the hand of the priest and make a feast for the servants of God, and in the feast [his penance] shall be ended and he shall be received to communion; he may then resume relations with his wife after his entire and complete penance, and if it is so decided he shall be joined to the altar....

---

[1] Laypeople, too, may be "joined to the altar" (e.g., see § 21 below), and thus "he shall join himself to the altar" seems to mean that the person will rejoin the congregation.

[2] Prov. 24:16.

[3] See Prov. 26:11.

[4] Heb. 8:11.

[5] "The fruit of his penance" refers to the savings that accrue from fasting.

2.10 A royal saint: *The Life of Queen Balthild* (c.680). Original in Latin.

The Merovingians based their power on land, treasure, prowess in battle, and alliances with major lay aristocrats and ecclesiastics (including monks) in Francia. Merovingian queens added to the prestige of the dynasty by cultivating often exceptional piety. Queen Balthild (d.*c.*680), wife of King Clovis II (r.639–657), was particularly devoted to the religious life. Although reported by her biographer to have risen from slavery, emphasizing her humility, she may well have belonged to a noble Anglo-Saxon family. In any event, once married, she quickly produced three sons, began distributing alms, and, as her biographer wrote, "prayed daily, ... fed the hungry, [and] clothed the naked with garments." After Clovis died, she took over as regent, acting in the name of her son Clothar III, who was around six-years-old at the time. She also lavished money and attention on the monasteries of the realm, founding Corbie and Chelles (to which she herself retired), and richly donating to others. Her biography was written shortly after her death by an anonymous writer, quite possibly a woman.

1. What Church reforms does Balthild's biographer credit her with, and why might these have seemed important at the time?
2. Comparing Balthild's virtues with those of Monegundis (above, p. 38), consider the different models of Merovingian female sanctity.

[Source: *Late Merovingian France: History and Hagiography (640–720)*, ed. and trans. Paul Fouracre and Richard A. Gerberding (Manchester: Manchester University Press, 1996), pp. 119–27, 129–32.]

Chapter 1

[The author declares his unworthiness to write about Queen Balthild, but he trusts that Christ will guide him and that his "straightforward words" will reveal the truth.]

Chapter 2

HERE BEGINS THE LIFE OF BLESSED QUEEN BALTHILD

Blessed be the Lord, "who wishes all men to be saved and to come to the recognition of truth,"[1] and "who causes them to will and to complete all in all."[2] And therefore His praise must be deservedly sung first in the merits and miracles of the saints, He "who makes great men out of those of low station, indeed, He who raises the poor man out of the dunghill and makes him to sit with the princes of His people,"[3] just as He has raised the present great and venerable woman, Lady Balthild, the queen. Divine providence called her from lands across the sea[4] and this precious and best pearl of God arrived here, having been sold at a low price. She was acquired by the late Erchinoald, the leader of the Franks and a man of illustrious standing, in whose service she dwelt as an adolescent most honorably so that her admirable and pious religious way of life pleased both the leader and all his servants. She was indeed kind in her heart, "temperate and prudent"[5] in her whole character, and provident. She contrived evil against no one. She was neither frivolous in her fine expression nor presumptuous in speaking, but most honorable in all her acts. And although she was from the race of the Saxons, the form of

---

[1] 1 Tim. 2:4.

[2] See Phil. 2.13, 1 Cor. 12:6 and Eph. 1:23.

[3] 1 Kings 2:8; Ps. 112:7–8.

[4] England.

[5] 1 Tim. 3:11.

her body was pleasing, very slender, and beautiful to see. Her expression was cheerful and her gait dignified. And, since she was thus, "she was exceedingly pleasing to the prince and she found favor in his eyes."[1] He engaged her to serve him the goblets in his chamber, and as a most honorable cupbearer she stood quite often present in his service. Nonetheless, from the favor of her position she derived no haughtiness but, based in humility, was loving and obedient to all her equals. With fitting honor she so served her seniors that she removed the shoes from their feet and washed and dried them. She fetched water for washing and promptly prepared their clothes. And she performed this service for them without muttering and with a good and pious heart.

Chapter 3

And from her noble way of life, greatest praise and love among her companions accrued to her, and she earned such a favorable reputation that, when the wife of the above-mentioned prince Erchinoald died, he decided to join the most honorable virgin, Balthild, to himself in the matrimonial bed. And, having learned this thing, she secretly and earnestly withdrew herself from his sight. And when she was called to the bedchamber of the prince, she hid herself in an out-of-the-way corner and threw cheap rags over herself so that no one would have thought anyone to be hiding there. Indeed, she was then still a shrewd and prudent virgin fleeing empty high positions and seeking humility. She tried, as she was able, to avoid human marriage so that she might deserve to come to her spiritual and heavenly groom. But indeed, beyond doubt, it was accomplished by divine providence that the prince did not find her, whom he sought, and then joined another matron to himself in marriage. And then the girl Balthild was finally found so that, by the true will of God who had shunned the nuptials of the prince, she would later have Clovis [II], son of the late King Dagobert [I], in marriage so that He could thus raise her to a higher station through the merit of her humility. And in this station divine dispensation decided to honor her so that, seeing that she had refused a follower of the king, she might obtain union with the king and, from her, royal progeny might come forth. And this has now come to pass, as it is obvious to everyone that the royal offspring reigning now is hers.

Chapter 4

But as she had the grace of prudence conferred upon her by God, with watchful eagerness she obeyed the king as her lord, and to the princes she showed herself a mother, to the priests as a daughter, and to the young and the adolescents as the best possible nurse. And she was friendly to all, loving the priests as fathers, the monks as brothers, the poor as a faithful nurse does, and giving to each generous alms. She preserved the honor of the princes and kept their fitting counsel, always exhorting the young to religious studies and humbly and steadfastly petitioning the king for the churches and the poor. While still in secular dress, she desired to serve Christ; she prayed daily, tearfully commending herself to Christ, the heavenly king. And the pious king [Clovis], taking care of her faith and devotion, gave his faithful servant, Abbot Genesius, to her as support, and through his hands she served the priests and the poor, fed the hungry, clothed the naked with garments, and conscientiously arranged the burial of the dead. Through him she sent most generous alms of gold and silver to the monasteries of men and women. And this servant of Christ, Lord Genesius, was later ordained bishop of Lyon at Christ's command. He was at that time regularly in the court of the Neustrians. And through him, as we said, the lady Balthild, along with the authority of King Clovis and at the petition of this servant of God [Genesius], provided the generous alms of the king to all the poor throughout many places.

Chapter 5

What more is there to say? At God's command, her husband, King Clovis, went forth from his body, leaving a lineage of sons with their mother. In his place after him, his son, the late King Clothar [III], took the throne of the Franks and then also with the excellent princes, Chrodbert, bishop of Paris, Lord Audoin, and Ebroin, mayor of the palace, along with the other great magnates and very many of the rest [of the aristocracy]. And, indeed, the kingdom of the Franks was maintained in peace. Then indeed, a little while ago, the Austrasians peacefully received her son Childeric [II] as king in Austrasia by the arrangement of Lady Balthild and, indeed, through the advice of the great magnates. But the Burgundians and the Neustrians were united. And we believe that, with God guiding, and in accordance with the great faith of

---

[1] Esther 7:3; 2:4; 9; and 5:8. Esther was also a royal spouse of low origins.

Lady Balthild, these three kingdoms kept the harmony of peace among themselves.

Chapter 6

At that time it happened that the heresy of simony stained the Church of God with its depraved practice in which they received the rank of bishop by paying a price for it.[1] By the will of God [acting] through her, and at the urging of the good priests, the above-mentioned Lady Balthild stopped this impious evil so that no one would set a price on the taking of holy orders. Through her, the Lord also arranged for another very evil and impious practice to cease, one in which many men were more eager to kill their offspring than to provide for them in order to avoid the royal exactions which were inflicted upon them by custom, and from which they incurred a very heavy loss of property. This the lady prohibited for her own salvation so that no one presumed to do it. Because of this deed, truly a great reward awaits her.

Chapter 7

Who, then, is able to say how many and how great were the sources of income, the entire farms and the large forests she gave up by donating them to the establishments of religious men in order to construct cells or monasteries? And she also built as God's own and private houses a huge nunnery for women consecrated by God at Chelles, near Paris where she placed the religious handmaiden of God, the girl Bertila, in the position of the first mother. And in this place the venerable Lady Balthild in turn decided to dwell under the pure rule of religion and to rest in peace. And in truth she fulfilled this with a devoted will.

Nor must we pass over what pertains to the praise of God, whatever God marvelously performs in his saints and elect, because as Scripture says, "God is miraculous in His saints,"[2] and His spirit, the Paraclete, works within through goodwill, as it is written: "God is the helper of

each willing good."[3] And it is known that it was truly thus with this great woman. As we said above, neither our tongue nor that of anyone, no matter how erudite, I do think, is able to relate all her good deeds. How many means of comfort and support did she give to the houses of God or to His poor for the love of Christ? And of what quality was the monastery called Corbie which she constructed at her own expense in the parish of Amiens? And here the venerable man, Lord Theudofred, who is now a bishop but who was then abbot, had charge of a large flock of brothers which the above-mentioned Lady Balthild sought from Luxeuil, from the late most reverend Lord Abbot Waldebert, and which she wonderfully directed to this monastery of brothers, and this is still known and praised.

Chapter 8

[She gave property to numerous monasteries including her own foundation at Chelles.]

Chapter 9

We certainly must not pass over [the fact] that throughout the senior basilicas of Lord Denis, Lord Germanus, Lord Medard, Saint Peter, Lord Anian, and Saint Martin[4] or wherever her precept reached, she ordered the bishops and abbots, by persuading them for the zeal of Christ, and sent them letters to this effect, that the monks dwelling in these places ought to live under a holy regular order.[5] And in order that they would freely acquiesce in this, she ordered a privilege to be confirmed for them and she also conceded them immunities[6] so that she might better entice them to exhort the clemency of Christ, the highest king, for the king and for peace. And this must be called to mind, because it pertains to the increase of her reward, that she forbade Christian men to become captives, and she issued precepts, throughout each region [ordering] that absolutely no one ought to transfer a captive Christian in the kingdom of the Neustrians. And in

---

1   The word simony derives from a person, Simon Magus, who in Acts 8:9–24 tries to buy Peter's holy powers. It refers to the practice of "buying" ecclesiastical offices. Although considered an abuse in the *Life of Balthild*, it did not become a focus of Church reform until the eleventh century.

2   Ps. 67:36; Douay Ps. 68:36.

3   Rom. 8:28.

4   These are the saints to whom "the senior basilicas"—the holiest places in the kingdom—were dedicated: the churches of Denis and Germanus were at Paris, that of Medard was at Soissons, Peter's at Sens, Anian's at Orléans, and Martin's at Tours.

5   In other words, under a rule, though not necessarily that of Benedict (for which see above, p. 20).

6   Immunities were documents that granted monasteries freedom from royal interference.

addition she paid the price and ordered many captives to be bought back and she released them as free. Others of them, especially from her own [Anglo-Saxon] race, men and also many girls, she sent into the monasteries as her own charges. However many she was able to attract, these she entrusted to the holy monasteries, and she ordered them to pray for her. She even often sent many generous gifts to Rome, to the basilicas of blessed Peter and Paul and to the Roman poor.

Chapter 10

It was, however, her holy vow that she ought to dwell in the monastery of religious women which we mentioned above, that is, at Chelles, which she herself built. But the Neustrians, for love of her, delayed in this especially, nor would they have permitted it to come about had not an insurrection arisen because of the wretched Bishop Sigobrand [of Paris] whose haughtiness among the Franks earned him mortal ruin. And from this a dispute arose because they killed him against her will. Fearing that the lady would hold it gravely against them and wish to vindicate his cause, they straightway permitted her to go into the monastery. And there is no probable doubt that it was not with a good heart that these princes then permitted this. But the lady considered it God's will that it was not so much their decision as a dispensation of God that her holy desire had been fulfilled, through whatever means, with Christ as her guide. And, having been escorted by certain noblemen, she came to her above-mentioned monastery at Chelles, and there, as is fitting, she was honorably and very lovingly received into the holy congregation by the holy maidens. Then, however, she had a complaint of no mean size against those whom she had kindly nurtured,[1] because they had erroneously considered her suspect and even repaid her with evil for her good deeds. But, discussing this quickly with the priests, she kindly forgave them everything and asked them to forgive her this disturbance of her heart. And thus, with the Lord as provider, peace was fully restored among them.

Chapter 11

Indeed, with a most pious affection she loved her sisters as her own daughters, she obeyed their holy abbess as

her mother, and rendered service to them as the lowest of handmaidens out of holy desire, just as [she had done] when she still ruled the royal palace and often visited her holy monastery. So strongly did she exhibit the example of great humility that she even served her sisters in the kitchen, and the lowest acts of cleaning, even the latrines, she herself did. All this she undertook with joy and a cheerful heart, in such humble service for Christ. For who would believe that the height of such power would serve in such lowly things if her most abundant and great love of Christ had not demanded it of her in every way? She remained incessantly in faithful prayer with tears and she very often attended divine reading; indeed, she occasioned constant consolation through her holy prayer and her frequent visitation of the infirm. For she grieved with the grieving through the eagerness of her love, she rejoiced with the joyful, and for the slaves she very often humbly beseeched the lady abbess that they might be consoled. And she [the abbess], as her mother, lovingly granted all things to her petition because there was truly for them, in the manner of the Apostles, "one heart and one soul"[2] because they loved each other tenderly and most fully in Christ....

Chapter 14

But when the lady sensed that her end was near, her holy heart was raised up toward heaven. And being informed of her great reward, of blessed repayment, she strongly prohibited those staying with her from notifying the other sisters or the lady abbess, who herself was gravely ill, lest she should also be endangered on account of the magnitude of her grief. There was at that time a certain child, her goddaughter, whom she wished to go with her, and she [the child] suddenly went out from her body and preceded her to the grave. Then, making the sign of the cross in faith, and with her faithful eyes and holy hands raised toward heaven, her holy soul was loosed from the chain of her body in peace. And suddenly a splendor from on high glistened most brightly in the little room. And without doubt this holy soul was gloriously received by a chorus of angels, and her very faithful friend, the late Lord Bishop Genesius, came out to meet her, as her great reward demanded.

---

1   The noblemen who forced her to retire to Chelles.

2   Acts 4:32.

Chapter 15

For a little while, those sisters, with the sigh of grief as their companion, kept this hidden under silence, just as she had ordered. so that it was reported only to the priests who were to commend her most blessed soul to the Lord. And when the abbess and the whole congregation later learned of the matter, with great weeping they demanded how [it had happened] so suddenly and unexpectedly, as the hour of her departure was not known to them. It was as if this gem which everybody wanted had been snatched from them. All were stunned and likewise lay prostrate there on the ground. There was a great profusion of tears: weeping with an immense groan of grief, giving thanks to the faithful Lord, and praising Him together, they commended her holy soul to Christ, the faithful king, that He might guide it to Saint Mary in the chorus and company of the saints. Then, as was fitting for her, they buried her with great honor and much reverence. Then the Lady Abbess Bertila, taking care because of the eagerness of her piety, requested the holy priests that her holy memory should be preserved constantly throughout many churches in holy sacrifices. And throughout many places deservedly her [memory] is still steadfastly celebrated....

Chapter 18

Indeed, we recall that other queens in the kingdom of the Franks have been noble and worshippers of God: Clothild, queen of the late King Clovis of old and niece of King Gundobad,[1] who, by her holy exhortations, led both her very brave and pagan husband and many of the Frankish nobles to Christianity and brought them to the Catholic faith. She also was the first to construct the churches in honor of Saint Peter at Paris and Saint George in the little monastery for virgins at Chelles, and she founded many others in honor of the saints in order to store up her reward, and she enriched them with many gifts. The same is said of Ultrogoda, queen of the most Christian King Childebert,[2] because she was a comforter of the poor and a helper of the servants of God and of monks. And [it is said] also of Queen Radegund, truly a most faithful handmaiden of God, queen of the late elder King Clothar,[3] whom the grace of the Holy Spirit had so inflamed that she left her husband while he was still alive and consecrated herself to the Lord Christ under the holy veil, and, with Christ as her spouse, accomplished many good things. These things are read in her Acts.[4]

Chapter 19

But it is pleasing, nevertheless, to consider this about her whom it here concerns: the Lady Balthild. Her many good deeds were accomplished in our times, and that these things were done by her herself we have learned in the best manner. Concerning these things, we have here commemorated a few out of the many, and we do not think her to be the inferior in merits of those earlier [queens]; rather we know her to have outdone them in holy striving. After the many good things which she did before her evangelical perfection, she gave herself over to voluntary holy obedience and as a true nun she happily completed her blessed life under complete religious practice.

HERE ENDS THE LIFE OF SAINT BALTHILD, QUEEN

2.11 Reforming the continental Church: *Letters to Boniface* (723–726). Original in Latin.

Born in Wessex, England, Boniface (672/675–754) entered a monastery at the age of seven, where he received an excellent education. In 716 he undertook the first of his missionary efforts by going to Frisia, where he followed in the footsteps of earlier English evangelists. In 717 he traveled to Rome, changing his name from the Anglo-Saxon "Wynfrith" to the

---

[1] The references are to the Merovingian king Clovis I (r.481/482–511) and the Burgundian king Gundobad (r.480–516).
[2] The Merovingian king Childebert I (r.511–558).
[3] The Merovingian king Clothar I (r.511–661).
[4] A reference to the hagiographical accounts of Radegund's life.

Latinate "Boniface" and receiving a commission from Pope Gregory II (715–731) to evangelize the people living east of the Rhine—in Bavaria and Thuringia. In fact, these regions had already been Christianized, and Boniface spent most of his time reforming churches already established rather than preaching the Word to pagans. In all of his work he was avidly supported by Charles Martel (d.741), the powerful mayor of the palace in Francia (as we may now call Gaul). After Charles's death, Boniface focused on reforming the Frankish Church itself, which he did through a series of Church councils that he called between 742 and 744. A year later he became archbishop of Mainz, but not long thereafter he returned to Frisia, which had not yet been Christianized, and there suffered a martyr's death in 754. The letters below come from Boniface's earliest period in Germany. In the first, Charles Martel offers him protection. In the second, Gregory II commends him to the Thuringians, whose Christianization he does not recognize. In the third, the pope instructs Boniface on particular matters of Christian practice.

1. Why did Gregory II support Boniface's missionary work?
2. What might explain Charles Martel's support of Boniface?

[Source: *The Letters of Saint Boniface*, trans. Ephraim Emerton (New York: W.W. Norton, 1940), pp. 47, 52–56.]

[CHARLES MARTEL COMMENDS BONIFACE TO ALL FRANKISH OFFICIALS, 723]

To the holy and apostolic bishops, our fathers in Christ, and to the dukes, counts, vicars, palace officials, all our lower agents, our circuit judges [*missi*] and all who are our friends, the noble Charles, mayor of the palace, your well-wisher, sends greeting.

Be it known to you that the apostolic man in Christ, Father Boniface, a man of apostolic character and a bishop, came to us with the request that we should take him under our guardianship and protection. Know that we have acquiesced with pleasure and, hence, have granted his petition before witnesses and commanded that this written order signed by our own hand be given him, that wheresoever he may choose to go, he is to be left in peace and protected as a man under our guardianship and protection to the end that he may render and receive justice. If he shall be in any need or distress which cannot be remedied according to law, let him and those dependent upon him come in peace and safety before our presence, so that no person may hinder or do him injury, but that he may rest at all times in peace and safety under our guardianship and protection.

And that this may the more surely be given credit, I have signed it with my own hand and sealed it with our ring.

[POPE GREGORY II COMMENDS BONIFACE TO THE THURINGIANS, DECEMBER 724]

Gregory, servant of the servants of God, to all the people of the Thuringians.

The Lord Jesus Christ, Son of God and very God, descended from Heaven, was made man, deigned to suffer and be crucified for us, was buried, rose from the dead on the third day, and ascended into Heaven. To His holy Apostles and disciples He said: "Go forth and teach all peoples, baptizing them in the name of the Father, the Son, and the Holy Spirit (Matt. 28:19)"; and He promised those who believed in Him eternal life.

We, therefore, desiring that you may rejoice with us forever where there is no ending, neither sorrow nor any bitterness, but eternal glory, have sent to you our most holy brother, Bishop Boniface, that he may baptize you and teach you the doctrine of Christ and lead you out of error into the way of safety, that you may win salvation and life eternal. But do you be obedient unto him in all things, honor him as your father, and incline your hearts to his instruction, for we have sent him to you, not for any temporal gain, but for the profit of your souls. Therefore love God and receive baptism in his name, for the Lord our God has prepared for those who love him things which the eye of man hath not seen, and which have never entered into the heart of man. Depart from evil doing, and do what is right. Worship not idols, neither sacrifice offerings of flesh to them, for God does not accept such things, but observe and do as our brother Boniface shall direct, and you and your children shall be in safety forever.

Build also a house where this your father and bishop may live and churches where you may offer up your prayers, that God may forgive your sins and grant you eternal life.

[REPLIES OF POPE GREGORY II TO QUESTIONS OF BONIFACE, NOVEMBER 22, 726]

Gregory, servant of the servants of God, to his most reverend and holy brother and fellow bishop Boniface.

Your messenger, the pious priest Denuald, has brought us the welcome news that you are well and prospering, with the help of God, in the service for which you were sent. He also brought a letter from you showing that the field of the Lord which had been lying fallow, bristling with the thorns of unbelief, has received the plowshare of your instruction, plowing in the seed of the word, and is bringing forth an abundant harvest of true belief.

In this same letter you inserted several paragraphs of inquiries as to the faith and teaching of this Holy and Apostolic Roman Church. And this was well done; for the blessed apostle Peter stands as the fountainhead of the apostolate and the episcopate. And to you who consult us about ecclesiastical matters we show what decision you have to take according to the teaching of apostolic tradition, and we do this not as if by our own personal authority, but by the grace of Him who opens the mouth of the dumb and makes eloquent the tongues of infants.

You ask first within what degrees of relationship marriage may take place. We reply: strictly speaking, in so far as the parties know themselves to be related they ought not to be joined together. But since moderation is better than strictness of discipline, especially toward so uncivilized a people, they may contract marriage after the fourth degree.

As to your question, what a man is to do if his wife is unable, on account of disease, to fulfill her wifely duty: it would be well if he could remain in a state of continence. But, since this is a matter of great difficulty, it is better for him who cannot refrain to take a wife. He may not, however, withdraw his support from the one who was prevented by disease, provided she be not involved in any grievous fault.

In regard to a priest or any cleric accused by the people: unless the evidence of the witnesses to the charge against him is positive, let him take oath before the assembly, calling as witness of his innocence Him to whom all things are plain and open; and so let him keep his proper standing.

In the case of one confirmed by a bishop, a repetition of this rite is prohibited.

In the celebration of the Mass, the form is to be observed which our Lord Jesus Christ used with his disciples. He took the cup and gave it to them, saying: "This cup is the new testament in my blood; this do ye as oft as ye take it." Wherefore it is not fitting that two or three cups should be placed on the altar when the ceremony of the Mass is performed.

As to sacrificial foods: You ask whether, if a believer makes the life-giving sign of the cross above them, it is permitted to eat them or not. A sufficient answer is given in the words of the blessed apostle Paul: "If any man say unto you, This is offered in sacrifice unto idols, eat not for his sake who showed it, and for conscience' sake."[1]

You ask further, if a father or mother shall have placed a young son or daughter in a cloister under the discipline of a rule, whether it is lawful for the child after reaching the years of discretion to leave the cloister and enter into marriage. This we absolutely forbid, since it is an impious thing that the restraints of desire should be relaxed for children offered to God by their parents.

You mention also that some have been baptized by adulterous and unworthy priests without being questioned whether they believe, as it is in the ritual. In such cases you are to follow the ancient custom of the Church. He who has been baptized in the name of the Father, Son, and Holy Spirit may on no account be baptized again; for he has received the gift of His grace not in the name of the one who baptizes, but in the name of the Trinity. Let the word of the Apostle be observed: "One God, one faith, one baptism."[2] We require you to convey spiritual instruction to such persons with especial zeal.

As to young children taken from their parents and not knowing whether they have been baptized or not, reason requires you to baptize them, unless there be someone who can give evidence in the case.

Lepers, if they are believing Christians, may receive the body and blood of the Lord, but they may not take food together with persons in health.

---

[1] 1 Cor. 10:28.

[2] Eph. 4:5.

You ask whether, in the case of a contagious disease or plague in a church or monastery, those who are not yet attacked may escape danger by flight. We declare this to be the height of folly; for no one can escape from the hand of God.

Finally, your letter states that certain priests and bishops are so involved in vices of many sorts that their lives are a blot upon the priesthood and you ask whether it is lawful for you to eat with or to speak with them, supposing them not to be heretics. We answer, that you by apostolic authority are to admonish and persuade them and so bring them back to the purity of church discipline. If they obey, you will save their souls and win reward for yourself. You are not to avoid conversation or eating at the same table with them. It often happens that those who are slow in coming to a perception of the truth under strict discipline may be led into the paths of righteousness by the influence of their table companions and by gentle admonition. You ought also to follow this same rule in dealing with those chieftains who are helpful to you.

This, my dear brother, is all that need be said with the authority of the Apostolic See. For the rest we implore the mercy of God, that He who has sent you into that region in our stead and with apostolic authority and has caused the light of truth to shine into that dark forest by means of your words may mercifully grant the increase, so that you may reap the reward of your labors and we may find remission for our sins.

God keep you in safety, most reverend brother.

Given on the tenth day before the Kalends of December, in the tenth year of our most pious and august Lord Leo, by God crowned emperor, in the tenth year of his consulship and the seventh of the Emperor Constantine his son, in the tenth indiction.[1]

2.12 Creating a Roman Christian identity for England: Bede, *The Ecclesiastical History of the English People* (731). Original in Latin.

A child of the cloister—he entered the monastery of Wearmouth-Jarrow in the north of England at the age of seven—Bede (673–735) was among the best-educated men of his day in the Roman, papal tradition and the expertise in Latin that went with it. Because his monastery was extraordinarily well stocked with books—brought back from the Continent (mainly Rome) by Wearmouth and Jarrow's founder, Benedict Biscop—Bede was able to consult a wide range of sources for his numerous writings. These included biblical commentaries, the lives of saints, liturgical works, sermons, scientific texts (his *Computation of Time* was particularly important for calculating the date of Easter and other movable feasts), and histories, including a *History of the Abbots of Wearmouth and Jarrow* and *The Ecclesiastical History*. Although Christianity came to England in a variety of ways, Bede emphasized the Roman contribution.

1. Why did Bede include letters from Gregory the Great in his *History*?
2. Why was the Council of Whitby held, and what was decided there?

[Source: Bede, *The Ecclesiastical History of the English People*, ed. Judith McClure and Roger Collins (Oxford: Oxford University Press, 1994), pp. 37–41, 55–57, 65, 70, 152–59, 370–75, 397 (notes modified).]

---

[1] The letter is thus dated by the reign of Byzantine emperor Leo III (r.717–741) and his son Constantine, for whom see *The Synod of 754* (above, p. 62).

Book 1

CHAPTER 23

In the year of our Lord 582 Maurice,[1] the fifty-fourth from Augustus, became emperor; he ruled for twenty-one years. In the tenth year of his reign, Gregory,[2] a man eminent in learning and in affairs, was elected pontiff of the apostolic see of Rome; he ruled for thirteen years, six months, and ten days. In the fourteenth year[3] of this emperor and about 150 years after the coming of the Angles to Britain, Gregory, prompted by divine inspiration, sent a servant of God named Augustine[4] and several more God-fearing monks with him to preach the word of God to the English race. In obedience to the pope's commands, they undertook this task and had already gone a little way on their journey when they were paralyzed with terror. They began to contemplate returning home rather than going to a barbarous, fierce, and unbelieving nation whose language they did not even understand. They all agreed that this was the safer course; so forthwith they sent home Augustine whom Gregory had intended to have consecrated as their bishop if they were received by the English. Augustine was to beg St. Gregory humbly for permission to give up so dangerous, wearisome, and uncertain a journey. Gregory, however, sent them an encouraging letter in which he persuaded them to persevere with the task of preaching the Word and trust in the help of God. The letter was in these terms:

Gregory, servant of the servants of God, to the servants of our Lord.

My dearly beloved sons, it would have been better not to have undertaken a noble task than to turn back deliberately from what you have begun: so it is right that you should carry out with all diligence this good work which you have begun with the help of the Lord. Therefore do not let the toilsome journey nor the tongues of evil speakers deter you. But carry out the task you have begun under the guidance of God with all constancy and fervor. Be sure that, however great your task may be, the glory of your eternal reward will be still greater. When Augustine your prior returns, now, by our appointment, your abbot, humbly obey him in all things, knowing that whatever you do under his direction will be in all respects profitable to your souls. May Almighty God protect you by His grace and grant that I may see the fruit of your labors in our heavenly home. Though I cannot labor with you, yet because I should have been glad indeed to do so, I hope to share in the joy of your reward. May God keep you safe, my dearly loved sons.

Given on July 23, in the fourteenth year of the reign of our most religious emperor Maurice Tiberius, and the thirteenth year after his consulship, and the fourteenth indiction.[5] [July 23, 596]

CHAPTER 24

The venerable pontiff at the same time also sent a letter to Etherius of Arles,[6] asking him to receive Augustine kindly on his return to Britain. This is the text:

To his most reverend and holy brother and fellow bishop Etherius, Gregory, servant of the servants of God.

Although religious men stand in need of no recommendation with those bishops who have that love which is pleasing to God, yet because a suitable occasion for writing presents itself, we think fit to send this letter to you our brother, informing you that we have directed thither the bearer of this document, Augustine, the servant of God, of whose zeal we are assured, together with other servants of God devoted to winning souls with the Lord's help. It is essential that your holiness should assist him with episcopal zeal and hasten to provide him with what he needs. And in order that you may be the more

---

[1] Emperor Maurice Tiberius (r.582–602).

[2] Pope Gregory the Great (590–604).

[3] August 595 to August 596.

[4] Augustine—who should not be confused with St. Augustine (d.430), the bishop of Hippo—had been prior (just below the abbot in administrative status) of the monastery that Gregory founded on his own family property on the Caelian Hill in Rome.

[5] "Indiction" was a regular cycle of fifteen years, used initially for tax-assessment purposes, but which remained a conventional way of dating documents in the late Roman Empire.

[6] Etherius was actually bishop of Lyon (r.586–602), not of Arles. Bede adopts the term "archbishop" used in the Anglo-Saxon Church, but the Frankish equivalents were called metropolitan bishops. Similar letters were sent to the bishops of Marseille, Arles, and Tours to secure assistance and safe passage for the mission.

prompt with your help, we have specially enjoined him to tell you of his mission. We are sure that when you know this you will be prepared with all zeal to afford him your help for the Lord's sake as the occasion requires. We also commend to your charity the priest Candidus,[1] a son of both of us, whom we have sent to take charge of a small patrimony of our church. God keep you safe, most reverend brother.

Given on July 23, in the fourteenth year of the reign of our most religious emperor, Maurice Tiberius, and the thirteenth year after his consulship and the fourteenth indiction. [July 23, 596]

CHAPTER 25

So Augustine, strengthened by the encouragement of St. Gregory, in company with the servants of Christ, returned to the work of preaching the word, and came to Britain. At that time Ethelbert, king of Kent [d.616], was a very powerful monarch. The lands over which he ruled stretched as far as the great river Humber, which divides the northern from the southern Angles. Over against the eastern districts of Kent there is a large island called Thanet which, in English reckoning, is 600 hides[2] in extent. It is divided from the mainland by the river Wantsum, which is about three furlongs wide,[3] can be crossed in two places only, and joins the sea at either end. Here Augustine, the servant of the Lord, landed with his companions, who are said to have been nearly forty in number. They had acquired interpreters from the Frankish race according to the command of Pope St. Gregory. Augustine sent to Ethelbert to say that he had come from Rome bearing the best of news, namely the sure and certain promise of eternal joys in heaven and an endless kingdom with the living and true God to those who received it. On hearing this the king ordered them to remain on the island where they had landed and be provided with all things necessary until he had decided what to do about them. Some knowledge about the Christian religion had already reached him because he had a

Christian wife of the Frankish royal family whose name was Bertha.[4] He had received her from her parents on condition that she should be allowed to practice her faith and religion unhindered, with a bishop named Liudhard whom they had provided for her to support her faith.

Some days afterwards the king came to the island and, sitting in the open air, commanded Augustine and his comrades to come there to talk with him. He took care that they should not meet in any building, for he held the traditional superstition that, if they practiced any magic art, they might deceive him and get the better of him as soon as he entered. But they came endowed with divine not devilish power and bearing as their standard a silver cross and the image of our Lord and Savior painted on a panel.[5] They chanted litanies and uttered prayers to the Lord for their own eternal salvation and the salvation of those for whom and to whom they had come. At the king's command they sat down and preached the word of life to himself and all his officials and companions there present. Then he said to them: "The words and the promises you bring are fair enough, but because they are new to us and doubtful, I cannot consent to accept them and forsake those beliefs which I and the whole people of the Angles have held so long. But as you have come on a long pilgrimage and are anxious, I perceive, to share with us things which you believe to be true and good, we do not wish to do you harm; on the contrary, we will receive you hospitably and provide what is necessary for your support; nor do we forbid you to win all you can to your faith and religion by your preaching." So he gave them a dwelling in the city of Canterbury, which was the chief city of all his dominions; and, in accordance with his promise, he granted them provisions and did not refuse them freedom to preach. It is related that as they approached the city in accordance with their custom carrying the holy cross and the image of our great King and Lord, Jesus Christ, they sang this litany in unison: "We beseech Thee, O Lord, in Thy great mercy, that Thy wrath and anger may be turned away from this city and from Thy holy house, for we have sinned. Alleluia."

---

[1] Candidus was being sent as Rector of the papal Patrimony, to take charge of the running of the estates owned by the Roman Church in southern Gaul.

[2] The "hide" was theoretically the amount of land that supported one family, its extent varying from place to place.

[3] A furlong is one-eighth of a mile.

[4] Bertha was the daughter of the Merovingian king Charibert I (r.561–567), whose short-lived realm had been centered on Paris. As Bede points out, she was a Catholic Christian who brought her own bishop, Liudhard, with her.

[5] How might Bede's emphasis on this image be an indirect critique of Byzantine iconoclasm? Bede was writing at the very beginning of that movement (see above, p. 62).

CHAPTER 26

As soon as they had entered the dwelling-place allotted to them, they began to imitate the way of life of the apostles and of the primitive church. They were constantly engaged in prayers, in vigils and fasts; they preached the word of life to as many as they could; they despised all worldly things as foreign to them; they accepted only the necessaries of life from those whom they taught; in all things they practiced what they preached and kept themselves prepared to endure adversities, even to the point of dying for the truths they proclaimed. To put it briefly, some, marveling at their simple and innocent way of life and the sweetness of their heavenly doctrine, believed and were baptized. There was nearby, on the east of the city, a church built in ancient times in honor of St. Martin,[1] while the Romans were still in Britain, in which the queen who, as has been said, was a Christian, used to pray. In this church they first began to meet to chant the psalms, to pray, to say mass, to preach, and to baptize, until, when the king had been converted to the faith, they received greater liberty to preach everywhere and to build or restore churches.

At last the king, as well as others, believed and was baptized, being attracted by the pure life of the saints and by their most precious promises, whose truth they confirmed by performing many miracles. Every day more and more began to flock to hear the Word, to forsake their heathen worship, and, through faith, to join the unity of Christ's holy Church. It is related that the king, although he rejoiced at their conversion and their faith, compelled no one to accept Christianity; though nonetheless he showed greater affection for believers since they were his fellow citizens in the kingdom of heaven. But he had learned from his teachers and guides in the way of salvation that the service of Christ was voluntary and ought not to be compulsory. It was not long before he granted his teachers a place to settle in, suitable to their rank, in Canterbury, his chief city, and gave them possessions of various kinds for their needs....

CHAPTER 29

Since Bishop Augustine had advised him that the harvest was great and the workers were few, Pope Gregory sent more colleagues and ministers of the word together with his messengers. First and foremost among these were Mellitus, Justus, Paulinus, and Rufinianus; and he sent with them all such things as were generally necessary for the worship and ministry of the Church, such as sacred vessels, altar cloths and church ornaments, vestments for priests and clerks, relics of the holy apostles and martyrs, and very many manuscripts....

CHAPTER 30

When these messengers had departed, St. Gregory sent after them a letter which is worth recording, in which he plainly showed his eager interest in the salvation of our race. This is what he wrote:

To my most beloved son, Abbot Mellitus, Gregory, servant of the servants of God.

Since the departure of our companions and yourself I have felt much anxiety because we have not happened to hear how your journey has prospered. However, when Almighty God has brought you to our most reverend brother Bishop Augustine, tell him what I have decided after long deliberation about the English people, namely that the idol temples of that race should by no means be destroyed, but only the idols in them. Take holy water and sprinkle it in these shrines, build altars and place relics in them. For if the shrines are well built, it is essential that they should be changed from the worship of devils to the service of the true God. When the people see that their shrines are not destroyed they will be able to banish error from their hearts and be more ready to come to the places they are familiar with, but now recognizing and worshiping the true God. And because they are in the habit of slaughtering many cattle as sacrifices to devils, some solemnity ought to be given them in exchange for this. So on the day of the dedication or the festivals of the holy martyrs, whose relics are deposited there, let them make themselves huts from the branches of trees around the churches which have been converted out of shrines, and let them celebrate the solemnity with religious feasts. Do not let them sacrifice animals to the devil, but let them slaughter animals for their own food to the praise of God, and let them give thanks to the Giver of all things for His bountiful provision. Thus while some outward rejoicings are preserved, they will be able more easily to share in inward rejoicings. It is doubtless impossible to

---

[1] The western section of the chancel (the space around the altar) of the extant church of St. Martin in Canterbury is thought to have formed part of the church of Queen Bertha. This reference, like that to Liudhard, hints at the survival of Christian worship in post-Roman lowland Britain prior to the arrival of Augustine.

cut out everything at once from their stubborn minds, just as the man who is attempting to climb to the highest place, rises by steps and degrees and not by leaps. Thus the Lord made Himself known to the Israelites in Egypt, yet he preserved in his own worship the forms of sacrifice which they were accustomed to offer to the devil and commanded them to kill animals when sacrificing to him. So with changed hearts they were to put away one part of the sacrifice and retain the other; even though they were the same animals as they were in the habit of offering, yet since the people were offering them to the true God and not to idols, they were not the same sacrifices. These things then, dearly beloved, you must say to our brother so that in his present position he may carefully consider how he should order all things. May God keep you in safety, most beloved son.

Given July 18 in the nineteenth year of the reign of our most religious emperor Maurice Tiberius, and in the eighteenth year after his consulship and in the fourth indiction. [July 18, 601]

Book 2

CHAPTER 1

About this time, in the year of our Lord 605,[1] Pope St. Gregory, who had reigned in great glory over the apostolic Roman see for thirteen years, six months, and ten days, died and was taken up to reign forever in the kingdom of heaven. Well indeed may we, the English nation converted by his efforts from the power of Satan to the faith of Christ, give a somewhat full account of him in this *History*. We can and should by rights call him our apostle, for though he held the most important see in the whole world and was head of Churches which had long been converted to the true faith, yet he made our nation, till then enslaved to idols, into a Church of Christ, so that we may use the apostle's words about him, "If he is not an apostle to others yet at least he is to us, for we are the seal of his apostleship in the Lord (see 1 Cor. 9:2)." [At this point, Bede relates Gregory's life and virtues.]

We must not fail to relate the story about St. Gregory which has come down to us as a tradition of our forefathers. It explains the reason why he showed such earnest solicitude for the salvation of our race. It is said that one day, soon after some merchants had arrived in Rome, a quantity of merchandise was exposed for sale in the market place. Crowds came to buy and Gregory too among them. As well as other merchandise, he saw some boys put up for sale, with fair complexions, handsome faces, and lovely hair. On seeing them he asked, so it is said, from what region or land they had been brought. He was told that they came from the island of Britain, whose inhabitants were like that in appearance. He asked again whether those islanders were Christians or still entangled in the errors of heathenism. He was told that they were heathen. Then with a deep-drawn sigh he said, "Alas that the author of darkness should have men so bright of face in his grip, and that minds devoid of inward grace should bear so graceful an outward form." Again he asked for the name of the race. He was told that they were called *Angli*. "Good," he said, "they have the face of angels [*angeli* in Latin], and such men should be fellow heirs of the angels in heaven." "What is the name," he asked, "of the kingdom from which they have been brought?" He was told that the men of the kingdom were called *Deiri*. "*Deiri*," he replied. "*De ira!* [=From anger!] good! snatched from the wrath of Christ and called to his mercy. And what is the name of the king of the land?" He was told that it was Ælle;[2] and playing on the name, he said, "Alleluia! the praise of God the Creator must be sung in those parts." So he went to the bishop of Rome and of the apostolic see, for he himself had not yet been made pope, and asked him to send some ministers of the word to the race of the Angles in Britain to convert them to Christ. He added that he himself was prepared to carry out the task with the help of the Lord provided that the pope was willing. But he was unable to perform this mission, because although the pope was willing to grant his request, the citizens of Rome could not permit him to go so far away from the city. Soon after he had become pope, he fulfilled the task which he had long desired. It is true that he sent other preachers, but he himself helped their preaching to bear fruit by his encouragement and prayers. I have thought it proper to insert this story into this Church *History*, based as it is on the tradition that we have received from our ancestors....

---

[1] Gregory died on March 12, 604; otherwise Bede is right about the length of his pontificate. But Bede's facts and dates are not always accurate.

[2] Ælle was king of the Deirans (in England) 559–588.

Book 3

CHAPTER 25

Meanwhile, after Bishop Aidan's death,[1] Finan succeeded him as bishop,[2] having been consecrated and sent over by the Irish. He constructed a church on the island of Lindisfarne suitable for an episcopal see, building it after the Irish method, not of stone but of hewn oak, thatching it with reeds; later on the most reverend Archbishop Theodore[3] consecrated it in honor of the blessed apostle Peter. It was Eadberht,[4] who was bishop of Lindisfarne, who removed the reed thatch and had the whole of it, both roof and walls, covered with sheets of lead.

In those days there arose a great and active controversy about the keeping of Easter. Those who had come from Kent or Gaul declared that the Irish observance of Easter Sunday was contrary to the custom of the universal church. One most violent defender of the true Easter was Ronan[5] who, though Irish by race, had learned the true rules of the church in Gaul or Italy. In disputing with Finan he put many right or at least encouraged them to make a more strict inquiry into the truth; but he could by no means put Finan right. On the contrary, as he was a man of fierce temper, Ronan made him the more bitter by his reproofs and turned him into an open adversary of the truth. James, once the deacon of the venerable Archbishop Paulinus, as we have already said,[6] kept the true and catholic Easter with all those whom he could instruct in the better way. Queen Eanfleda[7] and her people also observed it as she had seen it done in Kent, having with her a Kentish priest named Romanus who followed the Catholic observance. Hence it is said that in these days it sometimes happened that Easter was celebrated twice in the same year, so that the king had finished the fast and was keeping Easter Sunday, while the queen and her

people were still in Lent and observing Palm Sunday. This difference in the observance of Easter was patiently tolerated by all while Aidan was alive, because they had clearly understood that although he could not keep Easter otherwise than according to the manner of those who had sent him, he nevertheless labored diligently to practice the works of faith, piety, and love, which is the mark of all the saints. He was therefore deservedly loved by all, including those who had other views about Easter. Not only was he respected by the ordinary people but also by bishops, such as Honorius of Kent and Felix of East Anglia.

When Finan, Aidan's successor, was dead and Colman,[8] who had also been sent from Ireland, had become bishop, a still more serious controversy arose concerning the observance of Easter as well as about other matters of ecclesiastical discipline. This dispute naturally troubled the minds and hearts of many people who feared that, though they had received the name of Christian, they might have done so in vain. All this came to the ears of the rulers [of Northumbria] themselves, Oswiu [d.670] and his son Alhfrith. Oswiu, who had been educated and baptized by the Irish and was well versed in their language, considered that nothing was better than what they had taught. But Alhfrith had as his instructor in the Christian faith one Wilfrid, a most learned man who had once been to Rome to study church doctrine and had spent much time at Lyon with Dalfinus,[9] archbishop of Gaul, having received there his ecclesiastical tonsure in the form of a crown. So Alhfrith rightly preferred his teaching to all the traditions of the Irish and had therefore given him a monastery of forty hides in the place called Ripon. He had presented the site, a short time before, to those who followed Irish ways, but because, when given the choice, they preferred to renounce the site rather than

---

[1] Aidan (d.651) was the bishop of Lindisfarne (in northern England). He had come from Ireland to teach the Christian faith at the request of Oswald, king of Northumbria (d.642).

[2] Finan (d.661).

[3] Theodore was archbishop of Canterbury 668–690.

[4] Eadberht was bishop of Lindisfarne 688–698.

[5] Nothing else is known of Ronan. The Church in the south of Ireland had by this time largely adopted Continental practices with respect to the dating of Easter.

[6] Paulinus (d.644) was bishop of York and Rochester.

[7] Eanfleda (d.c.704) was the daughter of Edwin, king of Deira, and Ethelburg Tata, daughter of Ethelbert and Bertha of Kent. She married Oswiu, king of Bernicia (r.642–670).

[8] Colman was bishop of Lindisfarne 661–664.

[9] Bede confused Dalfinus, who was the prefect (secular ruler) of Lyon, with his brother Aunemundus, the bishop of Lyon (c.650–658). Wilfrid (d.709), bishop of York and Hexham, was the chief proponent of the Roman date for Easter.

change their customs, he gave it to one who was worthy of the place both by his doctrine and his way of life. At that time there had come to the kingdom of Northumbria Agilbert, bishop of the West Saxons, whom we have mentioned before, a friend of Alhfrith and of Abbot Wilfrid; he stayed some time with them and, at the request of Alhfrith, he ordained Wilfrid priest in his own monastery. Agilbert had with him a priest called Agatho.

When this question of Easter and of the tonsure and other ecclesiastical matters was raised, it was decided to hold a council [in 664] to settle the dispute at a monastery called *Streanæshealh* (Whitby), a name which means the bay of the lighthouse; at this time Hild, a woman devoted to God, was abbess.[1] There came to the council the two kings, both father and son, Bishop Colman with his Irish clergy, and Agilbert with the priests Agatho and Wilfrid. James and Romanus were on their side while the Abbess Hild and her followers were on the side of the Irish; among these also was the venerable Bishop Cedd, who, as has been mentioned, had been consecrated long before by the Irish and who acted as a most careful interpreter for both parties at the council.

First King Oswiu began by declaring that it was fitting that those who served one God should observe one rule of life and not differ in the celebration of the heavenly sacraments, seeing that they all hoped for one kingdom in heaven; they ought therefore to inquire as to which was the truer tradition and then all follow it together. He then ordered his bishop Colman to say first what were the customs which he followed and whence they originated. Colman thereupon said, "The method of keeping Easter which I observe, I received from my superiors who sent me here as bishop; it was in this way that all our fathers, men beloved of God, are known to have celebrated it. Nor should this method seem contemptible and blameworthy seeing that the blessed evangelist John, the disciple whom the Lord specially loved, is said to have celebrated it thus, together with all the churches over which he presided." When he had said all this and more to the same effect, the king ordered Agilbert to expound the method he observed, its origin, and the authority he had for following it. Agilbert answered, "I request that my disciple, the priest Wilfrid, may speak on my behalf, for we are both in agreement with the other followers of our church tradition who are here present; and he can explain our views in the English tongue better and more clearly than I can through an interpreter." Then Wilfrid,

receiving instructions from the king to speak, began thus: "The Easter we keep is the same as we have seen universally celebrated in Rome, where the apostles St. Peter and St. Paul lived, taught, suffered, and were buried. We also found it in use everywhere in Italy and Gaul when we traveled through those countries for the purpose of study and prayer. We learned that it was observed at one and the same time in Africa, Asia, Egypt, Greece, and throughout the whole world, wherever the Church of Christ is scattered, amid various nations and languages. The only exceptions are these men and their accomplices in obstinacy, I mean the Picts and the Britons, who in these, the two remotest islands of the Ocean, and only in some parts of them, foolishly attempt to fight against the whole world."

Colman answered, "I wonder that you are willing to call our efforts foolish, seeing that we follow the example of that apostle who was reckoned worthy to recline on the breast of the Lord; for all the world acknowledges his great wisdom." Wilfrid replied, "Far be it from me to charge John with foolishness: he literally observed the decrees of the Mosaic law when the Church was still Jewish in many respects, at a time when the apostles were unable to bring to a sudden end the entire observance of that law which God ordained in the same way as, for instance, they made it compulsory on all new converts to abandon their idols which are of devilish origin. They feared, of course, that they might make a stumbling-block for the Jewish proselytes dispersed among the Gentiles. This was the reason why Paul circumcised Timothy, why he offered sacrifices in the temple, and why he shaved his head at Corinth in company with Aquila and Priscilla; all this was of no use except to avoid scandalizing the Jews. Hence James said to Paul, 'Thou seest, brother, how many thousands there are among the Jews of them which have believed; and they are all zealous for the law (Acts 21:20).' But in these days when the light of the Gospel is spreading throughout the world, it is not necessary, it is not even lawful for believers to be circumcised or to offer God sacrifices of flesh and blood. So John, in accordance with the custom of the law, began the celebration of Easter Day in the evening of the fourteenth day of the first month, regardless of whether it fell on the sabbath or any other day. But when Peter preached at Rome, remembering that the Lord rose from the dead and brought to the world the hope of the resurrection on the first day of the week, he realized that Easter ought to be kept as follows: he

---

[1] Under Hild, Whitby was a double monastery with both men and women (in separate quarters). Hild presided over both.

always waited for the rising of the moon on the evening of the fourteenth day of the first month in accordance with the custom and precepts of the law, just as John did, but when it had risen, if the Lord's Day, which was then called the first day of the week, followed in the morning, he proceeded to celebrate Easter as we are accustomed to do at the present time. But if the Lord's Day was due, not on the morning following the fourteenth day of the moon but on the sixteenth or seventeenth or any other day until the twenty-first, he waited for it, and began the holy Easter ceremonies the night before, that is, on the Saturday evening; so it came about that Easter Sunday was kept only between the fifteenth day of the moon and the twenty-first. So this evangelical and apostolic tradition does not abolish the law but rather fulfils it, by ordering the observance of Easter from the evening of the fourteenth day of the moon in the first month up to the twenty-first of the moon in the same month. All the successors of St. John in Asia since his death and also the whole church throughout the world have followed this observance. That this is the true Easter and that this alone must be celebrated by the faithful was not newly decreed but confirmed afresh by the Council of Nicaea as the history of the Church informs us.[1] So it is plain, Colman, that you neither follow the example of John, as you think, nor of Peter, whose tradition you knowingly contradict; and so, in your observance of Easter, you neither follow the law nor the Gospel. For John who kept Easter according to the decrees of the Mosaic law, took no heed of the Sunday; you do not do this, for you celebrate Easter only on a Sunday. Peter celebrated Easter Sunday between the fifteenth and the twenty-first day of the moon; you, on the other hand, celebrate Easter Sunday between the fourteenth and the twentieth day of the moon. Thus you very often begin Easter on the evening of the thirteenth day of the moon, which is never mentioned in the law. This was not the day—it was the fourteenth, in which the Lord, the author and giver of the Gospel, ate the old passover in the evening and instituted the sacraments of the new testament to be celebrated by the church in remembrance of his passion. Besides, in your celebration of Easter you utterly exclude the twenty-first day, which the law of Moses specially ordered to be observed. So,

as I have said, in your celebration of the greatest of the festivals you agree neither with John nor Peter, neither with the law nor the Gospel."

Colman replied, "Did Anatolius, a man who was holy and highly spoken of in the history of the Church to which you appeal, judge contrary to the law and the Gospel when he wrote that Easter should be celebrated between the fourteenth and the twentieth day of the moon? Or must we believe that our most reverend father Columba and his successors,[2] men beloved of God, who celebrated Easter in the same way, judged and acted contrary to the holy scriptures, seeing that there were many of them to whose holiness the heavenly signs and the miracles they performed bore witness? And as I have no doubt that they were saints, I shall never cease to follow their way of life, their customs, and their teaching."

Wilfrid replied, "It is true that Anatolius was a most holy and learned man, worthy of all praise; but what have you to do with him since you do not observe his precepts? He followed a correct rule in celebrating Easter, basing it on a cycle of nineteen years, of which you are either unaware or, if you do know of it, you despise it, even though it is observed by the whole Church of Christ. He assigned the fourteenth day of the moon to Easter Sunday, reckoning after the Egyptian manner that the fifteenth day of the moon began on the evening of the fourteenth. So also he assigned the twentieth day to Easter Sunday, reckoning that after evening it was the twenty-first day. But it appears that you are ignorant of this distinction, in that you sometimes clearly keep Easter Day before full moon, that is on the thirteenth day of the moon. So far as your father Columba and his followers are concerned, whose holiness you claim to imitate and whose rule and precepts (confirmed by heavenly signs) you claim to follow, I might perhaps point out that at the judgment, many will say to the Lord that they prophesied in His name and cast out devils and did many wonderful works, but the Lord will answer that He never knew them. Far be it from me to say this about your fathers, for it is much fairer to believe good rather than evil about unknown people. So I will not deny that those who in their rude simplicity loved God with pious intent, were indeed servants of God and beloved by Him. Nor do I think that this observance

---

[1] This is a reference to the account of the First Council of Nicaea of 325 in Rufinus' translation and in the continuation in Eusebius' *History of the Church.*

[2] Columba (d.597) was an Irish monk who left his homeland to found the monastery of Iona (in Scotland), which he used as a base for missionary work. Though he was highly praised in the Irish world, Wilfrid seems to have known very little about him—or, at least, so Bede implies.

of Easter did much harm to them while no one had come to show them a more perfect rule to follow. In fact I am sure that if anyone knowing the Catholic rule had come to them they would have followed it, as they are known to have followed all the laws of God as soon as they had learned of them. But, once having heard the decrees of the apostolic see or rather of the universal Church, if you refuse to follow them, confirmed as they are by the holy Scriptures, then without doubt you are committing sin. For though your fathers were holy men, do you think that a handful of people in one corner of the remotest of islands is to be preferred to the universal Church of Christ which is spread throughout the world? And even if that Columba of yours—yes, and ours too, if he belonged to Christ—was a holy man of mighty works, is he to be preferred to the most blessed chief of the apostles, to whom the Lord said, 'Thou art Peter and upon this rock I will build my Church and the gates of hell shall not prevail against it, and I will give unto thee the keys of the kingdom of heaven'?"[1]

When Wilfrid had ended, the king said, "Is it true, Colman, that the Lord said these words to Peter?" Colman answered, "It is true, O King." Then the king went on, "Have you anything to show that an equal authority was given to your Columba?" Colman answered, "Nothing." Again the king said, "Do you both agree, without any dispute, that these words were addressed primarily to Peter and that the Lord gave him the keys of the kingdom of heaven?" They both answered, "Yes." Thereupon the king concluded, "Then, I tell you, since he is the doorkeeper I will not contradict him, but I intend to obey his commands in everything to the best of my knowledge and ability. Otherwise, when I come to the gates of the kingdom of heaven, there may be no one to open them, because the one who on your own showing holds the keys has turned his back on me." When the king had spoken, all who were seated there or standing by, both high and low, signified their assent, gave up their imperfect rules, and readily accepted in their place those which they recognized to be better.

---

[1]   Matt. 16:18.

TIMELINE FOR CHAPTER TWO

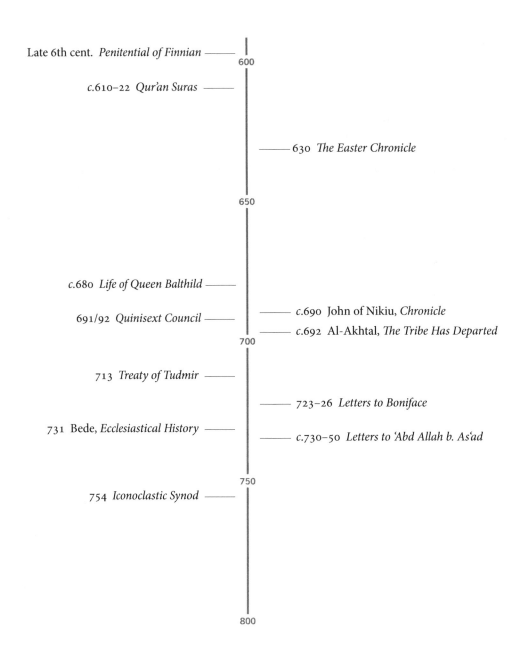

Late 6th cent. *Penitential of Finnian* ——

*c.*610–22 *Qur'an Suras* ——

600

—— 630 *The Easter Chronicle*

650

*c.*680 *Life of Queen Balthild* ——

691/92 *Quinisext Council* ——

—— *c.*690 John of Nikiu, *Chronicle*

—— *c.*692 Al-Akhtal, *The Tribe Has Departed*

700

713 *Treaty of Tudmir* ——

—— 723–26 *Letters to Boniface*

731 Bede, *Ecclesiastical History* ——

—— *c.*730–50 *Letters to 'Abd Allah b. As'ad*

750

754 *Iconoclastic Synod* ——

800

To test your knowledge and gain deeper understanding of this chapter, please go to **www.utphistorymatters.com** for Study Questions.

III

Creating New Identities (c.750–c.900)

THE MATERIAL BASIS OF SOCIETY

3.1 Manors in the West: *Polyptyque of the Church of Saint Mary of Marseille* (814–815). Original in Latin.

In the very year that Charlemagne died (814), an enterprising clerical scribe began to make an inventory of thirteen of the estates (*villae*; sing. *villa*) held by the cathedral of Marseille—Saint Mary, the seat of the bishop—and the monastery of Saint-Vincent of Marseille. Since the properties of Saint-Vincent were administered by the bishop of Marseille, there tended to be some overlap. The resulting register, called a *polyptyque*, provides a partial snapshot of some peasant households and the products and taxes that they owed. Each villa consisted of tenements, or small landholdings. In this polyptyque they are called *colonicae* (sing. *colonica*); in other regions they were called *mansi* (sing. *mansus*).

The entries (which are labeled A, B, and so on) follow a predictable pattern. First the villa is named, and then there are entries for each holding (*colonica*). First comes the holding's location, followed by the name and status of the male tenant (*colonus, mancipium*), the name of his wife and children, the age of the children (if under fourteen or fifteen) or indication that the child is grown (here translated as "adult"). Sometimes the entry indicates which of the children are in school (precious evidence of village schooling in the period) and which are in holy orders, that is, ordained as priests, deacons, and so on. The adult children's husbands and wives are sometimes named, and sometimes we learn whether they were "foreigners"—that is, from outside the village. Dues are mentioned occasionally, but sometimes not.

1. How does this document compare with a modern census?
2. What evidence does it provide for the size and composition of peasant households in early-ninth-century Provence?

[Source: *Carolingian Civilization: A Reader*, ed. Paul Edward Dutton, 2nd ed. (Toronto: University of Toronto Press, 2004), pp. 214–18 (slightly modified).]

B: Description of the Dependents of Saint Mary of Marseille from the Villa Domado of that Third Part, Made in the Time of the lord bishop Waldus [r.814–818], from the seventh indiction [814]

1. Holding [colonica] at Nemphas. Martinus, colonus. Wife Dominica. Bertemarus, an adult son. Desideria, an adult daughter. It pays the tax: 1 pig, 1 suckling [pig]; 2 fattened hens; 10 chickens; 40 eggs. Savarildis, an adult woman. Olisirga, a daughter 10 years old. Rica, a daughter 9 years old.

2. Holding of a colonus in vineyards. Ingoaldus, a dependent [mancipium]. Wife Unuldis. Martinus, a son; wife Magna. Onoria, a daughter, with a foreign husband. Deda, a daughter. Danobertus, an adult son. Ingolbertus, an adult son. Arubertus, an adult son.

3. Holding at Code: 1 lot without tenant.

4. Holding at Ruinolas: 1 lot without tenant.

5. In total these make 4 holdings.

6. Holding at Ursiniangas: 1 lot without tenant.

F. Description of the Dependents of Saint Mary of Marseille from the Villa of Betorrida,[1] Made in the Time of the lord bishop Waldus, from the seventh indiction

1. Holding in Cenazello. Dructaldus, tenant (*accola*); with his foreign wife. Dructomus, a son. Dutberta, an adult daughter. Drueterigus, a son at school. Sinderaldus, a son at school. Joannis. For pasturage: 1 denarius.[2]

2. Holding in Albiosco. Teodorus, colonus. Wife Eugenia. Marius, a deacon. Teobaldus, an adult son. Teodericus, a cleric. Ing... dus, a son 7 years old. Teodesia, a daughter 7 years old. For pasturage: 1 denarius.

3. Therein a holding: 1 lot without tenant. 2 denarii.[3]

4. Holding in Asaler. Candidus, colonus. Wife Dominica. Celsus, a son: information required. Mariberta, an adult daughter. Regitrudis, an adult daughter. Gennarius, a son, shepherd. Saviniana, a daughter: information required. It pays in tax: 1 pig, 1 sucking [pig]; 2 fattened hens; 10 chickens; 40 eggs; for pasturage: 1 castrated ram; in tribute: 1 denarius.

5. Holding without tenant in Nonticlo, which Bertarius, priest, holds in benefice. It pays tax and tribute similarly: [plus] a castrated ram.

6. Holding in the same place: 1 lot without tenant. Paulus and Valeriana, with their infants: information required. It pays tax and tribute similarly; for pasturage: 1 castrated ram.

7. Holding in Albiosco: information required.

8. Holding in Curia. Calumniosus, colonus, with a foreign wife. It pays tax: 1 denarius and similarly in tribute. Saumo, with his infants: information required.

9. Holding in the same place. Colonus Martinus. Wife Primovera. Felicis, an adult son. Deidonus, an adult son. Leobertga, an adult daughter. Martina, a daughter 6 years old. An infant at the breast. It pays tax and tribute similarly; for pasturage: 1 denarius.

10. Holding [in] Cusanulas, which Nectardus holds in benefice. It pays tax and tribute similarly.

11. Holding in Carmillo Sancto Promacio, held by the priest of the local church. It pays for pasturage: 1 denarius.

12. Holding in Cumbis: 1 lot without tenant, which Dructebertus has. For pasturage: 2 denarii.

13. Holding in Massimana. Donaldus, dependent. Wife Dominica. Domnildis, daughter. Bertarius, an adult son. Bertulfus, an adult son. Bertelaicus, an adult son. Saisa, an adult daughter. It pays for pasturage: 2 denarii.

14. Holding in Asinarius: 1 lot without tenant. For pasturage: 1 castrated ram.

15. Holding in Terciago, which Martinus holds in benefice. For pasturage: 2 denarii.

16. Holdings in Cenazellis: 2 lots without tenants. For pasturage: 1 castrated ram.

17. Holding in Tullo: 1 lot without tenant. For pasturage: 1 castrated ram. Vuarmetrudis, with her infants: information required.

18. Holding in Galiana. Cannidus, colonus. Wife Inguildis. An infant at the breast. Domecianus, a cleric. Laurada, a daughter 8 years old. It pays tax and tribute similarly. For pasturage: 2 denarii.

---

[1] Today Bezaudun, near Grasse.

[2] A denarius (pl. denarii) was a silver penny.

[3] Presumably this means that it pays two denarii when occupied by a tenant.

19. Holding in Cleo. Aquilo, an equitarius [a serf performing messenger duty on horseback]. Wife Vumiberga. Candidus, a son 6 years old. An infant at the breast. For pasturage: 1 denarius.
20. Holding in Gencianicus. Ursius, cleric. The dependent Lubus, son, with foreign wife, who ought to manage that holding.... Gencuonca, an adult daughter. Teodo, an adult son.
21. Holding in Nidis: 1 lot without tenant. Bernarius, cotidianus [owing daily service to the lord]. Wife Dominica. Magnildis, daughter: information required. Dominico, son. Bernardus, son. Teodranus, son: information required. In tribute: 1 denarius. Montigla, a female [serf], with foreign husband. Cenazello, son: information required.
22. Holding in Vencione. Ildebertus, a dependent. Wife Luborfolia. It pays tax: 2 denarii.
23. Holding in Cumbis: 1 lot without tenant. It pays for pasturage: 2 denarii.
24. Holding in Tasseriolas: 1 lot without tenant. For pasturage: 1 denarius.
25. Holding in Massimiana Sancto Promacio: belonging to the office of the local priest. Donobertus, Babilda: information required.
26. Holding in Camarjas, which Bertaldus, priest, holds.
27. We have a holding in Sugnone, a third part of that small village, and there are 10 holdings [there].
28. Holding in Camarja: 1 lot without tenant.
29. We have in Salo a third part of that small village, and there are three holdings without tenants.
30. Holding in Puncianicus: 1 lot without tenant.
31. Holding in Campellis: 1 lot without tenant.
32. Holding in Rosolanis: 1 lot without tenant.
33. Holding in Speluca: 1 lot without tenant.
34. Vualdebertus, Guirbertus, Ragnebertus: information required.
35. In total that makes 49 holdings.

3.2 The Byzantine countryside: Niketas, *The Life of Saint Philaretos* (821/822). Original in Greek.

Philaretos, a wealthy eighth-century Byzantine landowner, lost most of what he had and gave away the rest. His *Life* was composed by his grandson Niketas. It has many elements in common with Byzantine folktales, while Niketas himself made clear that it was modeled on the Bible's *Book of Job*. Just as the devil made a bargain with God to test the good man Job, so he did with Philaretos. Unlike most hagiographies, the *Life of Saint Philaretos* does not talk about the childhood of the saint nor his ascetic devotions (compare it with the *Life of St. Antony*, above, p. 30, which spends much time on both). Philaretos was a family man, and his eventual material success came with the marriage of Emperor Constantine VI (r.780–797) to Philaretos's granddaughter Maria, in a variant of the Cinderella story. In the course of his account, Niketas reveals much about the rural life of the eighth- and ninth-century Byzantine Empire.

1. What does the *Life* suggest were the resources held by a great Byzantine landowner?
2. What does the *Life* reveal about family life in rural Byzantium?

[Source: Lennart Rydén, ed. and trans., *The Life of St. Philaretos the Merciful Written by His Grandson Niketas* (Uppsala, 2002), pp. 61–89 (Greek omitted and notes modified).]

The Life and Conduct of Our Father Philaretos the Merciful Now among the Saints

1. PHILARETOS' WEALTH, FAMILY AND WAY OF LIFE

In the land of the Paphlagonians there was a man called Philaretos, and this man was the most noble of the men in Pontos and the Galatian region, the son of George, a farmer as the name says.[1] He was very rich and had many livestock: six hundred head of cattle, one hundred yoke of oxen, eight hundred mares in the pastures, eighty saddle horses and mules, twelve thousand sheep and he had forty-eight estates abounding in land, all separate, very beautiful and of great value, for in front of each one of them there was a well gushing forth from a hilltop, capable of watering everything that needed water from it in abundance.[2] And he had many slaves and very great possessions.

He also had a wife called Theosebo, who was likewise of noble birth and feared the Lord. They also had children, one very beautiful young boy called John and two daughters, one called Hypatia and the other Euanthia, they too very beautiful.

The man was very compassionate. When a beggar came to him asking for something, whatever it was, he first gladly offered him what he wanted from his table in satiety and then gave him what he was looking for, sending him away in peace, truly resembling the hospitable Abraham and Jacob.[3] Thus Philaretos did during many years. His compassion became famous in that region as well as in the whole East. And if through an accident somebody lost his ox or horse or some other beast, he went to the blessed man with confidence as if going to his own herd, and each man got what he needed. And whatever one lost from one's herd one could go to him and receive what one wanted. And the more he gave away, the more his possessions multiplied.

2. PHILARETOS TESTED BY THE DEVIL

When the devil saw the man's virtuous conduct, he became jealous of him as he once had been jealous of Job and demanded to have him, that he might make him poor and then see if he would show the same generosity. For, the devil said, the man does nothing marvellous when he gives to the poor out of his abundance.[4] He then obtained authority from God—for it was not possible for him to do this without God's permission, since the Lord makes poor, and makes rich; He brings low, and lifts up. He lifts up the poor from the earth, and raises the needy from the dunghill, according to the utterance of the prophetess Anna,[5] and while the man continued to distribute among the poor his cattle and the other things in which he abounded, God ceased to repay a hundredfold. At last, using his open-handedness, the cattle-lifting of the Ishmaelites[6] and numerous other methods, the devil managed to drive him to utter poverty so that he was left with no more than one yoke of oxen and one horse and one ass and one cow with its calf and one slave and one slave-girl, while all his farms were plundered by the neighbouring mighty and farmers, for, seeing that he was poor and unable to keep them and till his own soil, they divided his land among themselves, some using force, others entreating him, leaving him the property on which he lived and the house that he had inherited from his father.

Then, although he suffered all this, he never grieved nor blasphemed nor became angry, but as when a man who suddenly becomes rich is filled with joy, so this man rejoiced when he became poor, throwing off his wealth like a great burden, especially as he had in mind the utterance of the Lord: "It will be hard for those who have riches to enter the kingdom of God," and again: "It is easier for a camel to go through the eye of a needle than for a rich man to enter the kingdom of God."[7] Dispassionate and innocent wealth manifests itself in that we use it well when at hand and when lacking bear the loss without grieving, as it has been written: wealth is an asset to those who know how to handle it, while poverty is an asset to those who can endure it.[8]

---

[1] Paphlagonia was a region in northern Anatolia, on the coast of the Black Sea.

[2] It was important for the estates to be separate because of the limited water supply. That also explains the importance of the gushing wells.

[3] For Abraham, see Gen. 18:2–8. The reference to Jacob in this context is unclear.

[4] See Job 1:6–12.

[5] 1 Sam. 2:7–8.

[6] The Ishmaelites was another word for Muslims.

[7] The passages are from Mark 10:23 and 10:25.

[8] Perhaps quoting John Chrysostom, *De eleemosyna [On Almsgiving]*.

3. PHILARETOS GIVES AWAY HIS LAST PROPERTY, HIS HOUSE EXCEPTED

a. The yoke of oxen

One day he took his yoke of oxen and his plough and went himself to his field to plough. Ploughing and thanking God that he had been counted worthy of observing God's first penalty clause: "With difficulty and sweat you shall eat your bread,"[1] and the word of the Apostle: "By so toiling one must help the weak,"[2] and again: "If anyone will not work, let him not eat,"[3] respecting God's commands and becoming filled with complete joy, he drove his yoke beyond measure without growing weary himself because of his great joy. But as he saw his yoke being exhausted, he also remembered that it is written: "Blessed is he who has pity for the lives of his cattle,"[4] stopped the yoke and prayed to God, thanking Him for such poverty.

A poor peasant was also ploughing his field when suddenly his ox fell down and died. Not bearing the loss he began to grieve and cry. Under much wailing and lamenting he spoke to God: "Lord, I had nothing but this yoke, yet you deprived me of this too. With what shall I feed my wife and my nine small children? How shall I also be able to pay taxes to the emperor? With what shall I pay my debts? Lord, you know that the ox that died had been bought on credit. and I am at a loss what to do. Therefore, I shall leave home and run away to a far country before my creditors find out and fall upon me like wild beasts. O Lord, would that you had not impoverished Philaretos the Amnian, the friend of the poor, otherwise I would have gone to him with confidence and received another ox and put it under my yoke, forgetting about the death of my ox. But now he has also become dependent on others."

Absorbed in these thoughts he said to himself: "I shall go to him all the same and at least tell him, the onetime supporter of the strangers, of my disaster, so that he can at least share my sorrow and I may get some comfort in my distress (although I know that he cannot give me anything), since he has certainly not forgotten his old compassion. For when people notice that their friends share their distress when they are hit by disaster they usually get some consolation, and when they see those who share their joy when they are successful they feel even more joy and are inspired with more love for them. Therefore the apostle says, 'Rejoice with those who rejoice, weep with those who weep; live in harmony with one another; do not be haughty, but assist the lowly,'[5] that is, to be poor with the poor, to weep with those who weep, to help the weakly, to assist the sick, and not to set one's hope on uncertain wealth." Taking his ox-goad he went away to the once rich man, the real lover of virtue,[6] who had not yet forgotten his virtues.

Then when the peasant had gone away and found the righteous man ploughing he began in tears to tell him of the death of his ox. No sooner had the righteous man heard the beginning of the story of the ox than he at once hastily gave the peasant one from his own yoke, considering it better to make up for his loss with this gift than to weep with him. The peasant hesitated and said, "My lord, one thing I know, that you have no other ox, how then will you till your field?" He said to him. "At home I have another ox, very strong and big, that can support all my family. Only take this animal and hurry home, lest your other ox should be idle and your household should know and your wife start crying even more than you." The peasant took the ox and went his way with joy, praising God and blessing Philaretos.

The honourable and righteous man took his last and only ox and the yoke on his shoulder and returned home rejoicing. When his wife saw only one ox and the yoke on the old man's[7] shoulder, she said to him, "My lord, where is the other ox?" He answered, "I became giddy in the scorching heat of the sun and unharnessed the oxen so that they could graze. I rested a little, and as I fell asleep, the ox broke loose and ran away to the field."

His son went out to the field to look for the ox. As he searched he found the peasant ploughing with Philaretos' ox. Infuriated he began to abuse the peasant, saying, "How did you dare to put another man's ox under your yoke? Truly you have reckoned us among the dead, who from such wealth have been reduced to such poverty!" The peasant answered him, "My good son, your

---

[1] Gen. 3:19.

[2] Acts 20:35.

[3] 2 Thess. 3:10.

[4] See Prov. 12:10.

[5] See Rom. 12:15–16.

[6] The name "Philaretos" means "lover of virtue."

[7] The term does not necessarily mean literally "old" but rather expresses respect.

father gave me the ox." And he also told him of his own misfortune.

When the lad heard that his father had given away the ox he went home in sorrow and told his mother what had happened to it. When she heard this, she threw her kerchief from her head and began to tear her hair. She went to her husband, upbraided him and said, "You who have got a heart of steel. certainly you have no pity on me who was unlucky enough to make your acquaintance, but at least have pity on your children, who do not know how they shall be able to live without a yoke of oxen. But you, idler, grew tired of driving your team of oxen, and wanting to lie down in the shadow, for this reason you gave it to him, for it was certainly not for the sake of God."

But he listened meekly to his wife's reproaches with a smile on his face and made no answer, lest he would be carried away by anger and destroy what he had done out of charity. So admirable was the man that he not only devoted himself to charity but also, being full of discerning and humbleness, mixed his charity with these virtues. As she continued to reproach him in the bitterness of her soul, he answered her and said, "God is very rich and I hear Him saying: 'Look up to the birds in the sky: they neither sow nor reap nor gather into a barn, and yet your heavenly Father feeds them. How much more shall He not nourish us, who are superior to the birds?'[1] And further: 'Do not be anxious about tomorrow, what you shall eat or what you shall drink or what you shall put on, for the gentiles do all these things. but seek the kingdom of heavens, and all these things shall be yours as well.'[2] But I say: 'He promised to give a hundredfold to those who for His sake and for the Gospel distributed their riches, and to make them heirs of eternal life.'[3] Do you become distressed if for one ox we receive one hundred?" This he said not because he longed to receive a hundredfold in this world but to encourage the faintheartedness of his wife.[4] When the woman heard this, she became silent.

Then after five days, as the ox that had belonged to the peasant from the beginning was grazing, it did not escape the dangerous poison called the wolf's herb, but swallowed it and suddenly fell to the ground with a tremble and died. Taking the ox that he had received from the merciful man he went to him and said, "Because of the sin I committed against your children when I took the ox from you and starved them on purpose, for this reason God did not bear with my lack of concern but killed the other ox also."

But the man, being a real friend of God and a lover of virtue, got up at once and fetched his other and only ox, which he gave to the peasant, saying, "Take this as well and go and till your own soil, for I am going on a long journey so that the ox will be idle anyway." This he said, lest the peasant hesitate to accept the ox. But he took also this one and went his way filled with joy and praising God, marvelling at the man's generosity, that he had not forgotten his compassion, although he had lapsed into such poverty.

His children began to wail together with their mother, saying to each other. "It was to our misfortune that we made this man's acquaintance, for even if we had become poor, we could have consoled ourselves with our yoke of oxen and been spared from dying of hunger." But when the holy old man saw the moaning of his children and his wife, he started to assure them under oath, "My children, do not grieve, for I have money hidden in a certain place in such abundance that if you do not die but live one hundred years, it will suffice completely to feed and clothe you. For the cattle that you know we had in plenty, this I have sold in secret, since I foresaw this poverty and the spells of hunger to come, for I had learned from my parents that livestock is nothing worth: it disappears quickly, either because of the spells of winter weather or because of illness or because of robbery. When I heard this I decided that it would be better to sell it piecemeal and hide the payment in an uncorruptible chest. I often went there to make an estimate but could never count it."

When they heard this from their father. especially as he spoke under oath, they cheered up. For in his spirit the old man foresaw God's inexhaustible riches, and believing in the hundredfold reward in this age, he calculated that everything that he had distributed and given to the poor he carried in his bosom together with the eternal life. It was for this reason he had sworn without hesitating.

---

[1] See Matt. 6:26.

[2] See Matt. 6:34, 25, 32, 33.

[3] See Matt. 19:21.

[4] See 1 Thess. 5:14.

b. The horse

After a time there came imperial reinforcement[1] to the local troops for the purpose of a campaign against the Ishmaelites. As the commander of a thousand and the commander of a hundred and the commander of fifty mustered carefully the multitude of soldiers, scrupulously requiring their pairs of horses and their weapons,[2] there was one soldier, Mouselios by name, who was very poor, possessing only one horse and his weapon and nothing else; moreover, as the muster became urgent, his horse got the gripes, trembled and suddenly fell to the ground and died. The soldier got into trouble. As he could not afford another horse and the captain of hundreds refused to let him pass but rather threatened him with punishment and no little suffering, he hastened in despair to the great Philaretos and told him of his plight, asking him to give him his horse just for a moment so that he could get through the muster and escape disaster. The holy old man said to him, "Then after you have got through the muster and returned the horse to me, what do you plan to do?" He answered, "To begin with let me get through this day without being beaten by the captain of thousands; then I shall run away and go to a far country as fast as my legs can carry me, for I do not know what to do." As the venerable man heard this he immediately took out his horse with joy—it was both beautiful to look at and a good worker—and gave it to the soldier, saying, "Brother, take it as a gift and the Lord will be with you in every place and protect you from danger in the war." The soldier took the horse and went to the muster with joy, praising God and blessing the old man. But the truly God-fearing wife of the merciful man, believing with her children that he had plenty of money laid away, was no longer angry but sat silent.

c. The calf and the cow

Then only the heifer with its calf remained and the ass and his beehives, 250 in number. Another poor man came to Philaretos to beg, saying, "Servant of God, give me just one calf that I too may get a new start from your blessed gift, for your gift makes [people] cheerful, and where it entered into a man's house your blessed gift multiplied and made it rich." Philaretos took the calf and gave it to the poor man with joy. The man tied it and went his way, rejoicing. But the mother of the calf came to the door of the cattle shed, crying with a loud voice that even aroused the pity of the old man. When his wife heard the heifer crying her heart softened, since she knew what it means to give birth and to suckle. She said to her husband, "Even if you have surely taken no pity on your children, why don't you at least have pity on the heifer when it laments? How did you dare to separate it from its own offspring? Evidently, you will not even hesitate to separate me from you or from my own children." The man embraced his wife, blessed her and said, "Blessed be you by the Lord, because you rightly said this to me! I am truly merciless and pitiless, since I severed the calf from its mother. For this God will also be grieved with me." And he began to run after the poor man and cry with a loud voice, "Man, return the calf, for its mother is crying at the door of my house!" The poor man turned back with the calf, thinking that the old man no doubt repented so great a gift. When the mother saw her offspring, she ran to meet it, greeted it affectionately and began to give it suck. The God-fearing woman rejoiced greatly. Philaretos said to the poor man, "Brother, since my wife says that I committed a sin when I separated the calf from its mother, take its mother too and go your way, and the Lord shall bless you and make it multiply in your house as He once multiplied my herd." Which also came to pass, for so many cattle did the poor man receive from this blessed gift and so rich did he become, that his herd became even greater than the herd of the old man had been. But the woman blamed herself and said, "This served me right! If I had remained silent, I would not also have deprived my children of the mother of the calf."

d. The donkey

Then only the ass remained and the beehives. There was famine, and as the man did not know how to feed his children, he took his donkey and went into a far country and borrowed six bushels of grain, which he put on the donkey and carried home. At the same time as he unloaded the animal, a poor man appeared asking for one handful of grain. The merciful man said to his wife, who was sifting the grain together with her maid, "Woman, give one bushel of the grain to the poor man." She said to him, "Give this bushel to me, and one each to your children. and one to my daughter-in-law and the same to my maid, and if there is anything left, give it to whom it

---

[1] This refers to the *tagmata*, the mobile troops at the command of the emperor.

[2] The officer was trying to muster irregular troops because of the emergency. Note that the men were expected to provide their own horse and weaponry.

pleases you." He asked, "And what about my share?" She answered, "You are an angel and not a human being and do not need food, for if you had needed it, you would not have carried the grain you borrowed so many miles only to give it to others." And getting simply furious with him she said, "As far as Theosebo is concerned, give him two bushels."[1] The old man said, "Blessed be you by the Lord!" And he measured out two bushels and gave them to the poor man. But she became cross with him, as it were, and said, "If it had been me, I would have given him half of the load." He measured out the third bushel and gave him. As the poor man had no vessel in which to put the grain, he wanted to take off his garment but did not know how, since he had only one tunic, and became worried, being at a loss what to do. When the God-fearing woman noticed the poor man's perplexity and the venerable man's hurry to see him off, she said ironically to her husband, "If it had been me, I would have given him the sack as well." And he did so. But she threw the sieve on the ground, got up and said to her husband, "As far as Theosebo is concerned, give him also the other full sack." And he did so. As the poor man was leaving but was unable to carry all the six bushels he cried to the new Job,[2] "My Lord, let the grain stay here while I carry two bushels at a time to my home, for I cannot carry it all at once." When the God-fearing woman heard this, she sighed and said to her husband, "Give him also the donkey, lest the man makes his back ache." He blessed her, saddled and loaded the donkey, gave it to the poor man and sent him away gladly. And he began to cite the popular country saying, "A poor man should not worry; I myself came forth naked from my mother's womb, and naked shall I return thither."[3]

Then the mother sat hungry with her children, having no flour with which to bake bread to feed them, but since she could not stand seeing them starving, she got up and went to the neighbours, looking for bread to borrow. And having found one loaf she collected wild vegetables and brought it to her children. In the evening they ate and went to bed, but they did not invite the old man. He did not become angry but also went to their neighbour's house and ate and went to bed with gratitude.

4. THE BRIDE SHOW

a. The arrival of the envoys

At this time, when the Christ-loving *augusta* Irene reigned with her son the emperor Constantine, the empress was searching the whole land of the Romans from east to west for a girl to be chosen as consort for her son, the emperor.[4] Having in vain searched the whole west, south and north her men came to the region of Pontos. During their search they came to the merciful man's village, situated in inland Paphlagonia. The name of the village is Amnia, and it belongs to the jurisdiction of the city of Gangra. When the imperial envoys noticed the old man's house, which was old and very large and wholly pleasant, they thought that one of the great men lived in it and commanded their servants and billet-officers to make them lodge there. The elders of the village said to the imperial envoys, "No, Sirs, do not go to that house, for even if it looks great and honourable from the outside, it has nothing inside." But the imperial envoys, who thought that they said this by order of the master of the house, lest they take up their quarters there because he was rich and powerful, angrily told their servants, "Just go ahead, let us go to this house."

b. Philaretos' hospitality

The truly hospitable man and lover of God took his stick and met the imperial envoys outside his house, embraced them with great joy and said, "Welcome, my Lordships, whom God led to their servant's house! What made you do a poor man the honor of coming to his hut?" And he began anxiously to give instructions to his wife, saying, "Woman, make us a good meal, lest we be put to shame before such noble men!" But she answered, "The way you have run your house you have not left a single hen to me; now you can prepare wild plants and entertain the emperors' men with them!" But the man said to her, "Just make fire, put the great dining-room in order, wipe the old ivory table, and God will send food for their meal."[5] And she did so.

And look, the elders of the village came to the compassionate old man through the side door bringing him

---

[1] Theosebo is the name of Philaretos' wife. So, in effect she is saying, "As far as I am concerned, give him two bushels."

[2] The "new Job" is, of course, Philaretos.

[3] See Job 1:21, but apparently it was also a common saying.

[4] Irene was regent for her son Constantine VI (r.780–797) between 780 and 790 and ruled as emperor in her own name 797–802. The wedding between Constantine VI and Philaretos's granddaughter Maria took place in 788.

[5] It was unusual for Byzantine peasant families to have an ivory table; by mentioning it here, Niketas emphasizes how very rich the saint had been.

rams and lambs and hens and pigeons and choice wine and, in short, all that was needed. And from all this his wife prepared the most delicious dishes, as she had used to do earlier when they were rich. When the table had been laid in the great dining-room the imperial envoys entered, and when they saw that the dining-room was very beautiful and also that the table was of ivory, old, gilded all over, of round form, and so large that it could seat thirty-six men, and when they further saw that the food put on it was like that of a king and that the man was venerable and very handsome—for he was truly not only the very image of Abraham in hospitality but also like him in appearance—they were very pleased with him. When they had sat down at the table, the old man's son, John by name, entered. He was very handsome, for in his stature he was like Saul, and he had the hair of Abessalom and the beauty of Joseph.[1] His other offspring also came in, the sons of his sons, seven in number, all adorned with beauty. When the imperial envoys saw them, they were delighted by their beauty. They said to the merciful old man, "Venerable Father, have you got a wife?" He answered, "Yes, gentlemen, I have, and these young boys are my children and grandchildren." They said to him, "May your wife come here too and give us her blessing!" He called his wife, and she came out to the men. She was also handsome and so beautiful in appearance that her equal was not to be found in the whole region of Pontos. Seeing that she, too, was shining all around with such beauty, although she was in her old age, the imperial envoys said to them, "Do you have daughters?" The old man answered, "I have two daughters, mothers of the boys whom you see." The imperial envoys said, "Surely these boys also have sisters?" The old man answered, "My elder daughter has three daughters." The emperors's men said, "May the girls come out, that we may have a look at them according to the divine command of our great emperors, crowned by God, for they commanded us, their unworthy servants, that no girl in the whole land of the Romans should escape being seen by us." The old man said to the imperial envoys, "Gentlemen, let us eat and drink of what God has given us and be merry! And then, being tired after a long journey, go to sleep in tranquillity and let God's will be done tomorrow!" And it was so.

c. Maria qualifies for the competition. Departure for Constantinople

When they got up in the morning they asked for the girls again with great zest. But the old man said to them, "Gentlemen, even if we are poor, our daughters never left their chamber.[2] But if you like, my Lordships, go into their chamber and look at them!" The men got up and eagerly went into the chamber, and the old man's daughters met them together with their daughters. And when they saw the mothers and the daughters modestly dressed but radiating beauty more ravishing than the appearance of any other woman, they were amazed, and in their delight they were unable to distinguish the mothers from the daughters because of the equal beauty of their appearance and said to the old man, "Which are your daughters and which are your granddaughters?" He separated them, and at once they measured the size of the first with the imperial measure and found that it corresponded to what they were looking for. Comparing with the model portrait[3] they found that this also corresponded, and likewise measuring her foot by the shoe[4] they found that it fitted. And with great joy they took them with their mother and the venerable man and their whole household and left for Byzantium with joy, altogether thirty persons in number.

[Philaretos's granddaughter Maria is brought to Constantinople and is chosen by the emperor and his mother to be the imperial bride. Her whole family is honored and showered with gifts: jewels, lands, and houses. Philaretos persists in his generosity. Before he dies, he blesses his children and grandchildren, especially his grandson Niketas, the author of the *Life*. Niketas has a vision in which he sees Philaretos sitting on a golden throne in heaven, transformed into Abraham himself, the model of faith and trust in God.]

---

[1] For Saul, see 1 Sam. 9:2, for Abessalom (or Absalom), see 2 Sam. 4:26, and for Joseph, see Gen 39:6.

[2] Wealthy households had areas reserved to women, the *gynaikonitis*. Though poor, Philaretos claims to have clung to this practice.

[3] The imperial officials carried a laurel-wreathed portrait of the ideal empress.

[4] Unlike Cinderella's glass slipper, this was probably an imperial purple shoe.

3.3 The sale of a slave in Italy: *A Contract of Sale* (725). Original in Latin.

This is an absolutely ordinary record of a sale, much like many others drawn up at the same time in the Lombard kingdom of Italy for land and animals. In this case, however, the item sold was a boy.

1. To what degree did the female purchaser in this transaction have freedom to do business?
2. What does the document mean when it says that the seller will protect Satrelano "on behalf of the buyer"?

[Source: *Medieval Trade in the Mediterranean World*, trans. and ed. Robert S. Lopez and Irving W. Raymond (New York: Columbia University Press, 2001), pp. 45–46 (notes modified).]

Milan, June 6, 725

In the thirteenth year of the reign of our lord, most excellent man, King Liutprand,[1] on the eighth day before the Ides of June, eighth indiction; good fortune. I, Faustino, notary by royal authority, wrote this document of sale, invited by Ermedruda, honorable woman, daughter of Lorenzo, acting jointly with consent and will of that parent of hers, and being the seller. And she acknowledges that she has received, as indeed she at the present time is receiving from Totone, most distinguished man, 12 new gold solidi [coins] as the full price for a boy of the Gallic people named Satrelano, or by whatever other name the boy may be called. And she declared that it[2] had come to her from her father's patrimony. And she, acting jointly with her aforesaid father, promises from this day to protect that boy against all men on behalf of the buyer. And if the boy is injured or taken away and they [Ermedruda and Lorenzo] are in any way unable to protect it against all men, they shall return the solidi in the double to the buyer, [including all] improvements in the object.[3] Done in Milan, in the day, reign, and in the eighth indiction mentioned above.

The sign[4] of the hand of Ermedruda, honorable woman, seller, who declared that she sold the aforesaid Frankish boy of her own good will with the consent of her parent; and she asked this sale to be made.

The sign of the hand of Lorenzo, honorable man, her father, consenting to this sale.

The sign of the hand of Theoperto, honorable man, maker of cuirasses, son of the late Giovannace, relative of the same seller, in whose presence she proclaimed that she was under no constraint, giving consent.

The sign of the hand of Ratchis, honorable man, Frank, witness.

Antonino, devout man, invited by Ermedruda, honorable woman, and by her father giving his consent, undersigned as a witness to this record of sale.

I, the above Faustino, writer of this [record] of sale, after delivery gave [this record].

---

[1] Liutprand, king of the Lombards 712–744, ruled over much of northern Italy.

[2] A slave in Lombard as well as in Roman law was not considered as a person but as a thing (*res*); hence the document uses the neuter pronoun when referring to the boy.

[3] Again, the boy is considered as a thing. He may learn some skill and hence become more valuable.

[4] Ermedruda could not write her name, but she indicated her assent to the terms of the contract with a cross or other sign, recorded by the notary as her "sign." He himself supplied her name.

A MULTIPLICITY OF HEROES

3.4 Charlemagne as Roman emperor: Einhard, *Life of Charlemagne* (825–826?). Original in Latin.

Born to an elite Frankish family, Einhard (*c.*770–840) received a good education in biblical studies and Latin classics at the monastery of Fulda, which was founded in 744 by Saint Sturm, a disciple of Boniface, a religious reformer closely tied to the early Carolingians (see above, p. 92). Einhard was probably in his early twenties when he started to serve at the court of Charlemagne (r.768–814). There he was known by the other courtiers as "little Nard"—probably to rhyme with the "hard" of his name and to stress his tiny stature—and also as "Bezaleel," Moses' wonderful craftsman (see Exod. 31:1–5). But Einhard's expertise extended beyond the arts to elegant writing. This allowed him to serve as an ambassador and administrator under Charlemagne and also, for a time, under Charlemagne's heir, Louis the Pious (r.814–840). He did not produce any major writings while living at court, but later, after retiring with his wife, Emma, to the estates that he received for his service to the king, he began to write books. He was so taken with classical Latin models that his *Life of Charlemagne* was, to some degree, patterned on *The Lives of the Caesars*, portraits of the first Roman emperors written by the Roman writer and imperial official Suetonius (69–after 122).

1. What are the ways in which Einhard's good king is unlike a saint?
2. What is Einhard's attitude toward warfare?

[Source: *Charlemagne's Courtier: The Complete Einhard*, ed. and trans. Paul Edward Dutton (Toronto: University of Toronto Press, 1998), pp. 15–21, 23–24, 37, 39 (notes added).]

[Preface]

After I decided to describe the life and character, and many of the accomplishments, of my lord and foster father, Charles, that most outstanding and deservedly famous king, and seeing how immense this work was, I have expressed it in as concise a form as I could manage. But I have attempted not to omit any of the facts that have come to my attention, and [yet I also seek] not to irritate those who are excessively critical by supplying a long-winded account of everything new [I have learned]. Perhaps, in this way, it will be possible to avoid angering with a new book [even] those who criticize the old masterpieces composed by the most learned and eloquent of men.

And yet I am quite sure that there are many people devoted to contemplation and learning who do not believe that the circumstances of the present age should be neglected or that virtually everything that happens these days is not worth remembering and should be condemned to utter silence and oblivion. Some people are so seduced by their love of the distant past, that they would rather insert the famous deeds of other peoples in their various compositions, than deny posterity any mention of their own names by writing nothing. Still, I did not see why I should refuse to take up a composition of this sort, since I was aware that no one could write about these things more truthfully than me, since I myself was present and personally witnessed them, as they say, with my own eyes. I was, moreover, not sure that these things would be recorded by anyone else.

I thought it would be better to write these things down [that is, his personal observations], along with other widely known details, for the sake of posterity, than to allow the splendid life of this most excellent king, the greatest of all the men in his time, and his remarkable deeds, which people now alive can scarcely equal, to be swallowed up by the shadows of forgetfulness.

There is still another reason, an understandable one, I believe, which even by itself might explain why I felt compelled to write this account; namely, the foster care [Charlemagne] bestowed on me and the constant friendship [I had] with him and his children after I began living at his court. Through his friendship he so won me over to him and I owed him so much both in life and death, that I might both seem and be fairly criticized as ungrateful if I forgot the many kindnesses he conferred upon me. Could I keep silent about the splendid and exceedingly brilliant deeds of a man who had been so kind to me and could I allow his life to remain without record and proper praise, as if he had never lived? But to write and account [for such a life] what was required was [an almost] Ciceronian eloquence,[1] not my feeble talent, which is poor and small, indeed almost non-existent.

Thus [I present] to you this book containing an account of the most splendid and greatest of all men. There is nothing in it that you should admire but his accomplishments, except perhaps that I, a German with little training in the language of Rome, should have imagined that I could write something correct and even elegant in Latin. Indeed, it might seem [to you] that my headlong impudence is very great and that I have willfully spurned the advice of Cicero [himself], since in the first book of his *Tusculan* [*Disputations*], when speaking of Latin authors, he had said: "for people to set their thoughts down in writing when they cannot organize them, make them clear, or charm their readers with any style is a complete waste of time and energy."[2] Indeed, this opinion of the famous orator might have stopped me from writing [this book, at all], if I had not decided in advance that it was better to risk the criticisms of people and to endanger my own small reputation by writing [this book], than to neglect the memory of so great a man and [instead] say myself.

[The Life of Charlemagne]

1. The family of the Merovingians, from which the Franks used to make their kings, is thought to have lasted down to King Childeric [III], whom Pope Stephen [II] ordered deposed. His [long] hair was shorn and he was forced into a monastery. Although it might seem that the [Merovingian] family ended with him, it had in fact been without any vitality for a long time and [had] demonstrated that there was nothing of any worth in it except the empty name of 'king'. For both the [real] riches and power of the kingdom were in the possession of the prefects of the palace, who were called the mayors of the palace [*maiores domus*], and to them fell the highest command. Nothing was left for the king [to do] except sit on his throne with his hair long and his beard uncut, satisfied [to hold] the name of king only and pretending to rule. [Thus] he listened to representatives who came from various lands and, as they departed, he seemed to give them decisions of his own, which he had [in fact] been taught or rather ordered [to pronounce]. Except for the empty name of 'king' and a meager living allowance, which the prefect of the court extended to him as it suited him, he possessed nothing else of his own but one estate with a very small income. On that estate, he had a house and servants who ministered to his needs and obeyed him, but there were few of them. He traveled about on a cart that was pulled by yoked oxen and led, as happens in the countryside, by a herdsman to wherever he needed to go.[3] In this way he used to go to the palace and so also to the public assembly of his people, which was held annually for the good of the kingdom, and in this manner he also returned home. But it was the prefect of the court [the mayor of the palace] who took care of everything, either at home or abroad, that needed to be done and arranged for the administration of the kingdom.

2. When Childeric was deposed, Pepin [III, the Short], the father of King Charles, held the office [of mayor of the palace], as if by hereditary right. For his father Charles [Martel] had brilliantly discharged the same civil office, which had been laid down for him by his father Pepin [II, of Herstal]. This Charles overthrew those oppressors who claimed personal control over all of Francia and he so completely defeated the Saracens,[4] who were attempting to occupy Gaul, in two great battles—the first in Aquitaine near the city of Poitiers [in 732] and the

---

[1] In fact, Cicero (106–43 BCE), a Roman orator and writer whose Latin style was (and continues to be) greatly admired, was a major influence on Einhard. Note his reference to Cicero's *Tusculan Disputations* in the next paragraph.

[2] Cicero, *Tusculan Disputations*, 1.3.6.

[3] Although Einhard presents the Merovingians as ridiculous, in fact the cart as well as their right to wear long hair and beard had been signs of their royal and religious status.

[4] Muslims.

second near Narbonne on the River Berre [in 737]—that he forced them to fall back into Spain. For the most part, the people [that is, the Frankish nobles] only granted the office [of mayor of the palace] to those men who stood out above others because of the nobility of their birth and the magnitude of their wealth.

For a few years Pepin, the father of King Charles, had held, as if under that [Merovingian] king, the office [of mayor of the palace], which was left to him and his brother Carloman by his grandfather and father. He shared that office with his brother in splendid harmony. [Then in 747] Carloman walked away from the oppressive chore of governing an earthly kingdom. It is not clear why he did this, but it seems that he was driven by a desire to lead a contemplative life. [Hence] he went to Rome in search of a quiet life and there changed his way [of dress and life] completely and was made a monk. With the brothers who joined him there, he enjoyed for a few years the quiet life he so desired in the monastery [he] built on Mount Soracte near the church of St-Sylvester. But since many nobles from Francia frequently visited Rome in order to fulfill their solemn vows and did not wish to miss [seeing] the man who had once been their lord, they interrupted the peaceful life he so loved by constantly paying their respects and so forced him to move. For when he realized that this parade [of visitors] was interfering with his commitment [to the monastic life], he left Mount [Soracte] and retreated to the monastery of St. Benedict located on Monte Cassino in the province of Samnium. There he spent what was left of his earthly life [until 755] in religious contemplation.[1]

3. Moreover, Pepin, who had been mayor of the palace, was established as king [in 751] by the decision of the Roman pope [Zacharias] and he ruled the Franks by himself for fifteen years or more. When the Aquitainian war, which Pepin waged against Waifar, the duke of Aquitaine, for nine straight years, was over, he died of edema in Paris [in 768]. He was survived by two sons, Charles and Carloman, and upon them, by divine will, fell the succession of the kingdom. Indeed, the Franks at a general assembly solemnly established both of them as their kings, but on the condition, agreed to in advance, that they should divide up the entire territory of the kingdom equally. Charles was to take up and govern that part [of the kingdom] which their father Pepin had held and Carloman that part which their uncle Carloman had [once]

governed. Both of them agreed to these conditions and each of them received the portion of the kingdom allotted to him by the plan. That peaceful agreement of theirs held fast, but with the greatest strain, since many on Carloman's side sought to drive the brothers apart. Some went so far as to plot to turn them [against each other] in war. But the outcome of things proved that the threat [of war] was more suspected than real in this case, and when Carloman died [in 771] his wife and sons, along with some of his chief nobles, took refuge in Italy. For no reason at all, she spurned her husband's brother and placed herself and her children under the protection of Desiderius, the king of the Lombards. In fact, Carloman had died [naturally] from disease after ruling the kingdom for two years with his brother. After his death, Charles was established as king by the agreement of all the Franks.

4. I believe it would be improper [for me] to write about Charles's birth and infancy, or even his childhood, since nothing [about those periods of his life] was ever written down and there is no one still alive who claims to have knowledge of these things. Thus, leaving aside the unknown periods [of his life], I have decided to pass straight to the deeds, habits, and other aspects of his life that should be set forth and explained. Nevertheless, so that I might not skip anything either necessary or worth knowing, I shall first describe his deeds inside and outside [the kingdom], then his habits and interests, and finally his administration of the kingdom and his death.

5. Of all the wars he waged, [Charles] began first [in 769] with the one against Aquitaine, which his father had started, but left unfinished, because he thought that it could be quickly brought to a successful conclusion. His brother [Carloman] was [still] alive at the time and [Charles] even asked for his help. And despite the fact that his brother misled him [by not delivering] the promised help, he pursued the campaign with great energy. He refused to back away from a war already in progress or to leave a job undone, until he had by sheer determination and persistence completely achieved the goal he had set for himself. For he forced Hunold, who had tried to take possession of Aquitaine after Waifar's death and to revive a war that was almost over, to give up Aquitaine and seek [refuge in] Gascony. But [Charles], unwilling to allow him to settle there, crossed the River Garonne and through messengers commanded Lupus, the duke

---

[1] For the Rule that St. Benedict wrote for this monastery, see above, p. 20.

of the Gascons, to hand over the fugitive. If he did not do this quickly, [Charles] would demand his surrender by waging war. Lupus not only gave way to wiser counsel and returned Hunold, but he even entrusted himself and the territory he governed to [Charles's] power.

6. With things settled in Aquitaine and the war over, and since the co-ruler [of Francia, his brother Carloman] was now also dead, [Charles] took up war against the Lombards [in 773]. Hadrian [I], the bishop of the city of Rome, [had] asked and appealed to him to do this. Indeed, his father had previously taken up this war at the request of Pope Stephen [II], [but] with great trouble, since some of the chief Franks, whom he regularly consulted, were so opposed to his plan that they openly stated that they would abandon the king and return home. Despite that [threat], [Pepin] took up the war against King Haistulf and quickly finished it at that time. But, although [Charles] and his father seem to have had a similar or, rather, identical reason for taking up this war, all agree that the [actual] fighting and conclusion [of the two conflicts] were different. For in fact, after laying siege to King Haistulf for a short time [in 756] in Pavia, Pepin forced him to surrender hostages, to restore the cities and fortified places seized from the Romans, and to swear that he would not try to regain the things he had returned. But Charles after he had begun the war did not stop until he had, by means of a long siege [in 774], worn King Desiderius down and had accepted his complete surrender. He forced [Desiderius's] son Adalgis, on whom the hopes of all [the Lombards] seemed to rest, to depart not only from the kingdom, but also from Italy. [Charles] restored everything that had been seized from the Romans. He also overcame Rotgaud, the duke of Friuli, who was plotting new [uprisings in 776], and brought all Italy under his control. He set up his own son Pepin as the king of this conquered land.

I would relate here how difficult it was for one to enter Italy across the Alps and what a struggle it was for the Franks to overcome unmarked mountain ridges, upthrust rocks, and rugged terrain, were it not my intention in this book to record the manner of his life, rather than the details of the wars which he waged. Nevertheless, the end result of this war [against the Lombards] was that Italy was conquered, King Desiderius was sent into permanent exile, his son Adalgis was driven out of Italy, and the properties stolen by the Lombard kings were returned to Hadrian, the head of the Roman church.

7. At the conclusion of this campaign, the Saxon war, which had seemed merely postponed, was begun again.

No war taken up by the Frankish people was ever longer, harder, or more dreadful [than this one], because the Saxons, like virtually all the peoples inhabiting Germany, were naturally fierce, worshiped demons, and were opposed to our religion. Indeed, they did not deem it shameful to violate and contravene either human or divine laws. There were underlying causes that threatened daily to disturb the peace, particularly since our borders and theirs ran together almost everywhere in open land except for a few places where huge forests or mountain ridges came between our respective lands and established a clear boundary. Murder, theft, and arson constantly occurred along this border. The Franks were so infuriated by these [incidents], that they believed they could no longer respond [incident for incident], but that it was worth declaring open war on the Saxons.

Thus, a war was taken up against them, which was waged with great vehemence by both sides for thirty-three straight years [772–804]. But the damage done to the Saxons was greater than that suffered by the Franks. In fact, the war could have been brought to a close sooner, if the faithlessness of the Saxons had [but] allowed it. It is almost impossible to say how many times they were beaten and pledged their obedience to the king. They promised [on those occasions] to follow his orders, to hand over the hostages demanded without delay, and to welcome the representatives sent to them by the king. At different times, they were so broken and subdued that they even promised to give up their worship of demons and freely submit themselves to Christianity. But though they were on occasion inclined to do this, they were always so quick to break their promises, that it is not possible to judge which of the two ways [of acting] can be said to have come more naturally to them. In fact, since the start of the war with the Saxons there was hardly a single year in which they did not reverse themselves in this way. But the king's greatness [of spirit] and steadfast determination—both in bad times and good—could not be conquered by their fickleness or worn down by the task he had set himself. Those perpetrating anything of this sort were never allowed to go unpunished. He took vengeance on them for their treachery and exacted suitable compensation either by leading the army [against them] himself or by sending it under [the charge of] his counts. Finally, when all those who were in the habit of resisting had been crushed and brought back under his control, he removed ten thousand men who had been living with their wives and children along both sides of the Elbe river and he dispersed them here and there throughout Gaul and Germany in various [small] groups.

Thus, that war which had lasted for so many years ended on the terms laid down by the king and accepted by the Saxons, namely that they would reject the worship of demons, abandon their ancestral [pagan] rites, take up the Christian faith and the sacraments of religion, and unite with the Franks in order to form a single people....

13. Aside from the war against the Saxons, the greatest of all the wars waged by [Charles] was the one against the Avars or Huns, which came next [in 791]. He managed that war with greater attention and preparation than his other wars. Even then, he still led one campaign himself into Pannonia, a province then occupied by the Avars. He turned the other campaigns over to his son Pepin, to the governors of the provinces, and to the counts and even their representatives. These men very vigorously conducted this war and finally brought it to a close in its eighth year [it actually ended in 803]. How many battles occurred in that war and how much blood was spilled is indicated by the utter depopulation of Pannonia and the desertion of the khan's palace; in fact, there is hardly a trace [now] that people once lived there. All the nobility of the Huns died out in this war and all their glory vanished. All the wealth and treasure they had collected over many years was seized. No one can recall any war against the Franks that left them richer or better stocked with resources. Until then they had seemed almost impoverished. So much gold and silver was found in the [khan's] palace and so many precious objects were taken in this war, that it might be fairly said that the Franks had justly seized from the Huns what the Huns had unjustly seized from other peoples. Only two Frankish leaders died in that war: Eric, the duke of Friuli, who was ambushed by the people of Tersatto, a seaside city in Liburnia and Gerold, the governor of Bavaria....

14. Charles's final war was the one taken up against the Northmen who are called Danes. First they had operated as pirates, but then they raided the coasts of Gaul and Germany with larger fleets. Their king, Godefrid, was so filled with vain ambition, that he vowed to take control of all Germany. Indeed, he already thought of Frisia and Saxony as his own provinces and had [first] brought the Abodrites, who were his neighbors, under his power and [then] made them pay tribute to him. He even bragged that he would soon come to Aachen, where king [Charles] held court, with a vast army. Some stock was put in his boast, although it was idle, for it was believed that he was about to start something like this, but was suddenly stopped by death. For he was murdered by one of his own attendants and, thus, both his life and the war he had begun came to a sudden end [at the same time].

15. These [then] were the wars that that mighty king waged with great skill and success in many lands over the forty-seven years he reigned. In those wars he so splendidly added to the Frankish kingdom, which he had received in great and strong condition from his father Pepin, that he nearly doubled its size....

16. He also increased the glory of his kingdom by winning over kings and peoples through friendly means. In this way he so completely won over Alfonso [II], the king of Galicia and Asturias, that when he sent letters or emissaries to Charles, he ordered that in Charles's presence he was only to be referred to as his subject. By his generosity he had so impressed the Irish kings with his goodwill, that they publicly declared that he was certainly their lord and they were his subjects and servants. Some letters they sent to [Charles] still survive and testify to this sort of feeling toward him.

He had such friendly relations with Harun-al-Rashid, the king of the Persians,[1] who held almost all the east except India, that [Harun] counted the favor of his friendship as more valuable than that of all the kings and rulers in the world and thought that only [Charles] was worthy of receiving his honor and generosity. Indeed, when [Charles's] representatives, whom he had sent loaded with gifts for the most Holy Sepulcher of our Lord and Savior [in Jerusalem] and for the place of his resurrection, came before [Harun] and informed him of their lord's wishes, he not only allowed them to complete their mission, but even handed over that sacred and salvific place, so that it might be considered as under Charles's control.[2] [Harun] sent his own representatives back with [Charles's] and he sent magnificent gifts for him, among which were robes, spices, and other riches of the east. A few years before this he had sent an elephant, the only one he then possessed, to Charles who had asked him [for such an animal].

---

[1] Harun (r.786–809) was the caliph at Baghdad.

[2] One of Charlemagne's ambassadors had obtained the keys of the Holy Sepulcher from the Patriarch of Jerusalem in 799. Harun had nothing to do with this, and Jerusalem was never under Charlemagne's control.

The emperors of Constantinople, Nicephorus [I], Michael [I], and Leo [V], who were also voluntarily seeking friendship and an alliance with Charles, sent many representatives to him. But when he took up the title of emperor, [it seemed] to them that he might want to seize their empire. Thus, [Charles] struck a very strong treaty [with them], so that no [potential] source of trouble of any sort might remain between them. For the Romans and Greeks were always suspicious of Frankish power; hence that Greek proverb which still circulates: "Have a Frank as a friend, never as a neighbor."

17. Despite being so committed to increasing the size of the kingdom and to subduing foreign peoples and being so constantly preoccupied with business of this kind, [Charles] still took up many projects in different places to improve and beautify the kingdom. He achieved some of them, but not all. Probably the most outstanding of these [projects] are the church of the Holy Mother of God in Aachen, which is a remarkable edifice, and the bridge spanning the Rhine River at Mainz, which was half a mile long, the width of the river at that point. But that bridge burned down the year before Charles died. Although he thought of rebuilding it, this time in stone rather than wood, his sudden death prevented that. He also began [to build two] splendid palaces, one not far from the city of Mainz, on the [royal] estate of Ingelheim, and the other at Nijmegen on the River Waal, which passes along the south side of the island of the Batavians. Even then, if he learned that sacred churches had fallen into ruin because of their age anywhere in his kingdom, he ordered the bishops and priests responsible for them to repair them and charged his representatives with insuring that his orders had been followed.

He [also] constructed a fleet for use against the Northmen. Ships were built for this purpose near the rivers that flow from Gaul and Germany into the North Sea. Since the Northmen were constantly raiding and ravaging the coasts of Gaul and Germany, fortifications and guards were set up at all the ports and at the mouth of every river that seemed large enough to accommodate ships. With such fortifications he stopped the enemy from being able to come and go [freely]. He took the same [precautions] in the south, along the coasts of the province of Narbonne and Septimania and along the whole coast of Italy up to Rome, where the Moors[1] had recently taken to plundering. Through these measures, Italy suffered no

great harm from the Moors while [Charles] lived, nor did Gaul and Germany suffer from the Northmen. The Moors did, however, through betrayal capture and pillage Civitavecchia, a city of Etruria, and the Northmen raided some islands in Frisia not far from the German coastline.

18. It is widely recognized that, in these ways, [Charles] protected, increased the size of, and beautified his kingdom. Now I should begin at this point to speak of the character of his mind, his supreme steadfastness in good times and bad, and those other things that belong to his spiritual and domestic life.

After the death of his father [in 768], when he was sharing the kingdom with his brother [Carloman], he endured the pettiness and jealousy of his brother with such great patience, that it seemed remarkable to all that he could not be provoked to anger by him. Then [in 770], at the urging of his mother [Bertrada], he married a daughter of Desiderius, the king of the Lombards, but for some unknown reason he sent her away after a year and took Hildegard [758–783], a Swabian woman of distinct nobility. She bore him three sons, namely Charles, Pepin, and Louis, and the same number of daughters, Rotrude, Bertha, and Gisela. He had three other daughters, Theoderada, Hiltrude, and Rothaide, two by his wife Fastrada, who was an eastern Frank (that is to say, German), and a third by some concubine, whose name now escapes me. When Fastrada died [in 794], [Charles] married Liutgard, an Alemannian woman, who bore no children. After her death [in 800], he took four concubines: Madelgard, who gave birth to a daughter by the name of Ruothilde; Gersvinda, a Saxon, by whom a daughter by the name of Adaltrude was born; Regina, who bore Drogo and Hugh; and Adallinda who gave him Theoderic.

[Charles's] mother, Bertrada, also spent her old age in great honor with him. He treated her with the greatest respect, to the point that there was never any trouble between them, except over the divorce of King Desiderius's daughter, whom he had married at her urging. She died [in 783], not long after Hildegard's death, but [had lived long enough] to have seen three grandsons and the same number of granddaughters in her son's house. [Charles] saw to it that she was buried with great honor in St-Denis, the same church where his father lay.

He had only one sister, whose name was Gisela. She had devoted herself to the religious life from the time she was a girl. As he had with his mother, he treated her with

---

[1] Muslims.

the greatest affection. She died a few years before him [in 810] in the monastery [that is, the convent of Chelles where she was abbess] in which she had spent her life.

19. [Charles] believed that his children, both his daughters and his sons, should be educated, first in the liberal arts, which he himself had studied. Then, he saw to it that when the boys had reached the right age they were trained to ride in the Frankish fashion, to fight, and to hunt. But he ordered his daughters to learn how to work with wool, how to spin and weave it, so that they might not grow dull from inactivity and [instead might] learn to value work and virtuous activity.

Out of all these children he lost only two sons and one daughter before he himself died: Charles, his eldest son [who died in 811], Pepin, whom he had set up as king of Italy [died in 810], and Rotrude, his eldest daughter, who [in 781] was engaged to Constantine, emperor of the Greeks [she died in 810]. Pepin left behind only one surviving son, Bernard [who died in 818], but five daughters: Adelhaid, Atula, Gundrada, Berthaid, and Theoderada. The king displayed a special token of affection toward his [grandchildren], since when his son [Pepin] died he saw to it that his grandson [Bernard] succeeded his father [as king of Italy] and he arranged for his granddaughters to be raised alongside his own daughters. Despite the surpassing greatness [of his spirit], he was deeply disturbed by the deaths of his sons and daughter, and his affection [toward his children], which was just as strong [a part of his character], drove him to tears.

When he was informed of the death of Hadrian, the Roman pontiff [d.795], he cried so much that it was as if he had lost a brother or a deeply loved son, for he had thought of him as a special friend. [Charles] was, by nature, a good friend, for he easily made friends and firmly held on to them. Indeed, he treated with the greatest respect those he had bound closely to himself in a relationship of this sort.

He was so attentive to raising his sons and daughters, that when he was home he always ate his meals with them and when he traveled he always took them with him, his sons riding beside him, while his daughters followed behind. A special rearguard of his men was appointed to watch over them. Although his daughters were extremely beautiful women and were deeply loved by him, it is strange to have to report that he never wanted to give any of them away in marriage to anyone, whether it be to a Frankish noble or to a foreigner. Instead he kept them close beside him at home until his death, saying that he could not stand to be parted from their company.

Although he was otherwise happy, this situation [that is, the affairs of his daughters] caused him no end of trouble. But he always acted as if there was no suspicion of any sexual scandal on their part or that any such rumor had already spread far and wide.

20. Earlier I chose not to mention with the others [Charles's] son Pepin [the Hunchback] who was born to him by a concubine [named Himiltrude]. He was handsome in appearance, but hunchbacked. When his father had taken up the war against the Huns [in 792] and was wintering in Bavaria, [Pepin] pretended to be sick and entered into a conspiracy against his father with certain leading Franks who had enticed him with the false promise of a kingdom [of his own]. After the plot was uncovered and the conspirators were condemned, [Pepin] was tonsured and allowed to pursue the religious life he had always wanted in the monastery of Prüm [where he died in 811].

Another powerful conspiracy against Charles had arisen even earlier [in 785–786] in Germany, but all its perpetrators [led by Hardrad] were sent into exile; some blinded, others unharmed. Only three conspirators lost their lives, since to avoid arrest they had drawn their swords to defend themselves and had even killed some men [in the process]. They were cut down themselves, because there was [simply] no other way to subdue them. But it is [widely] believed that the cruelty of Queen Fastrada was the cause and source of these conspiracies, since in both cases these men conspired against the king because it looked as if [Charles] had savagely departed from his usual kind and gentle ways by consenting to the cruel ways of his wife. Otherwise, [Charles] passed his whole life with the highest love and esteem of everyone, both at home and abroad, and not the least charge of cruelty or unfairness was ever brought against him by anyone....

22. [Charles] had a large and powerful body. He was tall [at slightly over six feet or 1.83 meters], but not disproportionately so, since it is known that his height was seven times the length of his own foot. The crown of his head was round, his eyes were noticeably large and full of life, his nose was a little longer than average, his hair was grey and handsome, and his face was attractive and cheerful. Hence, his physical presence was [always] commanding and dignified, whether he was sitting or standing. Although his neck seemed short and thick and his stomach seemed to stick out, the symmetry of the other parts [of his body] hid these [flaws]. [When he walked] his pace was strong and the entire bearing of his body powerful. Indeed, his voice was distinct, but not as

[strong as might have been] expected given his size. His health was good until four years before he died, when he suffered from constant fevers. Toward the very end [of his life] he also became lame in one foot. Even then he trusted his own judgment more than the advice of his physicians, whom he almost loathed, since they urged him to stop eating roast meat, which he liked, and to start eating boiled meat [which he did not].

He kept busy by riding and hunting frequently, which came naturally to him. Indeed, there is hardly a people on earth who can rival the Franks in this skill. [Charles] also liked the steam produced by natural hot springs and the exercise that came from swimming frequently. He was so good at swimming that no one was considered better than him. For this reason [that is, the existence of the hot springs], he built his palace in Aachen and lived there permanently during the final years of his life until he died. He invited not only his sons to the baths, but also his nobles and friends. Sometimes he invited such a crowd of courtiers and bodyguards, that there might be more than a hundred people bathing together.

23. He normally wore the customary attire of the Franks. [Closest] to his body he put on a linen shirt and underwear, then a silk-fringed tunic and stockings. He wrapped his lower legs with cloth coverings and put shoes on his feet. In winter he covered his shoulders and chest with a vest made of otter or ermine skin, above which he wore a blue cloak. He was always armed with a sword, whose handle and belt were made of gold or silver. On occasion he bore a jeweled sword, but only on special feast days or if the representatives of foreign peoples had come [to see him]. He rejected foreign clothes, however gorgeous they might be, and never agreed to be dressed in them, except once in Rome when Pope Hadrian had requested it and, on another occasion, when his successor Leo had begged him to wear a long tunic, chlamys [a Greek mantle], and shoes designed in the Roman [that is to say, Greek] fashion. On high feast days he normally walked in the procession dressed in clothes weaved with gold, bejeweled shoes, in a cloak fastened by a golden clasp, and also wearing a golden, gem-encrusted crown. But on other days his attire differed little from people's usual attire.

24. [Charles] was moderate when it came to both food and drink, but he was even more moderate in the case of

drink, since he deeply detested [seeing] anyone inebriated, especially himself or his men. But he was not able to abstain from food, and often complained that fasting was bad for his health. He seldom put on [large] banquets, but when he did it was for a great number of people on special feast days. His dinner each day was served in four courses only, not including the roast, which his hunters used to carry in on a spit. He preferred [roast meat] over all other food. While eating, he was entertained or listened to someone read out the histories and deeds of the ancients. He was fond of the books of Saint Augustine, particularly the one called the *City of God*.[1]

He was so restrained in his consumption of wine and other drinks, that he seldom drank more than three times during a meal. After his midday meal in the summertime, he would eat some fruit and take a single drink. Then, after he had removed his clothes and shoes, just as he did at night, he would lie down for two or three hours. While sleeping at night, he would not only wake four or five times, but would even get up. [In the morning] while putting on his shoes and dressing, he not only saw friends, but if the count of the palace informed him that there was some unresolved dispute that could not be sorted out without his judgment, he would order him to bring the disputing parties before him at once. Then, as if he were sitting in court, he heard the nature of the dispute and rendered his opinion. He not only looked after cases such as this at that time, but also matters of any sort that needed to be handled that day or to be assigned to one of his officials.

25. [Charles] was a gifted and ready speaker, able to express clearly whatever he wished to say. Not being content with knowing only his own native tongue [German], he also made an effort to learn foreign languages. Among those, he learned Latin so well, that he spoke it as well as he did his own native language, but he was able to understand Greek better than he could speak it. Indeed, he was such a fluent speaker, that [at times] he actually seemed verbose.

He avidly pursued the liberal arts and greatly honored those teachers whom he deeply respected. To learn grammar, he followed [the teaching of] Peter of Pisa, an aged deacon. For the other disciplines, he took as his teacher Alcuin of Britain, also known as Albinus, who was a deacon as well, but from the [Anglo-]Saxon people. He was the most learned man in the entire world. [Charles] invested a great deal of time and effort studying

---

[1] See the excerpt from this book above, p. 16.

rhetoric, dialectic, and particularly astronomy with him. He learned the art of calculation [arithmetic] and with deep purpose and great curiosity investigated the movement of the stars. He also attempted to [learn how to] write and, for this reason, used to place wax-tablets and notebooks under the pillows on his bed, so that, if he had any free time, he might accustom his hand to forming letters. But his effort came too late in life and achieved little success.

26. With great piety and devotion [Charles] followed the Christian religion, in which he had been reared from infancy. For this reason he constructed a church of stunning beauty at Aachen and adorned it with gold and silver, with lamps, grillwork, and doors made of solid bronze. When he could not obtain the columns and marble for this building from any place else, he took the trouble to have them brought from Rome and Ravenna. As long as his health allowed him to, [Charles] regularly went to church both morning and evening, and also to the night reading and to the morning Mass. He was particularly concerned that everything done in the church should be done with the greatest dignity and he frequently warned the sacristans that nothing foul or unclean should be brought into the church or left there. He made sure that his church was supplied with such an abundance of sacred vessels made of gold and silver and with such a great number of clerical vestments, that, indeed, in the celebration of the Mass not even those looking after the doors, who hold the lowest of all ecclesiastical orders, found it necessary to serve in their normal clothes. He very carefully corrected the way in which the lessons were read and the psalms sung, for he was quite skilled at both. But he himself never read publicly and would only sing quietly with the rest of the congregation.

27. [Charles] was so deeply committed to assisting the poor spontaneously with charity, which the Greeks call alms, that he not only made the effort to give alms in his own land and kingdom, but even overseas in Syria, Egypt, and Africa. When he learned that the Christians in Jerusalem, Alexandria, and Carthage were living in poverty, he was moved by their impoverished condition and used to send money. It was chiefly for this reason that he struck up friendships with kings overseas, so that the poor Christians living under their rule might receive some relief and assistance.

He loved the church of St. Peter the Apostle in Rome more than all other sacred and venerable places and showered its altars with a great wealth of gold, silver, and even gems. He [also] sent a vast number of gifts to the popes. During his whole reign he regarded nothing as more important than to restore through his material help and labor the ancient glory of the city of Rome. Not only did he protect and defend the church of St. Peter, but with his own money he even embellished and enriched it above all other churches. Despite holding it in such high regard, he only traveled there four times during the twenty-seven years he reigned [in 774, 785, 787, and 800–801] to fulfill his vows and pray.

28. The reasons for his last visit [to Rome] were not just those [that is, his religious vows and for prayer], but rather because residents of Rome had attacked Pope Leo [III]. They had inflicted many injuries on him, including ripping out his eyes and cutting off his tongue.[1] This [attack] forced him to appeal to the loyalty of the king [in 799 at Paderborn]. Thus, [Charles] traveled to Rome to restore the state of the church, which was extremely disrupted, and he spent the whole winter there [until April 801]. It was at that time that he received the title of emperor and augustus, which at first he disliked so much that he stated that, if he had known in advance of the pope's plan, he would not have entered the church that day, even though it was a great feast day [Christmas 800]. But he bore the animosity that the assumption of this title caused with great patience, for the Roman [that is, Greek] emperors were angry over it. He overcame their opposition through the greatness of his spirit, which was without doubt far greater than theirs, and by often sending representatives to them and by calling them his brothers in his letters.

29. After assuming the imperial title, [Charles] realized that there were many deficiencies in the laws of his own people, for the Franks have two sets of laws that differ tremendously at a number of points. He decided, therefore, to fill in what was lacking, to reconcile the disagreements, and also to set right what was bad and wrongly expressed. He did nothing more about this than to add a few items to these laws, but even those were left in an imperfect state. But he did direct that the unwritten laws of all the peoples under his control should be gathered up and written down.

---

[1] The attackers attempted to mutilate the pope, but they did not in fact succeed.

[Charles] also [ordered] that the very old Germanic poems, in which the deeds and wars of ancient kings were sung, should be written down and preserved for posterity. He began [as well] a grammar of his native language. He even gave [German] names to the months, since before then the Franks were used to referring to them by a mix of Latin and Germanic names. He also assigned individual names to the twelve winds, since until then scarcely more than four of them had been named....

33. [Charles had] decided to draw up a will, so that he might make his daughters and illegitimate children heirs to some part of his estate. But the will was left too late and could not be completed. Nevertheless, three years before he died, he divided up his precious possessions, money, clothes, and other moveable goods in the presence of his friends and officials. He called on them to insure that, with their support, the division he had made would remain fixed and in force after his death. He described in a charter what he wanted done with the goods he had [so] divided....

After examining this same charter his son Louis, who succeeded by divine right, saw to it that [this division of properties] was fulfilled as quickly and faithfully as possible after his [father's] death.

3.5 An Abbasid victory in verse: Abu Tammam, *The sword gives truer tidings* (838). Original in Arabic.

Poetry, so important in pre-Islamic and Umayyad Arabic culture, continued to be a preeminent form of expression in the Abbasid period. Poets flourished even under Caliph al-Muʿtasim (r.833–842), who was renowned as a warrior, not a thinker. One of the most refined, subtle, and prolific of those poets was Abu Tammam (804–846).

The attack on Amorium, so highly praised in this poem, was justified as vengeance for an earlier assault by the Byzantines on the Muslim fortress of Zibatra. The poem (line 46) speaks of a "Zibatran woman's cry"; Islamic commentators explained that a captive Zibatran woman called on al-Muʿtasim for help. When he heard her call, he abandoned his wine cup and immediately began to prepare for battle. His destination was Amorium because, as lines 15–19 make clear, it was thought to be especially dear to the Byzantines.

The poem bears some resemblance to a Qurʾanic warning story. It begins with a veiled threat: the sword speaks louder than words. It continues with the enemy's pride and God's sudden justice. The end brings triumph on earth and at the Last Judgment. Stark opposites of good (al-Muʿtasim's army) against evil (the Byzantines) are at play. The various parts of the poem's argument are indicated in brackets.

Arabic poems were not read silently but rather were part of an oral performance. This one may well have been declaimed not so much to praise the taking of Amorium—the obvious topic—but to justify the caliph's mass executions carried out right after the victory in the wake of a conspiracy against him. There is a very vague allusion to the conspirators' treachery in line 62.

1. What is the poem referring to when it talks about fallacy, lies, and slander in lines 4–5?
2. Which passages reveal the poet's view of the Byzantines and their emperor?

[Source: Julia Bray, "Al-Muʿtasim's 'bridge of toil' and Abu Tammam's Amorium *qasida*," in *Studies in Islamic and Middle Eastern Texts and Traditions in Memory of Norman Calder*, ed. G.R. Hawting, J.A. Mojaddedi, and A. Samely, Journal of Semitic Studies Supplement 12 (Oxford: Oxford University Press, 2000), pp. 49–55 (notes modified).]

[Signs]

1. *The sword gives truer tidings than do scriptures;*[1]
its edge is what tells *zeal* from *vanity;*[2]

2. White blades, not the black letters on the page—these
reveal misguided doubts for what they are;

3. And knowledge flashes from the starry spears
when armies meet, not from the Pleiades.[3]

4. Where now the oracle, where now the stars
invoked to trump up fallacy and *lies*—

5. A slanderous tissue of apocrypha
that's fit for nothing when all's said and done.

6. Such marvels as they claimed! saying Fate itself
in that doomed month (which one?) would bolt from them,

7. Scaremongers who declared the western comet
would usher in a dark catastrophe,

8. Who said stability and revolution
are ordered by the zodiacal spheres,

9. *Indifferent* as they are, fixed or revolving;
yet from them they determine destiny!

10. *The idols and the cross and what befell them,*
if stars predict, this could not have been hid;[4]

11. A victory of victories, so sublime
prose cannot speak nor verse can utter it;

12. A victory at which Heaven threw wide its gates,
which Earth put on new dress to celebrate:[5]

13. O battle of Amorium, from which
our hopes returned engorged with milk and honey,

14. *The Muslims hast thou fixed in the ascendant,*
pagans and pagandom fixed in decline!

[The city in her pride]

15. This was their dear mother city; mothers
and fathers all they would have given for her;

16. Too bold she was for Chosroes to tame her,
and Abu Karib, King of Yemen, she shunned;[6]

17. A virgin undeflowered by misfortune,
whom mishap never ventured to approach

18. Since before Alexander; and thus Time
grew white-haired; but not so Amorium.

19. *So God with jealous parsimony churned*
the years, and she the cream of aeons was,

20. Till, dazzled, black disaster came upon them
whose city had been called Deliverer.

[The city warned and destroyed]

---

[1] Here as elsewhere, Abu Tamman's lines have more than one meaning. In this first line, he reverses the conventional "pen is mightier than the sword" antithesis. He also makes sly allusion to a letter sent by the Byzantines to al-Mu'tasim saying that Amorium would be taken only when the figs and grapes ripen. The siege took place during July and August, during Ramadan; apparently, the Byzantines had a different time of year in mind. More profoundly, the line seems to suggest that the sword is mightier than the Qur'an. Is this blasphemy? The rest of the poem progressively provides the answer: it is the Byzantines who misread Scripture and whose "doubts" about its true meaning are made clear by the Islamic victory at Amorium.

[2] "Vanity" translates an Arabic word that is related to those who deny the truth of God's Book.

[3] The Pleiades is a star cluster. Astrologers for the caliph predicted that the attack on Amorium would fail. That explains the next verse, which ridicules the "oracle" and the "scaremongers" who spoke it.

[4] Here the poem skips in time to the end of the siege, when the Muslims burned down a church (hence the reference to the idols and the cross) to which the Byzantine army had retreated, killing all inside.

[5] This implies rain and flowers, but in fact the siege was plagued by drought.

[6] Chosroes was the Persian ruler who fought with the Byzantines at the beginning of the seventh century. Abu Karib was a pre-Islamic Arab hero.

21. *Amorium drew an unlucky lot
at Ankara*, her courts left desolate,

22. And when she saw her sister now in ruins,
the rot spread to her faster than the mange.[1]

23. Within the city's battlements, how many
brave horsemen, red-locked with hot-flowing blood!

24. The sword prescribed that their own blood should be
their dye, not henna as Islam prescribes.

25. Commander of the Faithful, there you gave
defeated stone and wood up to *the flames*;

26. You left there *darkest night as broadest daylight*,
driven from the city's heart by a dawn of fire,

27. As if the cloak of darkness had forsworn
its color, and the sun had never set;

28. Brightness of burning in the clinging gloom,
and murk of smoke amid a sickly daylight,

29. Here the sun rises after it has set;
there the sun sinks away before its setting.

[The city in Muslim hands]

30. Clear as if clouds had parted over it,
Fate shows the battle both pure and uncleansed:

31. For on that day the sun did rise upon
no man but chaste, nor set upon a virgin.[2]

32. The city in her ruins looked as lovely
as Mayy's haunts in their heyday to Ghaylan,[3]

33. Her cheek, though streaked with grime, appeared as tempting
as cheeks aflush with maiden modesty.

34. Gazing on her disfigurement, no need
had we of beauty or of pleasant sights,

35. Seeing so smiling a reverse of fortune
follow upon such foul adversity.

[Destiny and history]

36. *Had it but known it, heathendom's deserts*
lay in wait down the ages in our weapons:

37. *Such was God's supplicant's, His devotee's,*
His champion's, al-Mu'tasim's, grand design.

38. With victory his daily bread, his spearheads,
undulled, beg audience of no shielded soul;

39. Wherever he campaigns, in holy warfare,
a host of terrors is his harbinger;

40. Were he not leader of a mighty squadron,
he alone would stand legion in the field.

41. God flung thee at the city's towers and razed her—
none but God casts with such unerring aim;[4]

42. With bristling garrison, in her they trusted,
but God unlocks the best-manned citadel.[5]

43. "They'll find no pasture for their beasts," their captain
declared, "nor water to sustain their siege"—[6]

---

[1] Before attacking Amorium, al-Mu'tasim's forces besieged the Byzantine city of Ankara, whose inhabitants fled, leaving the city empty. Mange is a skin disease common in camels.

[2] The sun did not "set upon a virgin" refers, among other things, to the rape of the Amorian women. From sunrise to sunset, the Muslim soldiers were required to remain chaste; after sunset, they raped their captives, thus becoming ritually (but not morally) unclean. This also explains the phrase "both pure and uncleansed," which refers to the Muslim warriors.

[3] Ghaylan was an Umayyad poet. He and Mayya were a proverbial pair of romantic lovers.

[4] This line recalls the Qur'an verse that speaks of the battle of Badr, which the poem refers to directly in line 70. In fact, the various siege engines that the Muslim army brought were ineffective. The walls were breached by a betrayal: a renegade Muslim married to an Amorian woman told the besiegers where the wall was weakest. See "Weapons and Warfare in the Middle Ages," in "Reading through Looking," pp. XII–XIV.

[5] In other words, the inhabitants of Amorium trusted in their fortifications.

[6] These were the vain taunts of the Byzantines.

44. Fond hopes of which our swords' edges despoiled them,
our spoiling lances made them all in vain.

45. For steel and javelins are twofold vessels,
of death, and of the wells and herbs of life.[1]

46. *Summoned by the Zibatran woman's cry,*
you poured away the wine of sleep and love,

47. In hot pursuit, cool lips, refreshing kisses,
spurned, in the teeth of your realm's frontier's wrongs,[2]

48. Your answer, with drawn sword and battle-cry—
only the sword can answer such a summons—

49. To fell the mainstay of the pagan tent,
not swerving to undo its pegs and guys.[3]

50. Now when Theophilus had looked on war,
which signifies wrath and expenditure,

51. With moneys he attempts to turn its course,
but cannot stem the ocean's heaving billows.[4]

52. Rather, *the very earth beneath his feet
quaked* at no plunderer's onslaught, but *a Reckoner's*,[5]

53. Who not for lack of golden coin had lavished
a store of gold beyond all measuring:

54. The lions, yea, the lions of the thicket

spoil for the kill alone, not for its spoils.[6]

55. The emperor fled. The spears had tied his tongue;
beneath his speechlessness his guts were clamouring;

56. He left his retinue to die, urged on
his fastest steed of cowardly desertion,

57. Seeking the trusty vantage of the hills
with fearful not with joyous nimbleness.

58. Though he runs like an ostrich from the heat,
the *hellish flames* you set spread with much kindling:

59. The ninety thousands like the fabled lions,
whose lifespan "*ripened ere the fig and grape.*"[7]

[The city in Muslim hands (ii)]

60. The Romans' root has been plucked out, and ah!
how sweet to Muslim souls no musk could sweeten,

61. Their anger dead, and by the sword restored
to lively satisfaction, the foe slain.

62. Our war stands firm, and holds the narrow pass
which brings all else who stand there to their knees.[8]

63. How many dazzling beauties in its glare,
embraces in its scowling gloom were taken;[9]

64. How many neck-cords there slit open, that

---

[1] In the pre-Islamic period, the spear was said to be a rope and bucket. In fact, the Muslim army carried water (in leather and goatskins), and it camped in places that had water and grass for the animals.

[2] For the Zibatran woman and the "wrongs" that the Byzantines had committed against the Muslims, see the introduction to this poem.

[3] The usual way to collapse a tent is to pull up its ground pegs and loosen the guy ropes.

[4] Theophilus was the Byzantine emperor (r.829–842). He tried to negotiate a peace—offering money, the poet says—but al-Mu'tasim would not meet with him until Amorium was taken.

[5] Al-Mu'tasim is here said to be the opposite of a plunderer; he is a Reckoner. This may be understood in three overlapping ways: he is settling scores with the emperor; he is dealing out God's reckoning; he is anticipating his own reward on the Day of Reckoning.

[6] Later Islamic commentators said that this line, which has the caliph reject money, made an impression on al-Mu'tasim, who used it to taunt a rebel who tried to bargain with gold for his life.

[7] The "fabled lions" refer to al-Shara, a proverbial place in Arabia once known for its many lions. The reference to the fig and grape recalls the false Byzantine prophecy (see p. 125, n. 1 above).

[8] A reference to the breach in the wall and the humbling of the Amorians. Rivalries over fighting in the breach brought to light a plot to murder al-Mu'tasim and to put another caliph on the throne.

[9] Many captives were taken; those who were salable were sold and the rest were burned.

the gently-nurtured virgin might be had;

65. How many a shapely form with quivering flanks
won by the quivering rapiers ready drawn.

66. White arms that, bared from out their sheaths, proved fitter
fellows to white-armed maidens than their veils![1]

[The true meaning of events]

67. Caliph of God! may God reward your labours
for faith's true stock, for Islam and renown;

68. *You looked upon the Peace of God and saw that
to reach it you must cross a bridge of toil.*

69. If it be that the haps of time bear kinship
in an unbroken line, or stand allied,

70. *Then surely this your triumph that God gave you
is of the noble lineage of Badr;*[2]

71. Whereby *the Paleface, yellow as his name,*[3]
is downcast, and the Arabs are exalted!

....

3.6 Mothers and fathers: Dhuoda, *Handbook for Her Son* (841–843). Original in Latin.

A precious document for the values of the Carolingian laity—or, more precisely, for aristocratic lay women of the time—Dhuoda's *Handbook for Her Son* was written in the time of crisis just before the Treaty of Verdun (843). Her husband, Bernard, count of the Spanish March (Septimania), had once been an important courtier under Louis the Pious, but, accused of adultery with the queen, he was expelled from the court by Louis's sons. Her son William, to whom she wrote, was being held hostage at the court of Charles the Bald, partly to guarantee his father's "good behavior" and partly to ensure William's own advancement at court. Dhuoda herself remained in the south of the Frankish kingdom, attempting, as she put it, "to defend the interests of my lord and master, Bernard." She had just given birth to another son. In her *Handbook*, motherhood, politics, and religion mingle as she tries to define a righteous and honorable rule of conduct for this life and the next. Just as Carolingian court scholars wrote "Mirrors of Princes" for kings to model themselves upon (see Einhard, p. 115 above), so Dhuoda wrote a "mirror" for her son in which he could "contemplate the health" of his soul, measuring it against the mirror's standard. We have no idea how William responded to Dhuoda's advice. Bernard was executed by the king shortly after she wrote, and William was executed in 850. Dhuoda may have died before she knew about these sad events.

1. What duties did Dhuoda think her son owed to his father and mother?
2. What does Dhuoda's writing suggest about place of women in the Carolingian empire?

[Source: *Handbook for William: A Carolingian Woman's Counsel for Her Son*, trans. Carol Neel (Washington, DC: Catholic University of America Press, 1991), pp. 1, 5–6, 21–23, and corresponding notes (notes slightly modified).]

---

[1] Many women were raped.

[2] "Haps of time" refers to the fortunes of the caliph, who is here said to be of the lineage of the Prophet Muhammad.

[3] The "Paleface" is the Byzantine, stereotyped as "sallow."

The little book before you branches out in three directions. Read it through and, by the end, you will understand what I mean. I would like it to be called three things at once, as befits its contents—rule, model, and handbook.[1] These terms all mirror each other. The rule comes from me, the model is for you, and the handbook is as much from me as for you—composed by me, received by you....

Here Begins the Prologue.

Things that are obvious to many people often escape me. Those who are like me lack understanding and have dim insight, but I am even less capable than they.[2] Yet always there is he at my side who "opened the mouths of the dumb, and made the tongues of infants eloquent."[3] I, Dhuoda, despite my weakness of mind, unworthy as I am among worthy women—I am still your mother, my son William, and it is to you that I now address the words of my handbook. From time to time children are fascinated by dice more than all the other games that they enjoy. And sometimes women are absorbed in examining their faces in mirrors, in order then to cover their blemishes and be more beautiful for the worldly intention of pleasing their husbands. I hope that you may bring the same care, burdened though you may be by the world's pressures, to reading this little book addressed to you by me. For my sake, attend to it—according to my jest—as children do to their dice or women to their mirrors.

Even if you eventually have many more books, read this little work of mine often. May you, with God's help, be able to understand it to your own profit. You will find in it all you may wish to know in compact form. You will find in it a mirror in which you can without hesitation contemplate the health of your soul, so that you may be pleasing not only in this world, but to him who formed you out of dust.[4] What is essential, my son William, is that you show yourself to be such a man on both levels that you are both effective in this world and pleasing to God in every way.

My great concern, my son William, is to offer you helpful words. My burning, watchful heart especially desires that you may have in this little volume what I have longed to be written down for you, about how you were born through God's grace. I shall best begin there.

Preface.

In the eleventh year of the imperial rule of our lord Louis, who then reigned by Christ's favor—on the twenty-ninth of June 824—I was given in marriage at the palace of Aachen to my lord Bernard, your father, to be his legitimate wife.[5] It was still in that reign, in its thirteenth year on the twenty-ninth of November,[6] that with God's help, as I believe, you were born into this world, my firstborn and much-desired son.

Afterward, as the wretchedness of this world grew and worsened, in the midst of the many struggles and disruptions in the kingdom, that emperor followed the path common to all men. For in the twenty-eighth year of his reign, he paid the debt of his earthly existence before his time.[7] In the year after his death, your brother was born on the twenty-second of March in the city of Uzès.[8] This child, born after you, was the second to come forth from my body by God's mercy. He was still tiny and had not yet received the grace of baptism when Bernard, my lord and the father of you both, had the baby brought to him in Aquitaine in the company of Elefantus, bishop of Uzès, and others of his retainers.

Now I have been away from you for a long time, for my lord [Bernard] constrains me to remain in this city. Nonetheless I applaud his success. But, moved by longing

---

[1] Dhuoda begins by describing her own work as threefold, reflecting the Trinity of the one Christian God—Father, Son, and Holy Spirit. In doing so, she affirms her adherence to this central element in Catholic doctrine.

[2] See 2 Cor. 11:23.

[3] Wisd. of Sol. 10:21.

[4] See Gen. 1:7.

[5] The marriage of Bernard and Dhuoda at the Carolingian capital, Aachen, suggests that they were children of families of great importance.

[6] The year was 826.

[7] Louis the Pious died in 840, in his late sixties, so Dhuoda's comment is polite.

[8] The year was 841. It is possible, given the long period between the births of Dhuoda's two sons, that she saw little of her husband in the interim. Bernard was heavily involved in politics and warfare across the Frankish dominions throughout their marriage.

for both of you, I have undertaken to have this little book—a work on the scale of my small understanding—copied down and sent to you. Although I am besieged by many troubles, may this one thing be God's will, if it please him—that I might see you again with my own eyes. I would think it certain that I would, if God were to grant me some virtue. But since salvation is far from me, sinful woman that I am,[1] I only wish it, and my heart grows weak in this desire.[2]

As for you, I have heard that your father, Bernard, has given you as a hostage to the lord king Charles.[3] I hope that you acquit yourself of this worthy duty with perfect good will. Meanwhile, as Scripture says, "Seek ye therefore the kingdom of God ... and all these things shall be added unto you,"[4] that is all that is necessary for the enjoyment of your soul and your body.

So the preface comes to an end.

[In Book One, Dhuoda expounds on William's primary task: to love God. In Book Two, she discusses the Trinity, the trinity of virtues (faith, hope, and charity), and the importance of prayer.]

Book Three

1. ON THE REVERENCE YOU SHOULD SHOW YOUR FATHER THROUGHOUT YOUR LIFE.

Now I must do my best to guide you in how you should fear, love, and be faithful to your lord and father, Bernard, in all things, both when you are with him and when you are apart from him. In this, Solomon is your teacher and your wisest authority. He chastises you, my son, and says

to you in warning, "For God hath made the father" who flourishes in his children "honorable."[5] And likewise: "He that honoreth his father shall have joy in his own children"[6] and "shall enjoy a long life. He that obeyeth the father shall be a comfort to his mother."[7] "As one that layeth up good things,"[8] so is he who honors his father. "He that feareth the Lord, honoreth his parents."[9] "So honor thy father," my son, and pray for him devoutly, "that thou mayest be longlived upon the land,"[10] with a full term of earthly existence. "Remember that thou hadst not been born" but through him.[11] In every matter be obedient to your father's interest and heed his judgment.[12] If by God's help you come to this, "support the old age of thy father and grieve him not in his life."[13] "Despise him not when thou art in thy strength."[14]

May you never do this last, and may the earth cover my body before such a thing might happen. But I do not believe that it will. I mention it not because I fear it but rather so that you may avoid it so completely that such a crime never comes to your mind, as I have heard that it indeed has done among many who are not like you.[15] Do not forget the dangers that befell Elias's sons, who disobediently scorned the commands of their father and for this met with a bitter death.[16] Nor should I fail to mention the tree of Absalom, who rebelled against his father and whom a base death brought to a sudden fall. Hung from an oak and pierced by lances, he ended his earthly life in the flower of his youth, with a groan of anguish. Lacking as he did an earthly kingdom, he never reached that highest of kingdoms promised to him.[17]

What of the many more who behave as he did? Their path is perilous. May those who perpetrate such evil suffer

---

[1] See Ps. 119:155; Douay Ps. 118:155.

[2] See Job 30:16.

[3] William had been entrusted to Charles the Bald after the battle of Fontenoy in 841.

[4] Matt. 6:33.

[5] Ecclus. 3:3. Dhuoda here assumes a traditional attribution of this Old Testament book to David's son Solomon.

[6] Ecclus. 3:6.

[7] Ecclus. 3:7.

[8] Ecclus. 3:5.

[9] Ecclus. 3:8.

[10] Exod. 20:12.

[11] Ecclus. 7:30.

[12] See Ecclus. 3:2.

[13] Ecclus. 3:14.

[14] Ecclus. 3:15.

[15] Dhuoda here clearly refers to the conflict among Louis the Pious and his sons.

[16] 1 Sam. 4:11.

[17] See 2 Sam 18:15.

accordingly. It is not I who condemn them, but Scripture that promises their condemnation, threatening them terribly and saying, "Cursed is he that honoreth not his father."[1] And again, "He who curseth his father, dying let him die"[2] basely and uselessly. If such is the punishment for harsh, evil words alone, what do you think will happen to those who inflict real injury upon their parents and insult the dignity of their fathers? We hear of many in our times who, thinking their present circumstances unjust, consider such crimes without taking into account the past. On them and on those like them fall hatred, jealousy, disaster, and calamity, and "nourishment to their envy."[3] They lose rather than keep those goods of others that they seek, and they are scarcely able even to keep their own property. I say these things not because I have seen them happen, but because I have read about such matters in books. I have heard of them in the past, you hear about them yourself, and I am hearing them even now. Consider what will happen in the future to those who treat others in this fashion. But God has the power to bring even these people—if there are such—to lament their evil ways and, in their conversion, to do penance and be worthy of salvation. May anyone who behaves so ill stay away from you, and may God give him understanding.

Everyone, whoever he may be, should consider this, my son: if the time comes that God finds him worthy to give him children of his own, he will not wish them to be rebellious or proud or full of greed, but humble and quiet and full of obedience, so that he rejoices to see them. He who was a son before, small and obedient to his father, may then be fortunate in his own fatherhood. May he who thinks on these things in the hope that they will happen consider too what I have said above. Then "all his limbs" will work "in concert, peacefully."[4]

Hear me as I direct you, my son William, and "listen carefully," follow the "instructions … of a father."[5] Heed the words of the holy Fathers, and "bind them in thy heart"[6] by frequent reading so that "years of life may be multiplied to thee"[7] as you grow continually in goodness. For "they that wait upon"[8] God, blessing him, obeying the Fathers and complying freely with their precepts—such men "shall inherit the land."[9] If you listen to what I say above and if you put it into worthy practice, not only will you have success here on this earth, but also you will be found worthy to possess with the saints what the Psalmist describes: "I believe to see the good things of the Lord in the land of the living."[10] So that this other land may be your inheritance, my son, I pray that he who lives eternally may deign to prepare you to dwell there.

2. ON THE SAME TOPIC, ON REVERENCE FOR YOUR FATHER.

In the human understanding of things, royal and imperial appearance and power seem preeminent in the world, and the custom of men is to account those men's actions and their names ahead of all others, as though these things were worthy of veneration and as though worldly power were the highest honor. This attitude is testified in the words of him who said, "whether it be to the king as excelling, or to the governors."[11] But despite all this, my wish is as follows, my son. In the smallness of my understanding—but also according to God's will—I caution you to render first to him whose son you are special, faithful, steadfast loyalty as long as you shall live. For it is a fixed and unchangeable truth that no one, unless his rank comes to him from his father, can have access to another person at the height of power.

So I urge you again, most beloved son William, that first of all you love God as I have written above. Then love, fear, and cherish your father. Keep in mind that your worldly estate proceeds from his. Recognize that from the most ancient times, men who have loved their fathers and have been truthfully obedient to them have been found worthy to receive God's benediction from those fathers' hands....

---

[1] Deut. 27:16.

[2] Lev. 20:9.

[3] Gen. 37:8.

[4] See *The Benedictine Rule*, chap. 34 above, p. 25: "all the members will be at peace." See as well 1 Cor. 12:12–30.

[5] Here Dhuoda recalls the opening words of *The Benedictine Rule*. See above, p. 21.

[6] Prov. 16:21.

[7] Prov. 4:10.

[8] Ps. 37:9; Douay Ps. 36:9.

[9] Ibid.

[10] Ps. 27:13; Douay Ps. 26:13.

[11] 1 Pet. 2:13–14.

3.7 A Christian hero in northern Iberia: *The Chronicle of Alfonso III* (early 880s). Original in Latin.

Although probably not the author of this text, King Alfonso III of Asturias (r.866–910) may have been involved in its composition. The *Chronicle* positions itself as a continuation of the story of the Visigoths. It starts with the seventh-century Visigothic king, Wamba (r.672–680), who, the chronicler claims, successfully parried a naval attack by the Muslims (there is no other evidence for this) and went on to numerous other victories. It traces the fall of the Visigothic kingdom to the wickedness of King Witiza (r.698–710), whose immorality offends God. Finally, it takes up the renewal of the Visigoths—although, in fact, there is little tying the new king of Asturias to the old Visigothic kings—and their gradual "reconquest" of the Iberian peninsula by the grace of God. The excerpt here begins with the reign of Witiza.

1. What does the chronicler see as the relationship between political success, human morality, and God's favor?
2. What sorts of names does the chronicler use for Muslims and what might be their significance?

[Source: *Conquerors and Chroniclers of Early Medieval Spain*, trans. Kenneth Baxter Wolf (Liverpool: Liverpool University Press, 1990), pp. 162–69 (notes modified).]

5. In the era 739 (701), after the death of Egica, Witiza returned to Toledo to the royal throne.[1] He was a reprobate and was disgraceful in his habits. He dissolved the councils. He sealed the canons. He took many wives and concubines. And so that no council would be convened against him, he ordered the bishops, priests, and deacons to take wives.[2] This, then, was the cause of Spain's ruin. Thus says the scripture, "Because iniquity abounded, charity grew cold."[3] And another passage from scripture says, "If the people sin, the priest prays, but if the priests sin, there will be a plague upon the people."[4] They withdrew from the Lord so that they did not walk in the paths of his precepts or attentively observe how the Lord prohibited priests from acting evilly when he said to Moses in Exodus, "Let the priests who come to the Lord God be sanctified lest the Lord forsake them."[5] And again: "When they approach to serve at the holy altar, let them not bring along any sin within them lest perchance they die."[6] And because the kings and priests forsook the Lord, all of the armies of Spain perished. Meanwhile, after the tenth year of his reign, Witiza passed away with a natural death in Toledo, in the era 749 (711).

7. After Witiza died, Roderic [r.710–711/12] was anointed as king. In his time Spain grew even worse in its iniquity. In the third year of his rule, the Saracens entered Spain on account of the treachery of the sons of Witiza.[7] When the king became aware of their invasion, he immediately went out with his army to fight against them. But, weighed down by the quantity of their sins and exposed by the treachery of the sons of Witiza, the Goths were

---

[1] The *Chronicle* used a dating system by "era" that does not quite correspond to modern dates.

[2] The chronicler considered this the worst of Witiza's sins, but the king may simply have been trying to implement the canons of the Quinisext Council (see p. 60) allowing clergymen to keep their wives if they had been married before their ordination.

[3] Matt. 24:12.

[4] Num. 8:19, 16, 46–48.

[5] Exod. 19:22.

[6] Lev. 12:33; Matt. 5:23.

[7] "Saracens" refer to Muslims.

put to flight.[1] The army, fleeing to its destruction, was almost annihilated. Because they forsook the Lord and did not serve him in justice and truth, they were forsaken by the Lord so that they could no longer inhabit the land that they desired. Concerning the aforementioned King Roderic, we know nothing certain about his death. But in our own unrefined times, when the city of Viseo and its suburbs were being settled by our order,[2] a monument was found in a certain basilica there, upon which was inscribed an epitaph in this manner: "Here lies Roderic, the last king of the Goths." But let us return to that time when the Saracens entered Spain on the third day before the Ides of November, era 752 (November 11, 714).

8. The Arabs, after oppressing the region along with the kingdom, killed many with the sword and subjugated the rest to themselves by mollifying them with a covenant of peace. The city of Toledo, victor over all peoples, succumbed, vanquished by the victories of the Ishmaelites; subjected, it served them.[3] They placed prefects throughout all the provinces of Spain and paid tribute to the Babylonian king for many years until they elected their own king and established for themselves a kingdom in the patrician city of Córdoba.[4] At almost the same time, in this region of the Asturians, there was in the city of Gijón a prefect by the name of Munnuza, a companion of Tariq.[5] While he held the prefecture, a certain Pelayo, the swordbearer of the kings Witiza and Roderic, oppressed by the dominion of the Ishmaelites, had come to Asturias along with his sister. On account of her, Munnuza sent Pelayo to Córdoba as his envoy.[6] Before Pelayo returned, Munnuza married his sister through some strategem. When Pelayo returned he by no means consented to it. Since he had already been thinking about the salvation of the church, he hastened to bring this about with all of his courage. Then the evil Tariq sent soldiers to Munnuza, who were to apprehend Pelayo and lead him back to Córdoba, bound in chains. When they came to Asturias, seeking to apprehend him treacherously in a village called Brece, the plan of the Chaldeans was made known to Pelayo by a friend.[7] Seeing that it would be impossible for him to resist the Saracens because they were so numerous, Pelayo escaped from among them, rushed off and came to the edge of the river Piloña.[8] He found it overflowing its banks, but by swimming with the help of the horse upon which he sat, he crossed to the opposite side and climbed a mountain. The Saracens stopped pursuing him. As he was heading into the mountains, Pelayo joined himself to as many people as he found hastening to assemble. He climbed a high mountain called Auseva and headed for a cave on the side of the mountain which he knew to be very safe.[9] From this great cave flows a stream called the Enna. After Pelayo sent an order to all of the Asturians, they gathered together in one group and elected him their leader.[10] Hearing this, the soldiers who had come to apprehend him returned to Córdoba and related everything to their king, saying that Pelayo, as Munnuza had suggested, was clearly a rebel. Hearing this, the king, moved by an insane fury, ordered a very large army from all over Spain to go forth and he placed Alqamah, his companion, in charge of it. He ordered Oppa, a certain bishop of the see of Toledo and son of King Witiza—on account of whose treachery the Goths had perished—to go with Alqamah and the army to Asturias. Alqamah was advised by his colleague Tariq that if Pelayo refused to come to terms with the bishop, he should be taken by force in battle and brought to Córdoba. Coming

---

[1] The "Goths" are the "Visigoths."

[2] The phrase "settled by our order" seems to imply that King Alfonso himself was the author of the *Chronicle*. Viseo is in northwest Spain, at that time part of the Kingdom of Asturias.

[3] The "Ishmaelites" are the Muslims.

[4] The "Babylonian king" refers to the caliph in Damascus. "Their own king" refers to Umayyad prince Abd al-Rahman I, who escaped the Abbasid revolution of 750 and established an independent Umayyad emirate in 756. In fact, the Muslims had no king; the chronicler is using a term borrowed from his own culture.

[5] Tariq led the original Islamic conquest of Spain.

[6] That is, as the text subsequently clarifies, on account of Munnuza's romantic interest in Pelayo's sister. Arab sources, however, claim that Pelayo was sent to Córdoba as a hostage in an effort to forestall unrest in Asturias.

[7] The "Chaldeans" refers to the Muslims. The precise location of Brece is not known.

[8] A location nearly on the northern coast of Asturias.

[9] Today Covadonga (cave of the lady), a few miles east of the river Piloña. The name reflects the presence of a shrine to the Virgin Mary in the cave.

[10] Pelayo ruled 718–737.

with an army of almost 187,000 soldiers, they entered Asturias.

9. Pelayo was on Mt. Auseva with his allies. The army advanced to him and set up countless tents before the mouth of the cave. Bishop Oppa ascended the hill in front of Covadonga and spoke to Pelayo, saying, "Pelayo, Pelayo, where are you?"

Pelayo, responding from an opening, said, "I am here."

The bishop said to him, "I think that it is not unknown to you, brother and son, how all of Spain a short time ago was organized according to one order under the rule of the Goths, and that it outshone all other lands in learning and knowledge. If when the entire army of the Goths was assembled, it was unable to sustain the attack of the Ishmaelites, how much better will you be able to defend yourself on this mountain top? To me it seems difficult. Rather, heed my warning and recall your soul from this decision, so that you may take advantage of many good things and enjoy the partnership of the Chaldeans."

To this Pelayo responded, "Have you not read in the divine scriptures that the church of God is compared to a mustard seed and that it will be raised up again through divine mercy?"[1]

The bishop responded, "It is indeed written thus."

Pelayo said, "Christ is our hope that through this little mountain, which you see, the well-being of Spain and the army of the Gothic people will be restored. I have faith that the promise of the Lord which was spoken through David will be fulfilled in us: "I will visit their iniquities with the rod and their sins with scourges; but I will not remove my mercy from them."[2] Now, therefore, trusting in the mercy of Jesus Christ, I despise this multitude and am not afraid of it. As for the battle with which you threaten us, we have for ourselves an advocate in the presence of the Father, that is, the Lord Jesus Christ, who is capable of liberating us from these few."

And the bishop turned to the army and said, "Go forth and fight. You heard how he responded to me. I can see by his determination that you will never have a covenant of peace with him unless it be achieved through the vengeance of the sword."

10. Then Alqamah ordered his men to engage in battle. They took up arms. The catapults were set up. The slings were prepared. Swords flashed. Spears were brandished. Arrows were shot incessantly. But on this occasion the power of the Lord was not absent. For when stones were launched from the catapults and they neared the shrine of the holy virgin Mary, which is inside the cave, they turned back on those who shot them and violently cut down the Chaldeans. And because the Lord does not count spears, but offers the palm of victory to whomsoever he will, when the Asturians came out of the cave to fight, the Chaldeans turned in flight and were divided into two groups. There Bishop Oppa was immediately captured and Alqamah was killed. In that same place 124,000 of the Chaldeans were killed. But the 63,000 who were left alive ascended to the summit of Mt. Auseva and came down to Liébana through Amuesa.[3] But they could not escape the vengeance of the Lord. For when they had reached the summit of the mountain, which is over the bank of a river called the Deva, next to a village called Cosgaya, it happened, by a judgement of God, that the mountain, quaking from its very base, hurled the 63,000 men into the river and crushed them all. There even now, when this river fills beyond its limit, it reveals many visible signs of these events. Do not think this to be unfounded or fictitious. Remember that he who parted the waters of the Red Sea so that the children of Israel might cross, also crushed, with an immense mass of mountain, the Arabs who were persecuting the church of God.[4]

11. When Munnuza learned what had happened, he sprang from the same coastal city of Gijón and fled. In a certain village called Olalies he was captured and killed along with his men. Then the country was populated, the church restored, and everyone together gave thanks to God, saying, "Blessed be the name of the Lord who strengthens those who believe in him and destroys wicked peoples." Within a short time, Alfonso, the son of Peter, who was the leader of the Cantabrians and was from the royal line, came to Asturias.[5] He received in marriage the daughter of Pelayo named Ermesinda and he brought about many victories with his father-in-law and also afterward. Finally, peace was restored to the land. To the extent that the dignity of the name of Christ grew, the derisive calamity of the Chaldeans wasted away. Pelayo lived as king for nineteen years. His life came to

---

[1] For the reference to the mustard seed, see Matt. 17:20.

[2] Ps. 89:32–33; Douay Ps. 88:33–34.

[3] The army apparently fled through the heart of the mountainous Picos de Europa region of eastern Asturias.

[4] The reference to the Red Sea is in Exod. 14:21–22. The chronicler equates the Arabs to the ancient Egyptians.

[5] The Cantabrians were just to the east of Asturias.

an end with a natural death at Cangas de Onís in the era 775 (737).

12. Afterwards, Favila [r.737–739], Pelayo's son, succeeded in the place of his father. He constructed, with marvellous workmanship, a basilica in honour of the Holy Cross. He lived only a short time. On a certain occasion of levity, he is reported to have been killed by a bear in the second year of his reign, in the era 777 (739).

13. After the death of Favila, Alfonso [r.739–757] was elected king by all the people, receiving the royal sceptre with divine grace. He always crushed the audacity of his enemies. Together with his brother, Fruela, he took many cities in battle, moving his army frequently. Specifically, he took: Lugo, Tuy, Oporto, Anegia, the metropolitan city of Braga, Viseo, Chaves, Ledesma, Salamanca, Numancia, which is now called Zamora, Avila, Astorga, León, Simancas, Saldaña, Amaya, Segovia, Osma, Sepúlveda, Arganza, Clunia, Mave, Oca, Miranda, Revenga, Carbonárica, Abeica, Cenicero, and Alesanco, with their fortresses, villas and villages.[1] Killing all the Arabs with the sword, he led the Christians back with him to his country.

3.8 Celebrating local leaders: Abbo of Saint-Germain-des-Prés, *Battles of the City of Paris* (late 9th cent.). Original in Latin and Greek.

The Viking invasions into Carolingian Europe necessitated immediate responses from local leaders, giving them new prestige and power. Abbo, a young monk at the monastery of Saint-Germain-des-Prés, at that time just outside Paris, composed a poem about the attacks on the city in the years 885–896, writing perhaps a decade later. Mingling Greek words with his mainly Latin text, Abbo enhanced his expressive choices, showed off his learning, and emphasized his major points. It was clear that Charles the Fat (r.881–887) was not going to revive the empire of Charlemagne. Attacked on every side, he did not have the forces to deal with all the challenges to his power, and thus he chose to negotiate rather than fight. Not he but Odo (*c.*860–898), count of Paris and duke of France, along with Gozlin, bishop of Paris (r.884–885), were the worldly heroes not only of the *Battles of the City of Paris* but also of the West Frankish nobility, who elected Odo king in 888. The heavenly heroes of Abbo's poem were Saint Germain and Sainte Genevieve, both associated with the city of Paris during their lifetimes. Moreover, Germain was the patron saint of Abbo's monastery, where his relics were housed.

1. How (in Abbo's view) were the attacks of the Vikings part of God's plan and what outcome did God have in mind?
2. How did the role of the Virgin Mary in Abbo's poem compare with her role in saving Constantinople against the Muslims in *The Easter Chronicle* (above, p. 55)?

[Source: *Viking Attacks on Paris: The* Bella parisiacae urbis *of Saint-Germain-des-Prés*, ed. and trans. Nirmal Dass (Peeters: Paris, 2007), pp. 23, 25, 27, 29, 31, 33, 35, 37, 39, 45 (notes modified).]

---

[1] This list of towns in the Duero and upper Ebro valleys reflects the geographical range of Asturian raids in the wake of the Berber rebellion and exodus from northern Spain in 740–741. Actual Asturian control over these areas probably dates from the next century, when the chronicle was written.

A Letter of Dedication by Abbo, the Most Humble, to His Beloved Brother Gozlin

Abbo, the least of God's creatures, unworthy deacon, embraces his brother Gozlin, with an affection that is pure, sincere, and higher than any found on earth, and wishes for him, in Christ, all the happiness that we are able to obtain both in this life and the next.[1] Your brotherly love, most dear to me, has impelled me, time and again, to dedicate to you this little work, devoted to the battles of Paris and to Odo, the most notable prince, the foremost of all the leaders of men that this kingdom has produced down to the present day;[2] this little work, as you well know, is born of our labor, and greatly testifies to your deep interest in my most meager talent, and demonstrates that you have not forgotten our brotherly love. Know then, O happiest of brothers, that a similar emotion urged me to address to you these simple pages, not only to ensure that so precious a love may not be disappointed on my account, but also to satisfy the very best friend among readers, so that these pages may fulfill to the very end the precious task for which they are being sent forth, and above all that your wise hand may clear up the imperfections found in them. Indeed, being preoccupied with my studies, to which I have devoted myself entirely, I have not found the leisure necessary to revise these pages. Thus, they are presented to you for the first time, such pages as now follow; only the parchment has changed. Skim through them with your wise judgment, like another Apollo.[3]

Having laid bare the purpose of this narration, it is good, I think, to make known the two reasons for which I decided to undertake this little work. The first was to embark on a literary exercise (for I was but a simple student of letters and had read the *Eclogues* of Virgil for the first time).[4] The second was my intention of leaving behind an enduring example to those who are guardians over other cities. As for the rest, I leave it to your benevolent love, and to that of other readers. Know that though I have undertaken to write this volume of verse, it is not meant to make me into a poet. Here you will see none of those fabrications often found in the work of grand poets. Indeed, nowhere have I gathered Fauns and wild animals dancing, singing, or frolicking, after the example of Silenus.[5] Nowhere have I forced rigid oak trees to rustle their tops. For the sake of charm, my song shall have neither forests, nor birds, nor even high walls, to keep company with my meters. None of my verses shall follow the example of Orpheus and seek to snatch away from Orcus, or from other infernal deities, the souls of those plunged into the darkness of Tartarus.[6] It is perfectly obvious that I have never had such a desire, nor do I have the ability to accomplish such an undertaking. Therefore, I do not take on the name of poet, and these are not fictions that I present. Rather, I have used the means available to me to complete my task.

I have divided these books into three, which are ornamented solely by those things that I saw and heard. Two of these books are notable for their account of the battles fought around Paris and those fought by King Odo, and also for the miracles, otherwise unknown, performed during the siege by my dear and most benevolent master Germain, who was once the bishop, without equal, of this city.[7] As for the third book, which completes the trinity, it is manifestly different from the story of the siege. Therefore, it takes up very little room, and it seeks to provide clerics with methods of effective literary adornment. It will be suitable for students who search for terms for their compositions. Allegory will also very briefly shine forth for those who admire such things. But, because allegory often works by way of obscure words, I have written the glosses on top with my own hand.[8] ...

---

[1] Perhaps this Gozlin was a fellow monk at Saint-Germain. He should not be mistaken for Bishop Gozlin.

[2] Odo, count of Paris and later king of the West Frankish Kingdom.

[3] Apollo was, among many other things, the patron of music and poetry and was known for his wise judgment. He was also the sun god, and is invoked as such in line 77.

[4] The Roman poet Virgil (d.19 BCE) was a model throughout the Middle Ages and indeed, into our own time.

[5] Here Abbo pokes fun at poems that describe wild parties; Silenus, while a Greek god, was also a notable drunkard.

[6] More fun at the expense of pagan Greek and Latin poetry. But Abbo is also making the point that his poem is serious history, not fanciful story-telling. Nevertheless, the *Battles of the City of Paris* includes some mythic elements, such as exaggerating the forces of the enemy in order to point up the heroism of the Christian defenders.

[7] Saint Germain (496–576) became bishop of Paris in 555. His bones were held as precious relics at Abbo's monastery, and (the poem claims) he continued to intervene in worldly affairs even after his death.

[8] Abbo's poem exists in full in only one manuscript, which is kept at the Bibliothèque nationale de France (MS lat. 13833); it may possibly be in his own hand.

May your joys and honors be many as the rays of Phoebus;
And may you come to find your end with God, who is without end.
HERE ENDS THE LETTER.

HERE BEGINS THE FIRST BOOK OF THE BATTLES OF THE CITY OF PARIS.

In the year 885.[1]
Shout with joy, Lutetia, you who were saved by God on high.
This is how you were known in days long ago, but now you take
Your name from Isia city that sat on the Danaan plain,[2]
Whose harbor shone forth as the brightest embellishment of all;⁣   5
That same Isia for whose treasures the greedy Argives yearned.[3]
A bastard name, indeed, a sort of metaplasm for you,
Isia's rival, but which describes you well, O Lutetia.
It is by this new name, that is Paris, that the world knows you;
This means you are Isia's twin; no difference between you both.   10

Now, in the region of Sequanus[4] is found the rich kingdom
Of the Franks. Raise yourself up high, now, so that you may sing forth:
"I am that city, dazzling like a queen over all cities."
And you too are renowned for your harbor, much praised by others.
Those that covet the wealth of the Franks come to pay you homage.   15
An island rejoices in you, and a river stretches out
Around you in a perfect embrace that caresses your walls.[5]
To your right, to your left, on your banks are bridges that hold back
The waves. Here and there are towers that guard the bridges;
Some of these face the city; others face out to the river.   20

Speak, most wondrous of cities, of the gift the Danes brought for you,
Those friends of Pluto, in the time when Gozlin, the Lord's bishop,
The sweetest of heroes, the mildest of shepherds, governed you.[6]
"Astonished am I," she said, "that no one has spoken of this.
Did you not see with your own eyes what came to pass? Speak of that."[7]   25
Indeed, I saw everything, and gladly I obey your will.

---

[1] Like a chronicle, the poem covers events year by year.

[2] Lutetia is the Roman name for Paris. Abbo thought that the name Paris derived from Isia (Hysia) a town in ancient Greece.

[3] Just as the Argives wanted the wealth of Hysia, so the Danes will lust after the riches of Paris. Abbo is right to call the Viking invaders of France "Danes," since they mainly came from what is Denmark today. The word "metaplasm" in the next line shows off Abbo's knowledge of Greek.

[4] Sequanus is the Gallo-Roman name for the Seine, which flowed (and flows) through Paris.

[5] The "island" is the Île-de-la-Cité, today right in the middle of Paris and the Seine River, and in Abbo's time constituting the heart of the city itself. In his battles with the Danes, Odo took advantage of its defensive walls.

[6] The "gift" of the Danes is meant to be ironic; if they are the "friends of Pluto," they come from Hell and are minions of the Devil. Bishop Gozlin (also known as Gauzlin) was related to the royal family. Chancellor for Emperor Charles the Bald (r.843–877), he was at the same time lay abbot of four monasteries including Saint-Germain itself. In 884 he became bishop of Paris; he died a year later.

[7] The city of Paris here asks Abbo to "speak"; she takes the role of his patron and audience.

Now, here are the gifts the cruel ones brought to offer you:
Seven hundred high-prowed ships and very many smaller ones,
Along with an enormous multitude of smaller vessels
The very ones that in the vulgar tongue are often called barques.[1] 30
The deep waters of Sequanus were so overly crowded,
For a distance that extended more than two leagues downriver,
That one asked in amazement, Where had the river vanished?
It could not be seen, hidden, as though by a veil of fir, oak,
Elm, and alder, each one entirely drenched by the water. 35
And when in two days these ships made landfall hard by the city,
Siegfried did make his way to the great hall of the famed shepherd;
Though king in name only, he still commanded many warriors.[2]
After bowing his head, he addressed the bishop in these words:
"O Gozlin, show mercy to yourself and the flock given you. 40
That you may come not to ruin, grant our plea, we ask you.
Give us your consent that we might go our way, well beyond
This city. Nothing in it shall we then touch, but shall preserve
And safeguard all the honors that belong to you and Odo,
Who is the noblest of all counts and who is the future king. 45
Guardian of this city, he shall become the kingdom's rampart."[3]

Then the Lord's bishop, in greatest loyalty, offered these words:
"By our king, Charles,[4] have we been given this city to guard;
By him, whose majestic realm spreads almost over the whole earth,
By the Lord's will, and who is King and Master of the mighty. 50
The realm must not suffer by the destruction of this city;
But rather this city must save the realm and preserve the peace.
Now, if by chance, these walls were entrusted to you, as they are
To us, and you were asked to do all that you have asked of us,
Would you deem it right and agree?" Siegfried said: "By my honor, 55
Rather my head were lopped off by a sword and thrown to the dogs.
However, if you do not agree to my requests, we shall
Have our siege engines, at daybreak, hurl poisoned darts at you;
With sunset you shall know hunger's curse. It shall go on for years."
Thus having spoken, he went his way and assembled his men. 60

Now, when dawn had nearly faded away, the battle began.
Jumping into their boats, the Danes headed for the tower,
And began to hurl stones at it and riddled it with arrows.
The city grew noisy; people grew fearful. Bridges swayed.
Everyone rushed about, trying to help defend the tower. 65
It was then that Count Odo did shine, along with his brother
Rotbert, as well as Count Ragenar. Then it was also that

---

[1] Abbo exaggerates the numbers of ships.

[2] Abbo picks up on the impermanence of Viking leadership. Siegfried was not a king but simply a leader of a group of raiders. Note that the raiders traveled with their families, as line 126, when the wives call out, makes clear.

[3] Here the wicked and pagan Siegfried is depicted as showing honor to the bishop and predicting Odo's future kingship.

[4] The reference is to Charles the Fat.

Ebolus, stalwart abbot, the bishop's nephew, proved worthy.[1]
At that place, the prelate was hit by a sharp-pointed arrow,
And at the same place, a young warrior, Frederick, was struck down 70
By a sword. The young warrior died, but the old man recovered,
Thanks to divine medicine, administered to him by God.
For many there, this was the last moment of their lives;
But others dealt out bitter wounds, and forced the Danes to fall back,
Who carried away with them many of their lifeless friends. 75
By now, Apollo, and all of Olympus, had veered westwards,
Soon sinking between ultimate Thule and the southern regions.[2]

Now the tower did not shine forth with all its magnificence,
For it was far from finished. But its foundations were solid
And stood firmly grounded. Proudly it rose; its crenels were sound.[3] 80
During the night that followed, after the battle had ended,
A wooden tier was built all the way around the tower,
Raised atop the old bastion, and half as high as before.
Thus, together, the sun and the Danes beheld this new tower.
The latter were soon locked in a frightful fight with the faithful. 85
Arrows flew here, there through the air; blood gushed and flowed;
Darts, stones, and javelins were hurled by ballistae and slingshots.[4]
Nothing was seen, between heaven and earth, but these projectiles.
The many arrows made the tower, built in the night, groan out;
It was the night that gave it birth, as I have chanted above. 90
Fear seized the city—people screamed, battle horns resounded
Calling everyone to come and protect the trembling tower.
Christians fought and ran about, trying to resist the assault.
Among all the warriors, there were two most outstanding
For their valor: one was a count, the other an abbot. 95
Victorious Odo was one, never routed in battle;
He fortified those who were exhausted; revived their strength,
And rushed about on the tower, striking down the enemy.
As for those who sought to dig beneath the walls with iron picks,
He served them up with oil and wax and pitch, which was all mixed up 100
Together and made into a hot liquid on a furnace,
Which burned the hair of the Danes; made their skulls split open.
Indeed, many of them died, and the others went and sought out
The river. And then our men, with one voice, loudly exclaimed:
"Right badly scorched are you! Run now quickly to the Sequanus. 105
Its current will allay your pain and restore your flowing manes."
Dauntless Odo struck down many. But what of the other one?
This other was Ebolus, his companion and his equal—

---

[1] Rotbert (also known as Robert) was Odo's younger brother. Ragenar (also known as Regnier) was the count of Hainault. Ebolus, nephew of Bishop Gozlin, was the abbot of Saint-Germain-des-Prés.

[2] That is, the sun set in the west, the "ultimate Thule" being a cliché for the far north.

[3] A crenel is a thin opening in a fortress, from which missiles or arrows can be fired.

[4] The Viking ballistae were "throwing engines" used to hurl either stones or javelins (heavy spears). Unlike traction and counter-weight trebuchets (see "Weapons and Warfare in the Middle Ages," in "Reading through Looking," pp. XII–XIV), ballistae were torsion catapults. They released projectiles by using the pulling force of a rope stretched between bow-shaped staves.

With a single spear, he pierced seven Danes all at once,
And in jest he said to his own to take them to the kitchen.[1]   110
In battle none outshone, equaled, or compared with these two men.
However, many did fight most courageously and scorned death.
But indeed what is a single drop for a thousand fires?

Among the faithful were no more than two hundred warriors;
The grim ones were a thousand times forty, or forty thousand;   115
They sent fresh troops dashing to the tower. O most horrid sight!
They only fought fiercely. A great, quaking clamor arose;
It could be heard on both sides—a mighty chorus of voices
Filled the air, as hurtling rocks thudded into painted shields.
These shields let forth groans and helmets clattered as swift arrows fell.   120
Some horsemen, returning from their pillaging, rode forward
To join the fight at the tower—well-rested and fed were they.
But many among them got no chance to hurtle their stones,
For they were struck down and killed; the rest ran back to their ships.
Before drawing their last anguished breath, the dying Danes tore   125
At their hair and shed tears. Then their wives cried out:
"So, you have run back from that furnace! I know, you Devil's son!
But not even one among you shall chance upon victory.
Was it all for nothing I gave you Ceres, Bacchus, boar meat?[2]
Why are you so quickly exhausted that you seek our shelter?   130
Were you hoping to have a second meal? Glutton! Is this why
The others return, too? A fine welcome they will also get!"[3]
These rude mouths drove them to make their own domed furnace near
The bottom of the tower, whose very name they greatly scorned.
The hard Danes ardently sought to breach the tower's foundations;   135
An immense breach appeared—wide-gaping beyond description.
As was readily seen, there appeared, at the bottom,
Those gallant warriors, whose names have already been mentioned,
With helms on their heads. They and the Danes beheld each other,
But the Danes held back, gripped by an insurmountable horror.   140
Suddenly, a huge wheel was thrown from the top of the tower
Right upon the Danes, laying low six, whose souls were sent to Hell;
They were dragged off by their feet and joined the throngs of the dead.
Then they set the gate alight with fire guarded by Vulcan,
By which they hoped to burn our men and destroy the tower.[4]   145
A dreadful pyre formed and smoke billowed up in ghastly clouds
That enveloped the warriors. And then, within an hour,
The fortress vanished completely in a great gloom, black as pitch.
Not wishing that we, who know Him, should suffer further torment,
Our Lord, filled with mercy for us, ordained that the dreadful   150
Smoke should fall upon the very ones that had created it.

---

[1] The joke is that the Danes were, so to speak, on a spit, ready to be roasted.

[2] Abbo has the wives complain that they have fed the best food to their husbands (Ceres is the god of grain, Bacchus of wine), but they have received only cowardice in return.

[3] In Viking sagas, too, the women often incite their men to violent deeds.

[4] Vulcan was the Roman god of fire.

Then Mars bestirred himself and aroused heated battle frenzy:[1]
And then, two standard-bearers rushed out of the good city.
Each one carried a lance, and they climbed up the tower, holding
The standards, tinted golden with saffron, that frightened the Danes;   155
A hundred of them were struck down by a hundred quick arrows—
The life of the Danes spurted away along with their blood—
Dragged off by the hair, to their ships—their last abode.
Thus was the surging of Lemnos overcome by the great might
Of Neptune—for the water soaked what the fire had ravaged.[2]   160
And there fell Rotbert, ever happy, joyful, struck down by
A cruel stroke, delivered by this most pernicious people;[3]
By God's grace, only some of our people perished with him.
Now, just as an overconfident wolf that is filled with shame,
For it seized no prey, seeks out the depths of the forest, thus did   165
The foe fall back and scurry away in great and furtive flight;
They mourned three hundred of their own, left lifeless for Charon.[4]
The night passed in fixing the damage done to the tower.
These two battles were fought just a few days before November
Grew frosty and ran its complete course, and just as December   170
Stood ready to wane and yield to the last days of the year.

Now as the sun began to fill the sky with reddening beams,
Over the See of the holy Dénis,[5] up along the banks
Of the Sequanus, indeed not far from Saint-Germain-le-Rond,[6]
The Danes assembled that they might set up their encampment,   175
Fashioning stakes, gathering stones and earth to pile in one heap.
Then, the cruel ones, both on horseback and on foot overran
The hills, the fields, forests, open pastures and the villages.
All infants, boys and girls, youths, and even those hoary with age,
The father and the sons and even mothers—they killed them all.   180
They slaughtered the husband before the very eyes of his wife;
Before the eyes of the husband, the wife fell prey to carnage.
The children perished right before the eyes of their parents.
The bondsman was set free, while the freeman was made a bondsman;
The slave was made the master, and the master became the slave.   185
Both the wine-grower and also the farmer, together with
The vineyards and the fields suffered the pitiless weight of death.
Then did the land of the Franks know grief, for masters and servants
Were gone; and gone the joy of heroes; only tears remained.
No more houses were left ruled over by a living master.   190
Alas! A rich land stripped of its treasures, left with bloody wounds,
Fully robbed, filled with grim murder—a frenzy beyond compare.

---

[1] Mars was the god of war.

[2] Lemnos was the Greek island where Vulcan kept his fiery forge; Neptune was the god of the sea.

[3] Not the Rotbert who was Odo's younger brother.

[4] Charon was the boatman who ferried the dead to the underworld.

[5] The See of the holy Dénis is a reference to Saint Denis, patron saint of Paris.

[6] Saint-Germain-le-Rond, today Saint-Germain-l'Auxerrois, was a church near Paris where the Vikings pitched their camp and set up fortifications. Today, like Saint-Germain-des-Prés, it is within the city of Paris.

The Danes ransacked and despoiled, massacred, and burned and ravaged;
They were an evil cohort, a deadly phalanx, a grim horde.
Nor did they tarry for long to do all that they sought to do,   195
Being driven by some blood-filled vision that was before them.
Valleys were worn down, befouled, that were once splendid as the Alps.
The men in arms, in their keenness to flee, sought out the woods.

No one stayed to be found; everyone fled. Alas! None fought back.
Ah, the Danes took away on their ships, all that was splendid   200
In this good realm, all that was the pride of this famous region!
Throughout this horrible conflict, Paris stood firm, fearless;
It remained cheerful, despite all the darts that fell around it.

...

Now when morning began to shine, the weapons of these hard men [the Danes] 205
Again clashed; they advanced, hard-packed, underneath a *testudo*.[1]
Many of them fought; others commenced to deal with the ditches
That encircled the tower; took to filling in the trenches:
They threw in clods of earth, and leaves torn from well-wooded forests,
And stalks that they had taken and stripped utterly of all grain.   210
Also, they flung in hay from meadows, scrub, and vines, grapes torn off;
Then they pushed in old oxen, and even lovely cows and calves;
And lastly, alas, they slaughtered the luckless captives they held;
All this they took and piled into the trenches to fill them in.[2]
This is what they did the whole day through on the field of battle.   215
Seeing everything, the holy bishop then shed bright tears.
In a loud voice, he besought the Mother of our Lord and
Savior: "Blessed Mother of our Redeemer—sole hope
Of this world, bright Star of the Sea, brighter far than all the stars—
Bend thine ear, in mercy, to my prayers and to my pleas.   220
If it is thy pleasure that I again celebrate the Mass,
Grant that this foe—impious, fierce, cruel and most wicked,
That has slain the captives—be led, I pray, into death's grim noose."
Then swiftly the bishop, Gozlin, with a tearful prayer,
From the high tower, let loose an arrow at a Dane below,   225
Sending that wretch, who had dispatched others, into death's dark bonds—
The luckless man held up his shield; sought to rush to his friends;
His mouth slackened and he fell heavily; gone was all courage;
He breathed out his soul, born of evil, and stretched out on the earth,
Filling the ditch just like the very victims of his cruel sword.   230

The city has honor through its love for Mary, most holy,
By whose grace we spend the days of our lives in harmony.
It is most fitting, while we are able, to render her thanks;
With our hymns of peace let us sing to her glory divine;
Let our voices ring on high; it is mere for so to do: 235

"O Mother most fair of our Savior. Hail, Queen of Heaven...."

---

[1] *Testudo:* a military formation that used shields above and on all sides to form a protected unit.

[2] The Parisians had built defensive trenches before the walls of the city.

RELIGION AND POLITICS

3.9 An early view of the Prophet: Muhammad ibn Ishaq, *Life of Muhammad* (754–767). Original in Arabic.

Writing under the patronage of the Abbasid Caliph al-Mansur, Ibn Ishaq (*c.*704–767), who was born in Medina, wrote the first extant life of Muhammad. It was soon attacked for including spurious poetry and for lacking sufficient *isnad*—the chains of named sources that were, by the end of the eighth century, considered essential to prove the authenticity of any narrative about the Prophet (hadith). (For hadith considered authoritative, see al-Bukhari, *On Fasting*, below, p. 147). Ibn Ishaq was also accused of Shi'ite sympathies. It is thus not surprising that his original work is lost. The version that we have today is an edition by Ibn Hisham (d.833), a scholar who, though somewhat critical of the original, also considered it of great value.

1. How and why does Ibn Ishaq show Muhammad, "the apostle of God," fulfilling the Christian and Jewish prophecies?
2. In what ways were the mission, virtues, and lifestyle of Muhammad in Ibn Ishaq's account similar to—and different from—those of saints in Christian hagiography, such as the *Life of St. Antony*, above, p. 30?

[Source: *The Life of Muhammad: A Translation of Ishaq's* Sirat Rasul Allah, trans. and ed. Alfred Guillaume (London: Oxford University Press, 1955), pp. 81–83, 104–7 (slightly modified).]

The apostle of God grew up, God protecting him and keeping him from the vileness of heathenism because he wished to honor him with apostleship, until he grew up to be the finest of his people in manliness, the best in character, most noble in lineage, the best neighbor, the most kind, truthful, reliable, the furthest removed from filthiness and corrupt morals through loftiness and nobility, so that he was known among his people as "The trustworthy" because of the good qualities which God had implanted in him. The apostle, so I was told, used to tell how God protected him in his childhood during the period of heathenism, saying, "I found myself among the boys of Quraysh[1] carrying stones such as boys play with; we had all uncovered ourselves, each taking his shirt and putting it round his neck as he carried the stones. I was going to and fro in the same way, when an unseen figure slapped me most painfully saying, 'Put your shirt on'; so I took it and fastened it on me and then began to carry the stones upon my neck wearing my shirt alone among my fellows." ...

The Apostle of God Marries Khadija

Khadija was a merchant woman of dignity and wealth. She used to hire men to carry merchandise outside the country on a profit-sharing basis, for Quraysh were a people given to commerce. Now when she heard about the prophet's truthfulness, trustworthiness, and honorable character, she sent for him and proposed that he should take her goods to Syria and trade with them, while she would pay him more than she paid others. He was to take a lad of hers called Maysara.

The apostle of God accepted the proposal, and the two set forth until they came to Syria. The apostle stopped in the shade of a tree near a monk's cell, when the monk came up to Maysara and asked who the man was who was resting beneath the tree. He told him that he was of Quraysh, the people who held the sanctuary; and the monk exclaimed: "None but a prophet ever sat beneath this tree."

---

[1] The tribe at Mecca to which Muhammad also belonged.

Then the prophet sold the goods he had brought and bought what he wanted to buy and began the return journey to Mecca. The story goes that at the height of noon, when the heat was intense as he rode his beast, Maysara saw two angels shading the apostle from the sun's rays. When he brought Khadija her property she sold it and it amounted to double or thereabouts. Maysara for his part told her about the two angels who shaded him and of the monk's words. Now Khadija was a determined, noble, and intelligent woman possessing the properties with which God willed to honor her. So when Maysara told her these things, she sent to the apostle of God and—so the story goes—said: "O son of my uncle I like you because of our relationship and your high reputation among your people, your trustworthiness and good character and truthfulness." Then she proposed marriage. Now Khadija at that time was the best born woman in Quraysh, of the greatest dignity and, too, the richest. All her people were eager to get possession of her wealth if it were possible.

Khadija was the daughter of Khuwaylid b. Asad b. 'Abdu'l-'Uzza b. Qusayy b. Kilab b. Murra b. Ka'b b. Lu'ayy b. Ghalib b. Fihr.[1] Her mother was Fatima bt. Za'ida b. al-Asamm b. Rawaha b. Hajar b. 'Abd b. Malis b. 'Amir b. Lu'ayy b. Ghalib b. Fihr. Her mother was Hala bt. 'Abd Manaf b. al-Harith b. 'Amr b. Munqidh b. 'Amr b. Ma'is b. 'Amir b. Lu'ayy b. Ghalib b. Fihr. Hala's mother was Qilaba bt. Su'ayd b. Sa'd b. Sahm b. 'Amr b. Husays b. Ka'b b. Lu'ayy b. Ghalib b. Fihr.

The apostle of God told his uncles of Khadija's proposal, and his uncle Hamza b. 'Abdu'l-Muttalib went with him to Khuwaylid b. Asad and asked for her hand and he married her.

She was the mother of all the apostle's children except Ibrahim, namely al-Qasim (whereby he was known as Abu'l-Qasim); al-Tahir, al-Tayyib, Zaynab, Ruqayya, Umm Kulthum, and Fatima.

Al-Qasim, al-Tayyib, and al-Tahir died in paganism. All his daughters lived into Islam, embraced it, and migrated with him to Medina.

Khadija had told Waraqa b. Naufal b. Asad b. 'Abdu'l-'Uzza, who was her cousin and a Christian who had studied the scriptures and was a scholar, what her slave Maysara had told her that the monk had said and how he had seen the two angels shading him. He said, "If this is true, Khadija, then truly Muhammad is the prophet of this people. I knew that a prophet of this people was to be expected. His time has come," or words to that effect. Waraqa was finding the time of waiting wearisome and used to say "How long?" Some lines of his on the theme are:

> I persevered and was persistent in remembering
> An anxiety which often evoked tears. And
> Confirmatory evidence kept coming from Khadija.
> Long have I had to wait, O Khadija,
> In the vale of Mecca in spite of my hope   5
> That I might see the outcome of thy words.
> I could not bear that the words of the monk
> You told me of should prove false
> That Muhammad should rule over us
> Overcoming those who would oppose him.   10
> And that a glorious light should appear in the land
> To preserve men from disorders.
> His enemies shall meet disaster
> And his friends shall be victorious.
> Would that I might be there then to see,   15
> For I should be the first of his supporters,
> Joining in that which Quraysh hate
> However loud they shout in that Mecca of theirs.
> I hope to ascend through him whom they all dislike
> To the Lord of the Throne though they are cast
>   down.   20
> Is it folly not to disbelieve in Him
> Who chose him Who raised the starry heights?
> If they and I live, things will be done
> Which will throw the unbelievers into confusion.
> And if I die, 'tis but the fate of mortals   25
> To suffer death and dissolution....

The Prophet's Mission

When Muhammad the apostle of God reached the age of forty, God sent him in compassion to mankind, "as an evangelist to all men."[2] Now God had made a covenant with every prophet whom he had sent before him that he should believe in him, testify to his truth, and help him against his adversaries. He required His prophets to transmit that to everyone who believed in them, and they carried out their obligations in that respect. God

---

[1] The abbreviation b. means "ibn," son of, while bt. means "bint," daughter of. Through this string of names, the author is authenticating Khadija's lineage. Compare a similar concern with genealogy in the case of Jesus, in Matt. 1:1–11.

[2] Sura 34:27.

said to Muhammad, "When God made a covenant with the prophets, [He said], 'This is the scripture and wisdom which I have given you; afterwards an apostle will come confirming what you know that you may believe in him and help him.' He said, 'Do you accept this and take up my burden?' i.e., the burden of my agreement which I have laid upon you. They said, 'We accept it.' He answered, 'Then bear witness and I am a witness with you.'"[1] Thus God made a covenant with all the prophets that they should testify to his truth and help him against his adversaries, and they transmitted that obligation to those who believed in them among the two monotheistic religions.

Al-Zuhri related from 'Urwa b. Zybayr that 'A'isha[2] told him that when Allah [God] desired to honor Muhammad and have mercy on His servants by means of him, the first sign of prophethood granted to the apostle was true visions, resembling the brightness of daybreak, which were shown to him in his sleep. And Allah, she said, made him love solitude so that he liked nothing better than to be alone.

'Abdu'l-Malik b. 'Ubaydullah b. Abu Sufyan b. al-'Ala' b. Jariya the Thaqafite, who had a retentive memory, related to me from a certain scholar that the apostle at the time when Allah willed to bestow His grace upon him and endow him with prophethood would go forth for his affair and journey far afield until he reached the glens of Mecca and the beds of its valleys where no house was in sight; and there was no stone or tree that he passed that didn't say, "Peace unto thee, O apostle of Allah." And the apostle would turn to his right and left and look behind him and he would see nothing but trees and stones. Thus he stayed seeing and hearing so long as it pleased Allah that he should stay. Then Gabriel came to him with the gift of God's grace while he was on Hira'[3] in the month of Ramadan.

Wahb b. Kaisan, a client of the family of al-Zubayr, told me: I heard 'Abdullah b. al-Zubayr say to 'Ubayd b. 'Umayr b. Qatada the Laythite, "O 'Ubayd tell us how began the prophethood which was first bestowed on the apostle when Gabriel came to him." And 'Ubayd in my presence related to 'Abdullah and those with him as

follows: The apostle would pray in seclusion on Hira' every year for a month to practice *tahannuth* as was the custom of Quraysh in heathen days. *Tahannuth* is religious devotion. Abu Talib said:

> By Thaur and him who made Thabir firm in its place
> And by those going up to ascend Hira' and coming down.[4]

Wahb b. Kaisan told me that 'Ubayd said to him: Every year during that month the apostle would pray in seclusion and give food to the poor that came to him. And when he completed the month and returned from his seclusion, first of all before entering his house he would go to the Ka'ba[5] and walk round it seven times or as often as it pleased God; then he would go back to his house until, in the year when God sent him, in the month of Ramadan in which God willed concerning him what He willed of His grace, the apostle set forth to Hira' as was his custom, and his family with him. When it was the night on which God honored him with his mission and showed mercy on His servants thereby, Gabriel brought him the command of God. "He came to me," said the apostle of God, "while I was asleep, with a coverlet of brocade whereon was some writing, and said, 'Read!' I said, 'What shall I read?' He pressed me with it so tightly that I thought it was death; then he let me go and said, 'Read!' I said, 'What shall I read?' He pressed me with it again so that I thought it was death; then he let me go and said 'Read!' I said, 'What shall I read?' He pressed me with it the third time so that I thought it was death and said 'Read!' I said, 'What then shall I read?'—and this I said only to deliver myself from him, lest he should do the same to me again. He said:

> Read in the name of thy Lord who created,
> Who created man of blood coagulated.
> Read! Thy Lord is the most beneficent,
> Who taught by the pen,
> Taught that which they knew not unto men.[6]

---

[1] Sura 3:75.

[2] One of Muhammad's wives.

[3] A nearby mountain.

[4] Thaur and Thabir are mountains near Mecca.

[5] This was Mecca's holy site. At this time, before Mecca became Muslim, it was filled with images of many gods.

[6] Sura 96:1–5. For a different translation, see "The Embryo" above, p. 68.

So I read it, and he departed from me. And I awoke from my sleep, and it was as though these words were written on my heart. When I was midway on the mountain, I heard a voice from heaven saying, 'O Muhammad! thou art the apostle of God and I am Gabriel.' I raised my head towards heaven to see (who was speaking), and lo, [there was] Gabriel in the form of a man with feet astride the horizon, saying, 'O Muhammad! thou art the apostle of God and I am Gabriel.' I stood gazing at him, moving neither forward nor backward; then I began to turn my face away from him, but towards whatever region of the sky I looked, I saw him as before. And I continued standing there, neither advancing nor turning back, until Khadija sent her messengers in search of me and they gained the high ground above Mecca and returned to her while I was standing in the same place; then he parted from me and I from him, returning to my family. And I came to Khadija and sat by her thigh and drew close to her. She said, 'O Abu'l-Qasim,[1] where have you been? By God, I sent my messengers in search of you, and they reached the high ground above Mecca and returned to me.' Then I told her of what I had seen; and she said, 'Rejoice, O son of my uncle, and be of good heart. Truly, by Him in whose hand is Khadija's soul, I have hope that you will be the prophet of this people.'" Then she rose and gathered her garments about her and set forth to her cousin Waraqa b. Naufal b. Asad b. 'Abdu'l-'Uzza b. Qusayy, who had become a Christian and read the scriptures and learned from those that follow the Torah and the Gospel. And when she related to him what the apostle of God told her he had seen and heard, Waraqa cried, "Holy! Holy! Truly, by Him in whose hand is Waraqa's soul, if you have spoken the truth to me, O Khadija, then the greatest Namus [i.e., Gabriel], who came to Moses in the past, has come to him [Muhammad], and lo, he is the prophet of this people. Bid him be of good heart." So Khadija returned to the apostle of God and told him what Waraqa had said. And when the apostle of God had

finished his period of seclusion and returned [to Mecca], in the first place he performed the circumambulation of the Ka'ba, as was his custom. While he was doing it, Waraqa met him and said, "O son of my brother, tell me what you have seen and heard." The apostle told him, and Waraqa said, "Surely, by Him in whose hand is Waraqa's soul, you are the prophet of this people. Unto you has come the greatest Namus, who came unto Moses. You will be called a liar, and they will use you spitefully and cast you out and fight against you. Truly, if I live to see that day, I will help God in such ways as He knows." Then he brought his head near to him and kissed his forehead; and the apostle went to his own house.

Isma'il b. Abu Hakim, a freedman[2] of the family of al-Zubayr, told me on Khadija's authority that she said to the apostle of God, "O son of my uncle, are you able to tell me about your visitor, when he comes to you?" He replied that he could, and she asked him to tell her when he came. So when Gabriel came to him, as he was wont, the apostle said to Khadija, "This is Gabriel who has just come to me." "Get up, O son of my uncle," she said, "and sit by my left thigh." The apostle did so, and she said, "Can you see him?" "Yes," he said. She said, "Then turn round and sit on my right thigh." He did so, and she said, "Can you see him?" When he said that he could she asked him to move and sit in her lap. When he had done this she again asked if he could see him, and when he said yes, she disclosed her form and cast aside her veil while the apostle was sitting in her lap. Then she said, "Can you see him?" And he replied, "No." She said, "O son of my uncle, rejoice and be of good heart, by God he is an angel and not a satan."

I told 'Abdullah b. Hasan this story and he said, "I heard my mother Fatima, daughter of Husayn, talking about this tradition from Khadija, but as I heard it she made the apostle of God come inside her shift, and thereupon Gabriel departed, and she said to the apostle of God, 'This truly is an angel and not a satan.'"

---

[1] Abu'l-Qasim means "Father of Qasim," and Muhammad was so called because Qasim was the name of his first-born son. It was Muhammad's "name of honor."

[2] I.e., a former slave who has been freed.

3.10 Muhammad's words in the hadith: Al-Bukhari, *On Fasting* (9th cent.). Original in Arabic.

The hadith are the traditions about the Prophet handed down by authoritative transmission. There are two parts to every hadith: the first consists in the chain of oral transmitters (*isnad*), with the most recent one listed first; the second part consists in the text of the tradition, which is always about the Prophet, his family, and his close associates. (Shi'ite hadith also include traditions about the imams—those few leaders who possessed the "Muhammadan light.") Numerous questions occurred to Muslims after the time of Muhammad; they attempted to answer them by recourse to "what the Prophet would do in such-and-such situation," for that was the guide to "right behavior" (*sunna*). By the early Abbasid period, numerous, sometimes conflicting, answers to these questions were circulating. Al-Bukhari (810–870) and other scholars who followed him attempted in their collections (though not entirely successfully) to include only the "authentic" hadith. The *isnad*—which should be unbroken and come from reliable sources close to Muhammad— were an important element in their winnowing process. The section below, on fasting, illustrates their attempt to account for every possible situation.

1. Why are there sometimes a variety of answers to a question?
2. What are the uses and benefits of fasting according to the hadith of al-Bukhari?

[Source: *A Reader on Islam: Passages from Standard Arabic Writings Illustrative of the Beliefs and Practices of Muslims*, ed. Arthur Jeffery ('S-Gravenhage: Mouton & Co., 1962), pp. 88–90, 92–94, 98–101.]

1. ON THE NECESSITY OF THE FAST OF RAMADAN, AND ON THE VERSE (II, 183/179): "O YOU WHO HAVE BELIEVED, FASTING IS PRESCRIBED FOR YOU, JUST AS IT WAS PRESCRIBED FOR THOSE WHO WERE BEFORE YOU. MAYBE YOU WILL SHOW PIETY."

Qutaiba related to us, saying: Isma'il b. Ja'far related to us from[1] Abu Suhail, from his father, from Talha b. 'Ubaidallah, that a nomad Arab came to the Apostle of Allah—on whom be Allah's blessing and peace—with dishevelled head, saying: "O Apostle of Allah, inform me of what Allah has laid on me as incumbent duty in the matter of saying prayers." He answered: "The five prayer-services, unless you would voluntarily add thereto." Then [the Arab] said: "O Apostle of Allah, inform me of what Allah has laid on me as incumbent duty in the matter of fasting." He answered: "The month of Ramadan, unless you would voluntarily add thereto." Said [the Arab]: "Inform me of what Allah has laid on me as incumbent duty in that matter of alms [i.e., charity]." So the Apostle of Allah informed him of the legal prescriptions of Islam [with regard to alms]. Said he: "By Him who has honored you with the truth, I will not voluntarily add anything, but neither will I come short of what Allah has prescribed as incumbent duties for me." Then the Apostle of Allah—upon whom be Allah's blessing and peace—said: "He will be one of the fortunate ones, if he means that." Or [according to another version, he said]: "He will be brought into Paradise, if he means that."

Musaddad related to us, saying: Isma'il related to us from Ayyub, from Nafi', from Ibn 'Umar, who said: "The Prophet—upon whom be Allah's blessing and peace—fasted 'Ashura'[2] and bade it be kept as a fast, but when Ramadan was made an incumbent duty [on the

---

[1] The particle *'an* used in these *isnads* really means "on the authority of," but as the transmission of the Tradition was "from" one authority to another, it is translated throughout by "from" for brevity's sake. The b. in names means "son of."

[2] A fast said to have been observed by the Jews and some of the Arabs in the pre-Islamic days as commemoration of their deliverance from their enemies.

Muslims], it was abandoned. 'Abdallah[1] used not to fast therein save when it happened to coincide with his [voluntary] fasts."

Qutaiba b. Sa'id said: al-Laith has related to us from Yazid b. Abi Habib, that 'Irak b. Malik related to him that 'Urwa informed him from 'A'isha[2] that the Quraysh[3] used to fast the Day of "Ashura" in the pre-Islamic days, and then the Apostle of Allah—upon whom be Allah's blessing and peace—bade it be kept as a fast, [which it was] till Ramadan was made an incumbent duty. Said the Apostle of Allah—upon whom be Allah's blessing and peace—: "If anyone so wishes, let him still keep it as a fast, but if anyone so wishes, let him eat thereon."

2. ON THE MERITS OF THE FAST.

'Abdallah b. Maslama related to us from Malik, from Abu'z-Zinad, from al-A'raj, from Abu Huraira,[4] that the Apostle of Allah—upon whom be Allah's blessing and peace—said: "Fasting is a protective covering [from the fires of Hell], so let there be no unseemly speech, no foolish acting [during it]. If a man is attacked or vilified [during it], let him say twice: 'I am fasting;' for by Him in whose hand is my soul, the odor from the mouth of him who fasts is sweeter to Allah than the perfume of musk. [Allah says to Himself]: 'He is giving up his food and his drink and his body lusts for My sake when he is fasting unto Me, so I shall reward him, and for each good deed [that he does] grant him the merit of ten.'"

3. ON FASTING AS AN EXPIATION.

'Ali b. 'Abdallah related to us, saying: Sufyan related to us, saying: several have related to us from Abu Wa'il, from Hudhaifa, who said: "Umar once asked: 'Who is there who has memorized a Tradition from the Prophet—upon whom be Allah's blessing and peace—about discord?' Hudhaifa answered: 'I heard him say that discord arises for a man from [three sources: from] his family, from his property, and from his neighbor; but prayer, fasting and gifts of charity may be its expiation.' Said ['Umar]: 'I am not asking about this [general matter of discord arising among men], but about that [which will come

at the Last Days] billowing like the billows of the sea.' 'Facing that,' said [Hudhaifa], 'there is a gate shut.' 'Will it be opened,' asked ['Umar], 'or broken down?' 'It will be broken down,' answered [Hudhaifa]. 'Then,' said he, 'it is not likely to be shut again until the Day of Resurrection.'" We said to Masruq: "Ask him if 'Umar knew who the 'Gate' would be?"[5] So he asked him, and he answered: "Yes, [he knew that] just as he knew that night is before morning." ...

8. ON HIM WHO DOES NOT GIVE UP SAYING FALSE WORDS AND DOING FALSE DEEDS DURING RAMADAN.

Adam b. Abi Iyas related to us, saying: Ibn Abi Dhi'b related to us, saying: Sa'id al-Maqburi related to us from his father, from Abu Huraira, who said: Said the Prophet—upon whom be Allah's blessing and peace—: "If one does not give up saying false words and doing false deeds in Ramadan, his giving up eating and drinking means nothing to Allah."

9. ON WHETHER, IF ONE IS REVILED, HE SHOULD SAY: "I AM FASTING."

Ibrahim b. Musa related to us, saying: Hisham b. Yusuf informed us from Ibn Juraij, who said: 'Ata' informed me from Abu Salih az-Zayyat, that he heard Abu Huraira say: The Apostle of Allah—upon whom be Allah's blessing and peace—said: "Allah, mighty and majestic is He, has said: 'Every deed of a child of Adam is his [and will be recorded and rewarded in due measure] save fasting, which is Mine, and which I will reward [in My own measure].' Fasting is a protective covering, so when the day comes for anyone of you to fast, let there be no unseemly speech, no clamoring. If anyone reviles such a person, or attacks him, let him say: 'I am fasting.' By Him in whose hand is my soul, the odor from the mouth of him who fasts is sweeter to Allah than the perfume of musk. He who fasts has two occasions of rejoicing. He will have joy when he breaks his fast, and when he meets his Lord he will have joy because of his fasting."

---

[1] Probably the companion of the Prophet 'Abdallah ibn 'Abbas.

[2] The Prophet's youngest wife, who is quoted as the source for a vast number of Traditions.

[3] The ruling Arab tribe in Mecca in the days of the Prophet.

[4] Abu Huraira was a highly celebrated "Companion" of the Prophet. Thousands of hadith named him as the final transmitter in the *isnad*.

[5] The technical word in this Tradition is *fitna*, "dissension," "discord," and in Muslim accounts of the events of the Last Days preceding the great Day of Judgment there are innumerable stories about the dissensions that will arise among the people. The "gate" (*bab*) is the individual who will usher in any particular dissension.

10. ON FASTING [AS A HELP] FOR ONE WHO FEARS [THE TEMPTATIONS OF ONE WHO REMAINS] CELIBATE.

'Ubdan related to us from Abu Hamza, from al-A'mash, from Ibrahim, from 'Alqama, [who said]: While I was walking with 'Abdallah he said: "I was once with the Prophet—upon whom be Allah's blessing and peace—when he said: 'Let him who is able to marry take a wife, for it is the best way of averting lascivious glances and of providing chaste enjoyment, but let him who is not able [to marry] fast, for it will be a remover [of unseemly passions] for him.'"

11. ON THE SAYING OF THE PROPHET—UPON WHOM BE ALLAH'S BLESSING AND PEACE—: "WHEN YOU SEE THE NEW MOON, FAST, AND WHEN YOU SEE IT, BREAK YOUR FAST."

Sila quoted from 'Ammar: "Whosoever fasts on a doubtful day is disobeying Abu'l-Qasim,[1]—upon whom be Allah's blessing and peace.

'Abdallah b. Maslama related to us from Malik, from Nafi', from 'Abdallah b. 'Umar, that the Apostle of Allah—upon whom be Allah's blessing and peace—mentioned Ramadan, and said: "Do not fast until you see the new moon, and do not break the fast until you see it, and if it is cloudy make a computation for it."

'Abdallah b. Maslama related to us, saying: Malik related to us from 'Abdallah b. Dinar, from 'Abdallah b. 'Umar, that the Apostle of Allah—upon whom be Allah's blessing and peace—said: "The month is twenty-nine nights, so do not fast till you see it (i.e., the new moon), and if it is cloudy then compute the number to thirty."

Abu'l-Walid related to us, saying: Shu'ba related to us from Jabala b. Suhaim, who said: "I heard Ibn 'Umar say that the Prophet—upon whom be Allah's blessing and peace—said: 'The month is so-and-so,' and he tucked in [his] thumb the third time."

Adam related to us, saying: Shu'ba related to us, saying: Muhammad b. Ziyad related to us, saying: I heard Abu Huraira say that the Prophet—upon whom be Allah's blessing and peace—said:—or maybe he said: Abu'l-Qasim, upon whom be, etc. said:—"Fast when it (i.e., the moon) becomes seeable, and break your fast when it becomes seeable, and if it is cloudy then complete the number of Sha'ban,[2] [i.e.,] thirty."

Abu 'Asim related to us from Ibn Juraij, from Yahya b. 'Abdallah b. Saifi, from 'Ikrima b. 'Abd al-Rahman from Umm Salama, that the Prophet—upon whom be Allah's blessing and peace—took an oath to abstain from his women for a month. When twentynine days had elapsed be came in the morning—or maybe it was in the evening—[to 'A'isha]. Someone objected, "But you swore that you would not enter for a month," and he replied: "A month has twentynine days."

'Abd al-'Aziz b. 'Abdallah related to us, saying: Sulaiman b. Bilal related to us from Humaid, from Anas, who said: "The Apostle of Allah—upon whom be Allah's blessing and peace—took an oath to abstain from his women. As his foot was injured he stayed in an upper chamber for twenty-nine nights. Then he came down, but they said: 'O Apostle of Allah, you took an oath for a month', whereat he said: 'The month is twenty-nine [days].'"

12. ON HOW THE TWO MONTHS OF FESTIVAL MAY NOT BE CURTAILED.

Musaddad has related to us, saying: Mu'tamir related to us, saying: I heard Ishaq b. Suwaid [quoting] from 'Abd al-Rahman b. Abi Bakra, from his father, from the Prophet—upon whom be Allah's blessing and peace—[or according to another *isnad*], Musaddad related to me, saying: Mu'tamir related to us from Khalid al-Hadhdha', who said: 'Abd al-Rahman b. Abi Bakra related to me from his father, from the Prophet—upon whom be Allah's blessing and peace—who said: "There are two months which may not be curtailed, the two months of festival, Ramadan and Dhu'l-Hijja."[3] Said Abu 'Abdallah: "Ishaq said: 'Twenty-nine complete days.' Ahmed b. Jundub said: 'If Ramadan is curtailed, complete Dhu'l-Hijja, and if Dhu'l-Hijja is curtailed, complete Ramadan.' Abu'l-Hasan said: 'Ishaq b. Rahuwaih used to say, 'Let neither be curtailed in [their] meritoriousness, whether it is twenty-nine or thirty [days].'" ...

22. ON THE FASTER WHO AWAKES IN THE MORNING IN A STATE OF SEXUAL POLLUTION.

---

[1] Abu'l-Qasim means "Father of Qasim," and Muhammad was so called because Qasim was the name of his first-born son. It was Muhammad's "name of honor."

[2] Sha'ban is the month that precedes the fasting month of Ramadan.

[3] Ramadan, the month of fasting, is the ninth month in the Islamic calendar, and Dhu'l-Hijja is the twelfth month, the month during which the annual pilgrimage to Mecca—the *hajj*—takes place.

'Abdallah b. Maslama related to us from Malik, from Sumayy, a client of Abu Bakr b. 'Abd al-Rahman b. al-Harith b. Hisham b. al-Mughira, that he heard Abu Bakr b. 'Abd al-Rahman say: "I was with my father when we entered to 'A'isha and Umm Salama," [or as another *isnad* has it], Abu'l-Yaman related to us, saying: Shu'aib informed us from al-Zuhri, who said: Abu Bakr b. 'Abd al-Rahman b. al-Harith b. Hisham informed me that his father 'Abd al-Rahman informed Marwan that 'A'isha and Umm Salama had both informed him, that the Apostle of Allah—upon whom be Allah's blessing and peace—would be overtaken by the dawn while he was still in a state of pollution from [sexual contact with] his wives, but he would bathe and then fast. Marwan said to 'Abd al-Rahman b. al-Harith: "I swear by Allah you shall surely [go and] disturb Abu Huraira by that [information]." Marwan was at that time [Governor] over Medina. Said Abu Bakr: "'Abd al-Rahman, however, disliked [the idea of doing] that, so it was decided among us that we would gather together at Dhu'l-Hulaifa, where Abu Huraira had some land. Then 'Abd al-Rahman said to Abu Huraira: 'I am about to mention to you a matter that I should never have mentioned to you had not Marwan sworn that I should.' Then he mentioned what 'A'isha and Umm Salama had said. Said [Abu Huraira]: 'That is so. Al-Fadl b. 'Abbas related [it] to me, and no one would know better than he.'" Said Hammam and Ibn 'Abdallah b. 'Umar [quoting] from Abu Huraira: "The Prophet—upon whom be Allah's blessing and peace—used to order [in such a case that] the fast be broken," but the first [version] has the better *isnad*.

23. ON THE [RESTRICTIONS OF] SEX RELATIONS FOR ONE WHO IS FASTING.

'A'isha said: "It is her vulva which is forbidden to him."

Sulaiman b. Harb related to us from Shu'ba, from al-Hakam, from Ibrahim, from al-Aswad, from 'A'isha, who said: "The Prophet—upon whom be Allah's blessing and peace—used to kiss and handle [his wives] while he was fasting, but he had more control over his *irb* than any of you." [As to this word *irb*], Ibn 'Abbas said that [the derivative from it] *ma'arib* means "need," and Tawus used to use the phrase "one who possesses no *irba*" for a defective who has no need of women. Jabir b. Zaid said: "If one looks [at a woman] and has an emission let him go on with his fast."

24. ON THE [LEGITIMACY OF] KISSING FOR ONE WHO IS FASTING.

Muhammad b. al-Muthanna related to us, saying: Yahya related to us from Hisham, who said: My father informed me from 'A'isha—with whom may Allah be pleased—from the Prophet—upon whom be Allah's blessing and peace—[or by another *isnad*], 'Abdallah b. Maslama related to us from Malik, from Hisham, from his father, from 'A'isha—with whom may Allah be pleased—who said: "There were times when the Apostle of Allah—upon whom be Allah's blessing and peace—would kiss certain of his wives while he was fasting." Then she laughed.

Musaddad related to us, saying: Yahya related to us from Hisham b. Abi 'Abdallah, who said: Yahya b. Abi Kathir related to us from Abu Salama, from Zainab daughter of Umm Salama, from her mother,[1] who said: "While I was with the Prophet—upon whom be Allah's blessing and peace—in bed, my menses started, so I slipped out and put on my menstrual clothes. He asked: 'What is the matter with you? has your period come on?' 'Yes,' I replied, and I entered the bed with him again." Now she and the Apostle of Allah—upon whom be Allah's blessing and peace—used both to bathe at the same [water] vessel, and he used to kiss her when he was fasting.

25. ON THE BATHING OF ONE WHO IS FASTING.

Ibn 'Umar soiled his garment with urine but put it on him while he was fasting. Ash-Sha'bi entered the [public] baths while he was fasting. Ibn Abbas said: "There is no harm in tasting [what is in] the cooking pot [while fasting] or [any other] thing." Al-Hasan said: "There is no harm in the faster gargling or cooling himself off" (i.e., provided he does not drink the water). Ibn Mas'ud said: "When the day comes around for any one of you to fast he may, as he rises in the morning, use oil and comb." Anas said: "I had a copper wash-basin in which I used to plunge even while I was fasting, and Ibn 'Umar used to brush his teeth at the beginning and at the end of the day [while he was fasting]." Ibn Sirin said: "There is no harm in the use of the tooth-brush if it is fresh." The objection was raised: "But it has taste," and [he replied]: "and so does the water have taste when you gargle with it, [yet that is not considered to be breaking the fast]. Anas, al-Hasan and Ibrahim also saw no harm in the faster making use of kohl [for the eyes].

Ahmad b. Salih related to us, saying: Ibn Wahb related to us, saying: Yunus related to us, from Ibn Shihab, from 'Urwa

---

[1] Her mother was one of the Prophet's wives.

and Abu Bakr, who said: 'A'isha—with whom may Allah be pleased—said: "The dawn used to overtake the Prophet in Ramadan when he was polluted—and not from an [erotic] dream—but he would bathe and [then commence the] fast."

Isma'il related to us, saying: Malik related to me from Sumayy, a client of Abu Bakr b. 'Abd al-Rahman b. al-Harith b. Hisham b. al-Mughira, that he heard Abu Bakr b. 'Abd al-Rahman say: "I was with my father and went along with him till we entered to 'A'isha—with whom may Allah be pleased—who said: 'I bear witness of the Apostle of Allah—upon whom be Allah's blessing and peace—that he used to wake up in the morning polluted [by sperm] from intercourse, not from dreaming, and then he would fast [that day].' Then we entered to Umm Salama, who said the same thing."

26. ON THE FASTER WHO EATS AND DRINKS FROM FORGETFULNESS.

'Ata' said: "If one snuffs up water and some of it enters the throat so that one is not able to reject it, no harm is done [thereby to one's fast]." Also al-Hasan said: "If a fly should get into one's throat, that is nothing," and al-Hasan and Mujahid both said: "If one should have sexual intercourse forgetfully, that is nothing."

'Abdan related to us [saying], Yazid b. Zurai' informed us, saying, Hisham related to us, saying: Ibn Sirin related to us from Abu Huraira, from the Prophet—upon whom be blessing and peace—that he said: "If anyone forgets and eats or drinks, let him complete his fast, for it was Allah who caused him thus to eat or drink."

27. ON THE FRESH AND THE DRY TOOTHBRUSH FOR HIM WHO IS FASTING.

It is reported from 'Amir b. Rabi'a, who said: "I have seen the Prophet—upon whom be Allah's blessing and peace—using the toothbrush while he was fasting more times than I can reckon or count." 'A'isha said, quoting the Prophet—upon whom be Allah's blessing and peace—: "The toothbrush is a purifier for the mouth and a thing well-pleasing to the Lord." 'Ata' and Qatada said: "One may swallow one's saliva [without thereby breaking one's fast]." Abu Huraira said, quoting the Prophet—upon whom be Allah's blessing and peace—: "Were it not that I might be causing distress to my community I should bid them use the toothbrush at every ablution." The like of this Tradition is transmitted from Jabir and Zaid b. Khalid from the Prophet—upon whom be Allah's blessing and peace—who [in this matter] did not particularize the one fasting from anyone else.

'Abdan related to us, saying: 'Abdallah informed us, saying: Ma'mar informed us, saying: al-Zuhri related to us from 'Ata' b. Yazid, from Humran, who said: "I saw 'Uthman [i.e., the third Caliph] performing ablutions. He poured [the water out] over his hands three times. Then he gargled and snuffed up [the water]. Then he washed his face three times. Then he washed his right arm up to the elbow three times. Then he washed his left arm up to the elbow three times. Then he rubbed his head [with his moist hands]. Then he washed his right foot three times. Then he washed his left foot three times. Then he said: 'I have seen the Apostle of Allah—upon whom be Allah's blessing and peace—performing ablution just like this ablution of mine, after which he [i.e., the Prophet] said: Whosoever performs [his] ablutions as I have done here, and prays a two-bow prayer, not allowing anything to distract him during them, will have all his past sins forgiven him.'"

3.11 The pope and the Carolingians: Pope Stephen II, *Letters to King Pippin III* (755–756). Original in Latin.

The letters from Pope Stephen II (752–757) to King Pippin III (r.752–768) are crucial sources for the commencement and early years of the Franco-papal alliance, the emergence of the Papal States, the development of the papal administration in and around Rome, and the political history of central Italy in the eighth century. Contained in the so-called *Codex Carolinus* (or "Charlemagne's Book"), these letters form part of a collection of ninety-nine letters sent by a series of popes to the Carolingian mayors of the palace and kings from 739 to about 791. The *Codex* survives in a single late-ninth-century manuscript prepared on the order of Archbishop Willibert of Cologne, but not all of the papal letters survive in the *Codex*. The excerpt here represents only some of the letters that Pope Stephen sent to Pippin.

1. Why did the pope put great emphasis on the role of Saint Peter?
2. What, exactly, did the pope want from the Carolingians?

[Source: *Codex Carolinus*, *Epistolae* 6–10, ed. Wilhelm Gundlach, Monumenta Germaniae Historica, Epistolae 3, Epistolae Merovingici et Karolini Aevi 1 (Berlin: Weidmann, 1892), pp. 488–503. Translated and introduced by Thomas F.X. Noble.]

1 (6): Stephen II to Pippin III (755)

Pope Stephen to the most excellent lords and sons, Pippin, king and our spiritual co-father,[1] and Charles and Carloman, likewise kings and all of them Patricians of the Romans.[2]

So long as your realm's reputation for sincere faith in blessed Peter will shine brilliantly among other peoples because of your sincere faith in the blessed Peter, prince of the apostles, it is crucial to pay particular attention that, even as all Christians declare that you are more glorious than other peoples in the service of blessed Peter, you should in the same way please the almighty Lord, "who gives salvation to kings,"[3] more perfectly in the defense of his holy church, so that you might have as a helper in all things the faith which you cherish for that same prince of the apostles.

Indeed, we had hoped, most exceptional sons, to delay a while longer amplifying our discourse, but because our heart is terribly worn down by sadness and our spirit grieves because of the many trials borne upon us by the wicked King Aistulf of the Lombards, so we have turned away from the wordiness of many speeches and we have been keen to bring one thing, because it is necessary, to the attention of your most excellent Christianity.

Our spiritual co-father, protected by God, and you, our sweetest sons, for the benefit of your souls, just as our merciful God has deigned to bestow victories upon you from heaven, you have been diligent to demand, as far as you could, the rights of blessed Peter, and through a charter of donation your goodness has confirmed that restitution should be made.[4] Now, however, just as we previously instructed your Christianity about the malice of this same wicked king, behold how his deceit and wicked perversity and perjury have been proclaimed recently. Indeed, the devil, the ancient enemy of the human race, has invaded his wicked heart and what was affirmed by the bond of an oath he has been seen to render worthless, and he has not suffered to return one hand's-breadth of land to blessed Peter and to his holy church, the Republic of the Romans.[5] Indeed, since that day when we [the pope and Pippin] parted from one another, he has attempted to afflict us and to hold the holy church of God in great disgrace to such an extent that the tongues of men cannot describe it, since the very stones themselves, if it may be said, cry out with great lamentation at our tribulation.[6] And he has been seen to afflict us to such a degree that our weakness has been renewed in us once again. For I deeply lament, most excellent sons, that not hearing the words of our unhappiness, you, deceiving yourselves and mocking, have chosen to believe falsehood [spread by Aistulf] rather than truth. Whence even without having achieved the justice of blessed Peter we have returned to our own flock and to the people committed to us.

Finally, all Christians used to believe so firmly that blessed Peter, the prince of the apostles, would now have received his justice through your most potent right arm, since through the intercession of his prince of the apostles

---

[1] Stephen anointed Pippin's sons Charles and Carloman as kings of the Franks and thus entered a spiritual relationship that made Stephen and Pippin "co-fathers" of the two boys. Compaternity was normally associated with baptismal sponsorship.

[2] "Patrician" was a Roman honorific title that conferred no specific rights. In principle, only the Roman (i.e., Byzantine) emperor could confer this title, but the popes began conferring it on the Carolingians.

[3] Ps. 144:10; Douay Ps. 143:10.

[4] Stephen refers to the so-called "Quierzy Document" (754), which spelled out the lands that Pippin would make Aistulf restore to the pope.

[5] Historically only the Roman Empire could be designated this way; the pope is calling the lands assigned to him by Pippin the "Republic" of the Romans.

[6] See Luke 19:40.

the Lord God and Savior Jesus Christ has displayed such a great and resplendent miracle in your most blessed times and has deigned to bestow such an immense victory upon you for the defense of his holy church. But nevertheless, good sons, trusting that same wicked king in what he promised through the bond of an oath, by your own will you have confirmed by a charter of donation that the cities and localities of blessed Peter and of the republic of the holy church of God ought to be restored. But he, having forgotten the Christian faith and the God who ordered him to be born, has been seen to have rendered empty what was confirmed by an oath. Wherefore "his iniquity falls upon his own head";[1] indeed, the trap that he has dug has been revealed, and he is caught in it for his mendacity and perjury.

I implore you most excellent and God-protected sons, through the Lord our God and his holy, glorious and ever virgin mother Mary, our lady, and all the powers of heaven, and through blessed Peter the prince of the apostles, who anointed you as kings, that you grieve for the holy church of God, and that according to that donation which you ordered to be offered to your very protector, our lord, the blessed Peter, you eagerly restore and hand over everything to the holy church of God, and that by no means would you now trust the seductive words or lying illusion of that most wicked king, or his representatives. Behold, his mendacity is indeed manifest such that it ought not by any means to have any further capacity to attract belief but rather, his wicked spirit and wicked will being known, his treachery is uncovered. Indeed, what you once promised blessed Peter, and what was confirmed through a donation in your own hand, for the good of your soul, hasten to restore and hand over to blessed Peter. Finally, the blessed apostle Paul says "It is better not to make a vow than, having made a vow, not to fulfill it."[2]

For truly we commend to your heart all the causes of the holy church of God, and you will render account to God and to blessed Peter on the day of the fearful judgment for exactly how you struggled in the cause of that same prince of the apostles and for the restoration his cities and localities. For ultimately this good work

has been reserved for you already for a long period of time now, so that through you the holy church might be exalted, and the prince of the apostles might obtain his justice. None of your ancestors merited such a magnificent gift, but God chose and foreknew you before all time, just as is written "Those whom he foreknew and predestined, those he also called; and those whom he called, he also justified."[3] You have been called. Attend with all haste to effect the justice of this very prince of the apostles because it is written "Faith is justified by works."[4]

Concerning all our tribulations, which we have suffered or are yet suffering, with God's help, let our son Fulrad,[5] your counselor, and his associates inform you. And so act then in the cause of blessed Peter so that in this life you may be victorious with the Lord's favor and, in the future life, through the intercession of that very same prince of the apostles, blessed Peter, you may possess eternal joys.

Farewell, most excellent sons.

3 (8) Stephen II to Pippin (c.Feb. 24, 756)

Pope Stephen to his most excellent lord son and spiritual co-father Pippin, king of the Franks and patrician of the Romans.

We believe that the very creation of the whole universe would declare by what great, mournful, and extremely bitter sadness we are on every side surrounded, and by what great anxiety and difficulty we are hemmed in, and what great tears our streaming eyes pour forth as unceasing evils increase. Who, seeing these tribulations, would not mourn? Who, hearing of the calamities weighing upon us, would not wail? Wherefore we speak in the words of a certain good and modest woman, Susannah: "Difficulties lie upon our every side and we do not know what to do."[6] O, most excellent and Christian sons, just as the almighty creator of all things, the Lord, in former times had sent the prophet Habakkuk, carried thence suddenly by an angel to revive and console the distinguished prophet Daniel who was concealed in the lion's den, so also now, if I may say so, if only his most merciful

---

[1] Ps. 7:17; Douay Ps. 6:17.

[2] Actually, not Paul but Eccles. 5:4.

[3] A paraphrase of Rom. 8:29–30.

[4] James 2:24.

[5] Abbot of Saint-Denis and key adviser to Pippin and later to his son Charlemagne.

[6] Dan. 13:22.

patience had made your God-preserved excellence present here even for the space of a single hour so that you might behold the miserable and mournful hardships and tribulations which we are suffering helplessly at the hands of the Lombard people and their wicked king! Behold, the days of hardship have come upon us. Days of weeping and bitterness, the day of anxiety and groans of grief are at hand, for what we feared is happening, and what we dreaded is coming to pass. And so, attacked, afflicted, and overwhelmed and surrounded on every side by their most wicked king and their Lombard people, shedding tears and beating our breast we say, calling upon the Lord with the prophet "Help us, Lord of our salvation, and for the honor of your name, deliver us."[1] And again "Take up arms and a shield and rise up in our assistance; Lord, condemn those who are harming us and defeat those who are attacking us."[2] Indeed, though we seem often to bring our tribulations to the attention of your goodness, now however we have taken care to relate the perils of the evils that we have suffered from that same shameless king and his Lombard people, since the magnitude of the danger compels us.

We believe, most Christian and excellent son, and spiritual co-father, that everything is already known to your nobility: How the peace treaty has been overthrown by the wicked King Aistulf and his people; and how we have been able to obtain nothing in the way that he agreed to and which was confirmed through the bond of an oath; and even that no gain has come to us but instead after the desolation of our whole region even more murders have been perpetrated by that same people. And now may you recognize what we are saying with great tears and sorrow in our heart, most excellent son and spiritual co-father. On the very first of January the entire army of that same King Aistulf of the Lombards mustered from the area of Tuscany against this Roman city and camped right at the gate of Saint Peter, and the gate of Saint Pancras, and the gate of Portuensis. Indeed Aistulf himself joined with other troops from a different area and pitched his tents at the Salarian gate and at other gates too and he sent to us,

saying "Open the Salarian Gate to me that I might enter the city, and hand over to me your pontifical office, and I might have mercy on you.[3] Otherwise, overturning the walls, I shall kill you with a single sword and we shall see who can rescue you from my hands." And indeed all the Beneventans as a whole mustering against this Roman city have taken up a position at the gate of blessed John the Baptist, at the gate of blessed Paul the apostle, and at the rest of the gates of this Roman city.

To be sure, they have laid waste with fire and sword all the estates far and wide outside the city and, burning up all the houses, they have razed them almost to their foundations. They have set fire to the churches of God, and, casting the most holy images of the saints into the fire, they have destroyed them with their swords. And as for the holy gifts, that is the body of our Lord Jesus Christ, they have put them in their foul vessels that they call bags, and stuffed with abundant food of flesh, they eat those same gifts.[4] Carrying off the veils or all the ornaments of the churches of God, which it is too cruel to have to relate, they have used them for their own purposes. Beating the monks, the servants of God who live in monasteries for the sake of the divine office,[5] with immense blows, they have mutilated quite a few. They have dragged away and polluted with great cruelty the nuns and recluses who, for the love of God, handed themselves over to be cloistered from infancy or the age of puberty, and they seem in that same contamination even to have killed some of them. They have put to the torch all the *Domuscultae*[6] of blessed Peter or, as is reported, they have utterly destroyed by fire the houses of all the Romans outside the city, stolen all the flocks, cut the vines almost to the roots, and completely destroyed the crops by grinding them down. Neither to the house of our holy church nor to anyone living in this Roman city has there remained any hope of surviving because, as it is reported, they have destroyed everything with fire and sword and have killed many. And they have also slain the abundant family[7] of blessed Peter and of all the Romans, both men and women, and they have led away many others as captives. These same

---

[1] Ps. 78:9; Douay Ps. 77:9 (slightly paraphrased).

[2] See Ps. 34:2; Douay Ps. 33:2.

[3] The Latin is tortured here but it seems that Aistulf was asking Stephen to resign.

[4] This is a reference to the consecrated bread of the altar, the Eucharist.

[5] Monks gathered several times each day to pray the *Opus Divinum*, the Divine Office. See *The Benedictine Rule* above, p. 20.

[6] Beginning with Pope Zachary (741–752) the papacy began reorganizing some of its scattered rural estates into large-scale farms called *Domuscultae*.

[7] *Familia* means household more than a small group of related people. The word here relates to the peasants who worked the lands of the Roman Church.

wicked Lombards have killed the innocent little children whom they have snatched from their mothers' breasts as well as the mothers themselves, whom they have polluted by force. Indeed they have committed such evils in this Roman province as certainly not even the pagan peoples ever before perpetrated so that, as one could say, even the very stones, seeing our losses, cry out with us.[1]

Besieging this suffering Roman city and surrounding it on every side for five and fifty days, they have waged the fiercest battles against us at the walls of this Roman city incessantly, day and night, and they do not stop attacking us with the aim of subjecting all the people to his power—may God prevent it!—so that wicked king Aistulf may kill them with a single sword. For in such a way, mocking us with great fury, they were proclaiming: "Behold, you are surrounded by us and you will not escape our hands. Let the Franks come now and save you from our hands."

Now they have seized the city of Narni, which your Christianity conceded to us, and they have taken certain cities of ours. Afflicted in such a way, we have barely been able, through great cleverness and by using a sea route, to send our envoys and our present letter, which we have written with great tears, to your excellent Christianity. We even—we speak with the truth bearing us out—would express through each and every letter tears mixed with blood; and if only the Lord would grant it to us, at the moment when you read our mournful exhortation a tear filled with blood might flow in your presence through every letter of this message.

Whence, most excellent son and spiritual co-father, I ask you, and as though appearing in your very presence bowed down upon the ground and prostrating myself at your feet, with the divine mysteries, I adjure you before the living and true God and blessed Peter his prince of the apostles, that you come to our assistance with all possible haste and the greatest speed, lest we perish, for after God, it is in your hands that we have placed all our souls, those of all the Romans. Do not abandon us; so also may the Lord not abandon you in all your works and deeds. Do not spurn us; so also may the Lords not spurn you when you call upon his power. Do not withdraw your aid from us, most Christian son and spiritual co-father; so also may the Lord not withdraw his aid and protection from you and your people when you have marched out to fight against your enemies. Come to our assistance and

help us with great speed, most Christian one: Thus may you receive support from almighty God who anointed you into kingship above all the masses of the peoples through the disposition of blessed Peter. Hasten, hasten, son, hasten to help us before the enemy's sword reaches our heart; I plead with you, lest we perish, lest the peoples who are in all the earth have occasion to say "What has become of the trust of the Romans which they used to place, after God, in the kings and people of the Franks?" Do not suffer us to perish and do not hold back or delay to relieve us or cut us off from your support; thus may you not be a stranger from the kingdom of God and be cut off by force from your dearest wife, the most excellent queen and our spiritual co-mother. Do not permit us to be worried and endangered any further and to continue in mourning and weeping, fine excellent son and spiritual co-father; in the same way, may sorrow not come upon you over your and my sweetest sons, the lords Charles and Carloman, most outstanding kings and patricians. Do not shut your ear from hearing us and do not turn your face from us lest we be disappointed in our petitions and we be imperiled to the very extremity. In the same way, may the Lord not shut his ear from hearing your prayers and may he not turn his face from you on that day of judgment to come when, with the blessed Peter and with the rest of his apostles, he shall sit to judge through fire every order, both sexes, and every human and worldly power and—God forbid it!—may he not say to you "I do not know you because you have not helped to defend the church of God and you scarcely took any care to rescue his special people in their time of danger."

Hear me, son, hear me and come to our assistance. Behold, the time for saving us has arrived. Save us, before we perish, most Christian king. For what could be better, or finer, or more outstanding than to save those who are in grave danger and caught in dire straits? For it is written: "He who saves is like he who builds up."[2] On this point indeed the eminent prophet Isaiah said: "Relieve the oppressed."[3] For all peoples who are located all around you and have sought protection from your people of the Franks, most mighty through the power of God, have been made safe, and if you do not hesitate to bestow assistance upon all peoples and they are made safe by you, you ought much more to have freed the holy church of God and his people from the attack of their

---

[1]   See Luke 19:40.

[2]   Although reminiscent of passages in Psalms and Proverbs, this quotation cannot be identified.

[3]   Isa. 1:17.

enemies. O how much confidence there was in our heart when we were worthy to behold your honeyed countenance and we were bound and connected in a bond of love that we would remain in great peace and comfort! But while we were expecting to see the light from you, darkness burst forth[1] and our new situation became worse than the former one. Consider, son, consider and reflect deeply, I adjure you through the living God, how our soul and the souls of all the Roman people, committed to you by God, depend, after God and his prince of the apostles, upon your God-protected excellence and the people of the Franks, for as has already been related, we have committed our souls into your keeping. And if it should happen that we perish—let it not be so and may divine mercy prevent it—weigh carefully, I beseech you, and in every way consider upon whose soul the sin shall lie. Believe with all certainty, most Christian one, that if some perilous disaster shall befall us—may it not happen—you, of all people, protected by God, and most beloved to us, will be destined to give account before the tribunal of God with all your officials because, as has been related, we have, through the precept of God and of blessed Peter, committed the holy church of God and our people of the republic of the Romans for protection to no one else but only to your most beloved excellence and to your sweetest sons and to the whole people of the Franks.

Behold, we have made known all our sorrows and anxieties and difficulties to your God-protected goodness. As for you, most excellent son and spiritual co-father, act, and after God, free those who are fleeing to you so that, bearing good fruit, on the day of future judgment you shall be worthy to say "My lord, blessed Peter, prince of the apostles, behold I, your unworthy servant, having run the race, having kept faith with you, having defended the church of God commended to you by heavenly mercy, I freed it from the hands of its persecutors and, standing unblemished before you, I offer you the sons whom you committed to me for the purpose of rescuing them from the hands of enemies, standing here now unharmed and safe." Then, both holding the helm of the kingdom in this present life and also reigning with Christ in the world to come, you would deserve to obtain the joys of heavenly rewards, hearing without doubt that longed-for fatherly voice of the one who says "Come, blessed of my father,

and receive the kingdom that has been prepared for you from the beginning of the world."[2]

May heavenly grace keep your Excellency safe and sound.

4 (9) Pope Stephen II to Pippin, Charles, and Carloman (c.Feb. 24, 756)

To the most excellent lords Pippin, Charles, and Carloman, three kings and our patricians of the Romans, and also to all the bishops, abbots, priests and monks, and to the glorious dukes, counts, and to the entire army of the kingdom and provinces of the Franks, Pope Stephen and all the bishops, priests, deacons, and dukes, soldiers, counts, tribunes, and the whole people and army[3] of the Romans, all placed in affliction.

[The rest of this letter repeats the previous one almost verbatim. What is different is the address to all the officials of the Frankish world and the letter's dispatch from all the religious and secular officials of Rome.]

5 (10) Pope Stephen II writes in the name of Saint Peter to Pippin, Charles, and Carloman (c.Feb. 24, 756)

Peter, called to be an apostle by Jesus Christ the son of the living God who, reigning before all time with the Father in the unity of the Holy Spirit, in the last days became incarnate and was made a man for the salvation of us all and redeemed us by his precious blood through the will of the Father's glory, just as he ordained through his holy prophets in the holy scriptures; and through me the entire catholic and apostolic Roman church of God, the head of all the churches of God, founded by the blood of our very redeemer upon a solid rock, and Stephen, prelate of that same nourishing church: May Grace, peace, and strength for rescuing from the hands of its persecutors that same holy church of God and its Roman people committed to me, be bestowed fully upon you by our Lord God, most excellent men, Pippin, Charles, and Carloman, all three kings, and also upon the most holy bishops, abbots, priests and all the religious monks, as well as upon the

---

[1] See Job 30:26.

[2] Matt. 25:34.

[3] The presence of these military figures may be surprising, but the popes seem to have retained something of the military establishment of the formerly Byzantine Duchy of Rome. They were neither numerous nor effective, as these letters make clear.

dukes, counts, and all the rest of the armies and people living in Francia.

I, Peter the Apostle, when I was called by Christ, the son of the living God, by the will of divine clemency, was foreordained as the teacher of the whole world by his power, as that very same Lord our God confirmed: "Go, teach all nations, baptizing them in the name of the Father and of the Son and of the Holy Spirit";[1] and again "Receive the Holy Spirit; whose sins you shall remit, they are remitted for them."[2] And commending his sheep in particular to me, his meager servant yet called as an apostle, he said: "Feed my sheep, feed my lambs." And again "You are Peter and upon this rock I shall build my church, and the gates of Hell will not prevail against it, and I shall give you the keys of the kingdom of heaven; whatever you will have bound on earth will also be bound in heaven and whatever you will have loosed on earth will also be loosed in heaven."[3] Wherefore, let all those who, hearing my teaching, fulfill it, believe with certainty that in this world their sins are forgiven by the precept of God and they shall proceed clean and without blemish into that life. Thus, because the inspiration of the Holy Spirit has shone forth in your gleaming hearts and you have been made lovers of his unique and holy Trinity by receiving the word through the preaching of the Gospel, your hope of future reward is held bound up in this holy Roman church of God that has been committed to us.

Therefore, I, Peter, the apostle of God, who regard you as adopted sons, appealing to the love of all, I implore you to defend from the hands of its enemies this Roman city and the people committed to me by God, and also to rescue the house where I lie at rest according to the flesh from the defilement of the nations, and bearing witness I warn you to liberate the church of God commended to me by the divine power of God because they are suffering immense afflictions and oppressions from the awful nation of the Lombards. May you by no means believe otherwise, most beloved, but instead trust in it as a certainty: Through my very own self, just as if I were standing alive in the flesh before you, we constrain and bind with mighty adjurations through this exhortation because, according to the promise which we received from that same Lord God, our redeemer, we consider all you peoples of the Franks to be a special people among all the nations. So I bear witness and I warn you as if

through a mysterious vision and with firm obligation I adjure you, most Christian kings Pippin, Charles, and Carloman, and also all the archbishops, bishops, abbots, priests, and all the religious monks, and all the officials, and the dukes, counts, and the whole people of the kingdom of the Franks, and believe, all of you, just as firmly that the words of the exhortation are addressing you as you would if I, Peter, the apostle of God, were standing before you alive in the flesh in person, because, even if I am not there in the flesh, I am not absent from you spiritually, for it is written: "He who receives a prophet in the name of a prophet, receives the prophet's reward."[4]

And also our mistress, the mother of God, the ever-virgin Mary, bears witness, warns, and commands you, along with us, adjuring by great obligations, likewise also thrones and dominions, and all the troops of the heavenly host, not to mention the martyrs and confessors of Christ, and everyone wholly pleasing to God. And these, urging and imploring along with us, testify to how much you grieve for this Roman city committed to us by the Lord God, and for the Lord's flocks dwelling within it, and also for the holy church of God commended to me by the Lord. So, defend and free it, with great haste, from the hands of the persecuting Lombards, lest—may it never be!—my body which suffered torments for the sake of the Lord Jesus Christ, and my house, where by God's command it lies at rest, be contaminated by them and lest my special people be further maimed or they be butchered by that very people of the Lombards who stand guilty of such a great crime of treachery and are proven to be transgressors of the divine scriptures. Offer therefore to my Roman people, committed to me by God in this life, your own brothers, protection with all your strength, with the Lord assisting you, so that I, Peter, called to be an apostle of God, may extend in turn patronage to you in this life and on the day of future judgment, so that in the kingdom of God the most shining and distinguished tents may be prepared for you and that I, giving my word, may bestow upon you in turn the rewards of eternal recompense and the endless joys of paradise, provided that you will have defended my Roman city and my special people, your brothers, the Romans, with great swiftness, from the hands of the wicked Lombards.

Hasten, hasten, I urge and protest by the living and true God, hasten and assist, before the living font whence you

---

[1]   Matt. 28:19.

[2]   John 20:22–23.

[3]   Matt. 16:18–19.

[4]   Matt. 10:41.

were nourished and reborn dries up; before that little spark that remains from the most blazing flame, from which you have known your light, is extinguished; before your spiritual mother, the holy church of God, in which you hope to receive eternal life, is humiliated, overwhelmed, and is violated and contaminated by the impious. I witness before you, my most beloved adoptive sons, through the grace of the Holy Spirit, I bear witness and I greatly urge and admonish before God the terrible creator of all, I, the apostle of God, Peter, and together with me the holy, catholic, and apostolic church of God, which the Lord committed to me: Do not suffer this Roman city to perish in which the Lord laid my body and which he commended to me and established as the foundation of the faith.

Free it and its Roman people, your brothers, and in no way permit it to be invaded by the people of the Lombards; thus may your provinces and possessions not be invaded by peoples of whom you know nothing. Let me not be cut off from my Roman people; thus may you not be foreign and cut off from the kingdom of God and eternal life. In whatever you have demanded of me, I shall come to your aid, that is to say, I shall also bestow my patronage. Come to the aid of my Roman people, your brothers, and struggle more perfectly and achieve final success in freeing them. For no one receives the crown except he who has genuinely struggled. And you, struggle bravely for the liberation of the holy church of God lest you perish for eternity. I adjure you, I adjure you, most beloved, as I have already said, by the living God, and I stand true witness: Do not in the slightest permit this my Roman city and the people living in it to be mutilated any further by the people of the Lombards; thus may your bodies and souls not be slashed and tormented in the eternal and inextinguishable fire of Tartarus with the devil and his stinking angels. And let not the sheep of the Lord's flock, committed to me by God, that is the Roman people, be further scattered; may the Lord not scatter and drive you out just as the Israelite people has been scattered.

For it has been declared that your people of the Franks is devoted to me, to the apostle of God, Peter, beyond all peoples who are under heaven; thus I have commended to you through the hand of my vicar the church, which the Lord handed to me, so that you might free it from the hands of its enemies. Believe most confidently that I, the servant of God, called to be an apostle, have lent my aid in all your needs when you have called on me, and I have bestowed victory upon you, through the power of God, over your enemies, and in the future I shall bestow no less, believe me, if you make haste with great dispatch to free this my Roman city. Remember this as well: How I also caused the enemies of the holy church of God to be struck down by you when they threatened battle against you who were few in number against them. Therefore, struggle; fulfill this warning of mine quickly, that you may more perfectly deserve to obtain my help through the grace that has been given to me by Christ, our Lord God.

Behold, dearest sons, for in preaching I have warned you. If you shall have obeyed quickly it will lead to great reward for you and assisted by my intercession you will overcome your enemies in the present life and you will endure to a great age, and you will have the goods of the earth at your disposal and beyond doubt you will enjoy eternal life. If not, however, which we do not believe, you will have made some delay or excuse for making no haste to fulfill this our exhortation to defend this Roman city of mine and the people living in it and the holy apostolic church of God committed to me by the Lord, and likewise his prelate, then know this: That by the authority of the holy and unique Trinity, through the grace of the apostolic office, a grace that has been given to me by the Lord Christ, we disinherit you from the kingdom of God and from eternal life for your transgression of our exhortation.

But may our God and Lord Jesus Christ who, redeeming us by his precious blood, has led us to the light of truth and established us as preachers and teachers for the whole world, grant it to you to judge these things wisely, and to understand and to make arrangements concerning them exceedingly quickly so that you may more swiftly hasten to rescue this Roman city and its people and the holy church of God committed to me by the Lord and, with my intercession intervening on your behalf, may he keep you safe and victorious with the mercy he shows to those who are faithful to his power, and in the world to come may he make you worthy many times over of the gifts of his reward with his saints and chosen ones.

Farewell.[1]

---

[1] Soon after this letter Pippin mustered his army, marched into Italy, defeated Aistulf, and drew up the Second Peace of Pavia, better known as the "Donation of Pippin."

3.12 Modeling the state on Old Testament Israel: *The Admonitio Generalis* (789). Original in Latin.

Eleven years before he was crowned emperor, King Charlemagne drew up a set of general instructions, *The Admonitio Generalis*, for the great men of his realm, both lay and ecclesiastical, "to lead the people of God to the pastures of eternal life." He took as his model the biblical King Josiah, who discovered a copy of "the book of the law," realized how badly his people deviated from what was written therein, and immediately took steps to reform his kingdom (see 2 Kings 22–23). In effect, the many laws set forth by *The Admonitio Generalis*, only some of which are excerpted here, were Charlemagne's attempts to govern his kingdom according to the laws of God.

1. What must the clergy have been doing that needed reform?
2. Why are weights and measures included in the *Admonitio*'s reforms?

[Source: *Christianity through the Thirteenth Century*, ed. Marshall W. Baldwin (New York: Harper and Row, 1970), pp. 115–19.]

Our Lord Jesus Christ ruling forever.

I, Charles by the grace of God and the gift of His mercy, king and ruler of the kingdom of the Franks, devout defender and humble supporter of holy church, give greetings of lasting peace and beatitude to all grades of the ecclesiastical order and to all ranks of the secular power, in Christ our Lord, eternal God. Reflecting with dutiful and calm consideration, along with our priests and councilors, on the abundant mercy of Christ the King toward us and our people, we have considered how necessary it is not only with our whole heart and voice to offer thanks for His goodness unceasingly, but also to persist in the continuous exercise of good works in His praise so that He who has given our kingdom such honors may deign to preserve and protect us and our kingdom forever. Accordingly it has pleased us to solicit your efforts, O pastors of the churches of Christ and leaders of His flock and distinguished luminaries of the world, to strive to lead the people of God to the pastures of eternal life by watchful care and urgent advice and stir yourselves to bring back the wandering sheep within the walls of ecclesiastical constancy on the shoulders of good example or exhortation, lest the wolf, plotting against anyone who transgresses the canonical laws or evades the fatherly traditions of the ecumenical councils—which God forbid!—find him and devour him. Thus they must be admonished, urged, and even forced by the great zeal of piety, to restrain themselves within the bonds of paternal sanctions with staunch faith and unrelenting

constancy. Therefore, we have sent our missi who by the authority of our name are to correct along with you what should be corrected. And we append herewith certain chapters from canonical ordinances which seem to us to be particularly necessary.

Let no one judge this admonition to piety, by which we endeavor to correct errors, remove superfluous matter, and condense those things which are right, to be presumptuous. I entreat him rather to accept it with a benevolent spirit of charity. For we read in the book of Kings how the holy Josiah, traveling around the kingdom bestowed on him by God, correcting and admonishing, labored to recall it to the worship of the true God: not that I hold myself equal to his holiness, but because the examples of the saints are always to be followed by us, and we must bring together whomsoever we can to a devotion to the good life in the praise and glory of our Lord Jesus Christ....

Chapter 70, to the Clergy

Bishops should carefully see to it that throughout their dioceses (*parochiae*) the priests observe their Catholic faith and baptism and understand well the prayers of the mass; and that the psalms are chanted properly according to the divisions of the verses and that they understand the Lord's Prayer and preach that it is to be understood by all, so that each person may know what he is asking of

God; and that the "Glory be to the Father" be sung with all dignity by everyone and that the priest himself with the holy angels and all the people of God with one voice intone the "Holy, Holy, Holy." And it should in every way be made clear to priests and deacons that they should not bear arms but trust in the protection of God rather than in arms.

Chapter 71, Something to the Priest, Something to People

It is likewise our will to urge your reverences that each throughout his diocese see that the church of God is held in His honor and the altars venerated with suitable dignity, and that the house of God is not used as a pathway for dogs and that the vessels consecrated to God are kept with great care or used with honor; and that secular or mundane affairs are not transacted in churches because the house of God must be a house of prayer and not a den of thieves;[1] and that the people when they come to the solemnities of the mass are attentive and do not leave before the completion of the priest's blessing.

Chapter 72, to the Clergy

And we also demand of your holiness that the ministers of the altar of God shall adorn their ministry by good manners, and likewise the other orders who observe a rule and the congregations of monks. We implore them to lead a just and fitting life, just as God himself commanded in the Gospel. "Let your light so shine before men that they may see your good works and glorify your Father which is in heaven,"[2] so that by their example many may be led to serve God; and let them join and associate to themselves not only children of servile condition, but also sons of free men. And let schools be established in which boys may learn to read. Correct carefully the Psalms, the signs in writing (notas), the songs, the calendar, the grammar in each monastery or bishopric, and the catholic books; because often some desire to pray to God

properly, but they pray badly because of the incorrect books. And do not permit your boys to corrupt them in reading or writing. If there is need of writing the Gospel, Psalter, and Missal, let men of mature age do the writing with all diligence.

Chapter 73, to the Clergy

We have likewise taken pains to ask that all, wherever they are, who have bound themselves by the vow of a monastic life live in every way regularly in a monastic manner according to that vow. For it is written, "Render your vows to the Lord God";[3] and again, "it is better not to vow than not to fulfill."[4] And let those coming to monasteries according to the regular manner be first tested in the examination room and so accepted. And let those who come to the monastery from the secular life not be sent immediately on monastic tasks outside before they are well educated within. And monks are not to seek worldly pleasures. Likewise, those who are admitted to that clerical state which we call the canonical life, we desire that they live such a life canonically and in every way according to its rule; and the bishop should govern their life as the abbot does the monks.

Chapter 74, to All

Let all have equal and correct weights and just and equal measures, whether in the towns or in the monasteries, whether in giving in them or in receiving, as we have the command in the law of the Lord,[5] and likewise in Solomon, when the Lord says, "[Different] weight and [different] measure, my soul abhors."[6] ...

Chapter 80, to All the Clergy

Let them teach fully the Roman chant and let the office be followed according to the direction of the nocturnal or gradual as our father Pepin, of blessed memory, ordered

---

[1] See Matt. 21:13.

[2] Matt. 5:16.

[3] Deut. 23:21.

[4] Eccles. 5:4.

[5] See Lev. 19:35–36.

[6] Prov. 20:10.

done when he suppressed the Gallican use for the sake of unity with the apostolic see and the peaceful harmony of the holy church of God.[1]

Chapter 81, to All

And we also decree, according to what the Lord ordained in the law,[2] that there be no servile work on Sundays, as my father, of good memory, ordered in the edicts of his synods, that is: that men do no farm work, either in plowing fields or in tending vineyards, in sowing grain or planting hedges, in clearing in the woods or in cutting trees, in working with stone or in building houses, or in working in the garden; nor are they to gather for games or go hunting. Three tasks with wagons may be performed on Sunday, the arms' cart or the food wagon, or if it is necessary to bear someone's body to the grave.

Likewise, women are not to work with cloth nor cut out clothes, nor sew or embroider; nor is it permissible to comb wool or crush flax or wash clothes in public, or shear sheep, to the end that the honor and quiet of the Lord's day be kept. But let people come together from all places to the church for the solemnities of the mass and praise God on that day for all the good things He has done for us.

Chapter 82, to All

And you are to see to it, O chosen and venerable pastors and rulers of the church of God, that the priests whom you send through your dioceses (*parochiae*) for ruling and preaching in the churches to the people serving God, that they rightly and justly preach; and you are not to allow any of them to invent and preach to the people new and unlawful things according to their own judgment and not according to Holy Scripture. And you too are to preach those things which are just and right and lead to eternal life, and instruct others that they are to preach these same things.

3.13 The Slavic conversion: Constantine-Cyril, *Prologue to the Gospel* (863–867). Original in Old Church Slavonic.

In 863 the brothers Constantine and Methodius were sent to Moravia at the behest of the Byzantine Patriarch Photius and at the invitation of the Moravian ruler Ratislav. They stayed about four years, translating the Scriptures into the Slavic dialect they had learned in Macedonia, which was not the language of Moravia but was nevertheless comprehensible to the people living there. Today this language is called Old Church Slavonic. In the *Prologue* to his translation of the Gospels, Constantine speaks of the importance of literacy: "The soul lacking letters / Grows dead in human beings."

1. How does the *Prologue* make the conversion of the Slavs seem inevitable?
2. How does the *Prologue* employ the five senses to make its point?

[Source: Roman Jakobson, "St. Constantine's Prologue to the Gospel," *St. Vladimir's Seminary Quarterly* 7 (1963): 16–19.]

---

[1] The "Gallican use" refers to the words and melodies used in Church liturgy in Francia under the Merovingians. Although Charlemagne here attributes the suppression of this liturgy to his father, Pippin III (d.768), in fact it was Charlemagne himself who was most instrumental in reforming the chants used in his kingdom along Roman models.

[2] See Exod. 20:8–10.

I am the Prologue to the Holy Gospels:
As the prophets prophesied of old—
"Christ comes to gather the nations and tongues,
Since He is the light of the world"[1]—
So it has come to pass in this seventh millennium. 5
Since they have said, "The blind shall see,
The deaf shall hear the Word of the Book,
For it is proper that God be known."[2]
Therefore hearken, all ye Slavs!
For this gift is given by God, 10
The gift on God's right hand,
The incorruptible gift to souls,
To those souls that will accept it.
Matthew, Mark, Luke, and John
Teach all the people, saying: 15
"If you see and love the beauty of your souls,
And hence are striving
To dispel the darkness of sin,
And to repel the corruptness of this world,
Thus to win paradise life 20
And to escape the flaming fire,
Then hear now with your own mind,
Since you have learned to hear, Slavic people,
Hear the Word, for it came from God,
The Word nourishing human souls, 25
The Word strengthening heart and mind,
The Word preparing all to know God."
As without light there can be no joy—
For while the eye sees all of God's creation,
Still what is seen without light lacks beauty— 30
So it is with every soul lacking letters,
Ignorant of God's law,
The sacred law of the Scriptures,
The law that reveals God's paradise.
For what ear not hearing 35
The sound of thunder, can fear God?
Or how can nostrils which smell no flower
Sense the Divine miracle?
And the mouth which tastes no sweetness
Makes man like stone; 40
Even more, the soul lacking letters
Grows dead in human beings.
Thus, considering all this, brethren,
We speak fitting counsel
Which will divide men 45

From brutish existence and desire,
So that you will not have intellect without intelligence,
Hearing the Word in a foreign tongue,
As if you heard only the voice of a copper bell.
Therefore St. Paul has taught: 50
"In offering my prayer to God,
I had rather speak five words
That all the brethren will understand
Than ten thousand words which are
incomprehensible."[3] 55
What man will not understand this?
Who will not apply the wise parable,
Interpreting to us the true message?
As corruption threatens the flesh,
Decaying and rotting everything worse than pus 60
If there is no fit nourishment,
So each soul no longer lives
Deprived of Divine Life,
Hearing not the Divine Word.
Let another very wise parable
Be told, ye men that love each other 65
And wish to grow toward God!
Who does not know this true doctrine?
As the seed falls on the field,
So it is upon human hearts
Craving the divine shower of letters 70
That the fruit of God may increase.
What man can tell all the parables
Denouncing nations without their own books
And who do not preach in an intelligible tongue?
Even one potent in all tongues 75
Lacks power to tell their impotence.
Let me add my own parable
Condensing much sense into few words:
Naked indeed are all nations without their own books
Who being without arms cannot fight 80
The Adversary of our souls
And are ripe for the dungeon of eternal torments.
Therefore, ye nations whose love is not for the Enemy
And who truly mean to fight him:
Open eagerly the doors of your intelligence— 85
You who have now taken up the sturdy arms
That are forged through the Lord's Books,
And who mightily crush the head of the Enemy.
Whoever accepts these letters,

---

[1] See Isa. 66:8 and John 8:12.

[2] See Isa. 29:18.

[3] See 1 Cor. 14:19.

To him Christ speaks wisdom,	90	Standing on the right hand of God's throne,	100
Feeds and strengthens your souls,		When He judges the nations with fire,	
And so do the Apostles with all the Prophets.		And rejoicing throughout the ages with the angels,	
Whoever speak their words		Eternally praising God the merciful,	
Will be fit to slay the Foe,		Always with songs from the holy books,	
Bringing God good victory,	95	Singing to God who loves man:	105
Escaping the suppurant corruption of flesh—		To Him befits all glory,	
Flesh that lives as in a sleep;		To the Son of God, honor and praise forever,	
These will not fall but hold fast,		With the Father and the Holy Ghost,	
And come forth before God as men of valor,		Unto the ages of ages, from all creatures!	

3.14 The Bulgarian khan in Byzantine guise: *Seal of Boris-Michael* (864–889).

The Bulgars established themselves in Bulgaria in the 670s, as Byzantine control over the region south of the Danube weakened. The Bulgar khans and nobles subjected both Slavs and Greek-speaking Byzantines to their rule, employing the Greek speakers in their administration. Influenced by Byzantine practices, these administrators affixed seals to official documents sent out in the name of the seal's owner. The seals were made of lead, a common metal. They were locally stamped and decorated with monograms or inscriptions or even human heads. Lead was used not only because it was malleable but also to indicate the low-level and routine nature of the correspondence involved. Use of the inferior metal also acknowledged the lower status of the Bulgarian ruler within the Byzantine political hierarchy. Only the Byzantine emperor had the right to use gold seals, while notables with the highest titles were allowed, in exceptional circumstances, to use silver. Lower-ranking rulers who recognized the superior position of the emperors used lead.

When Khan Boris (r.852–889) converted to the Christian religion and adopted the name Michael and the title of "prince," he had lead seals made to advertise his new faith. On the seal shown here, the "obverse"—or "heads," as in "heads or tails"—side of the seal has a circle with the inscription, "Christ help your servant Michael ruler of Bulgaria." Inside the circle is the head of a long-haired and bearded Christ with a cross nimbus (halo) behind him. His right hand gives a sign of blessing, while his left hand holds the Gospels. On the "reverse"—or tails—side is, again, a circle with an inscription, this time reading: "Mother of God help your servant Michael ruler of Bulgaria." Inside the circle is the head of Mary, mother of God, wearing a *maphorion* (a mantle with a hood), her hands upraised in prayer. Note that, influenced by Byzantine notions of rulership, the seal presents Boris-Michael as a territorial ruler (over "Bulgaria") rather than ruler of the Bulgar people (the "Bulgarians").

See Plate 1, "Reading through Looking," p. II, for a color reproduction of the seal.

1. How did seals such as this function as political advertisements?
2. How did the seal suggest the role of religion in Boris-Michael's administrative decisions?

[Kiril Petkov, ed. and trans., *The Voices of Medieval Bulgaria, Seventh–Fifteenth Century: The Records of a Bygone Culture* (Leiden: Brill, 2008), p. 33. Images courtesy of Dr. Ivan Jordanov.]

3.15 The Bulgarians adopt Christianity: Pope Nicholas I, *Letter to Answer the Bulgarians' Questions* (866). Original in Latin.

Christians mingled with Bulgars in the Bulgar state, and more arrived gradually in the course of the ninth century via Greek captives and deserters. In *c.*864 Khan Boris converted to the Byzantine form of Christianity, taking the baptismal name of Michael, after Emperor Michael III (r.842–867). (See one of his seals in Plate 1, "Reading through Looking," p. II.) But Boris-Michael did not intend to be subservient to the emperor. Thus in 866, seeking to reconcile Bulgar with Christian practices, he turned to Pope Nicholas I to clarify various points of the faith and how they should apply to the Bulgarians. His original questions have been lost, but the pope's advice suggests what they were.

1. What daily religious practices did the pope prescribe?
2. What did Nicholas think of Boris-Michael's treatment of the people who "rose up against" him?

[Source: Nicholas I, *Epistola* 99, in *Epistolae* 6, ed. Ernest Perels, Monumenta Germaniae Historica (Berlin, 1925), pp. 568–600. Translated by William L. North.]

Not much needs to be said in response to your inquiries nor have we considered it necessary to pause long over each question, since we, with God's aid, are going to send to your country and to your glorious king,[1] our beloved son, not only the books of divine law but also suitable messengers of ours[2] who will instruct you concerning

---

[1] Boris-Michael. Note that the pope bestows the title of king on him.
[2] Paul, bishop of Populonia, and Formosus, bishop of Porto.

the details insofar as time and reason dictate; to them, as well, we have committed books that we thought they would need.

Chapter I.

Now then, at the very beginning of your questions, you state in excellent and praiseworthy fashion that your kind seeks the Christian law. If we tried to explain this law fully, countless books would have to be written. But in order to show briefly in what things it chiefly consists, you should know that the law of Christians consists in faith and good works....

Chapter IV.

We do not think we need to explain to you, who are rough and in some ways children in the faith, how many times or days in the course of a year one should abstain from meat. For the time being, on the days of fasting when one should especially supplicate the Lord through abstinence and the lamentation of penance, one should completely abstain from meat. For, although it is fitting to pray and abstain at all times, one should nevertheless be even more of a slave to abstinence during times of fasting. This is to say that he who recalls that he has committed illicit deeds, should abstain on these days even from licit things in accordance with the sacred decretals, namely during Lent, which is before Easter, on the fast before Pentecost, at the fast before the assumption of the holy mother of God and the ever virgin Mary, our Lady, as well as on the fast before the feast of the birth of our Lord Jesus Christ: these are the fasts which the holy Roman church received in antiquity and maintains. But on the sixth day of every week, and on all the vigils of famous feasts one should cease from eating meat and should apply oneself to fasting....

Chapter VII.

You further inquire, whether a clean or unclean person is allowed to kiss or carry the cross of the Lord when he holds it. [We answer] that for the person who is clean, it is completely permissible; for what is indicated in a kiss if not the love with which someone burns for these things? And in carrying it, what else is expressed if not the mortification or fellow-suffering of the flesh? Indeed, the Lord also ordered him to carry this cross, but in his mind; but when it is performed with the body, one is more easily reminded that it should also be performed in the mind....

Chapter IX.

You ask whether you should partake of the body and blood of the Lord every day during greater Lent.[1] We humbly pray to omnipotent God and exhort you all most vehemently that you do so, but not if your mind is disposed towards sin, or if your conscience—because it is unrepentant or unreconciled perhaps—accuses your mind of criminal sins; or if one of you is not reconciled to a brother through his own fault....

Chapter X.

You wish to know if anyone is permitted to perform any labor on Saturday or Sunday. Concerning this matter the oft-remembered holy Pope Gregory said, while addressing the Romans: "It has come to my attention that certain men of a perverse spirit have sowed some depraved things among you which are contrary to the holy faith, so that they forbid anything to be done on Saturday. What else should I call such people except preachers of the Antichrist, who shall, when he comes, make Saturday and Sunday be kept free from any work? ... But on Sundays one should cease from earthly labor and devote oneself to prayers in every way, in order that whatever act of negligence has been committed during the other six days, may be expiated with prayers throughout the day of the Lord's resurrection.[2]

Chapter XI.

You ask whether you should cease from earthly work on the feast days of these apostles, martyrs, confessors, and virgins. Yes, [you should cease from work] on the feasts of the blessed virgin Mary, of the twelve apostles, of the evangelists and of their precursor, the lord John, of St. Stephen the Protomartyr as well as on the birthdays of those

---

[1] The forty days preceding Easter.

[2] Here Nicholas is thinking of a letter of Gregory the Great to the citizens of Rome.

saints whose celebrated memory and feast day shall be held among you by God's favor. You should know clearly, that worldly work should cease on feast days in order for Christians to attend church more easily; to engage in psalms, hymns, and spiritual songs; to spend time in prayer; to offer oblations; to share in the remembrance of the saints; to rise to imitate them; to concentrate on divine scriptures, and to distribute alms to the needy....

Chapter XII.

Because you ask whether it is permitted to carry out judgment on the feasts of the saints, and whether the person, if he deserves it, should be sentenced to death on this same day, you should know that on those feasts when, as we have shown, one should cease from all worldly labor, we think that one should abstain all the more from secular affairs and especially from executions...

Chapter XIII.

Among your questions and inquiries, you said that you are requesting secular laws.[1] Regarding this matter, we would willingly have sent the volumes that we thought you might need at present, if we had learned that one among you could interpret them for the rest; if we have given some books concerning secular law to our messengers, we do not want them to be left [with you] when they return, lest by chance someone interpret them for you in a perverse way or violate them with some falsehood....

Chapter XVII.

Now then, you have told us about how you received the Christian religion by divine clemency and made your entire people be baptized, and how these people, after they had been baptized, fiercely rose up against you with one spirit, claiming that you had not given them a good

law and wishing to kill you and establish another king. [You then recounted] how you, prepared to oppose them with the help of divine power, conquered them from the greatest to the least and held them captives in your hands, and how all the leaders and magnates along with every one of their children were slaughtered by the sword, though the mediocre and lesser persons suffered no evil. Now you desire to know whether you have contracted any sin on account of those who were deprived of their lives. Clearly what did not escape sin nor could have happened without your fault was that a child who was not privy to their parents' plot nor is shown to have born arms against you, was slaughtered along with the guilty, even though he was innocent.... You also should have acted with greater mildness concerning the parents who were captured, that is, [you should have] spared their lives out of love for the God Who delivered them into your hands. For thus you might be able to say to God without hesitation in the Lord's Prayer: "Forgive us our debts, as we forgive our debtors."[2] But you also could have saved those who died while fighting, but you did not permit them to live nor did you wish to save them, and in this you clearly did not act on good advice; for it is written: "There shall be judgment without mercy for the person who does not exercise mercy."[3] ... But because you erred more because of your zeal for the Christian religion and your ignorance than because of any other vice, with subsequent penance seek mercy and indulgence for these sins through the grace of Christ....

Chapter XXVI.

With regard to those who have slaughtered their kinsman, that is, someone related by blood such as a brother, cousin, or nephew, the venerable laws [of the Bulgarians] should be properly enforced. But if they have fled to a church, they should be saved from the laws of death but they should also submit without hesitation to the penance which the bishop or priest of the place has decided. "I do not want the death of the sinner," says the Lord, "but rather wish that he be converted and live."[4] ...

---

[1] Note the close association that newly converted kings made between becoming Christian and gaining written lawbooks and codes. See, for example, King Stephen's *Laws* for Hungary (below, p. 213). But the Bulgarians, who (as Nicholas implies) were more familiar with Greek than with Latin, did not write down a law code until the ninth century. It was based on an eighth-century Byzantine code that in turn depended on the law codes sponsored by Justinian.

[2] Matt. 6:12.

[3] James 2:3.

[4] Ezek. 33:11.

Chapter XXXIII.

When you used to go into battle, you indicated that you carried the tail of a horse as your military emblem, and you ask what you should carry now in its place. What else, of course, but the sign of the cross? ...

Chapter XXXIV.

You also asked, if, when a messenger arrives, you should set off immediately in order to get to the fighting or whether there are any days when it is not fitting to go forth into battle. On this matter we answer: there is no day which should be kept completely free from beginning or carrying out any kind of business, except (if too great a necessity does not compel you) the most celebrated days mentioned above, which are venerated by all Christians. But this is not because it is forbidden to do such things on these days. For our hope should be placed not in days nor determined by days, but all salvation should be expected absolutely from the true and living God alone. Rather it is because on these days, if the necessity is not unavoidable, one should spend time in prayer and the mysteries of so great a festival should be attended more zealously than usual....

Chapter XXXV.

You say that when you went forth into battle, you used to watch the days and hours and perform incantations, games, songs and some auguries, and you wish to be instructed on what you should do now. Regarding this matter, we would of course instruct you, if we did not think that you have been divinely instructed on this matter; for atop the divine foundation, we cannot build anything. Therefore, when you decide to go forth into battle, do not fail to do what you yourselves have recalled, i.e. go to the churches, carry out prayers, forgive sinners, be present at the solemnities of the Mass, offer oblations, make a confession of your sins to the priests, receive the reconciliation and communion, open the jails, loose the fetters and grant liberty to servants and especially to those who are broken and weak and captives, and distribute alms to the needy, so that you may fulfill what the Apostle admonishes when he says: "Do everything,

whether it be in word or deed, do it all in the name of the Lord Jesus."[1] For the things that you mentioned, that is, the observations of days and hours, the incantations, the games, iniquitous songs, and auguries are the pomp and workings of the devil, which you already renounced, thank God, in baptism and you cast off all these things completely along with the old man and his actions, when you put on the new....

Chapter XLI.

With regard to those who refuse to receive the good of Christianity but instead sacrifice to and bow down before idols, we can write nothing more to you than that you win them over to the correct faith with warnings, exhortations, and reason rather than with force. For they have knowledge but it is in vain: although they are people with capable intellects, they adore the products of their own hands and senseless elements, or to speak more truly, they bend their necks and sacrifice to demons....

Chapter XLVII.

You ask whether it is permitted to play games during Lent. Christians are not permitted to do this not only during Lent but also at any other time. But you are weak and are not yet strong enough to climb to the mountain to receive the highest commandments of God but instead have been placed in the flatlands like the former children of Israel, so that you may at least receive some of the simpler, lesser commandments. Therefore, because we cannot yet to convince you to refrain from games at all times, you should at least abstain from games, from the vain conversation and scurrility that do not befit the occasion, and idle chatter during the time of Lent and fasting when you should be spending more time and be more intent on prayer, abstinence, and every kind of penance....

Chapter XLIX.

Furthermore, you ask whether you are permitted to show your wives gold, silver, cattle, horses, etc. as dowry just as [you did] before. Because it is no sin and the laws do not forbid it, we, too, do not forbid this from occurring;

---

[1] Col. 3:17.

and not only this, but also whatever else you did before baptism, you are now clearly permitted to do....

Chapter LI.

You ask if you are permitted to have two wives at the same time; if this is not permitted, you know what the person in this situation should do at this point. Neither the origin of the human condition nor any Christian law allows a man to have two wives at once. For God, Who made the human being, made one male and one female at the very beginning. Of course, he could have given him two wives, if he wished but he did not want to do so....

Chapter LVII.

You claim that the Greeks forbid eunuchs to kill your animals, so that they assert that anyone who has eaten [meat] from animals killed by them has committed a grave sin. This sounds truly strange and silly to us. But because we have not heard the reasoning of the people who say these things, we cannot decide anything definitive concerning their assertion, since it is not yet fully known....

Chapter LXIV.

The number of days after a woman gives birth to a child that a man should abstain from [having intercourse] with her is proclaimed not by the products of our own wit but by the words of the Roman Pope and apostle of the English nation, Gregory [the Great] of blessed memory. Among other things, he says when he writes to Bishop Augustine, whom he had sent to [the Anglo-Saxons]: "A woman's husband should not come to lie with her

until the infants to whom she has given birth, have been weaned...."[1]

Chapter XCV.

You ask what we think should be done about those who flee to a church because of certain crimes. Now then, although the sacred canons require that the decrees of the worldly laws be upheld and these laws appear to be without mercy towards certain persons, we who do not accept the spirit of this world nevertheless say that if someone flees to a church, he should not be removed unless he wishes [to come out] voluntarily. For if long ago robbers and those guilty of various crimes fled to the Temple of Romulus for asylum and received protection from harm, so much more should those who flee to the Temple of Christ receive remission for their sins and be restored to their original state of complete safety, once the suspect has offered an oath on his own behalf.

[Closing]

... We have given these responses to your questions and proposals, insofar as the Lord has given them to us. It is not as much as we could say but rather as much as we thought could satisfy you for the time being. But when, by God's concession, you shall possess a bishop through the ministry of our prelacy, he shall teach you everything that pertains to his office. And if there are things that he does not understand, he shall receive them again from the authority of the apostolic see. May God, who has worked the greatest salvation among you, bring this to completion, make it solid, and give it stability and strength to the end [of time]. Amen.

---

[1] Gregory the Great, in a set of letters transmitted by Bede (see above, pp. 96–99).

TIMELINE FOR CHAPTER THREE

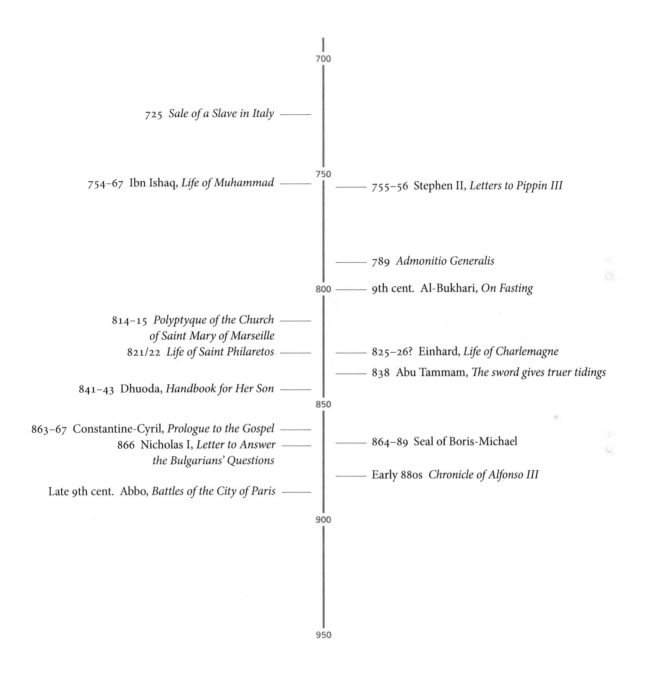

700

725 *Sale of a Slave in Italy* ———

750

754–67 Ibn Ishaq, *Life of Muhammad* ——— ——— 755–56 Stephen II, *Letters to Pippin III*

——— 789 *Admonitio Generalis*

800 ——— 9th cent. Al-Bukhari, *On Fasting*

814–15 *Polyptyque of the Church* ———
of Saint Mary of Marseille
821/22 *Life of Saint Philaretos* ——— ——— 825–26? Einhard, *Life of Charlemagne*
——— 838 Abu Tammam, *The sword gives truer tidings*

841–43 Dhuoda, *Handbook for Her Son* ———

850

863–67 Constantine-Cyril, *Prologue to the Gospel* ———
866 Nicholas I, *Letter to Answer* ——— ——— 864–89 Seal of Boris-Michael
the Bulgarians' Questions
——— Early 880s *Chronicle of Alfonso III*

Late 9th cent. Abbo, *Battles of the City of Paris* ———

900

950

To test your knowledge and gain deeper understanding of this chapter, please go to **www.utphistorymatters.com** for Study Questions.

IV

Political Communities Reordered (c.900–c.1050)

REGIONALISM: ITS ADVANTAGES AND ITS DISCONTENTS

4.1 Fragmentation in the Islamic world: Al-Tabari, *The Defeat of the Zanj Revolt* (*c*.915). Original in Arabic.

Al-Tabari (839–923) was born in Amul, on the southern shore of the Caspian Sea. His education took him to Baghdad, Basra, and Egypt before he returned to Baghdad (*c*.870) to write and teach. He was a prolific author, producing works on jurisprudence, the Qur'an, and history. His universal history, from which the excerpt below comes, began with Creation and continued to 915. He modestly called this extremely long work *The Short Work on the History of Messengers, Kings, and Caliphs*. The section printed here covers the last part of the reign of Caliph al-Mu'tamid (r.870–892), a period through which al-Tabari himself lived. Key to the events of this period was the revolt of the Zanj, black slaves who were put to work removing the salt from the marshes formed by the Tigris and Euphrates rivers. Led by 'Ali b. Muhammad, whom al-Tabari calls "the abominable" and "the traitor," the Zanj pillaged the cities around Basra and incited some local groups to challenge the caliph's authority. In response, al-Mu'tamid called on his brother al-Muwaffaq Abu Ahmad and Abu Ahmad's son Abu al-'Abbas (later Caliph al-Mu'tadid) to wage war against the Zanj. The passage here begins in 880 with a victory by Abu al-'Abbas. Although ruthlessly killing all the captives in this instance, father and son also offered amnesty and "robes of honor" to those who deserted the Zanj cause, severely dividing and weakening the opposition. They ultimately won the war against the Zanj in 883, but al-Tabari hints of other local defections from the caliphate, presaging its eventual decline.

Let us use this document to discuss how to read a primary source. Al-Tabari's account of the Zanj revolt is a very different kind of source from *The Edict of Milan* in Chapter 1, which was earlier used to explore reading methods. Nevertheless, it should be subjected to the same series of questions. The answers lead to new questions that work just for al-Tabari (and perhaps for a small cluster of similar documents as well), in the same way as the answers to the questions about *The Edict of Milan* led to questions largely pertinent to it alone.

Who wrote it, and for what audience was it written? In this case, the answer is quite simple: the author was al-Tabari, and you know a bit about his career from the introductory note above. You can easily guess that his audience was meant to be his students and other educated readers in the Islamic world.

When was it written? Your editor has given you the date *c.*915. At this point in your studies, you need not worry much about how this date was arrived at. It is more important to consider the circumstances and historical events in the context of which a date such as 915 takes on meaning. Here you should be considering how, even as the caliphate was weakening, the Islamic world was open to scholars keenly interested in the causes and effects of its decline.

Where was it written? The answer is, no doubt, Baghdad. But you should not be content with that. You should consider Baghdad's significance at the time. Was it still the capital of the Islamic world? If not, why do you suppose al-Tabari settled there?

Why was it written? Al-Tabari begins this voluminous history with an extended passage in praise of God. He then says that he intends to begin with the Creation of the world and to continue by chronicling all the kings, messengers, and caliphs that he has heard about. But the first topic that he addresses in some detail is philosophical: "What is Time?" Thus, although al-Tabari does not say precisely why he wrote, he clearly wished to produce both a comprehensive chronicle about the powerful men in the world and a reflective work on the nature of history itself. But you should go beyond this answer to ask what other motives might have been at work. For example, might al-Tabari have thought that there were moral, practical, and religious—even doctrinal—lessons to be learned from history? Might he have been interested in legitimizing the Abbasids or other dynasties?

What is it? Clearly it is a history; the word is in the title. But what sort of history? Al-Tabari was careful to document many of his facts by citing the chain of sources (*isnad*) that attested to them. This technique was important in Islamic hadith (see above, p. 147) and legal works as well. Al-Tabari's work thus assimilates history with the scholarly traditions of other disciplines. Moreover, his history might be called "universal," given its huge time frame. On the other hand, it is not a history of everything but rather of certain key figures.

What does it say? This is the most important question of all. To answer it, you need to analyze the text (or, here, the excerpt) carefully, taking care to understand what the author is describing and seeking further information (if necessary) about the institutions that he takes for granted.

What are the implications of what it says? This requires you to ask many questions about matters that lie behind the text. Important questions to ask are: *What does the document reveal about such institutions as family, power, social classes and groups, religion, and* *education and literacy in the world that produced it? What are its underlying assumptions about gender; about human nature, agency, and goals; about the nature of the divine?*

How reliable is it? Certainly al-Tabari's citations of his sources suggest that he was interested in reliability. On the other hand, you may ask if al-Tabari included everything that he knew, or if he had a certain "slant" on the events.

Are there complicating factors? In the Middle Ages authors often dictated their thoughts and then reworked them over time. Al-Tabari apparently finished lecturing on his *History* in about 915, but he continued to rework it. After his death, the work was copied numerous times—by hand. Paper was prevalent in the Islamic world, and it was cheaper and more abundant than parchment, which the West and the Byzantine Empire relied on. Nevertheless, today we have no complete manuscript of al-Tabari's history, and scholars have had to reconstruct the full text from the various parts that are extant.

If you compare the questions and answers here with those introducing the *Edict of Milan*, you should be convinced that reading primary sources is both complex and fascinating.

[Source: *The History of al-Tabari*, vol. 37: *The 'Abbasid Recovery*, trans. Philip M. Fields, annotated by Jacob Lassner (Albany: State University of New York Press, 1987), pp. 24–27, 65–66, 132–36.]

Abu Ahmad remained in al-Firk for several days to permit his troops, and any others who wanted to proceed with him, to join on. He had prepared the barges, galleys, ferries and boats. Then, on Tuesday, the second of Rabi' I [October 11, 880], he and his clients, pages, cavalry and infantry reportedly left al-Firk, bound for Rumiyat al-Mada'in. From there they journeyed on, stopping at al-Sib, Dayr al-'Aqul, Jarjaraya, Qunna, Jabbul, al-Silh and a place one *farsakh* [about four miles] from Wasit.[1] He remained at the latter for one day and one night and was met by his son Abu al-'Abbas and a squadron of cavalry including his leading officers and men. Abu Ahmad inquired about the state of his men, and getting from his son a picture of their gallantry and devotion in fighting, he ordered that robes of honor be bestowed upon them and Abu al-'Abbas. Thereupon, the son returned to his camp at al-'Umr where he remained throughout the day. In the early morning of the next day, Abu Ahmad took to the water where he was met by his son, Abu al-'Abbas, and all his troops in military formation, as fully equipped as they would be when confronting the traitor's forces. Abu Ahmad sailed on until he reached his camp on the waterway called Shirzad, where he stopped. On Thurs-

day, the twenty-eighth of Rabi' I [November 6, 880], he departed from there and stopped at the canal called Nahr Sindad, opposite the village called 'Ab-dallah. He instructed his son Abu al-'Abbas to halt on the eastern side of the Tigris, opposite the mouth of the Barduda, and put him in charge of the vanguard. Then he allotted the soldiers' allowances and paid them. Following that, he instructed his son to advance in front of him with the equipment that he had in his possession, toward the mouth of the Bar Musawir Canal.

Abu al-'Abbas set out with the best of his officers and troops, including Zirak al-Turki, the commander of his vanguard, and Nusayr Abu Hamzah, the commander of the barges and galleys. After this it was Abu Ahmad who set out with his selected cavalry and infantry, leaving the bulk of his army and many of his horsemen and foot soldiers behind in his place of encampment.

His son Abu al-'Abbas met him with a show of captives, heads and bodies of slain enemies from among the troops of al-Sha'rani. For, on that same day, before the arrival of his father Abu Ahmad, Abu al-'Abbas had been attacked by al-Sha'rani who came upon the former's camp. Abu al-'Abbas dealt him a severe blow,

---

[1] The places mentioned in this document are in or near Iraq.

killing a great many of his men and taking captives. Abu Ahmad ordered that the captives be beheaded, which was done. Then Abu Ahmad descended to the mouth of the Bar Musawir, where he stayed for two days. From there, on Tuesday, the eighth of Rabi' II [November 17, 880], he departed from Suq al-Khamis with all his men and equipment bound for the city which the leader of the Zanj had named al-Mani'ah bi-Suq al-Khamis. He proceeded with his ships along the Bar Musawir while the cavalry marched before him along the eastern side of the waterway until they reached the waterway called Baratiq, which led to Madinat al-Sha'rani. Abu Ahmad preferred to begin fighting against Musa al-Sha'rani before he fought Sulayman b. Jami' because he feared that al-Sha'rani, who was to his rear, might attack and thus divert him from the adversary in front of him. That is why he set out against al-Sha'rani. He ordered the cavalry to cross the canal and proceed along both banks of the Baratiq. Abu Ahmad also instructed his son Abu al-'Abbas to advance with a flotilla of barges and galleys, and he himself followed with barges along with the bulk of his army.

When Sulayman, his Zanj troops and others noticed the cavalry and infantry proceeding on both banks of the canal and the ships advancing along the waterway—this was after Abu al-'Abbas had met them and engaged them in a skirmish—they fled and scattered. The troops of Abu al-'Abbas climbed the walls killing those who opposed them. When the Zanj and their supporters scattered, Abu al-'Abbas and his forces entered the city, killed a great many of its people, took many prisoners and laid hold of whatever was there. Al-Sha'rani and the others who escaped with him fled; they were pursued by Abu Ahmad's men up to the marshes where many drowned. The rest saved themselves by fleeing into the thickets.

Thereupon, Abu Ahmad instructed his troops to return to their camp before sunset of that Tuesday, and he withdrew. About five thousand Muslim women and some Zanj women, who were taken in Suq al-Khamis, were saved. Abu Ahmad gave instructions to take care of all the women, to transfer them to Wasit and return them to their families.

Abu Ahmad spent that night opposite the Baratiq Canal and in the early morning of the next day, he entered the city and gave the people permission to take all the Zanj possessions there. Everything in the city was seized. Abu Ahmad ordered the walls razed, the trenches filled, and the remaining ships burned. He left for his camp at Bar Musawir with booty taken in the districts and villages previously possessed by al-Sha'rani and his men; this included crops of wheat, barley and rice. He ordered that the crops be sold and the money realized from the sale be spent to pay his mawla's pages,[1] the troops of his regular army, and other people of his camp.

Sulayman al-Sha'rani escaped with his two brothers and others, but he lost his children and possessions. Upon reaching al-Madhar he reported to the traitor [that is, the leader of the Zanj] what had befallen him and that he had taken refuge in al-Madhar.

According to Muhammad b. al-Hasan—Muhammad b. Hisham, known as Abu Wathilah al-Kirmani: I was in the presence of the traitor—he was having a discussion—when the letter from Sulayman al-Sha'rani arrived with the news of the battle and his flight to al-Madhar. As soon as he had the letter unsealed and his eye fell on the passage describing the defeat, his bowel muscles loosened and he got up to relieve himself, then he returned. As his Assembly came to order, he took the letter and began reading it again, and when he reached the passage which had disturbed him the first time, he left once more. This repeated itself several times. There remained no doubt that the calamity was great, and I refrained from asking him questions. After some time had elapsed, I ventured to say, "Isn't this the letter from Sulayman b. Musa?" He replied, "Yes, and a piece of heartbreaking news, too. Indeed, those who fell upon him dealt him a crushing blow 'that will not spare nor leave unburned.' He has written this letter from al-Madhar, and he has barely saved his own skin."

I deemed this news momentous and only God knows what a joy filled my heart, but I concealed it and refrained from rejoicing at the prospect of the approaching relief. However, the traitor regained self-control in face of vicissitude, and showed firmness. He wrote to Sulayman b. Jami', cautioning him against al-Sha'rani's fate and instructing him to be vigilant and watchful concerning what might lie before him....

On Tuesday, the first day of al-Muharram [August 12, 881], Ja'far b. al-Ibrahim, who was known as al-Sajjan, sought safe-conduct from Abu Ahmad al-Muwaffaq. It is mentioned that the reason for this was Abu Ahmad's battle at the end of Dhu al-Hijjah 267 [July 3–31, 881], to which we have referred above, as well as the flight of Rayhan b. Salih al-Maghribi and his men from the camp

---

[1] A mawla could mean either master or servant. Here it undoubtedly refers to a servant or dependent.

of the deviate, and their linking up with Abu Ahmad. The abominable one became completely discouraged at this; al-Sajjan was, reportedly, one of his trustworthy associates.

Abu Ahmad conferred on this al-Sajjan robes of honor, various gifts, as well as a military allotment, and a place of lodging. Al-Sajjan was assigned to Abu al-ʿAbbas, who was ordered to transport him in a barge to a position in front of the abominable one's fortress so his [former] compatriots could see him. Al-Sajjan addressed them and told them that they were misled by the abominable one; he informed them what he had experienced because of the latter's lies and immoral behavior. The same day that al-Sajjan was placed in front of the abominable one's camp, a great many Zanj officers and others sought guarantees of safety; all of them were treated kindly. One after another the enemy sought safety and abandoned the abominable one.

After that battle which I have mentioned as having taken place on the last day of Dhu al-Hijjah of the year 267 [July 31, 881], Abu Ahmad did not cross over to fight the abominable one, thus giving his troops a respite until the month of Rabiʿ II [November 9–December 7, 881].

In this year, ʿAmr b. al-Layth went to Fars to fight Muhammad b. al-Layth, his own governor in this province. ʿAmr routed Muhammad b. al-Layth and auctioned off the spoils of his camp; the latter escaped with a small group of his men. ʿAmr entered Istakhr, which was looted by his troops, and then sent a force to chase after Muhammad b. al-Layth. They seized him, and then delivered him to ʿAmr as a prisoner. Thereupon, ʿAmr went to Shiraz where he remained....

Now [August 883] Abu Ahmad was sure of victory, for he saw its signs, and all the people rejoiced at what God had granted—namely, the rout of the profligate and his men. They rejoiced as well at God's having made it possible to expel the enemy from their city, and seize everything in it, and distribute what had been taken as booty—that is the money, treasures and weapons. Finally there was the rescue of all the captives held by the rebels. But Abu Ahmad was angry at his men because they disobeyed orders and abandoned the positions in which he had placed them. He ordered that the commanders of his mawlas and pages and the leading men among them be gathered together. When they were assembled for him, he scolded them for what they had done, judging them weak and castigating them in harsh language. Then they made excuses; they supposed that he had returned, and they had not known about his advance against the profligate, nor about his having pressed so far into the rebel's camp.

Had they known this, they would have rushed toward him. They did not leave their places until they had taken a solemn oath and covenant that, when sent against the abominable one, none of them would withdraw before God had delivered him into their hands; and should they fail, they would not budge from their positions until God had passed judgment between them and him. They requested of al-Muwaffaq that, after they had left al-Muwaffaqiyyah to fight, he order the ships transporting them to return and, thus, eliminate any temptation to those who might seek to leave the battle against the profligate.

Abu Ahmad accepted their apologies for their wrongdoing and again took them into his favor. Then he ordered them to prepare for crossing and to forewarn their troops just as they themselves had been forewarned. Abu Ahmad spent Tuesday, Wednesday, Thursday and Friday preparing whatever he would need. When this was completed, he sent word to his entourage and the officers of his pages and mawlas, instructing them as to their tasks when crossing [into combat]. Friday evening he sent word to Abu al-ʿAbbas and the officers of his pages and mawlas to set out for places which he, that is, Abu Ahmad, had specified.

Al-Muwaffaq instructed Abu al-ʿAbbas and his troops to set a course for a place known as ʿAskar Rayhan, which lay between the canal known as Nahr al-Sufyani and the spot where the rebel sought refuge. He and his army were to follow the route along the canal known as Nahr al-Mughirah, so that they would exit where the canal intersects the Abu al-Khasib and reach ʿAskar Rayhan from this direction. He forwarded instructions to an officer of his black pages to reach the Nahr al-Amir and cross at its center. At the same time, he ordered the rest of his officers and pages to pass the night on the eastern side of the Tigris, opposite the profligate's camp, and be prepared to attack him in the early morning.

During Friday night, al-Muwaffaq made the rounds among the officers and men in his barge. He divided amongst them key positions and locations which he had arranged for them in the profligate's camp. According to the assigned plan, they were to march towards these places in the morning. Early Saturday morning, on the second of Safar, 270 [August 11, 883], al-Muwaffaq reached the Abu al-Khasib Canal in his barge. He remained there until all his men had crossed [the waterway] and disembarked from their vessels, and the cavalry and infantry had assumed their positions. Then, after giving instructions for the vessels and ferries to return to the eastern side, he gave the troops the go-ahead to march against the profligate. He himself preceded them until he reached the spot where he estimated the profligates would make a stand in an attempt to repel the government army. Meanwhile, on Monday, after the army had withdrawn, the traitor and his men returned to the city and stayed there, hoping to prolong their defense and repel the attack.

Al-Muwaffaq found that the fastest of his cavalry and infantry among the pages had preceded the main force of the army and had attacked the rebel and his companions, dislodging them from their positions. The enemy force fled and dispersed without paying attention to one another, and the government army pursued them, killing and capturing whomever they managed to catch. The profligate, with a group of his fighting men, was cut off from [the rest] of his officers and troops—among them was al-Muhallabi. Ankalay, the rebel's son, had abandoned him, as had Sulayman b. Jami'. Moving against each of the contingents which we have named was a large force of al-Muwaffaq's mawlas, and cavalry and infantry drawn from his pages. Abu al-'Abbas's troops, assigned by al-Muwaffaq to the place known as 'Askar Rayhan, met the rebel's fleeing men and put them to the sword. The officer assigned to the Amir Canal also arrived there, and having blocked the rebels' path he attacked them. Encountering Sulayman b. Jami', he took the fight to him, killing many of his men and seizing Sulayman. He made Sulayman a captive and delivered him to al-Muwaffaq without conditions. The people were glad to learn of Sulayman's capture, and there were many cries of "God is Great!" and great clamor. They felt certain of victory, since Sulayman was known to be the most able of the rebel's companions. After him, Ibrahim b. Ja'far al-Hamdani, one of the field commanders of the rebel's army, was taken captive; then Nadir al-Aswad, the one known as al-Haffar, one of the earliest companions of the rebel, was captured.

Upon al-Muwaffaq's order, precautionary measures were taken, and the captives were transferred in barges to Abu al-'Abbas.

Following this, those Zanj who had separated from the main body, together with the profligate, assaulted the government force, dislodging them from their positions and causing them to lose the initiative. Al-Muwaffaq noticed the loss of initiative, but he pressed on with the search for the abominable one, advancing quickly in the Abu al-Khasib Canal. This bolstered his mawlas and pages, who hastened to pursue (the enemy) with him. As al-Muwaffaq reached the Abu al-Khasib Canal, a herald arrived with the good news of the rebel's death; before

long another herald arrived carrying a hand, and claimed that this was the hand of the rebel. This seemed to lend credence to the report of the rebel's demise. Finally a page from Lu'lu''s troops arrived, galloping on a horse and carrying the head of the abominable one. Al-Muwaffaq had the head brought closer, and then showed it to a group of former enemy officers who were in his presence. They identified it, and al-Muwaffaq prostrated himself in adoration to God for both the hardships and bounties He had conferred upon him. Abu al-'Abbas, the mawlas and the officers of al-Muwaffaq's pages then prostrated themselves, offering much thanks to God, and praising and exalting Him. Al-Muwaffaq ordered the head of the rebel raised on a spear and displayed in front of him. The people saw it and thus knew that the news of the rebel's death was true. At this, they raised their voices in praise to God.

It is reported that al-Muwaffaq's troops surrounded the abominable one after all his field commanders had abandoned him save al-Muhallabi; the latter now turned away from him and fled, thus betraying the rebel. The rebel then set off for the canal known as Nahr al-Amir and plunged into the water, seeking safety. Even before that, Ankalay, the son of the abominable one, had split off from his father and fled in the direction of the canal known as Nahr al-Dinari, where he entrenched himself in the swampy terrain.

Al-Muwaffaq retired, with the head of the abominable one displayed on a spear mounted in front of him on a barge. The vessel moved along the Abu al-Khasib Canal, with the people on both sides of the waterway observing it. When he reached the Tigris, he took his course along the river and gave the order to return the vessels, with which he had crossed to the western side of the Tigris at daylight, to the eastern side of the river. They were returned to ferry the troops [back] across the river.

Then al-Muwaffaq continued his trip, with the abominable one's head on the spear before him, while Sulayman b. Jami' and al-Hamdani were mounted for display. When he arrived at his fortress in al-Muwaffaqiyyah, he ordered Abu al-'Abbas to sail the barge, keeping the rebel's head and Sulayman b. Jami' and al-Hamdani in place, and to take his course to the Jatta Canal where the camp of al-Muwaffaq began. He was to do this so that all the people of the camp could have a look at them. Abu al-'Abbas did this, and then returned to his father, Abu Ahmad, whereupon the latter imprisoned Sulayman b. Jami' and al-Hamdani and ordered that the rebel's head be properly prepared and cleaned.

4.2 The powerful in the Byzantine countryside: Romanus I Lecapenus, *Novel* (934). Original in Greek.

In Byzantine legal terms, a "novel" is a "new law." Emperor Romanus I Lecapenus (r.920–944) issued one such law on behalf of the poor in the countryside in 934. Newly powerful provincial landowners, known as *dynatoi*, were taking advantage of a recent famine to buy up whole villages, enhancing both their economic and social positions. Romanus tried to set back the clock—he wanted the land to stay in the hands of the original peasant families or at least in the hands of their village neighbors. He insisted that the powerful "return [the land] without refund to the owners."

1. What reasons did Romanus give for issuing his *Novel*?
2. What benefits might the emperor himself have gained from this new law?

[Source: *The Land Legislation of the Macedonian Emperors*, trans. and ed. Eric McGeer (Toronto: Pontifical Institute of Mediaeval Studies, 2000), pp. 53–56, 59–60 (notes modified).]

Novel of the Lord Emperor Romanus the Elder

PROLOGUE

To dispose the soul in imitation of the Creator is the desire and ardent endeavor of those for whom it is a great and blessed thing to regard and to call themselves the work of the all-creating hand. As for those by whom this has not been accounted great and holy, they have the task of denying the Creation and the reckoning of Judgment, and, as with persons wholly content with life on earth and who choose to live their lives upon the earth alone, the display of their choice has been left in their wake.[1] Hence the great confusion of affairs, hence the great tide of injustices, hence the great and widespread oppression of the poor, and the great sighing of the needy, for whose sake the Lord rose from the dead. For He says, "For the oppression of the poor, for the sighing of the needy, now will I arise, saith the Lord."[2] If God, our Creator and Savior, Who made us emperor, rises in retribution, how will the poor man, who awaits only the eyes of the emperor for intercession, be neglected and altogether forgotten by us? Therefore, not only upon examination of the actions taken against them in the recent past or attempts to make amends, but also administering a common and lasting remedy to the matter, we have issued the present law to avenge them, having prepared this as a purgative and a cleansing of the predilection of greed. We have considered it advantageous that now no longer will anyone be deprived of his own properties, nor will a poor man suffer oppression, and that this advantage is beneficial to the common good, acceptable to God, profitable to the treasury, and useful to the state. Careful attention to this subject, for the sake of which decrees and judgments restraining the wickedness of the will and curtailing the reach of the grasping hand have streamed down to all the officials under our authority, has not been long neglected, nor has [our concern] arisen inappropriately. But since evil is versatile and multifarious, and all evils—not least greed, if indeed not even more so—contrive to evade the grip of laws and edicts and to regard the inescapable eye of divine justice as of no account, these measures, ejecting and excising the crafty workings of the will of the evildoers, have as a result now warranted more secure and rigorous codification.

---

[1] The general sense seems to be this: people who see themselves as part of God's Creation try to act in accordance with God's ways, while people who do not venerate the Creation will have to reckon with the Last Judgment; such people have left ample evidence behind them of their choice to ignore divine justice and to lead their lives in pursuit of earthly, not eternal, rewards.

[2] Ps. 12:5; Douay Ps. 11:6.

177

1.1. We ordain therefore that those living in every land and district, where after God our rule extends, are to keep the domicile which has come down to them free and undisturbed. If time continues to preserve this arrangement, let the subsequent acquisition by the offspring or relatives through testamentary disposition, or the intention of the owner's preference, be fulfilled. If, though, given the course of human life and the ebb and flow of time, the pressure of necessity or even the prompting of the will alone, be it as it may, the owner embarks on the alienation of his own lands either in part or in whole, the purchase must first be set before the inhabitants of the same or adjacent fields or villages. We do not introduce this legislation out of animosity or malice towards the powerful; but we issue these rulings out of benevolence and protection for the poor and for public welfare. Whereas those persons who have received authority from God, those risen above the many in honor and wealth, should consider the care of the poor an important task, these powerful persons who regard the poor as prey are vexed because they do not acquire these things more quickly. Even if such impious conduct is not true of all, let adherence to the law be common to all, lest the tare [weeds] brought in with the wheat escape notice.[1]

1.2. As a result, no longer shall any one of the illustrious *magistroi*[2] or *patrikioi*,[3] nor any of the persons honored with offices, governorships, or civil or military dignities, nor anyone at all enumerated in the Senate,[4] nor officials or ex-officials of the themes nor metropolitans most devoted to God, archbishops, bishops, *higoumenoi* [abbots], ecclesiastical officials, or supervisors and heads of pious or imperial houses,[5] whether as a private individual or in the name of an imperial or ecclesiastical property, dare either on their own or through an intermediary to intrude into a village or hamlet for the sake of a sale, gift, or inheritance—either whole or partial—or on any other pretext whatsoever. As this sort of acquisition has been ruled invalid, the acquired properties, along with the improvements since added, are to return without refund to the owners or, if they or their relatives are no longer alive, to the inhabitants of the villages or hamlets.

For the domination of these persons has increased the great hardship of the poor, bringing upheavals, persecutions, coercion, and other concomitant afflictions and difficulties through the multitude of their servants, hirelings or other attendants and followers, and, to those able to see it, will cause no little harm to the commonwealth unless the present legislation puts an end to it first. For the settlement[6] of the population demonstrates the great benefit of its function—the contribution of taxes and the fulfillment of military obligations—which will be completely lost should the common people disappear. Those concerned with the stability of the state must eliminate the cause of disturbance, expel what is harmful, and support the common good.

2.1. Let time hereafter maintain these measures for the common benefit and settled order of our subjects; but it is necessary to apply the approved remedy not only to the future, but also to the past. For many people seized upon the indigence of the poor—which time bringer of all things brought, or rather, which the multitude of our sins, driving out divine charity, caused—as the opportunity for business instead of charity, compassion, or kindness; and when they saw the poor oppressed by famine, they bought up the possessions of the unfortunate poor at a very low price, some with silver, some with gold, and others with grain or other forms of payment. Harsher than the duress at hand, in those times which followed they were like a pestilential attack of disease to the miserable inhabitants of the villages, having entered like gangrene into the body of the villages and causing total destruction....

EPILOGUE It is our desire that these regulations remain in force for the safety of our subjects for whose sake great and constant care is our concern. For if we have expended so much care for those under our authority, so as to spare nothing that contributes to freedom, on account of which lands, towns, and cities have, with the help of God, come into our hands from the enemy, some as the result of war, while others have passed over to us by the example [of the conquered towns] or through fear of capture and were taken before the trumpet's call to battle; and if we have

---

[1] Echoing the parable of the wheat and the tares related in Matt. 13:24–30; 36–43.

[2] Those holding the highest possible dignity conferred on non-imperial family members.

[3] Those who hold a high dignity conferred on governors of themes (military districts) or military leaders.

[4] The Byzantine Senate was an advisory body whose members were high civil officials and dignitaries.

[5] Philanthropic foundations administered by crown officials.

[6] The Greek word for "settlement" also embraces the notions of stability and prosperity among the rural populace.

striven, with the help of God, to provide our subjects with such great freedom from enemy attack, setting this as the goal of our prayers and exertions, how will we, after accomplishing so much against the onslaught of external enemies, not rid ourselves of our own enemies within, enemies of the natural order, of the Creation, and of justice, by reviling and repressing insatiety [endless desire], by excising the greedy disposition, and by liberating our subjects from the yoke of the tyrannical, oppressive hand and mind with the righteous intention to free them with

the cutting sword of the present legislation? Let each of those to whom judicial authority has fallen see to it that these provisions remain in force in perpetuity [forever], for the service of God and for the common benefit and advantage of our empire received from Him.

In the Month of September of the eighth indiction in the year 6443 from the creation of the world, Romanus, Constantine, Stephanus, and Constantine, emperors of the Byzantines and faithful to God.

....

4.3 Evanescent centralization in al-Andalus: Ibn ʿAbd Rabbihi, *Praise Be to Him* (929–940). Original in Arabic.

Al-Andalus (Islamic Spain) was politically independent long before Abbasid power diminished elsewhere. In the ninth century, like so many other polities of the day, al-Andalus broke up into regional lordships. That situation was reversed by ʿAbd al-Rahman III (r.912–961), who took the title of "caliph" in 929. When he first came to the throne, his power, like that of most Western rulers, extended only locally, around Córdoba. He had to contend not only with regional Islamic lords but also with the threat of the Shiʿite Fatimids to the south and Christian kingdoms to the north. ʿAbd al-Rahman waged constant wars during the first twenty years of his reign, working to unify al-Andalus under his rule and to turn the Christian kingdoms into vassals. His ambitions were largely realized—although they proved evanescent, as regional rulers reasserted themselves in the next century. The new caliph took Baghdad as a model, and his poets and writers cast a glowing light on him. One of these, Ibn ʿAbd Rabbihi (860–940), wrote a grand encyclopedia, *The Unique Necklace*, in which he included a long epic poem, *Praise Be to Him*. Much as Abu Tammam had celebrated the ninth-century Abbasid Caliph al-Muʿtasim (see above, p. 124), so Ibn ʿAbd Rabbihi glorified an Islamic leader's military campaigns. Like a chronicle in that it recounted events year by year (compare it to *The Easter Chronicle*, above p. 55, for example), *Praise Be to Him* was also a work of art, written in rhyming couplets and full of color, sound, and feeling.

1. What qualities does Ibn ʿAbd Rabbihi invoke to prove that ʿAbd al-Rahman was rightfully called caliph?
2. What sorts of forces did the Islamic leader command and what tactics did he use to fight his wars?

[Source: James T. Monroe, "The Historical Arjuza of Ibn ʿAbd Rabbihi, a Tenth-Century Hispano-Arabic Epic Poem," *Journal of the American Oriental Society*, 91:1 (1971): 80–81, 86–88, 89–90 (some notes added from James T. Monroe, "[Reading 1:] Ibn ʿAbd Rabbihi," in *Hispano-Arabic Poetry: A Student Anthology* [Berkeley: University of California Press, 1974], pp. 74–128).]

1. Praise be to Him who is not contained in any region nor reached by any vision;

2. Before whose countenance all faces are lowered in submission, for He has no rival or equal;

3. Praise be to Him for He is a mighty Creator, well informed about His creation; far-seeing.

4. [He is] a first principle having no beginning and a last one having no end.

5. His kindness and excellence have favored us, while it would be impossible to find His like,

6. Since He is far too illustrious for eyes to perceive or imagination and opinion to grasp,

7. Although He may be perceived by the mind, the intellect and by rational proofs,

8. Since these are the most solid means of knowing subjects that are abstruse and fine.

9. The knowledge grasped by man's intellect is more solid than that gained from ocular evidence,

10. Therefore may God be praised most plentifully for His blessings and favors;

11. And after praising and glorifying God, and thanking the Creator and Quickener of the dead,

12. I shall speak about the battle-days of the best of men; one who has been adorned with generosity and courage;

13. One who has destroyed unbelief and rebellion and sundered sedition and schism.

14. For we were experiencing a moment of darkness intense as the night, as well as a civil war; being like the scum and rubbish [swept] by the torrent,

15. Until that worshipper of the Clement who is the most eminent of the Banu Marwan[1] was invested with power.

16. Being supported [by God] he appointed a sword from the edges of which death flowed, to judge over his enemies.

17. While he saluted royal power at dawn along with the new moon, so that they both arose in the morning like two rivals in beauty.

18. He bore [signs of] piety on his forehead and religious and secular authority upon his right hand.

19. The land was illuminated by his light and the stirring up of evil and mischief was interrupted,

20. During a time rife with rebellion when the breaking of alliances as well as apostasy were rampant,

21. And the earth had straitened its inhabitants while war had kindled the blaze of its fires,

22. When we were enfolded in a pitch-black night-blindness and a gloom without equal,

23. Such that every day we were attacked by mourning so that no eye could enjoy sleep.

24. Thus during 'Id we have even had to pray under the protection of guards out of fear for an enemy intent upon revenge,[2]

25. Until we were given in rescue, like a light putting heaven and earth next to each other,

26. The Caliph of God, whom He elected and chose over all creation ...

The Year 308 [920–921]

192. Then the Imam campaigned against the land of the infidel and what a momentous affair that was![3]

---

[1] The Banu Marwan: i.e., the Umayyads.

[2] 'Id refers to an Islamic festival.

[3] The Imam (signifying a religious leader) refers to the caliph, 'Abd al-Rahman III. The "land of the infidel" is the land of the Christians. The campaign of Muez, which this section of the poem narrates, was 'Abd al-Rahman's first foray into Christian territory.

193. To this end the chiefs of the provinces were mustered around him as well as those who enjoyed honor and rank among men,

194. Including ministers, generals, all those who were connected to marks of distinction,

195. Everyone who sincerely obeyed [the law of] the Clement both in secret and in public,

196. And everyone determined to wage a Holy War or whom a saddle could hold on a generous steed.

197. So what a troop it was!—One made up of every freeborn man among us as well as every slave.

198. Thus you would have thought that the people were "locusts scattered abroad" as our Lord says of those who will be assembled [at Doomsday].[1]

199. Then the one rendered victorious, aided [by God], upon whose forehead lies [the imprint of] the Message and the Light, set forth

200. While before him went troops of angels seizing or sparing for their Lord's sake,

201. Until, when he went in among the enemy, the Clement made him avoid all harm,

202. While he was able to impose the poll-tax and dire misfortunes upon those who had associated partners to God.[2]

203. Thus their feet quaked in terror and they were scared away out of fear for the blaze of war,

204. Rushing blindly through mountain passes and into places of concealment, surrendering fortresses and towns,

205. So that no church or monastery belonging to any Christian monk remained in any of the provincial districts

206. But that he made it go up in smoke like a fire that has come in contact with [dry] stubble,

207. While the cavalry of the Sultan knocked down all the buildings in them.

208. One of the first fortresses they knocked down and [one of the first] enemies within it whom they attacked, was

209. A town known as Osma which they left behind like a blackened piece of charcoal.

210. Then they ascended from there to certain towns which they left behind like a yesterday that has elapsed.

211. Then they moved forward with the infidel following them with his army, fearing and imitating their [movements].

212. Until they came directly to the river Dayy[3] where orthodoxy effaced the paths of error,

213. When they met in *Majma' al-Jawzayn*, for the squadrons of the two unbelievers had been collected

214. From the people of León and Pamplona, and those [of] Arnedo and Barcelona.[4]

215. The infidels were helping one another in spite of their unbelief, having gathered together from various lands;

216. Yet they were milling around at the foot of a lofty mountain, forming their ranks for battle

217. So [our] vanguard, raised high on their raiding horses, ran up to them,

218. And its swell was followed by another swell stretching out like an ocean of vast expanse.

219. In this way the two infidels were put to flight in the company of [their] infidels, having donned a robe of dust.

---

[1] A reference to Qur'an 54:7: "They will come forth, their eyes humbled, from their graves, [torpid] like locusts scattered abroad."

[2] "Those who had associated partners to God" are those who believed in the Trinity rather than God's oneness.

[3] The river Dayy is the Duero River.

[4] Majma' al-Jawzayn has not been identified. The "two unbelievers" were Ordoño II (d.924), king of Galicia and later king of Galicia and León; and Sancho I (d. by 925), king of Pamplona.

220. Each of the two looks back at times, yet in every face he sees his death,

221. Fine white [swords] and tawny [lances] are on their track, while killing and capturing penetrate deeply into their [ranks].

222. There is no fleeing for them, and heads were carried [aloft] on spears,

223. Because the Amir[1] gave orders for putting to rout and [our] army was swift to rush against [the enemy].

224. It came upon their multitude when they had been put to flight, and watched as their commanders were destroyed.

225. For when they wished to enter their fortress, they entered one of death's enclosures.

226. O, what an enclosure, O!—In it their souls paid up the debt to death which had fallen due.

227. When they saw the waves [of our army] before them, they entrenched themselves in a stronghold which became a tether for them;

228. A rock which became a dire misfortune for them, since they turned from it to Hellfire;

229. They fell one by one asking for water, yet their souls were taken from them while they were still athirst.

230. Therefore, how many a man was present at the feast of the crows and vultures, who had fallen prey to God's sword!

231. And how many priests who summon [their followers] to crosses and bells were killed by it!

232. Then the Amir departed, while all around him shouts of "There is no God but one God!" and "God is very great!" could be heard,

233. For he was determined to wage war on the land of the infidels, and [moved forward] preceded by squadrons of Arab cavalry.

234. Hence he trampled it underfoot as well as imposing on it ignominy, disgrace, bloodshed and a smashing destruction.

235. Moreover they burned down and destroyed fortresses, and afflicted their inhabitants,

236. So look right and left and all you will see is the fierce blaze of fire;

237. In the morning their habitations appeared devastated and all you could see was a spreading pall of smoke,

238. While in the midst of them all, the Imam, [God's] elect, was granted victory, for he had quenched [his thirst for vengeance] upon the enemy and could rejoice at the evil lot that had befallen them....

The Year 312 [924–925]

269. Afterwards the campaign of the year twelve took place. How many misfortunes and warning examples occurred during its course!

270. The Imam campaigned with his squadrons around him, like the full moon surrounded by its stars;

271. He campaigned with the sword of victory in his right hand and the rising star of good fortune on his forehead,

272. While the officer in charge of the army and the government was the eminent Musa, the Amir's chamberlain.

273. He destroyed the fortresses of Todmir and made the wild animals descend from the rocky peaks.[2]

274. So that the people unanimously agreed [to obey] him and the leaders of the rebellion acknowledged him as chief,

---

[1] The Amir (signifying a secular leader) is 'Abd al-Rahman III, as is the Sultan referred to in line 207. By using these various epithets for 'Abd al-Rahman, the poet indirectly argues for both his religious and secular authority.

[2] Todmir (or Tudmir), a province more-or-less corresponding to present-day Murcia (in Spain's southeast), was the region won by the Islamic conquerors through diplomacy in *The Treaty of Tudmir* (above, p. 78).

275. Until, when he had taken all of their fortresses and inscribed the truth elegantly on their texts,

276. There set forth, travelling in the shadow of the army, under the banner of the great lion,

277. The men of Todmir and their kinfolk, of every tie that could trace back its lineage to them.

278. Until, when he occupied Tudela, it was mourning over its blood that had gone unavenged;[1]

279. Over the magnitude of what it had suffered at the hands of the enemy, and over the constant warring, evening and morning.

280. Therefore he became anxious to humiliate the land of the infidel and that supporting [troops] should occupy the mountain pass.

281. Next he consulted those of his friends and of the frontiersmen who were endowed with wisdom and intelligence,

282. But they all advised him not to invade [the enemy territory] through the mountain pass, nor to cross through the densely-tangled mountain,

283. For he was accompanied by an army weakened by the loss of all the officers and [main] troops,

284. And they spread the rumor that fifty thousand of the infidel's men were stationed beyond the ravine.

285. Yet he declared: "I will most definitely enter [the pass], there being no road for me but the one leading to it,

286. And to my subduing the territory of Pamplona and the plain of that accursed city."

287. Yet no one but the chamberlain supported him in this decision.

288. Thus he asked God for assistance, set his troops in battle formation and entered, following which a victory without equal ensued.

289. Once he had set out and was crossing the mountain passes, wearing the breastplate of war,

290. A certain infidel placed his squadrons of cavalry in battle formation to attack him, and they plunged over the ravines.

291. Therefore the Imam asked for the assistance of the Lord of mankind, after which he sought the help of generosity and courage.

292. Then he took refuge in both private oration and prayer, to bring victory down from heaven.

293. Next he put the commanders at the head of the [main] troops, making auxiliaries follow one after another.

294. In this way the infidel was put to rout, while a slaughter took place in which the rearguard outdid the vanguard,

295. So that they were massacred in such a way as to be reduced to nought; moreover the white [swords] were abundantly watered with blood.

296. Then he turned toward Pamplona and the army rushed blindly upon the city

297. Until, when "they entered to search the very inmost parts of its homes"[2] and ruin rushed into the flourishing state of its civilization,

298. Onlookers wept over what befell it, when hooves first began to pound on it,

299. For the loss of its men who were slaughtered, and for the abasement of its children who were orphaned.

300. How many uncircumcised ones [lie dead] in and around it, over whom the eye of the bishop sheds [bitter] tears:[3]

301. And how many churches in it have been held in contempt, while their bells have been replaced by the muezzin's call;

---

[1] The poem here moves back to the north; Tudela was claimed by the Christians of Navarre/Pamplona.

[2] Qur'an 17:5.

[3] The "uncircumcised ones" are the Christians.

302. Both bell and cross weep over [Pamplona], for to each of them weeping is a [last remaining] duty!

303. Meanwhile the Imam departed with success, victory, divine support and prosperity;

304. Then, while on his way back, he turned the banners in the direction of the Banu Dhi n-Nun, because of his success,[1]

305. So that after a period of prosperity, the latter entered one of hardship, while their cheeks were glued to the ground,

306. Until they appeared before him with hostages consisting of both the eldest of the parents and of the offspring.

307. Therefore let there be great praise to God for supporting him and giving him right guidance!

4.4 Donating to Cluny: Cluny's *Foundation Charter* (910) and various charters of donation (10th–11th cent.). Originals in Latin.

William, duke of Aquitaine (875–918), and his wife Ingelberga, anxious to ensure their eternal salvation, founded the monastery of Cluny on family property in the region of Mâcon (Burgundy, France). Soon the monastery gained an astonishing reputation for piety, and the prayers of its monks were praised for sending souls to heaven. Local donors, ranging from small peasants to rich aristocrats, gave land to Cluny in order to associate themselves with the monks' redemptive work. The donations were recorded in charters. Those below are, first, the original donation made by William and Ingelberga; and, second, a group of charters drawn up for one family, later known as the Grossi (see Genealogy 4.1).

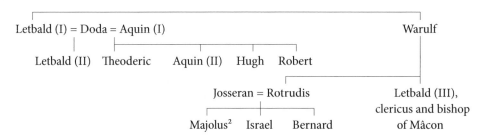

Genealogy 4.1 The Grossi

1. What reasons did people give for donating to the monastery of Cluny?
2. What roles did women have in supporting the monastery?

[Source: Patrick J. Geary, ed., *Readings in Medieval History*, 4th ed. (Toronto: University of Toronto Press, 2010), pp. 315–22 (slightly modified).]

---

[1] The Banu Dhi n-Nun were lords of Toledo, in the heart of al-Andalus.

[2] The Majolus of this family was not the same person as the Majolus who was abbot of Cluny 954–994.

[The Foundation Charter of Cluny: Charter # 112 (September 11, 910)]

To all right thinkers it is clear that the providence of God has so provided for certain rich men that, by means of their transitory possessions, if they use them well, they may be able to merit everlasting rewards. As to which thing, indeed, the divine word, showing it to be possible and altogether advising it, says: "The riches of a man are the redemption of his soul."[1] I, William, count and duke by the grace of God, diligently pondering this, and desiring to provide for my own salvation while I am still able, have considered it advisable—nay, most necessary, that from the temporal goods which have been conferred upon me I should give some little portion for the gain of my soul. I do this, indeed, in order that I who have thus increased in wealth may not, perchance, at the last be accused of having spent all in caring for my body, but rather may rejoice, when fate at last shall snatch all things away, in having reserved something for myself. Which end, indeed, seems attainable by no more suitable means than that, following the precept of Christ: "I will make his poor my friends"[2] and making the act not a temporary but a lasting one, I should support at my own expense a congregation of monks. And this is my trust, this my hope, indeed, that although I myself am unable to despise all things, nevertheless, by receiving despisers of the world, whom I believe to be righteous, I may receive the reward of the righteous. Therefore be it known to all who live in the unity of the faith and who await the mercy of Christ, and to those who shall succeed them and who shall continue to exist until the end of the world, that, for the love of God and of our Savior Jesus Christ, I hand over from my own rule to the holy apostles, Peter, namely, and Paul, the possessions over which I hold sway, the villa[3] of Cluny, namely, with the court and demesne mansus,[4] and the chapel in honor of St. Mary the mother of God and of St. Peter the prince of the apostles, together

with all the things pertaining to it, the villas, indeed, the chapels, the serfs of both sexes, the vines, the fields, the meadows, the woods, the waters and their outlets, the mills, the incomes and revenues, what is cultivated and what is not, all in their entirety. Which things are situated in or about the county of Mâcon, each one surrounded by its own bounds. I give, moreover, all these things to the aforesaid apostles—I, William, and my wife Ingelberga—first for the love of God; then for the soul of my lord king Odo;[5] of my father and my mother; for myself and my wife—for the salvation, namely, of our souls and bodies;—and not least for that of Ava who left me these things in her will;[6] for the souls also of our brothers and sisters and nephews, and of all our relatives of both sexes; for our faithful ones who adhere to our service; for the advancement, also, and integrity of the catholic religion. Finally, since all of us Christians are held together by one bond of love and faith, let this donation be for all,—for the orthodox, namely, of past, present or future times.

I give these things, moreover, with this understanding, that at Cluny a regular monastery shall be constructed in honor of the holy apostles Peter and Paul, and that there the monks shall congregate and live according to the rule of St. Benedict,[7] and that they shall possess, hold, have and order these same things unto all time, provided that the venerable house of prayer which is there shall be faithfully filled with vows and supplications, and that celestial converse shall be sought and striven after with all desire and with the deepest ardor; and also that there shall be diligently directed to God prayers, beseechings and exhortations both for me and for all, according to the order in which mention has been made of them above. And let the monks themselves, together with all the aforesaid possessions, be under the power and dominion of the abbot Berno, who, as long as he shall live, shall preside over them according to the Rule and consistent with his knowledge and ability. But after his death, those same monks shall have power and permission to elect any one

---

[1] See Prov. 13:8.

[2] Luke 16:9.

[3] In this instance, the word *villa* means an estate, which included an enclosed area (the "court"), land, waste, meadow and various other appurtenances. In many of the other charters of Cluny, however, the word *villa* refers to a small district in which many landowners held land.

[4] A *mansus* (pl. *mansi*) was a farming unit. A "demesne *mansus*" was an outsize farming unit belonging to the lord (in this case William, and soon the monastery of Cluny), which included the *mansi* of dependent peasants.

[5] Odo, related to the later Capetians, was king of the west Franks 888–898.

[6] Ava was a sister of the donor.

[7] For *The Benedictine Rule* see above, p. 20.

of their order whom they please as abbot and rector, following the will of God and the rule promulgated by St. Benedict,—in such a way that neither by the intervention of our own or of any other power may they be impeded from making a purely canonical election. Every five years, moreover, the aforesaid monks shall pay to the church of the apostles at Rome ten *solidi*[1] to supply them with lights; and they shall have the protection of those same apostles and the defense of the Roman pontiff; and those monks may, with their whole heart and soul, according to their ability and knowledge, build up the aforesaid place. We will, further, that in our times and in those of our successors, according as the opportunities and possibilities of that place shall allow, daily, works of mercy towards the poor, the needy, strangers, and pilgrims will be performed with the greatest zeal. It has pleased us also to insert in this document that, from this day, those same monks there congregated shall be subject neither to our yoke, nor to that of our relatives, nor to the sway of any earthly power. And, through God and all his saints, and by the awful day of judgment, I warn and abjure that no one of the secular princes, no count, no bishop whatever, not the pontiff of the aforesaid Roman see, shall invade the property of these servants of God, or alienate it, or diminish it, or exchange it, or give it as a benefice to any one, or constitute any prelate over them against their will. And that such unhallowed act may be more strictly prohibited to all rash and wicked men, I subjoin the following, giving force to the warning. I adjure you, oh holy apostles and glorious princes of the world, Peter and Paul, and you, oh supreme pontiff of the apostolic see, that, through the canonical and apostolic authority which you have received from God, you remove from participation in the holy church and in eternal life, the robbers and invaders and alienators of these possessions which I do give to you with joyful heart and ready will; and be protectors and defenders of the aforementioned place of Cluny and of the servants of God abiding there, and of all these possessions—on account of the clemency and mercy of the most holy Redeemer. If anyone—which Heaven forbid, and which, through the mercy of the God

and the protection of the apostles I do not think will happen—whether he be a neighbor or a stranger, no matter what his condition or power, should, through any kind of wild attempt to do any act of violence contrary to this deed of gift which we have ordered to be drawn up for the love of almighty God and for reverence of the chief apostles Peter and Paul; first, indeed, let him incur the wrath of almighty God, and let God remove him from the land of the living and wipe out his name from the book of life, and let his portion be with those who said to the Lord God: Depart from us; and, with Dathan and Abiron whom the earth, opening its jaws, swallowed up, and hell absorbed while still alive, let him incur everlasting damnation.[2] And being made a companion of Judas let him be kept thrust down there with eternal tortures, and, lest it seem to human eyes that he pass through the present world with impunity, let him experience in his own body, indeed, the torments of future damnation, sharing the double disaster with Heliodorus and Antiochus, of whom one being coerced with sharp blows and scarcely escaped alive; and the other, struck down by the divine will, his members putrefying and swarming with worms, perished most miserably.[3] And let him be a partaker with other sacrilegious persons who presume to plunder the treasure of the house of God; and let him, unless he come to his senses, have as enemy and as the one who will refuse him entrance into the blessed paradise, the key-bearer of the whole hierarchy of the church,[4] and, joined with the latter, St. Paul; both of whom, if he had wished, he might have had as most holy mediators for him. But as far as the worldly law is concerned, he shall be required, the judicial power compelling him, to pay a hundred pounds of gold to those whom he has harmed; and his attempted attack, being frustrated, shall have no effect at all. But the validity of this deed of gift, endowed with all authority, shall always remain inviolate and unshaken, together with the stipulation subjoined. Done publicly in the city of Bourges. I, William, commanded this act to be made and drawn up, and confirmed it with my own hand.

---

[1] A *solidus* was a coin, in this case silver.

[2] For Dathan and Abiron, Hebrews who challenged Moses in the desert and were swiftly swallowed up by the earth, see Num. 16:12–15, 25–34.

[3] Judas is the betrayer of Christ. In 2 Macc. 3:7–27, Heliodorus, minister of King Seleusis of Syria, is sent to plunder the Temple at Jerusalem but is beaten up by mysterious persons sent by divine will. In 2 Macc. 9:7–9, King Antiochus of Syria falls from a chariot and suffers horribly thereafter.

[4] The "key-bearer of the whole hierarchy of the church" is Saint Peter.

[Here follow the names of Ingelberga and 42 other people, mainly bishops, nobles, and members of William's family.]

[Charters of the Grossi Family: Charter # 802 (March 951)]

To all who consider the matter reasonably, it is clear that the dispensation of God is so designed that if riches are used well, these transitory things can be transformed into eternal rewards. The Divine word showed that this was possible, saying "Wealth for a man is the redemption of his soul," and again, "Give alms and all things will be clean unto you."[1]

We, that is, I, Doda, a woman, and my son Letbald [II], carefully considering this fact, think it necessary that we share some of the things that were conferred on us, Christ granting, for the benefit of our souls. We do this to make Christ's poor our friends, in accordance with Christ's precept and so that He may receive us, in the end, in the eternal tabernacle.

Therefore, let it be known to all the faithful that we—Doda and my son Letbald—give some of our possessions, with the consent of lord Aquin [I], my husband, for love of God and his holy Apostles, Peter and Paul,[2] to the monastery of Cluny, to support the brothers [i.e., monks] there who ceaselessly serve God and His apostles. [We give] an allod[3] that is located in the pagus[4] of Mâcon, called Nouville.[5] The serfs [servi] that live there are: Sicbradus and his wife, Robert, Eldefred and his wife and children, Roman and his wife and children, Raynard and his wife and children, Teutbert and his wife and children, Dominic and his wife and children, Nadalis with her children, John with his wife and children, Benedict with his wife and children, Maynard with his wife and children, another Benedict with his wife and children, and a woman too...[6] with her children.

And we give [land in] another villa[7] called Colonge and the serfs living there: Teotgrim and his wife and children, Benedict and his wife and children, Martin and his children, Adalgerius and his wife and children, [and] Sicbradus.

And [we give] a mansus[8] in Culey and the serfs there: Andrald and his wife and children, Eurald and his wife and children. And [we give] whatever we have at Chazeux along with the serf Landrad who lives there. We also give a little harbor on the Aar river and the serfs living there: Agrimbald and Gerald with their wives and children.

In addition, we give an allod in the pagus of Autun, in the villa called Beaumont and the serfs living there, John, Symphorian, Adalard and their wives and children, in order that [the monks] may, for the love of Christ, receive our nephew, Adalgysus, into their society.[9]

[We give] all the things named above with everything that borders on them: vineyards, fields, buildings, serfs of every sex and age, ingress and egress, with all mobile and immobile property already acquired or to be acquired, wholly and completely. We give all this to God omnipotent and His apostles for the salvation of our souls and for the soul of Letbald [I], the father of my son, and for the salvation of Aquin [I], my husband, and of all our relatives and finally for all the faithful in Christ, living and dead.

Moreover, I, the aforesaid Letbald, uncinch the belt of war, cut off the hair of my head and beard for divine love, and with the help of God prepare to receive the monastic habit in the monastery [of Cluny]. Therefore, the property that ought to come to me by paternal inheritance I now give [to Cluny] because of the generosity of my mother and brothers. [I do so] in such a way that while [my mother and brothers] live, they hold and possess it. I give a mansus in Fragnes, along with the serf Ermenfred and his wife and children, to [my brother] Theoderic, clericus,[10] and after his death let it revert to [Cluny]. And I give another mansus at Verzé with the serf Girbald and

---

[1] Prov. 13:8 and Luke 11:41.

[2] As William's foundation charter stipulated, Cluny had been handed over to the apostles Saints Peter and Paul.

[3] An allod in this region was land that was owned outright, in contrast to land held in fief, for example.

[4] A pagus was a Roman administrative subdivision.

[5] Almost all the places mentioned in these charters are within about ten miles of the monastery of Cluny.

[6] Effaced in the manuscript.

[7] Here the word villa refers to a district.

[8] The reference here is no doubt to a demesne mansus.

[9] Possibly Adalgysus is to become a monk; but it is more likely that he is to become a special "friend" of the monastery for whom prayers will be said.

[10] I.e., a priest.

his wife and children to my brother Hugo. In the *pagus* of Autun I give to [my brother] Aquin [II] the allod that is called Dompierre-les-Ormes, and the serf Benedict and his wife and their son and daughter. [I give Aquin also] another allod in Vaux, and the serfs Teutbald and his wife and children and Adalgarius. [I give all this] on condition that, if these brothers of mine [Hugh and Aquin], who are laymen, die without legitimate offspring, all these properties will go to the monastery as general alms.

If anyone (which we do not believe will happen) either we ourselves (let it not happen!) or any other person, should be tempted to bring a claim in bad faith against this charter of donation, let him first incur the wrath of God, and let him suffer the fate of Dathan and Abiron and of Judas, the traitor of the Lord. And unless he repents, let him have the apostles [Peter and Paul] bar him from the celestial kingdom. Moreover, in accordance with earthly law, let him be forced to pay ten pounds. But let this donation be made firm by us, with the stipulation added. S[ignum][1] of Doda and her son Letbald, who asked that it be done and confirmed. S. of Aquin, who consents. S. of Hugo. S. of Evrard. S. of Walo. S. of Warembert. S. of Maingaud. S. of Giboin. S. of Leotald. S. of Widald. S. of Hemard. S. of Raimbald. Dated in the month of March in the 15th year of the reign of King Louis.[2] I, brother Andreas, *levite*,[3] undersign at the place for the secretary.

[Charter # 1460 (November 12, 978–November 11, 979)[4]]

I, Majolus, humble abbot [of Cluny] by the will of God, and the whole congregation of brothers of the monastery of Cluny. We have decided to grant something from the property of our church to a certain cleric, named Letbald [III] for use during his lifetime, and we have done so, fulfilling his request.

The properties that we grant him are located in the *pagus* of M,con, in the *ager*[5] of Grevilly, in a *villa* called Collonge: *mansi*, vineyards, land, meadows, woods, water, and serfs of both sexes and whatever else we have in that place, which came to us from Raculf.[6] And we grant two *mansi* at Boye and whatever we have there. And in Massy, one *mansus*. And in "Ayrodia" [not identified], in a place called Rocca, we give *mansi* with vineyards, land, woods, water, and serfs of every sex and age; and we grant all the property of Chassigny [a place near Lugny that has disappeared]: vineyards, land, meadows, woods, water, mills and serfs and slaves. And at "Bussiacus" [near Saint-Huruge], similarly [we grant] *mansi*, vineyards, lands, meadows, and woods. And at "Ponciacus" [not identified] [we give] *mansi*, vineyards, and land. Just as Raculf gave these things to us in his testament, so we grant them to [Letbald] on the condition that he hold them while he lives and after his death these things pass to Cluny. And let him pay 12 dinars every year to mark his taking possession.

We also grant to him other property that came from lord Letbald [I], his uncle: a *mansus* at La Verzé and another at Bassy and another at Les Légères, and again another in Fragnes and another in Chazeux. And again a *mansus* in the *pagus* of Autun, at Dompierre-les-Ormes and another in Vaux and the serfs and slaves of both sexes that belong to those *mansi*. Let him hold and possess these properties as listed in this *precaria*[7] for as long as he lives. And when his mortality prevails—something no man can avoid—let this property fall to [Cluny] completely and without delay. [Meanwhile] let him pay 12 dinars every year, on the feast day of Apostles Peter and Paul.

I have confirmed this decree with my own hand and have ordered the brethren to corroborate it, so that it will have force throughout his lifetime. S. of lord Majolus, abbot. S. of Balduin, monk. S. of Vivian. S. of John. S. of Arnulf. S. of Costantinus. S. of Tedbald. S. of Joslen. S.

---

1 Usually laypeople did not sign charters; rather they made a mark or sign (their *signum*) that was indicated by the scribe in front of their name. The S refers to this sign.

2 This was King Louis D'Outremer (r.936–954), one of the last of the Carolingians.

3 A *levite* was a deacon.

4 This charter has this range of dates because the scribe dated it in the twenty-fifth year of the reign of King Lothar, the son of King Louis, whose rule began on November 12, 954.

5 The *pagus* of Mâcon was divided into subdivisions called *agri* (sing. *ager*). There were perhaps ten or more *villae* in each *ager*.

6 Raculf was probably a member of the Grossi family.

7 This document is a "precarial" donation. A *precaria* was a conditional grant of land *by* a monastery to someone outside of the monastery for his or her lifetime.

of Grimald. S. of Hugo. S. of Rothard. S. of Ingelbald. S. of Achedeus. S. of Vuitbert. S. of Ingelman. Dated by the hand of Rothard, in the 25th year of the reign of King Lothar.

[Charter # 1577 (Nov. 12, 981–Nov. 11, 982)]

To this holy place, accessible to our prayers [et cetera].[1] I, Rotrudis, and [my husband] Josseran, and my sons, all of us give to God and his holy Apostles, Peter and Paul and at the place Cluny, half of a church[2] that is located in the *pagus* of Mâcon, named in honor of St. Peter, with everything that belongs to it, wholly and completely, and [property in] the *villa* that is called Curtil-sous-Buffières. There [we give] a field and a meadow that go together and have the name *ad Salas*. This land borders at the east on a *via publica*[3] and a manmade wall; at the south on a meadow; at the west on a *via publica*, and similarly at the north. [I make this gift] for the salvation of the soul of my husband Josseran, and [for the soul of my son] Bernard. Done at Cluny. Witnesses: Rotrudis, Josseran, Bernard, Israel, Erleus, Hugo, Odo, Raimbert, Umbert. Ingelbald wrote this in the 28th year of the reign of King Lothar.

[Charter # 1845 (990–991)]

By the clemency of the Savior a remedy was conceded to the faithful: that they could realize eternal returns on His gifts if they distributed them justly. Wherefore, I, Majolus,[4] in the name of God, give to God and his holy apostles Peter and Paul and at the place Cluny some of my property which is located in the county of Lyon, in the *villa* "Mons" [not identified]. It consists of a demesne *mansus* with a serf named Durannus and his wife, named

Aldegard, and their children, and whatever belongs or appears to belong to this *mansus*, namely fields, vineyards, meadows, woods, pasturelands, water and water courses, that is already acquired or will be acquired, whole and complete. I make this donation first for my soul and for my burial [in Cluny's cemetery] and for the soul of my father Josseran and of my mother Rotrudis and of my brothers, and for the souls of my *parentes*[5] and for the salvation of all the departed faithful, so that all may profit in common. [I give it] on the condition that I may hold and possess it while I live, and that every year I will pay a tax of 12 dinars on the feast day of the Prince of the Apostles [i.e., St. Peter]. After my death, let [the property] go to Cluny without delay.

But if anyone wants to bring any bad-faith claim against this donation, let him first incur the wrath of the Omnipotent and all His saints; and unless he returns to his senses, let him be thrust into Hell with the devil. As in the past, let this donation remain firm and stable, with the stipulation added. Done publicly at Cluny. S. of Majolus, who asks that it be done and confirmed. S. of Bernard, S. of Israel, S. of Arleius, S. of Bernard, S. of Hubert. Aldebard, *levita*, wrote this in the 4th year of the reign of Hugh [Capet].

[Charter # 2508 (994–1030?)[6]]

Notice of a quitclaim[7] that took place at Cluny in the presence of lord Rainald, venerable prior at that place; and of other monks who were there, namely Walter, Aymo, Amizon, Warner, Lanfred, Locerius, Giso; and of noblemen: Witbert, Robert, Ildinus, Gislebert, Bernard, and Hugo. In the first place, let all, present and future, know that a long and very protracted quarrel between the monks of Cluny and Majolus[8] finally, by God's mercy, came to this

---

[1] This charter began with a formula considered so commonplace that it did not need to be fully written out.

[2] Churches could be given in whole or in part—since the revenues could be divided—and with or without their tithes (which often belonged not to the holder of the church but to the local bishop).

[3] In this region, a *via publica* was a dirt road. There was a very extensive network of roads in the area around Cluny left over from the Roman period.

[4] Not the Cluniac abbot but rather a member of the Grossi family.

[5] The *parentes* were much broader than the nuclear family but perhaps not quite as large as a clan.

[6] The scribe did not give a date. But we know that Rainald was prior at Cluny beginning in 994 and that Majolus died c.1030. These give us, respectively, the *terminus post quem* [time after which] and the *terminus ante quem* [the time before which] the document must have been drawn up.

[7] That is, this gives notice that a claim has been dropped ("quit").

[8] The donor from the Grossi family.

end result: first that he [Majolus] quit his claim to the land which Oddo and Teza [Oddo's] daughter[1] destined for us and handed over by charter: the woods in *Grandi Monte* with its borders [as follows]: on the east [it borders on] its own inheritance [namely] passing between mountains and through wasteland and across the castle of Teodoric; on the south [it borders on] *terra francorum*;[2] on the west and north [it borders on] land of St. Peter. [Majolus] draws up this notice at this time so that he may reunite himself with the favor of St. Peter and the brothers, and so that he may persevere in future as a faithful servant in the service of St. Peter. S. Hugo, S. Witbert, S. Robert, S. Ildinus, S. Gislebert, S. Bernard.

[Charter # 2946 (1018–1030?)[3]]

In the name of the incarnate Word. I, Raimodis, formerly the wife of the lord Wichard, now dead, and now joined in matrimony to lord Ansedeus, my husband; with the consent and good will [of Ansedeus], I give or rather give again some land which is called Chazeux to St. Peter and Cluny. [I give it] for the soul of my husband Wichard. This land once belonged to St. Peter and Cluny. But the abbot and monks gave it as a precarial gift to lord Letbald [III], a certain cleric who afterwards became bishop of Mâcon. Letbald, acting wrongly, alienated [the land] from St. Peter and gave it to Gauzeran to make amends for killing Gauzeran's relative, Berengar.

Therefore I give it again to St. Peter for the soul of my husband Wichard, and for Gauzeran, Wichard's father. I also give a slave named Adalgarda and her children, and [I give] the whole inheritance for the soul of my husband Wichard, and of my daughter Wiceline, and for my own soul.

If anyone wants to bring false claim against this donation, let him not prevail, but let him pay a pound of gold into the public treasury. S. of Raimodis, who asked that this charter be done and confirmed. S. of Ansedeus. S. of another Ansedeus. S. of Achard. S. of Walter. S. of Costabulus. S. of Ugo.

4.5 Love and complaints in Angoulême: *Agreement between Count William of the Aquitainians and Hugh IV of Lusignan* (1028). Original in Latin.

This document of a series of disputes and their eventual settlement is written from the point of view of Hugh, who was the castellan (the lord of a castle and its garrison) of Lusignan, although he here calls himself Chiliarch—"leader of one thousand." The events described may be dated between about 1022 and 1028. The chief protagonists of Hugh's drama are Hugh himself and William, whom he calls "count of the Aquitainians" but who was, more importantly, count of Poitou (he ruled from c.995–1030). The center of his county was Poitiers, which included Lusignan (about fifteen miles southwest of Poitiers) and many of the other locations mentioned in this document. Other characters who appear are mainly laymen, laywomen, and a few bishops. The *Agreement* presents an admittedly one-sided picture of the activities of the French aristocracy in the early eleventh century. As you read this document, consider what it meant to be the "man" of a lord.

1. In what ways were legal and quasi-legal proceedings essential institutions in the Poitou?

---

[1] Oddo and Teza were probably relatives of Majolus.
[2] This probably refers to land of free peasants.
[3] This date, which is quite uncertain, is suggested on the basis of other charters that tell us at what date Raimodis, the donor in this charter, became a widow.

2. What are the meanings of "love," "anger," and "sorrow" in this early eleventh-century account?

[Source: Jane Martindale, "Conventum inter Guillelmum Aquitanorum comitem et Hugonem Chiliarchum," *English Historical Review* 84/332 (1969): 528–48. Translated by Thomas Greene and Barbara H. Rosenwein from the Latin text, in consultation with translations by George Beech, "Hugh of Lusignan: Agreement between Lord and Vassal," in *Readings in Medieval History*, ed. Patrick J. Geary, 4th ed. (Toronto: University of Toronto Press, 2010), pp. 377–81; Martindale, "Conventum," pp. 541–48; and Paul Hyams and others, "Agreement between Duke William V of Aquitaine and Hugh IV of Lusignan" at http://falcon.arts.cornell.edu/prh3/436/texts/conventum.htm.]

William, called count of the Aquitainians, had an agreement with Hugh the Chiliarch that when Viscount Boso died, William would give Boso's honor in commendation to Hugh.[1] Bishop Roho saw and heard this and kissed the arm of the count.[2] But Viscount Savary seized from Hugh land which Hugh held from Count William.[3] When the viscount died the count promised Hugh that he would make no agreement or accord with Ralph, the brother of the dead viscount, until the land had been restored. He said this in the presence of all, but afterwards he secretly gave the land to Ralph. For that land itself, or for a larger one, or for other things, Hugh had an agreement with Viscount Ralph that he would accept Ralph's daughter as his wife. When the count heard this, he was greatly angered and he went humbly to Hugh and said to him, "Don't marry Ralph's daughter. I will give to you whatever you ask of me, and you will be my friend before all others except my son." Hugh did what the count ordered, and out of love and fidelity for the count he secretly rejected the woman.

At that time it happened that Joscelin of Parthenay castle died.[4] The count said that he would give Joscelin's honor and wife to Hugh, and if Hugh refused to accept them, he would no longer have confidence in him. Hugh did not entreat or request this from the count, either for himself or for anyone else. Thinking it over, he said to the count, "I will do all that you have ordered." The count, however, after holding a public meeting with Count Fulk,[5] promised to give Fulk something from his own benefices, and Fulk promised that he would give Hugh what belonged to him. At the meeting, the count called for Viscount Ralph and said to him: "Hugh will not keep the agreement he has with you because I forbid him to. But Fulk and I have an agreement that we will give to Hugh the honor and wife of Joscelin. We do this to mess up your life, because you are not faithful to me." When he heard this, Ralph was very hurt and he said to the count, "For God's sake do not do that." So the count said, "Pledge to me that you will not give Hugh your daughter, nor keep your agreement with him, and in turn I will arrange that he not possess the honor and wife of Joscelin." And they so acted that Hugh got neither the one nor the other. Ralph went to Count William, who was at Montreuil castle, sending a message to Hugh that they should talk together. That was done. And Ralph said to Hugh, "I tell you this in confidence so that you will not give me away. Pledge to me that you will help me against Count William, and I will keep your agreement for you and will aid you against all men." But Hugh refused all of this out of his love for Count William. Hugh and Ralph

---

[1] Boso (d. by 1033) was viscount of Chatellerault, twenty miles northeast of Poitiers. An "honor" referred to property.

[2] Roho was bishop of Angoulême (r.1020–1036). Formal agreements were often concluded by a kiss of peace; sometimes witnesses participated in this gesture of concord and, as here, the kiss might function as well as a sign of deference.

[3] Savary was viscount of Thouars.

[4] The "castles" that this document refers to were not luxurious chateaux but rather strongholds or fortresses. Some of them were thrown up haphazardly and minimally fortified; others were built more solidly and sometimes included a stone tower. Armed garrisons of horsemen guarded the castles and were important players—as victims, hostages, and guarantors—in the disputes and negotiations between regional lords. Included in the notion of the castle was the surrounding district that it dominated.

[5] Fulk was count of Anjou (r.987–1040).

parted unhappily. Then Ralph began to prosecute a public dispute with Count William, while Hugh, out of love for the count, started one with Ralph. And Hugh suffered great harm.

When Ralph died, Hugh asked the count to restore to him the land which Ralph had seized from him. Moreover, the count said to Hugh, "I will not make an agreement with Viscount Josfred, the nephew of Ralph, nor with the men of Thouars castle, until I return your land." Yet none of this was done, and the count went and made an agreement with Viscount Josfred and with the men of Thouars castle. He never made an agreement with Hugh, and Hugh did not get his land. And because of the misdeeds which Hugh committed on the count's behalf, Josfred got into a dispute with Hugh, and he burned Mouzeuil castle and captured Hugh's horsemen and cut off their hands and did many other things. The count did not help Hugh at all nor did he broker a good agreement between Josfred and Hugh, but Hugh even now has lost his land, and for the sake of the count he has lost still other land that he was holding peacefully. And when Hugh saw that he was not going to get his land he took forty-three of the best horsemen of Thouars. He could have had peace and his land and justice for the wrongdoing; and if he had been willing to accept a ransom he could have had 40,000 *solidi*.[1]

When the count heard this, he should have been glad, but he was sad and sent for Hugh, saying to him, "Give me back the men." Hugh answered him, "Why do you ask these things of me, Lord? I am a loser only because of my loyalty to you." Then the count said, "I do not ask this of you to hurt you, but in fact because you are mine to do my will. And as all will know by our agreement, I will take over those men on condition that I make a settlement with you that your lands will be secured and the wrongdoing compensated, or I will return the men to you. Do this without doubting my credibility and good faith, and if anything should turn out badly for you, you can be sure that I will hand them over to you." Hugh put

his trust in God and the count and handed the men over to the count according to this agreement. Later on Hugh got neither the men nor justice, and he lost his land.

The count of the Poitevins[2] and Bishop Gilbert[3] had an agreement among themselves with Joscelin, Hugh's uncle.[4] It was about the castle at Vivonne, and it said that after the death of Bishop Gilbert it was to be Joscelin's castle. During his lifetime, the bishop made the men of that castle commend themselves to Joscelin, and he gave Joscelin the tower. And after the death of both men, the count made an agreement between Hugh and Bishop Isembert[5] that Hugh would get half of the castle and half of the demesne and two shares of the vassals' fiefs.[6] Then the count made Hugh commend himself to Bishop Isembert—but now he has taken the better estate from them.

A certain official named Aimery seized the castle called Civray from Bernard, his lord, but this castle was rightly Hugh's, as it had been his father's. Because of his anger at Aimery, Count William urged Hugh to become the man[7] of Bernard for the part of the castle that had belonged to his father, so that together they might wage a dispute with Aimery. But it seemed wrong to Hugh that he become Bernard's man, and he did not want to do it. The count persisted in this admonition for a year, and the more he got angry, the more he urged Hugh to become the man of Bernard. After a year passed, the count came to Hugh as if in anger and said to him, "Why don't you make an agreement with Bernard? You owe so much to me that if I should tell you to make a peasant into a lord you should do it. Do what I say, and if it should turn out badly for you, come and see me about it." Hugh believed him and became the man of Bernard for the fourth part of Civray castle. But Bernard made the count a guarantor to Hugh, as well as four hostages. The count said to Hugh, "Commend those hostages to me under such conditions that if Bernard does not faithfully keep your agreements, I will turn them over to your custody and I will faithfully aid you." How strongly the count promised this to Hugh he himself knows very well. Hugh trusted in his lord and

---

[1] A *solidus* (pl. *solidi*) is here a silver coin.

[2] That is, Count William.

[3] Gilbert was bishop of Poitiers (r.975–1023/1024).

[4] This is presumably a different Joscelin from the one of Parthenay.

[5] Isembert was Gilbert's successor as bishop of Poitiers.

[6] It was possible to have "half a castle" because what was at stake were the revenues due to the castle, not the stronghold itself. The "demesne" was land belonging to the fortress directly; other land pertaining to it was granted out in fief.

[7] The word used here is *homo*, which may be translated as "man" or "vassal," depending on one's view of the relations among these aristocrats and the implications of these words.

began a fierce dispute on account of Civray castle and suffered great losses in men and many other things. The count started to build a castle, which he called Couhé, but he did not finish it for Hugh. Instead, he talked it over with Aimery, abandoned the castle, and in no way aided Hugh.

Afterwards the count grew even more unhappy with Aimery on account of the castle called Chizé, which Aimery had seized, and Hugh and the count joined together in a dispute against Aimery. The count besieged the castle called Mallevault because of the injuries that Aimery had done to him and captured it, and Hugh aided him as best he could. Before Hugh left the count, the count promised him—just as a lord ought rightly to promise to his man—that he would make no agreement or alliance with Aimery without Hugh, and that Mallevault would not be rebuilt without his advice. But the count did make an agreement with Aimery and allowed him to rebuild Mallevault without the advice of Hugh. As long as Aimery lived, none of the property mentioned above came to Hugh.

After the death of Aimery a great dispute began between his son Aimery and Hugh. At the same time, Hugh went to the count and said to him, "Things are going badly for me now, my Lord, because I have none of the property that you acquired for me." The count answered him, "I am going to hold a public hearing with them so that if they act well, good; if not, I will turn over to you the castle which I started." And the castle was constructed on the advice of Bernard, who thus far had helped Hugh in the dispute. When they saw the heavy demands Hugh was making on them, the men of Civray were not able to hold out, and they made an agreement with Bernard and returned the castle to him. He received it without the advice of Hugh. Now both Bernard and Aimery were in dispute with Hugh, and he was alone against them. Coming to the count, Hugh said to him, "Lord, I am doing very badly because the lord whom I got upon your advice has just taken away my property. I beg and urge you by the faith which a lord owes to aid his man: either let me have a proper public hearing or my property, just as you pledged to me; or return to me the hostages which I commended to you; and above all help me as you pledged to me." The count, however, neither aided him, nor made an agreement with him, nor returned the hostages but released them and gave them back to Bernard. And after that the dispute between Bernard and Aimery and Hugh increased.

And since Hugh saw that the count aided him in no way, he went to seek the advice of Gerald, the bishop of Limoges. Gerald and Hugh went together into La Marche

against Bernard and built a castle. But the count, who ought to have aided Hugh, seized the castle from him and burned it. And the count and his son ordered all their men not to help Hugh unless they wished to die. Then Bernard accepted the council of his men that they should do harm to Hugh on the advice of the count, and they appointed a deadline fifteen days away. During those fifteen days the count arranged a truce between Bernard and Hugh. Three days into the truce the count took Hugh along with his army to Apremont castle, and a meeting was held in his castle. From there the count went to Blaye, where he was to have a meeting with Count Sancho, and he told Hugh that he should come along. And Hugh responded, "Lord, why do you ask me to go with you? You yourself know how short the truce is which I have with Bernard, and he himself is threatening to do me harm." The count said to him: "Do not fear that they will do anything to you as long as you are with me." And the count took Hugh with him by force and against Hugh's will.

While they were staying at the meeting place, Hugh's men heard that Bernard was coming against him; they sent a message to Hugh to come. Then Hugh said to the count, "Bernard is attacking me." And the count said, "Don't be afraid that they will dare attack you; and, besides, you need them to attack so that I can destroy them and aid you." In that same hour the count sent orders through his men, and he told Hugh to go on ahead, and he followed him. When Hugh reached Lusignan, Bernard was at Confolens castle. He had captured the suburb and the outskirts and burned everything; he had taken spoils, captured men, and done plenty of other evil deeds. A messenger ran up to Hugh and said to him, "Bernard has your wife besieged in the old castle which survived the fire." Hugh came to the count and said to him: "My lord, help me now, because my wife is now being besieged." But the count gave him no aid or advice at all. And Bernard turned back, and he and his men did so much harm to Hugh and his men that 50,000 *solidi* would not have paid for it. And Hugh suffered this damage during the truce that the count offered to him at Blaye.

Not long after this Hugh went to Gençay castle and burned it and seized the men and women and took everything with him. Hastening to the count, he said to him, "Lord, give me permission to build the castle which I burned." And the count said to him, "You are the man of Fulk, how can you build the castle? Fulk will demand it of you, and you will not be strong enough to keep it from him." Hugh said, "Lord, when I became Fulk's man I told him that his men were seizing what was my right and that if I was able to regain possession of them, I would do it, but I would only hold it in his fealty, which is what I want to do. And Fulk said to me, 'If you take anything from them, don't take from me.'" When the count heard that Fulk and Hugh had such an agreement, he was pleased. And the count said to Hugh: "Build the castle under such an agreement that if I am able to negotiate with Count Fulk about my price and yours, one part will be mine and the other yours."

And Hugh built the castle. Then Fulk asked the count for it. The count responded to him, "Ask Hugh for it." And Fulk did that. Hugh answered him, "When I became your man, I said to you that if I would be strong enough to take castles from my enemies, I should take them and hold them in your fealty, and I wanted to do that because the castle which you are demanding belonged to my relatives, and I have a better right to it than those who were holding it." But Fulk said, "You who are mine, how can you hold against my will something I didn't give to you?" And Hugh sought advice from the count. The count told him, "If he is willing to give you guarantees that your enemies will not have the castle, then you cannot keep it. If not, keep it, because he will not be able to accuse you of anything." Hugh asked that Fulk give hostages to him, and Fulk gave him nothing, but said, "I will make my demands known to the count and give hostages to him and he will give you some of his own." Then the meeting turned angry. Fulk demanded Hugh's castle from the count. Hugh said, "I will not give it up without assurances." The count said to him, "I will give an assurance, and he has told me what sort to give." Hugh said, "Take what you want from Count Fulk and give me what I'm asking for. Give me the man who has custody of the tower at Melle, so that if Aimery should get the castle without my advice, and harm should befall me, that man will turn the tower over to me." The count said to him, "I will not do this, because I cannot." Hugh said, "If you don't want to do this with Melle, make the same agreement with regard to Chizé." But the count didn't want to do either.

It seemed to Hugh and his men that the count was treating him badly. And they parted in anger. Then Hugh sent all kinds of necessities into the castle and intended to hold it against all comers if they would not give him assurances. The count came out of the city,[1] asked Hugh to come to him, and commanded through Count William of Angoulême that he submit himself to the mercy of the count, because the count could not change the fact that he had to aid Fulk; and he was afraid to lose either Fulk or Hugh. Then Hugh committed himself to the trust and friendship of the count his lord, and he did this out of love for him because he was assured that he would not suffer harm at Fulk's hands. And the count said: "Let Hugh do this for me and I will keep the faith with him that a lord ought to keep with his man. If he suffers harm, he will know that I have betrayed him, and he will never trust me again." And Hugh said, "My lord has spoken similarly to me about many things by which he has deceived me." And not a single one of Hugh's men would advise him to trust the count. But the count reminded Hugh of all the good things which he had done for him, and Hugh, holding back the count by his love and entreaties—that is by their common oath—said to the count, "I will put all my trust in you, but watch out that you do not do me wrong, for if you do, I will not be faithful to you nor will I serve you, nor will I render fidelity to you. But, on account of the fact that I will be separated from you and you are not able to give me guarantees, I want you to give me my fief as a pledge that then I will no longer serve you, and release me from the oath which I have made to you." The count answered, "Gladly."

Hugh returned the castle to the count, against the wishes of his men, on condition that Aimery would not have it without Hugh's advice and that Hugh would suffer no harm. On account of hearing those lies, Hugh accepted his fief as a pledge, and the count gave it to him on condition that if he should suffer harm because of the agreement about Gençay, Hugh would never again serve him. And the count released him from his oaths, so that he would no longer do anything for the count on account of them, but not out of ill will. [But] the count handed over Gençay without the advice of Hugh and got money and some demesne land. It went very badly for Hugh, with men killed, houses burned, booty taken, land seized and many other things which in truth cannot be enumerated. When this had ended, the count gave Hugh a respite and promised that he would give him a benefice either of something that was his by right or something that would be pleasing to him. But when this period passed the count did nothing for Hugh. He sent an order to him: "Don't wait, because I am not going to do anything for you. Even if the whole world were mine I would not give you as much as a finger could lift with regard to this matter."

---

[1] Presumably Poitiers.

When Hugh heard this, he went to the court of the count and made the case for his rights, but it did him no good. This saddened Hugh, and in the hearing of all he renounced his fealty[1] to the count, except what he owed for the city [of Poitiers] and his own person. Before either Hugh or his men did any harm, the men of the count seized a benefice from Hugh's men in the name of war. When Hugh saw this, he went to Chizé castle, which had been his uncle's but which Peter[2] was holding unjustly, and from which much harm was being done to Hugh. He seized the tower and threw out Peter's men. Hugh did this because he thought he had the right—because it had belonged to his father or others of his relatives—which he was losing. When the count heard of this he was greatly saddened and sent an order to Hugh that he turn over the tower that he had taken away from Peter. Hugh demanded that the count return the honor of his father and the other things which belonged to his relatives and to which he had right, and he would surrender the tower and all the things that he had taken within it, and in addition the entire honor which had belonged to Joscelin[3] and which the count had given him. The count thought this over and they arranged for a hearing. And the count said to Hugh, "I will not give you those honors which you ask of me, but I will give you that honor which was your uncle's—the castle, the tower and the entire honor—on condition that you no longer demand of me that honor which was your father's, or others of your relatives, nor anything which you claim as your right."

When he heard this Hugh greatly mistrusted the count, because through evil trickery in the past the count had deceived Hugh in many things. He said to the count, "I don't dare do this, because I fear that you will threaten me with harm, as you have done with regard to many other things." The count said to Hugh, "I will give such assurances to you that you will no longer distrust me."

Hugh said to him, "What kind of assurances?" The count said, "I will produce a serf who will undergo an ordeal for you so that you will not doubt that the agreement which we make among ourselves will be good and firm. And with regard to all the affairs of the past, no harm will ever again be done to you, but the agreement will be kept firmly without any evil trickery." When Hugh heard what the count was saying in this way, he said, "You are my lord. I will not take a guarantee from you, but I will simply rely on the mercy of the Lord and yourself." The count said to Hugh, "Give up all those claims that you have demanded from me in the past and swear fidelity to me and my son, and I will give you your uncle's honor or something else of equal value in exchange for it." And Hugh said, "Lord, I beg you by God and this blessed crucifix which is made in the figure of Christ that you do not make me do this if in future you and your son intend to threaten me with evil trickery." The count said, "My son and I will do this in faith and without evil trickery." Hugh said, "And when I have sworn fidelity to you, you will ask me for Chizé castle, and if I should not turn it over to you, you will say that it is not right that I deny you the castle which I hold from you; but if I should turn it over to you, you and your son will take it away from me because you will have given me no guarantee except the mercy of God and yourself." The count said, "We will not do that, but if we should demand it of you, don't turn it over to us."

They received Hugh as their man in faith and trust under the terms of the agreement as it was finally pronounced: that the count and his son should bear faith to Hugh without evil trickery. And they made Hugh give up everything that he claimed from the past. And he swore fidelity to them, and they gave him the honor of his uncle Joscelin, just as Joscelin held it one year before he died.

Here end the agreements between the count and Hugh.

---

[1] The Latin word here is *defidavit*, which means defied. The root of the word is "faith"; a man declares his faith (*fides*=fidelity) to his lord, but if he formally renounces that fealty, as here, he "defies"—"de-fealties"—him.

[2] Peter has not been identified.

[3] This Joscelin was Hugh's uncle.

4.6 The Peace of God at Bourges: Andrew of Fleury, *The Miracles of St. Benedict* (1040–1043). Original in Latin.

The Peace of God was a movement initiated by bishops, and eventually declared by kings as well, to protect unarmed people (including clerics) and property (including Church property) from armed predators. At Church synods, laypeople and churchmen alike met to proclaim the Peace. Those who fought (the *bellatores* or *milites*: the knights) swore oaths not to violate the Peace. In the late 1030s, at one such synod, Aimon, the archbishop of Bourges from 1030 to 1070, organized a militia consisting of clergy, peasants, and a few nobles that succeeded in forcing most of the nobility of the region to take the oath. The militia even enforced the Peace by going to war against breakers of the oath. But it ran into opposition from one holdout, Odo, lord of Déols, who defeated it soundly. Andrew, a monk at the monastery of Fleury, recounted the incident in the course of his work on the *Miracles of St. Benedict*, written 1040–1043. He praised the militia's initial promise but berated it for its "ambition" and confidence in its own power rather than God's.

1. Why were common people enthusiastic about the Peace of God?
2. How might the sorts of disputes described in the *Agreement between Count William and Hugh* (above, p. 190) have contributed to the Peace of God movement?

[Source: *The Peace of God: Social Violence and Religious Response in France around the Year 1000*, ed. Thomas Head and Richard Landes (Ithaca, NY: Cornell University Press, 1992), pp. 339–42.]

5.1 In the 1038th year after the incarnation of the Lord, on the eighth day of August, in the middle of the day, the sun was darkened and hid the rays of its splendors for a space of almost two hours. Again the following morning it remained under the same appearance for the entire day and unremittingly gave off bloody flames.

5.2. At this very same time, Archbishop Aimon of Bourges wished to impose peace in his diocese through the swearing of an oath. After he had summoned the fellow bishops of his province and had sought advice from these suffragans, he bound all men of fifteen years of age and over by the following law: that they would come forth with one heart as opponents of any violation of the oath they had sworn, that they would in no way withdraw secretly from the pact even if they should lose their property, and that, what is more, if necessity should demand it, they would go after those who had repudiated the oath with arms. Nor were ministers of the sacraments excepted, but they often took banners from the sanctuary of the Lord and attacked the violators of the sworn peace with the rest of the crowd of laypeople. In this way they many times routed the faithless and brought their castles

down to the ground. With the help of God they so terrified the rebels that, as the coming of the faithful was proclaimed far and wide by rumor among the populace, the rebels scattered. Leaving the gates of their towns open, they sought safety in flight, harried by divinely inspired terror. You would have seen [the faithful] raging against the multitude of those who ignore God, as if they were some other people of Israel. Presently they trampled [the rebels] underfoot so that they forced them to return to the laws of the pact which they had ignored.

We thought it fitting to insert in writing that which was agreed to in the pact which the archbishop himself, along with various fellow bishops, promised under oath in the following way: "I Aimon, by the gift of God archbishop of Bourges, promise with my whole heart and mouth to God and to his saints that I shall discharge with my whole spirit and without any guile or dissimulation everything that follows. That is, I will wholeheartedly attack those who steal ecclesiastical property, those who provoke pillage, those who oppress monks, nuns, and clerics, and those who fight against holy mother church, until they repent. I will not be beguiled by the enticement of gifts, or moved by any reason of bonds of kinship or neighborliness, or in any way deviate from the path of righteousness. I promise to move with all my troops against those who dare in any manner to transgress the decrees and not to cease in any way until the purpose of the traitor has been overcome."

He swore this over the relics of Stephen, the first martyr for Christ, and urged the other [bishops] to do likewise. Obeying with one heart, his fellow bishops made among everyone age fifteen or older (as we already said) in their separate dioceses subscribe [the pact] with the same promise. Fear and trembling then struck the hearts of the unfaithful so that they feared the multitude of the unarmed peasantry as if it were a battle line of armored men. Their hearts fell so that, forgetting their status as knights and abandoning their fortified places, they fled from the humble peasants as from the cohorts of very powerful kings. The prayer of David fitted the situation most aptly: "For thou dost deliver a humble people, but the haughty eyes thou dost bring down, for who is God but the Lord?"[1] ... Odo of Déols remained alone among the whole multitude [of rebels], reserved by the judgment of God for the punishment of evil doers.

5.3. When by the will of God they had, trusting in the help of divine strength, established peace in every direction, ambition (the root and aid of all evil) began to seep along the stalks of such good works. They forgot that God is the strength and rampart of his people and ascribed the power of God to their apostate power.... Thus the aforementioned bishop was touched by the sting of mammon[2] and raged around and around in blind ambition. Unmindful of his episcopal dignity, he attacked Beneciacum, the castle of one Stephen, along with a multitude of the people of Bourges. He reproached Stephen for the fault of having ignored the peace, he tried to burn the castle with flames and ordered it to be leveled to the ground, as if he were exacting the vengeance of God upon it. They burned the castle, which was hemmed in on all sides by the siege, with more than one thousand four hundred people of both sexes inside. Stephen alone of that great number escaped, although his brothers, wife, and sons were all consumed by the fire, and he placed the laurel wreath of his great victory on their wretched heads. The inhabitants of that region for a radius of fourteen miles had fled to this castle and, since they feared the theft of

their possessions, they had brought them along. The cruel victors were hardly moved by the laments of the dying, they did not take pity on women beating their breasts; the crowd of infants clinging to their mothers' breasts did not touch any vein of mercy.... And so the just bore responsibility for the crime of the iniquitous and the just perished in place of the impious. Having been granted this great triumph, the people returned to their homes dancing with a pitiable joy. Stephen was placed under guard in a prison in Bourges.

5.4. Almighty God wished to avenge the blood of his servants and, not long after this, set the aforesaid bishop against Odo, the sole rebel. The bishop sought to force Odo to join in the pact common to all, but he would not delay in making an armed attack. Discovering that Odo's spirit remained inflexible, as was God's will, Aimon began—while the blood of the innocents was not yet dry—to collect allies together from all sides, including a large contingent of God's ministers. Confiding in lesser things, he directed his battleline against the enemy. When both armies stood almost at grips, a sound was made heavenward [indicating that Aimon's forces should] retreat, since they no longer had the Lord with them as a leader. When they made no sign of following this advice, an enormous globe of flashing light fell in their midst. Thus it came to pass, as it is said, "Flash forth the lightning and scatter them, send out the arrows and rout them!"[3] Then the people perceived that they were much inferior to their adversaries, since those exceeded in number the sands of the sea. They decided that some foot soldiers should be mounted on various animals and mixed into the cohorts of mounted warriors [*milites*] so that they would be judged mounted warriors by their opponents, more because of the appearance of their being mounted than because of the setting of their weapons. Without delay up to two thousand of the plebeian rabble were mounted on asses and arrayed as knights among the order of knights. But these men were terrified and they took flight along the banks of the Cher. They were killed in such numbers that they blocked the river in such a way that they made a bridge out of the bodies of the dying over which their enemies proceeded. More fell by their own swords than by those of their pursuers.... The number of the dying could not be comprehended: in one valley seven hundred clerics fell. Thus the most tempered

---

1 Ps. 18:27, 31; Douay Ps. 17:28, 32.

2 The false god personifying riches and avarice.

3 Ps.144:6; Douay Ps. 143:6.

judgment of God made those people—who had refused obedience to any requests for mercy, and had not been moved by the smell of their brothers' being burned, and had rejoiced more than was just to have their hands in an unfortunate victory—lost their lives along with that victory.

BYZANTIUM IN ASCENDANCE

4.7 Patronage of the arts: "Theophanes Continuatus," *Constantine VII Porphyrogenitus* (before 963). Original in Greek.

Although Constantine VII (r.945–959) was known as the Porphyrogenitus because he was born in the purple porphyry-paneled imperial bed chambers, he was shunted aside by Romanus I Lecapenus (whose *Novel* appears above, p. 177). Constantine ascended to the throne by deposing Romanus's sons. To ensure his power and reputation, he hired the most able military generals and patronized the finest scholars and artists. "Theophanes Continuatus" is the name given to a collection of imperial biographies written by various writers. The one for Constantine—whose real author is much disputed—includes an admiring assessment of the emperor's artistic and architectural achievements, excerpted here.

1. What did "Theophanes" admire most about Constantine's patronage of the arts?
2. What role did the emperor himself have in the art and architecture produced during his reign, at least according to "Theophanes"?

[Source: *The Art of the Byzantine Empire, 312–1453*, ed. Cyril Mango (Toronto: University of Toronto Press, 1986), pp. 207–9 (notes modified).]

15. Furthermore, he restored the imperial vestments as well as the crowns and diadems that had been damaged for a long time. He also embellished the Bucoleon[1] with statues which he gathered from different places, and he installed a fish-pond there.... 20. We ought also to mention the roof of [the hall of] the Nineteen Couches.[2] For perceiving it to be rotten, altogether unsightly and about to collapse, he restored it, and chose to make new and splendid the gilded ceiling which had fallen apart with the passage of time. He contrived in it octagonal cavities which he embellished with perforations and various carved shapes resembling the tendrils and leaves of the vine and the form of trees, and these he sprinkled with gold, making [the ceiling] so beautiful as to amaze the beholder. 21. And for his son, the Emperor Romanus, he built more palaces than previous emperors had done.... At the Tetraconch of the apostle Paul[3] which had lost its ancient beauty, he, with a view to instilling a new beauty into it, set up various golden figures and images.

22. This man [Constantine] was, I believe, more thoroughly versed in the art of painting than anyone before him or after him. He often corrected those who labored

---

[1] Enclosed within the complex of the Great Palace, the Bucoleon was a group of buildings comprising a harbor, a quay, and a palace overlooking the Sea Walls.

[2] A ceremonial dining hall in the Great Palace.

[3] A tetraconch is a church with a central bay framed by four walled "conches"—semicircular lobes.

at it and appeared to be an excellent teacher—indeed, he not only appeared as such, but was universally admired as a prodigy in an art that he had never learned. Who could enumerate all the instances in which the Porphyrogenitus set craftsmen right? He corrected stone carvers and builders, workers in gold leaf, silver-smiths and iron-smiths and in every case he showed his excellence. 23. Being a lover of beautiful things, the same Constantine constructed the silver doors of the Chrysotriklinos;[1] furthermore, with much industry, he made a silver table for the reception of guests and the adornment of the dining-room, which table, in addition to its natural color, he beautified with materials and plaques of various other hues, thus affording a greater pleasure to his guests than they would have derived [solely] from the savor of the repast.

24. He also built a guardhouse of porphyry[2] in front of his chamber, wherein he contrived a receptacle of water surrounded by marble columns shining smooth. And what else did his noble mind [invent]? He set upon the water pipe a silver eagle, looking not ahead but sideways, his neck high and proud as if he had caught a prey, while stifling a serpent that was coiled round his feet. In the vestibule or the imperial chamber he also put up artful mosaic images, a spectacle of diverse colors, materials, and forms....

28. Who would be able to describe the sacred objects and hangings which he presented to the common propitiatorium (I mean the great and admirable one)?[3] Each time he came, he wished not to appear empty-handed in the sight of God, and so repaid his debt by lavish offerings of objects wrought in gold, of pearls, precious stones and cloths. These adorn the holy of holies and proclaim [the name of] Constantine who offered them....

33. It is also fitting that we should speak of the Chrysotriklinos which the ingenious Emperor turned into a blooming and sweet-smelling rose-garden by means of minute, variegated mosaic cubes imitating the colors of freshly opened flowers. Enclosed by spiral convolutions and shaped by the composition itself, these [cubes?] are altogether inimitable. He girded [the hall] with silver, encompassing it as with a border (*antux*),[4] and so offered the spectator a source of inexhaustible delight.

4.8 The toils of war: *The Epitaph of Basil II* (1025). Original in Greek.

Powerful provincial families known as *dynatoi* confronted the Byzantine emperor Basil II (r.976–1025). His harsh measures against them culminated in 988, when he defeated a revolt led by some *dynatoi* and confiscated their estates. Meanwhile, on Byzantium's frontiers, Basil pursued expansionist policies in every direction. These wars created the image of himself that he most valued, as his epitaph makes clear. The epitaph was placed, along with Basil's sarcophagus, in a church in the Hebdomon Palace, just outside Constantinople.

1. What activities did Basil want remembered?
2. What role did God play in Basil's conception of himself?

[Source: Paul Stephenson, *The Legend of Basil the Bulgar-Slayer* (Cambridge: Cambridge University Press, 2003), p. 49 (notes added).]

---

[1] The Chrysotriklinos was the main reception hall of the imperial palace at Constantinople.

[2] Purple marble. Porphyry was the imperial color.

[3] Hagia Sophia, the great church constructed by Emperor Justinian in the sixth century.

[4] This probably refers to a decorative silver molding running along the entire interior of the hall.

Other past emperors
previously designated for themselves other burial places.
But I Basil, born in the purple chamber,[1]
place my tomb on the site of the Hebdomon[2]
and take sabbath's rest from the endless toils   5
which I fulfilled in wars and which I endured.[3]
For nobody saw my spear at rest,
from when the Emperor of Heaven called me
to the rulership of this great empire on earth,[4]

but I kept vigilant through the whole span of my life   10
guarding the children of New Rome[5]
marching bravely to the West,
and as far as the very frontiers of the East.
The Persians and Scythians bear witness to this
and along with them Abasgos, Ismael, Araps, Iber.[6]   15
And now, good man, looking upon this tomb
reward it with prayers in return for my campaigns.

4.9 Imperial rule under two sisters: Michael Psellus, *Zoe and Theodora* (before 1063). Original in Greek.

Michael Psellus (1018–1078), probably born and certainly educated in Constantinople, was a teacher, a prolific writer, and a courtier in the service of many of the emperors and empresses during the second half of the eleventh century. Among his many writings was the *Chronographia*, a book containing the biographies of Byzantine emperors and empresses from the time of Basil II (r.976–1025) to Michael VII (r.1071–1078). The first and longest part of the text was written before 1063; later, Psellus added a section that took the story to 1078. He knew Zoe and Theodora, and his "take" on them has influenced historians ever since. Only recently have some tried to understand these two sisters apart from the very male point of view of their biographer. They were daughters of Basil II's older brother Constantine, who took the emperorship after Basil, ruling as Constantine VIII (r.1025–1028). Brought up at the imperial palace, both were at first pliant tools of imperial ambition. Zoe, the eldest of the two (a still older sister had entered a monastery), was married (at the age of fifty) to her father's designated heir, Romanus, who gained the throne as her husband. But, unable to have children, Zoe and Romanus III (r.1028–1034) became estranged, and Zoe took up with an ambitious courtier, Michael, who eventually drowned Romanus in his private pool, perhaps with Zoe's assent. In any event, Zoe quickly married Michael, who became Michael IV (r.1034–1041). Ill and fearful that Zoe would betray him in turn, Michael stepped down and handed the throne to his nephew, Michael V (r.1041–1042), who could claim the emperorship because Zoe had earlier adopted him as her son. The new emperor had Zoe's hair cut (a disfigurement that religious women usually chose voluntarily) and sent her into exile. But a popular rebellion on her behalf in Constantinople (including

---

[1] "Born in the purple chamber" means that he was born after his father became emperor and refers to the imperial bedchamber, the walls of which were lined with purple (porphyry) marble.

[2] A palace just outside Constantinople, a place for imperial retreats.

[3] A Sabbath is meant to be a day of rest.

[4] God is the "Emperor of Heaven," and the Byzantine emperor is his counterpart on earth.

[5] The first Rome was in Italy; Constantinople was the "New (or Second) Rome."

[6] Byzantine authors used "the Persians" for a variety of people to the east of the empire, while the Scythians referred to any northern barbarian. The emphasis here is on Basil's conquests to the east: Abasgos and Iber referred to peoples living along the eastern shore of the Black Sea; the Ismael were the Ismaelites, the Muslims; the Araps were the Arabs.

even noble women!) forced Michael to bring her back. Ultimately, he was blinded and Zoe and her sister Theodora became joint rulers. The excerpt from Psellus below picks up the story from this point.

1. Why could Zoe and Theodora not have remained rulers in their own right?
2. If Zoe had written her own story, what would she have said about her rulership and her marriages?

[Source: Michael Psellus (1018–after 1078) *Chronographia*, trans. Edgar R.A. Sewter (New Haven: Yale University Press, 1953), Book 6, pp. 113–25, at https://sourcebooks.fordham.edu/basis/psellus-chrono06.asp (excerpted and some notes added or modified).]

Book 6

1. So the Empire passed into the hands of the two sisters, and for the first time in our lives we saw the transformation of a *gynaeconitis*[1] into an emperor's council chamber. What is more, both the civilian population and the military caste were working in harmony under empresses, and more obedient to them than to any proud overlord issuing arrogant orders. In fact, I doubt if any other family was ever so favored by God as theirs was—a surprising thing, when one reflects on the unlawful manner in which the family fortune was, so to speak, rooted and planted in the ground, with murder and bloodshed.[2] Yet the plant blossomed out and sent forth such mighty shoots, each with its royal fruit, that no others could be compared with it, either in beauty or grandeur.[3] But this is a mere digression from my main story.

2. For a while the sisters preferred to govern alone. The Empire was administered without the appointment of new officials, and no immediate reforms were brought in to affect the constitution already established. After dismissing only the members of the rebel family, Zoe and Theodora maintained in their position of authority the other ministers of state, who were men of proved loyalty and known for their traditional allegiance to themselves. These men, because they were afraid lest at some future

time they should be accused of introducing new ideas into the constitution, or of making foolish decisions, or of acting illegally, were meticulously careful in their conduct of state affairs, both military and civil, and as far as possible, they treated the empresses with all due honor.

3. Court procedure, in the case of the sisters, was made to conform exactly to the usual observance of the sovereigns who had ruled before them. Both of them sat in front of the royal tribunal, so aligned that Theodora was slightly behind her sister. Near them were the Rods and Sword-bearers and the officials armed with the *rhomphaia*.[4] Inside this circle were the special favorites and court officials, while round them, on the outside of the circle, was the second rank of the personal bodyguard, all with eyes fixed on the ground in an attitude of respect. Behind them came the Senate and the privileged class, then persons of the second class and the tribes, all in ranks and drawn up at proper intervals. When all was ready, the other business was carried on. There were lawsuits to be settled, questions of public interest, or contributions of money, audiences with ambassadors, controversies or agreements, and all the other duties that go to fill up an emperor's time. Most of the talking was done by the officials concerned, but sometimes, when it was necessary, the empresses also gave their instructions in a calm voice or made their replies, sometimes being

---

[1] Women's quarters.

[2] "Murder and bloodshed": When Basil I (r.867–886) came to the throne as the first Macedonian emperor, he did so by ordering the murder of the reigning emperor. His successors variously gained and lost the emperorship until Basil II (r.976–1025) secured it and defeated the powerful *dynatoi* (regional aristocrats) who challenged his rule. When Basil died without heirs, there was further foul play, as discussed in the introduction above.

[3] Psellus's patron was Constantine IX, the third husband of Zoe, which helps explain why, for Psellus, he was a "mighty shoot" of the Macedonian dynasty.

[4] A large sword or scimitar.

prompted and taking their cue from the experts, sometimes using their own discretion.

4. For those who did not know them it may be instructive if I give here some description of the two sisters. The elder, Zoe, was the quicker to understand ideas, but slower to give them utterance. With Theodora, on the other hand, it was just the reverse in both respects, for she did not readily show her inmost thoughts, but once she had embarked on a conversation, she would chatter away with an expert and lively tongue. Zoe was a woman of passionate interests, prepared with equal enthusiasm for both alternatives—death or life, I mean. In that she reminded me of sea-waves, now lifting a ship on high and then again plunging it down to the depths. Such characteristics were certainly not found in Theodora: in fact, she had a calm disposition, and in one way, if I may put it so, a dull one. Zoe was open-handed, the sort of woman who could exhaust a sea teeming with gold-dust in one day; the other counted her *staters*[1] when she gave away money, partly, no doubt, because her limited resources forbade any reckless spending, and partly because inherently she was more self-controlled in this matter.

5. To put it quite candidly (for my present purpose is not to compose a eulogy, but to write an accurate history) neither of them was fitted by temperament to govern. They neither knew how to administer nor were they capable of serious argument on the subject of politics. For the most part they confused the trifles of the harem with important matters of state. Even the very trait in the elder sister which is commended among many folk today, namely, her ungrudging liberality, dispensed very widely over a long period of time, even this trait, although it was no doubt satisfactory to those who enjoyed it because of the benefits they received from her, was after all the sole cause, in the first place, of the universal corruption and of the reduction of Roman fortunes to their lowest ebb.[2] The virtue of well-doing is most characteristic of those who govern, and where discrimination is made, where the particular circumstances and the fortune of the recipients and their differing personal qualities are taken into account, there the distribution of largess is to be commended. On the contrary, where no real discernment is exercised in these questions, the spending of money is wasted.

6. Such were the differences that marked the sisters in character. In personal appearance there was an even greater divergence. The elder was naturally more plump, although she was not strikingly tall. Her eyes were large, set wide apart, with imposing eyebrows. Her nose was inclined to be aquiline, without being altogether so. She had golden hair, and her whole body was radiant with the whiteness of her skin. There were few signs of age in her appearance: in fact, if you marked well the perfect harmony of her limbs, not knowing who she was, you would have said that here was a young woman, for no part of her skin was wrinkled, but all smooth and taut, and no furrows anywhere. Theodora, on the other hand, was taller, more taper [slender] of form. Her head was small, and out of proportion with the rest of her body. She was more ready with her tongue than Zoe, as I have said, and quicker in her movements. There was nothing stern in her glance; on the contrary, she was cheerful and smiling, eager to find any opportunity for talk.

7. So much for the character and physical appearance of the two empresses. I will return to the government. In those days, it seems to me, a peculiar magnificence and an added prestige attached itself to the executive power. The majority of the officials underwent a sudden change, as if they were playing parts on a stage and had been promoted to a role more glorious than any they had acted before. Largess was poured out as never in the past. Zoe, in particular, opened the coffers of the imperial treasury. Any trifles hidden away there were distributed by her with generous abandon. These monies had not been contributed voluntarily, but were the fruits of robbery and plunder. In fact, all this squandering, together with the high standard of living, was the beginning of the utter decline in our national affairs and the cause of our subsequent humiliation. But that was clear only to the prophets: only the wise saw what was really happening.

8. The prize-money for the soldiers and the revenues devoted to army expenditure were quite unnecessarily diverted and put aside for the use of other persons—a crowd of sycophants and those who at that time were deputed to guard the empresses—as if the emperor Basil [II] had filled the imperial treasuries with wealth for this very purpose.

9. Most men are convinced that the nations around us have made their sudden incursions against our borders, these wild unexpected inroads, for the first time in our day, but I myself hold a different view. I believe the

---

[1] Coins.

[2] The Byzantines called themselves Romans, and Byzantium was the New Rome.

house is doomed when the mortar that binds its bricks together becomes loose, and although the start of the trouble passed unnoticed by the majority, there is no doubt that it developed and gathered strength from that first cause. In fact, the gathering of the clouds in those days presaged the mighty deluge we are suffering today. But I must not speak of that yet.

THE AUGUSTA ZOE DELIBERATES WHOM TO PROMOTE TO THE THRONE

10. In the description of the events that follow I will speak with greater authority and more personal knowledge. The affairs of state urgently demanded vigorous and skillful direction. The country needed a man's supervision—a man at once strong-handed and very experienced in government, one who not only understood the present situation, but also any mistakes that had been made in the past, with their probable results. We wanted a man who would make provision for the future and prepare long beforehand against all possible attacks or likely invasions from abroad.[1] But the love of power, or the lack of power, the apparent freedom and the absence of supervision and the desire for ever greater power—these were the things that made the emperor's apartment into a *gynaeconitis*.

11. Even so, most people had no settled convictions. One rumor after another was bruited abroad, either favorable or otherwise to Zoe (for there were some who thought that Theodora should rightly be empress, on the ground that she had championed the cause of the people; moreover, they said, she had never married; others, again, believed the elder sister was more suited to rule, because she had previous experience of power, and power exercised a peculiar fascination on her). While these rumors were spreading, first one way, then another, among the people, Zoe anticipated their decision and seized all power for herself a second time.[2] The next move was to search for and decide on the man of the most illustrious descent and of the most distinguished fortune, whether he held a seat in the senate or served in the army....

14. Fate, indeed, decreed that the new master of the Empire should be Constantine, the son of Theodosius.[3] He was the last scion of the ancient family of the Monomachi, in the male line. A long account of him will be given by me later, when I launch out into the

description of his reign—a long account, because he was emperor for more years than any of Basil's successors, and because there was more to relate. Constantine was more active than his predecessors, although it must be admitted that he was not uniformly more successful. Indeed, in some ways he was greatly inferior. There is no reason why I should not be candid about this and tell the true story. Immediately after his accession I entered his service, served throughout his reign, was promoted to the Senate, entrusted with the most honorable duties. Thus there was nothing that I did not know, no overt act, no secret diplomacy. Naturally, therefore, I shall devote more space to him than to the other emperors.

THE MANNER IN WHICH AUGUSTA INTRODUCED THE EMPEROR CONSTANTINE INTO THE PALACE

15. But this is not the time to speak of these things. Our present task is to describe how, and for what reasons, and by what turn of fate, he came to power. Because of his family this man held very high rank in the Empire. He had the additional advantage of great wealth, and his personal appearance was singularly charming. Beyond all doubt, he seemed a fit person to marry into the most illustrious families. In the first place, he became son-in-law to the most prominent member of court society, but his wife fell ill and died. He was forced into a second alliance. At the time Romanus, the future emperor,[4] was still a private citizen, although high hopes were entertained that he would eventually be promoted and the people treated him with the greatest respect, because of his position. Romanus had conceived a deep affection for Constantine—a young man in the flower of his manhood and scion of a most noble family—and he grafted this fine young cutting on his own rich fertile olive. The lady in question was none other than the daughter of his sister Pulcheria, who in the past had been married to Basil Sclerus (he had the misfortune later to be deprived of his sight) and she had become the mother of this one child, a daughter. Alliance with this family conferred on the young man extraordinary brilliance, but he still held no important office. Basil's advisers, because of the hatred they nursed for the father, vented their spite on the son, and Sclerus's revolutionary designs had an unfortunate

---

[1] The use of "we" here implies that Psellus and other courtiers were pushing Zoe to find a suitable military man to wed.

[2] Zoe ousted her sister only temporarily.

[3] Theodosius Monomachus (d.1029) had been an important official under Basil II. Constantine would become Constantine IX (r.1042–1055).

[4] He was to become Emperor Romanus III (r.1028–1034).

effect on the emperor's relations with Constantine.[1] That was the reason why neither Basil [II] nor Constantine [VIII], his brother, ever promoted him to any responsible post in the government. Actually, they did him no harm, but he was slighted, and they certainly never dreamed that the man had a glorious future.

16. Even the accession of Romanus did little to help Constantine in his career, so mistaken was the new emperor in his estimate of the young man's qualities. However, Romanus did at least keep him at the imperial court, and if for no other reason, he was very much in the public eye through his near relationship with the emperor. His fresh complexion (to the men of our generation he was as unspoiled as spring fruit) and his graceful manners and his conversation, in which he excelled all others, these were the things that won the heart of the empress. She delighted in his company again and again. He for his part made himself thoroughly agreeable to her, and by cleverly adapting himself to please her on all occasions, he captivated her completely. By these arts he obtained favors from her, but at the same time both he and she were assailed with calumny from the court. There were times when their clandestine meetings were not much to the liking of most courtiers.

17. At any rate, these activities made him a likely candidate for promotion to the throne, and Michael,[2] who succeeded Romanus, viewed him with suspicion. In fact, Michael, even after his own accession, remained stubbornly jealous, although not unfriendly at first. Later he trumped up false accusations, suborning witnesses unjustly, and Constantine was driven from the city. His punishment was relegation to a certain determined area, in this case the island of Mitylene, and there for seven years—the exact length of Michael's reign—he endured his misfortune. Michael Calaphates, like Paphlagon, inherited the emperors' hatred of the young man.

18. Zoe's first reaction, when for the second time she found herself at the head of the Empire, was, as I have already said, to protect herself against any sudden reversal of fortune in the future. To strengthen her position, she proceeded to look for a husband, not a man from abroad, but someone in the court circle. However, as one had been discredited through misfortune, another rejected because of his ignoble lineage, a third suspected

as dangerous, and stories had been invented one after another to bring into disrepute her various suitors, she renounced all of them and again considered the claims of Constantine. She spoke openly on the subject to her personal bodyguard and household staff, and when she saw that they were unanimous in their support of Constantine as the future emperor—their agreement seemed almost preconcerted—she informed the senate also of her designs. There too her plan was greeted as an inspiration from God. So Constantine was recalled from his exile, and he set out, still a private citizen and without the paraphernalia of his new dignity.

19. When he drew near the city, however, a more sumptuous lodging was prepared for his reception and an imperial tent was pitched for him, surrounded by an imperial guard. In front of the palace there met his eyes a vision of magnificent splendor. People of all ages and conditions poured out in a flood to meet him. There were salutations and addresses of congratulation and good wishes. The city wore all the appearance of a popular festival; perhaps it would be nearer the mark to say that there were two cities, for beside the Queen of Cities there had been hastily erected a second city and the townsfolk had poured out right up to the walls, with markets, and fairs. When all was ready and the preparations for his official entry had been completed, the signal to go forward was given, and with great magnificence Constantine entered the courts of the palace.

20. Since the common laws respecting marriage could hardly be flouted, the patriarch Alexius settled the question of the wedding.[3] He made concessions to expediency—or shall we say that he bowed to the will of God in the whole affair? Certainly he did not himself lay his hands upon them in blessing at the coronation, but he did embrace them after the marriage ceremony and the act of crowning had been performed. Whether this was done in accordance with priestly tradition, or was a bit of flattery and done to suit the occasion, I do not know.

21. For the empresses, these events marked the end of their authority and personal intervention in the affairs of state; for Constantine, the beginning of his reign. His power was now for the first time established. So, after a joint rule of three months, the sisters retired from public life and the emperor—but we must not speak of him yet.

---

1 Basil Sclerus led a revolt against Emperor Basil II. This is why there were strained relations between Basil and Constantine, who was married to the daughter of Sclerus and Pulcheria.

2 Michael IV, Zoe's second husband.

3 Third marriages were prohibited by the Byzantine Church. This would be the third marriage for both Zoe and Constantine.

First I have some brief remarks to make, for the benefit of those who may be interested.

22. Several persons, on more than one occasion, have urged me to write this history. Among them were not only men in authority and leaders in the senate, but also students of theology, who interpret the mysteries of Holy Writ, and men of great sanctity and holiness. Through the passing of time the historical evidence has already proved inadequate for the writing of a proper record. There is a danger that events may be hidden in the remote past, so forgotten that our knowledge of bygone days rests on no sure foundation.

These gentlemen, therefore, asked me to do what I could to remedy those deficiencies: it was not right, they argued, that our own contemporary history should be concealed and utterly obscured, while events that took place before our time were thought worthy of record by succeeding generations. Such was the pressure and such the arguments with which they urged me to take up this task, but for myself I was not particularly enthusiastic for the undertaking. It was not that I was lazy, but I was afraid of two alternatives, either of which could not be disregarded: I might pass over, for reasons which I will explain later, things done by certain individuals, or distort my account of them, and so be convicted not of writing a history, but of mere fabrication, as if I were composing a play. That was one alternative. The other was that I might go to extreme lengths in hunting down the truth, and so become a laughing-stock to the critics. They would think me, not a lover of history, but a scandalmonger.

23. For these reasons I was not very eager to tackle the history of our times, especially as I knew that in many things I would clash with the emperor Constantine, and I would be ashamed of myself if I did not seize every opportunity of commending him. I should be ungrateful and altogether unreasonable if I did not make some return, however small, for his generosity to me, a generosity which showed itself not only in positive acts, but in the indirect ways in which he helped me to better my condition. It would be shameful if I did not prove my gratitude in my writings. It was therefore because of this man that I consistently refused to compose the history. I was most anxious to avoid imputing any blame to him. I did not want to reveal by my words any actions not to his credit and things it is better to keep dark. I was loath to put before the public a dishonest story, yet at the same time I was unwilling to shame the hero of my former eulogy. In my opinion, it was wrong to exercise literary talents, which I had perfected because of his encouragements to do him harm....

28. Naturally, I would have wished that my favorite emperor had been perfect, even if such a compliment was impossible for all the others, but the events of history do not accommodate themselves to our desires. So, divine soul, forgive me, and if sometimes in describing your reign I speak immoderately, concealing nothing and telling the truth, pardon me for it. Not one of your nobler deeds shall be passed over in silence. They shall all be revealed. Likewise, whatever derives not from the same nobility, that too shall be made manifest in my history. And there we must leave the matter and return to our narrative.

[At this point, Psellus takes up the story of Constantine.]

SCHOLARSHIP AND THE ARTS ACROSS THE ISLAMIC WORLD

4.10 Political theory: Al-Farabi, *The Perfect State* (*c*.940–942). Original in Arabic.

Abu Nasr al-Farabi (872–950) was born in Turkestan, spent most of his adulthood in Baghdad, where he made a very modest living as a philosopher and writer, and joined the court of the emir of Aleppo in Syria toward the end of his life. His *Perfect State* engaged a long tradition of Greek thought on a great variety of spiritual, biological, and social topics; al-Farabi wanted to show their importance for a Muslim audience. His work thus began with God, angels, the heavens, the "bodies below the heavens," and so on, leading to the chapters below, which deal with human societies and their different degrees of excellence.

1. How does al-Farabi's view of the "excellent and ignorant cities" compare with Augustine's notion of the "cities of God and Man" in *The City of God*, above, p. 16?
2. What, in the view of al-Farabi, justified social and political hierarchies?

[Source: *Al-Farabi on the Perfect State*, ed. and trans. Richard Walzer (Oxford: Clarendon Press, 1985), pp. 231, 235, 239, 241, 253, 255, 257, 259.]

Chapter 15
Perfect Associations and Perfect Ruler; Faulty Associations

... §3. The most excellent good and the utmost perfection is, in the first instance, attained in a city, not in a society which is less complete than it. But since good in its real sense is such as to be attainable through choice and will and evils are also due to will and choice only, a city may be established to enable its people to cooperate in attaining some aims that are evil. Hence felicity is not attainable in every city. The city, then, in which people aim through association at cooperating for the things by which felicity in its real and true sense can be attained, is the excellent city, and the society in which there is a cooperation to acquire felicity is the excellent society; and the nation in which all of its cities cooperate for those things through which felicity is attained is the excellent nation. In the same way, the excellent universal state will arise only when all the nations in it cooperate for the purpose of reaching felicity.

§4. The excellent city resembles the perfect and healthy body, all of whose limbs cooperate to make the life of the animal perfect and to preserve it in this state. Now the limbs and organs of the body are different and their natural endowments and faculties are unequal in excellence, there being among them one ruling organ, namely the heart, and organs which are close in rank to that ruling organ, each having been given by nature a faculty by which it performs its proper function in conformity with the natural aim. So, too, the parts of the city are by nature provided with endowments unequal in excellence which enable them to do one thing and not another. But they are not parts of the city by their inborn nature alone but rather by the voluntary habits which they acquire such as the arts and their likes; to the natural faculties which exist in the organs and limbs of the body correspond the voluntary habits and dispositions in the parts of the city.

§5. The ruling organ in the body is by nature the most perfect and most complete of the organs in itself and in its specific qualification, and it also has the best of everything of which another organ has a share as well; beneath it, in turn, are other organs which rule over organs inferior to them, their rule being lower in rank than the rule of the first and indeed subordinate to the rule of the first; they rule and are ruled. In the same way, the ruler of the city is the most perfect part of the city in his specific qualification and has the best of everything which anybody else shares with him; beneath him are people who are ruled by him and rule others.

The heart comes to be first and becomes then the cause of the existence of the other organs and limbs of the body, and the cause of the existence of their faculties in them and of their arrangement in the ranks proper to them, and when one of its organs is out of order, it is the heart which provides the means to remove that disorder. In the same way the ruler of this city must come to be in the first instance, and will subsequently be the cause of the rise of the city and its parts and the cause of the presence of the voluntary habits of its parts and of their arrangement in the ranks proper to them; and when one part is out of order he provides it with the means to remove its disorder.

The parts of the body close to the ruling organ perform of the natural functions, in agreement—by nature—with the aim of the ruler, the most noble ones; the organs beneath them perform those functions which are less noble, and eventually the organs are reached which perform the meanest functions. In the same way the parts of the city which are close in authority to the ruler of the city perform the most noble voluntary actions, and those below them less noble actions, until eventually the parts are reached which perform the most ignoble actions. The inferiority of such actions is sometimes due to the inferiority of their matter, although they may be extremely useful—like the action of the bladder and the action of the lower intestine in the body; sometimes it is due to their being of little use; at other times it is due to their being very easy to perform. This applies equally to the city and equally to every whole which is composed by nature of well-ordered coherent parts: they have a ruler whose relation to the other parts is like the one just described.

§6. This applies also to all existents.[1] For the relation of the First Cause to the other existents is like the relation of the king of the excellent city to its other parts.[2] For the ranks of the immaterial existents are close to the First [Cause]. Beneath them are the heavenly bodies, and beneath the heavenly bodies the material bodies. All these existents act in conformity with the First Cause, follow it, take it as their guide and imitate it; but each existent does that according to its capacity, choosing its aim precisely on the strength of its established rank in the universe: that is to say the last follows the aim of that which is slightly above it in rank, equally the second existent, in turn, follows what is above itself in rank, and in the same way the third existent has an aim which is above it. Eventually existents are reached which are linked with the First Cause without any intermediary whatsoever. In accordance with this order of rank all the existents permanently follow the aim of the First Cause. Those which are from the very outset provided with all the essentials of their existence are made to imitate the First [Cause] and its aim from their very outset, and hence enjoy eternal bliss and hold the highest ranks; but those which are not provided from the outset with all the essentials of their existence, are provided with a faculty by which they move towards the expected attainment of those essentials and will then be able to follow the aim of the First [Cause]. The excellent city ought to be arranged in the same way: all its parts ought to imitate in their actions the aim of their first ruler according to their rank.

§7. The ruler of the excellent city cannot just be any man, because rulership requires two conditions: (a) he should be predisposed for it by his inborn nature, (b) he should have acquired the attitude and habit of will for rulership which will develop in a man whose inborn nature is predisposed for it. Nor is every art suitable for rulership, most of the arts, indeed, are rather suited for service within the city, just as most men are by their very nature born to serve. Some of the arts rule certain [other] arts while serving others at the same time, whereas there are other arts which, not ruling anything at all, only serve. Therefore the art of ruling the excellent city cannot just be any chance art, nor due to any chance habit whatever. For just as the first ruler in a genus cannot be ruled

by anything in that genus—for instance the ruler of the limbs cannot be ruled by any other limb, and this holds good for any ruler of any composite whole—so the art of the ruler in the excellent city of necessity cannot be a serving art at all and cannot be ruled by any other art, but his art must be an art towards the aim of which all the other arts tend, and for which they strive in all the actions of the excellent city....

[Al-Farabi now explores the qualities of the ruler of the excellent city: his Passive Intellect (the only sort of intellect that human beings have) learns all the intelligibles—all that can be understood by the intellect alone—from the Active Intellect, which is God.]

§15. In opposition to the excellent city are the "ignorant" city, the wicked city, the city which has deliberately changed its character and the city which has missed the right path through faulty judgment. In opposition to it are also the individuals who make up the common people in the various cities.

§16. The "ignorant" city is the city whose inhabitants do not know true felicity, the thought of it never having occurred to them. Even if they were rightly guided to it they would either not understand it or not believe in it. The only good things they recognize are some of those which are superficially thought of as good among the things which are considered to be the aims in life such as bodily health, wealth, enjoyment of pleasures, freedom to follow one's desires, and being held in honor and esteem. According to the citizens of the ignorant city each of these is a kind of felicity, and the greatest and perfect felicity is the sum total of all of them. Things contrary to these goods are misery such as deficiency of the body, poverty, no enjoyment of pleasures, no freedom to follow one's desires, and not being held in honor.

§17. The ignorant city is divided into a number of cities. One of them is the city of necessity, that is the city whose people strive for no more food, drink, clothes, housing and sexual intercourse than is necessary for sustaining their bodies, and they cooperate to attain this. Another is the city of meanness; the aim of its people is to cooperate in the acquisition of wealth and riches, not in order to enjoy something else which can be got through wealth, but because they regard wealth as the sole aim in life. Another is the city of depravity and baseness; the aim of its people is the enjoyment of

---

[1] I.e., that which exists, whether thing, action, or quality.

[2] The First Cause is God. The term "First Cause" is found in Aristotle's *Physics*, book 8, and his *Metaphysics*, book 12. However, the hierarchy of being that al-Farabi describes here is neo-Platonic.

the pleasure connected with food and drink and sexual intercourse, and in general of the pleasures of the senses and of the imagination, and to give preference to entertainment and idle play in every form and in every way. Another is the city of honor; the aim of its people is to cooperate to attain honor and distinction and fame among the nations, to be extolled and treated with respect by word and deed, and to attain glory and splendor either in the eyes of other people or among themselves, each according to the extent of his love of such distinction or according to the amount of it which he is able to reach. Another is the city of power; the aim of its people is to prevail over others and to prevent others from prevailing over them, their only purpose in life being the enjoyment which they get from power. Another is the "democratic" city: the aim of its people is to be free, each of them doing what he wishes without restraining his passions in the least.

§18. There are as many kings of ignorant cities as there are cities of this kind, each of them governing the city over which he has authority so that he can indulge in his passion and design.

We have herewith enumerated the designs which may be set up as aims for ignorant cities.

§19. The wicked city is a city whose views are those of the excellent city; it knows felicity, God Almighty, the existents of the second order, the Active Intellect and everything which as such is to be known and believed in by the people of the excellent city; but the actions of its people are the actions of the people of the ignorant cities.

The city which has deliberately changed is a city whose views and actions were previously the views and actions of the people of the excellent city, but they have been changed and different views have taken their place, and its actions have turned into different actions.

The city which misses the right path [the "erring" city] is the city which aims at felicity after this life, and holds about God Almighty, the existents of the second order, and the Active Intellect pernicious and useless beliefs, even if they are taken as symbols and representations of true felicity. Its first ruler was a man who falsely pretended to be receiving "revelation"; he produced this wrong impression through falsifications, cheating and deceptions.

§20. The kings of these cities are contrary to the kings of the excellent cities: their ways of governing are contrary to the excellent ways of governing. The same applies to all the other people who live in these cities.

4.11 A Jewish poet in al-Andalus: Dunash ben Labrat, *There Came a Voice* (mid-10th cent.). Original in Hebrew.

Born in Fez (today Morocco), Dunash ben Labrat (*fl.* mid-10th cent.) became a rabbi in Spain (perhaps at Córdoba). He was one of many scholars and writers to flourish under the patronage of Hasdai ibn Shaprut, the first Jew to be an important figure at the Islamic Spanish court. Under these favorable conditions, Dunash ben Labrat and others debated Hebrew grammar, compiled Hebrew dictionaries, and created a new, secular form of Hebrew poetry. Mastering the traditions of Arabic poetic meter and rhyme, Dunash ben Labrat took up many of the same themes as the Arabic poets while invoking a very specific Jewish identity.

1. What is Dunash ben Labrat's attitude toward sensual pleasures?
2. What lines of this poem articulate the anxieties of an unwelcome minority?

[Source: *Wine, Women, & Death: Medieval Hebrew Poems on the Good Life*, trans. and ed. Raymond P. Scheindlin (Oxford: Oxford University Press, 1986), pp. 41–42.]

There came a voice: "Awake!
Drink wine at morning's break.
'Mid rose and camphor make
A feast of all your hours,

'Mid pomegranate trees   5
And low anemones,
Where vines extend their leaves
And the palm tree skyward towers,

Where lilting singers hum
To the throbbing of the drum,   10
Where gentle viols thrum
To the plash of fountains' showers.

On every lofty tree
The fruit hangs gracefully.
And all the birds in glee   15
Sing among the bowers.

The cooing of the dove
Sounds like a song of love.
Her mate calls from above—
Those trilling, fluting fowls.   20

We'll drink on garden beds
With roses round our heads.
To banish woes and dreads
We'll frolic and carouse.

Dainty food we'll eat.   25
We'll drink our liquor neat,
Like giants at their meat,
With appetite aroused.

When morning's first rays shine
I'll slaughter of the kine[1]   30
Some fatlings; we shall dine
On rams and calves and cows.

Scented with rich perfumes,
Amid thick incense plumes,
Let us await our dooms,   35
Spending in joy our hours."

I chided him: "Be still!
How can you drink your fill
When lost is Zion hill[2]
To the uncircumcised.   40

You've spoken like a fool!
Sloth you've made your rule.
In God's last judgment you'll
For folly be chastised.

The Torah, God's delight   45
Is little in your sight,
While wrecked is Zion's height,
By foxes vandalized.

How can we be carefree
Or raise our cups in glee,   50
When by all men are we
Rejected and despised?"

---

[1] Cows of every sort.

[2] A reference to the land of Israel, "lost" to the Jews of the Diaspora.

4.12 Education: Al-Qabisi, *A Treatise Detailing the Circumstances of Students and the Rules Governing Teachers and Students* (before 1012). Original in Arabic.

Abu al-Hasan Ali ibn Khalaf al-Qabisi (935–1012) was an important leader of one school of Islamic legal thought, the Maliki, named after its founder, Malik ibn Anas (d.796). After studying with scholars at Mecca and Cairo, al-Qabisi settled in Tunisia. Among his many writings were collections of hadith (traditions about the Prophet: see above, p. 147) and commentaries on the Qur'an. Above all, al-Qabisi was interested in law, and his treatise on students, parents, and teachers, some of which is presented here, formed part of his legal corpus.

Teachers were under contract to parents and students, so al-Qabisi was concerned to clarify their mutual obligations and to justify payments for instruction. (In the thirteenth century, western scholastics would take up similar issues.) His treatise was written in the form of a response to "an urgent questioner"; the views of al-Qabisi and other authorities were given in the third person embedded in chains of transmission in the same way that the hadith were transmitted by *isnad*. In al-Qabisi's view, it was the obligation of parents and guardians to teach their children (usually by sending them to a teacher), and if they could not do that, it was up to the state to educate the young.

1. What made education of the young an essential part of Islamic upbringing?
2. How did al-Qabisi restrict the kinds of education girls should have?

[Source: *Classical Foundations of Islamic Education Thought*, ed. Bradley J. Cook with Fathi H. Malkawi (Provo, UT: Brigham Young University Press, 2010), pp. 45–51, 54. Translated by Michael Fishbein. (Notes modified.)]

In the name of God, the Merciful, the Compassionate; God Bless Muhammad.

25. Abu al-Hasan [al-Qabisi] said: What I have told you about the merit a father can be expected to acquire from teaching his child the Qur'an should serve to encourage the father to teach his young child who, being unable to help or harm himself and unable to distinguish for himself what to take up and what to turn away, has only his father as a refuge, whose duty it is to provide his means of support....

27. Muslims throughout their history have diligently taught their children the Qur'an and provided them with teachers. This is something that no father refrains from doing for his child if he has the means to do so, unless he is following his soul's avarice. The latter is no excuse for him, for God, who is praised, has said: "Souls are very prone to avarice."[1] And, "whosoever is guarded against the avarice of his own soul—they are the prosperers."[2] Not one father would leave off doing this, deeming its omission trivial and insignificant, except a coarse father with no desire for good....

28. A child's religious status, as long as he is a minor, is the status of his father. Will the father then leave his minor child, not teaching him religion, when his teaching him the Qur'an will make his knowledge of religion firm?

---

[1] Qur'an 4:128.

[2] Qur'an 64:16.

Has he not heard the words of the Messenger of God, on whom be peace? "Every infant is born in a state of nature; then his parents make him a Jew or a Christian. It is just as camels are brought forth as beasts intact. Do you discern any that are mutilated?"[1] ...

29. If the children of unbelievers experience harm from their parents, it behooves the children of believers to benefit religiously from their parents. The first generations of believers had no need to trouble themselves arguing about this; they made do with the desire that had been placed in their hearts; they acted according to it, and they left it as customary practice that each generation passed on from the previous one. No father was ever reproved regarding this, nor did any father ever turn out to have omitted to do so from desire or from negligence. That is no attribute of a believing Muslim! Had it ever become evident that someone had omitted to teach his child the Qur'an out of negligence, his condition would have been deemed one of ignorance, ugliness, and deficiency, beneath that of people of contentment and satisfaction. Sometimes, however, lack of means causes parents to lag behind in this matter; then their behavior is excusable—depending on how sound their excuse turns out to be.

30. If the child has property, his father or his guardian (if his father has died) should not leave him. Let him enter the primary school and engage the teacher to teach him the Qur'an from his wealth, as is due. If the orphan has no guardian, the ruler[2] of the Muslims should oversee his affairs and proceed with his instruction as the father or guardian would have proceeded. If the child is in a town where there is no ruler, oversight would be exercised for him in a matter such as this if the town's righteous people came together to oversee the interests of the town's people, for overseeing this orphan is one of those interests.

31. If the orphan has no property, his mother or next of kin should be encouraged to take charge of teaching him the Qur'an. If someone else volunteers to bear the burden for them, that person shall have his reward. If the orphan has no kin to care for him, any Muslim who cares for him shall have his reward. If the teacher, reckoning on a heavenly reward, teaches him solely for God's sake, bearing it patiently, his reward for it, God willing, shall be doubled, especially since it is his craft from which he supports himself....

32. As for teaching a female the Qur'an and learning, it is good and of benefit to her. However, her being taught letter-writing or poetry is a cause for fear. She should be taught only things that can be expected to be good for her and protect her from temptation. It would be safer for her to be spared learning to write. When the Prophet (may God bless him and grant him peace) permitted women to attend the festival, he commanded them to bring out adolescent girls and those who normally are secluded behind a curtain.[3] At the same time he commanded menstruating women to avoid the place where people pray. He said, "Let women be present where there is blessing and at the prayers of Muslims." On this basis it is acceptable to teach them good things that are safe for them; as for things from which harm to them can be feared, it is preferable that such things be kept away from them, and this is the duty of their guardian. Understand what I have explained to you. Seek guidance from God, and He will guide: He is a sufficient guide and helper for you.

33. Know that God, who is mighty and exalted, has imposed certain duties on believing women, just as He has imposed certain duties on believing men. This may be inferred from God's words: "It is not for any believer, man or woman, when God and His Messenger have decreed a matter, to have the choice in the affair."[4] And, "The believers, the men and the women."[5] In more than one verse of His Book He has joined men and women together in being well rewarded. For example, "God has promised the believers, men and women, gardens underneath which rivers flow, forever therein to dwell, and goodly dwelling-places in the Gardens of Eden; and greater God's good pleasure, that is the mighty triumph."[6] And He commanded the wives of His Prophet (on whom be peace) to remember what they had heard from the Prophet: "And remember that which is recited in your houses of the signs of God and the Wisdom."[7] How should they not

---

[1] After they were born, the ears of camels were notched (and thus mutilated) to brand them.

[2] The word used here was *hakim*, which could refer to a leader of any sort, from the ruler of a country to a judge to a community official.

[3] An "adolescent girl" (*awatiq*) had begun puberty and was kept behind the curtain in the tent of her family, but she was not yet married.

[4] Qur'an 33:36.

[5] Qur'an 9:71.

[6] Qur'an 9:72.

[7] Qur'an 33:34.

be taught the good and what helps to its attainment? But whoever is in charge of them should turn from them anything of which one should beware on their behalf, since he is their protector and responsible for them....

37. Know that there was not one of the religious leaders[1] of the Muslims in the first days of this community but who gave thought to what would be of benefit to Muslims in all their affairs, private and public. We have never heard that any of them appointed teachers to teach people's children in elementary schools[2] during their childhood or gave such teachers a share from the public treasury, as they did for anyone they charged to serve the Muslims either by judging between them in lawsuits, calling them to prayer in the mosque, or anything else that they established to protect Muslims and guard their affairs. They could not have neglected the business of teachers for young children. However—and God only knows—they thought it was a matter that concerned each individual personally, inasmuch as what a person taught his child was part of his own welfare that was of special concern to him. They therefore left it as one of the tasks of fathers, something that it was not fitting for someone else to do for them if they were able to do it themselves. Since the religious leaders of the Muslims had made no provision for the matter and it was one that Muslims had to carry out for their children and without which they would not feel at ease, they got themselves a teacher for their children, someone to devote himself to them on a regular basis and to care for them as he would care for his own young children. Since it was unlikely that anyone could be found to volunteer for the Muslims, teach their children for them, devote himself entirely to them, and give up seeking his own livelihood and his profitable activities and other needs, it was appropriate for Muslims to hire someone to take care of teaching their children on a constant basis, to the exclusion of any other business. Such a teacher would relieve the children's parents of the burden of educating them; he would make them understand how to live upright lives, and he would increase their understanding of the good and turn them away from evil.

38. This is an occupation that few people volunteer to perform free of charge. If one had waited for people to volunteer to teach young children the Qur'an, many children would have been neglected and many people would not have learned the Qur'an. This would necessarily have led to loss of the Qur'an from people's hearts. It would have caused Muslim children to be confirmed in ignorance.

39. Yet there is no good reason to cause a shortage where there is no scarcity, and no injunction to abstain [from being paid to teach the Qur'an] has been confirmed as coming from the Messenger of God (may God bless him and grant him peace).

40. Al-Harith ibn Miskin,[3] in a report dated to the year [789–90], said: "Ibn Wahb gave us the following report: 'I heard Malik say, "None of the scholars I have known saw anything wrong with paying teachers—teachers of the Qur'an school."'"[4]

41. The following is also attributed to Ibn Wahb in his *Muwatta* from 'Abd al-Jabbar ibn 'Umar: "No one I asked in Medina sees anything wrong in teachers teaching for pay." ...

53. The aforementioned people disagreed only about paying the teacher to teach something other than the Qur'an and writing. They did not disagree about subjects meant to reinforce the Qur'an, such as writing and penmanship.

54. Ibn Sahnun[5] mentioned: "It is fitting for the teacher to teach his students [the correct reading of] the case-endings of [the words of] the Qur'an—it is his duty to do so—and vocalization, spelling, good handwriting, good reading, when to pause [in recitation], and how to articulate clearly; it is his duty to do so. It is his duty to teach them the good reading that has become well-known, namely the reading of Nafi',[6] but there is no harm in his having them read according to another [authority] if [the reading] is not considered disagreeable. There is no harm in his teaching them homilies, if they desire.

55. "He should teach them good manners, for it his duty toward God to give good advice, protect them, and care for them. The teacher should command them to

---

[1] The word used here was *a'immah*, the plural of *imam*, a religious scholar and especially the founder of a legal school.

[2] The word used here was *katatib*, the plural of *kuttab*, a school in which students learned to read the Qur'an.

[3] Al-Harith ibn Miskin was an earlier scholar of the Maliki school.

[4] Because ibn Wahb (743–812) here transmitted the words of Malik ibn Anas, founder of the Maliki school, this passage and others like it linked al-Qabisi himself to the founder.

[5] Ibn Sahnun (817–870) was an earlier scholar of the Maliki school and a student of ibn Wahb. Al-Qabisi was much influenced by ibn Sahnun's writings on education and quoted him extensively.

[6] The Maliki school considered the reading of Nafi', i.e., the Qur'anic text cited as correct by Nafi' of Medina, to be best.

perform the ritual prayer when they are seven years old and beat them for [omitting to pray] when they are ten. That is what Malik said...."

56. [Malik also said:] "Let him take care to teach them supplications,[1] that they may make their humble petitions to God; and let him teach them God's greatness and majesty, that they may magnify Him for it. If the people suffer from drought and the imam leads them in prayers for rain, I would have the teacher bring the children out [those of them who know how to pray], and let them beseech God with supplications and make their humble petitions to Him, for I have been told that when the people to whom Jonah was sent (may God's blessing be upon our Prophet and upon him) saw the chastisement with their own eyes, they brought out their children and entreated God by means of them, and the chastisement was lifted. He should teach them arithmetic, but it is not his duty unless it has been stipulated for him; and likewise poetry, obscure words, Arabic language, and the whole of grammar—in these matters he acts voluntarily. There is no harm in his teaching them poetry—words and reports of the [ancient] Arabs that contain nothing indecent—but it is not incumbent upon him." According to Sahnun there is nothing wrong if the person who teaches Qur'an and writing teaches all this, whether voluntarily or by stipulation. However, as for paying the teacher to teach these things with no intent to teach the Qur'an and writing, Sahnun, as mentioned previously, rejects it based on Malik's saying that he did not like payment for the teaching of poetry.

57. Ibn Habib, on the other hand, said: "There is nothing wrong with paying a teacher to teach poetry, grammar, letter-writing, the Days of the Arabs, and similar things, such as the knowledge of famous men and of chivalrous knights: there is nothing wrong with paying for the teaching of all this. I, however, am opposed to the teaching, learning, or recitation by an adult or child of any poetry containing accounts of unbridled violence, obscenity, or foul satire."

KINGDOMS IN EAST CENTRAL EUROPE

4.13 Hungary as heir of Rome: King Stephen, *Laws* (1000–1038). Original in Latin.

The Bulgarians entered a largely Byzantine orbit when they settled in the region just south of the Danube. By contrast, the Magyars (called Hungarians in the rest of Europe), entered a region contested by both the Byzantines and the Germans. When they arrived in the Pannonian plains (north of the Danube), they contributed to the dismantling of the formerly powerful Moravian empire, which had kept its independence from Germany, in part by converting to Christianity under the aegis of the Byzantines (it was for the Moravians that Constantine-Cyril and Methodius—see above, p. 161—first made their translations). The Hungarians, by contrast, eventually allied themselves with Germany and with the Catholicism that its emperor represented. Hungarian prince Géza (r.972–997) converted under the auspices of German churchmen and invited German priests to spread the religion, using Christianity to enforce his rule. His son Stephen (r.997–1038), married to the sister of Duke Henry IV of Bavaria (who later became Emperor Henry II), defeated his chief rival for rule with the help of German warriors, and around the year 1000, with the approval of Emperor Otto III, received a royal crown and a blessing from Pope Sylvester II. As king, Stephen adopted many of the institutions of the post-Roman successor states, including written laws. Those excerpted below are from the oldest of the laws that he promulgated.

---

[1] That is, prayers on various occasions that were not part of the five obligatory times of ritual prayers.

1. Compare the justifications for and provisions of Stephen's *Laws* with Charlemagne's *Admonitio Generalis* (above, p. 159).
2. What were the various classes of Hungarian society that are revealed by these laws?

[Source: *The Laws of the Medieval Kingdom of Hungary*, vol 1: 1000–1301, trans. and ed. János M. Bak, György Bónis, and James Ross Sweeney (Bakersfield, CA: Charles Schlacks, Jr. Publisher, 1989), pp. 1, 3–8, 80–83 (slightly modified).]

Preface to the Royal Law

The work of the royal office subject to the rule of divine mercy is by custom greater and more complete when nourished in the Catholic faith than any other office. Since every people use their own law, we, governing our monarchy by the will of God and emulating both ancient and modern caesars, and after reflecting upon the law, decree for our people too the way they should lead an upright and blameless life. Just as they are enriched by divine laws, so may they similarly be strengthened by secular ones, in order that as the good shall be made many by these divine laws so shall the criminals incur punishment. Thus we set out below in the following sentences what we have decreed....

6. ROYAL CONCESSIONS OF FREE DISPOSITION OF GOODS.

We, by our royal authority have decreed that anyone shall be free to divide his property, to assign it to his wife, his sons and daughters, his relatives, or to the church;[1] and no one should dare to change this after his death.

7. THE PRESERVATION OF ROYAL GOODS.

It is our will that just as we have given others the opportunity to master their own possessions, so equally the goods, warriors,[2] bondmen,[3] and whatever else belongs to our royal dignity should remain permanent, and no one should plunder or remove them, nor should anyone dare to obtain any advantage from them.

8. THE OBSERVANCE OF THE LORD'S DAY.

If a priest or *ispán* [local lord], or any faithful person find anyone working on Sunday with oxen, the ox shall be confiscated and given to the men of the castle to be eaten;[4] if a horse is used, however, it shall be confiscated, but the owner, if he wishes, may redeem it with an ox which should be eaten as has been said. If anyone uses other equipment, this tool and his clothing shall be taken, and he may redeem them, if he wishes, with a flogging.

9. MORE ON THE SAME.

Priests and *ispánok*[5] shall enjoin village reeves[5] to command everyone both great and small, men and women, with the exception of those who guard the fire, to gather on Sundays in the church. If someone remains at home through their negligence let them be beaten and shorn.

10. THE OBSERVANCE OF EMBER DAYS.[6]

If someone breaks the fast known to all on the Ember day, he shall fast in prison for a week.

---

[1] The king seems to have wanted to transform the undivided property of clans into the personal property of freemen and nobles, as was the case in western European societies of the time. But he was not successful.

[2] The Latin word used here was *milites* (sing. *miles*), the same word for "fighters" or "warriors" that was used in the Peace Movement (see above, Andrew of Fleury, *Miracles of St. Benedict*, p. 196). In the *Laws of Hungary*, the *milites* seem to have been armed servants of the king and magnates.

[3] The Latin word used here was *servi*, (sing. *servus*), which could mean either "slave" or "serf." Since the meaning here is not clear, the neutral term "bondmen" is used.

[4] The "men of the castle" (*cives* in Latin) were dependent men attached to the castles of the royal *ispánok* (the plural of *ispán*) for their defense and maintenance, much like the garrisons that guarded the castles in the document about Hugh of Lusignan and his lord (above, p. 190).

[5] In this period, the reeves (*villici* in Latin) were free peasants in charge of enforcing some laws.

[6] The observance of three days' fast during the weeks following Ash Wednesday, Pentecost, the Exaltation of the Holy Cross, and the feast of St. Lucy was widespread in the Carolingian realm and, as we see here, adopted in Hungary.

11. THE OBSERVANCE OF FRIDAY.

If someone eats meat on Friday, a day observed by all Christianity, he shall fast incarcerated during the day for a week.

12. THOSE WHO DIE WITHOUT CONFESSION.

If someone has such a hardened heart—God forbid it to any Christian—that he does not want to confess his faults according to the counsel of a priest, he shall lie without any divine service and alms like an infidel. If his relatives and neighbors fail to summon the priest, and therefore he should die unconfessed, prayers and alms should be offered, but his relatives shall wash away their negligence by fasting in accordance with the judgment of the priests. Those who die a sudden death shall be buried with all ecclesiastical honor, for divine judgment is hidden from us and unknown.

13. THE OBSERVANCES OF CHRISTIANITY.

If someone neglects a Christian observance and takes pleasure in the stupidity of his negligence, he shall be judged by the bishops according to the nature of the offense and the discipline of the canons.[1] If he rebelliously objects to suffer the punishment with equanimity, he shall be subject to the same judgment seven times over. If, after all this, he continues to resist and remains obdurate, he shall be handed over for royal judgment, namely to the defender of Christianity.[2]

14. ON HOMICIDE.

If someone driven by anger and arrogance, willfully commits a homicide, he should know that according to the decrees of our [royal] council he is obliged to pay one hundred ten gold *pensae*,[3] from which fifty will go to the royal treasury, another fifty will be given to relatives, and ten will be paid to arbiters and mediators. The killer himself shall fast according to the rules of the canons.

MORE ON THE SAME.

If someone kills a person by chance, he shall pay twelve *pensae* and fast as the canons command.

THE KILLING OF SLAVES.

If someone's slave kills another's slave, the payment shall be a slave for a slave, or he may be redeemed and do penance as has been said.

MORE ON THE SAME.

If a freeman kills the slave of another, he shall replace him with another slave or pay his price, and fast according to the canons.

15. THOSE WHO KILL THEIR WIVES.

If an *ispán* with a hardened heart and a disregard for his soul—may such remain far from the hearts of the faithful—defiles himself by killing his wife, he shall make his peace with fifty steers[4] to the kindred of the woman, according to the decree of the royal council, and fast according to the commands of the canons. And if a warrior or a man of wealth commits the same crime he shall pay according to that same council ten steers and fast, as has been said. And if a commoner has committed the same crime, he shall make his peace with five steers to the kindred and fast.

16. DRAWING THE SWORD.

In order that peace should remain firm and unsullied among the greater and the lesser of whatever station, we forbid anyone to draw the sword with the aim of injury. If anyone in his audacity should put this prohibition to the test, let him be killed by the same sword.

17. ON PERJURY.

If a powerful man of stained faith and defiled heart be found guilty of breaking his oath by perjury, he shall atone for the perjury with the loss of his hand; or he may redeem it with fifty steers. If a commoner commits perjury, he shall be punished with the loss of his hand or may redeem it by twelve steers and fast, as the canons command.

18. ON MANUMISSION.

If anyone, prompted by mercy, should set his male and female slaves free in front of witnesses, we decree that no one out of ill will shall reduce them to servitude after his

---

[1] This chapter in fact authorizes the introduction of canon (Church) law into Hungary.

[2] The "defender of Christianity" was Stephen himself.

[3] The *pensa auri* was a gold coin equivalent to the contemporary Byzantine gold *solidus*.

[4] Steers were valued at one gold *pensa* each; hence fifty oxen, that is fifty *pensa*, here reflect the cost of legal compensation for the death of a woman by a man of the *ispán* class.

death. If, however, he promised them freedom but died intestate, his widow and sons shall have the power to bear witness to this same manumission and to render *agape*[1] for the redemption of the husband's soul, if they wish.

19. GATHERING AT CHURCH AND THOSE WHO MUTTER OR CHATTER DURING MASS.

If some persons, upon coming to church to hear the divine service mutter among themselves and disturb others by relating idle tales during the celebration of mass and by being inattentive to Holy Scripture with its ecclesiastical nourishment, they shall be expelled from the church in disgrace if they are older, and if they are younger and common folk they shall be bound in the narthex of the church[2] in view of everyone and punished by whipping and by the shearing off of their hair.

20. INADMISSIBILITY OF ACCUSATIONS AND TESTIMONY OF BONDMEN OR BONDWOMEN AGAINST THEIR MASTERS OR MISTRESSES.

In order that the people of this kingdom may be far removed and remain free from the affronts and accusations of bondmen and bondwomen, it is wholly forbidden by decree of the royal council that any servile person be accepted in accusation or testimony against their masters or mistresses in any criminal case.

21. THOSE WHO PROCURE LIBERTY FOR BONDMEN OF OTHERS.

If anyone thoughtlessly brings the bondman of another, without the knowledge of his master, before the king or before persons of higher birth and dignity in order to procure for him the benefits of liberty after he has been released from the yoke of servitude, he should know that if he is rich, he shall pay fifty steers of which forty are owed to the king and ten to the master of the bondman, but if he is poor and of low rank, he shall pay twelve steers of which ten are due to the king and two to the master of the bondman.

22. THOSE WHO ENSLAVE FREEMEN.

Because it is worthy of God and best for men that everyone should conduct his life in the vigor of liberty, it is established by royal decree that henceforth no *ispán* or warrior should dare to reduce a freeman to servitude. If, however, compelled by his own rashness he should presume to do this, he should know that he shall pay from his own possessions the same composition, which shall be properly divided between the king and the *ispánok*, as in the other decree above.

SIMILARLY ON THE SAME.

But if someone who was once held in servitude lives freely after having submitted to a judicial procedure[3] held to consider his liberty, he shall be content with enjoying his freedom, and the man who held him in servitude shall pay nothing.

23. THOSE WHO TAKE THE WARRIORS OF ANOTHER FOR THEMSELVES.

We wish that each lord have his own warriors and no one shall try to persuade a warrior to leave his longtime lord and come to him, since this is the origin of quarrels.

24. THOSE WHO TAKE GUESTS OF ANOTHER FOR THEMSELVES.[4]

If someone receives a guest with benevolence and decently provides him with support, the guest shall not leave his protector as long as he receives support according to their agreement, nor should he transfer his service to any other.

25. THOSE WHO ARE BEATEN WHILE LOOKING FOR THEIR OWN.

If a warrior or a bondman flees to another and he whose warrior or man has run away sends his agent to bring him back, and that agent is beaten and whipped by anyone, we decree in agreement with our magnates that he who gave the beating shall pay ten steers.

---

[1] The *agape* was a memorial meal shared by the manumitted (those released from slavery) or an offering made in memory of the dead.

[2] The entrance hall or porch.

[3] The "judicial procedure" refers to the ordeal by hot iron: the subject (in this case a person claiming to be free) must carry a hot iron for a few paces, and then put it down. His hand is bandaged. After three days, the wound is inspected. If "clean," he is judged to have told the truth (or, in criminal cases, he is judged not guilty); if discolored or infected, he is judged to have lied.

[4] The "guests" were foreigners, most of whom were Western clerics and knights.

26. WIDOWS AND ORPHANS.

We also wish widows and orphans to be partakers of our law in the sense that if a widow, left with her sons and daughters, promises to support them and to remain with them as long as she lives, she shall have the right from us to do so, and no one should force her to marry. If she has a change of heart and wants to marry and leave the orphans, she shall have nothing from the goods of the orphans except her own clothing.[1]

MORE ABOUT WIDOWS.

If a widow without a child promises to remain unmarried in her widowhood, she shall have the right to all her goods and may do with them what she wishes. But after her death her goods shall go to the kin of her husband, if she has any, and if not, the king is the heir.

27. THE ABDUCTION OF GIRLS.

If any warrior debased by lewdness abducts a girl to be his wife without the consent of her parents, we decree that the girl should be returned to her parents, even if he raped her, and the abductor shall pay ten steers for the abduction, although he may afterwards have made peace with the girl's parents. If a poor man who is a commoner should attempt this, he shall compensate for the abduction with five steers.

28. THOSE WHO FORNICATE WITH BONDWOMEN OF ANOTHER.

In order that freemen preserve their liberty undefiled, we wish to warn them. Any transgressor who fornicates with a bondwoman of another, should know that he has committed a crime, and he is to be whipped for the first offense. If he fornicates with her a second time, he should be whipped and shorn; but if he does it a third time, he shall become a slave together with the woman, or he may redeem himself. If, however, the bondwoman should conceive by him and not be able to bear but dies in childbirth, he shall make compensation for her with another bondwoman.

THE FORNICATION OF BONDMEN.

If a bondman of one master fornicates with the bondwoman of another, he should be whipped and shorn, and if the woman should conceive by him and dies in childbirth, the man shall be sold and half of his price shall be given to the master of the bondwoman, the other half shall be kept by the master of the bondman.

29. THOSE WHO DESIRE BONDWOMEN AS WIVES.

In order that no one who is recognized to be a freeman should dare commit this offense, we set forth what has been decreed in this royal council as a source of terror and caution so that if any freeman should choose to marry a bondwoman of another with her master's consent, he shall lose the enjoyment of his liberty and become a slave forever.

30. THOSE WHO FLEE THEIR WIVES BY LEAVING THE COUNTRY.

In order that people of both sexes may remain and flourish under fixed law and free from injury, we establish in this royal decree that if anyone in his impudence should flee the country out of loathing for his wife, she shall possess everything which her husband rightfully possessed, so long as she is willing to wait for her husband, and no one shall force her into another marriage. If she voluntarily wishes to marry, she may take her own clothing leaving behind other goods, and marry again. If her husband, hearing this, should return, he is not allowed to replace her with anyone else, except with the permission of the bishop.

31. THEFT COMMITTED BY WOMEN.

Because it is terrible and loathsome to all to find men committing theft, and even more so for women, it is ordained by the royal council, that if a married woman commits theft, she shall be redeemed by her husband, and if she commits the same offense a second time, she shall be redeemed again; but if she does it a third time, she shall be sold.

32. ARSON OF HOUSES.

If anyone sets a building belonging to another on fire out of enmity, we order that he replace the building and whatever household furnishings were destroyed by the fire, and also pay sixteen steers which are worth forty *solidi*.[2]

---

[1] Here women apparently did not have a right to their dower—the gift that a husband gave his new wife—after the death of their husbands, though in later laws that right was recognized.

[2] In this particular case, Bavarian silver *solidi* are meant; twenty-five of them were equal to a Byzantine gold *solidus*.

33. ON WITCHES.

If a witch is found, she shall be led, in accordance with the law of judgment into the church and handed over to the priest for fasting and instruction in the faith. After the fast she may return home. If she is discovered in the same crime a second time, she shall fast and after the fast she shall be branded with the keys of the church in the form of a cross on her bosom, forehead, and between the shoulders. If she is discovered on a third occasion, she shall be handed over to the judge [of the secular court].

34. ON SORCERERS.

So that the creatures of God may remain far from all injury caused by evil ones and may not be exposed to any harm from them—unless it be by the will of God who may even increase it—we establish by decree of the council a most terrible warning to magicians and sorcerers that no person should dare to subvert the mind of any man or to kill him by means of sorcery and magic. Yet in the future if a man or a woman dare to do this he or she shall be handed over to the person hurt by sorcery or to his kindred, to be judged according to their will. If,

however, they are found practicing divination as they do in ashes or similar things, they shall be corrected with whips by the bishop.

35. THE INVASION OF HOUSES.

We wish that peace and unanimity prevail between great and small according to the Apostle: Be ye all of one accord, etc.,[1] and let no one dare attack another. For if there be any *ispán* so contumacious that after the decree of this common council he should seek out another at home in order to destroy him and his goods, and if the lord of the house is there and fights with him and is killed, the *ispán* shall be punished according to the law about drawing the sword.[2] If, however, the *ispán* shall fall, he shall lie without compensation. If he did not go in person but sent his warriors, he shall pay compensation for the invasion with one hundred steers. If, moreover, a warrior invades the courtyard and house of another warrior, he shall pay compensation for the invasion with ten steers. If a commoner invades the huts of those of similar station, he shall pay for the invasion with five steers.

4.14 Coming to terms with Catholic Poland: Thietmar of Merseburg, *Chronicle* (1013–1018). Original in Latin.

Poland, like Hungary, became a state in the wake of Moravia's collapse. Mieszko I (r.*c*.960–992) was the first leader to unite a region that was (roughly speaking) between the Oder and Vistula rivers. Baptized in 966, he expanded his duchy by taking advantage of Bohemian and German rivalries. In 990 or 991 he placed Poland under the direct protection of the pope. Mieszko's son and successor, Boleslaw the Brave (r.992–1025), maintained good relations with Emperor Otto III (r.996–1002) and helped him destabilize Bohemia, which was in the interest of both rulers. The major sources for this early history come not from Poland but from Germany. An example is the *Chronicle* of Thietmar of Merseburg (975–1018). Thietmar came from a prominent Saxon family. Educated in the classics and Christian texts at Magdeburg, Thietmar was (like Ruotger and his hero Bruno of Cologne, see below, p. 224) a product of the Ottonian Renaissance, groomed to serve the king as well as to preside in a high Church office. In 1009, he became bishop of Merseburg, a key bishopric created by the Ottonians to strengthen the empire's control over its eastern border. Thietmar wrote mainly about events in Germany, but he was well aware of what was happening in Poland and had strong opinions about it.

---

[1] See Phil. 2:2–4.

[2] See above, chapter 16 of this law code.

The passage below begins with the arrival in Poland of the body of Saint Adalbert (956–997). Born in Bohemia but educated, like Thietmar, at Magdeburg, Germany, Adalbert was made bishop of Prague in 983 but, clashing with factions there in 988, fled to Rome. After a stint in a monastery there, he made trips to Germany, Hungary, and Poland, benefiting from his excellent relations with the rulers in each place. In 997 he went as a missionary to Prussia, where he was martyred. His body was eagerly purchased as a precious relic by Boleslaw. When in the year 1000 Otto III came on pilgrimage to see those relics at Gniezno, Poland's capital city, Boleslaw orchestrated a synod that raised Gniezno to an archbishopric.

1. Why was a German bishop like Thietmar interested in Poland?
2. Why might you not believe Thietmar's description of the customs of Poland?

[Source: *Ottonian Germany: The Chronicon of Thietmar of Merseburg*, trans. David A. Warner (Manchester: Manchester University Press, 2001), pp. 171–72, 191–93, 361–63 (notes modified).]

4.28 In the beginning of the summer, Adalbert, bishop of the Bohemians, arrived. He had received the name Woyciech at his baptism, the other name, at his confirmation, from the archbishop of Magdeburg. He was educated in letters, in that same city.... As he was unable to separate his flock from the ancient error of wickedness through godly teaching, he excommunicated them all and came to Rome to justify himself before the pope. For a long time, with the pope's permission, he lived an exemplary life according to the strict rule of Abbot Boniface.[1] With the same pope's permission, he later tried to subdue the Prussians, their thoughts still estranged from Christ, with the bridle of holy preaching. On 23 April, pierced by a spear and beheaded, he alone received the best martyrdom, without a groan. This occurred just as he himself had seen it in a dream and had predicted to all the brothers, saying: "I thought I saw myself celebrating mass and communicating alone." Seeing that he had now died, the authors of this wicked crime increased both their wickedness and the vengeance of God by throwing the blessed body in the water. His head, however, they scornfully transfixed with a stake. They returned home in great joy. After learning of this, Boleslaw, Mieszko's son, immediately purchased both the martyr's celebrated body and his head. In Rome, after the emperor [Otto III] had been informed, he humbly offered praises to God because, during his lifetime, he had taken such a servant for himself through the palm of martyrdom....

4.55 I cannot place in its correct order everything that ought to be treated within the context of this book. In what follows, therefore, I will not be embarrassed to add a few recollections. Indeed, I rejoice in the change of pace much as the traveler who, because of its difficulty or perhaps from ignorance, leaves the course of the more direct road and sets out on some winding secondary path. Hence, I will relate the remaining deeds of Mieszko [I], the celebrated duke of the Poles, who has already been treated in some detail in the previous books. He took a noble wife from the region of Bohemia, the sister of Boleslaw the Elder. Her life corresponded to her name—she was called Dobrawa in Slavic, which, in German, means 'the good'. For this one, faithful to Christ, and realizing that her husband was mired in various heathen errors, turned her humble spirit to the task of binding him to the faith as well. She tried in every way to conciliate him, not because of the threefold appetite of this evil world but rather for the sake of the admirable and, to all the faithful, desirable fruit of future salvation.[2]

4.56 She sinned willingly for a while, that she might later be good for a long time. For during Lent, which closely followed her marriage, though she intended to offer an acceptable tithe to God by abstaining from meat and through the affliction of her body, her husband asked and tried to coax her into giving up her plan. She consented, thinking that he might therefore be more willing to listen

---

[1] That is, Adalbert spent time at the monastery of Santi Bonifacio e Alessio in Rome. That Boniface was a martyr saint of the early Church, not the English missionary of the eighth century.

[2] For the "three-fold" appetites, see 1 John 2:16.

to her on some other occasion. Some say that she only ate meat during a single Lenten period, others say three. Now, O reader, you have heard her sin, now also consider the attractive fruit of her pious will. She labored for the sake of her husband's conversion and was heard by the Creator in his kindness; and through his infinite goodness that most zealous persecutor came to his senses. After being admonished frequently by his beloved wife, he vomited out the poison of his unbelief and, in holy baptism, wiped away the stain of his birth. Immediately, members of his hitherto reluctant people followed their beloved head and lord and, after accepting the marriage garments, were numbered among the wards of Christ. Jordan, their first bishop, labored much with them, while he diligently invited them by word and deed to the cultivation of the heavenly vineyard. Then the couple rightly rejoiced, namely the man and the noble woman, and all who were subject to them rejoiced at their marriage in Christ. After this, the good mother gave birth to a son who was very different from her and the misfortune of many mothers. She named him Boleslaw [the Brave], after her brother. He first revealed his innate evil to her and then raged against his own flesh and blood, as I will reveal in the following.

4.57 But when his mother died [977], his father married Margrave Dietrich's daughter, a nun at the convent called Calbe, without the approval of the church. Oda was her name and great was her presumption. She rejected her celestial spouse in favor of a man of war, which displeased all the pastors of the church but most of all her own bishop, the venerable Hildeward.[1] But the welfare of the land, and the need to strengthen the peace, kept this from leading to a break; rather it provided a healthy and continuous incentive for reconciliation. For she increased the service of Christ in every way: many captives were returned to their homeland, prisoners were released from their chains, and the prisons of those who had been accused were opened. I hope that God will forgive her the magnitude of her sin, since such love of pious deeds was revealed in her. We read, however, that he who does not entirely abandon the evil he has begun, will try in vain to placate the Lord. She bore her husband three sons: Mieszko, Swentepulk and [...]. She

passed her life there, highly honored, until her husband's death. She was beloved among those with whom she lived and useful to those from whom she had come.

4.58 But on 25 May, in the year of the Incarnation 992, in the tenth year of Otto III's kingship,[2] the aforementioned duke [Mieszko], now old and feverish, went from this place of exile to his homeland,[3] leaving his kingdom to be divided among many claimants. Yet, with fox-like cunning, his son Boleslaw unified it once more in the hands of one ruler, after he had expelled his stepmother and brothers, and had their familiars Odilien and Przibiwoj blinded. That he might be able to rule alone, he ignored both human and divine law. He married the daughter of Margrave Rikdag, but later sent her away and took a Hungarian woman as his wife. She bore him a son, named Bezprym, but he also sent her away. His third wife was Emnilde, a daughter of the venerable lord, Dobromir. Faithful to Christ, she formed her husband's unstable character completely for the better and strove unceasingly to wash away both of her sins through the generous dispersal of alms and abstinence. She bore two sons, Mieszko and another one whom the father named after his beloved lord.[4] She also produced three daughters of whom one was an abbess, the second married Count Herman, and the third the son of King Vladimir. I will say more about them later....

8.1 In the year 1018 of the Incarnation, in the second indiction, in the sixteenth year of Lord Henry's reign, and his fourth as emperor, the same Henry celebrated the Circumcision and Epiphany of the Lord in Frankfurt, with great solemnity.[5] On 25 January, Ezzelin the Lombard was granted his liberty. He had been held in custody for four years. Afterwards, on 30 January, Bishops Gero and Arnulf, the counts Herman and Dietrich, and the emperor's chancellor Frederick agreed to a sworn peace at the burg Bautzen. The agreement was made at the emperor's order and in response to Boleslaw's constant supplications. This was not as it should have been, however. Rather, it was the best that could be accomplished under the circumstances. In the company of a select group of hostages, the aforesaid lords returned. After four days,

---

[1] A nun was supposed to be married to Christ and thus could not take another husband.

[2] In fact, the ninth year.

[3] I.e., he died.

[4] Referring to Otto III.

[5] Thietmar here refers to Emperor Henry II (r.1014–1024), the successor of Otto III.

Oda, Margrave Ekkehard's daughter, whom Boleslaw had long desired, was escorted to Zützen by Otto, the duke's son.[1] When they arrived, they were greeted by a large crowd of men and women, and by many burning lamps, since it was night-time. Contrary to the authority of the canons, Oda married the duke after Septuagesima.[2] Until now, she has lived outside the law of matrimony and thus in a manner worthy only of a marriage such as this one.

8.2 In her husband's kingdom, the customs are many and varied. They are also harsh, but occasionally quite praiseworthy. The populace must be fed like cattle and punished as one would a stubborn ass. Without severe punishment, the prince cannot put them to any useful purpose. If anyone in this land should presume to abuse a foreign matron and thereby commit fornication, the act is immediately avenged through the following punishment. The guilty party is led on to the market bridge, and his scrotum is affixed to it with a nail. Then, after a sharp knife has been placed next to him, he is given the harsh choice between death or castration. Furthermore, anyone found to have eaten meat after Septuagesima is severely punished, by having his teeth knocked out. The law of God, newly introduced in these regions, gains more strength from such acts of force than from any fast imposed by the bishops. There are also other customs, by far inferior to these, which please neither God nor the inhabitants, and are useful only as a means to inspire terror. To some extent, I have alluded to these above. I think that it is unnecessary for me to say any more about this man whose name and manner of life, if it please Almighty God, might better have remained concealed from us. That his father and he were joined to us, through marriage and great familiarity, has produced results so damaging that any good preceding them is far outweighed, and so it will remain in the future. During false periods of peace, Boleslaw may temporarily regard us with affection. Nevertheless, through all kinds of secret plots, he constantly attempts to sow dissension, diminish our inborn freedom, and, if time and place permit, rise up and destroy us.

8.3 In the days of his father,[3] when he still embraced heathenism, every woman followed her husband on to the funeral pyre, after first being decapitated. If a woman was found to be a prostitute, moreover, she suffered a particularly wretched and shameful penalty. The skin around her genitals was cut off and this 'foreskin', if we may call it that, was hung on the door so that anyone who entered would see it and be more concerned and prudent in the future. The law of the Lord declares that such a woman should be stoned, and the rules of our ancestors would require her beheading.[4] Nowadays, the freedom to sin dominates everywhere and to a degree that is not right or normal. And so it is not just a large number of frustrated girls who engage in adultery, having been driven by the desire of the flesh to harmful lust, but even some married women and, indeed, with their husbands still living. As if this were not enough, such women then have their husbands murdered by the adulterer, inspiring the deed through furtive hints. After this, having given a wicked example to others, they receive their lovers quite openly and sin at will. They repudiate their legal lord in a most horrible fashion and prefer his retainer, as if the latter were sweet Abro or mild Jason.[5] Nowadays, because a harsh penalty is not imposed, I fear that many will find this new custom more and more acceptable. O you priests of the Lord, forcefully rise up and let nothing stop you! Take a sharp ploughshare and extirpate this newly sprouted weed, down to the roots! You also, lay people, do not give aid to such as these! May those joined in Christ live innocently and, after these supplanters have been rooted out, forever groan in shame. Unless these sinners return to their senses, may our helper, Christ, destroy them with a powerful breath from his holy mouth and scatter them with the great splendor of his second coming.[6]

---

[1] This Oda was Boleslaw's fourth wife.

[2] Septuagesima was supposed to inaugurate a period of fasting before Easter and was therefore not an appropriate time to celebrate a marriage.

[3] I.e., in the days of Mieszko I.

[4] For the "law of the Lord," see John 8:5.

[5] Abro was a rich ancient Greek proverbially known for high living; Jason was the mythological leader of the Argonauts.

[6] For the image of the Lord slaying sinners with his breath, see 2 Thess. 2:8.

4.15 Poland's self-image: *Boleslaw's Coin* (992–1000).

Although we have few written sources from tenth-century Poland, we do have material sources, including this coin, which was issued by Boleslaw the Brave (r.992–1025) either right after 992, when he ousted his half brothers and ascended to rulership, or around the year 1000, when Emperor Otto III met Boleslaw at Gniezno and the city was established as an archbishopric. In the emperor's eyes, Boleslaw was subservient to Germany. But Boleslaw clearly had other ideas about himself. His coin shows him (on the obverse) in profile, like a Roman emperor. He wears a helmet with earflaps, cultivating a martial image. On the other side of the coin (reverse) is a cross, proclaiming his Christian religion, and the Latin inscription reads "Gnezdun civitas" (City of Gniezno), elevating the status of his chief city to a Christian center (whether or not the coin was struck after Gniezno was declared an archbishopric by Otto).

See Plate 2, "Reading through Looking," p. III, for a color reproduction of the coin.

1. Why is a coin a good way for a ruler to advertise himself?
2. Why did a Polish king consider a Roman emperor to be a good model for his own self image?

[From the collection of the National Museum in Kraków]

4.16 Kievan Rus': *The Russian Primary Chronicle* (c.1113, incorporating earlier materials). Original in Russian.

The Russian Primary Chronicle is one of the earliest sources that we have for Russian history. Composed *c.*1113 by an anonymous monk of the Crypt Monastery near Kiev, it was clearly tied to the history of the princes of Kiev. In the excerpt below, Kievan Prince Yaroslav the Wise (r.1019–1054) is portrayed as following the model of the Christian ruler, especially the Byzantine emperor, even to the point of naming the church that he founded "St. Sophia," after Hagia Sophia, the church built by Justinian at Constantinople. Russian dates counted the years from the time of the Creation, a system that followed the Byzantine dating system. In parentheses are the corresponding dates CE.

1. In what ways did Rus' imitate Byzantium?
2. In what ways was Rus' like Poland and Hungary, even though its Christianity did not come from Rome?

[Source: *The Russian Primary Chronicle: Laurentian Text*, trans. and ed. Samuel Hazzard Cross and Olgerd P. Sherbowitz-Wetzor (Cambridge, MA: Medieval Academy of America, 1953), pp. 136–38 (slightly modified).]

6544 (1036) Thereafter Yaroslav assumed the entire sovereignty, and was the sole ruler in the land of Rus'. Yaroslav went to Novgorod, where he set up his son Vladimir as prince, and appointed Zhidyata bishop.[1] At this time, a son was born to Yaroslav, and he named him Vyacheslav. While Yaroslav was still at Novgorod, news came to him that the Pechenegs were besieging Kiev.[2] He then collected a large army of Varangians[3] and Slavs, returned to Kiev, and entered his city. The Pechenegs were innumerable. Yaroslav made a sally from the city and marshaled his forces, placing the Varangians in the center, the men of Kiev on the right flank, and the men of Novgorod on the left. When they had taken position before the city, the Pechenegs advanced, and they met on the spot where the metropolitan church of St. Sophia now stands. At that time, as a matter of fact, there were fields outside the city. The combat was fierce, but toward evening Yaroslav with difficulty won the upper hand. The Pechenegs fled in various directions, but as they did not know in what quarter to flee, they were drowned, some in the Setoml',[4] some in other streams, while the remnant of them disappeared from that day to this. In the same year, Yaroslav imprisoned his brother Sudislav in Pskov because he had been slanderously accused.

6545 (1037). Yaroslav built the great citadel at Kiev, near which stands the Golden Gate. He founded also the metropolitan Church of St. Sophia, the Church of the Annunciation over the Golden Gate, and also the Monastery of St. George and the convent of St. Irene. During his reign, the Christian faith was fruitful and multiplied, while the number of monks increased, and new monasteries came into being. Yaroslav loved religious establishments and was devoted to priests, especially to monks. He applied himself to books, and read them continually day and night. He assembled many scribes, and translated from Greek into Slavic. He wrote and collected many books through which true believers are instructed and enjoy religious education. For as one man plows the land, and another sows, and still others reap and eat food in abundance, so did this prince. His father Vladimir[5] plowed and harrowed the soil when he enlightened Rus' through baptism, while this prince sowed the hearts of the faithful with the written word, and we in turn reap the harvest by receiving the teaching of books. For great is the profit from book-learning.

Through the medium of books, we are shown and taught the way of repentance, for we gain wisdom and continence from the written word. Books are like rivers that water the whole earth; they are the springs of wisdom. For books have an immeasurable depth; by them we are consoled in sorrow. They are the bridle of self-restraint. For great is wisdom. As Solomon said in its praise, "I (wisdom) have inculcated counsel; I have summoned reason and prudence. The fear of the Lord is the beginning of wisdom. Mine are counsel, wisdom, constancy, and strength. Through me kings rule, and the mighty decree justice. Through me are princes magnified and the oppressors possess the earth. I love them that love me, and they who seek me shall find grace."[6] If you seek wisdom attentively in books, you obtain great profit for your

---

[1] The first bishop of Novgorod died in 1030 after designating his successor. Yaroslav, however, insisted on Luka Zhidyata, who presided over the see from 1036 to 1055.

[2] The Pechenegs were a Turkic nomadic people who in the tenth century occupied the region between the Don and the Danube but, squeezed by other nomadic groups and the expanding Byzantines and Rus, raided into Rus' only to be repulsed by Yaroslav.

[3] The Varangians were the Scandinavian settlers of Rus'.

[4] The Setoml' was a small stream in Kiev.

[5] Saint Vladimir I (r.c.980–1015) converted to Christianity under the influence of Byzantine emperor Basil II, took the baptismal name of Basil, and married Basil's sister.

[6] Prov. 8:12, 13, 14–17.

spirit. He who reads books often converses with God or with holy men. If one possesses the words of the prophets, the teachings of the evangelists and the apostles, and the lives of the holy fathers, his soul will derive great profit therefrom. Thus Yaroslav, as we have said, was a lover of books, and as he wrote many, he deposited them in the Church of Saint Sophia which he himself had founded. He adorned it with gold and silver and churchly vessels, and in it the usual hymns are raised to God at the customary seasons. He founded other churches in the cities and districts, appointing priests and paying them out of his personal fortune. He bade them teach the people, since that is the duty which God has prescribed them, and to go often into the churches. Priests and Christian laymen thus increased in number. Yaroslav rejoiced to see the multitude of his churches and of his Christian subjects, but the devil was afflicted, since he was now conquered by this new Christian nation.

6546 (1038). Yaroslav attacked the Yatvingians.[1]
6547 (1039). The Church of the Blessed Virgin, which had been founded by Vladimir, Yaroslav's father, was consecrated by the Metropolitan Theopemptos.
6548 (1040). Yaroslav attacked Lithuania.
6549 (1041). Yaroslav attacked the Mazovians by boat.

NORTHERN EUROPE

4.17 An Ottonian courtier-bishop: Ruotger, *Life of Bruno, Archbishop of Cologne* (late 960s). Original in Latin.

Bruno (925–965) was the youngest of the three sons of King Henry I of Saxony (r.919–936). Destined from an early age for the Church, Bruno first studied in Utrecht, a city in the present-day Netherlands. In the tenth century Utrecht was part of Lotharingia, a turbulent territory that Henry occupied the year Bruno was born. In his teens, Bruno was summoned by his brother, Henry's successor Otto I (r.936–973), to be a member of the royal court. The court had no fixed capital; rather, the king and his entourage were constantly on the move. In effect, the king ruled on horseback! Bruno continued his studies as he met learned people across his brother's realm. At age twenty-eight, he became archbishop of Cologne, in Lotharingia, and a few months later Otto made him duke of Lotharingia, the highest civilian authority there, amidst a rebellion against Otto. Bruno served his brother as general and chief administrator of Lotharingia while he served the Church as archbishop of Cologne, pastor, and reformer, until his death at the age of forty.

By contrast, little is known about Bruno's biographer Ruotger. He was a monk in Cologne; from comments in the *Life of Bruno*, it is clear that he knew Bruno personally. Certainly, Ruotger was staggeringly learned, likely a member of Bruno's intellectual circle, and perhaps his student. Besides more than twenty biblical citations or echoes, the excerpts from the *Life of Bruno* below include allusions to eight pagan Roman authors, nine Latin Christian authors, mentions of the pagan Roman orator and statesman Cicero (106–43 BCE) and Christian Latin poet Prudentius (348–after 405), and a paraphrase of the Roman historian Sallust (86–35/34 BCE). Highly conscientious, Ruotger produced a reliable account of a prince who was unique: at one and the same time a courtier, a warrior, and an archbishop.

---

[1] The Yatvingians were a Lithuanian people. Attacks on them and on Lithuania and the Mazovians (below) were evidently designed both to protect the northwest flank of Rus' and to keep open access to eastern Poland, on which Yaroslav made claim.

1. What was the nature of Bruno's education and how did it compare with the education of a Muslim child described by al-Qabisi (above, p. 210)?
2. How did Ruotger justify the warlike activities of Bishop Bruno?

[Source: *Ruotgers Lebensbeschreibung des Erzbischofs Bruno von Köln* (*Ruotgeri Vita Brunonis Archiepiscopi Coloniensis*), ed. Irene Ott, Monumenta Germaniae Historica, Scriptores rerum Germanicarum, Nova series, 10 (Cologne: Böhlau-Verlag, 1958), pp. 3–4, 5–7, 11, 20–21, 23–24, 31–32, 33–34, 38–39, 55. Translated and introduced by Bruce L. Venarde.]

2. ... He was born in the time when his father, the glorious king Henry, was very zealously rebuilding what had been destroyed after he had quelled the ferocity of the barbarians and subdued the menace of civil strife.[1] Now at last Henry ruled a willing people with the reins of justice and, now at last, amidst a most secure and long-awaited peace. Thus the time of Bruno's birth already heralded, as it were, the future signs of his good will. For since he always approached every good thing very vigorously, he very carefully sought out the gift of peace as the nourishment and adornment of other virtues, because he knew it would benefit all good things. In tranquil times, virtues can be nourished and strengthened. Then in any disturbance, they will not allow a man to be weakened in the force of his power....

4. When he was about four years old, the noble progeny of kings was sent to Utrecht and to the venerable Bishop Baldric (who still survives) to be steeped in study of the liberal arts.[2] There, while he progressed as befits a boy of good character, with excellent discipline and according to a wise nature, at long last, as if by a considerable siege on the hateful tyranny of the Normans,[3] churches and other buildings of which scarcely ruins had survived were restored on this occasion.

Thus he passed through no stage of his life without benefit to the holy Church of God. Through him, although he did not know it yet, the Christian populace, freed from its enemies, rejoiced in the praise of God. When he had learned the first rudiments of grammar—as we often heard from him as he meditated on the glory of the almighty God—next he began to read the poet Prudentius as taught by his master.[4] Because Prudentius is catholic in faith and purpose, outstanding in eloquence and truth, and most elegant in the variety of his meters and his books, such sweetness was so immediately pleasing to the taste of Bruno's heart that he drank in with greater eagerness than can be described not only knowledge of the external words but also the marrow of inner meaning and its purest nectar, if I may put it that way.

After that there was nearly no type of liberal study in Greek or Latin that escaped the vitality of his genius. Never, which is unusual, did great riches or the abundance of clamoring crowds or the approach of any other bother turn his spirit from this noble leisure. Perpetual meditation and tireless eagerness for mental exercise testified to the purity of his heart, since already nearly all disposition of this sort became habit, as it is written: "A boy is known from his inclinations, if his behavior is pure and righteous" [Prov. 20:11]. It reached the point that just as he did not allow the fire of his soul to be put out by the idleness and frivolity of others nor be corrupted by empty and unnecessary conversation, he bore it very sorrowfully if the books he was studying or any that were in his sight were carelessly handled or creased or treated in any way with too little attention. Indeed, he considered that nothing that pertained to him should be neglected since indeed, as Solomon says, "He who neglects the small things dies little by little" [Eccles. 19:1].

---

[1] The "barbarians" are the Vikings, who had frequently raided Utrecht and its vicinity. A less partisan description of civil strife would emphasize the struggles King Henry had in establishing full authority in Lotharingia.

[2] Bishop Baldric of Utrecht, a relative of Bruno's mother, lived for several years after the composition of Ruotger's account; he was bishop from 918 to 975! Utrecht was a center of learning.

[3] I.e., the Vikings (Norsemen).

[4] The Spanish poet Prudentius was a highly placed imperial official who withdrew to the ascetic life in his forties. It was during this period that he wrote the Christian epics for which he was best known, including the *Psychomachia*, an allegory of the duels between personified virtues and vices.

5. After his father, Henry, who had founded and pacified his realm to the last detail, went the way of all flesh, his first-born son Otto, blessed by the Lord and anointed with the oil of happiness, with the full will and consent of his chief men began to reign in the 188th lustrum and the 63rd cycle of the indiction since the birth of our lord Jesus Christ.[1] Otto was a man on whom the spirit of God had conferred a gift of singular truthfulness and faithfulness. If I promised that I would catalogue his virtues, I would take too much on myself and be tolerated little, for praise and glory owed him exceed whatever eloquence Cicero himself might offer. Otto honorably called his brother Bruno, dedicated to God, still a youth but as if an equal, from the schools to his court, a place fitting for such a bright mirror where whatever was unseemly in almost the whole world showed itself more clearly through studies.[2] From all of Otto's borders came everything that seemed important. Likewise, all harassed by any accusation sought this sole refuge [Otto's court]. For there presided a model of wisdom, piety, and justice beyond human memory. Returning from the court, those who just before had seemed to themselves very learned, blushingly approached the rudiments of the liberal arts as if saying, "Now I begin." When nothing stirred on the left side of the breast, he thereafter modestly abstained from that high tribunal, so to speak.[3] The Lord filled this his vessel with the spirit of wisdom and thoughtfulness. It did not suffice to him to gather what he had ready at hand in the treasury of his own heart; he additionally considered foreign puzzles, and whatever philosophic matter he thought remote from earthly understanding he drew forth from wherever it came. He unveiled the seven liberal arts long forgotten. Whatever historians, orators, poets, and philosophers trumpeted was the great new thing he examined with great diligence along with teachers of whatever language it was in, and there where a master exceled in genius, he humbly offered himself as a student....

11. Then Wicfrid,[4] shepherd of the holy church of Cologne, for a long time quite feeble, yet faithful to the majesty of the kingdom and fatherland, at last returning his exhausted body to earth, was joined with heavenly spirits. The people, deprived of a shepherd, in grief chose for consolation, neither ambivalently nor wavering among candidates, the one solely hoped for: Lord Bruno, a splendid and most experienced man, following the counsel of great men and the whole clergy.[5] Youthful in body, he was mature in habits, humble and gentle despite the greatest nobility, at the height of his wisdom, which had taught him not to think himself wiser than is fitting to think, but wise in measure. Sparing of himself in his royal affluence, he was a rich man to his friends....

20. The emperor, disturbed about this event,[6] so sudden and unforeseen, and grieving more for the misery of its citizens than his own loss, lifted the siege of Mainz, having finally gotten the treaty he wanted. Turning from his camp toward the east along with those he knew to be loyal, Otto decided quickly to make a plan for the region he was leaving [i.e., Lotharingia] and made his brother [Bruno] the guardian and supervisor in the west, an archduke, so to speak, in such dangerous times. He gave him these orders. [The king said to Bruno,] "How much I rejoice, my dearest brother, that we have always understood matters as one and the same, and that it cannot be said we ever had different desires in any matter. It is the thing that greatly comforts me most of all in bitter times: I see royal priesthood, by the grace of almighty God, come into our kingdom. Both priestly religion and royal power are mighty in you, in that you know how to give everyone his due, which is justice, and you are able to withstand the dread and deceit of enemies, which is power and justice. For a long time now you have investigated the very mother of the liberal arts and truly its virtue, philosophy, which has trained you in modesty and greatness of spirit...."

---

[1] Ruotger's dating method, which derived from ancient Rome, refers only to a range of years. The precise date is July 2, 936.

[2] The summons was in 939 or 940, when Bruno was a teenager. Otto's itinerant court allowed Bruno to travel widely during the next dozen or so years. The unseemliness here apparently refers to poor Latin, since the rest of the paragraph focuses on Bruno's intellectual pursuits, as teacher and learner, while a member of his brother's entourage.

[3] The right side of the breast is the seat of wisdom; here Ruotger is paraphrasing the Latin poet Juvenal. The meaning appears to be that if a line of study did not seem fruitful for him, he left it to others.

[4] Archbishop of Cologne (r.924–953).

[5] Bruno became archbishop of Cologne in 953.

[6] Bruno was elected amidst a rebellion against Otto I led by his son Liudolf and Duke Conrad (duke since 944 and also Otto's son-in-law), as described in chapters 18 and 19, omitted here. Chapter 20 picks up with Otto besieging rebels in Mainz. Although Otto did not take the title of emperor until 962, Ruotger calls him such retrospectively.

23. Some people ignorant of divine will may object: why did a bishop assume public office and the dangers of war when he had undertaken only the care of souls? If they understand any sane matter, the result itself will easily satisfy them, when they see a great and very unaccustomed (especially in their homelands) gift of peace spread far and wide through this guardian and teacher of a faithful people, lest in this matter those objecting further stumble around in darkness where there is no light. Nor was governing this world new or unusual for rectors of the holy Church, previous examples of which, if someone needs them, are at hand. But we, moving on to other things, leave it to the judgment of each what he wants to say concerning this pious man, in the knowledge that nobody of sound mind would strive to blacken the most evident blessing with the curse of reproach. Everything that Bruno did was honorable and useful for our republic.[1] In his deeds he by no means had as object that by gaining favor, news of his actions should fly through the mouths of men, but rather he lived this way: he regulated all his works before men so that they would be a horror to the worst and a reward for the best. He made it clear to all that in the episcopate he sought a good work, in which he could not easily be censured by the hostile and jealous, but that it worked even more to his credit that he displeased such people. Therefore, engaged in this wonderful occupation, the ever watchful manager of the highest head of the household and chief priest, bearing in his hands a burning lamp, namely an example of good work, he led some willing and dragged others unwilling to the ways of God....

31. Bruno gathered from everywhere the bodies of the saints and relics and other kinds of monuments in order to increase protection for his people and by means of this glory spread the glory of the Lord among peoples near and far. He arranged places and service for them very copiously, at great expense and in great sumptuousness, concerning each of which many things could be said if my promised brevity would allow it. These are signs of invincible faith, through which he sought not what was his but what was Jesus Christ's. Everyone knows with what care, fervor, and joy he brought the staff and chain of St. Peter to Cologne, the former from Metz and the latter from Rome. In honor of St. Peter, he wondrously expanded his most honorable house, which he changed from beautiful to very beautiful.[2] ...

33. Meanwhile, in many places in the parishes of his diocese, this faithful and wise servant of the Lord built churches, monasteries and other buildings suited for the service of his one lord God and in honor of God's saints. Certain other structures already founded he enlarged and others long ruined he restored. With the foreseeing skill of his nature, he placed in each one those who would serve almighty God by the rule of canonical life, and in so doing generously provided for them, lest anything be lacking to carry out this way of life.[3] The memorials of his work and most salutary zeal, lasting as the air, remain fixed in place where he put them, so that for the praise and glory of Jesus Christ the memory of such a great man never suffer a time of obscurity. He poured out the same effort for foreign people; in the kingdom entrusted to his wisdom he provided sometimes by example, sometimes through his works, sometimes through qualities in other people and in repeated exhortation.[4] He did not allow any of his people to be occupied in vain or be inactive in lazy leisure, specifying, as he often said, that a lazy beast ought to be blocked from the trough and that according to the apostle [Paul], he who does not work does not eat [see 2 Thess. 3:10]. All the good things he did, taught, and loved cannot be written out one by one. So much material would remain for those attending to it that they would quickly leave off in exhaustion before finishing what they had undertaken. In preaching the word of God and in the subtlety of his debates concerning the truth of the scriptures, we can marvel at such and so great a man, but we cannot sum him up....

37. The merciful shepherd Bruno, champion of truth, sower of the Gospel, with the greatest care sought out zealous and diligent men who would keep watch over the republic, in loyalty and strength, each in his own place. He took great care that neither advice nor resources would be lacking to them. At Bruno's most beneficial urgings, all the princes and regional chiefs and others who had to do with the interests of the kingdom agreed to treaties in full

---

[1] Ruotger does not distinguish between kingdom and republic, which in the Roman tradition he knew so well meant simply "public sphere."

[2] That is, the cathedral of Cologne, which was dedicated to St. Peter. The chain was from Peter's imprisonment in Rome before his execution.

[3] The canonical rule was *The Benedictine Rule*, for which see p. 20.

[4] Bruno's rebuilding, reforming, and evangelizing efforts, then, went beyond his diocese and into other parts of Lotharingia.

faith for the common good of the property of all people. He considered them among the highest men and his intimates, and especially won over his brother the emperor to them, thinking—not foolishly—about a maxim of a wise man: "A good man gets slower when you ignore him, but a bad one is made more wicked." He cherished above all with great honor Archbishop Henry of Trier, a man of great merit and the highest integrity, who succeeded the great prelate Ruotbert, who died during a serious epidemic at Cologne when the emperor, too, was there; and also William of Mainz, an archbishop of most brilliant and agreeable excellence, Bruno's nephew and successor to Frederick: both of them outstanding men, both wholly trained in the Lord's law, both closely connected in friendship, the one through blood relation to the emperor, the other for his integrity.[1] Bruno often turned for advice to these two very illustrious men, so wise and religious and learned in all the good arts, lest he alone chance to stray anywhere off the path of truth, as is the way in human affairs. We saw them together with him not only in reading, counsel, and debate, but even in the line of battle, caring for good not only before God but before men. For there was in the western parts of Lotharingia a nearly untamable barbarism, which seemed a race of the church, begrudging the salvation of others no less than their own, scornful of gentle paternal admonition, nearly without fear of power.[2] Had they been allowed their own judgment, they would have seemed evil to their own and the worst thing for themselves. Bruno before all things practiced a forethoughtful way of governing, so that according to the nature of times and places, he pondered the rule of our very wise emperor in the elevation of shepherds for the peace and harmony of the Lord's flock.[3] He preferred those who understood several matters fully: a shepherd's duty, the vice of hirelings, the taking up of ministry, and what should be done or hoped for in this service. Some, like richly dyed curtains, would adorn the interiors of the Lord's house and others, like hair shirts, would guard against the violence of external storms....

49. [A lament for the now deceased Bruno]

Hearts, pour out prayers, send forth tearful words
Behold the father of his fatherland shut up in stone.
Royal stock to be remembered in all lands,
Bruno the peacemaker, a good and pious man.
Archbishop whose seat was famed Cologne,
He seemed dear to all good people everywhere.
His long-lasting light struck out against foul darkness.
The envious tongue falls silent; only true praise
    satisfies.
This world was not worthy of so rare a gift:
Taken from this world's shortcomings, he now rejoices
    in the company of the Lord.
On the ides of October in his twelfth year as bishop[4]
He gave up this life, hope his loving companion.

4.18 Law: King Æthelred II, *Law Code* (1008). Original in Old English.

Written law codes were, among other things, a way for early medieval kings to signal that their realms were part of the "Roman" tradition. That is why *The Theodosian Code* (see above, p. 4) was of enduring importance. Although these codes were drawn up to seem timeless, they were very much products of local conditions and circumstances. Æthelred II the Unready's reign (978–1016) was beset by Viking invasions (see *The Anglo-Saxon Chronicle* below, p. 233) and internal feuds. The nickname "Unready" came from the

---

[1] Cologne, Trier, and Mainz were the seats of the three archbishops of Lotharingia. Ruotbert was Bruno and Otto's uncle, and William was the natural son of Otto and thus Bruno's nephew. Frederick was archbishop of Mainz from 937 to 954, not unstintingly loyal to Otto, which explains why Otto's son succeeded him.

[2] That is, they were nominally Christians but so savage and destructive to themselves and others as to be Christians in name only.

[3] This sentence refers to Bruno's consultation with Otto about the appointment of bishops in the cities of western Lotharingia.

[4] I.e., October 15, 965.

Anglo-Saxon word *unræd*, meaning "no-counsel." Despite the disorder, Æthelred's code was, as it says, issued with the approval of his "ecclesiastical and lay councilors." In fact, one of those councilors was the most distinguished churchman of his age, Archbishop Wulfstan of York (r.1002–1023), whose handwriting may be detected in several of the entries in the manuscripts of this code. Inspired by Roman legal models, this law code was written up in two languages: Latin and Old English (or Anglo-Saxon). This, too reflected local conditions: on the Continent, such codes were written only in Latin, but in the British Isles, the spoken language had prestige as well.

1. What evidence can you find in this code of military crisis?
2. What concerns were common to both Æthelred's code and the roughly contemporary law code of King Stephen of Hungary (above, p. 213)?

[Source: *English Historical Documents*, vol. 1: *c.*500–1042, ed. Dorothy Whitelock, 2nd ed. (London: Routledge, 1979), pp. 442–46 (slightly modified).]

PROLOGUE. This is the ordinance which the king of the English and both ecclesiastical and lay councilors have approved and decreed.

1. First, namely, that we all shall love and honor one God and zealously hold one Christian faith and entirely cast off every heathen practice; and we all have confirmed both with word and with pledge that we will hold one Christian faith under the rule of one king.

1.1. And it is the decree of our lord and his councilors that just practices be established and all illegal practices abolished, and that every man is to be permitted the benefit of law;

1.2. and that peace and friendship are to be rightly maintained in both religious and secular concerns within this country.

2. And it is the decree of our lord and his councilors that no Christian and innocent men are to be sold out of the country, and especially not among the heathen people, but care is earnestly to be taken that those souls be not destroyed which God bought with his own life.

3. And it is the decree of our lord and his councilors that Christian men are not to be condemned to death for all too small offences.

3.1. But otherwise life-sparing punishments are to be devised for the benefit of the people, and God's handiwork and his own purchase which he paid for so dearly is not to be destroyed for small offences.

4. And it is the decree of our lord and his councilors that men of every order are each to submit willingly to that duty which befits them both in religious and secular concerns.

4.1 And especially God's servants—bishops and abbots, monks and nuns, priests and women dedicated to God—are to submit to their duty and to live according to their rule and to intercede zealously for all Christian people.

5. And it is the decree of our lord and his councilors that every monk who is out of his monastery and not heeding his rule, is to do what behooves him: return readily into the monastery with all humility, and cease from evil-doing and atone very zealously for what he has done amiss; let him consider the word and pledge which he gave to God.

6. And that monk who has no monastery is to come to the bishop of the diocese, and pledge himself to God and men that from that time on he will at least observe three things, namely his chastity, and monastic garb, and serve his Lord as well as ever he can.

6.1. And if he keeps that, he is then entitled to the greater respect, no matter where he dwells.

7. And canons,[1] where there is property such that they can have a refectory and dormitory, are to hold their minster [church] with right observance and with chastity, as their rule directs; otherwise it is right that he who will not do that shall forfeit the property.

---

[1] Canons here refer to priests who live together in common.

8. And we pray and instruct all mass-priests to protect themselves from God's anger.

9. They know full well that they may not rightly have sexual intercourse with a woman.

9.1. And whoever will abstain from this and preserve chastity, may he have God's mercy and in addition as a secular dignity, that he shall be entitled to a thegn's wer-gild and a thegn's rights, in life as well as in the grave.[1]

9.2. And he who will not do what belongs to his order, may his dignity be diminished both in religious and secular concerns.

10. And also every Christian man is zealously to avoid illegal intercourse, and duly keep the laws of the Church.[2]

10.1. And every church is to be under the protection of God and of the king and of all Christian people.

10.2. And no man henceforth is to bring a church under subjection, nor illegally to traffic with a church,[3] nor to expel a minister of the church without the bishop's consent.

11. And God's dues are to be readily paid every year.

11.1. Namely, plough-alms 15 days after Easter, and the tithe of young animals by Pentecost, and of the fruits of the earth by All Saints' Day, and "Rome money" by St. Peter's day and light-dues three times a year.[4]

12. And it is best that payment for the soul be always paid at the open grave.

12.1. And if anybody is buried elsewhere, outside the proper parish, the payment for the soul is nevertheless to be paid to the minster to which it belonged.

12.2. And all God's dues are to be furthered zealously, as is needful.

12.3. And festivals and fasts are to be properly observed.

13. The Sunday festival is to be diligently observed, as befits it.

13.1. And one is readily to abstain from markets and public meetings on the holy day.

14. And all the festivals of St. Mary are to be diligently observed, first with a fast and afterwards with a festival.

14.1. And at the festival of every Apostle there is to be fasting and festivity, except that we enjoin no fast for the festival of St. Philip and St. James, because of the Easter festival.

15. Otherwise other festivals and fasts are to be kept diligently just as those kept them who kept them best.

16. And the councilors have decreed that St. Edward's festival is to be celebrated over all England on March 18th.[5]

17. And there is to be a fast every Friday, except when it is a feast day.

18. And ordeals and oaths are forbidden on feast days and the legal Ember days, and from the Advent of the Lord until the octave of Epiphany, and from Septuagesima [Lent] until 15 days after Easter.

19. And at these holy seasons, as it is right, there is to be peace and unity among all Christian men, and every suit is to be laid aside.

20. And if anyone owes another a debt or compensation concerning secular matters, he is to pay it readily before or after [these seasons].

21. And every widow who conducts herself rightly is to be under the protection of God and the king.

21.1. And each [widow] is to remain unmarried for twelve months; she is afterwards to choose what she herself will.

22. And every Christian man is to do what is needful for him, heed zealously his Christian duties, form the habit

---

[1] The wergild was the price of compensation, which varied with the status of the victim. Thegns were noblemen, and they had the high wergild of 1200 shillings.

[2] This provision involves not marrying within six degrees of relationship, or with the widow of so near a kinsman, or a close relative of a previous wife, or a nun, or anyone related by spiritual affinity, or a deserted woman.

[3] This refers to buying an ecclesiastical office or bartering a church.

[4] "Rome money" refers to Peter's Pence, dues sent to Rome to support the papacy. "Light-dues" were revenues to pay for church candles.

[5] St. Edward was the martyred King Edward (r.975–978), the brother of Æthelred.

of frequent confession, and freely confess his sins and willingly atone for them as he is directed.

22.1. And everyone is to prepare himself often and frequently for going to communion;

22.2. and to order words and deeds rightly and keep carefully oath and pledge....

34. We must all love and honor one God and entirely cast out every heathen practice.

35. And let us loyally support one royal lord, and all together defend our lives and our land, as well as ever we can, and pray Almighty God from our inmost heart for his help.

....

4.19 Christianity comes to Denmark: *The Jelling Monument* (960s).

The Jelling Monument is a large boulder with writing and carvings on it. It is important for understanding how Christianity became incorporated into the networks of power and prestige in Scandinavia.

Powerful people with great resources had long lived in Jelling, close to what is today Vejle, on the Jutland peninsula. During the Bronze Age, before 500 BCE, they built an earthen mound, and, just south of the mound, they lined up several large standing stones to suggest the outline of a ship.

In 958 the Viking king Gorm died at Jelling. His son Harald Bluetooth buried his father in the old mound, adding more soil to make it taller. He also constructed another mound a short distance to the south, in the process destroying the "ship." The construction of mounds was a newly resuscitated custom in the tenth century. It was a self-conscious appeal to old traditions in the face of Christian practices spreading from Denmark's southern neighbors, the Germans. Accompanying Gorm in his tomb were a horse, riding gear, an elegant silver cup, a chest, a small wooden cross, and other artifacts. A powerful man or woman was not to arrive in the afterlife without suitable equipment. This was entirely the opposite of Christian traditions, which by the tenth century prohibited burying goods with bodies: the Christian afterlife was supposed to be immaterial.

Harald took over his father Gorm's kingdom. Then, in the 960s, he became a Christian. The reminders in Jelling of his pagan past, including his father, became an embarrassment, so Harald built a large wooden church close to the northern mound. He dug up the body of his father and moved him to an honored place in the middle of the church, thus posthumously Christianizing Gorm. The centerpiece of the new Christian compound was a piece of art, a large granite boulder situated exactly at the midpoint between the two mounds— the "Jelling Monument." Harald had the boulder inscribed on three sides with large pictures and a text in runic characters, a special alphabet. When they were new, the pictures and the text would have been painted in bright colors. The stone proudly proclaimed that this was a Christian site. One side depicts a great rampant animal (a dragon? a lion?) entwined by a snake. Another side (see photo) portrays Christ crucified. Remarkably, the cross itself is lacking. Instead, interlacing bands surround Christ.

The inscription reads: "King Harald had this monument made in memory of his father Gorm and in memory of his mother Thyre; that Harald who won for himself all of Denmark and Norway and made the Danes Christian." The last words are visible under the figure of Christ.

Thousands of runestones still dot the landscape of Scandinavia, most put up in the eleventh century, when the majority of the population had converted to Christianity. The text of these runestones was usually along the lines of the formula of Jelling: "X had this stone made/raised in memory of Y, his/her mother/father/brother/companion-at-arms." Many stones added "God save his (or her) soul," and others had crosses.

These inscriptions may appear to be selfless acts of remembrance of loved ones, but they served at least as much to remind all who passed of the power and wealth of the sponsor of the inscription, the person who was able to afford such a great monument. Certainly, Harald did not hide behind any false humility; he forthrightly included his name twice to drive the point home. Harald, no one else, was the powerful conqueror and the religious benefactor of those he conquered. In this he appeared both as a traditional Viking warlord and as a good Christian ruler.

The Jelling compound was part of Harald's efforts to consolidate his power, which also included the construction of forts all over his kingdom. It did not help. His son Svein Forkbeard rebelled against him in 986 or 987. Harald had to go into exile, where he soon died. The tomb that he had reserved for himself in the church next to his father Gorm is still empty.

See Plate 3a, "Reading through Looking," p. IV, for a color photo of *The Jelling Monument* today and Plate 3b, p. V, as it was probably painted originally.

1. In what ways does this monument suggest how Christianity was—and was not—compatible with pre-Christian forms of kingship?
2. Why, do you suppose, interlace was used in place of the cross?

[Caption by Anders Winroth. Image courtesy of the Nationalmuseet, Denmark]

4.20 The Vikings as enemies: *The Anglo-Saxon Chronicle* (*c.*1048?). Original in Anglo-Saxon.

There are many versions of the *Anglo-Saxon Chronicle*, each taking up the history of England year by year (or nearly), each written in the vernacular (Anglo-Saxon, or Old English), and each treating events from its own point of view. The first version probably took shape in the ninth century under King Alfred the Great (r.871–899); it was circulated and copied during Alfred's reign, and various centers of manuscript production added to it. Different as the versions are, all focus on the Viking invasions and their effects. The version excerpted here, from the so-called C manuscript, was produced either at Abingdon, a monastery in southern England, or, even more likely, at Christ Church, Canterbury, an archbishopric in the same region but about 130 miles southeast of Abingdon. Seven eleventh-century scribes worked on the C manuscript, beginning their account with the year 60 BCE and ending with 1066 CE. One scribe wrote the bulk of it, however, beginning with 491 and ending with 1048. The passages here are concerned with a few years during the reign of Æthelred II (r.978–1016), for whose *Law Code*, see above p. 228. Many of the places named are in southern England (see Map 4.1), which may reflect the concerns of the chronicler.

1. How did the English respond to the Viking attacks?
2. Are there any heroes in this section of the *Chronicle*?

[Source: Margaret Ashdown, ed. and trans., *English and Norse Documents Relating to the Reign of Ethelred the Unready* (Cambridge: Cambridge University Press, 1930), pp. 45–47 (notes added).]

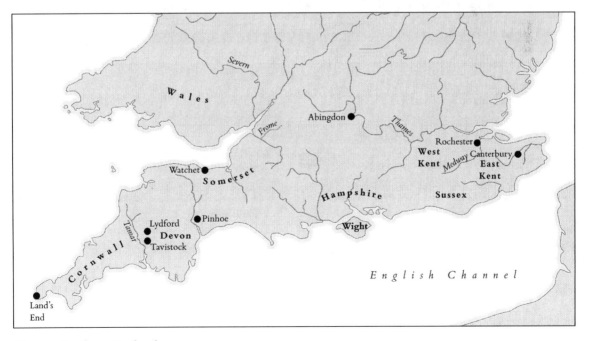

Map 4.1 Southern England

996. In this year Ælfric was consecrated Archbishop at Christ Church [Canterbury].

997. In this year the enemy host[1] went round Devonshire [Devon] into the mouth of the Severn, and harried round about, in Cornwall, Wales and Devon, and went ashore at Watchet, and wrought great havoc in burning and in the slaughter of men, and after that went back round Land's End to the southern side, and entered the mouth of the Tamar and so up until they came to Lydford. There they burned and slew all that they met, and Ordulf's monastery at Tavistock they burned to the ground, and took an indescribable amount of booty with them to the ships.

998. In this year the enemy host turned eastward again, and into the mouth of the Frome, and pushed up into Dorset in whatever direction they pleased. Many a time an army was assembled to oppose them, but as soon as they were to join battle, always for some cause it was agreed to disperse, and always in the end they [the Vikings] had the victory. Then for another period they took up their quarters in Wight, and drew their supplies from Hampshire and Sussex.

999. In this year the host again came round into the Thames, and so up the Medway to Rochester. Then the Kentish levies came against them, and a sharp encounter took place. But alas! all too quickly they turned and fled! And the Danes held the field, and then got horses and rode far and wide in whichever direction they would, and ravaged and laid waste almost the whole of West Kent. Then the king decided with his counsellors to advance against the host with both a naval and a land force, but when the ships were ready, there was delay from one day to another, causing distress to the unhappy folk who were stationed on the ships, and, time after time, the more urgent a thing was the more it was behindhand, and all the while they were allowing the enemy forces to increase, and all the while they were retreating from the sea, with the enemy following in their tracks. And then in the end this naval and land campaign effected nothing, except the afflicting of the people, waste of money and the encouragement of their enemies.

1000. In this year the king marched into Cumberland,[2] and laid waste very nearly the whole of it. And his ships went round by Chester and should have come to meet him, but were not able. Then they ravaged Man. The enemy fleet had gone during the summer over to Richard's realm.[3]

1001. In this year the enemy host came to the mouth of the Exe, and so up to the town, and attacked it stubbornly, but they were met with a fierce defense. Then they went about the land, and did just as their wont was, slaying and burning. Then an immense army was assembled of the people of Devon and Somerset, and they joined battle at Pinhoe, and as soon as they met, the home force drew back, and they (the enemy) caused great loss of life, and then went riding over the land, and each inroad was worse than the last, and they took much booty with them to their ships. Thence they made for Wight and there went about at will in any direction and nothing stopped them. Neither fleet by sea nor land force dared approach them, went they never so far inland. Then was it lamentable in every way, for they never ceased from their evil deeds.

1002. In this year the king and his counsellors decided that tribute should be paid to the fleet and peace made, on condition that they should cease from their evil deeds. Then the king sent Ealdorman Leofsige to the fleet, and he, in accordance with the word of the king and his counsellors, arranged a truce with them, and that they should receive maintenance and tribute. This they accepted, and were paid twenty-four thousand pounds. Then in the midst of these events Ealdorman Leofsige slew Æfic, the king's reeve, and the king banished him from the realm. In the same spring landed the Lady, Richard's daughter, and in the summer of the same year died Archbishop Ealdulf, and in this year the king gave orders for all Danish men who were in England to be slain. This was done on the festival of (Saint) Brice [November 13th]. The reason was that it was told the king that they meant to entrap and slay him, and all his counsellors after him, and then possess this realm.

---

[1]   The Vikings from Denmark.

[2]   All the places in this paragraph are located to the north and are therefore not on Map 4.1.

[3]   King Æthelred was at war with "Cumberland," that is, the kingdom of Strathclyde. "Richard's realm": Richard II (r.996–1026) was the duke of Normandy.

4.21 The Vikings as heroes: *Egil's Saga* (10th cent./13th cent.). Original in Old Norse.

Egil's Saga was written down in Iceland in the thirteenth century, long after the Scandinavian world had been Christianized and brought into the European orbit. But it drew on stories and poetry that its hero, Egil Skallagrimsson (*c.*910–990) composed in the tenth century; these tales remained alive through oral performance. *Egil's Saga* praises the exploits of its hero, and since its hero was a Viking, it provides a very different "take" on the sorts of attacks that *The Anglo-Saxon Chronicle* (above, p. 233) deplored. Indeed, the *Saga* reveals many of the motivations and values of Viking culture. While there were no kings of Iceland in the tenth century, the kings of Norway and other strong men dominated Iceland's thirteenth-century history. The written form of the *Saga* celebrates a long-lost past, when powerful farmer chieftains were fiercely independent and zealous about their honor. The excerpt here begins with Kveldulf, Egil's grandfather, who resists the demands of King Harald Fairhair (r.*c.*858–*c.*930; king of a unified Norway from the mid-870s).

1. What constituted male honor in the world of *Egil's Saga*?
2. What roles did kings have in the *Saga*?

[Source: *Egil's Saga*, trans. Bernard Scudder, ed. and notes by Svanhildur Óskarsdóttir (London: Penguin, 1997, 2004), pp. 3–5, 7–8, 52–56, 67–69, 88–89 (some notes added, some modified).]

1. Kveldulf and his wife had two sons. The elder one was named Thorolf and the younger one Grim, and they both grew up to be big, strong men like their father. Thorolf was an attractive and highly accomplished man. He took after his mother's side of the family, a cheerful, generous man, energetic and very eager to prove his worth. He was popular with everyone. Grim was swarthy and ugly, resembling his father in both appearance and character. He turned out to be an active man; he was gifted at working in wood and iron, and grew to be a great craftsman. In winter he would often set off on a fishing boat to lay nets for herring, taking many farmhands with him.

When Thorolf was twenty, he made ready to go raiding, and Kveldulf gave him a longship. Kari's sons Eyvind and Olvir joined him, with a large band of men and another longship.[1] In the summer they went raiding and took plenty of booty which they shared out among themselves. They went raiding for several summers, spending the winters at home with their fathers. Thorolf brought many precious things back to give to his parents, for in those days it was easy to win both wealth and renown. Kveldulf was very old by then, and his sons had reached full manhood.

3. King Harald inherited the titles of his father Halfdan the Black and swore an oath not to cut or comb his hair until he had become sole king of Norway. He was called Harald Tangle-hair.[2] He did battle with the neighboring kings and defeated them, as is told in long accounts. Afterwards he took over Oppland, and proceeded northwards to Trondheim where he fought many battles before gaining full control of all Trondheim district.

After that he intended to go north to Naumdal and take on the brothers Herlaug and Hrollaug, who were kings there, but when they heard that he was on his way, Herlaug and eleven of his men went into the [funeral] mound they had spent the past three years building, and had it closed upon them. Hrollaug tumbled from power and took the title of earl instead, then submitted to Harald and handed over his kingdom. King Harald

---

[1] Kari was a long-time companion of Kveldulf; when young, they went raiding together.

[2] A reference to Harald's oath to his betrothed, Bytha, that he would not have his hair cut until he had subdued all of Norway. Once Harald became sole ruler of Norway, he was known as Harald Fairhair.

thereby took over Naumdal province and Halogaland and appointed men to govern there in his name.

4. Once King Harald had taken over the kingdoms he had recently won, he kept a close watch on the landholders and powerful farmers and everyone else he suspected would be likely to rebel, and gave them the options of entering his service or leaving the country, or a third choice of suffering hardship or paying with their lives; some had their arms and legs maimed. In each province King Harald took over all the estates and all the land, habited or uninhabited, and even the sea and lakes. All the farmers were made his tenants, and everyone who worked the forests and dried salt, or hunted on land or at sea, was made to pay tribute to him.

Many people fled the country to escape this tyranny and settled various uninhabited parts of many places, to the east in Jamtland and Halsingland, and to the west in the Hebrides, the shire of Dublin, Ireland, Normandy in France, Caithness in Scotland, the Orkney Isles and Shetland Isles, and the Faroe Islands. And at this time, Iceland was discovered.

5. King Harald stayed with his army in Fjordane, and sent out messengers through the countryside to meet the people that he felt he had reason to contact but who had not joined him.

The king's messengers went to Kveldulf's and received a warm welcome.

They told him their business, saying that the king wanted Kveldulf to go to see him: "He has heard that you are a man of high birth and standing," they said. "You have the chance to receive great honor from the king, because he is eager to be joined by people who are renowned for their strength of body and heart."

Kveldulf replied that he was too old for going on fighting ships: "So I will stay at home now and give up serving kings."

"Then let your son go to see the king," the messenger said. "He's a big and brave man. The king will make you a landholder if you serve him."

"I don't want to be a landholder while my father is still alive," Grim said, "because he is my superior for as long as he lives."

The messengers departed, and when they reached the king they told him everything Kveldulf had said to them. The king grew surly, remarking that these must be arrogant people, and he could not tell what their motivation was.

[King Harald reconciled with Kveldulf because Thorolf offered him his service. Thorolf became very rich in land, men, and goods as tax collector for the king. He paid rich tribute to the king in return. But Thorolf's enemies slandered him to the king, who came to suspect him of treason. He seized some of Thorolf's land, reassigned the tax collection to others, and ultimately ran him through with a sword. The king then had a falling out with Thorolf's brother, Grim, now called Skallagrim. Kveldulf, Skallagrim and his wife, Bera, fled to Iceland along with many ships and all their dependents, including men, women, and children. Kveldulf died on the journey.]

30. King Harald Fairhair confiscated all the lands left behind in Norway by Kveldulf and Skallagrim and any other possessions of theirs he could come by. He also searched for everyone who had been in league with Skallagrim and his men, or had even been implicated with them or had helped them in all the deeds they did before Skallagrim left the country. The king's animosity towards Kveldulf and his son grew so fierce that he hated all their relatives or others close to them, or anyone he knew had been fairly close friends. He dealt out punishment to some of them, and many fled to seek sanctuary elsewhere in Norway, or left the country completely.

Yngvar, Skallagrim's father-in-law, was one of these people. He opted to sell all the belongings he could, procure an oceangoing vessel, man it and sail to Iceland, where he had heard that Skallagrim had settled and had plenty of land available. When his crew were ready to sail and a favorable wind got up, he sailed out to the open sea and had a smooth crossing. He approached Iceland from the south and sailed into Borgarfjord and entered the river Langa, all the way to the waterfall, where they unloaded the ship.

Hearing of Yngvar's arrival, Skallagrim went straight to meet him and invited him to stay with him, along with as many of his party as he desired. Yngvar accepted the offer, beached his ship and went to Borg with his men to spend the winter with Skallagrim. In the spring, Skallagrim offered him land, giving him the farm he owned at Alftanes and the land as far inland as the brook at Leirulaek and along the coast to Straumfjord. Yngvar went to that outlying farm and took it over, and turned out to be a highly capable man, and grew wealthy. Then Skallagrim set up a farm in Knarrarnes which he ran for a long time afterwards.

Skallagrim was a great blacksmith and worked large amounts of bog-iron during the winter. He had a forge built by the sea a long way off from Borg, at the place called Raufarnes, where he did not think the woods were too far away.[1] But since he could not find any stone suitably hard or smooth to forge iron against—because there was nothing but pebbles there, and small sands along the shore—Skallagrim put out to sea one evening in one of his eight-oared boats, when everyone else had gone to bed, and rowed out to the Midfjord islands. There he cast his stone anchor off the prow of his boat, stepped overboard, dived and brought up a rock which he put into his boat. Then he climbed into the boat, rowed ashore, carried the rock to his forge, put it down by the door and always forged his iron on it. That rock is still there with a pile of slag beside it, and its top is marked from being hammered upon. It has been worn by waves and is different from the other rocks there; four men today could not lift it.

Skallagrim worked zealously in his forge, but his farmhands complained about having to get up so early. It was then that Skallagrim made this verse:

The wielder of iron must rise
early to earn wealth from his bellows,
from that sack that sucks in
the sea's brother, the wind.
I let my hammer ring down
on precious metal of fire,
the hot iron, while the bag
wheezes greedy for wind.

31. Skallagrim and Bera had many children, but the first ones all died. Then they had a son who was sprinkled with water and given the name Thorolf.[2] He was big and handsome from an early age, and everyone said he closely resembled Kveldulf's son Thorolf, after whom he had been named. Thorolf far excelled boys of his age in strength, and when he grew up he became accomplished in most of the skills that it was customary for gifted men to practise. He was a cheerful character and so powerful in his youth that he was considered just as able-bodied as any grown man. He was popular with everyone, and his father and mother were very fond of him.

Skallagrim and Bera had two daughters, Saeunn and Thorunn, who were also promising children.

Skallagrim and his wife had another son who was sprinkled with water and named Egil. As he grew up, it soon became clear he would turn out very ugly and resemble his father, with black hair. When he was three years old, he was as big and strong as a boy of six or seven. He became talkative at an early age and had a gift for words, but tended to be difficult to deal with in his games with other children.

That spring Yngvar visited Borg to invite Skallagrim out to a feast at his farm, saying that his daughter Bera and her son Thorolf should join them as well, together with anyone else that she and Skallagrim wanted to bring along. Once Skallagrim had promised to go, Yngvar returned home to prepare the feast and brew the ale.

When the time came for Skallagrim and Bera to go to the feast, Thorolf and the farmhands got ready as well; there were fifteen in the party in all.

Egil told his father that he wanted to go with them.

"They're just as much my relatives as Thorolf's," he said.

"You're not going," said Skallagrim, "because you don't know how to behave where there's heavy drinking. You're enough trouble when you're sober."

So Skallagrim mounted his horse and rode away, leaving Egil behind disgruntled. Egil went out of the farmyard and found one of Skallagrim's pack-horses, mounted it and rode after them. He had trouble negotiating the marshland because he was unfamiliar with the way, but he could often see where Skallagrim and the others were riding when the view was not obscured by knolls or trees. His journey ended late in the evening when he arrived at Alftanes. Everyone was sitting around drinking when he entered the room. When Yngvar saw Egil he welcomed him and asked why he had come so late. Egil told him about his conversation with his father. Yngvar seated Egil beside him, facing Skallagrim and Thorolf. All the men were entertaining themselves by making up verses while they were drinking the ale. Then Egil spoke this verse:

I have come in fine fettle to the hearth
of Yngvar, who gives men gold from the glowing
curled serpent's bed of heather;[3]

I was eager to meet him.

---

[1] Bog-iron was a precious resource in the Viking Age. Found in peat bogs with mountain streams, it was used to make weapons and tools. Charcoal is used in the smelting process, explaining Skallagrim's decision to move the forge closer to woodland.

[2] Baptism with water is a detail that would make sense only after the Viking period.

[3] This is a reference to a hoard of treasure guarded by a mythical serpent.

Shedder of gold rings bright and twisted
from the serpent's realm, you'll never
find a better craftsman of poems
three winters old than me.

Yngvar repeated the verse and thanked Egil for it. The next day Yngvar rewarded Egil for his verse by giving him three shells and a duck's egg. While they were drinking that day, Egil recited another verse, about the reward for his poem:

The skillful hardener of weapons[1]
that peck wounds gave eloquent
Egil in reward three shells
that rear up ever-silent in the surf.
That upright horseman of the field
where ships race knew how to please Egil;
he gave him a fourth gift,
the brook-warbler's favorite bed.

Egil's poetry was widely acclaimed. Nothing else of note happened during that journey, and Egil went home with Skallagrim.

40. Skallagrim took a great delight in trials of strength and games, and liked talking about them. Ball games were common in those days, and there were plenty of strong men in the district at this time. None of them could match Skallagrim in strength, even though he was fairly advanced in age by then.

Thord, Grani's son from Granastadir, was a promising young man, and was very fond of Egil Skallagrimsson. Egil was a keen wrestler; he was impetuous and quick-tempered, and everyone was aware that they had to teach their sons to give in to him.

A ball game was arranged early in winter on the plains by the river Hvita, and crowds of people came to it from all over the district. Many of Skallagrim's men attended, and Thord Granason was their leader. Egil asked Thord if he could go to the game with him; he was in his seventh year then. Thord let him, and seated Egil behind him when he rode there.

When they reached the games meeting, the players were divided up into teams. A lot of small boys were there as well, and they formed teams to play their own games.

Egil was paired against a boy called Grim, the son of Hegg from Heggsstadir. Grim was ten or eleven years old, and strong for his age. When they started playing the game, Egil proved to be weaker than Grim, who showed off his strength as much as he could. Egil lost his temper, wielded the bat and struck Grim, who seized him and dashed him to the ground roughly, warning him that he would suffer for it if he did not learn how to behave. When Egil got back on his feet he left the game, and the boys jeered at him.

Egil went to see Thord Granason and told him what had happened.

Thord said, "I'll go with you and we'll take our revenge."

Thord handed Egil an axe he had been holding, a common type of weapon in those days. They walked over to where the boys were playing their game. Grim had caught the ball and was running with the other boys chasing him. Egil ran up to Grim and drove the axe into his head, right through to the brain. Then Egil and Thord walked away to their people. The people from Myrar seized their weapons, and so did the others. Oleif Hjalti rushed to join the people from Borg with his men. Theirs was a much larger group, and at that the two sides parted.

As a result, a quarrel developed between Oleif and Hegg. They fought a battle at Laxfit by the river Grimsa, where seven men were killed. Hegg received a fatal wound and his brother Kvig died in the battle.

When Egil returned home, Skallagrim seemed indifferent to what had happened, but Bera said he had the makings of a true Viking when he was old enough to be put in command of warships. Then Egil spoke this verse:

My mother said
I would be bought
a boat with fine oars,
set off with Vikings,
stand up on the prow,
command the precious craft,
then enter port,
kill a man and another.

When Egil was twelve, he was so big that few grown men were big and strong enough that he could not beat them at games. In the year that he was twelve, he spent

---

[1]   In this verse, Yngvar is the "hardener," the wielder or maker of weapons that "peck wounds"; then he is the "horseman"—the captain—of the sea, "the field where ships race"; and finally, he is the man who provides little Egil with the duck's favorite "bed," its egg.

a lot of time taking part in games. Thord Granason was in his twentieth year then, and strong too. That winter Egil and Thord often took sides together in games against Skallagrim.

Once during the winter there was a ball game at Borg, in Sandvik to the south. Egil and Thord played against Skallagrim, who grew tired and they came off better. But that evening after sunset, Egil and Thord began losing. Skallagrim was filled with such strength that he seized Thord and dashed him to the ground so fiercely that he was crushed by the blow and died on the spot. Then he seized Egil.

Skallagrim had a servant woman named Thorgerd Brak, who had fostered Egil when he was a child. She was an imposing woman, as strong as a man and well versed in the magic arts.

Brak said, "You're attacking your own son like a mad beast, Skallagrim."

Skallagrim let Egil go, but went for her instead. She fled, with Skallagrim in pursuit. They came to the shore at the end of Digranes, and she ran off the edge of the cliff and swam away. Skallagrim threw a huge boulder after her which struck her between the shoulder blades. Neither the woman nor the boulder ever came up afterwards. That spot is now called Brakarsund (Brak's Sound).

Later that evening, when they returned to Borg, Egil was furious. By the time Skallagrim and the other members of the household sat down at the table, Egil had not come to his seat. Then he walked into the room and went over to Skallagrim's favorite, a man who was in charge of the workers and ran the farm with him. Egil killed him with a single blow, then went to his seat. Skallagrim did not mention the matter and it was let rest afterwards, but father and son did not speak to each other, neither kind nor unkind words, and so it remained through the winter.

[Egil joins his brother and his men on his brother's ship.]

50. In the days of King Harald Fairhair of Norway, Alfred the Great reigned over England, the first of his kinsmen to be sole ruler there. His son Edward succeeded him on the throne; he was the father of Athelstan the Victorious, who fostered Hakon the Good.[1] At this time, Athelstan succeeded his father on the throne. Edward had other sons, Athelstan's brothers.

After Athelstan's succession, some of the noblemen who had lost their realms to his family started to make war upon him, seizing the opportunity to claim them back when a young king was in control. These were British,[2] Scots and Irish. But King Athelstan mustered an army, and paid anyone who wanted to enter his service, English and foreign alike.

Thorolf and Egil sailed south past Saxony and Flanders, and heard that the king of England was in need of soldiers and that there was hope of much booty there. They decided to go there with their men. In the autumn they set off and went to see King Athelstan. He welcomed them warmly and felt that their support would strengthen his forces greatly. In the course of their conversations he invited them to stay with him, enter his service, and defend his country. It was agreed that they would become King Athelstan's men.

England had been Christian for a long time when this happened. King Athelstan was a devout Christian, and was called Athelstan the Faithful. The king asked Thorolf and Egil to take the sign of the cross, because that was a common custom then among both merchants and mercenaries who dealt with Christians. Anyone who had taken the sign of the cross could mix freely with both Christians and heathens, while keeping the faith that they pleased. Thorolf and Egil did so at the king's request, and both took the sign of the cross. Three hundred of their men entered the king's service.

---

[1] Alfred the Great (r.871–899); Edward the Elder (r.899–924); Athelstan or Æthelstan (r.924–939). Hakon the Good was a son of Harald Fairhair and Æthelstan's foster son, ruler in Norway *c*.934–960.

[2] The "British" were the Welsh.

TIMELINE FOR CHAPTER FOUR

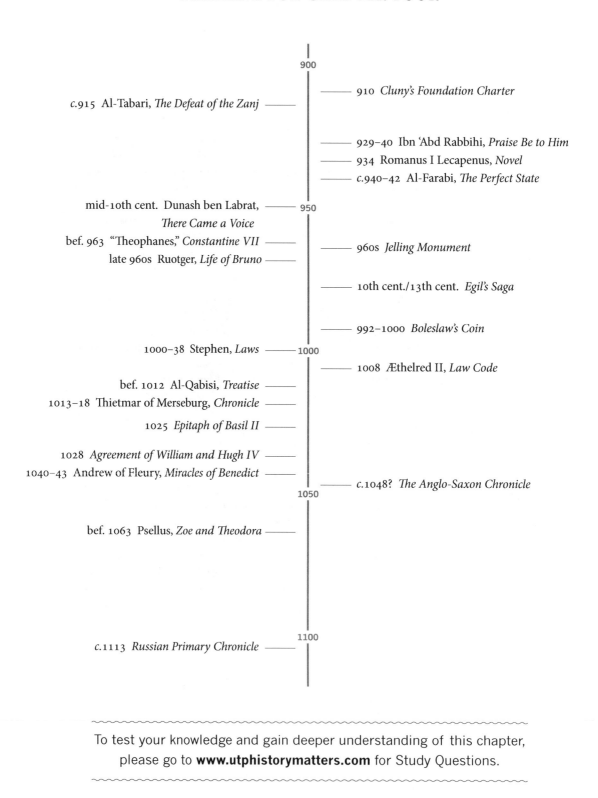

900

—— 910 *Cluny's Foundation Charter*

c.915 Al-Tabari, *The Defeat of the Zanj* ——

—— 929–40 Ibn 'Abd Rabbihi, *Praise Be to Him*
—— 934 Romanus I Lecapenus, *Novel*
—— c.940–42 Al-Farabi, *The Perfect State*

mid-10th cent. Dunash ben Labrat, —— 950
There Came a Voice
bef. 963 "Theophanes," Constantine VII —— —— 960s *Jelling Monument*
late 960s Ruotger, *Life of Bruno* ——

—— 10th cent./13th cent. *Egil's Saga*

—— 992–1000 *Boleslaw's Coin*

1000–38 Stephen, *Laws* —— 1000
—— 1008 Æthelred II, *Law Code*

bef. 1012 Al-Qabisi, *Treatise* ——
1013–18 Thietmar of Merseburg, *Chronicle* ——
1025 *Epitaph of Basil II* ——

1028 *Agreement of William and Hugh IV* ——
1040–43 Andrew of Fleury, *Miracles of Benedict* ——
—— c.1048? *The Anglo-Saxon Chronicle*

1050

bef. 1063 Psellus, *Zoe and Theodora* ——

1100

c.1113 *Russian Primary Chronicle* ——

To test your knowledge and gain deeper understanding of this chapter,
please go to **www.utphistorymatters.com** for Study Questions.

V

New Configurations (c.1050–c.1150)

THE SELJUK TRANSFORMATION

5.1 The Seljuks as enemies: Abu'l-Fazl Beyhaqi, *The Battle of Dandanqan* (before 1077). Original in Persian.

Abu'l-Fazl Beyhaqi (995–1077) served as a secretary at the courts of several Ghaznavid rulers, whose sultanates included eastern Iran and Afghanistan. Throughout his career, he kept careful notes of the events taking place around him, and when he retired, he wrote them up in a massive multi-volume history, of which only a small portion remains today. As an active player at court and in the army, he was present at the disastrous battle of Dandanqan (1040), led by Emir (or Sultan) Mas'ud (r.1030–1041) against the Seljuk Turks. (See Map 5.1.) With that decisive victory, the Seljuks, a Turkic group from the Kazakh steppe, found the way open for them to conquer much of the eastern half of the Islamic world and part of the Byzantine as well. The excerpt from Beyhaqi's *History* given here opens with the Ghaznavid army approaching Merv to fight the Seljuks, whose leader, Toghril Beg Mohammad (r.1040–1063), became the founder of the Great Seljuk sultanate. Against the advice of his generals, Mas'ud insisted on launching the expedition from Sarakhs to Merv across hot desert lands with exhausted troops. The army, waylaid at Dandanqan, never quite got there.

1. Why was food so central to Beyhaqi's account?
2. If the army was "well-equipped and in formation," as Beyhaqi says, why did it lose the battle?

[Source: Abu'l-Fazl Beyhaqi, *The History of Beyhaqi (The History of Sultan Mas'ud of Ghazna, 1030–1041),* trans. C.E. Bosworth, rev. Mohsen Ashtiany, 3 vols. (Boston and Washington, DC: Ilex Foundation and Center for Hellenic Studies, 2011), 2: 327–30 (notes added).]

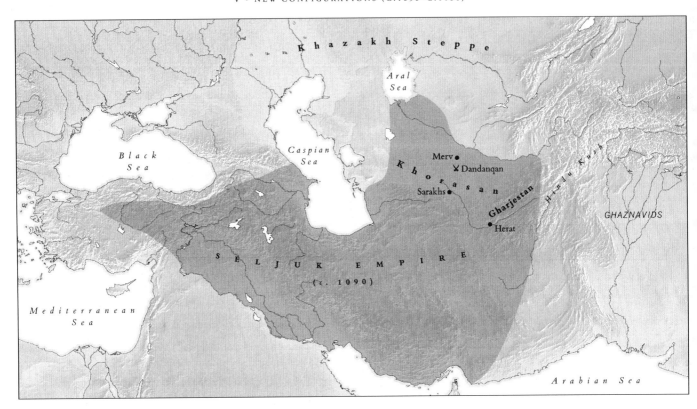

Map 5.1 The Early Seljuk Empire

When we arrived [at Sarakhs] it was the beginning of Ramadan. We found those regions devastated, with no crops or beasts there and barren, uncultivated fields. The situation there had reached the point that a tiny amount of hay, for instance, could not be had even for a dirham.[1] Prices had risen so high that the old were saying that such high prices had not been known for over a hundred years. A *man*[2] [of flour] had gone up to ten dirhams, but none could be found. There was not a blade of straw or of barley to be seen anywhere, and as a result, the mounted troops and the entire army suffered greatly. Bearing in mind that even our personal guards, despite their many mounts and supplies, were in grave trouble, one can imagine how the rest of the leading court figures and retainers and mass of troops fared. The situation reached such a pitch that there were continuous and ubiquitous arguments and public disputes amongst the various elements of the army, and the troops at large and the palace guards bickered over

food, fodder and beasts, so that finally this quarrelling passed from the level of verbal exchanges to that of the sword. Our confidants told us about this, and those we had selected ourselves to be our counsellors and advisers were telling us in both plain and in diplomatic language that, "The correct course of action is for us to head for Herat, since food and fodder can be found there in abundance, and it is near to all the parts of the province and is the pivotal point of Khorasan." The right course was indeed as they said; but we were overcome by a sense of sullen belligerence and obstinacy. Also, it would have meant that the problem of those upstarts[3] would still remain tangled and unresolved, and we were keen to go to Merv in order to get the whole affair straightened out. Moreover, Fate was driving us forward and making us confront unsuccessfully that unforeseen disaster which was about to happen.

---

[1] Dirhams were silver coins. They were Persian in origin but adopted by Persia's Islamic conquerors to use for large payments.

[2] A measure of weight.

[3] The Seljuk Turks.

We went towards Merv, and we could feel it in our bones that we were committing a grave error. The road was not as it should have been; there was no food or fodder and no water, and we had to face heat and the sand dunes of the desert. When we had gone three or four stages, violent arguments broke out among all sections of the army about the length of the stages, fodder, our mounts, food, etc. The commanders of the troops who had been appointed over the center, the right and left wings, and other places of the army's line of deployment tried to calm down the situation, but the dispute had flared up to such an extent that it could not be damped down sufficiently and was becoming more intense by the hour. Then on a certain day, when we moved from a certain stage at the time of the afternoon worship with the intention of seeking to encamp at a further place, a detachment of the enemy appeared on the fringes of the sandy wastes of the desert. They sprang a daring attack on us and tried to carry off plunder. The troops gave them a severe beating, and they failed to achieve their aim. Sporadic fighting continued late into the day. Our troops maintained their battle formation as they travelled on, and there were some clashes and skirmishes, but no fierce battle occurred, and the enemy steered clear of close encounters and intense fighting. If our troops, our best warriors, had reacted more robustly to these clashes, they would have been able to chase the enemy away in all directions. We encamped at nightfall in a certain place; there had been no mishaps and no prominent commander had been lost. We took all the usual precautions, including posting guards and sending out scouts so that nothing unexpected and untoward should happen to us in the darkness of the night. The next day was spent in the same way until we reached near Merv.

On the third day, we set out with the army well-equipped and in formation in tune with the occasion. The guides had told us that once we passed the fortress of Dandanqan and travelled one parasang[1] further, we would get to flowing water. We set off. When we reached the fortress of Dandanqan before noon, the enemy had filled up and blocked the wells at the gate of the fortress to make it impossible to encamp there. The inhabitants of Dandanqan shouted down that there were five wells within the fortress which would yield ample water for the army, and that if we were to encamp there they would open up once more the wells outside the fortress; there would then be sufficient water and no cause for a crisis. The day was extremely hot, and the only sensible course was to encamp there. But foreordained Fate had to fulfill its brief, and so we set off. A parasang further on, dried-up and deeply hollowed-out beds of streams came into view. The guides were perturbed, because they had thought that there would be water there since no-one could remember a time when those streams had run dry.

The lack of water there worried the troops, and they became dismayed and disorderly. The enemy launched a fierce attack from all four sides, and I myself had to ride out from the center and confront the enemy. We made strenuous attacks, and we thought that the compact formations of the right and left wings were still intact. We did not know that a detachment of the palace gholams mounted on camels had dismounted and were stealing the horses from anyone in sight so that they themselves might ride them into battle.[2] This tussle over horses, and the forcing of one another to dismount, became so intense that they started fighting among themselves and leaving their own stations. The enemy exploited this opportunity, and the situation became intractable, so that neither we nor our leading men could see a way out. We had thus to abandon our equipment and baggage to our opponents and leave the scene, and they became busy with plundering the captured baggage.

We rode on a parasang or so until we reached a large pool of standing water, and all the retainers and troops stationed at court, comprising our brothers and our sons, the leading men and the subordinate ranks, reached there in good shape, such that there were no casualties among the leading figures. It was suggested to us that we should go away, since the situation was irretrievable. This seemed to us a fair assessment, and we set off. On the eighth day, we came to the main town of Gharjestan, and spent two days there until the palace gholams and the rest of the army caught up, so that no person of note was left behind. The only people who were left behind were some members of the palace infantry and others of no note and significance.

---

[1] A parasang was an Iranian unit of distance equal to about three and one-half miles.

[2] The "gholams" were slave soldiers, usually Turks. The "palace gholams" were the personal bodyguards of the sultan.

5.2 Shi'ites vilified: Nizam al-Mulk, *The Book of Policy* (1091). Original in Persian.

Nizam al-Mulk (1018–1072) was officially the vizier, a sort of prime minister, for Great Seljuk Sultans Alp Arslan (r.1063–1072) and Malikshah (r.1072–1092). But under Malikshah, at least at first, he was in effect the ruler. He wrote *The Book of Policy* for Malikshah late in life, when he felt his power over the sultan slipping in favor of his arch-rival, Taj al-Mulk. *The Book of Policy* very subtly accuses Taj al-Mulk of being a secret Ismaili, an adherent of a radical branch of Shi'ism. In the passage below, Nizam al-Mulk ridicules Ismailism while nevertheless warning of its dire dangers, associating it with the "Qarmatis" and "Batinis" whom he accuses of fomenting unrest. It is true that some of the Seljuk elites flirted with Ismailism, but it was only after the time of Malikshah that the Ismailis tried to take power. In the event, they did not succeed.

1. How did Nizam al-Mulk explain the origins and spread of the form of Shi'ism known as Ismailism?
2. What did he object to in Ismaili doctrine?

[Source: *The Book of Government or Rules for Kings. The siyasat-nama or Siyar al-Muluk of Nizam al-Mulk,* trans. Hubert Darke (New Haven: Yale University Press, 1960), pp. 213–16 (notes added).]

Chapter Forty-Six

ON THE RISINGS OF THE QARMATIS [CARMATHIANS] AND BATINIS IN KUHISTAN, 'IRAQ AND KHURASAN[1]

1. The origin of the Qarmati religion was as follows. Ja'far al-Sadiq had a son whose name was Isma'il; he died before his father leaving a son named Muhammad; and this Muhammad lived until the time of [Caliph] Harun al-Rashid [r.786–809]. Now one of the Zubairis suggested to Harun al-Rashid that Muhammad was plotting a revolt and preaching in secret with the intention of seizing the caliphate.[2] Harun al-Rashid brought Muhammad from Medina to Baghdad and put him in prison, and during this confinement he died, and was buried in the cemetery of the Quraish.[3] Muhammad had a certain Hijazi page called Mubarak, and he was a calligrapher in the fine script known as *muqarmat*; for this reason he used to be called Qarmatwaih. This Mubarak had a friend in the city of Ahwaz whose name was 'Abd Allah ibn Maimun al Qaddah. The latter was one day sitting with him in private and said, "Your master Muhammad ibn Isma'il was my friend and he used to tell me his secrets." Mubarak was deceived and impatient to know what they were. Then 'Abd Allah ibn Maimun made Mubarak swear not to disclose what he was going to tell him except to persons fit to hear it. He then made several statements, introducing obscure words from the language of the imams, mixed up with sayings of the naturalists and utterances of the philosophers, and consisting largely of mention of The Prophet and the angels, the tablet and pen, and heaven and the throne. After that they parted; Mubarak went towards Kufa, and 'Abd Allah to Kuhistan and 'Iraq; and they sought to win over the people of the Shi'a.

---

[1] The Qarmatis split from the Ismailis, who supported the Fatimids. Batinis was another word for "Ismailis." Nizam al-Mulk did not differentiate between the two; for him they were equally heretical. Kuhistan refers to a part of Khurasan, both lying in Iran and beyond, to the east. Nizam al-Mulk's power was centered in Iran and Iraq. Almost all the place names in this excerpt refer to cities or regions in Iran.

[2] The Zubairis (or Zubayrids) were members of an elite family that had been Companions of Muhammad and momentary rulers of a break-away state in Iraq in the time of the Umayyads.

[3] The Quraish (Quraysh) was the tribe of the Prophet Muhammad.

2. This was at the time when Musa ibn Ja'far was in prison. Mubarak carried on his activities in secret, and disseminated his propaganda in the district around Kufa. Of the people who accepted his teaching, the Sunnis called some of them Mubarakis and others Qarmatis. Meanwhile 'Abd Allah ibn Maimun preached this religion in Kuhistan. Incidentally he was a very clever conjuror, and Muhammad ibn Zakariyya [Razi] has mentioned his name in his book *Makhariq al Anbiya* [Frauds of the Prophets].[1] He then appointed a man called Khalaf to succeed him and said to him, "Go in the direction of Rayy, for thereabouts in Rayy, Qum and Kashan the people are all Rafidis, professing Shi'a beliefs; so they will accept your teaching." 'Abd Allah himself departed in fear towards Basra.

So Khalaf went to Rayy. In the district of Fashabuya there is a village which they call Kilin. There he stayed and practised embroidery at which craft he was expert. He remained there some time without being able to reveal his secrets to anybody, till at last by dint of great efforts he managed to find a suitable person, and instructed him in the religion. He made out that the religion was that of the house [of the Prophet] and had been kept hidden; and said, "When the Qayim [Mahdi] appears the religion will be revealed, and the time of his coming is near. It behooves you to learn now, so that when you see him you will not be ignorant of the religion."[2] So he began secretly to instruct the people of this village in the religion. One day the headman of Kilin was passing outside the village when he heard a voice corning from a ruined mosque. He approached the mosque and listened. This Khalaf was expounding his religion to some of the people. On returning to the village he said, "O people, thwart this man's business. Do not go near him. Judging by what I have heard him say, I am afraid that our village may suffer through his activities." Incidentally Khalaf's speech was imperfect and he could not pronounce the letters *ta* and *ha*. When he knew that he had been discovered, he fled from that village and went to Rayy where he died. He had converted a few of the inhabitants of Kilin, and his son Ahmad ibn Khalaf took his place and continued to foster his father's religion. Ahmad ibn Khalaf found a man named Ghiyath who was well versed in literature and grammar. He made him his successor as propagandist.

3. This Ghiyath then embellished the elements of their religion with verses from the Qur'an, traditions of The Prophet (upon him be peace), Arab proverbs, and various verses and stories. He composed a book entitled *Kitab al Bayan* [The Book of Explanation] and in it he described in the manner of a lexicon the meaning of such terms as "prayer," "fasting," and other religious precepts. Then he held argument with people of the Sunna,[3] and news spread to Qum and Kashan that a man called Ghiyath had come forth from the village of Kilin as a missionary, and was giving glad tidings and teaching religion. The people of these cities flocked to Ghiyath and began to learn the new religion. Eventually the jurist 'Abd Allah Za'farani was informed of this, and he knew that the religion was a heresy. So he urged the people of Rayy to attack the heretics; some of the latter were known by the people of the Sunna as Khalafis, and others as Batinis. By the year 200 (from the hijra) [815/816 CE] the religion was widespread. This was the year in which a man called Sahib al Hal [The Master of the Situation] led a revolt in Syria and captured most of that country. Ghiyath had been forced to flee from Rayy and he went to Khurasan, and stayed at Marv-al-Rud, where he proselytized the emir Husain ibn 'Ali.[4] Husain was converted; his command extended over Khurasan, especially Taliqan, Maimana, Paryab, Gharchistan and Ghur. After adopting the new religion, he converted a number of people in these districts.

4. Ghiyath then nominated a successor at Marv-al-Rud to maintain the converts in the religion and to extend their numbers, while he himself returned to Rayy and began to preach again there. Then he left someone else to carry on the propaganda—a man from the district of Fashabuya called Abu Hatim, who was well versed in Arab poetry and strange tales. Even before he went to Khurasan he had already promised that before long in such-and-such a year the Qayim (whom they call the Mahdi) would appear, and the Qarmatis had trusted in this promise. The people of the Sunna found out that Ghiyath had returned and was once more calling the people to the religion of the Batinis (Allah curse them); and now he continued to promise that at a certain time, the Mahdi would appear, and he kept up this deceit in his

---

[1] Al-Razi (*c.*854–925/935) was a physician, courtier, and philosopher who famously debated with an Ismaili. In fact, al-Razi was against all revealed religion.

[2] The Mahdi, the "rightly guided one," refers to the one who will rule before the world ends.

[3] The "people of the Sunna" are the Sunni Muslims.

[4] Emirs were local governors.

preaching for some time. However, it chanced that the promised time for the coming of the Mahdi arrived, and he was proved false. The Shi'ites then turned against him, and reviled and renounced him; the Sunnis sought to kill him; but he fled and nobody could find him.

A PROFIT ECONOMY

5.3 Cultivating new lands: *Frederick of Hamburg's Agreement with Colonists from Holland* (1106). Original in Latin.

The commercial revolution took place in both town and countryside. In rural areas, it depended on the enterprise of peasants and the support of people in power. In this charter of agreement, the archbishop of Hamburg-Bremen, Frederick (r.1105–1123), granted swamp land in his diocese to colonists from Holland willing to undertake the backbreaking, collective work of drainage. (They were used to this sort of effort; much of Holland itself was swampland.) The archbishop required payments in return, not only for the produce from the land but also for granting the colonists the right to hear their own court cases. His call to settlers was part of a wider movement: Hamburg-Bremen was on the Slavic frontier, and bringing Christians to settle it was one way that German leaders meant to subdue the polytheistic natives.

1. What did the archbishop gain from this agreement?
2. How was settlement and colonization mingled with religion?

[Source: *Ausgewählte Urkunden zur Erläuterung der Verfassungsgeschichte Deutschlands im Mittelalter*, ed. Wilhelm Altmann and Ernst Bernheim, 5th ed. (Berlin: Weidmannsche Buchhandlung, 1920), pp. 161–62, no. 80. Translated by Barbara H. Rosenwein.]

[1] In the name of the holy and individual Trinity, Frederick, bishop of the church of Hamburg by grace of God, [gives] to all the faithful in Christ, present and future, perpetual benediction. We wish to notify all of a certain agreement that certain people living on this side of the Rhine, who are called Hollanders, made with us.

[2] The aforementioned men came to Our Majesty resolutely asking us to concede to them territory for them to cultivate. This land is situated in our bishopric and has hitherto been uncultivated, marshy, and useless to our locals. And so, having taken counsel with our vassals (*fideles*) and thinking it would be beneficial for us and our successors not to refuse their petition, we gave [our] assent.

[3] Moreover, the agreement of their petition was that they give to us a single denar [a silver coin] each year for every manse of this land.[1] We have thought it necessary to write down here the dimensions of a manse, lest there be a dispute later on among the people: a manse is 720 royal rods long and 30 wide, including the streams which flow through the land, which we grant in similar manner.

[4] Finally, they promised to give us a tithe according to our decree, that is, the eleventh part of the fruit of the earth, the tenth of the lambs, similarly of pigs, similarly of goats, the same of geese, and also they will give in the same way a tenth of the amount of honey and flax. They will render a dinar for each foal on the feast of St. Martin

---

[1] A manse (*mansus*) was a farming unit: it often included a house, waste, meadow, a garden, and, of course, land for crops. Here its dimensions are standardized and declared because the land is considered "virgin" and ready to be parceled out at will.

[November 11], and an obol [a coin worth less than a dinar] for each calf.

[5] They promised that they would obey us always in all matters pertaining to ecclesiastical law according to the decrees of the holy fathers, canon law, and the customs of the church of Utrecht [the home diocese of the colonists].

[6] With regard to judgments and court hearings involving secular law, they affirm that they will pay 2 marks [a gold or silver coin worth a substantial amount] each year for every 100 manses so that they may try all disputes themselves, lest they suffer from the prejudice of foreign [judges]. If they are unable to settle the more serious hearings or judgments, they shall refer them to the tribunal of the bishop. If they bring him with them to decide the case, for however long he remains [with them] they shall provide for him at their own expense in this manner: they shall keep two thirds of the court fees and give the last third to the bishop.

[7] We have allowed them to construct churches on said territory wherever it seems appropriate to them. We have offered to each church, for the express use of the priests serving God there, a tithe from our tithes of those parish churches. They confirm that the parishioners of each church will give no less than one manse to each church as an endowment for the use of the priest.

[8] The names of the men who came together to make and confirm this agreement are: Heinricus, the priest, to whom we have granted the aforesaid churches for life, and other laymen: Helikinus, Arnoldus, Hiko, Fordoltus, and Referic. To them and their heirs after them we concede the said land according to the secular laws and abovementioned agreement.

[9] The affirmation of this agreement was made in the year of our Lord's incarnation 1106, in the sixth indiction,[1] in the reign of Lord Henry IV, Emperor Augustus of the Romans. To confirm this document with our affirmation, it pleases us that the charter be affixed with the impression of our seal. If anyone says anything against it, let him be anathema.

[10] In confirmation of this document, I, Bishop Wernherus was present and signed. I, Bishop Marquardus. I, Bishop Hasoko. I, Bishop Hujo. I, Adelbero. I, Thieto was present and signed. I, Gerungus, *advocatus* [a lay protector of a church] was present and witnessed. I, Hericus, was present. I, Thidericus. I, Willo, was present. I, Erpo, was present and witnessed. I, Adelbertus. I, Gerwardus. I, Ermbertus. I, Reinwardus. I, Ecelinus.

5.4 Urban commerce: Ibn 'Abdun, *Regulations for the Market at Seville* (early 12th cent.). Original in Arabic.

Al-Andalus, the Islamic part of Iberia, was urbanized before most other Western regions and, as the document here demonstrates, its economic life was integrated into its notions of religion and morality. Ibn 'Abdun may well have been a market inspector—a *muhtasib*—responsible not only for making sure that products sold were up to a certain standard and that prices were legitimate but also for regulating relations between Christians, Muslims, and Jews and enforcing Muslim rules regarding sexuality and purity.

1. Why did the market need to be regulated?
2. Which provisions were meant for good health, and which were meant to enforce ritual purity?

[Source: Bernard Lewis, ed. and trans., *Islam: From the Prophet Muhammad to the Capture of Constantinople*, vol. 2: *Religion and Society* (New York: Oxford University Press, 1987), pp. 157–65 (some notes added).]

---

[1] Indictions were used for dating Roman imperial documents. Why do you suppose it was invoked here?

Shopkeepers must be forbidden to reserve regular places for themselves in the forecourt of the great mosque or elsewhere, for this amounts to a usurpation of property rights and always gives rise to quarrels and trouble among them. Instead, whoever comes first should take his place.

The *muhtasib* [market inspector] must arrange the crafts in order, putting like with like in fixed places. This is the best and most orderly way.

There must be no sellers of olive oil around the mosque, nor of dirty products, nor of anything from which an irremovable stain can be feared.

Rabbits and poultry should not be allowed around the mosque, but should have a fixed place. Partridges and slaughtered barnyard birds should only be sold with the crop plucked, so that the bad and rotten can be distinguished from the good ones. Rabbits should only be sold skinned, so that the bad ones may be seen. If they are left lying in their skins, they go bad.

Egg sellers must have bowls of water in front of them, so that bad eggs may be recognized.

Truffles should not be sold around the mosque, for this is a delicacy of the dissolute.[1]

Bread should only be sold by weight. Both the baking and the crumbs must be supervised, as it is often "dressed up." By this I mean that they take a small quantity of good dough and use it to "dress up" the front of the bread which is made with bad flour....

The cheese which comes from al-Madāin[2] should not be sold, for it is the foul residue of the curds, of no value. If people saw how it is made, no one would ever eat it. Cheese should only be sold in small leather bottles, which can be washed and cleaned every day. That which is in bowls cannot be secured from worms and mold.

Mixed meats should not be sold on one stall, nor should fat and lean meat be sold on one stall. Tripe should only be sold dry on boards, for water both spoils it and increases its weight. The entrails of sheep must be taken out, so that they should not be sold with the meat and at the same price, which would be a fraud. The heads of sheep should not be skinned, except for the young. The guts must always be removed from the bodies of animals, except lambs, and should not be left there, for this too would be an occasion for fraud.

No slaughtering should take place in the market, except in the closed slaughterhouses, and the blood and refuse should be taken outside the market. Animals should be slaughtered only with a long knife. All slaughtering knives should be of this kind. No animal which is good for field work may be slaughtered, and a trustworthy and incorruptible commissioner should go to the slaughterhouse every day to make sure of this; the only exception is an animal with a defect. Nor should a female still capable of producing young be slaughtered. No animal should be sold in the market which has been brought already slaughtered, until its owner establishes that it is not stolen....

Women should be forbidden to do their washing in the gardens, for these are dens for fornication.

Grapes in large quantities should not be sold to anyone of whom it is known that he would press them to make wine. This is a matter for supervision.

Fruit must not be sold before it is ripe for this is bad, except only for grapes, which are good for pregnant women and for the sick....

The seller of grapes should have baskets and nets in which to arrange them, as this is the best protection for them.

Cakes should be properly baked and should only be made wide, as thin ones are good only for the sick.

If someone assays gold or silver coins for a person, and later it emerges that there is base metal in them, the assayer must make good, for he deceived and betrayed the owner of the coins, who placed his trust in him. Swindlers when detected must be denounced in all crafts, but above all in assaying coin, for in this case the swindler can only be a person who is expert in matters of coin.

Women should not sit by the river bank in the summer if men appear there.

No barber may remain alone with a woman in his booth. He should work in the open market in a place where he can be seen and observed.

The cupper.[3] He should only let blood into a special jar with graduation marks, so that he can see how much blood he has let. He should not let blood at his discretion, for this can lead to sickness and death.

---

[1] Apparently a common view. A Spanish Arabic proverb includes the large consumption of truffles among the signs by which the dissolute may be recognized.

[2] A term applied to the fertile islands in the lower Guadalquivir, below Seville.

[3] Muslims practiced "wet" bloodletting. A cup was applied to the skin to create a mild suction, and then the swollen area was cut with the proper tools. A second application of the cup drew out the blood.

The water wheel. Most of the holes for the spindles should be wedged, as this is best for its working.

No one may be allowed to claim knowledge of a matter in which he is not competent, especially in the craft of medicine, for this can lead to loss of life....

Only a skilled physician should sell potions and electuaries and mix drugs. These things should not be bought from the grocer or the apothecary whose only concern is to take money without knowledge; they spoil the prescriptions and kill the sick, for they mix medicines which are unknown and of contrary effect....

Only good and trustworthy men, known as such among people, may be allowed to have dealings with women in buying and in selling. The tradespeople must watch over this carefully. The women who weave brocades must be banned from the market, for they are nothing but harlots.

On festival days men and women shall not walk on the same path when they go to cross the river....

The basins in the public baths should be covered. If they are left uncovered, they cannot be protected from pollution, yet this is a place of purity. The bath attendant, the masseur, and the barber should not walk about in the baths without a loincloth or drawers.

A Muslim must not massage a Jew or a Christian nor throw away his refuse nor clean his latrines. The Jew and the Christian are better fitted for such trades, since they are the trades of those who are vile. A Muslim should not attend to the animal of a Jew or of a Christian, nor serve him as a muleteer, nor hold his stirrup. If any Muslim is known to do this, he should be denounced.

Muslim women shall be prevented from entering their abominable churches for the priests are evil-doers, fornicators, and sodomites. Frankish[1] women must be forbidden to enter the church except on days of religious services or festivals, for it is their habit to eat and drink and fornicate with the priests, among whom there is not one who has not two or more women with whom he sleeps. This has become a custom among them, for they have permitted what is forbidden and forbidden what is permitted. The priests should be ordered to marry, as they do in the eastern lands. If they wanted to, they would....

A Jew must not slaughter meat for a Muslim. The Jews should be ordered to arrange their own butcher's stalls.

A garment belonging to a sick man,[2] a Jew, or a Christian must not be sold without indicating its origin; likewise, the garment of a debauchee. Dough must not be taken from a sick man for baking his bread. Neither eggs nor chickens nor milk not any other foodstuff should be bought from him. They should only buy and sell among themselves.

The sewer men must be forbidden to dig holes in the streets, as this harms them and causes injury to people, except when they are cleaning the entire street.

Itinerant fortune-tellers must be forbidden to go from house to house, as they are thieves and fornicators.

A drunkard must not be flogged until he is sober again.

Prostitutes must be forbidden to stand bareheaded outside the houses. Decent women must not bedeck themselves to resemble them. They must be stopped from coquetry and party making among themselves, even if they have been permitted to do this [by their husbands]. Dancing girls must be forbidden to bare their heads.

No contractor,[3] policeman, Jew, or Christian may be allowed to dress in the costume of people of position, of a jurist, or of a worthy man. They must on the contrary be abhorred and shunned and should not be greeted with the formula, "Peace be with you," for the devil has gained mastery over them and has made them forget the name of God. They are the devil's party, "and indeed the devil's party are the losers."[4] They must have a distinguishing sign by which they are recognized to their shame.

Catamites[5] must be driven out of the city and punished wherever any one of them is found. They should not be allowed to move around among the Muslims nor to participate in festivities, for they are debauchees accursed by God and man alike.

When fruit or other foodstuffs are found in the possession of thieves, they should be distributed in prisons and given to the poor. If the owner comes to claim his goods and is recognized, they should be returned to him.

---

[1] That is, Christians from outside Spain and from those parts of Spain not under Muslim rule.

[2] Probably lepers are meant.

[3] I.e., tax farmer.

[4] Qur'an 57:22.

[5] A young man who has sexual relationships with men.

5.5 The role of royal patronage: Henry I, *Privileges for the Citizens of London* (1130–1133). Original in Latin.

Towns were permanent commercial centers, and their citizens often demanded and received special privileges that gave them considerable autonomy. In this charter, Henry I, king of England (r.1100–1135), grants privileges to the citizens of London c.1130, basing them on grants handed out by previous kings. The Londoners have the right to the "farm" or revenues of their own borough, Middlesex. They hold it from the king and his heirs as a vassal might hold a fief. The citizens are also allowed to have their own courts and freedom from various duties and tolls (e.g., passage and lestage—all called "customs" here). The reference to "sokes" in this text means "jurisdictions," which, among other things, were sources of revenues.

1. How do the freedoms granted by King Henry compare with those granted by Archbishop Frederick in his *Agreement with Colonists*, p. 246 above?
2. What might Henry have gained from granting these privileges?

[Source: *English Historical Documents*, vol. 2: 1042–1189, ed. David C. Douglas and George W. Greenaway, 2nd ed. (London: Routledge, 1981), pp. 1012–13 (slightly modified).]

Henry, by the grace of God, king of the English, to the archbishop of Canterbury, and to the bishops and abbots, and earls and barons and justices and sheriffs, and to all his liegemen, both French and English, of the whole of England, greeting. Know that I have granted to my citizens of London that they shall hold Middlesex at "farm" for 300 pounds "by tale" for themselves and their heirs from me and my heirs, so that the citizens shall appoint as sheriff from themselves whomsoever they may choose, and shall appoint from among themselves as justice whomsoever they choose to look after the pleas of my crown and the pleadings which arise in connection with them. No other shall be justice over the men of London. And the citizens shall not plead outside the walls of the city in respect of any plea; and they shall be quit of scot and of Danegeld and the murder-fine.[1] Nor shall any of them be compelled to offer trial by battle.[2] And if any one of the citizens shall be impleaded [sued] in respect of the pleas of the crown, let him prove himself to be a man of London by an oath which shall be judged in the city. Let no one be billeted within the walls of the city, either of my household, or by the force of anyone else. And let all the men of London and their property be quit and free from toll and passage and lestage and from all other customs throughout all England and at the seaports. And let the churches and barons and citizens hold and have well and in peace their sokes, with all their customs, so that those who dwell in these sokes shall pay no customs except to him who possesses the soke, or to the steward whom he has placed there. And a man of London shall not be fined at mercy[3] except according to his "were,"[4] that is to say, up to 100 shillings: this applies to an offence which can be punished by a fine. And there shall no longer be "miskenning"[5] in the hustings court, nor in the folk-moot,[6] nor in other pleas within the city. And the hustings court shall sit once a week, to wit, on

---

[1] The "murder-fine" (*murdrum*) penalized an entire community for the death of any Norman. It dated from the period after the Norman Conquest, when feelings ran high against the invaders. The Londoners are here exempt from paying this.

[2] This was a duel to determine which party was in the right; the tradesmen of London preferred other forms of trial.

[3] I.e., fined at discretion, and to an unlimited amount.

[4] The "were" was the wergild, the price a murderer had to pay as compensation to the kin of his victim. In this case, the price of 100 shillings is slightly higher than the "were" of a commoner but lower than that of a thegn.

[5] A "miskenning" was a verbal error in reciting the formal oaths protesting innocence; this entailed the loss of the case.

[6] The "hustings court" and the "folk-moot" were both judicial assemblies, but the folk-moot was slightly larger.

Monday. I will cause my citizens to have their lands and pledges and debts within the city and outside it. And in respect of the lands about which they make claim to me, I will do them right according to the law of the city. And if anyone has taken toll or custom from the citizens of London, then the citizens of London may take from the borough or village where toll or custom has been levied as much as the man of London gave for toll, and more also may be taken for a penalty. And let all debtors to the citizens of London discharge their debts, or prove in London that they do not owe them; and if they refuse either to pay or to come and make such proof, then the citizens to whom the debts are due may take pledges within the city either from the borough or from the village or from the county in which the debtor lives. And the citizens shall have their hunting chases, as well and fully as had their predecessors, namely, in Chiltern and Middlesex and Surrey. Witness: the bishop of Winchester; Robert, son of Richer; Hugh Bigot; Alfred of Totnes; William of Aubigny; Hubert the king's chamberlain; William of Montfiquet; Hagulf "de Tani"; John Belet; Robert, son of Siward. Given at Westminster.

CHURCH REFORM

5.6 The pope's challenge: Gregory VII, *Admonition to Henry IV* (1075). Original in Latin.

Both popes and emperors initially supported the movement for Church reform, which demanded that the clergy be celibate and gain their offices according to canon law—that is, without lay interference. But as the issue of Church leadership came to the fore, the two powers inevitably clashed, for kings did not consider themselves mere laymen. When, in 1075, King Henry IV (r.1056–1106) "invested"—put into office—his episcopal candidate at Milan, Tedald, Pope Gregory VII (1073–1085) complained bitterly in a letter of admonition to Henry. Although the Investiture Conflict was long in the making, this letter may be said to have crystallized it.

1. What did Gregory have in mind when he demanded that Henry "obey the Apostolic See as becomes a Christian king"?
2. How did Gregory understand his relationship to Saint Peter?

[Source: *The Correspondence of Pope Gregory VII: Selected Letters from the Registrum*, trans. Ephriam Emerton (New York: Columbia University Press, 1969), pp. 86–90 (notes added).]

Gregory, bishop, servant of God's servants, to King Henry, greeting and the apostolic benediction—but with the understanding that he obeys the Apostolic See as becomes a Christian king.

Considering and weighing carefully to how strict a judge we must render an account of the stewardship committed to us by St. Peter, prince of the Apostles, we have hesitated to send you the apostolic benediction, since you are reported to be in voluntary communication with men who are under the censure of the Apostolic See and of a synod.[1] If this is true, you yourself know that you cannot receive the favor of God nor the apostolic blessing unless you shall first put away those excommunicated persons and force them to do penance and shall yourself obtain

---

[1] "Under the censure": Gregory is referring to the Roman Lenten Synod of 1075, where five of Henry's advisors had been excommunicated. It was a sin for a Christian to associate with excommunicates.

absolution and forgiveness for your sin by due repentance and satisfaction.[1] Wherefore we counsel Your Excellency, if you feel yourself guilty in this matter, to make your confession at once to some pious bishop who, with our sanction, may impose upon you a penance suited to the offense, may absolve you, and with your consent in writing may be free to send us a true report of the manner of your penance.

We marvel exceedingly that you have sent us so many devoted letters and displayed such humility by the spoken words of your legates, calling yourself a son of our Holy Mother Church and subject to us in the faith, singular in affection, a leader in devotion, commending yourself with every expression of gentleness and reverence, and yet in action showing yourself most bitterly hostile to the canons and apostolic decrees in those duties especially required by loyalty to the Church. Not to mention other cases, the way you have observed your promises in the Milan affair, made through your mother and through bishops, our colleagues, whom we sent to you and what your intentions were in making them is evident to all.[2] And now, heaping wounds upon wounds, you have handed over the sees of Fermo and Spoleto—if indeed a church may be given over by any human power—to persons entirely unknown to us, whereas it is not lawful to consecrate anyone except after probation and with due knowledge.

It would have been becoming to you, since you confess yourself be a son of the Church, to give more respectful attention to the master of the Church, that is, to Peter, prince of the Apostles. To him, if you are of the Lord's flock, you have been committed for your pasture, since Christ said to him: "Peter, feed my sheep," and again: "To thee are given the keys of Heaven, and whatsoever thou shalt bind on earth shall be bound in Heaven and whatsoever thou shalt loose on earth shall be loosed in Heaven." Now, while we, unworthy sinner that we are, stand in his place of power, still whatever you send to us, whether in writing or by word of mouth, he himself receives, and while we read what is written or hear the voice of those who speak, he discerns with subtle insight from what spirit the message comes. Wherefore Your Highness should beware lest any defect of will toward the Apostolic See be found in your words or your messages and should

pay due reverence, not to us but to Almighty God, in all matters touching the welfare of the Christian faith and the status of the Church. And this we say although our Lord deigned to declare: "He who heareth you heareth me; and he who despiseth you despiseth me."

We know that one who does not refuse to obey God in those matters in which we have spoken according to the statutes of the holy fathers does not scorn to observe our admonitions even as if he had received them from the lips of the Apostle himself. For if our Lord, out of reverence for the chair of Moses, commanded the Apostles to observe the teaching of the scribes and pharisees who sat thereon, there can be no doubt that the apostolic and Gospel teaching, whose seat and foundation is Christ, should be accepted and maintained by those who are chosen to the service of teaching.

At a synod held at Rome during the current year, and over which Divine Providence willed us to preside, several of your subjects being present, we saw that the order of the Christian religion had long been greatly disturbed and its chief and proper function, the redemption of souls, had fallen low and through the wiles of the Devil had been trodden under foot. Startled by this danger and by the manifest ruin of the Lord's flock we returned to the teaching of the holy fathers, declaring no novelties nor any inventions of our own, but holding that the primary and only rule of discipline and the well-trodden way of the saints should again be sought and followed, all wandering paths to be abandoned. For we know that there is no other way of salvation and eternal life for the flock of Christ and their shepherds except that shown by him who said: "I am the door and he who enters by me shall be saved and shall find pasture." This was taught by the Apostles and observed by the holy fathers and we have learned it from the Gospels and from every page of Holy Writ.

This edict,[3] which some who place the honor of men above that of God call an intolerable burden, we, using the right word, call rather a truth and a light necessary for salvation, and we have given judgment that it is to be heartily accepted and obeyed, not only by you and your subjects but by all princes and peoples who confess and worship Christ—though it is our especial wish and would be especially fitting for you, that you should excel others

---

[1] Christians are to confess each sin to a prelate, who then assigns them penance (for example fasting on bread and water for some length of time) and absolves and forgives the sin.

[2] The promises, made at Easter in 1074, were not to appoint Tedald bishop of Milan.

[3] It is not clear what edict Gregory is referring to.

in devotion to Christ as you are their superior in fame, in station and in valor.

Nevertheless, in order that these demands may not seem to you too burdensome or unfair we have sent you word by your own liegemen not to be troubled by this reform of an evil practice but to send us prudent and pious legates from your own people. If these can show in any reasonable way how we can moderate the decision of the holy fathers [at the council] saving the honor of the eternal king and without peril to our own soul, we will condescend to hear their counsel. It would in fact have been the fair thing for you, even if you had not been so graciously admonished, to make reasonable inquiry of us in what respect we had offended you or assailed your honor, before you proceeded to violate the apostolic decrees. But how little you cared for our warnings or for doing right was shown by your later actions.

However, since the long-enduring patience of God summons you to improvement, we hope that with increase of understanding your heart and mind may be turned to obey the commands of God. We warn you with a father's love that you accept the rule of Christ, that you consider the peril of preferring your own honor to his, that you do not hamper by your actions the freedom of that Church which he deigned to bind to himself as a bride by a divine union, but, that she may increase as greatly as possible, you will begin to lend to Almighty God and to St. Peter, by whom also your own glory may merit increase, the aid of your valor by faithful devotion.

Now you ought to recognize your special obligation to them for the triumph over your enemies which they have granted you, and while they are making you happy and singularly prosperous, they ought to find your devotion increased by their favor to you. That the fear of God, in whose hand is all the might of kings and emperors, may impress this upon you more than any admonitions of mine, bear in mind what happened to Saul after he had won a victory by command of the prophet, how he boasted of his triumph, scorning the prophet's admonitions, and how he was rebuked by the Lord, and also what favor followed David the king as a reward for his humility in the midst of the tokens of his bravery.[1]

Finally, as to what we have read in your letters and do not mention here we will give you no decided answer until your legates, Radbod, Adalbert and Odescalcus, to whom we entrust this, have returned to us and have more fully reported your decision upon the matters which we commissioned them to discuss with you.

5.7 The royal response: Henry IV, *Letter to Gregory VII* (1075). Original in Latin.

Henry reacted vigorously to Gregory's challenge. He immediately met with his bishops at the city of Worms, and the assembly denounced Gregory (calling him by his old name, Hildebrand) as a usurper of the papal throne. The letter below, which was circulated within Germany, charges Gregory with throwing the Church into chaos and calls upon him to resign. A milder version was sent to the pope himself.

1. How did Henry try to undermine Gregory's understanding of Saint Peter?
2. By what right did Henry demand that Gregory "descend"?

[Source: *Imperial Lives and Letters*, ed. Robert L. Benson; trans. Theodor E. Mommsen and Karl F. Morrison (New York: Columbia University Press, 2000), pp. 150–51.]

---

[1] After Saul's victory against the Ammonites (1 Sam. 11:15), he refused to listen to Samuel's admonitions and therefore lost his crown to David (1 Sam. 16:1–13).

Henry, King not by usurpation, but by the pious ordination of God,[1] to Hildebrand, now not Pope, but false monk:

You have deserved such a salutation as this because of the confusion you have wrought; for you left untouched no order of the Church which you could make a sharer of confusion instead of honor, of malediction instead of benediction.

For to discuss a few outstanding points among many: Not only have you dared to touch the rectors of the holy Church—the archbishops, the bishops, and the priests, anointed of the Lord as they are[2]—but you have trodden them under foot like slaves who know not what their lord may do.[3] In crushing them you have gained for yourself acclaim from the mouth of the rabble. You have judged that all these know nothing, while you alone know everything. In any case, you have sedulously used this knowledge not for edification, but for destruction,[4] so greatly that we may believe Saint Gregory, whose name you have arrogated to yourself, rightly made this prophesy of you when he said: "From the abundance of his subjects, the mind of the prelate is often exalted, and he thinks that he has more knowledge than anyone else, since he sees that he has more power than anyone else."[5]

And we, indeed, bore with all these abuses, since we were eager to preserve the honor of the Apostolic See. But you construed our humility as fear, and so you were emboldened to rise up even against the royal power itself, granted to us by God. You dared to threaten to take the kingship away from us—as though we had received the kingship from you, as though kingship and empire were in your hand and not in the hand of God.

Our Lord, Jesus Christ, has called us to kingship, but has not called you to the priesthood. For you have risen by these steps: namely, by cunning, which the monastic profession abhors, to money; by money to favor; by

favor to the sword. By the sword you have come to the throne of peace, and from the throne of peace you have destroyed the peace. You have armed subjects against their prelates; you who have not been called by God have taught that our bishops who have been called by God are to be spurned; you have usurped for laymen the bishops' ministry over priests, with the result that these laymen depose and condemn the very men whom the laymen themselves received as teachers from the hand of God, through the imposition of the hands of bishops.

You have also touched me, one who, though unworthy, has been anointed to kingship among the anointed. This wrong you have done to me, although as the tradition of the holy Fathers has taught, I am to be judged by God alone and am not to be deposed for any crime unless—may it never happen—I should deviate from the Faith. For the prudence of the holy bishops entrusted the judgment and the deposition even of Julian the Apostate not to themselves, but to God alone. The true pope Saint Peter also exclaims, "Fear God, honor the king."[6] You, however, since you do not fear God, dishonor me, ordained of Him.

Wherefore, when Saint Paul gave no quarter to an angel from heaven if the angel should preach heterodoxy,[7] he did not except you who are now teaching heterodoxy throughout the earth. For he says, "If anyone, either I or an angel from heaven, preach any other Gospel unto you than that which we have preached unto you, let him be accursed."[8] Descend, therefore, condemned by this anathema and by the common judgment of all our bishops and of ourself. Relinquish the Apostolic See which you have arrogated. Let another mount the throne of Saint Peter, another who will not cloak violence with religion but who will teach the pure doctrine of Saint Peter.

I, Henry, King by the grace of God, together with all our bishops, say to you: Descend! Descend!

---

[1] Rom. 13:2.

[2] Ps. 105:15; Douay Ps. 104:15; 2 Sam. 1:14.

[3] See John 15:15.

[4] See 2 Cor. 10:8, 13:10.

[5] Gregory I, *Pastoral Care* 2.6.

[6] 1 Pet. 2:17.

[7] That is, doctrine that diverges from correct belief.

[8] Gal. 1:18.

5.8 The papal view: Gregory VII, *Letter to Hermann of Metz* (1076). Original in Latin.

Soon after receiving Henry's letter, the pope met with *his* bishops and excommunicated Henry. Many of Henry's supporters abandoned the king, and Bishop Hermann of Metz, one of a handful of bishops at Worms who had opposed the condemnation of Gregory, was important in fomenting the resulting war. Yet Hermann needed arguments to back up the actions of the pope and convince others to separate themselves from the excommunicated king. Gregory supplied some reasons in this letter, downgrading the dignity of kingship and maintaining that the act of excommunicating kings had a long and illustrious history.

1. How did Gregory justify his excommunication of Henry IV?
2. What reasons did Gregory give for considering the "episcopal dignity"—that is, the dignity of bishops—to be greater than the "royal dignity."

[Source: Herbert E.J. Cowdrey, *The Register of Pope Gregory VII, 1073–1085: An English Translation* (Oxford: Oxford University Press, 2002), pp. 208–11 (notes modified).]

Gregory, bishop, servant of the servants of God, to Hermann, bishop of Metz, greeting and apostolic blessing.

By your questioning you are seeking many things of me who am exceedingly busy, and you send a messenger who presses me too much at his own pleasure. Accordingly, if I do not reply sufficiently, I ask you to bear it with patience.

Therefore how I am in my bodily health, or how the Romans and the Normans[1] who are proving themselves to be with regard to me, the bearer of this letter may tell you. But as regards the other matters about which you have questioned me, would that blessed Peter[2] might answer through me, for he is often honored or suffers injury in me, his servant such as I am.

Now, who the excommunicated bishops, priests, or laymen are there is no need that you should inquire of me, for undoubtedly they are those who are known to have held communion with the excommunicated King Henry, if it is right that he should be called king. For they do not scruple to set human favor or fear before the precept of the eternal King, nor do they fear by their support to drive their king towards the wrath of Almighty God. He, however, by communicating with his own courtiers who were excommunicated for the simoniac heresy[3] has not feared to incur excommunication, and has not been ashamed to draw others to be excommunicated by communicating with him. Concerning such men, what else is there that we might think except what we have learnt in the Psalms: "The fool has said in his heart, 'There is no God,'" and again, "All have together been made unprofitable" in their intentions?[4]

Now, as for those who say, "it is not right that the king should be excommunicated," although in view of their great folly we have no need so much as to answer them, yet lest we seem to pass impatiently over their foolishness we direct them to the words or deeds of the holy fathers, in order that we may call them back to sound teaching. Let them, therefore, read what blessed Peter commanded to the Christian people at the ordination of St. Clement about him whom they knew not to have

---

[1] When Gregory spoke of the Romans, he meant the people—and above all the nobles—of Rome. By the Normans he meant the rulers of Southern Italy, with whom the papacy had been allied since 1059.

[2] This refers to St. Peter, whose "servant" but also spokesman Gregory considered himself.

[3] Gregory called the purchasing of Church offices "simony" or the "simoniac heresy" after Simon Magus, who in Acts 8:18–24 offered money to Peter and John if they would give him the power to confer the Holy Spirit.

[4] Ps. 14:1–3; Douay Ps. 13:1–3.

the favor of the pontiff.[1] Let them learn why the Apostle says, "Ready to avenge every act of disobedience,"[2] and of whom he says, "With such a man not even to take food."[3] Let them ponder why Pope Zacharias deposed the king of the Franks and absolved all the Frankish people from the bond of the oath that they had taken to him.[4] Let them also learn in the Register of blessed Gregory that in privileges that he drew up for certain churches he not only excommunicated kings and dukes who contravened his words but also adjudged that they should forfeit their office.[5] Nor let them overlook that blessed Ambrose not only excommunicated Theodosius—not only a king but indeed an emperor in habitual conduct and power, but even debarred him from remaining in church in the place of the priests.[6]

But perhaps these men wish to have it thought that, when God three times committed his church to blessed Peter saying, "Feed my sheep,"[7] he made an exception of kings. Why do they not take notice, or rather shame-facedly confess, that, when God gave principally to blessed Peter the power of binding and loosing in heaven and upon earth,[8] he excepted nobody and withheld nothing from his power. For when a man denies that he can be bound by the chain of the church, it remains that he must deny that he can be loosed by its power; and whoever brazenly denies this altogether separates himself from Christ. And if the holy apostolic see, deciding through the pre-eminent power that is divinely conferred upon it, settles spiritual matters, why not also secular matters? In truth, as for the kings and princes of this world who place their own honor and temporal gains before the righteousness of God, and who by neglecting his honor seek their own, whose members they are or to whom

they cleave your charity is not in ignorance. For just as those who set God before their own entire will and obey his command rather than men[9] are members of Christ,[10] so also those of whom we have been speaking above are members of Antichrist. If, then, spiritual men are judged when it is necessary, why are not secular ones the more under constraint concerning their wicked deeds?

But perhaps they think that the royal dignity excels the episcopal. From their origins they can gather how greatly they each differ from the other. For human pride has instituted the former; divine mercy has instituted the latter. The former ceaselessly snatches at vain glory; the latter always aspires to the heavenly life. And let them learn what the blessed Pope Anastasius wrote to the Emperor Anastasius about these dignities,[11] and how blessed Ambrose distinguished between these dignities in his pastoral letter: "The episcopal honor and excellence," he said, "if you compare them with the splendor of kings and the diadem of emperors, leave them much more inferior than if you compare the metal of lead with the splendor of gold."[12] Being not unaware of these things, the Emperor Constantine the Great chose not the principal but the least place to sit amongst the bishops; for he knew that "God resists the proud, but he gives favor to the humble."[13]

Meanwhile, brother, we are letting you know that, having received letters from certain of our brother bishops and dukes, by the authority of the apostolic see we have given licence to these bishops to absolve those excommunicated by us who are not afraid to keep themselves from communion with the king. As regards the king himself, [Henry IV] we have absolutely forbidden that anyone should venture to absolve him until his assured penitence

---

[1] *Epistola Clementis prior*, chapter 18.

[2] 2 Cor. 10:6.

[3] 1 Cor. 5:11.

[4] In 751, Pope Zacharias (741–752) sanctioned the deposition of Childeric III (r.743–c.751), the last of the Merovingian kings.

[5] This refers to the letters of Pope Gregory the Great (590–604).

[6] The reference is to St. Ambrose's measures against Emperor Theodosius I (r.379–395) after the emperor responded to a revolt at Thessalonica by massacring its inhabitants.

[7] John 21:15–17.

[8] See Matt. 16:19. The power of binding and loosing, as interpreted by the papacy, was the priestly power to impose penance and to administer absolution.

[9] See Acts 5:29.

[10] See 1 Cor. 6:15.

[11] This refers to a letter from Pope Anastasius II (496–498) to Emperor Anastasius I (r.491–518).

[12] We now know that the work in question was not written by St. Ambrose.

[13] James 4:6. The reference is to Emperor Constantine I (r.306–337) at the Council of Nicaea (325).

and sincere satisfaction shall have been reported to us by trustworthy witnesses, so that we may at the same time ascertain how, if divine mercy shall look upon him, we may absolve him to the honor of God and to his own salvation. For it is not hidden from us that there are some of you who, seizing any pretext that might seem to come from us, would be led astray by fear or human favor and presume to absolve him if we were not to forbid, and to add wound to wound in place of medicine. If any who are bishops in truth should forbid them, they would conclude that they were not defending righteousness but pursuing enmities.

Now, as for the ordination and consecration of bishops who venture to communicate with the excommunicated king, as blessed Gregory testifies, before God they become an execration.[1] For when they proudly resist to obey the apostolic see, as Samuel is witness, they fall into the crime of idolatry.[2] For if he is said to be of God who is stirred up by the zeal of divine love to destroy vices, he assuredly denies that he is of God who refuses, so far as he is able, to reprove the life of carnal men. And if he is accursed who withholds his sword from blood,[3] that is, the word of preaching from the slaying of carnal life, how much more is he accursed who from fear or favor drives the soul of his brother to eternal perdition [damnation]? In sum, that the accursed and excommunicated can bless and bestow upon anyone the divine grace that they do

not fear to deny by their own works, can be discovered in no ruling of the holy fathers.

Meantime, we order you to have a word with the venerable archbishop of Trier,[4] our brother that is, who is to forbid the bishop of Toul[5] from intruding into the affairs of the abbess of the monastery of Remiremont,[6] and who, in concert with you, is to annul whatever he has decided against her. Now, as regards Matilda,[7] the daughter of us both and the faithful handmaid of blessed Peter, what you wish, I wish. But in what state of life she should continue under God's direction, I do not yet grasp for certain. But of Godfrey her late husband,[8] you may know for a certainty that I, although a sinner, frequently make memorial before God; for neither his enmity nor any vain consideration holds me back and, moved by your own brotherly love and Matilda's pleading, I long for his salvation.

May Almighty God, by the intercession of the queen of heaven, Mary ever-virgin, and by the authority of the blessed apostles Peter and Paul which is granted by him to them, absolve from all sins both you and all our brothers in whatever order who are defending the Christian religion and the dignity of the apostolic see; and, giving to you the increase of faith, hope, and charity, may he make you strong in the defense of his law, so that you may deserve to attain to eternal salvation. Given at Tivoli on August 25th, in the fourteenth indiction.

THE CLERGY IN ACTION

5.9 Dressing for the liturgy: *Vesting Prayers* (*c.*1000?). Original in Latin.

Even before the Gregorian reform, clerics themselves developed devotions to prepare spiritually for their sacramental duties. One practice used the special garments that the priest wore to celebrate the Mass to help him cultivate purity and virtue, prescribing prayers to be said as each liturgical vestment was put on. These vesting prayers developed into a

---

[1] This is a reference to a letter of Gregory the Great.

[2] See 1 Sam. 15:23.

[3] See Jer. 48:10.

[4] Bishop Udo.

[5] Bishop Pibo.

[6] Gisela.

[7] Matilda was countess of Tuscany and a staunch supporter of Gregory.

[8] Godfrey, duke of Lorraine, was killed on February 26, 1076.

pre-Mass ritual performed in the sacristy: the clerics participating in the liturgy chanted a few psalms to put them in the proper frame of mind and then recited prayers as they donned their vestments. This clerical devotion emerged in response to ninth-century Carolingian reforms (as the manuscript excerpted below, dated to the late tenth century or the beginning of the eleventh, demonstrates), but was more widely disseminated through the eleventh-century Gregorian movement. Vesting prayers proved incredibly popular with clerics and were required until the Second Vatican Council in 1965 made them optional. Brief prayers such as these were sometimes recorded before the text or *ordo* of the Mass, but they were also copied into margins and on blank spaces at the beginning and ends of liturgical manuscripts. Often, as in the example below, variant prayers are given so that clerics could choose versions that spoke to them.

1. Why and how did clothing have moral significance for the clergy?
2. How was each prayer suited to the garment item associated with it?

[Source: Biblioteca Apostolica Vaticana, Ottoboniensis Latinus 6, fol. 9v. Translated and introduced by Maureen C. Miller.]

Here begins the rite (*ordo*) for a bishop or priest to prepare himself to say Mass.

First, chant the psalms "Quam dilecta," "Benedixisti," "Inclina," and "Credidi."[1] Then recite the "Kyrie eleison" and the Lord's Prayer.[2] Then pray,

Let your mercy, O God, be upon us
You will turn, O God, and bring us to life
Show us, O Lord, your mercy
And enter not into judgment with your servant
Hear, O Lord, my prayer.[3]

To the amice:[4] Rend, O Lord, my garment and wrap me in joy. To the same: Protect my shoulders, O Lord, with the grace of the Holy Spirit and gird my spirit, all sins having been removed, [so that I might] sacrifice to you, O God, [who] lives and reigns forever.

To the alb:[5] Clothe me, O Lord, in the vestment of salvation and gird me with the breastplate of fortitude. To the same: Gird me, O Lord, with the armor of faith, so that having been shielded from the arrows of iniquity, I might have the strength to preserve righteousness and justice. To the same: Omnipresent and eternal God, I humbly beseech you in order that having cast off the deception of all evasions and put on this white garment, I might be worthy to follow you into the realm of true joy.

To the cincture:[6] Equip me, O Lord, with a watchfulness for my soul, lest my mind be warped by a prideful spirit. To the same: Gird me, O Lord, with virtue and make my soul immaculate. To the same: Fasten most powerfully upon my thigh, O Lord, your sword, so that I may be able manfully to vanquish your enemies with the steadfast hope of eternal truth.

---

[1] Psalms 84, 85, 86, and 116; Douay Ps. 83, 84, 85, and 115, here identified by their opening word or words in the Latin in which they would have been chanted.

[2] The "Kyrie eleison" is a brief Greek prayer incorporated into the Latin Mass during the early Middle Ages. Meaning "Lord have mercy," the phrase appears in the Greek translation of the Old Testament (the Septuagint) and in the New Testament. The Lord's Prayer is thus called because the Gospels of Matthew (6:9–15) and Luke (11:2–4) describe Jesus teaching it to his disciples. It is also known by its opening phrase as the Our Father (in Latin, *Pater noster*).

[3] All of these are lines from the Psalms: 33:22, 85:7–8, 143:2, 143:1; Douay Ps. 32:22, 84:7–8; 142:2; 142:1.

[4] The amice, the first vestment to be put on, was a rectangular piece of linen or cotton with ties extending from the long ends of one side. It was draped over the shoulders with the ties crossing the chest, crossing again in back, and then tied in front. It likely served to protect the neckline of other vestments from grime (the amice being more easily washable).

[5] A white linen or cotton long-sleeved tunic that was the base garment worn for the Mass and other ceremonies.

[6] A belt worn over the alb and used to adjust its length by pulling fabric up over the belt.

To the stole:[1] Place the stole of justice around my neck, O Lord, and purify my soul of all sinful corruption; break the chain of my sins, so that having taken up the yoke of your service, I might be worthy to attend you with fear and reverence.

To the chasuble:[2] Robe me, O Lord, with the ornament of humility, love, and peace so that having been completely fortified with virtues I might be able to withstand sins and enemies of mind and body, through you, Jesus Christ.

5.10 Keeping tabs: *A Visitation Record* (1268). Original in Latin.

Reformers not only disseminated "best practices" for the clergy, but they also made more rigorous and systematic efforts to enforce these standards. An important tool was the visitation of parishes. Church councils from the fifth century set out the requirement that bishops, or their delegates, visit the churches of their dioceses to inspect their physical condition, their equipment (the books and ceremonial objects essential to delivering pastoral care), their ministers, and more generally the spiritual and moral condition of both clergy and laity. Sporadic prescriptive and documentary sources reveal episcopal attempts to carry out visitations from the ninth through the twelfth centuries, but it is only in the thirteenth century that we begin to get detailed records produced by visitations. Usually the checklist or questionnaire that the prelate carried into the field does not survive, but the notes taken down by the scribe or notary accompanying the visitor reveal ecclesiastical concerns and the standards being enforced. Translated below are the records of a visitation of the churches in the deanery (an ecclesiastical district within a large diocese) of Demouville in the Norman see of Bayeux. It was conducted in 1268 by Henri de Vézelay, then archdeacon of Bayeux, on behalf of his bishop. Henri went on to have a brilliant career in royal administration, serving as chancellor and advisor to French kings Louis IX (Saint Louis, r.1226–1270) and his son Philip III the Bold (r.1270–1285).

1. Why did Henri de Vézelay care about a church gate, an old Missal, and an unsecured baptismal font?
2. What sorts of moral issues did Henri care about?

[Source: L. Delisle, "Visites pastorales de maître Henri de Vezelai, archidiacre d'Hiémois en 1267 et 1268," *Bibliothèque de l'École des Chartres* 54 (1893): 465–67. Translated and introduced by Maureen C. Miller.]

---

[1] A sort of liturgical scarf worn by deacons and priests, but especially associated with priestly status. Usually eight to ten feet long and two to three inches wide, the stole was put on over the alb, resting on the neck with both ends falling down straight over the front of the body.

[2] The chasuble was the outermost vestment worn by a Christian priest during the Mass. It was a poncho-like garment, often made of a precious fabric such as silk, and highly ornamented.

1268, ON THE MONDAY BEFORE THE FEAST OF BLESSED MICHAEL [24 SEPTEMBER 1268], DEANERY OF DEMOUVILLE.

At Robehomme the *chrismatorium*[1] should be restored and a Gradual and Psalter[2] ought to be bought. The spider cloth[3] above the altar ought to be removed, the blessed altar renewed and repaired, and thus we ordered the people of the place and their treasurers to do this. Garinus Hayche, a married man, is defamed[4] of Johanna, the unmarried daughter of William Viel.

TUESDAY [25 SEPTEMBER 1268]

At Bavent a few things are lacking in the church and its ornaments. A lantern ought to be bought for doing the viaticum.[5] Henry Hemet, a cleric, is defamed of Maltide, daughter of the deceased Noel and he has a child by her. Henry Prestrel is defamed of the wife of Hormont, she whom he had abjured, and he threw out his own wife. Master Gelscuel of Bigarz, a cleric, keeps his own concubine at home.

At Petiville the church gate is falling down and very dangerous. Neither the tabernacle where the body of the Lord [is kept] nor the font are secured due to the negligence of the priest.

At Varaville the Missal[6] is old and unreadable.

At Sallenelles we did not enter the church because the priest was absent and the key to the church could not be found.

At Amfreville the priest was absent, however we visited the church and came upon the chalice in a bag without any other cloth [protecting it]. The church was uncovered[7] through the negligence of the priest. Neither the receptacle where the body of the Lord is kept nor the [baptismal] font was secured. The vestments are very dirty and horrible. Finally, the priest arrived and everything was shown [to us] by him. He was ordered on pain of suspension to get a key for the receptacle for the body of Christ by the following Monday and to correct other things.

At Colombelles the church is being re-roofed; books are lacking.

At Giberville nothing is lacking in the church's ornaments, [but] the church is uncovered. The two chaplains frequent taverns. Thomas Diaconus, a cleric, is denounced for usury and for keeping a kitchen maid. William Synemande, an excommunicate, has been excommunicated several times for a long time. The cleric Aliotus keeps a kitchen maid. Regnaudus Basile, a cleric, is defamed of Petronilla, the widow of the deceased Martin son of Philip.

At Demouville nothing is lacking in the church or its ornaments. The cleric Henry, brother of the dean, is defamed of the widow Florencia. Herbert Boet has a child by Matilda. The cleric Richard Boti still has Marieta. Richard Carsanoz is defamed of Juliana, wife of Selle Guerart and took her to his native land.[8] The cleric Robert Biquet has Matilda and has a child with her. Men don't keep feast days.

---

[1] A *chrismatorium* is a vessel for storing chrism, a mixture of olive oil and balsam consecrated by the bishop that is used in the administration of several sacraments.

[2] The Gradual was a book containing the chants to be sung by the choir at Mass. It takes its name from the step (*gradus*) on which the cantor stood to lead the responsorial psalms intoned after the reading of the Epistle and before the Gospel. The Psalter was a book of the psalms used to recite the cycle of daily prayer known as the Divine Office, a devotion increasingly enjoined on priests from the twelfth century. It was also used to teach reading.

[3] A cloth protecting the altar from spiders and other potential sources of contamination.

[4] The visitor's inquiries allowed parishioners to comment on the conduct and morals of their pastor, but they also brought their own behavior under scrutiny. The passive verb *diffamatur* (here translated "defamed"), from *diffamo*, to accuse or slander, indicates that someone made an accusation of immoral, usually sexual, conduct.

[5] The viaticum was the Eucharist administered to those on the verge of death. The term originally denoted traveling provisions and in Christian usage conveyed the idea that the Eucharist would aid believers on the journey into eternal life. The concern registered here seems to be that if the clergy were summoned in the middle of the night to administer the viaticum, they would have a lamp to light their way while carrying the sacrament.

[6] The Missal is the liturgical book containing all the texts (prayers, readings) needed for saying Mass.

[7] *Ecclesia discooperta* likely comments on the state of the building's roofing.

[8] The text uses *patria*—fatherland, country—suggesting that Richard was not from Normandy.

THURSDAY [27 SEPTEMBER 1268]

At Banneville-la-Campagne the ornaments, corporals,[1] and vestments are dirty. The Breviary[2] is old and unreadable.

At Guillerville the church is poor. The ornaments are good enough.

At ... Émiéville [the church] lacks a key for the font and chrismatorium; the cemetery is not enclosed. These things ought to be corrected within three years. A Psalter and Manual[3] are also lacking. The person assigned to the church does not want to live here so the bishop holds the church. Robert Hardiz still has Luceta au Tabour, whom he is unable to have as his wife because of their consanguinity.

At Manneville the chrismatorium lacks a key through the priest's negligence. He also owes the church treasury three *sextaria* [of grain].

At Cagni all that was lacking in the church has been corrected.

At Vimont the person assigned to the church is still defamed of Petronilla, his blood relative whom he had abjured, and she goes about with him. We ordered a person to remove his straw from the church.

THE FIRST CRUSADE

5.11 Calling the crusade: Robert the Monk, *Pope Urban II Preaches the First Crusade* (1095). Original in Latin.

Byzantine emperors often sent letters or deputations to recruit mercenaries to help fight their wars. To counter the Seljuks, Emperor Alexius (r.1081–1118) sent two delegations to Pope Urban II asking for help. Urban chose to interpret the request in his own way; he left Rome to make a very long trip across the Alps. Among his many activities—stopping at various monasteries and churches, consecrating altars, giving sermons—he attended the Council of Clermont. There, after declaring the Truce of God and reminding the audience of laymen and clergy of their duty to keep the peace, Urban made a new sort of appeal; he called for a new—a holy—way to use arms: in a pilgrimage to the Holy Land. Later historians came to call the result of his call the First Crusade. We do not have Urban's exact words at Clermont. Rather we have a number of accounts of his sermon there, all written a bit later. The one by Robert the Monk (d.1122), who claims to have been an eyewitness, was probably written between 1106–1110 partly to drum up interest in a new crusading expedition.

1. What connection did Urban make between peace in Europe and war against the Seljuks?
2. What are the implications of Urban's appeal to "wrest that land from the wicked race, and subject it to yourselves"?

---

[1] A corporal is a piece of linen upon which the chalice and paten are placed on the altar.

[2] The Breviary is a liturgical book containing all the texts (psalms, antiphons, hymns, lessons) needed to recite the Divine Office. It appears to date from the eleventh century, and Pope Gregory VII is often credited with this abridged and simplified form of the hours suited to the active lives of secular clerics. Since it could replace several books—the Psalter, Antiphonary, Lectionary—the Breviary was well suited to rural churches.

[3] A Manual is a book containing ceremonial directions for performing various liturgies or services.

[Source: Dana C. Munro, ed., *Urban and the Crusaders*, University of Pennsylvania, Translation and Reprints from the Original Sources of European History, vol. 1, no. 2 (Philadelphia: University of Pennsylvania Press, 1895), pp. 5–8 (notes added).]

Oh, race of Franks, race from across the mountains,[1] race chosen and beloved by God—as shines forth in very many of your works—set apart from all nations by the situation of your country, as well as by your catholic faith and the honor of the holy church! To you our discourse is addressed and for you our exhortation is intended. We wish you to know what a grievous cause has led us to your country, what peril threatening you and all the faithful has brought us.

From the confines of Jerusalem and the city of Constantinople a horrible tale has gone forth and very frequently has been brought to our ears, namely, that a race from the kingdom of the Persians,[2] an accursed race, a race utterly alienated from God, a generation forsooth which has not directed its heart and has not entrusted its spirit to God, has invaded the lands of those Christians and has depopulated them by the sword, pillage and fire; it has led away a part of the captives into its own country, and a part it has destroyed by cruel tortures; it has either entirely destroyed the churches of God or appropriated them for the rites of its own religion. They destroy the altars, after having defiled them with their uncleanness. They circumcise the Christians, and the blood of the circumcision they either spread upon the altars or pour into the vases of the baptismal font. When they wish to torture people by a base death, they perforate their navels, and dragging forth the extremity of the intestines, bind it to a stake; then with flogging they lead the victim around until the viscera having gushed forth the victim falls prostrate upon the ground. Others they bind to a post and pierce with arrows. Others they compel to extend their necks and then, attacking them with naked swords, attempt to cut through the neck with a single blow. What shall I say of the abominable rape of the women? To speak of it is worse than to be silent. The kingdom of the Greeks is now dismembered by them and deprived of territory so vast in extent that it can not be traversed in a march of two months.[3] On whom therefore is the labor of avenging these wrongs and of recovering this territory incumbent, if not upon you? You, upon whom above other nations God has conferred remarkable glory in arms, great courage, bodily activity, and strength to humble the hairy scalp of those who resist you.

Let the deeds of your ancestors move you and incite your minds to manly achievements; the glory and greatness of king Charles the Great, and of his son Louis,[4] and of your other kings, who have destroyed the kingdoms of the pagans, and have extended in these lands the territory of the holy church. Let the holy sepulchre of the Lord our Saviour, which is possessed by unclean nations, especially incite you, and the holy places which are now treated with ignominy and irreverently polluted with their filthiness. Oh, most valiant soldiers and descendants of invincible ancestors, be not degenerate, but recall the valor of your progenitors.

But if you are hindered by love of children, parents, and wives, remember what the Lord says in the Gospel, "He that loveth father or mother more than me, is not worthy of me." "Every one that hath forsaken houses, or brethren, or sisters, or father, or mother, or wife, or children, or lands for my name's sake shall receive an hundred-fold and shall inherit everlasting life."[5] Let none of your possessions detain you, no solicitude for your family affairs, since this land which you inhabit, shut in on all sides by the seas and surrounded by the mountain peaks, is too narrow for your large population; nor does it abound in wealth; and it furnishes scarcely food enough for its cultivators. Hence it is that you murder and devour one another, that you wage war, and that frequently you perish by mutual wounds. Let therefore hatred depart from among you, let your quarrels end, let wars cease, and let all dissensions and controversies slumber. Enter upon the road to the Holy Sepulchre; wrest that land

---

[1] "Across the mountains": Urban is thinking of the Franks from his own perspective: he had to cross the Alps to get to France from Rome.

[2] Urban is speaking of the Seljuk Turks, who did not stem from Persia at all, but seemed to Western eyes to come from there.

[3] "The Kingdom of the Greeks" is a reference to Byzantium.

[4] A reference to Charlemagne (d.814) and his son Louis the Pious (d.840).

[5] Quotes from Matt. 10:37 and 19:29.

from the wicked race, and subject it to yourselves. That land which as the Scripture says "floweth with milk and honey,"[1] was given by God into the possession of the children of Israel.

Jerusalem is the navel of the world; the land is fruitful above others, like another paradise of delights. This the Redeemer of the human race has made illustrious by His advent, has beautified by residence, has consecrated by suffering, has redeemed by death, has glorified by burial. This royal city, therefore, situated at the centre of the world, is now held captive by His enemies, and is in subjection to those who do not know God, to the worship of the heathens.[2] She seeks therefore and desires to be liberated, and does not cease to implore you to come to her aid. From you especially she asks succor, because, as we have already said, God has conferred upon you above all nations great glory in arms. Accordingly undertake this journey for the remission of your sins, with the assurance of the imperishable glory of the kingdom of heaven.

When Pope Urban had said these and very many similar things in his urbane discourse, he so influenced to one purpose the desires of all who were present, that they cried out, "It is the will of God! It is the will of God!" When the venerable Roman pontiff heard that, with eyes uplifted to heaven he gave thanks to God and, with his hand commanding silence, said:

Most beloved brethren, to-day is manifest in you what the Lord says in the Gospel, "Where two or three are gathered together in my name there am I in the midst of them."[3] Unless the Lord God had been present in your spirits, all of you would not have uttered the same cry.

For, although the cry issued from numerous mouths, yet the origin of the cry was one. Therefore, I say to you that God, who implanted this in your breasts, has drawn it forth from you. Let this then be your war-cry in combats, because this word is given to you by God. When an armed attack is made upon the enemy, let this one cry be raised by all the soldiers of God: It is the will of God! It is the will of God!

And we do not command or advise that the old or feeble, or those unfit for bearing arms, undertake this journey; nor ought women to set out at all, without their husbands or brothers or legal guardians. For such are more of a hindrance than aid, more of a burden than advantage. Let the rich aid the needy; and according to their wealth, let them take with them experienced soldiers. The priests and clerks of any order are not to go without the consent of their bishop; for this journey would profit them nothing if they went without permission of these. Also, it is not fitting that laymen should enter upon the pilgrimage without the blessing of their priests.

Whoever, therefore, shall determine upon this holy pilgrimage and shall make his vow to God to that effect and shall offer himself to Him as a living sacrifice, holy, acceptable unto God, shall wear the sign of the cross of the Lord on his forehead or on his breast. When, truly, having fulfilled his vow he wishes to return, let him place the cross on his back between his shoulders. Such, indeed, by the two-fold action will fulfill the precept of the Lord, as He commands in the Gospel, "He that taketh not his cross and followeth after me, is not worthy of me."[4]

5.12 Jewish martyrs: Solomon bar Samson, *Chronicle* (*c*.1140). Original in Hebrew.

In the spring of 1096, irregular crusader armies, inspired by popular preachers such as Peter the Hermit, responded to Pope Urban II's call to regain the Holy Land from the Muslim "infidels" who ruled it by first attacking the "infidels in their midst"—the Jews. Thus, on their way to Jerusalem, they made a "detour" to the cities of the Rhineland, where Jews were flourishing under the protection of local bishops and the emperor. City by city, they

---

[1] Scripture speaks of the land flowing "with milk and honey" in many passages, e.g., Lev. 20:24.

[2] Jerusalem had been under Islamic rule since 637.

[3] Matt. 18:20.

[4] Matt. 16:24.

rounded up the Jews and gave them the alternatives of conversion or death. At Speyer, many Jews were saved by the local bishop, but at Worms most were massacred. When an army led by Emico, a German nobleman, attacked Mainz, many of the city's Jews not only refused to convert but also actively sought martyrdom, some by their own hands. These suicide-martyrdoms became a rallying image for northern European Jews over the next century, inspiring accounts like that of Solomon bar Samson.

1. Why did the Jews of Mainz kill themselves?
2. Comparing this reading with the account of the martyrdom of Bishop Adalbert in Thietmar of Merseburg's *Chronicle* (above, p. 218), discuss the diverse attitudes toward martyrdom in medieval Christian and Jewish cultures.

[Source: Jacob Rader Marcus and Marc Saperstein, eds., *The Jews in Medieval Europe: A Source Book, 315–1791* (Pittsburgh: Hebrew Union College and University of Pittsburgh Presses, 2015), pp. 75–78 (notes and trans. by Jacob Marcus).]

It was on the third day of Sivan ... at noon [Tuesday, May 27], that Emico the wicked, the enemy of the Jews, came with his whole army against the city gate, and the burghers opened it up for him. Then the enemies of the Lord said to each other: "Look! They have opened up the gate for us. Now let us avenge the blood of 'the hanged one.'"[1]

The children of the holy covenant were there, martyrs who feared the Most High, although they saw the great multitude, an army numerous as the sand on the shore of the sea, still clung to their Creator. Then young and old donned their armor and girded on their weapons, and at their head was Rabbi Kalonymus ben Meshullam, the chief of the community. Yet because of the many troubles and the fasts which they had observed they had no strength to stand up against the enemy.[2] Then came gangs and bands, sweeping through like a flood, until Mainz was filled from end to end.

The foe Emico proclaimed in the hearing of the community that the enemy be driven from the city and be put to flight. Panic was great in the town. Each Jew in the inner court of the bishop girded on his weapons, and all moved towards the palace gate to fight the crusaders and the burghers. They fought each other up to the very gate, but the sins of the Jews brought it about that the enemy overcame them and took the gate.

The hand of the Lord was heavy against His people. All the gentiles were gathered together against the Jews in the courtyard to blot out their name, and the strength of our people weakened when they saw the wicked Edomites overpowering them.[3] The bishops' men, who had promised to help them, were the very first to flee, thus delivering the Jews into the hands of the enemy. They were indeed a poor support; even the bishop himself fled from his church for it was thought to kill him also because he had spoken good things of the Jews....[4]

When the children of the holy covenant saw that the heavenly decree of death had been issued and that the enemy had conquered them and had entered the courtyard, then all of them—old men and young, virgins and children, servants and maids—cried out together to their Father in heaven and, weeping for themselves and for their lives, accepted as just the sentence of God. One to another they said, "Let us be strong and let us bear the yoke of the holy religion, for only in this world can the

---

[1] "The hanged one" (*ha-talui*), echoing the use of the word in Deut. 21:23, is a demeaning way of referring to Jesus in medieval Jewish texts. Obviously, this could not have been a direct quotation from the crusaders.

[2] Fasting was a traditional manner of Jewish repentance in the hope of appeasing divine anger and receiving protection. Ironically, in this case the narrator claims that the fasts interfered with the Jews' more practical armed resistance.

[3] The Edomites were the traditional foes of the Jews; here, Christians are meant.

[4] Archbishop Ruthard had been paid to remain and defend the Jews. He was later accused of having received some of the plunder taken from them. It is clear that local bishops were not instigators of the violence, and in many cases they made a good-faith effort to protect the Jews of their cities.

enemy kill us—and the easiest of the four deaths is by the sword. But we, our souls in paradise, shall continue to live eternally, in the great shining reflection [of the divine glory]."[1]

With a whole heart and with a willing soul they then spoke: "After all it is not right to criticize the acts of God—blessed be He and blessed be His name—who has given to us His Torah and a command to put ourselves to death, to kill ourselves for the unity of His holy name.[2] Happy are we if we do His will. Happy is anyone who is killed or slaughtered, who dies for the unity of His name, so that he is ready to enter the World to Come, to dwell in the heavenly camp with the righteous—with Rabbi Akiba and his companions, the pillars of the universe, who were killed for His name's sake.[3] Not only *this*; but he exchanges the world of darkness for the world of light, the world of trouble for the world of joy, and the world that passes away for the world that lasts for all eternity." Then all of them, to a man, cried out with a loud voice: "Now we must delay no longer, for the enemy are already upon us. Let us hasten and offer ourselves as a sacrifice to the Lord. Let him who has a knife examine it that it not be nicked, and let him come and slaughter us for the sanctification of the Only One, the Everlasting, and then let him cut his own throat or plunge the knife into his own body."[4]

As soon as the enemy came into the courtyard they found some of the very pious there with our brilliant master, Isaac ben Moses. He stretched out his neck, and his head they cut off first. The others, wrapped in their fringed praying-shawls, sat by themselves in the courtyard, eager to do the will of their Creator. They did not care to flee into the chamber to save themselves for this temporal life, but out of love they received upon themselves the sentence of God.[5] The enemy showered stones and arrows upon them, but they did not care to flee; and "with the stroke of the sword, and with slaughter, and destruction"[6] the foe killed all of those whom they found there. When those in the chambers saw the deed of these righteous ones, how the enemy had already come upon them, they then cried out, all of them: "There is nothing better than for us to offer our lives as a sacrifice."[7]

The women there girded their loins with strength and slew their sons and their daughters and then themselves. Many men, too, plucked up courage and killed their wives, their sons, their infants. The tender and delicate mother slaughtered the babe she had played with; all of them, men and women arose and slaughtered one another.[8] The maidens and the young brides and grooms looked out of the windows and in a loud voice cried: "Look and see, O our God, what we do for the sanctification of Thy great name in order not to exchange you for a hanged and crucified one...."

Thus were the precious children of Zion, the Jews of Mainz, tried with ten trials like Abraham, our father, and like Hananiah, Mishael, and Azariah.[9] They bound their sons as Abraham bound Isaac his son, and they received upon themselves with a willing soul the yoke of the fear of God, the King of the Kings of Kings, the Holy One, blessed be He, rather than deny and exchange the religion of our King for "an abhorred offshoot,"[10] a bastard born of menstruation and lust.[11] They stretched out their necks

---

[1] In Jewish law the four death penalties were stoning, burning, beheading, and strangulation.

[2] While traditional martyrdom to avoid the sin of idolatry is understood to be a mandate from the Torah, there is no commandment that could be understood to justify suicide in this context, and certainly not the killing of other Jews, as the narrative will describe.

[3] The Romans martyred Akiba during the Bar Kokba revolt, about 135 CE.

[4] The taking of their own lives by Jews is presented as a reenactment of the ancient Temple sacrifices, for which a knife without blemishes was required.

[5] This is a description of traditional, passive martyrdom, in which the martyr makes no attempt to resist.

[6] Esther 9:13.

[7] The outnumbered Jews had no chance to prevail: Emico is reported to have had about twelve thousand men.

[8] The narrator does not appear to recognize that such behavior is far more problematic in Jewish law. It is said here to be initiated not by the rabbis but by ordinary Jews.

[9] Who were thrown into a fiery furnace (Dan. 3:21).

[10] Isa. 14:19.

[11] This contemptuous reference to Jesus is based on the assertions in the birth narrative of Matthew's Gospel: Mary and Joseph were betrothed, Mary was pregnant, Joseph was not the father. Jewish readers concluded that the pregnancy was therefore the result of an adulterous relationship.

to the slaughter and they delivered their pure souls to their Father in heaven. Righteous and pious women bared their throats to each other, offering to be sacrificed for the unity of the Name. A father turning to his son or brother, a brother to his sister, a woman to her son or daughter, a neighbor to a neighbor or a friend, a groom to a bride, a fiancé to a fiancée, would kill and would be killed, and blood touched blood. The blood of the men mingled with their wives', the blood of the fathers with their children's, the blood of the brothers with their sisters', the blood of the teachers with their disciples', the blood of the grooms with their brides', the blood of the leaders with their cantors', the blood of the judges with their scribes', and the blood of infants and sucklings with their mothers'. For the unity of the honored and awe-inspiring Name were they killed and slaughtered.

The ears of one who hears these things will tingle, for who has ever heard anything like this? Inquire now and look about, was there ever such an abundant sacrifice as this since the days of the primeval Adam? Were there ever eleven hundred offerings on one day, each one of them like the sacrifice of Isaac, the son of Abraham?

For the sake of Isaac who was ready to be sacrificed on Mount Moriah, the world shook, as it is said, "Behold their valiant ones cry without; [the angels of peace weep bitterly],"[1] and "the heavens grow dark."[2] Yet see what these martyrs did! Why did the heavens not grow dark and the stars not withdraw their brightness? Why did not the moon and the sun grow dark in their heavens when on one day, on the third of Sivan, on a Tuesday, eleven hundred souls were killed and slaughtered, among them so many infants and sucklings who had never transgressed nor sinned, so many poor, innocent souls?

Wilt Thou, despite this, still restrain Thyself, O Lord? For Thy sake it was that these numberless souls were killed.

Avenge quickly the blood of Thy servants which was spilt in our days and in our sight. Amen.

5.13 A Westerner in the Holy Land: Stephen of Blois, *Letter to His Wife* (March 1098). Original in Latin.

The crusaders had moderate success in their war against the Muslims. During the long siege of Antioch, which began in October 1097 and was not over until July 1098, one of the crusade leaders, Count Stephen of Blois (d.1102), dictated a letter to his wife, Adela. Full of love, bravado, false claims (e.g., that he was the leader of the "whole expedition"), and pious sentiments, the letter betrays little sign that Stephen was about to desert the army and return home. The letter is a good illustration of what a crusader was supposed to think about the enterprise, whether he did or not.

1. What does the letter suggests about the relations between husbands and wives (at least those of the French nobility)?
2. What is Stephen's opinion of the Crusade in this letter?

[Source: *The Crusades: A Reader*, ed. S.J. Allen and Emilie Amt (Toronto: University of Toronto Press, 2003), pp. 63–66, revised from *Translations and Reprints from the Original Sources of European History*, ed. Dana C. Munro, Ser. 1, Vol. 1 (Philadelphia: University of Pennsylvania Department of History, 1895), no. 4, pp. 5–8.]

---

[1] Isa. 33:7.

[2] Jer. 4:28.

Count Stephen to Adela, his sweetest and most amiable wife, to his dear children, and to all his vassals of all ranks—his greeting and blessing.

You may be very sure, dearest, that the messenger whom I sent to give you pleasure, left me before Antioch safe and unharmed, and through God's grace in the greatest prosperity. And already at that time, together with all the chosen army of Christ, endowed with great valor by him, we had been continuously advancing for twenty-three weeks toward the home of our Lord Jesus. You may know for certain, my beloved, that of gold, silver and many other kind of riches I now have twice as much as your love had assigned to me when I left you. For all our princes, with the common consent of the whole army, against my own wishes, have made me up to the present time the leader, chief and director of their whole expedition.

You have certainly heard that after the capture of the city of Nicaea we fought a great battle with the perfidious Turks and by God's aid conquered them. Next we conquered for the Lord all Romania[1] and afterwards Cappadocia. And we learned that there was a certain Turkish prince Assam, dwelling in Cappadocia; thither we directed our course. All his castles we conquered by force and compelled him to flee to a certain very strong castle situated on a high rock. We also gave the land of that Assam to one of our chiefs and in order that he might conquer the above-mentioned Assam, we left there with him many soldiers of Christ. Thence, continually following the wicked Turks, we drove them through the midst of Armenia, as far as the great river Euphrates. Having left all their baggage and beasts of burden on the bank, they fled across the river into Arabia.

The bolder of the Turkish soldiers, indeed, entering Syria, hastened by forced marches night and day, in order to be able to enter the royal city of Antioch before our approach. The whole army of God, learning this, gave due praise and thanks to the omnipotent Lord. Hastening with great joy to the aforesaid chief city of Antioch, we besieged it and very often had many conflicts there with the Turks; and seven times with the citizens of Antioch and with the innumerable troops coming to its aid, whom we rushed to meet, we fought with the fiercest courage, under the leadership of Christ. And in all these seven battles, by the aid of the Lord God, we conquered and most assuredly killed an innumerable host of them. In those battles, indeed, and in very many attacks made upon the city, many of our brethren and followers were killed and their souls were borne to the joys of paradise.

We found the city of Antioch very extensive, fortified with incredible strength and almost impregnable. In addition, more than 5,000 bold Turkish soldiers had entered the city, not counting the Saracens, Publicans, Arabs, Turcopolitans, Syrians, Armenians and other different races of whom an infinite multitude had gathered together there. In fighting against these enemies of God and of our own we have, by God's grace, endured many sufferings and innumerable evils up to the present time. Many also have already exhausted all their resources in this very holy passion. Very many of our Franks, indeed, would have met a temporal death from starvation, if the clemency of God and our money had not succored them. Before the above-mentioned city of Antioch indeed, throughout the whole winter we suffered for our Lord Christ from excessive cold and enormous torrents of rain. What some say about the impossibility of bearing the heat of the sun throughout Syria is untrue, for the winter there is very similar to our winter in the west.

When truly Caspian,[2] the emir of Antioch—that is, prince and lord—perceived that he was hard pressed by us, he sent his son Sensodolo[3] by name, to the prince who holds Jerusalem, and to the prince of Calep, Rodoam[4] and to Docap prince of Damascus.[5] He also sent into Arabia for Bolianuth[6] and to Carathania for Hamelnuth.[7] These five emirs with 12,000 picked Turkish horsemen suddenly came to aid the inhabitants of Antioch. We, indeed, ignorant of all this, had sent many of our soldiers away to the cities and fortresses. For there are 165 cities and fortresses throughout Syria which are in our power. But a little before they reached the city, we attacked them

---

[1] "Romania" here refers to the Byzantine Empire; at the time Stephen was writing, much of Anatolia had been taken by the Seljuk Turks.

[2] This was Yaghi Siyan, appointed emir in 1087.

[3] Shams ad-Daulah.

[4] This was Ridwan of Aleppo.

[5] Docap was Duqaq, Seljuk ruler of Damascus (r.1095–1104).

[6] This was Kerbogha, the Turkish governor of Mosul (d.1102).

[7] Carathania refers to Khorasan, today in Iran.

at three leagues' distance with 700 soldiers, on a certain plain near the "Iron Bridge."[1] God, however, fought for us, his faithful, against them. For on that day, fighting in the strength that God gives, we conquered them and killed an innumerable multitude—God continually fighting for us—and we also carried back to the army more than two hundred of their heads, in order that the people might rejoice on that account. The emperor of Babylon also sent Saracen messengers to our army with letters, and through these he established peace and concord with us.[2]

I love to tell you, dearest, what happened to us during Lent. Our princes had caused a fortress to be built before a certain gate which was between our camp and the sea. For the Turks, daily issuing from this gate, killed some of our men on their way to the sea. The city of Antioch is about five leagues' distance from the sea. For this reason they sent the excellent Bohemond[3] and Raymond, count of St. Gilles,[4] to the sea with only sixty horsemen, in order that they might bring mariners to aid in this work. When, however, they were returning to us with those mariners, the Turks collected an army, fell suddenly upon our two leaders and forced them to a perilous flight. In that unexpected flight we lost more than 500 of our footsoldiers—to the glory of God. Of our horsemen, however, we lost only two, for certain.

On that same day truly, in order to receive our brethren with joy, and ignorant of their misfortunes, we went out to meet them. When, however, we approached the above-mentioned gate of the city, a mob of horsemen and footsoldiers from Antioch, elated by the victory which they had won, rushed upon us in the same manner. Seeing these, our leaders sent to the camp of the Christians to order all to be ready to follow us into battle. In the meantime our men gathered together and the scattered leaders, namely, Bohemond and Raymond, with the remainder of their army came up and narrated the great misfortune which they had suffered.

Our men, full of fury at these most evil tidings, prepared to die for Christ and, deeply grieved for their brethren, rushed upon the sacrilegious Turks. They, the enemies of God and of us, hastily fled before us and attempted to enter their city. But by God's grace the affair turned out very differently; for, when they wanted to cross a bridge built over the great river Moscholum,[5] we followed them as closely as possible, killed many before they reached the bridge, forced many into the river, all of whom were killed, and we also slew many upon the bridge and very many at the narrow entrance to the gate. I am telling you the truth, my beloved, and you may be very certain that in this battle we killed thirty emirs, that is princes, and, three hundred other Turkish nobles, not counting the remaining Turks and pagans. Indeed, the number of Turks and Saracens killed is reckoned at 1,230, but of ours we did not lose a single man.

While on the following day (Easter) my chaplain Alexander was writing this letter in great haste, a party of our men, lying in wait for the Turks, fought a successful battle with them and killed sixty horsemen, whose heads they brought to the army.

These which I write to you are only a few things, dearest, of the many which we have done, and because I am not able to tell you, dearest, what is in my mind, I charge you to do right, to carefully watch over your land, to do your duty as you ought to your children and your vassals. You will certainly see me just as soon as I can possibly return to you. Farewell.

---

[1] The "Iron Bridge" crossed the Orontes River, about seven miles north of Antioch.

[2] A reference to an offer of neutrality by the Fatimid caliph of Egypt, who was Shi'ite, and thus hostile to the Sunni Turks.

[3] Bohemond of Taranto (d.1111), leader of the Norman contingent.

[4] Raymond of St. Gilles (d.1105) was the count of Toulouse and an important crusade leader.

[5] The Orontes River; this was another battle at the Iron Bridge.